Programming with

Java™

A Multimedia Approach

Radhika S. Grover

Santa Clara University

ES & BARTLETT
ARNING

World Headquarters
Jones & Bartlett Learning
5 Wall Street
Burlington, MA 01803
978-443-5000
info@jblearning.com
www.jblearning.com

Jones & Bartlett Learning books and products are available through most bookstores and online booksellers. To contact Jones & Bartlett Learning directly, call 800-832-0034, fax 978-443-8000, or visit our website, www.jblearning.com.

Substantial discounts on bulk quantities of Jones & Bartlett Learning publications are available to corporations, professional associations, and other qualified organizations. For details and specific discount information, contact the special sales department at Jones & Bartlett Learning via the above contact information or send an email to specialsales@jblearning.com.

Production Credits
Publisher: Cathleen Sether
Senior Acquisitions Editor: Timothy Anderson
Managing Editor: Amy Bloom
Director of Production: Amy Rose
Associate Marketing Manager: Lindsay White
Online Products Manager: Dawn Mahon Priest
V.P., Manufacturing and Inventory Control: Therese Connell
Composition: Northeast Compositors, Inc.
Cover and Title Page Design: Kristin E. Parker
Cover and Title Page Images: Wave in background: © Joel Calheiros/Dreamstime.com
    Photos: © Italianestro/Dreamstime.com
Printing and Binding: Malloy, Inc.
Cover Printing: Malloy, Inc.

To order this product, use ISBN: 978-1-4496-3861-0

Library of Congress Cataloging-in-Publication Data
Grover, Radhika S.
  Programming with Java : a multimedia approach / Radhika S. Grover.
    p. cm.
  Includes bibliographical references and index.
  ISBN 978-0-7637-8433-1 (pbk.)
1. Java (Computer program language) 2. Multimedia systems. I. Title.
QA76.73.J38G784 2012
006.7'6—dc22
                    2011008939

6048

Printed in the United States of America
15 14 13 12 11   10 9 8 7 6 5 4 3 2 1

Dedication

To my parents Deepa and Lokesh Kumar Singhal

Contents

Preface

Programming with Java: A Multimedia Approach is an introduction to computer science programming that utilizes Java as the programming language. The audience for this book includes those with little or no programming experience who are looking for an easy-to-understand, in-depth treatment of Java. It can be used as a textbook for career and introductory undergraduate courses, as well as a reference textbook for graduate courses.

Features

- To keep the reader engaged and thinking creatively, this book uses multimedia-based programs as a means of instruction. With this book, the reader will learn Java using programs that draw graphics and images, perform animation, read and play audio files, display video, and more.

- Each chapter contains several example programs, and a project is developed in the relevant chapters.

- This book uses example programs to highlight the applications of computers in various fields such as engineering, business, and science.

- Comprehensive exercises are provided at the end of each chapter.

- Instructor's supplements, including Solutions to Exercises, a Test Bank, PowerPoint lecture outlines, and program source code, are available for instructors who adopt this textbook. In addition, instructors have the opportunity to assign additional online programming activities to their students with Turing's Craft CodeLab. (A complete description of this online service and how to get started can be found after this preface.) A CodeLab student access code and log-in instructions are located on the inside front cover of this text.

■ The CD included with this text offers source code, video, audio, and image files from the text, as well as links to download the Java Platform, Standard Edition and Apple QuickTime™.

About This Book

The conventional approach that is followed in most other books on Java is to use a console output in programs. In this book, a multimedia-based approach is used right from the beginning, creating examples that are imaginative and interesting. The assumption is that the reader has no prior programming experience or knowledge of media APIs. Java has media APIs that are well integrated into the language, such as AWT, Java 2D and Swing for graphics, and Java Sound for audio. In addition, there are other software libraries available for media such as QuickTime for Java (QTJ), developed by Apple Inc., for audio and video. This book leverages these toolkits to aid in learning Java. Basic and advanced concepts are explained by providing the reader with simple frameworks that he or she can use to write programs. Initially, the reader can write programs without complete understanding of the details of these frameworks. Once the reader has gathered sufficient background to grasp it fully, the media API is explained in more detail.

This book begins with a gentle introduction to the Java 2D API using examples that can be easily understood by a reader who is new to programming. These examples show how to create objects using preexisting Java 2D classes and use these objects to display graphics on the computer screen. After the reader gains familiarity with Java basics that are discussed next, he or she will then learn how to write new classes. The approach used is objects-first, in which objects are used early, but writing classes comes later.

Every chapter contains code snippets and stand-alone examples. In some chapters, a large project is developed incrementally to help explain new concepts as well as demonstrate how these tie in with previously discussed material. An essential (and sometimes neglected) part of programming is writing algorithms. The algorithms for several programs are provided using flowcharts and/or systematic explanations.

Outline of Chapters

Chapter 1 provides a general overview of how computers execute programs and explains how to compile and run a Java program. Chapter 2 describes how to create objects using Java 2D classes and display text, images, and graphical shapes in a window on the computer screen. Chapter 3 explains basic concepts such as data types, variables, literals, strings, and operators. Near the end of the chapter, applications of computers in engineering are discussed.

Chapter 4 covers conditional statements and loops. Flowchart-based explanations are used throughout this chapter to explain the different constructs in detail. Chapter 5 explains how to write custom classes. A class called *Lamp* is developed in this chapter as an example. The methods in this class are used to draw and color a lamp shape on the screen. Chapter 6 explores inheritance in detail. A class called *Vehicle* is developed, and animation is added to display moving shapes such as cars and airplanes. Chapter 6 also describes the applications of computers in business and includes a program to calculate credit card finance charges.

Chapter 7 explains how to use arrays and strings. In this chapter, a two-player game called *Crystals* is developed, the objective of which is to grow imaginary crystals on a grid of squares using a set of rules. This chapter also contains a section on how computers are used in science with an example program from the field of bioengineering. Chapter 8 covers interfaces and nested classes in detail. A program called *Palette* that mixes colors to create new colors is developed here. Chapter 9 explores how to create Graphical User Interfaces using Swing. A photo editing GUI application called *PhotoOp* is developed. The application demonstrates how various components can be added to a GUI and used to modify a photograph.

Chapter 10 covers the exception-handling mechanism, and provides many examples on how to catch and handle exceptions. Chapter 11 describes classes for reading textual and binary data from files, and for serialization. A program called *AudioMixer* is written to read the content of WAV audio files and modify them. The examples show how to merge the contents of two audio files and reverse the contents of an audio file, among others.

Chapter 12 describes generics and the Java Collections framework. A multimedia information system called *PhotoFinder* is developed in this chapter. This program shows how to create data structures for efficient retrieval of the photographs stored on a user's disk using keyword-based searches.

Chapter 13 explains how mouse and key events are handled as well as how the swing timer mechanism is used. A simple two-dimensional animation game called *BallGame* is developed here. Chapter 14 explores thread programming basics using video and audio. The *MoviePlayer* class is provided to play media using the QuickTime player and QuickTime for Java.

Acknowledgments

I would like to thank the wonderful editorial and production team at Jones & Bartlett Learning: Tim Anderson, Senior Acquisitions Editor; Amy Bloom, Managing Editor; and Amy Rose, Director of Production. Tim and Amy Rose provided invaluable guidance and help in this project. Amy Bloom provided help with the supplementary materials. I also thank the following for their excellent contributions: Jennifer Bagdigian for copyediting the manuscript, Beth Kohler for proofreading, Northeast Compositors for the composition and layout, Kristin E. Parker for the cover design, Laurel Muller for the artwork, and Nancy Fulton for preparing the index. I am very grateful to the reviewers and to Elizabeth Sugar Boese of Colorado State University for a thorough review and technical edit of this textbook, and for making detailed suggestions that have improved this book immensely.

Many thanks to my husband Puneet, and sons Rohan and Pranav, for their incredible support and help. This book could not have been completed without help from Rohan, who composed the music in the files groovy.wav and audio.wav and reviewed several chapters of the book. Pranav tested the games and other programs and provided helpful suggestions on how to improve them. Finally, I would like to thank my parents for their constant support and encouragement.

Turing's Craft CodeLab Student Registration Instructions

 turingscraft

CodeLab is the web-based interactive programming exercise service that accompanies this text. It is designed to reduce attrition and raise the overall level of the class. Since 2002, CodeLab has analyzed over twenty-two million exercise submissions from more than 75,000 students.

CodeLab has over 300 short exercises, each focused on a particular programming idea or language construct. The student types in code and the system immediately judges its correctness, offering hints when the submission is incorrect. Through this process, the student gains mastery over the semantics, syntax, and common usage of the language elements.

For the Students

CodeLab offers a tree-based table of content navigation system augmented by prev/next buttons that permit sequential traversal. Exercises are organized within a hierarchy of topics that match the textbook's organization and can be reconfigured as needed by the instructor. The student interface offers three tabs for each exercise: a work-area tab containing the instructions of the exercise and a text area for typing in a submission; a results tab that indicates the correctness of the student's submission and provides an analysis of the submission code in the event of an error; and a solutions tab which, by default, is invisible but may be made available at the discretion of the instructor. The solutions tab contains one or more solutions to the exercise; the results tabs contains one or more of the following: correctness indicator, ad hoc hints, marked-up submission indicating possible errors, compiler messages, table of passed and failed test cases. In addition, the usual online amenities of preferences, account management, documentation, and customer support options are provided.

A unique student access code can be found at the beginning of this textbook. Length of student access is 52 weeks for this edition of the textbook.

Students can also purchase the access code online at

jblearning.turingscraft.com.

For the Instructors

CodeLab provides the preceding student interface and in addition provides

- a **Course Manager** that permits the instructor to rearrange, rename, and/or omit topics and exercises. It also allows instructors to assign deadlines, specify dates when solutions can be seen by students, dates past which student work will not be "counted," and dates prior to which the exercises will be invisible to students.

- a **Grading Roster** that presents a graphical spreadsheet view of student work, where each row corresponds to a student and each column to an exercise. It is also possible to mail and/or download rosters in CSV format.

- an **Exercise Creation Tool** that permits instructors to create their own exercises.

Custom CodeLab

CodeLab is customized to this textbook as follows:

1. The organization of the CodeLab matches the organization of the textbook.

2. For each chapter that covers an appropriate standard introductory programming topic, the CodeLab offers CodeLab exercises, taken from either the standard set of existing CodeLab exercises or added to fill in any gaps in coverage.

Demonstration Site for CodeLab

A Jones & Bartlett Learning demonstration site is available online at

jblearning.turingscraft.com

Visitors to this site will be directed to a landing page that provides an overview of the product. By clicking on the selected Jones & Bartlett Learning textbook cover, you will be led to more detailed product description pages. In the detailed product description pages there are further descriptions, examples of or links to examples of specific examples of custom CodeLab tie-ins with this textbook, and a link to a fully functional demo version of the Custom CodeLab. The latter offers full functionality and contains all of the exercise content of the particular Custom CodeLab. To make use of this link, instructors will need a unique Section Creation access code provided by their Jones & Bartlett Learning Computer Science Account Specialist at 1-800-832-0034, or online at www.jblearning.com.

Using this CodeLab Section Creation Code permits instructors to use the online tool to create their own unique CodeLab sections based on the Custom CodeLab. This permits instructors to have instructor accounts that enable access to the Course Manager, roster, and exercise creation tools described on the previous page.

Additonally Turing's Craft provides online documentation and support for both prospective adopters and actual faculty users of this text. In creating sections for classroom adopting, instructors will receive CodeLab Section Access Codes that should be provided to their students—enabling their students to associate their accounts (i.e., join their instructor's CodeLab section).

System Requirements: CodeLab runs on recent versions of most browsers (e.g., Internet Explorer, Firefox, Safari) on Windows and MacOS and on many versions of Linux. CodeLab does require the installation of the latest Flash Reader, available from www.adobe.com. (Most systems come with Flash pre-installed.) More details about CodeLab browser compatibility can be found at:

www.turingscraft.com/browsers.html

CHAPTER 1

Introduction

CHAPTER CONTENTS

1.1 A Brief History of Java

Originally named Oak, the Java language was developed by James Gosling and his team at Sun Microsystems in the early 1990s. Since its release in 1995, Java has grown tremendously in popularity. It is now used in providing a wide variety of services: applications for small devices, such as portable digital assistants (PDAs) and cell phones; web applications that run in a browser; application servers that provide business services to the clients of a company; and more.

There have been significant changes to Java since the first version, called JDK 1.0, was released. Newer versions of Java include 1.5 and 1.6 (also known as Java 5 and Java 6, respectively). Many features in the original version are no longer used. The language has grown much bigger as new features have been introduced in subsequent versions. Examples include the Swing and Java 2D graphical toolkits introduced in Java 2, and the generics framework introduced in Java 5.

This chapter begins with the basics that are essential to understanding how to write and run a simple Java program. It describes the components of a computer and explains how computers execute programs. It also discusses the software development method and shows how you can apply it to develop your programs.

1.2 What Is a Program?

Computers are ubiquitous in our everyday lives. We use **laptop** and **desktop computers** for email, web browsing, video game playing, scientific applications, and much more. Another category of computers that is more common than laptop and desktop computers is **embedded computer systems**. Embedded computers are enclosed in appliances and devices and perform specific tasks. They are used inside devices such as personal digital assistants (PDAs), cell phones, household appliances, traffic light controllers, and medical equipment. The various tasks performed by computers are accomplished by different programs running within them.

A **program** is a set of instructions that tells the computer what to do. It is used to solve a specific problem. For example, consider the following problem:

Display an image on the computer screen.

The following steps describe how this can be accomplished:

1. Create a window in the computer.

2. Draw an image in the window.

3. Set the window size.

4. Make the window visible on the computer screen.

Steps 1 to 4 describe a particular sequence of operations known as an **algorithm**. The algorithm is then written using a computer language to create a program. Thousands of programming languages, such as Java, Pascal, FORTRAN, COBOL, and Lisp, are used to write programs. These languages, known as **high-level languages**, contain instructions consisting of English words and algebraic expressions that hide the underlying details of the computer architecture from the programmer. After the program has been written, it can be run on a computer. In the next section, we look at how computers execute programs.

1.3   How Computers Work

Although the architecture, size, and cost of computers can vary significantly, most of them contain the following components:

- One or more processors

- Memory

- Secondary memory, such as hard drives

- Input devices, such as a keyboard and a mouse

- Output devices, such as monitors and speakers

A computer has a **processor** (also called the **central processing unit**, or **CPU**) and **memory** (also called **RAM**, or **main memory**). The processor is responsible for executing instructions in a program. The RAM stores programs temporarily while they are running on the processor. Besides the RAM, another place where computers store information is in the **hard drive** (also called the **hard disk**). For example, you can create a document using a word processor and store it in the hard drive. This is *nonvolatile* computer memory, which means that the computer stores information even after it is powered down. RAM, on the other hand, is *volatile* memory. Any information stored in the RAM is lost when the computer is turned off.

Unfortunately, computers do not speak English, Mandarin Chinese, Swahili, or any other language that humans use to communicate. Computers use **machine language**, a binary language composed of only two digits, 0 and 1 (a lot simpler than English, with its 26 letters, or Chinese, which has more than 47,000 characters). Each digit is called a **bit**. A specific sequence of bits forms an instruction that tells the computer what to do. For example, the instruction "10101111" might instruct a computer to add two numbers. A set of eight bits is called a **byte**. Instructions can contain from one byte to several bytes, and they differ between processors.

Machine language is composed of these instructions. It would be a tedious and error-prone process to write a program directly in machine language. (Can you imagine writing 0 and 1 a few billion times?) Thus, programs are written in a high-level language, such as Java or Pascal. These programs are then translated into machine language using a **compiler**, which is a program that converts a high-level language program into a machine language program that a computer can understand. (The machine code generated is specific to the processor in the computer.) The machine language program is then loaded into memory; the processor examines the instructions in the program and carries them out.

Some compilers translate a program into an intermediate language instead of a machine language. Java compilers use this approach and translate Java programs into a special binary code called **Java bytecode**. Unlike machine language, Java bytecode is not dependent upon which type of processor the computer uses. You will see why this is useful in the next section.

1.4   Compiling and Running a Java Program

The first step of compiling and running a Java program is to write the text of your program in a document and save it on the hard drive. This document is called a **source file**, and you must name it with a **.java** extension. Next, compile this program using a Java compiler. The compiler checks the program for errors and, if no errors are found, it generates a new document containing Java bytecode. This document is called a **class file**, and its name ends with a **.class** extension.

Although a processor can run machine code directly, it cannot execute Java bytecode. Instead, a special program called the **Java virtual machine** (or **JVM**) is used for this purpose. Unlike processors that are built from hardware components, the JVM is software that does the work of a processor. The JVM contains a **class loader** that loads the program into memory, and an **interpreter** that is responsible for executing Java bytecode. The JVM must be installed on the computer where you want to run Java programs. A **platform** refers to the type of processor and/or the operating system in a computer. Different JVMs are available for different platforms. Figure 1–1 shows how the program stored in the source file HelloWorld.java is compiled and run.

The advantage of using Java bytecode is that it is portable—that is, you can run the bytecode for a program on any platform that has a JVM installed on it. For this reason, Java is a "compile once, run anywhere" language. On

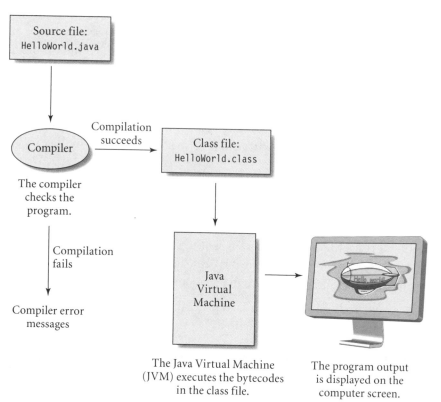

Figure 1–1

Compiling and running a Java program.

the other hand, programs written in a language such as C or C++ are usually compiled each time they are run on a different platform. The compilers for these languages directly generate machine code for the platform on which the program will be run.

1.5   The Software Development Method

To develop a software product, it is necessary to complete the following set of tasks, which is collectively referred to as the "software development method":

1. Define the problem.

2. Design an algorithm to solve the problem.

3. Develop the program code from the algorithm.

4. Test the code and verify its correctness.

5. Maintain the code.

First, you must clearly define the problem. Next, you collect all pertinent information related to the problem. This information is used to design an algorithm that outlines which steps must be taken to solve the problem. Each step in the algorithm can be a subproblem that is further broken down into simpler steps. (It is important to verify that the algorithm works correctly by running some test cases through it manually.) Then, you use this algorithm to develop a program. This is accomplished by using statements in a programming language to describe the work done in the various steps of the algorithm.

Test the program by running it several times and checking that the outputs are correct. Use different sets of data each time the program is run. If the output contains errors, you will have to repeat the previous steps. After the testing is completed, the software is sent to customers, but it may still contain errors that are detected while it is being used. Maintenance involves correcting these errors and adding enhancements to improve the software.

In the next section, we write a Java program to explain how the software development method should be used.

1.6   A Java Program: HelloWorld

In Section 1.2 *What Is a Program?*, we defined the following problem and designed an algorithm to solve it:

Display an image on the computer screen.

Each step in this algorithm is converted into a Java statement. The resulting Java program, called HelloWorld, is shown here. We will explain it in more detail a little later.

```java
// Program HelloWorld
import javax.swing.*;

public class HelloWorld {
  public static void main(String[] args) {
    JFrame frame = new JFrame("My First Program");
    frame.getContentPane().add(new JLabel(new ImageIcon("blimp.png")));
    frame.pack();
    frame.setVisible(true);
  }
}
```

You must compile and run the program after it has been written. There are many tools available for compiling Java programs, such as javac, GCJ, and ECJ. The **javac** compiler is available from Oracle Corporation (www.oracle.com) and comes bundled in the **Java Development Kit** (JDK), along with other Java programming tools. **GCJ** is a GNU (a collection of free software tools and libraries) compiler for Java. It can generate Java bytecode as well as machine code for various processors. **ECJ** is a Java compiler in Eclipse, a software development environment that supports programming in various languages, such as Java, C, C++, and Perl. Besides javac, the JDK contains the Java Runtime Environment, libraries, and other tools. The **Java Runtime Environment** (JRE) implements the Java virtual machine that executes bytecode.

Download and install JDK if it is not already installed on your PC. Macintosh computers come preinstalled with Java, and thus no download or installation is required.

1.6.1   Compiling the HelloWorld Program

In this section, we describe how you can compile the HelloWorld program using the javac compiler. Before compiling the program, it is important to correctly place the files in specific directories. (To simplify matters, we assume that this program and all the code examples in the rest of the book are placed in a directory called JavaBook.)

Create the JavaBook directory on your computer. (We assume it is created in the C: drive on a PC, but you can create it in a different directory.) Next, create two new directories, called src and bin, inside JavaBook. All the source code files (that is, files with the .java extension) will be placed in the src directory. The bin directory contains class files (files with the .class extension). It is important to keep the class files and source files separate so that you can delete the class files without accidentally deleting source files. Copy the HelloWorld.java file from the JavaBook\src directory on the CD-ROM into the C:\JavaBook\src directory on your computer. This file contains the HelloWorld program. In addition, copy the file blimp.png from the JavaBook directory on the CD-ROM to the C:\JavaBook directory. This file contains an image that will be displayed on your computer screen when you run the program. Figure 1–2 shows the directory structure.

After the directories have been set up, change the working directory to C:\JavaBook using the cd (change directory) command:

```
C:\> cd JavaBook
```

This sets the current directory to C:\JavaBook. To compile HelloWorld.java on a PC, type the following statement at the command prompt:

```
C:\JavaBook> javac -d bin src\HelloWorld.java
```

You should not get any error messages upon running this program; if you do, check that you have typed the statement correctly. The -d option tells the compiler that the destination directory for the class files is bin. Examine the contents of the bin directory and note that a file called

Figure 1–2

Directory structure for the source and class files.

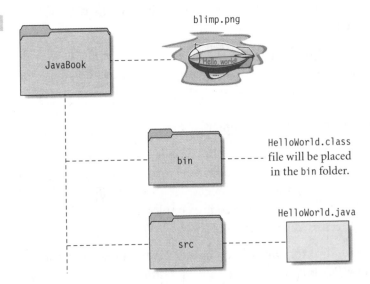

`HelloWorld.class` has been created in it. This file contains the bytecodes for the `HelloWorld` program.

To compile the program on a Macintosh computer, you must first open a terminal window (by selecting *Applications* → *Utilities* → *Terminal*). The prompt will be similar to this:

`computer:~YourName$`

Then navigate to the `JavaBook` directory (assume that this directory is in the `/Users/YourName` directory) using the `cd` command:

`computer:~YourName$ cd JavaBook`

You can compile the program after you have set the working directory to `JavaBook`. This is similar to how a program is compiled on a PC, except that in this case, you use a forward slash (/) instead of a backslash (\):

`computer:~/JavaBook YourName$ javac -d bin src/HelloWorld.java`

The final step in this exercise is to run the program using this file, a process that is described next.

1.6.2 Running the `HelloWorld` Program

The `java` tool loads the JVM and runs the specified program. To run the `HelloWorld` program on a PC, invoke the `java` command in the `C:\JavaBook` directory as follows:

`C:\JavaBook> java -classpath bin HelloWorld`

If you are using a Macintosh, type the same command:

`computer:~/JavaBook YourName$ java -classpath bin HelloWorld`

The name of the directory containing the class files (`bin`) is placed after the `-classpath` option. This is followed by the name of the class file that is to be executed (`HelloWorld.class`), except that the `.class` extension should not be specified. The JVM will execute the bytecodes in the `HelloWorld.class` file, and you will see the picture in Figure 1–3 appear on the computer screen. This output consists of a window with the title "My First Program" and the picture of a blimp within it.

If a window appears but there is no picture, it means that the `blimp.png` file is not in the `C:\JavaBook` directory. Move the file to this directory and run the program again. Alternately, replace the following line in the `HelloWorld.java` file:

`frame.getContentPane().add(new JLabel(new ImageIcon("blimp.png")));`

Figure 1–3

Output of the HelloWorld **program.**

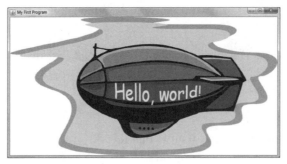

blimp.png courtesy of iclipart.com

with this one:

```
frame.getContentPane().add(new JLabel("Hello, World! "));
```

Compile and run the program again. This will bring up a window containing the words "Hello, World!" instead of a picture.

You can also run the program from another directory instead of C:\JavaBook. For example, to run the program from the C:\Users\YourName directory on a PC, copy the blimp.png file to this directory and provide the complete pathname to the bin directory:

```
C:\Users\YourName> java -classpath C:\JavaBook\bin HelloWorld
```

This will bring up the same picture shown in Figure 1–3.

1.7   The Parts of a Java Program

A Java program defines a class that contains methods and statements. A class is declared using the keyword class. **Keywords** are reserved words in Java that are used to create a program and must be specified in lowercase. For example, the keyword public is used to specify that the contents are visible to everybody, whereas the private keyword restricts access. Java supports the concept of information hiding, so that a class, or parts of it, can be hidden. The name of the class, which is HelloWorld for this program, follows the class keyword:

```
public class HelloWorld {
}
```

A class is made up of **methods**. A method consists of a group of statements enclosed within braces { }. There can be any number of methods in a class. A **statement** specifies an action to be performed. Each statement ends with a semicolon. The words in each statement can be separated by any number of spaces; in general, though, only a single space is used. Note that a space should never be used *within* a word.

A special method called `main` is also present. The interpreter calls this method first, and thus it is always executed before any other method in the class:

```
public class HelloWorld {
  public static void main(String[] args) {
  }
}
```

The statements in a method are executed sequentially. This first statement in the `main` method of `HelloWorld` creates a window with the title "My First Program":

```
JFrame frame = new JFrame("My First Program");
```

The next statement adds a picture stored in the file `blimp.png` to this window:

```
frame.getContentPane().add(new JLabel(new ImageIcon("blimp.png")));
```

The last two statements set the window size and make the window visible on the computer screen:

```
frame.pack();
frame.setVisible(true);
```

Note that the order of the statements is important. If we rearrange them in some other way—say, by moving the last statement to the beginning—we create errors in the program. Try rearranging the sentences in this chapter randomly. Do they make any sense? Reorder the statements in the `HelloWorld` program, try to compile it, and note the errors.

Java programs also contain **comments**, which are statements ignored by the compiler. There are two types of comments. The first type starts with the symbol "//", which means that all words following this symbol to the end of the line should be ignored.

```
// compiler ignores the words in this line
but not the words in this line
```

The second type of comment starts with "/*" and ends with "*/." This type of comment can span several lines.

```
/* compiler ignores all the
words in these
three lines */
```

The following HelloWorld program has comments inserted:

```java
import javax.swing.*;

public class HelloWorld {
  public static void main(String[] args) {
    // create a window with the title "My First Program"
    JFrame frame = new JFrame("My First Program");

    // add the picture in file "blimp.png" to this window
    frame.getContentPane().add(new JLabel(new ImageIcon("blimp.png")));

    // set the window size so that the contents fit
    frame.pack();

    // make the window visible on the computer screen
    frame.setVisible(true);
  }
}
```

As you can see, comments make it easier to understand what a program does. By inserting meaningful comments, you can make it easier for others (and yourself) to read and use your programs.

1.8   Errors in Programs

As you begin to write programs, you will encounter three main types of errors (also called **bugs**): compiler errors, run-time errors, and logic errors. It is important to understand how to identify and correct these errors in your program. These errors are discussed in more detail next.

1.8.1   Compiler Errors

The compiler generates a class file only if it does not find any errors in the source code. Otherwise, the compiler prints out corresponding error messages and halts. These error messages are called **compiler errors**, **compile-time errors**, or **compilation errors**. For example, Java statements are terminated with a semicolon. If we incorrectly omitted a semicolon at the end of the statement, we would get a compiler error:

```java
frame.setVisible(true)    // ERROR!
```

Another example of a compiler error is a comment that is not closed correctly due to a space between the * and /, as shown here:

```
/* this comment has an error * /
```

Other causes of compiler errors include misspelled keywords, class, and method names, and incorrect punctuation. The compiler produces error messages that describe the locations and types of errors. The programmer must then correct the errors, recompile the program, and repeat the process until the program compiles successfully.

Some errors have been introduced intentionally into the HelloWorld program. The modified program follows:

```
/ * Program with errors */
import javax.swing.*;

public class HelloWorld {
  public static void main(String[] args) {
    JFrame frame = new JFrame(My First Program");
    frame.getContentPane().add(new JLabel(new ImageIcon("blimp.png")))
    frame.pack();
    frame.setVisible(true);
  }
```

When you compile this program, it will produce several errors. We next discuss each compiler error message, its meaning, and how it can be resolved.

Compiler Output 1

```
src\HelloWorld.java:1: class, interface, or enum expected
/ * Program with errors */
```

What the Compiler Means

There is an unidentified error on line 1.

What You Should Do

This compiler error message does not clearly describe that the error on line 1 of the program is caused by a badly formed comment. You need to determine what is wrong by examining the code on line 1. In this case, you must correct the open-comment sequence that has been mistyped with a space between the / and *.

Compiler Output 2

```
src\HelloWorld.java:6: ')' expected
    JFrame frame = new JFrame(My First Program");
src\HelloWorld.java:6: unclosed string literal
    JFrame frame = new JFrame(My First Program");
src\HelloWorld.java:6: not a statement
    JFrame frame = new JFrame(My First Program");
```

What the Compiler Means

There are three errors on line 6: a missing '),' an unclosed string literal, and an invalid statement.

What You Should Do

Sometimes the compiler can complain a little too much. There is a single error here, but multiple error messages are produced. A pair of quotes needed at the beginning of the words *My First Program* is missing on line 6. This single error creates three compiler error messages. Instead of attempting to resolve all of the error messages at one time, it is usually better to fix the errors corresponding to the first few error messages only and then recompile the program again.

Compiler Output 3

```
src\HelloWorld.java:7: ';' expected
    frame.getContentPane().add(new JLabel(new ImageIcon("blimp.png")))
```

What the Compiler Means

There should be a semicolon at the end of line 7.

What You Should Do

Insert a semicolon at the end of line 7.

Compiler Output 4

```
src\HelloWorld.java:10: reached end of file while parsing
    }
```

What the Compiler Means

It is likely that a closing brace is missing at the end of the program.

What You Should Do

Insert a closing brace after the last line of the program.

Compiler messages can be vague and confusing at times. As you gain experience in programming, you will learn how to interpret compiler error messages and correct your programs, as well as learn how to avoid these types of errors.

1.8.2   Run-Time Errors

An error that occurs while the program is executing is a run-time error. The computer can detect some types of run-time errors and terminate a program prematurely to display a diagnostic message. Other types of run-time errors do not stop program execution but produce incorrect program output. For example, in the HelloWorld program, if the file blimp.png cannot be found, an empty window is displayed. This is an example of a run-time error. A subtle error can occur in the program if you forget to insert the square brackets in the following statement:

```
public static void main(String[] args)
```

This omission does not produce a compiler error, but the program fails to run and crashes after displaying this mysterious error message:

```
Exception in thread "main" java.lang.NoSuchMethodError: main
```

1.8.3   Logic Errors

Logic errors occur when the algorithm used in the program is incorrect. With logic errors, the program executes normally, but its output is not correct. This type of error can be detected by manually computing the result and comparing it with the output of the program.

A **debugger** is a program that is used to identify the errors in another program. With a debugger, you can "step" through the program by executing one statement at a time and examining the results of each step. Debuggers have other sophisticated features as well, such as executing multiple statements at a time by setting breakpoints. Another way to debug a program is to trace the output by printing out intermediate results at different points in the program. However, you can prevent logic errors by designing and coding the algorithm carefully.

1.9   Summary

After reading this chapter, you will have gained a better understanding of what is inside a computer and how programs are executed. The structure and syntax of Java programs was explained briefly. An example program called HelloWorld was provided, which displayed a picture on the computer screen. The HelloWorld program gives you only a glimpse of what you can do with Java. As we dig deeper in subsequent chapters, you will get a better appreciation of how rich the Java language is and how powerful its programs are.

Exercises

1. Give examples of programs that you can use on your computer.

2. Explain each of these terms:
   a.   Algorithm
   b.   Java bytecode
   c.   Machine language
   d.   High-level programming language

3. What does a compiler do?

4. What is the JVM, and what does the Java interpreter do?

5. How is a .class file different from a .java file?

6. What is the software development method?

7. Explain the steps for creating and running a Java program.

8. Describe the three types of errors that can be present in a program.

9. Modify the HelloWorld program so that it displays a different picture on the screen.

10. List some applications that use Java. (You can search the Web for information on this.)

CHAPTER 2

Introduction to Classes and Objects

CHAPTER CONTENTS

The world is made up of objects, and Java programs are no different. In this chapter, you learn how to create objects from existing classes. We use Java 2D classes to create shapes such as rectangles, ellipses, curves, and lines. In subsequent chapters, you learn how to write your own classes.

Early on in this chapter, we will use a class called DrawingKit to create a window and display graphics on this window. The DrawingKit class has been provided for you to make it easy to display graphics on the screen as you start learning Java and is not a part of Java's standard class libraries. By the time you have completed Chapter 9, on GUI (Graphical User Interface) programming, you will be able to write code to display graphics without needing to use this class. So let's dive in, starting with the basics.

2.1   Thinking Objectively

Java is an *object-oriented* language. An object-oriented language allows a programmer to create and use *objects*. This, naturally, brings up the following question: What are objects?

An object is something that is real or *exists*—it has characteristics called *states*, and things it can do called *behaviors*. Each behavior changes the object's state. If you look around your room, what are some of the things that you see? Your list might include computers, books, cups, lamps, pencils—all of these are *objects*. A ball can have *states* such as its shape, color, and current position. It can have *behavior*, such as bouncing and rolling. A lamp can have certain states such as height, wattage, type, and whether it is lighted. It can possess behaviors such as turning on or off. Figure 2–1 gives more examples of states and behaviors.

In Java, objects exist while the program is running. As the program runs, an object can change state depending on its behavior. In addition, objects can interact with each other to do useful work.

2.2   Creating Objects

A **class** contains information that is needed to create an object. Suppose that you are working on a project. First, you will need to write down the project specifications—this is similar to writing a class. Next, you will use these specifications to build the project. Similarly, the class can be used to

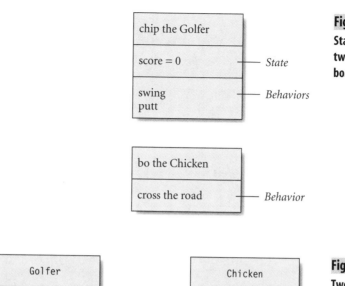

Figure 2–1

State and behaviors of two objects—chip and bo.

Figure 2–2

Two classes—Golfer and Chicken.

create an object. Figure 2–2 shows two classes: *Golfer* and *Chicken*. Java refers to states and behaviors as **fields** and **methods** respectively. A pair of parentheses () is added at the end of each method name in Figure 2–2 to indicate that this is a method.

There is an important difference between the classes in Figure 2–2 and the objects in Figure 2–1: *A class does not have specific values assigned to its fields, whereas an object does*. Therefore, the object *chip* has a value assigned to its *score* field. Different objects of the same class can have different field values. Figure 2–3 shows several objects created from the *Golfer* class.

The following statement creates an object (called *chip*) of the *Golfer* class:

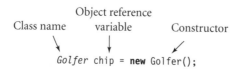

Figure 2–3

Creating three objects (chip, sally, and phil) from class Golfer.

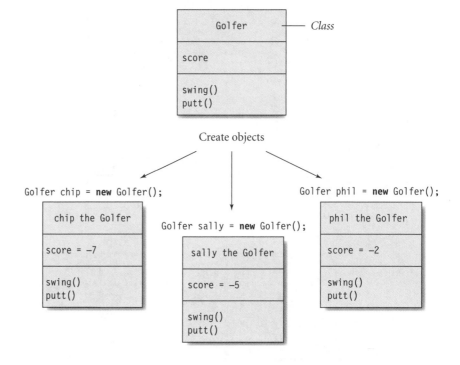

The keyword new is reserved in Java and is used along with a *constructor* to create a new object. The **constructor** is a special method that knows how to create an object. The name of the constructor is the same as the name of the class and is followed by a pair of parentheses. The new object is put in a part of the computer's memory known as the **heap**.

> The **heap** is an area in the computer's memory that can be used by a program when it executes. A program creates an object and stores it on the heap using the new operator. A special program called "garbage collector" runs periodically to remove objects that are no longer needed by the program.

You cannot see the object named *chip* because it is stored inside the computer; however, you can interact with this object by printing some information about it or sending it some data through the console. Later in this chapter, you will learn how to use the DrawingKit class to draw graphics objects on the screen so that you can view them. Here, *chip* is called an **object reference variable** (or more simply, a **reference variable**) because it refers to a particular object. An object of a class is also called an **instance** of that class. Figure 2–3 shows three instances of the *Golfer* class that are assigned to the reference variables *chip*, *sally*, and *phil*. Fields are also known as **instance variables** because each instance keeps a separate copy of its field values.

2.3 How Methods Work

An object calls its methods to do some work. For example, the object *chip* calls its *swing* method, and *bo* calls its *crossTheRoad* method, as shown here:

chip.swing();

bo.crossTheRoad();

Objects can call their methods as follows:

dot

objectName.methodName();

The names of the object and the method are separated by a dot. When a method is called, some data might be displayed on the screen, or changes might be made to the object's fields. For example, after *chip* calls the method *swing*, its *score* field is updated.

Java 2D is a Java toolkit that is used for drawing two-dimensional graphical shapes. It has several classes, a few of which are `Rectangle2D.Float`, `RoundRectangle2D.Float`, `Line2D.Float`, `Ellipse2D.Float`, `BasicStroke`, and `Font`. In the following sections, you will learn how to use these classes to create graphical objects such as rectangles and lines. We start by discussing some basics about how graphics are drawn.

2.4 The Computer Screen

The screen on a computer monitor contains millions of **pixels**. A pixel is a tiny, colored dot that is used to display a point in an image. The pixels are arranged very closely together in the form of a grid. Although a single pixel is hardly visible, groups of these can be combined to form images and text on the computer screen. In Figure 2–4, suppose that each square represents

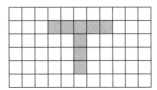

Figure 2–4

An enlarged view of pixels on a computer screen.

a pixel. The squares that are colored blue form the letter "T." Colored pixels form graphics and text similarly on the screen.

Graphics are drawn inside a *window* on the screen. Later in the chapter, you will learn how to draw a window using the class DrawingKit. To draw a graphical shape, you must specify the location and size of this shape inside the window. We discuss window coordinates next.

2.4.1   Window Coordinates

The window uses the Cartesian coordinate system, in which the x- and y-coordinates of points must be specified. A point in the window is represented by its x- and y-coordinates as (x, y). The top-left corner of the window is the origin $(0, 0)$. The values of the x-coordinates increase from left to right as in a typical graph, whereas the values of the y-coordinates increase from top to bottom. Figure 2–5 represents a window 300 pixels wide and 300 pixels high. The bottom-right corner of this window is the point $(300, 300)$. Using this coordinate system, you can calculate the coordinates of the points in the window where you want to draw the graphics.

This leads to an important question: How large is this window on the screen in inches? This depends on the screen **resolution**, which is the number of pixels in a given area on the screen. For example, 300 pixels will be displayed as 12 inches on a 25 pixels/inch screen, but only 3 inches on a 100 pixels/inch screen. This means that a window that is 500 pixels high and

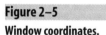

Figure 2–5

Window coordinates.

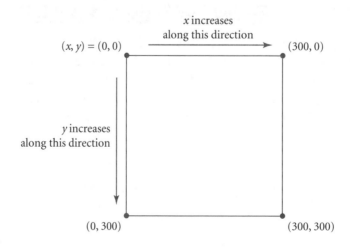

500 pixels wide will have a height and width of 5 inches on a 100 pixels/inch screen.

In the examples in this chapter, we draw objects in a square window with a width and height of 500 pixels. Later, you will see how to create a window of a specific size.

Example 1

Find the (x, y) coordinates of the points labeled A, B, and C in Figure 2–6. How many inches long is a line joining the points A and B on a screen with a resolution of 72 pixels/inch?

Solution: Apply basic graph theory. For each point, check its x- and y-coordinates. For example, the x- and y-coordinates of point A are 100 and 200, respectively. Similarly, read the values of the coordinates of points B and C from the grid. The coordinates are A (100, 200), B (100, 400), and C

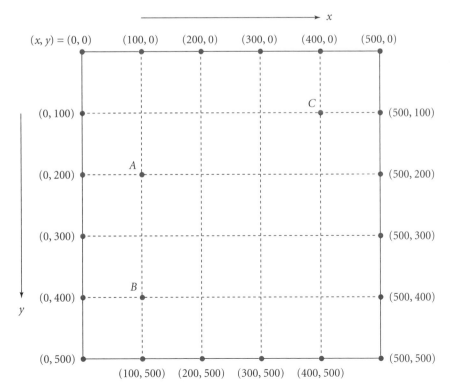

Figure 2–6

Points *A*, *B*, and *C* on a grid.

(400, 100). The line joining *A* and *B* is 200 pixels, and there are 72 pixels in one inch; thus its length is 200/72, or about 2.78 inches. ■

2.5   Creating a Rectangle Object

Java 2D's `Rectangle2D.Float` class is used to create rectangles. Figure 2–7(a) shows the fields in this class. Figure 2–7(b) shows how an instance can be created using a constructor in this class. (This class also has several methods, which are not shown here.)

The fields x and y are the (*x*, *y*) coordinates of the rectangle's top-left corner inside the window. For example, to create a rectangle called rect with its top-left corner at the point (50, 100), and a width and height of 200 and 300, respectively, we can write:

```
Rectangle2D.Float rect = new Rectangle2D.Float(50, 100, 200, 300);
```

This is similar to how we created the objects named *chip* and *bo*, except that we are also assigning some values to rect's fields when creating it. The Rectangle2D.Float constructor takes four numbers as input, called **arguments**. Using arguments, we can create objects with different values for their instance variables. By changing the arguments 50, 100, 200, and 300 of the constructor, you can create a rectangle of a different size at another position in the window.

```
Rectangle2D.Float rect = new Rectangle2D.Float(5, 10, 400, 300);
```

Rectangle2D.Float	
x y width height	

(a)

(*x*, *y*)

Height

←Width→

rect the Rectangle2D.Float
x = 5 y = 10 width = 400 height = 300

(b)

Figure 2–7

(a) Fields in the `Rectangle2D.Float` class, and (b) creating an instance of this class.

The order in which the arguments appear is very important! The first argument is the value of x, the second argument is the value of y, and the remaining two arguments are the values of width and height, in that order. The name of this object is rect, but you can choose another name. The names of each of the reference variables in a program should be unique. We discuss the rules and conventions for naming variables in the next chapter.

2.6   The DrawingKit Class

A class called DrawingKit is provided for you in the JavaBook\com\programwith-java\basic folder on the CD-ROM. Using this class, you can draw a window on the screen and add graphics to it. Internally, DrawingKit uses existing classes in Swing and Java 2D to create a window and add graphics to it. (Swing is a Java toolkit that is used to create graphical user interfaces, or GUIs.) You have to know only how to use the methods in the DrawingKit class, and not its internal details.

Figure 2–8(a) shows a constructor and some of the methods in DrawingKit. Figure 2–8(b) shows a window. You can use an instance of class DrawingKit to create a window, and draw and color graphical shapes on this window.

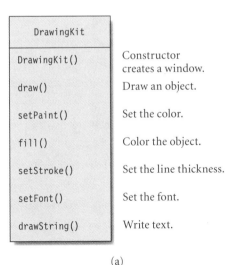

DrawingKit	
DrawingKit()	Constructor creates a window.
draw()	Draw an object.
setPaint()	Set the color.
fill()	Color the object.
setStroke()	Set the line thickness.
setFont()	Set the font.
drawString()	Write text.

(a)

(b)

Figure 2–8

(a) A constructor and some methods in class DrawingKit. (b) You can create this window, and then draw and color shapes on it using an instance of class DrawingKit.

Note that when you click at any point in this window, the *x*- and *y*-coordinates of that point will be displayed on the console.

2.6.1   Compiling and Running Your Program with Class DrawingKit

To run the programs correctly, you must put the DrawingKit.java file in the correct directory. We set up the JavaBook directory in the previous chapter to run the HelloWorld program. Create a directory named com inside src, and another directory named programwithjava inside com, and finally a directory named basic inside programwithjava. Copy the file DrawingKit.java from the CD-ROM into the JavaBook\src\com\programwithjava\basic directory in your computer. The directory structure is shown in Figure 2–9.

Copy the program shown in Example 2 into a file called RectangleDemo.java. Place this file in the src folder. This program uses the DrawingKit class in the DrawingKit.java file. You should provide the names of both files when you compile the program. On a PC, use:

```
C:\JavaBook> javac -d bin src\com\programwithjava\basic\DrawingKit.java
src\RectangleDemo.java
```

Figure 2–9

The directory structure to use for your programs.

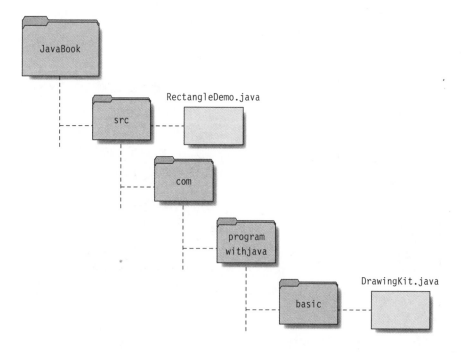

You will compile it similarly on a Macintosh:

```
computer:~/JavaBook YourName$ javac -d bin
src/com/programwithjava/basic/DrawingKit.java  src/RectangleDemo.java
```

If you get any compilation errors, check the directory structure. Also, check that you are running the preceding command in the JavaBook directory. If there are no errors, look inside the bin directory. You will see that a com\programwithjava\basic directory has been created and that the DrawingKit.class file has been placed in it. In addition, the bin directory should contain the RectangleDemo.class file. To run this program on a PC, type the following into the JavaBook directory:

```
C:\JavaBook> java -classpath bin RectangleDemo
```

Use the same command to run the program on a Macintosh.

It is important to note that the name of the file should match that of the class defined in it. Thus, if the class is called Foo, it should be placed in a file named Foo.java.

Example 2

This example shows how to draw and display a rectangle with its top-left corner at (50, 100) and a width and height of 200 and 100, respectively. The following code draws a window on the computer screen, and then displays the rectangle inside this window. When you compile and run this program, you will see a rectangle inside the window similar to the one in Figure 2–10.

```java
import java.awt.*;
import java.awt.geom.*;
import com.programwithjava.basic.DrawingKit;

public class RectangleDemo {
   public static void main(String[] args) {
     DrawingKit dk = new DrawingKit("Rectangle");
     Rectangle2D.Float rect = new Rectangle2D.Float(50, 100, 200, 100);
     dk.draw(rect);
   }
}
```

Congratulations! You have started on an exciting journey to create fantastic artwork.

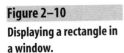

Figure 2–10

Displaying a rectangle in a window.

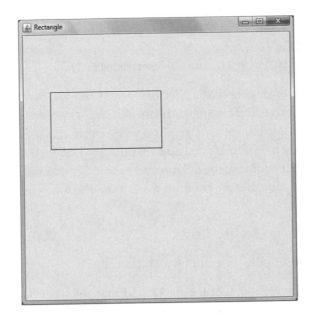

2.6.2   Nuts and Bolts of the Program

We used several new Java keywords, such as **public**, **static**, and **class**, in Example 2. Rest assured that these are explained in detail in later chapters. For now, a brief explanation of the Java statements used in this program follows.

Java contains many classes that have the necessary information for implementing graphics. These classes are organized into *packages* for convenience. To use a class, you have to specify the package in which it is placed. For example, the `java.awt.geom` package contains the class `Rectangle2D.Float` and many others that are used to create geometrical shapes. The `import` keyword lets you use the classes in this package:

```
import java.awt.geom.*;
```

This imports the `DrawingKit` class from the `com.programwithjava.basic` package:

```
import com.programwithjava.basic.DrawingKit;
```

A commonly used package is `java.awt`, which contains many Java 2D classes (such as `BasicStroke`, `Color`, and `Font`). We will use it in our programs when required.

The next statement declares a class named RectangleDemo:

```
public class RectangleDemo
```

You can change the name of the class to another if you wish. Two keywords used here are public and class. Remember that keywords must be copied *exactly* as shown with all letters in lowercase because Java is case-sensitive.

Every program must contain a method called main. The computer starts executing the program from the start of the main method. It has to be declared as shown here:

```
public static void main(String[] args) { }
```

A bare-bones Java program that does not perform any actions contains an empty main method inside a class, as shown here:

```
public class RectangleDemo {
  public static void main(String[] args) {
      // your code goes here
  }
}
```

Now let us examine the code inside the example's main method. These lines create the various graphical objects such as the window and the graphics inside this window. The following statement creates a window on the computer screen using the DrawingKit constructor:

```
DrawingKit dk = new DrawingKit("Rectangle");
```

We use this instance dk of class DrawingKit to draw and color graphics inside this window. The title on the window is Rectangle. You can change this title, and the new title will appear on the window. For example, to give the window a title of My First Program, you write:

```
DrawingKit dk = new DrawingKit("My First Program");
```

The next statement creates a rectangle:

```
Rectangle2D.Float rect = new Rectangle2D.Float(50, 100, 200, 100);
```

The last statement draws the rectangle rect in the window:

```
dk.draw(rect);
```

Here, the instance dk of class DrawingKit calls its draw method to draw the object in the window. The variable that references the object to be drawn is used as an argument to the draw method. It should be specified within parentheses, as shown.

2.6.3   Coloring a Rectangle

A shape can be colored by using DrawingKit's setPaint and fill methods. The object dk calls the setPaint method with a color as the argument. It then calls the fill method with the variable that references the object to be colored as its argument.

Suppose you would like to color the rectangle created in the previous example with the color *red*. To do so, you must add these two lines to the code in the RectangleDemo.java file below the dk.draw statement:

```
dk.setPaint(Color.red);
dk.fill(rect);
```

The argument Color.red is a constant value defined in Java 2D's Color class. After adding these two lines, compile and run the program again. You will see the rectangle is colored red on the screen.

There are many other colors that can be used, such as white, gray, lightGray, black, pink, yellow, green, orange, cyan, blue, darkGray, and magenta. If you want to color the rectangle gray instead, the code becomes:

```
dk.setPaint(Color.gray);
dk.fill(rect);
```

Try using other colors and see how the rectangle's color changes!

2.7   Creating and Displaying Graphics Objects

The Rectangle2D.Float class has been used to draw rectangles with sharp corners. Another useful class is RoundRectangle2D.Float. This class is used to draw rectangles with *rounded* corners. Like the Rectangle2D.Float class, this class also takes the x- and y-coordinates, which specify the position of the rectangle's top-left corner, as well as its width and height as arguments. The difference is that RoundRectangle2D.Float takes two additional arguments called *corner width* and *corner height*, which specify the width and height of each corner, respectively. Thus, the following line of code creates a rectangle called rectRounded positioned at (10, 20) with width 30, height 40, corner width 15, and corner height 25:

```
RoundRectangle2D.Float rectRounded = new RoundRectangle2D.Float(10, 20, 30,
40, 15, 25);
```

As an exercise, modify the RectangleDemo class to create rectangles with different corner widths and heights.

2.7.1 Drawing and Coloring an Ellipse

Next, you learn how to draw an ellipse (oval). The class that can be used to create this shape is called Ellipse2D.Float. In this statement, four arguments are passed to the Ellipse2D.Float constructor:

```
Ellipse2D.Float myellipse = new Ellipse2D.Float(50, 100, 300, 200);
```

This creates an ellipse called myellipse that fits perfectly in a rectangle that has its top-left corner at (50, 100) and has a width of 300 and a height of 200. The first two arguments are the *x*- and *y*-coordinates of the rectangle's top-left corner, and the third and fourth arguments are the *width* and *height* of the ellipse, respectively. The relation between the arguments to the Ellipse2D.Float constructor and the resulting shape are shown in Figure 2–11.

If the width is set equal to height, the resulting shape is a circle. The ellipse can be drawn on the screen by using DrawingKit's draw method:

```
dk.draw(myellipse);
```

Like the rectangle shape drawn earlier, it can be colored by using the setPaint and fill methods. For example, to color the ellipse magenta, use these two lines:

```
dk.setPaint(Color.magenta);
dk.fill(myellipse);
```

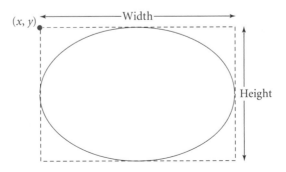

Figure 2–11

Drawing an ellipse using the Ellipse2D.Float constructor.

2.7.2   Drawing a Line

A line can be drawn using the Line2D.Float class. The *x*- and *y*-coordinates of the endpoints must be specified. The following code shows how to use the Line2D.Float constructor to create a Line2D.Float object called myLine that joins the points (10, 20) and (40, 50):

```
Line2D.Float myLine = new Line2D.Float(10, 20, 40, 50);
```

The first two arguments specify the coordinates of the starting point, and the next two arguments give the coordinates of the ending point. To display a line of a particular color (say, magenta), use the setPaint and draw methods:

```
dk.setPaint(Color.magenta);
dk.draw(myLine);
```

Attempting to fill a line will display the same result as drawing it.

2.7.3   Changing the Line Thickness

The thickness of a line (and other details) can be set using a class called BasicStroke. The only argument to the BasicStroke constructor is the width of a line. The following code shows how to create a stroke called myStroke with a width of 10:

```
BasicStroke myStroke = new BasicStroke(10);
dk.setStroke(myStroke);
```

After these statements are executed, graphics objects will be drawn with a line thickness of 10. If the number 10 is changed to a larger value, a thicker line will be drawn.

Example 3

This program shows how to change the line width using the constructor of class BasicStroke, and the setStroke method of DrawingKit. The first ellipse is drawn with a line width of 1.0, which is the default width. The second ellipse has the line width set to 8.0 using setStroke.

```
import java.awt.*;
import java.awt.geom.*;
import com.programwithjava.basic.DrawingKit;
```

```
public class TwoEllipsesDemo {
  public static void main(String[] args) {
    DrawingKit dk = new DrawingKit("Two Ellipses");

    // create and draw the first ellipse with the default line width
    Ellipse2D.Float one = new Ellipse2D.Float(50, 100, 50, 60);
    dk.draw(one);

    Ellipse2D.Float two = new Ellipse2D.Float(300, 100, 50, 60);

   // change the line thickness to 8
    BasicStroke s2 = new BasicStroke(8);
    dk.setStroke(s2);

    // draw the second ellipse with the new line width
    dk.draw(two);
  }
}
```

The ellipses are shown in Figure 2–12.   ∎

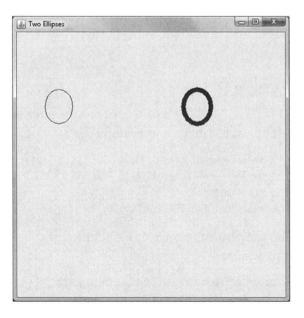

Figure 2–12
Two ellipses drawn using lines of different widths.

2.7.4   Writing Text

Text can be written on the screen using DrawingKit's drawString method. The arguments to this method are the text that you want to write and the coordinates of the starting location. For example, to write the word "Hello" starting at the point (50, 100) on the window, use the following statement:

```
dk.drawString("Hello", 50, 100);
```

Note that the word to be displayed is enclosed in double quotes. A group of words that is enclosed in double quotes is called a **string literal**. The name, style, and size of the font used for the string literal should be specified. To do this, create a new font using a constructor in a class called Font:

```
Font myFont = new Font("Times New Roman", Font.ITALIC, 12);
```

This creates a new font object of the given name, style, and size. The first argument is the name of a font, such as "Times New Roman", "Arial", "Lucida Sans Regular", "Lucida Sans Bold", or some other font. The second argument is the style, and it can be Font.PLAIN, Font.ITALIC, Font.BOLD, or Font.ITALIC | Font.BOLD. The third argument is the font size. The setFont method is called by dk to set the font to this new font:

```
dk.setFont(myFont);
```

The following example shows how you can use it in your code.

Example 4

This example shows how to write to the screen. Insert the following code after the last statement in Example 3:

```
// Write the words "Two Ellipses"
Font myfont = new Font("ARIAL", Font.BOLD, 32);
dk.setFont(myfont);
dk.drawString("Two Ellipses", 100, 300);
```

You can also color the ellipses in different colors by adding the following statements:

```
// color ellipse called "one" with magenta
dk.setPaint(Color.magenta);
```

```
dk.fill(one);

// color ellipse called "two" with yellow
dk.setPaint(Color.yellow);
dk.fill(two);
```

When you run your program, the window shown in Figure 2–13 appears on the screen. ∎

2.7.5 Drawing a Curve

A quadratic curve can be drawn using the QuadCurve2D.Float class. The setCurve method of this class takes the *x*- and *y*-coordinates of three points as arguments. These statements draw a curve joining the points (10, 20) and (100, 200) through the point (80, 90):

```
QuadCurve2D.Float curve1 = new QuadCurve2D.Float();
curve1.setCurve(10, 20, 80, 90, 100, 200);
dk.draw(curve1);
```

We use this method in the next example to draw a spaceship.

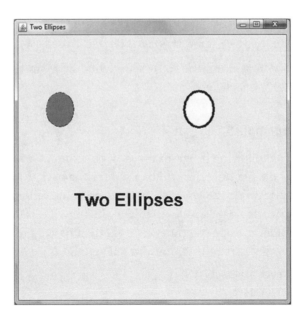

Figure 2–13
Writing the words "Two Ellipses" in a window.

2.7.6 Drawing an Image Stored in a File

It is easy to draw an image from a file using DrawingKit. You must use the drawPicture method of this class and specify the name of the file as an argument to this method. For example, the following statement draws the picture in the file clouds.jpg on the screen:

```
dk.drawPicture("clouds.jpg");
```

This file should be present in the working directory, where you are compiling your program. The working directory can be different on different computers (for example, C:\JavaBook on a PC or /Users/YourName/JavaBook on a Macintosh), but Java will pick up the file from the correct directory. This way the program will run correctly on different computers without your having to change the file pathname. We are using the **relative pathname** of the file because it is specified relative to the working directory. For example, if you moved the file into the C:/JavaBook/image directory, you would use the relative pathname image/.

The next example shows how you can use the drawPicture method.

2.7.7 Changing the Window Size

The default window size is 500 by 500. If you want to create a window of a different size (say, 800 by 200), you can do so by specifying it in the following manner using a DrawingKit constructor:

```
DrawingKit dk = new DrawingKit("title", 800, 200);
```

The first number (800) is the window's width and the second number (200) is its height.

Example 5

The following program draws a spaceship in a window. The picture stored in the file space.jpg will be used for the background. Create a folder called image inside the JavaBook directory on your computer. Copy the space.jpg file from the JavaBook/image folder on the CD-ROM into the JavaBook/image folder in your computer. We will then draw graphical shapes on this background using the various Java 2D methods we discussed earlier.

```
import java.awt.*;
import java.awt.geom.*;
import com.programwithjava.basic.DrawingKit;

public class SpaceShip {
```

```
public static void main(String[] args) {
  DrawingKit dk = new DrawingKit("Spaceship", 1200, 900);

  // draw the picture
  dk.drawPicture("image/space.jpg");

  // draw the body
  BasicStroke stroke1 = new BasicStroke(2);
  dk.setStroke(stroke1);
  dk.setPaint(Color.red);
  QuadCurve2D.Float curve1 = new QuadCurve2D.Float();
  curve1.setCurve(500, 500, 600, 400, 700, 500);
  dk.draw(curve1);
  QuadCurve2D.Float curve2 = new QuadCurve2D.Float();
  curve2.setCurve(500, 500, 600, 610, 700, 500);
  dk.draw(curve2);
  dk.setPaint(Color.yellow);
  dk.fill(curve1);
  dk.fill(curve2);

  // draw a window
  dk.setPaint(Color.lightGray);
  Ellipse2D.Float curve3 = new Ellipse2D.Float(580, 425, 50, 60);
  dk.fill(curve3);
  dk.setPaint(Color.red);
  dk.draw(curve3);

  // draw the wings
  Ellipse2D.Float ellipse1 = new Ellipse2D.Float(660, 495, 80, 15);
  dk.fill(ellipse1);
  BasicStroke stroke2 = new BasicStroke(22);
  dk.setStroke(stroke2);
  Line2D.Float line1 = new Line2D.Float(685, 475, 700, 455);
  dk.draw(line1);
  Line2D.Float line2 = new Line2D.Float(685, 530, 710, 555);
  dk.draw(line2);

  // name the spaceship
  Font font1 = new Font("ARIAL", Font.ITALIC, 13);
  dk.setFont(font1);
  dk.drawString("STARSHIP", 570, 520);
  }
}
```

Compile and run the program. This draws the spaceship in a window, as shown in Figure 2–14.

Figure 2–14

Drawing a picture and graphical shapes in a window using DrawingKit.

space.jpg © Adrian Neiderhäuser, 123RF.com

2.8   Writing to the Console

We have only seen examples of graphical programs so far. The next program that we explore does not use graphics; it simply displays text messages on the console. This type of console output is especially useful for debugging a program. To display the string literal "This is text output," you can write:

```
System.out.print("This is text output");
```

Here, System.out refers to the console. This calls the print method to display messages on the console. Another way to display messages is to use the println method. If there are multiple calls to this method, each message is displayed on a new line.

Example 6

Write a program to display the following two lines of text:

> Text output is useful for debugging programs.

> Graphics are more fun, though.

Solution: Note that only two println statements are needed to print out these two lines, and they can be placed directly inside main. We do not have to create the window here because no graphics are being drawn. If you replace the println method with print, the output will be displayed on a single line. Be sure to place the text within quotes on a single line, because a compiler error will occur otherwise.

```
public class ConsoleOutputDemo {
  public static void main(String[] args) {
    System.out.println("Text output is useful for debugging programs.");
    System.out.println("Graphics are more fun, though.");
  }
}
```

2.9 Summary

This chapter described a subset of Java 2D graphics to create simple graphical shapes and text in different fonts. These shapes are rectangles, lines, ellipses, and curves. You can create a window, and display and color graphical shapes using the DrawingKit class. Furthermore, DrawingKit also lets you load images from files into a window. We will use this background in Java 2D to explore Java in subsequent chapters, using colorful and fun examples.

Graphics Statements

A summary of the Java statements discussed in this chapter to draw a window and other graphics is provided here for your reference.

Create a window   The following statement creates a window with a default width and height of 500:

```
DrawingKit dk = new DrawingKit();
```

The following statement creates a window with the specified string literal set as the title of the window:

```
DrawingKit dk = new DrawingKit("Two Ellipses");
```

The following statement creates a window with the specified title, width, and height:

```
DrawingKit dk = new DrawingKit("Two Ellipses", width, height);
```

Draw a rectangle   To draw a rectangle called rect1 of the given width and height with its top-left corner coordinates at the point (x, y), use the following statement:

```
Rectangle2D.Float rect1 = new Rectangle2D.Float(x, y, width, height);
dk.draw(rect1);
```

Draw an ellipse   The following statements draw an ellipse called myellipse of the specified width and height and positioned at (x, y):

```
Ellipse2D.Float myellipse = new Ellipse2D.Float(x, y, width, height);
dk.draw(myellipse);
```

Draw a line   The following statements draw a line called myLine:

```
Line2D.Float myLine = new Line2D.Float(x1, y1, x2, y2);
dk.draw(myLine);
```

The first two arguments (x1, y1) specify the coordinates of the starting point, and the next two arguments (x2, y2) give the coordinates of the ending point.

Draw a rounded rectangle   To draw a rectangle with rounded corners called rectRounded having the given width and height, with its top-left corner coordinates at the point (x, y) and the specified corner width and height, use the following statement:

```
RoundRectangle2D.Float rectRounded = new RoundRectangle2D.Float(x, y,
width, height, cornerWidth, cornerHeight);
```

Color a shape   To color a Java 2D graphics object called shape1 a given color (say, red), use the following statements:

```
dk.setPaint(Color.red);
dk.fill(shape1);
```

Write text   Write the string literal "Hello there" starting at the position (x, y) with the following statements:

```
dk.drawString("Hello there", x, y);
```

Change font   To change the font to Arial with style Bold and size 12, use the following statements:

```
Font myfont = new Font("ARIAL", Font.BOLD, 12);
dk.setFont(myfont);
```

Change line thickness   The following statements change the thickness of the lines used to draw shapes:

```
BasicStroke myStroke = new BasicStroke(thickness);
dk.setStroke(myStroke);
```

Draw an image   The following statement draws an image from the specified file on the window:

```
dk.drawPicture("space.jpg");
```

Exercises

1. Explain briefly:

   a.   What is a class?

   b.   How can you create an object of a class?

   c.   What is a reference variable?

   d.   How is a class different from an object?

   e.   What is an instance of a class?

   f.   What is a method?

   g.   What is a constructor?

   h.   What is a package?

   i.   What is the main method?

2. Write a program that uses the System.out.println method to print out your first and last names on different lines.

3. Write a program that uses the System.out.print method to print out the current date and time.

4. Fix the errors in the following program so that it compiles and runs correctly:

```
public class ProgramWithErrors {
    public void main(String[] args) {
        System.out.println("Program runs correctly")
      }
    }
```

5. Fix the errors in the following program so that it compiles and runs correctly:

```
public class AnotherProgramWithErrors {
    public static void main(String args) {
        System.out.println("Program runs correctly");
}
```

Graphics Problems

6. Give the statements needed to create an object of the following classes:

    a. `Rectangle2D.Float`

    b. `Ellipse2D.Float`

    c. `Line2D.Float`

    d. `QuadCurve2D.Float`

7. What do the following methods do?

    a. `draw` method of `DrawingKit`

    b. `fill` method of `DrawingKit`

    c. `drawPicture` method of `DrawingKit`

    d. `setCurve` method of `QuadCurve2D.Float`

8. Fix the order of statements in the following program so that it draws a red ellipse on the screen:

```
import java.awt.*;
import java.awt.geom.*;
import com.programwithjava.basic.DrawingKit;

public class EllipseDemo {
    public static void main(String[] args) {
        DrawingKit dk = new DrawingKit("Ellipse");
        dk.draw(rect);
        Ellipse2D.Float rect = new Ellipse2D.Float(50, 100, 200, 100);
        dk.fill(rect);
        dk.setPaint(Color.red);
    }
}
```

9. Fix the compilation errors in this program:

```
import java.awt.*;
import java.awt.geom.*;
import com.programwithjava.basic.DrawingKit;

public class RectangleDemo {
    DrawingKit dk = new DrawingKit("Ellipse");
    Rectangle2DFloat rect = new Rectangle2DFloat(50, 100, 200);
    dk.draw(rect1);
    BasicStroke stroke = new BasicStroke(22);
    dk.setStroke(stroke);
```

```
        dk.setPaint(Color = blue);
        line1 = new Line2D.Float(285, 175, 300, 155);
        dk.draw(line1);
    }
```

10. Write a program to draw a rectangle inside a window with its top-left corner at (30, 50) and a width and height of 100 and 300, respectively. Color this rectangle yellow.

11. Repeat the previous problem to create the rectangle with rounded corners.

12. Write a program to draw a line inside a window joining the points (0, 0) and (500, 500) with thickness 7. Color this line blue.

13. Write a program to draw an ellipse having width 50 and height 60 that just fits in a rectangle with its top-left corner at (100, 100).

14. Write a program to draw a curve inside a window joining the points (30, 100) and (100, 300), and passing through the point (50, 150).

15. Write a program to write your name inside a window in italics using Arial font of size 15.

16. Write a program to draw a robot using the Java statements discussed in this chapter, and your imagination.

17. Repeat the previous problem to draw a vehicle of your choice.

Further Reading

For more information on Java, the interested reader can consult the references [1–5]. [1] is a set of online Java tutorials. You can find detailed information on other Java 2D classes and advanced graphics techniques in [6].

References

1. "The Java™ Tutorials." Web.
   <http://download.oracle.com/javase/tutorial/>.

2. Guzdial, Mark, and Barbara Ericson. *Introduction to Computing and Programming in Java: A Multimedia Approach.* Upper Saddle River, NJ: Pearson Prentice Hall, 2007. Print.

3. Eckel, Bruce. *Thinking in Java.* Upper Saddle River, NJ: Prentice Hall, 2006. Print.

4. Anderson, Julie, and Herve Franceschi. *Java 6 Illuminated: An Active Learning Approach.* Sudbury, MA: Jones and Bartlett, 2008. Print.

5. Sierra, Kathy, and Bert Bates. *Head First Java.* Sebastopol, CA: O'Reilly, 2005. Print.

6. Knudsen, Jonathan. *Java 2D Graphics.* Beijing: O'Reilly, 1999. Print.

CHAPTER 3

Programming Basics

CHAPTER CONTENTS

In this chapter, we present some vocabulary and fundamental concepts concerning Java programs. These will help you gain a deeper understanding of the graphical programs written in the previous chapter, as well as lay the foundation for new material that will be covered in subsequent chapters. We also provide some background on digital images: how image data is stored in a computer, and some of the classes that can be used to display and manipulate an image.

3.1   Primitive Data Types

You saw examples of object reference variables in the previous chapter. These variables store references to objects. You can create a different type of variable in your program to store a simple value (such as a number, alphabet letter, or symbol) that is not an object by using Java's built-in data types called **primitive data types**. The primitive data types are **int**, **byte**, **short**, **long**, **float**, **double**, **char**, and **boolean**. A variable of any of these data types is called a **primitive variable**. We explain primitive data types in more detail as follows:

> **Integers:** An integer is a number that can be written without using a decimal point or a fraction. Examples of integers are numbers such as 23, −51, and 200. Integers can be represented using these primitive data types: `int`, `byte`, `short`, and `long`.
>
> **Floating-point numbers:** Numbers such as 3.2 and 5.41 that contain a decimal point are floating-point numbers, not integers. Just as there are different data types for integer numbers, there are two types for floating-point numbers: `float` and `double`.
>
> **Characters:** A character is a single letter of the alphabet, such as "A," a digit, such as "1," or a symbol, such as "%." The `char` data type is used to hold a character.
>
> **True/false values:** The `boolean` type is different from all of the others because it does not hold a number or a character. Instead, it represents one of two values: `true` or `false`.

You might be wondering why multiple types such as `byte`, `short`, `int`, and `long` are used for integers, and `float` and `double` are used for floating-point numbers. The difference between them lies in the *size* of data they can hold.

For bytes, the numbers must lie within the range −128 to 127. This requires only 8 bits of memory. The short data type is used for integers that lie in the range −32,768 to 32,767, and it takes up 16 bits of memory. A variable of type int can hold integer numbers in the range −2,147,483,648 to 2,147,483,647. It takes 32 bits to store numbers in this range. The long data type is used for very large integers, with a size of up to 64 bits, in the range −9,223,372,036,854,775,808 to 9,223,372,036,854,775,807! A float takes less memory (32 bits) than a double (64 bits), and the range varies. A char takes up 16 bits. When a primitive variable is declared, a specific amount of memory is reserved for it depending on its type. If you know the range of values that a variable will hold in your program, you can declare it with the appropriate data type for that range. The most commonly used data types are int for integer values and double for floating-point numbers.

3.1.1 Declaring and Initializing Primitive Variables

A primitive variable is declared by specifying its data type followed by its name. The following statement declares an integer variable called num1:

```
int num1;
```

Note that the new keyword is not needed for primitives, and memory is reserved automatically for the variable num1 when it is declared.

Before a variable can be used, it must be assigned an initial value—this is known as **initialization**. The following statement initializes the variable num1 to the value 10:

```
num1 = 10;
```

A variable can be declared and initialized in a single statement. So we can also write:

```
int num1 = 10;
```

The following statement declares a floating-point variable of type float called num2 and initializes it to the value 1020.43:

```
float num2 = 1020.43f;
```

Although a float requires a suffix of letter "f" after the number, a double does not. Therefore, the following is valid:

```
double num3 = 32.56;
```

A `long` requires a suffix of letter "L" after the number:

```
long num4 = 9000000000L;
```

Character data must be enclosed in single quotes. In the following statement, the letter A is stored in a variable called ch1 of type `char`:

```
char ch1 = 'A';
```

You cannot store multiple characters in a `char` variable. The following statement is incorrect:

```
char ch2 = 'AB'; // error
```

A `boolean` variable can be either true or false. The variable `flag` is declared and initialized to the value `true` in the following statement:

```
boolean flag = true;
```

These variables `num1`, `num2`, `num3`, `num4`, `ch1`, and `flag` are primitive variables.

3.2   Identifiers

An **identifier** is the name given to a variable, class, method, or package. It can contain any number of digits and alphabetic letters, but there are a few simple rules that must be followed:

- An identifier cannot contain spaces.
- An identifier should start with a letter and not a number or symbol; an exception to this rule is that an identifier can begin with the symbols _ or $. For example, the identifiers `star4` and `_4star` are valid, but `4star` is invalid.
- You can use underscore characters within identifiers, as in `my_score`.
- Identifiers are case sensitive: `upper` is not the same as `uPper`.
- You cannot use a Java keyword as an identifier. These keywords are shown in Table 3–1.

In addition to the preceding rules, you should follow these conventions as well:

- Use identifiers that are short and meaningful.
- Do not use a $ or _ to start an identifier, even though this is allowed.
- When you create an identifier by combining multiple words, capitalize the first letter of each of the words that follow, such as in `myPicture`, `pixelColor`, and `numberOfPixels`.

TABLE 3–1 Java Keywords		
abstract	final	public
assert	finally	return
boolean	float	short
break	for	static
byte	goto	strictfp
case	if	super
catch	implements	switch
char	import	synchronized
class	instanceof	this
const	int	throw
continue	interface	throws
default	long	transient
do	native	try
double	new	void
else	package	volatile
enum	private	while
extends	protected	

3.3   Literals

A **literal** is a fixed value used in a program, such as a number or character. For example, the literals are the values on the right-hand side of the following assignments:

```
int index = 10;
float win = 1033.45f;
boolean isCorrect = true;
char modulus = '%';
```

The values 10, 1033.45f, true, and % are literals.

3.4   Strings

A char variable can hold only a single character. To reference one or more characters using a single variable, you must use strings. A *string literal* is a set of characters on a single line that is enclosed within double quotes. A **string** is an instance of class String and it represents a string literal. Some examples of string literals are shown here:

"Hello!"

"Current Score: 100"

"5 % 3"

You can initialize a String object with a string literal:

```
String str = "This is a string literal";
String firstName = "Joan";
String lastName = "Wright";
String randomValue = "a1z$_2345";
```

As with other objects, instances of String can also be created using a constructor of this class. However, the preferred way of creating strings is without using the new operator, as shown previously.

You can combine multiple strings using the + operator (known as the **concatenation operator**):

```
String fullName = firstName + " " + lastName;
System.out.println(fullName);     // prints out: Joan Wright
```

String literals cannot span multiple lines. To remedy this, you can use + when a string literal does not fit on a single line. The following creates a string representing "Hippopotomonstrosesquipedaliophobia," which (ironically) is the fear of long words:

```
String fearOfLongWords = "Hippopotomonst" +
                         "rosesquipedaliophobia";
```

We will discuss String and other related classes (such as StringBuilder) in detail in Chapter 7, *Arrays and Strings*.

3.5   Constants

Unlike variables, a constant has a fixed value that cannot be changed anywhere in the program. Constants are declared using the `final` and `static` keywords. By convention, constant names are in uppercase letters. This initializes a constant called `MAX_SIZE` with the value 100:

```
static final int MAX_SIZE = 100;
```

It is a compile-time error to declare a constant and not initialize it. Java has a `Math` class, which stores high precision values of type `double` for the constants `E` and `PI`:

```
static final double E;
static final double PI;
```

When you use these constants in your programs as `Math.E` and `Math.PI`, they will be replaced by their numeric values.

In the previous chapter, you used the `Font` constructor to create new fonts. This constructor is defined in the `Font` class in the `java.awt` package. This class also contains the following constants to represent different font styles:

```
static final int PLAIN;
static final int BOLD;
static final int ITALIC;
```

Before reading further ahead, test yourself on the problems in the next example.

Example 1

(a) Declare variables and initialize them with the following literals:

   (i) 23.5 (ii) 4354 (iii) $ (iv) "Hello"

(b) Which identifiers are invalid?

   (i) `alpha1` (ii) `orang3` (iii) `5year` (iv) `switch`

Solution: (a) Any valid identifiers can be selected:

   (i) `float num1 = 23.5f;`

   (ii) `int num2 = 4354;`

   (iii) `char c = '$';`

(iv) `String s = "Hello";` Note that you could have also declared `num1` as type `double`, and `num2` as type `short` or `long`.

(b) (i) and (ii) are valid. (iii) is invalid because you cannot start an identifier with a digit. (iv) is invalid because `switch` is a keyword.   ■

3.6   Assignment Statements

In the preceding sections, you learned how to assign a value to a variable when it is declared. This value can then be changed by using **assignment statements**. For example, suppose that you declared a variable called `length` of type `int` as follows:

```
int length = 10;
```

The variable `length` is initialized to the number 10. This value can be changed to 5 by using the following assignment statement:

```
length = 5;// length holds the value 5
```

You can use any number of assignment statements to change the value of a variable in a program. However, remember that the left side of the equation should *always* be a variable, which represents a memory location. The following assignment is wrong because 5 is not a memory location, and thus a value cannot be stored in it:

```
5 = length;// error!
```

The following statement declares another variable called `width` and initializes it with the value in `length`:

```
int width = length;
```

You can change the values stored in both variables `width` and `length` to 20 using a single statement:

```
width = length = 20;
```

In general, an assignment statement has three parts: **variable**, **equal sign**, and **expression**:

variable = expression;

An *expression* can contain variables and **operators**. Operators change the values stored in variables. Later in this chapter, we will discuss these four types of operators in detail: **arithmetic**, **increment**, **decrement**, and

assignment. Arithmetic operators are the simplest to understand. Examples of these operators include "+" and "–". In the following statement, 5 is subtracted from the value of length and assigned to width:

```
width = length - 5;
```

If length is 20, width will be assigned 15.

3.7   Conversion and Casting

An assignment can involve variables of different types. In some cases, the data type of the *expression* is changed *automatically* to the *variable*'s data type. For example, suppose that i is an integer variable declared as follows:

```
int i = 10;
```

Even though d is a variable of type double, the following assignment is valid:

```
double d = i; // valid, i is converted to type double
```

Java changes i from int to double, and then assigns it to d. This conversion does not cause any loss of information because the double data type is 64 bits wide and thus is wider than the int data type that has 32 bits. This is called a **widening conversion** because a narrower type is converted to a wider type, and it takes place implicitly. Here are some more examples of when widening conversions occur:

```
short s = 10;
int num = s;      // conversion of s from short to int
float f = num;    // conversion of num from int to float
double d = f;     // conversion of f from float to double
```

Figure 3–1 summarizes the conversion rules: A conversion occurs from a given data type to any of the data types on its right. For example, a conversion from byte to any one of the following can take place: short, int, long, float, and double; however, a float can be converted only to a double.

Cast is needed to convert to the narrower type on the left

| byte | short | int | long | float | double |

Conversion to the wider type on the right takes place implicitly

Figure 3–1
Conversion and casting rules.

On the other hand, assigning a value of type double to an int causes a compilation error:

```
double d = 100.5;
int i = d; // error!
```

Java does not allow this assignment because a double can hold a larger range of values than an int, and it could result in an inadvertent loss of data if d is larger than the largest value that can be stored in an int, or if it is smaller than the smallest value that can be stored in an int. To allow this type of assignment, it is necessary for the programmer to force a conversion from double to int using a *cast*.

> A **cast** is a data type enclosed within parentheses. Casting is used to convert a wider type, such as a double, to a narrower type, such as an int.

For example, a cast is used here to force a conversion of the variable d to type int and then assign it to i:

```
int i = (int) d;   // i = 100
```

Note that this assignment **truncates** (not rounds) the fractional part so that it assigns 100 to i.

Figure 3–1 also depicts all cases when casting is needed; a cast must be used to convert a particular type to any of the types on its *left*. Thus, a cast is needed to convert from type float to type byte, short, int, or long:

```
float f = (float) 10.5;  // cast a literal of type double to float
byte b = (byte) f;       // cast a float to byte
short s1 = (short) f;    // cast a float to short
int i = (int) f;         // cast a float to int
long l = (long) f;       // cast a float to long
```

A boolean variable can be assigned only values of type boolean. Conversely, a variable of any of the other data types cannot be assigned a boolean value.

3.8   Using Constructors and Methods

In the previous chapter, you created various graphical shapes by giving different arguments to constructors. To use a particular constructor or method, you must look up its declaration in the class that contains it. For example, the `Rectangle2D.Float` constructor is declared in class `Rectangle2D.Float` in the `java.awt.geom` package as shown here:

`Rectangle2D.Float(float x, float y, float w, float h)`—a constructor that creates a rectangle at the coordinates (`x, y`) with width `w` and height `h`.

The variables used in a constructor or method declaration are called **parameters**. Thus, the variables `x`, `y`, `w`, and `h` are parameters of the `Rectangle2D.Float` constructor. Each of these parameters is of type `float`. To use this constructor or method in your code, you must call it using arguments (known as **passing arguments**). When the program runs, the arguments are copied into the parameters.

The following statement creates an object called `rect` of type `Rectangle2D.Float`:

```
Rectangle2D.Float rect = new Rectangle2D.Float (50, 100, 200, 300);
```

The object referenced by the `rect` variable is located at coordinates (50, 100) and has a height and width of 300 and 200, respectively. It is created by passing the arguments 50, 100, 200, and 300 to this constructor. The parameter `x` is assigned the value 50, `y` is assigned 100, and `w` and `h` are assigned 200 and 300, respectively, as shown in Figure 3–2. A widening conversion converts the four integer arguments in the `Rectangle2D.Float` constructor to type `float`.

Consider how you use a calculator: You simply input the data and it provides the result. You do not have to know what circuitry is inside the calculator or how it computes the result. Similarly, you need to know how a constructor or method is declared, and not the internal details, to use it.

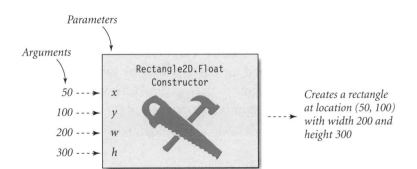

Figure 3–2

Passing arguments to a constructor.

> You need to know the **data type** and **order** of the parameters in the constructor or method, and pass in arguments that match that type and order.

In addition to primitive types, reference-type arguments can also be passed into constructors and methods. The setFont method of the DrawingKit class takes an object reference of type Font as an argument:

setFont(Font f)—a method in DrawingKit class that sets the font that will be displayed on the screen to f.

Based on this declaration of the method, you cannot pass the method an object reference of a different type (say, Rectangle2D.Float).

As another example, consider the Font constructor defined in the Font class. It takes three parameters of types String and int:

Font(String name, int style, int size)—a constructor that creates a Font object with the given name, style, and size.

This statement creates a Font object by passing these three arguments to the Font constructor—the string literal "ARIAL," the integer constant Font.Bold, and the integer literal 32:

```
Font myfont = new Font("ARIAL", Font.BOLD, 32);
```

The declarations for the constructors and methods used in the previous chapter to create lines, ellipses, and other graphical objects are provided at the end of this chapter for your reference.

3.8.1   Using Variables as Arguments

You can also pass variables instead of literals as arguments to a method or constructor. The Rectangle2D.Float constructor requires arguments of type float. Define four variables of type float to represent the *x*- and *y*-coordinates, height, and width of the rectangle as follows:

```
float x = 50, y = 100, width = 200, height = 300;
```

Note that a widening conversion occurs here, and the four integer numbers are converted to float and then assigned to the variables. When you pass these variables as arguments to the Rectangle2D.Float constructor, they will be copied into the corresponding parameters of the constructor:

```
Rectangle2D.Float rect_same = new Rectangle2D.Float (x, y, width, height);
```

This rectangle rect_same has the same position and size as the rectangle called rect we created earlier.

The next example demonstrates why variables are so useful.

Example 2

This example creates a stick figure with a **reference point** (x, y) shown as a small dot near the figure's head. All of the graphical objects in the figure have their starting point defined relative to this reference point. The reference point is located at the coordinates (100, 100) in this example. By changing its value, you can move the stick figure to a different location. In this way, you do not have to individually change the coordinates of each shape that builds the stick figure. You can select any point as a reference point. We will use the concept of reference points later to do animation in Chapter 6, *Inheritance.*

```java
import java.awt.*;
import java.awt.geom.*;
import com.programwithjava.basic.DrawingKit;

public class StickFigure {
  public static void main(String[] args) {
    DrawingKit dk = new DrawingKit("Stick Figure");
    int x = 100, y = 100;

    BasicStroke s = new BasicStroke(5);
    dk.setStroke(s);
    Font f = new Font("Arial", Font.ITALIC, 50);
    dk.setFont(f);
    // Watch the dot. The stick figure moves with it.
    dk.drawString(".", x, y);

    // draw the head
    Ellipse2D.Float head = new Ellipse2D.Float(x, y, 80, 80);
    dk.draw(head);

    // draw the body
    Line2D.Float body = new Line2D.Float(x+40, y+80, x+40, y+200);
    dk.draw(body);
```

```
    // draw the hands
    Line2D.Float hand1 = new Line2D.Float(x+40, y+110, x-20, y+160);
    dk.draw(hand1);
    Line2D.Float hand2 = new Line2D.Float(x+40, y+110, x+100, y+160);
    dk.draw(hand2);

    // draw the legs
    Line2D.Float leg1 = new Line2D.Float(x+40, y+200, x+20, y+300);
    dk.draw(leg1);
    Line2D.Float leg2 = new Line2D.Float(x+40, y+200, x+70, y+300);
    dk.draw(leg2);
  }
}
```

You should use variables instead of the literals passed into the constructors in this program (although we have not done so in order to highlight the use of the reference point). Also, note that the identifiers of both primitive and reference variables must be unique inside the main method; otherwise, a compilation error will result. The program output is shown in Figure 3–3.   ■

Figure 3–3

Creating a graphical shape by passing variables as arguments to constructors and methods.

You can move this figure to a different location in the window by changing the coordinates of this reference point

3.8.2   Methods That Return Values

Like constructors, methods are also declared using a parameter list. You are familiar with the drawString method in the DrawingKit class used to write text in a window. This method is declared as follows:

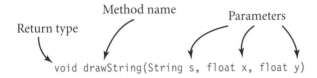

In addition to the parameter list, a *return type* must be specified for methods. A method can perform some calculations to obtain a result and return it to the calling method. This result can be of a primitive type or a reference type. The **return type** refers to this data type of the result. A method returns either a *single* value or none at all. A method that does not return a result has a return type of void. Constructors do not return any values, and thus they do not have a return type.

The Scanner class contains several methods that return values. The following section shows you how to use these methods.

3.9   The Scanner Class

In the previous chapter, you learned how to print out textual data on the console using the methods println and print. By using the Scanner class in package java.util, you can *read* textual data typed in at the console into a program. Figure 3–4 shows some of the methods in class Scanner.

Scanner	
int nextInt()	Returns the next integer value in the input.
long nextDouble()	Returns the next floating-point value in the input.
String next()	Returns the next word in the input as a String.
String nextline()	Returns one line of data in the input.

Figure 3–4
Some methods in the Scanner class.

The nextShort, nextFloat, and nextLong methods in Scanner work similarly. Each of these methods (except nextLine) reads a set of consecutive characters until a *whitespace* (such as a blank or a tab) is encountered. The nextLine method reads all of the data that a user typed on a line before pressing the Enter key on a keyboard.

We can create a scanner that reads data from the console by using a System.in argument to the Scanner constructor:

```
Scanner scanner = new Scanner(System.in);
```

The value returned by a method can be copied into a variable whose data type matches that of the returned value. For instance, the integer value that is returned by the nextInt method is copied into another variable called number1 using an assignment statement:

```
int number1 = scanner.nextInt();
```

If the user enters a value that is different from the type expected (such as a floating-point number), a run-time error will result.

The following statement reads a string from the console by using the next method and stores it in the variable named string1:

```
String string1 = scanner.next();
```

The variables number1 and string1 can be used as needed in the rest of the program. In the next section, you will learn how to use a scanner in a program.

3.10 Operators

Operators are used to modify the information stored in a variable. We look at three types of operators in this section: arithmetic, unary, and special assignment.

3.10.1 Arithmetic Operators

Arithmetic operators are used for simple arithmetic operations. The various operators are represented by the symbols: +, −, *, / and %.

```
+   add        1 + 1 = 2
-   subtract   2 - 1 = 1
*   multiply   2 * 3 = 6 (same as 2 X 3 = 6)
```

```
/   divide      6 / 2 = 3
%   modulus     7 % 2 = 1
```

The modulus operator gives the remainder when a division operation is performed.

When the operands of an arithmetic operator are of different types, they must be changed to the same type before the operation is performed. **Type promotion** automatically converts the data type of the narrower operand to the type of the wider operand. For example, if d and i are operands of type double and int, respectively, i is promoted to double in the following expression:

```
double v = d * i;
```

Example 3

This example shows how the minus arithmetic operator is used. The program prompts the user to enter two numbers on the console and reads them in using the scanner. The second number is subtracted from the first, and the result is displayed on the console.

```java
import java.util.Scanner;

public class Calculator {
  public static void main(String[] args) {
    Scanner scanner = new Scanner (System.in);
    System.out.print("Enter a number:");
    // read the number from the console into variable number1
    double number1 = scanner.nextDouble();
    System.out.print("Enter another number:");
    // read the number from the console into variable number2
    double number2 = scanner.nextDouble();
    System.out.println("The result is:" +(number1 - number2) );
  }
}
```

The program output is:

```
Enter a number:10
Enter another number:30.5
The result is:-20.5
```

The output shows that the user entered the numbers 10 and 30.5, and the program displayed the result: -20.5.

The + operator can be used in a different context in print statements—to concatenate different types. For example, the following statement concatenates the string "The result is:" with the result of the subtraction number1 − number2:

```
"The result is:" +(number1 - number2)
```

You can also pass primitive types as arguments to the print and println methods. Therefore, the following arguments are all valid:

```
int x = 10, y = 20; String s = "30";
System.out.println(x);      // prints out 10
System.out.println(x + y + x);    // prints out 40
System.out.println(s + x + x);    // prints out 301010
```

In the last statement, the + operator performs a concatenation because the first argument s is of type String.

Modify the program so that it uses a different arithmetic operator and rerun it. Use different input values and check the program output. ∎

3.10.2   Unary Operators

Whereas arithmetic operators take two operands, **unary** operators take a single operand. The unary operators are:

  ++   increment

  --   decrement

  +   plus

  –   minus

The **increment** operator is used to increase the value of a variable by 1, and the **decrement** operator to decrease a variable's value by 1.

This statement increases the value of alpha by 1:

```
++alpha;       // increment operator used in prefix position
```

This is the same as writing:

```
alpha = alpha + 1;
```

When the operator appears before the variable name, it is known as **prefix** notation. The statement can also be written as follows:

```
alpha++;       // increment operator used in postfix position
```

Conversely, when the operator is applied after the variable name, the notation is called **postfix** notation. In this case as well, the value of alpha is increased by 1.

The following statements use the **decrement** operator. Each statement decreases the value of variable beta by 1:

```
beta = beta - 1;    // reduce the value of variable beta by 1
--beta;             // decrement operator used in prefix position
beta--;             // decrement operator used in postfix position
```

All three statements are equivalent.

When the decrement and increment operators are used in assignment statements, the position of the operator affects the value of the expression. For example, suppose that the variable length has the increment operator placed in the postfix position:

```
float breadth = length++ - 5.0f;
```

This means that length is incremented *after* the expression is evaluated using its original value. Hence, the preceding statement is equivalent to the following two statements:

```
float breadth = length - 5.0f;
length = length + 1;
```

When the operator appears in the prefix position as in the following statement, it means that the variable length is incremented first, and the value of the expression is evaluated using this incremented value. The statement shows the operator in prefix notation:

```
float breadth = ++length - 5.0f;
```

The preceding statement is equivalent to the following two statements:

```
length = length + 1;
float breadth = length - 5.0f;
```

The **unary minus** operator is prefixed before an expression to negate it:

```
int x = 10;
int y = -(x - 5);
```

The expression in parentheses is a single operand $(x - 5)$ with the value 5. The value of y is -5. This is the same as writing:

```
int x = 10;
int y = -x + 5;
```

The **unary plus** operator has no effect on an expression:

```
int x = 10;
int y = +(-(x - 5));
```

The value of y is still -5.

3.10.3   Assignment Operators

Earlier in this chapter, you used the assignment operator =. This operator can be combined with the arithmetic operators +, –, *, /, and % to give a new set of assignment operators: +=, –=, *=, /=, and %=. These new operators are used to represent assignment statements in an abbreviated form. For example, the following two statements are equivalent, and you can use either one of them:

```
length = length + 5;
length += 5;              // increment length by 5
```

The following two statements are also equivalent:

```
length = length * 10;
length *= 10;             // multiply length by 10
```

The advantage of the second statement is that it is shorter because `length` appears only once instead of twice. The other operators are used similarly:

```
radius /= 5.5;           // radius = radius / 5.5;
x %= 10;                 // x = x % 10;
```

Note that if the variable on the right is different from the variable on the left, the abbreviated form cannot be used. The following statement uses two different variables:

```
size = breadth * 10;
```

This statement *cannot* be written as:

```
size *= 10;    // incorrect, as it does not contain variable breadth
```

3.10.4   Operator Precedence

In the assignment statements we've examined so far, we have used only one arithmetic operator at a time. If more than one arithmetic operator is used, the result depends on the order in which the operators are applied. This order is determined by importance of the operators, known as **operator precedence**. For example, what is the value of d, if a = 6, b = 4, and c = 2?

```
d = a * b + c;
```

The value of d depends on which operator is more important. Suppose that * is more important than +; this means the variables a and b are multiplied first, to give the value 24, which is then added to the value of c. The value of d becomes 26.

```
d = (6 * 4) + 2  // if multiplication is done first, d = 26
```

On the other hand, if + is applied *before* *, then b and c are added together first to give 6, which is multiplied by a. The resulting value of d is 36.

```
d = 6 * (4 + 2)  // if addition is done first, d = 36
```

So, which value should be used for d, 26 or 36? According to the operator precedence rules, * is more important than +, and so multiplication should be done before addition. The resulting value of d is 26, not 36.

We could have written the assignment statement for d using parentheses as follows:

```
d = (a * b) + c; // using parentheses makes it clearer!
```

This statement shows that the operation inside the parentheses should be done first. In general, use parentheses generously in assignment statements in order to make it clear how the expression should be evaluated or to override the operator precedence order.

The following is a mnemonic to help you remember the precedence order, from highest to lowest: **PUMAS**.[1]

P   **P**arentheses ( ), **P**ostfix a++ a--

U   **U**nary operators (except postfix) + (positive) − (negative) ++a --a

M   **M**ultiplication, division and **M**odulus * / %

A   **A**ddition and subtraction + −

S   **S**pecial assignments = += −= *= /= %=

We apply this precedence order to evaluate the values of expressions. The following example should help clarify this:

```
d = a * b++ + c;
```

Adding parentheses to this statement will make it clear as to how it should be evaluated. The steps are as follows:

1. The ++ operator is the most important of the operators in this expression. Add parentheses around b++:

   ```
   d = a * (b++) + c;
   ```

---

[1]A puma is a mountain lion or cougar found in many parts of North and South America.

2. Among the *remaining* operators *, +, and =, * has greater importance. Add parentheses around * and the two variables that use this operator:

```
d = (a * (b++)) + c;
```

3. The operator + has higher importance than =, so add parentheses as follows:

```
d = ((a * (b++)) + c);
```

4. The expression is now fully parenthesized. Next, the values in the inner parentheses must be evaluated before those in the outer parentheses. Assume that a = 5, b = 3, and c = 1; then the value of d is (5 * 3) + 1 = 16.

> Use the mnemonic PUMAS to help you remember the operator precedence order.

First, you must parenthesize an expression fully using the operator precedence order. Then, evaluate the expression starting from the innermost parentheses and moving toward the outermost parentheses. If there are multiple operators with the *same* priority or importance in the expression, evaluate these from *left to right*.

3.11   Classes and Packages

Similar to primitive data types, classes also represent a data type, but they provide greater functionality. We have been using built-in classes such as `Rectangle2D.Float`, `Line2D.Float`, and others to create shapes. In Chapter 5, *User-Defined Classes,* you will learn how to write your own classes.

In order to make it easier for the programmer to use these classes, related classes are placed into *packages*. A **package** is simply a directory containing a group of Java source files. All packages whose names begin with `java` or `javax` are a part of Java. There are many packages in Java, including `java.lang`, `java.util`, `java.math`, and `java.text`. A **subpackage** is a package that is inside another package. Thus, the package `java.awt.geom` is a subpackage of `java.awt`. The class `DrawingKit` is a custom class and is not a part of stan-

TABLE 3–2 Some Packages and Classes	
Package	**Some Classes in This Package**
java.awt.geom	Ellipse2D.Float, Ellipse2D.Double, Line2D.Double, Line2D.Float, Rectangle2D.Double, Rectangle2D.Float, RoundRectangle2D.Double, RoundRectangle2D.Float, QuadCurve2D.Float, QuadCurve2D.Double
java.awt	BasicStroke, Button, Color, Font
java.awt.image	BufferedImage
java.lang	Math, String
com.programwithjava.basic	DrawingKit
java.util	Scanner, Random

dard Java. It is in the com.programwithjava.basic subpackage, and is provided by the author of this text. Some packages and classes are listed in Table 3–2.

3.11.1   Using Packages

You can use a class that is in a different package from your program in two ways:

- *Prefix the package name to the class name:* If you want to use the class Rectangle2D.Float in the java.awt package in your program, you can write it as java.awt.Rectangle2D.Float every time you use it. The disadvantage of this approach is the extra typing that is required. The second option, described next, is easier to use.

- *Use an* import *statement:* You can use an import statement at the start of the source code file to specify which class you want to use. This is the preferred approach, and the one that we are using. To use the class Rectangle2D.Float class, specify the package name and class name after the import keyword as follows:

  import java.awt.geom.Rectangle2D.Float;

Note that there is no need to prefix `Rectangle2D.Float` with the package name `java.awt` anywhere else in that file.

Multiple `import` statements can also be specified in the same file. Thus, to use class `Ellipse2D.Float` in the same file, add another `import` statement:

```
import java.awt.geom.Ellipse2D.Float;
```

When several classes have to be imported from the same package, it is not necessary to specify every class. Instead, a wildcard operator (*) can be used to import all classes in that package by using a single statement:

```
import java.awt.geom.*;
```

Note that this does not import any of the classes in the subpackages. Therefore, the following statement does *not* import the classes in the subpackage `java.awt.geom`:

```
import java.awt.*;
```

The `java.lang` package containing the `Math` and `String` classes is loaded automatically by the JVM, and thus you do not have to import the classes in this package into your programs.

3.12   Introduction to Digital Images

In this section, we will discuss the basics of digital images: representation, color models, file formats, and other information that is needed to modify them.

Digital images (photographs and graphics) are stored as **two-dimensional arrays** of color values. Each color value is called a **pixel**. The term pixel is used for both pixels on the computer screen as well as the pixels of an image. A pixel on a computer screen is a physical entity used to display an image on the screen, whereas the pixel in a digital image is a numeric value representing a color. It is not necessary that a one-to-one correspondence exist between the two. Figure 3–5(a) shows an enlarged view of the pixels in a black and white image on the screen. Figure 3–5(b) shows how the pixels are stored for this image in an array comprising rows and columns. A particular pixel can then be accessed by specifying its column-row pair. An important point to note is that the rows and columns are numbered starting from zero. Thus, the pixels at (0, 0) and (0, 2) are the colors white and black, respectively.

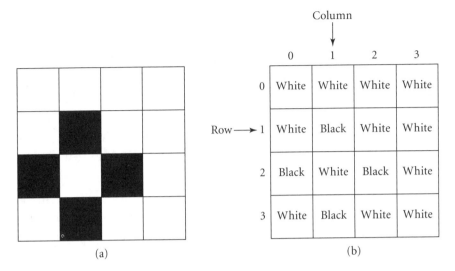

How is the color information stored in the pixel of an image displayed as a color on a screen pixel? To answer this question, we must understand what a color model is. You are probably familiar with the term **primary colors**—these are a set of three colors that can be combined together to make a large number of new colors. A **color model** consists of a specific set of primary colors. The **RGB color model**, used in computers and televisions, has *red*, *green*, and *blue* as its primary colors. Combining these colors in different proportions produces other shades, such as yellow, orange, brown, cyan, white, and many others. For example, mixing green and red in equal amounts produces yellow. When the amount of red is double the amount of green, it produces orange. The RGB color model is based on how we perceive color. The retina of the human eye contains special cells called **cones**. There are three types of cones, each of which is sensitive to a particular wavelength of light: short, medium, or long. When the light falls on the eye, it stimulates these cones. The information from the cones is combined in the brain, which enables us to perceive color.

In a colored digital image, each pixel has three values, one for each of the red, blue, and green components. These values are called **samples**. An RGB color image has three samples for every pixel, whereas a grayscale image has one sample per pixel. The term *channel* is commonly used when working with digital images. A **channel** refers to one particular component of *every* pixel in a picture. An RGB image has three channels. If the image is displayed using the red channel, all the samples corresponding to the red component of the image will be shown on the screen.

Some images have a fourth channel, called alpha. The **alpha** channel specifies the transparency of pixels in an image. Suppose that we draw an image over some text. If the image is fully transparent, only the text will be visible and not the image itself, whereas if the image is **opaque** (that is, not transparent), the text will not be visible and only the image will show. In some types of images, you can specify the level of transparency so that the text and the image are both partly visible.

It is particularly important to understand how the samples are stored in the computer. Recall from our discussion in Chapter 1 that all information in a computer is stored in a binary format composed of bits. The number of bits needed to store a sample is called **bit depth**. It is common for images to have a bit depth of 8 bits. Each sample is a number in the range 0 to 255 and it can be stored in 8 bits. For example, a white pixel in an 8-bit RGB color image has samples (255, 255, 255), and a black pixel has samples (0, 0, 0). A pixel has three samples in an RGB image; thus, a total of 24 bits is used to represent the color of each pixel. If the alpha channel is also present, each pixel has 32 bits.

Example 4

Java 2D has a class called Color in the package java.awt. The values of the red, blue, and green components for several colors such as white, black, and others are stored in constants defined in this class. For example, the color white is declared as follows:

```
public static final Color white;
```

The following program shows how you can print out the values of these components for several colors.

```
import java.awt.Color;

public class ColorComponentDisplay {
  public static void main(String[] args) {
    System.out.println("White:  " +Color.WHITE);
    System.out.println("Black:  " +Color.BLACK);
    System.out.println("Red:    " +Color.RED);
    System.out.println("Green:  " +Color.GREEN);
    System.out.println("Blue:   " +Color.BLUE);
```

```
    System.out.println("Yellow: " +Color.YELLOW);
    System.out.println("Orange: " +Color.ORANGE);
    System.out.println("Pink:   " +Color.PINK);
  }
}
```

The program output is:

```
White:  java.awt.Color[r=255,g=255,b=255]
Black:  java.awt.Color[r=0,g=0,b=0]
Red:    java.awt.Color[r=255,g=0,b=0]
Green:  java.awt.Color[r=0,g=255,b=0]
Blue:   java.awt.Color[r=0,g=0,b=255]
Yellow: java.awt.Color[r=255,g=255,b=0]
Orange: java.awt.Color[r=255,g=200,b=0]
Pink:   java.awt.Color[r=255,g=175,b=175]
```

Note in the output that the color white has the value 255, whereas black has the value 0 for each of its components. The intensity and proportion of each component varies in the other colors.   ∎

Example 5

A color image using the RGB color model has a bit depth of 8 bits per channel. What is the total number of colors that can be displayed using this model?

Solution: 256 different shades can be stored in 8 bits for each of the three components (red, green, and blue). These can be mixed together in 256 × 256 × 256 = 16,777,216 ways, which is the total number of colors that can be represented in this model.   ∎

An important characteristic of a digital image is its *resolution*. The **resolution** is the total number of pixels in an image. An image that is 300 pixels wide and 400 pixels high has a resolution of 120,000 pixels. As the number of pixels increases, the clarity of the image improves, but correspondingly, the size of the image also increases so that it needs more storage space.

Example 6

Calculate the size of an RGB color image that has a resolution of 700 × 400. Assume that the bit depth is 8 bits and that the alpha channel is present.

Solution: The total number of pixels in the image is 280,000. Each pixel needs 32 bits to store color information (8 bits for each of the red, green, and blue samples, and another 8 bits for alpha). The total size of the image is 280,000 $\times$ 32 = 8,960,000 bits, which is 1.068 MB. (Note that 1 byte = 8 bits, 1 kilobyte (KB) = 1024 bytes, and 1 megabyte (MB) = 1024 KB.)   ■

3.12.1   File Formats

Although a large number of file formats are available for digital images, the most commonly used ones are GIF (Graphics Interchange Format), JPEG (Joint Photographic Experts Group), PNG (Portable Networks Graphics), and TIFF (Tagged Image File Format). An image file can be large—up to several megabytes in size—and so these formats employ **compression** to reduce the file size. There are two types of compression methods: lossless and lossy. **Lossless compression** methods reduce the size of the file without discarding any information, whereas **lossy compression** methods discard data from the file while attempting to preserve its quality. In general, lossy compression methods result in a smaller file size, but the quality of the resulting image is also lower. JPEG uses lossy compression, whereas the GIF, PNG, and TIFF formats employ lossless compression.

GIF files are commonly used on the Internet in web browsers because of their small size, but only a limited range of colors (256) is supported. PNG files use the RGB color model, and may contain an alpha channel to support transparency. JPEG does not support transparency, but JPEG files storing photographs generally have a smaller size than PNG files. GIFs have limited transparency; they are either fully transparent (which makes them invisible) or fully opaque. This is unlike PNG files in which a pixel can be made partially transparent. PNG files have extension .png or .PNG; JPEG files have extension .jpg or .jpeg; GIF files have a .gif extension; and TIFF files have .tiff extension.

3.12.2   Java 2D Classes for Handling Images

Java 2D supports the GIF, PNG, and JPEG file formats, among others. It has a BufferedImage class in the `java.awt.image` package that can be used to store images in the computer's memory, and to retrieve information about and manipulate these images. Two methods in BufferedImage used to get the size of an image are shown in Figure 3–6.

Another useful Java 2D class is Color. We will explore a few other methods in BufferedImage and Color a little bit later.

BufferedImage	
int getHeight()	Returns the number of pixels in a column of the image.
int getWidth()	Returns the number of pixels in a row of the image.

Figure 3-6
**Methods in class
BufferedImage to get the
size of an image.**

3.12.3 Displaying an Image with DrawingKit

Displaying an image is a two-step process. First, the image is loaded from a
file into the computer's memory. Next, the image is transferred from memory onto the screen. The image can be modified while it is stored in memory and before it is displayed. For example, the transparency and the colors of the image may be manipulated—you will learn how to do this in the next chapter. The DrawingKit class contains the two methods shown in Figure 3-7 for displaying an image. The loadPicture method returns an object reference of type BufferedImage.

DrawingKit	
BufferedImage loadPicture(String f)	Loads the picture stored in the file f into the computer's memory.
void drawPicture(BufferedImage picture, int x, int y)	Draws picture at coordinates (x, y) in the window.

Figure 3-7
**Methods in class
DrawingKit to load a
picture from a file and
display it.**

Example 7

So, why is it important to know all this information about colors and pixels
in digital images? With this knowledge, you can start modifying digital
images' colors and displaying them on the screen. The following program
shows how you can display a picture stored in the JPEG file daffodils.jpg.
Copy this file from the JavaBook/image directory on the CD-ROM into the
JavaBook/image directory on your computer.

```java
import java.awt.image.*;
import com.programwithjava.basic.DrawingKit;

public class DisplayPicture {
  public static void main(String[] args) {
```

```
        DrawingKit dk = new DrawingKit("Daffodils", 850, 850);

    // transfer the image from daffodils.jpg file into computer's memory
        BufferedImage pict = dk.loadPicture("image/daffodils.jpg");

        // draw the image referenced by pict on the screen
        dk.drawPicture(pict, 25, 50);
    }
}
```

The program output is shown in Figure 3–8. The loadPicture method in DrawingKit reads the data in the daffodils.jpg file, stores it in the computer's memory as a BufferedImage, and returns a reference called pict to this BufferedImage object. The reference variable pict is then passed as an argument to the drawPicture method, which will display the image stored in memory on the screen. You can write a similar program to display images in other formats, such as GIF and PNG.   ■

3.12.4   Retrieving Samples from an Image File

You may want to retrieve information about the color of a particular pixel in an image and/or modify it. The BufferedImage class contains two methods for this, which are shown in Figure 3–9.

Figure 3–8

Displaying an image stored in a file using DrawingKit.

daffodils.jpg © Monika Adamczyk, 123RF.com

BufferedImage	
int getRGB(int x, int y)	Returns the encoded color value of a pixel at location (x, y).
void setRGB(int x, int y, int rgbvalue)	Sets the color of a pixel at location (x, y) to an encoded color value rgbvalue.

Figure 3–9

Methods in class BufferedImage to retrieve and modify the samples of a particular pixel in an image.

The getRGB method returns an **encoded** value, meaning that if you print it out on the screen, it will be meaningless. You must extract the red, green, and blue samples that are stored inside this encoded value. This can be done easily using Java 2D's Color class, which we discuss next.

Java 2D's Color class in the java.awt package comes in handy when working with color in images. You can create new colors using this class, determine the values of the various components of an existing color, and perform several other operations. Two constructors for this class are shown in Figure 3–10. You can pass the encoded color value of a pixel to the second Color constructor. The resulting Color object contains red, blue, and green components whose values can be displayed separately. The next example explains this in more detail.

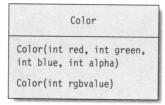

Color	
Color(int red, int green, int blue, int alpha)	Creates a new color using the specified values for each of its components.
Color(int rgbvalue)	Creates a new Color object using the encoded color value rgbvalue.

Figure 3–10

Two constructors in the Color class.

Example 8

Display the contents of the file daffodils.jpg in a window, and print out the samples of a pixel at location (500, 80) in the window.

```
import java.awt.image.*;
import java.awt.geom.*;
import java.awt.*;
import com.programwithjava.basic.DrawingKit;

public class PixelColorDemo {
```

```
public static void main(String[] args) {
  int x = 500, y = 80;
  DrawingKit dk = new DrawingKit("Daffodils", 800, 800);
  BufferedImage pict = dk.loadPicture("image/daffodils.jpg");

  // get pixel value at location (500, 80)
  int encodedPixelColor = pict.getRGB(x, y);
  Color pixelColor = new Color(encodedPixelColor);
  System.out.println(pixelColor);

  // display the approximate location of the pixel
  dk.drawPicture(pict, 0, 0);
  BasicStroke s = new BasicStroke(3);
  dk.setStroke(s);
  Ellipse2D.Float e = new Ellipse2D.Float(x-3, y-3, 8, 8);
  dk.draw(e);
  dk.drawString("(500, 80)", x-3, y-5);
  }
}
```

The modified image is displayed in Figure 3–11.

The samples for the pixel with coordinates (500, 80) are output on the console:

```
java.awt.Color[r=253,g=252,b=195]
```

Figure 3–11

Displaying color information about the pixels in an image.

daffodils.jpg © Monika Adamczyk, 123RF.com

We have only printed out the samples of one pixel. It would be impractical to use the statements shown in this example to print out the samples for every pixel in this image. In the next chapter, we will discuss a control structure called a *loop*, with which you can display all samples with only a few statements.   ■

3.13   Computers in Engineering: GPS Receivers

Computer software is widely used in various facets of engineering for product development, analysis, and testing. Computer programs are used to perform a myriad of tasks: controlling household appliances and electronics; patient monitoring and therapy in medical devices such as pacemakers; improved control of industrial systems, such as for oil drilling; simulaton of models of systems, such as transportation; driving cars, flying aircrafts, and operating satellites; and much more. In this section, we will explore how GPS receivers determine the location of a specific place using a technique called **3D trilateration** and develop a program for the similar (but simpler) **2D trilateration** method.

The **Global Positioning System (GPS)**, established in 1973, is used to determine the accurate location of a place anywhere in the world. This system consists of 24 satellites that circle the earth continuously. The satellites contain atomic clocks that provide a very accurate measurement of time. Every satellite transmits signals that contain the precise location of the satellite above the earth, as well as the time. A GPS receiver combines signals from three or more satellites—using a technique called 3D trilateration—to determine the location of a place. The 2D trilateration method is similar to, but easier to understand, than 3D trilateration, and so we will discuss it first.

3.13.1   2D Trilateration

The basic idea behind 2D trilateration is that if the coordinates of three points (A, B, and C) are known, and their distances from a fourth point U (with unknown coordinates) are also known, then we can determine the coordinates of point U (using simple geometry and algebraic manipulation). We explain this procedure next. Figure 3–12(a) shows three points, A, B, and C, with coordinates (a_1, b_1), (a_2, b_2), and (a_3, b_3), respectively, and their distances from point U are r_1, r_2, and r_3, respectively.

Figure 3–12
(a) Points A, B, and C have known coordinates, whereas point U does not; the distances of A, B, and C from U are known. (b) The three circles with centers at A, B, and C and the given radii intersect at point U.

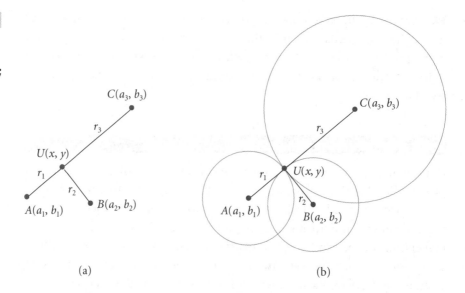

(a)　　　　　　　　　　　　　(b)

Draw a circle that has center A and radius r_1, where r_1 is the distance between A and U. This circle will pass through U. Draw a second circle with center B and radius r_2, where r_2 is the distance between U and B. These two circles intersect at two points, one of which is U. Draw a third circle with center C and radius r_3, which is the distance between U and C. All three circles intersect at exactly one point, which is U, as shown in Figure 3–12(b). Using geometry, the equations of the three circles are given by:

$$(x-a_1)^2 + (y-b_1)^2 = r_1^2$$
$$(x-a_2)^2 + (y-b_2)^2 = r_2^2$$
$$(x-a_3)^2 + (y-b_3)^2 = r_3^2$$

Solving the preceding equations for x and y gives:

$$y = \frac{[(a_2-a_1)(a_3^2+b_3^2-r_3^2)+(a_1-a_3)(a_2^2+b_2^2-r_2^2)+(a_3-a_2)(a_1^2+b_1^2-r_1^2)]}{2[b_3(a_2-a_1)+b_2(a_1-a_3)+b_1(a_3-a_2)]}$$

$$x = \frac{[r_2^2+a_1^2+b_1^2-r_1^2-a_2^2-b_2^2-2(b_1-b_2)y]}{2(a_1-a_2)}$$

We will use these equations for x and y in our program. We begin by working out an example by hand. Assume that the coordinates of the points are

$A = (4, 8)$, $B = (11, 7)$, and $C = (16, 17)$, and the distances of these points from U are $r_1 = 5$, $r_2 = 5$, and $r_3 = 10$, respectively. Plugging these values into the preceding equation gives the coordinates of $U = (8, 11)$. You can plot these points on graph paper and verify this result.

3D trilateration is similar, except that it uses spheres instead of circles, and the position of each point is given not only by its (x, y) coordinates (representing the latitude and longitude of a place), but also by its altitude. The GPS receiver determines the positions of four or more satellites and their distance from the receiver. It then uses this information to calculate the current position of the receiver.

3.13.2   2D Trilateration Program

First, we will develop an algorithm to solve the preceding problem, and then we will convert it to Java code. The algorithm is as follows:

1. Prompt the user to enter the coordinates of points A, B, and C.

2. Read the coordinates of these three points and store them in variables.

3. Prompt the user to enter the distances of points A, B, and C from point U.

4. Read the three distance values and store them in variables.

5. Calculate the coordinates of U using the formulas for y and x.

6. Display the coordinates of point U.

This algorithm is converted to Java code. We use a scanner to read the data entered by the user on the console.

```java
import java.util.Scanner;

public class Trilateration2D {
  public static void main(String[] args) {
    // declare variables to store the coordinates of A, B, C and U.
    double a1, b1, a2, b2, a3, b3, x, y;
    // declare variables to store the distances of A, B and C from U.
    double r1, r2, r3;

    // Prompt user to enter coordinates of A, B and C and read them.
    Scanner scanner = new Scanner(System.in);
    System.out.print("Enter the x and y coordinates of point A:");
    a1 = scanner.nextDouble();
```

```
    b1 = scanner.nextDouble();
    System.out.print("Enter the x and y coordinates of point B:");
    a2 = scanner.nextDouble();
    b2 = scanner.nextDouble();
    System.out.print("Enter the x and y coordinates of point C:");
    a3 = scanner.nextDouble();
    b3 = scanner.nextDouble();

    // Prompt user to enter the distances and read them.
    System.out.print("Enter the distance between point A and U:");
    r1 = scanner.nextDouble();
    System.out.print("Enter the distance between point B and U:");
    r2 = scanner.nextDouble();
    System.out.print("Enter the distance between point C and U:");
    r3 = scanner.nextDouble();

    // Calculate coordinates of U using the formulas for y and x
    double a1Sq = a1 * a1, a2Sq = a2 * a2, a3Sq = a3 * a3, b1Sq = b1 * b1,
b2Sq = b2 * b2, b3Sq = b3 * b3, r1Sq = r1 * r1, r2Sq = r2 * r2, r3Sq = r3 *
r3;

    double numerator1 = (a2 - a1) * (a3Sq + b3Sq - r3Sq) + (a1 - a3) *
(a2Sq + b2Sq - r2Sq) + (a3 - a2) * (a1Sq + b1Sq - r1Sq);
    double denominator1 = 2 * ( b3 * (a2 - a1) + b2 * (a1 - a3) + b1 *
(a3 - a2));
    y = numerator1/denominator1;

    double numerator2 = r2Sq - r1Sq + a1Sq - a2Sq + b1Sq - b2Sq - 2 *
(b1 - b2) * y;
    double denominator2 = 2 * (a1 - a2);
    x = numerator2/denominator2;

    // Display the coordinates of U
    System.out.println("The coordinates of point U are " +x + " " +y);
  }
}
```

Compile and run this program. Test it by providing the input values that were used in the example we did by hand earlier, and then verify that the program output is correct.

```
Enter the x and y coordinates of point A:4 8
Enter the x and y coordinates of point B:11 7
Enter the x and y coordinates of point C:16 17
Enter the distance between point A and U:5
```

```
Enter the distance between point B and U:5
Enter the distance between point C and U:10
The coordinates of point U are 8.0 11.0
```

The program output matches the values that were calculated by hand.

3.14   Summary

In this chapter, we discussed the basic concepts for writing Java programs. These include primitive data types, literals, constants, strings, conversion and casting, and various operators. Using several examples, we showed how arguments can be passed to constructors and methods, and how values returned by methods are stored in variables. We presented some fundamental concepts and terminology related to digital images, and introduced the BufferedImage and Color classes. This chapter lays the foundation for building interesting programs to modify photographs, animate graphics, and more in subsequent chapters.

Key Constructors and Methods

Here, we present a summary of the constructors and methods discussed in this chapter.

Java 2D Constructors for Graphics Objects

Ellipse2D.Float(float x, float y, float w, float h)—a constructor that creates an ellipse object at coordinates (x, y) with the specified width w and height h. It is defined in the Ellipse2D.Float class.

Line2D.Float(float x1, float y1, float x2, float y2)—a constructor that creates a line object joining the points (x1, y1) and (x2, y2). It is defined in the Line2D.Float class.

Rectangle2D.Float(float x, float y, float w, float h)—a constructor that creates a rectangle object at coordinates (x, y) with the specified width w and height h. It is defined in the Rectangle2D.Float class.

RoundRectangle2D.Float(float x, float y, float w, float h, float cw, float ch)—a constructor that creates a rectangle with rounded corners object at coordinates (x, y) with the specified width w and height h. The width and height of the corners is given by cw and ch, respectively. It is defined in the RoundRectangle2D.Float class.

QuadCurve2D.Float(float x1, float y1, float x2, float y2, float x3, float y3)—a constructor that creates a curve object joining the points (x1, y1) and (x3, y3) and passing through the point (x2, y2). It is defined in the QuadCurve2D.Float class.

BasicStroke(float w)—a constructor that creates a stroke object with the specified width w. It is defined in the BasicStroke class.

Font(String n, int s, int r)—a constructor that creates a font object with the given name n, style s, and size r. This constructor is defined in the Font class.

Java 2D Color Class   These constructors in the Color class create a new color object:

Color(int red, int green, int blue, int alpha)—a constructor that creates a new color using the specified values for each of its components.

Color(int rgbvalue)—a constructor that creates a new Color object using the encoded rgbvalue.

Java 2D BufferedImage Class   The methods in the BufferedImage class retrieve useful information about an image:

int getHeight()—a method that returns the number of pixels in a column of the image.

int getWidth()—a method that returns the number of pixels in a row of the image.

int getRGB(int x, int y)—a method that returns the encoded color value of a pixel at location (x, y).

void setRGB(int x, int y, int rgbvalue)—a method that sets the color of a pixel at location (x, y) to an encoded color value rgbvalue.

DrawingKit Class   Any of these four constructors can be used to create a DrawingKit object:

DrawingKit()—a constructor that creates a window with a default width and height of 500.

DrawingKit(String title)—a constructor that creates a window with the specified title and a width and height of 500.

DrawingKit(int width, int height)—a constructor that creates a window with the specified width and height.

DrawingKit(String title, int width, int height)—a constructor that creates a window with the specified title, width, and height.

`DrawingKit` has the following methods:

> **void drawPicture(BufferedImage picture, int x, int y)**—a method that draws a `picture` of type `BufferedImage` at coordinates (x, y).

> **public void drawPicture(String s)**—a method that draws the picture contained in the file with filename s at coordinates $(0, 0)$.

> **void drawString(String s, float x, float y)**—a method that writes the string s at coordinates (x, y).

> **BufferedImage loadPicture(String f)**—a method that loads the image from file f into the computer's memory.

> **void setFont(Font f)**—a method that sets the font to f.

> **void setPaint(Color c)**—a method that sets the current color to c.

> **void setStroke(BasicStroke s)**—a method that sets the line thickness to s.

> **void draw(Shape obj)**—a method that draws the Java 2D graphics object obj on the window.

> **void fill(Shape obj)**—a method that fills the Java 2D graphics object obj with the current color.

The `draw` and `fill` methods take an argument of a type that we have not discussed yet (`Shape`). Narrower types, such as `Rectangle2D.Float`, `Line2D.Float`, `Ellipse2D.Float`, and `RoundRectangle2D.Float`, are converted automatically to the wider type `Shape`. This automatic conversion of reference types is known as **upcasting**. We discuss this in Chapter 6, *Inheritance*.

Exercises

1. State whether the following statements are correct or not, and correct the errors if any occur:

    a. `Double I, j;`

    b. `float k = 200.0;`

    c. `double m = 14;`

    d. `int 123_alpha = 10;`

    e. `10 = b + c;`

    f. `int b, c, a; b + c = a;`

2. Which of the following are Java keywords?

    a. `main`

    b. `class`

    c.   `static`

    d.   `Rectangle2D`

    e.   `New`

3. Declare variables to hold numbers in the following ranges:

    a.   from -10 to $+100$

    b.   from 10,000 to 30,000

    c.   from 101.5 to 150.5

4. Declare a variable to hold the character "c".

5. Declare a `boolean` variable initialized to `true`.

6. Explain the differences between each of the following terms:

    a.   Primitive and object reference variables

    b.   Literals and constants

    c.   Parameters and arguments

    d.   Conversion and casting

7. Explain these terms:

    a.   Pixel in a digital image

    b.   Primary colors

    c.   RGB color model

    d.   Sample

    e.   Component

    f.   Lossy compression

    g.   Lossless compression

    h.   Channel

    i.   Alpha channel

    j.   Bit depth

8. Give the values of variable f after each of the following statements (using arithmetic operators) is executed.

```
int a = 5, b = 10, f;
```

    a.   `f = a + b;`

    b.   `f = a % b;`

    c.   `f = a / b;`

9. Give the values of variable f after each of the following statements (using increment and decrement operators) is executed.

```
int a = 5, b = 10, f;
```

 a. f = ++a - b;

 b. f = a-- - b;

 c. f = ++a + b--;

10. Give the values of variable f after each of the following statements (using special assignment operators) is executed:

```
int a = 10, b = 50, f = 5;
```

 a. f += a + 10;

 b. f *= b / a;

 c. f %= b + a;

11. Find the values of the variables fee and rem after the following statements are executed:

```
double fee = 5.5;
int rem = 150;
fee *= 10.5;
rem %= 10;
```

12. Find the value of variable g after each of the following statements is executed. Use the mnemonic PUMAS to help you parenthesize the expression correctly:

```
int a = 1, b = 2, c = 3, d = 4, e = 5, f = 6, g;
```

 a. g = ++a * b / c - d * e % f;

 b. g = a++ * b / (c - d) * e % f;

 c. g = ++a * b / c - d * (e % f);

13. Give the values of variable f after each of the following statements using different types of operators is executed. Use the mnemonic PUMAS to help you parenthesize the expression correctly:

```
int a = 5, b = 4, c = 3, d = 2, e = 1, f = 0;
```

 a. f += a % b++ - (c / d) * e;

 b. f += a % b++ - c / d * e;

 c. f %= a % b++ - c / d * e--;

d. f -= a % b++ - c / d * e--;

e. f %= a + b - c * d + e;

f. f %= a + (b - c)* d + e;

14. Identify the errors, if any, in the following statements:

```
int x = 10, y = 20; float z = 30.5f;
```

a. int index = (float) z;

b. float salary = (int) (x * 1000.5f);

c. int value = (int) z;

d. boolean isRed = 10;

e. x = x - 100++;

f. y = --(x * y);

g. System.out.println("x =" x);

15. Give Java statements to describe the formulas that follow:

a. Area of a circle with radius $R = \pi R^2$

b. Surface area of a sphere with radius $R = 4\pi R^2$

c. Volume of a sphere with radius $R = 4\pi R^3/3$

16. Write a program that prompts the user to enter a value for radius. Read this value from the console using an instance of class Scanner. Next, compute the surface area and volume of a sphere using the value of radius entered by the user and print them out on the console.

17. a. Write a program to calculate the value of gravity g of a planet using the following equation:

$$g = (G \times M)/R^2$$

where M is the mass of the planet, R is the radius of the planet, and the gravitational constant $G = 6.67 \times 10^{-11} \mathrm{m^3 kg^{-1} s^{-2}}$. The program should prompt the user to enter the mass of the planet and its radius, and print out its gravity. Use this program to determine the value of gravity of the planet Mercury ($R = 2.43 \times 10^6$m, $M = 0.33 \times 10^{24}$kg) and Jupiter ($R = 71.49 \times 10^6$m, $M = 1.89 \times 10^{27}$kg).

b. Modify the program developed in part (a) to print out the weight of a person on that planet as well. The program reads the weight of a person on Earth, and calculates his or her weight on a different planet using the formula:

$$w_{planet} = w \times \frac{g}{g_e}$$

where w is the person's weight on Earth, g is the gravity on the planet calculated in part (a), and $g_e = 9.81\text{ms}^{-1}$ is the value of gravity on earth.

Graphics Problems

18. The following code segment draws a figure that has a circle inside a rectangle. Rewrite this code so that the position of the figure is represented by the reference point (x, y). The figure can be moved to a new position in the window by changing the values of x and y. Use variables, not literals, as arguments to the constructors.

```
DrawingKit dk = new DrawingKit();
Ellipse2D.Float e1 = new Ellipse2D.Float(100, 150, 100, 50);
dk.draw(e1);
Rectangle2D.Float r1 = new Rectangle2D.Float(100, 150, 100, 50);
dk.draw(r1);
```

19. Rewrite the following code segment so that the position of the figure is represented by the reference point (x, y). By changing the values of x and y, the figure is moved to a new position in the window. Use variables, not literals, as arguments to the constructors.

```
int x = 200; int y = 250;
Ellipse2D.Float e1 = new Ellipse2D.Float(100, 150, 100, 50);
dk.draw(e1);
Ellipse2D.Float e2 = new Ellipse2D.Float(100, 165, 50, 20);
dk.draw(e2);
Rectangle2D.Float r1 = new Rectangle2D.Float(100, 150, 100, 50);
dk.draw(r1);
```

20. Modify the code in the StickFigure class provided earlier in this chapter to create a different stick figure using your imagination. When the reference point (x, y) is changed, the figure should move to another position in the window. Use variables instead of literals in the constructors and methods in your program.

21. Draw a robot inside a window using the graphics classes discussed so far. The position of the robot should be represented by a reference point (x, y). Changing the values of x and y (and making no other changes in the code) should move the robot to a new position in the window. Remember to use variables instead of literals in the constructors and methods in your program.

22. Java 2D's `Color` class also defines other colors, such as magenta and pink. These are declared as constants in the following manner:

```
static final Color MAGENTA;
static final Color PINK;
```

Write a program to print out the values of the red, green, and blue components of the colors *magenta* and *pink* on the console.

Image Manipulation Problems

23. Modify the `DisplayPicture` class (see Example 7 in this chapter) to display the image in the file `blimp.png`.

24. Modify the `PixelColorDemo` class (see Example 8 in this chapter) to display only the red component of the pixel at location (500, 260) on the console. Update the text displayed on the window.

25. Modify the `PixelColorDemo` class (see Example 8 in this chapter) to display the pixel at location (400, 210). Update the text displayed on the window.

Further Reading

For a detailed overview of the techniques employed to store and manipulate digital images and other media, see [2]. You can find out more about how GPS works, as well as view videos on this topic, by visiting the website listed in [3].

References

1. "The Java™ Tutorials." Web. <http://download.oracle.com/javase/tutorial/>.

2. Brinkmann, Ron. *The Art and Science of Digital Compositing: Techniques for Visual Effects, Animation and Motion Graphics, Second Edition.* Burlington, MA: Morgan Kaufmann/Elsevier, 2008. Print.

3. "GPS Overview." *GPS.gov*. Web. <http://www.gps.gov/systems/gps/>.

4. *Java™ Platform, Standard Edition 6, API Specification*. Web. <http://download.oracle.com/javase/6/docs/api/>.

5. Guzdial, Mark, and Barbara Ericson. *Introduction to Computing and Programming in Java: A Multimedia Approach*. Upper Saddle River, NJ: Pearson Prentice Hall, 2007. Print.

6. Eckel, Bruce. *Thinking in Java*. Upper Saddle River, NJ: Prentice Hall, 2006. Print.

7. Anderson, Julie, and Herve Franceschi. *Java 6 Illuminated: An Active Learning Approach*. Sudbury, MA: Jones and Bartlett, 2008. Print.

8. Sierra, Kathy, and Bert Bates. *Head First Java*. Sebastopol, CA: O'Reilly, 2005. Print.

9. Knudsen, Jonathan. *Java 2D Graphics*. Beijing: O'Reilly, 1999. Print.

CHAPTER 4

Control Flow Statements

CHAPTER CONTENTS

In this chapter, we discuss structures that control the sequence in which statements are executed in a program: selection statements, branching statements, and loops. We use graphical examples such as "magic" shapes and a "crystal ball" to explain how selection statements and loops work. You will also learn how to use these various control structures to modify pictures by changing the colors, transparency, and brightness of a picture.

4.1   Selection Statements and Loops

In the programs that we have written so far, statements are executed sequentially. Thus, if statements *i* and *j* appear in the code in the order shown here, statement *j* is executed after *i*:

statement i;

statement j;

Selection statements and **loops** alter this sequential flow of execution. (They are also referred to as **control flow** statements.) Selection statements are used to perform one out of many possible operations, depending on which condition in a given set is true. Loops are useful when certain operations must be performed repeatedly. There are three types of selection statements: if, if-else, and switch, and three types of loops: while, do-while, and for. We discuss each of these in detail in this chapter.

4.2   Flowcharts

Flowcharts use symbols to describe an algorithm. Figure 4–1 shows the different symbols that can be used in a flowchart, where each symbol represents a particular type of operation. In a flowchart, these symbols are connected together to describe a sequence of actions that is used to solve a problem. Flowcharts are not unique; there can be different flowcharts for the same problem.

We will use flowcharts with many examples in this chapter. Initially, you may find it helpful to draw a flowchart before you write a program. However, as you gain experience programming, you will be able to write code without needing to draw a flowchart.

Symbol	Explanation	
		Figure 4–1 **Flowchart symbols.**

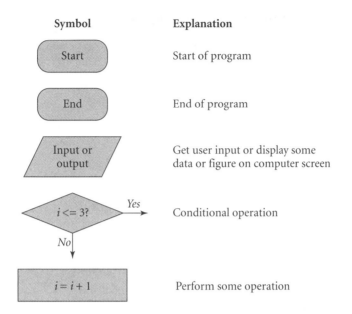

Symbol	Explanation
Start	Start of program
End	End of program
Input or output	Get user input or display some data or figure on computer screen
$i <= 3?$	Conditional operation
$i = i + 1$	Perform some operation

4.3 Conditions

A **condition** is a boolean expression that evaluates to either true or false. Here are some more examples of conditions:

```
5 > 4 // true
3 < 1 // false
```

In the previous chapter, we discussed assignment, arithmetic, and unary operators. We will now introduce another operator, known as the *relational operator*. **Relational operators** are used to formulate a condition. The six relational operators are shown in Table 4–1.

For example, suppose that Picture 1 has p_1 pixels and Picture 2 has p_2 pixels. Then, we can formulate the condition "Picture 1 has fewer pixels than Picture 2" as follows:

```
p₁ < p₂
```

This condition is true if p_1 is less than p_2; otherwise, it is false. A condition must contain a relational operator. Here are more examples of conditions:

```
x > 2 // true if x is greater than 2
y < z + 3  // true if y is less than z + 3
```

TABLE 4–1   Relational Operators

Relational Operator	Definition
<	Less than
<=	Less than or equal to
>	Greater than
==	Equal to
!=	Not equal to
>=	Greater than or equal to

The result depends upon the values of the variables and literals used in these conditions. For example, the condition x > 2 is true if x has the value 10, and false if x has the value 2.

Each operator consists of two characters: <=, >=, ==, !=. There should not be a space between these characters. So, the symbol > = is invalid as there is a space between the > and = symbols. The operator >= returns true if the value on the left is *greater than or equal to* the value on the right:

```
x >= 2  // true if x is greater than or equal to 2
```

Thus, the condition x >= 2 is true if x has the value 2. Examine the following conditions:

```
y != z  // true if y is not equal to z
w == g * 2 // true if w is equal to g * 2
m <= -3 // true if m is less than or equal to -3
```

The equality operator (==) contains two equal signs. We can write the condition "x is equal to 200" using the equality operator as:

```
x == 200     // true if x is equal to 200
```

A common mistake is to use a single equal sign in a condition:

```
x = 200     // error! not a condition
```

This will assign the value 200 to x instead of performing a comparison to determine whether x equals 200.

Conditions can also be more complex, containing two or more relational operators. Later in this chapter, we discuss logical operators (*AND*, *OR*, and

NOT) and how they can be used to create these types of conditions. Conditions are used in selection statements, which are discussed next.

4.4   Selection Statements

We use conditions to decide our behavior in everyday life. An example is:

if "*book is available*"

   I will read it

If the condition "book is available" is true, then the action that is taken is to read the book. This does not specify what should be done if the condition is false.

Consider another example:

if "*it is raining*"

   I will drive

else

   I will walk

Here, the condition is "it is raining." If this condition is true, then the action taken is to drive; otherwise, if the condition is false, the action taken is to walk.

A flowchart can contain a conditional operation box. This contains a condition that is evaluated to be either true or false. If the condition is true, the set of statements following the "Yes" path are executed; otherwise, the statements on the "No" path are executed. Figure 4–2 shows a flowchart with a conditional operation box.

Conditional statements in Java programs are similar. A condition is evaluated and the action taken depends on whether this condition is true or false. Here we discuss three types of conditional statements: `if`, `if-else`, and `switch`.

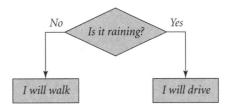

Figure 4–2

A simple flowchart with a conditional operation box.

4.4.1   The if Statement

The if statement checks whether a condition evaluates to true or false, and executes a given set of statements if this condition is true. The general form of this construct is as follows:

```
if (condition)  {
  // statements
}
```

It is necessary to enclose the condition within parentheses (). Multiple statements following the "if" clause should be enclosed within braces {}. A set of statements within braces is referred to as a **block**. The braces are typically omitted if there is a single statement in a block. Indent the statements inside the block by a few spaces so that the program is easier to read.

The condition can be simple, such as checking whether the value of a variable is greater than a certain number. For example, the statements in this block are executed only if ratio has a value greater than 1.0:

```
if (ratio > 1.0) {
  ratio = 1.0;
  width++;
}
```

The braces are omitted here because only a single statement will be executed if the condition is true:

```
if (radius > 5.0)
  height = 1.0;
```

4.4.2   The if-else Statement

The if-else statement specifies alternate actions to be carried out when the "if" clause evaluates to false. The general form of an if-else statement follows:

```
if (condition) {
  // statements
} else {
  // statements
}
```

If *condition* evaluates to true, the statements in the if block are executed and the else block is skipped; otherwise, the statements in the if block are skipped, and the else block is executed. A compilation error occurs if a statement is placed between the two blocks:

```
if (length != 550){
  // do something here
}
int y = 5; // error
else {
  // do something else
}
```

The braces are left out here because there is a single statement following each of the "if" and "else" clauses:

```
if (length != 550)
   width = 10;
else
   width = 20;
```

A variant of the if-else statement checks more than one condition. This is written using multiple else-if clauses, each of which specifies a different condition to be tested:

```
if (condition_1) {
   // statements to be executed if condition_1 is true
} else if (condition_2) {
   // statements to be executed if condition_2 is true
}
...
} else if (condition_i) {
   // statements to be executed if condition_i is true
} else {
   // statements to be executed if
   // none of the above conditions is true
}
```

First, *condition_1* is checked. If it is true, the statements in the first block are executed, and the remaining conditions are skipped. If *condition_1* is false, *condition_2* is checked next. This procedure of checking conditions continues until a condition evaluates to true, and the statements in the corresponding block are then executed. If none of the conditions is true, the statements in the else block are executed. The else block is optional and can be omitted. Figure 4–3 shows the flowchart when if, else-if, and else blocks are present.

Figure 4–3
**Flowchart of a statement
with** if, else-if, **and**
else **blocks.**

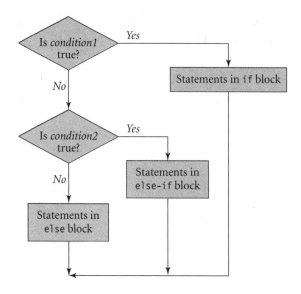

Example 1

Compile and run this program several times. Each time a different shape or
color appears. Can you figure out the "magic"?

```
import java.awt.*;
import java.awt.geom.*;
import java.util.Random;
import com.programwithjava.basic.DrawingKit;

public class MagicShapes {
  public static void main(String[] args) {
    int x = 75, y = 75, w1 = 200, h1 = 300, w2 = 300, h2 = 300;

    // draw the window
    DrawingKit dk = new DrawingKit("Magic Shapes");

    // magicShape gets a random integer value of 0, 1, 2 or 3.
    Random rand = new Random();
    int magicShape = rand.nextInt(4);

    // magicColor gets a random integer value of 0, 1 or 2
    int magicColor = rand.nextInt(3);

    if (magicColor == 0) {
      // magicColor is 0, set color to red
      dk.setPaint(Color.red);
```

```
    } else if (magicColor == 1) {
        // magicColor is 1, set color to cyan
        dk.setPaint(Color.cyan);
    } else {
        // magicColor is 2, set color to magenta
        dk.setPaint(Color.magenta);
    }

    if (magicShape == 0) {
        // magicShape is 0, draw and color a rectangle
        Rectangle2D.Float shape = new Rectangle2D.Float(x, y, w1, h1);
        dk.fill(shape);
    } else if (magicShape == 1) {
        // magicShape is 1, draw and color an ellipse
        Ellipse2D.Float shape1 = new Ellipse2D.Float(x, y, w1, h1);
        dk.fill(shape1);
    } else if (magicShape == 2) {
        // magicShape is 2, draw and color a circle
        Ellipse2D.Float shape2 = new Ellipse2D.Float(x, y, w2, h2);
        dk.fill(shape2);
    } else {
        // magicShape is 3, draw a square
        Rectangle2D.Float shape3 = new Rectangle2D.Float(x, y, w2, h2);
        dk.draw(shape3);
    }
  }
}
```

How does the program create different shapes with different colors each time it runs? Let us examine the program closely. We begin with two lines:

```
Random rand = new Random();
int magicShape = rand.nextInt(4);
```

These two lines create a **pseudorandom** integer number and assign it to magicShape. The number generator used here creates numbers based on some initial starting value known as the *seed*. For a given seed, the numbers that are produced are always the same, and are therefore not truly random (instead, they are known as pseudorandom). The class Random is defined in the java.util package, and an instance of this class is used to generate pseudorandom numbers. The nextInt method in this class, shown in Figure 4–4, creates pseudorandom integers. The argument to the nextInt method is 4; thus, the pseudorandom number assigned to magicShape will have a value of 0, 1, 2, or 3.

Figure 4–4

A constructor and method of class Random.

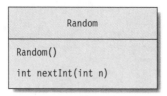

Random	
Random()	Constructor.
int nextInt(int n)	Returns a pseudorandom integer number in the range 0 to n−1.

This statement assigns a pseudorandom integer selected from 0, 1, and 2 to magicColor:

```
int magicColor = rand.nextInt(3);
```

In the following if else-if else statement, the value of magicColor decides what the color of the figure will be. If magicColor is 0, the color is set to red; if it is 1, the color is set to cyan, and so forth.

The next if else-if else statement checks the value of magicShape. This determines which shape is drawn. If magicShape is 0, a rectangle is drawn and filled with the color that was set using magicColor; a value of 1 for magicShape draws and colors an ellipse, and so forth.

You can display the values of magicColor and magicShape in the window using the drawString method of class DrawingKit:

```
dk.drawString("magicShape is " +magicShape, 50, 50);
dk.drawString("magicColor is " +magicColor, 175, 50);
```

The drawString method shown here has a slightly different format from the one we used earlier. In addition to the text, the values of the variables magicShape and magicColor are also displayed using the concatenation operator +. Add these two lines to the program after the random numbers have been assigned to the variables magicShape and magicColor, and compile and run the program again. One possible output is shown in Figure 4–5. You can now see the values of magicShape and magicColor in this window. ∎

4.4.3 The switch Statement

Similar to the if-else statement, the switch statement is used to select one out of many conditions. The general form of a switch statement is as follows:

```
switch(var) {
  case value1:
      // execute these statements if var is equal to value1
      break;
```

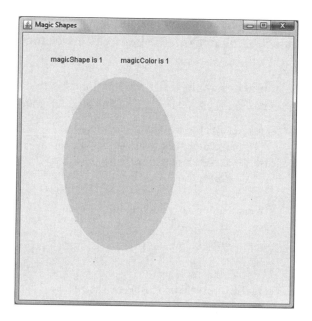

Figure 4–5

The output of program MagicShapes **depends on the pseudorandom integer values assigned to** magicShape **and** magicColor.

```
    case value2:
        // execute these statements if var is equal to value2
        break;
...
    default:
        // execute these statements if var does not match any value
        break;
}
```

The switch keyword is followed by a variable *var* within parentheses. The values placed after the case keywords (such as *value1* and *value2*) must be constants. First, *var* is compared to the first case constant, namely *value1*. If they are equal, the following statements are executed until the break statement is encountered. After a break statement is executed, all of the remaining statements in the switch structure are skipped. Otherwise, if *var* is not equal to *value1*, it is compared to the next case constant *value2*, and so on. If there is no match with any of the case constants, the statements in the default clause are executed. There can be only a single default clause and it is optional. The case constants must be unique; otherwise, a compilation error results.

A common mistake made by beginners is to forget to insert break statements. For instance, if you forget to insert break statements in the switch block shown previously, and the value of *var* is equal to *value1*, then every statement in this block will be executed even though *var* is not equal to any of the other case constants.

As another example, let us rewrite the code that checks the value of magic-Color in the previous program using a switch statement:

```java
switch(magicColor) {
    // if magicColor is 0, set color to red
    case 0: dk.setPaint(Color.red);
            break;

    //if magicColor is 1, set color to cyan
    case 1: dk.setPaint(Color.cyan);
            break;

    // set color to magenta
    default: dk.setPaint(Color.magenta);
            break;
}
```

The next example also shows how you can use a switch statement in a program.

Example 2

This is the program for a crystal ball. Run the program and see what the ball says.

```java
import java.awt.*;
import java.util.Random;
import java.awt.image.*;
import com.programwithjava.basic.DrawingKit;

public class CrystalBall {
  public static void main(String[] args) {
    DrawingKit dk = new DrawingKit("Crystal Ball");
    int x1 = 120, y1 = 0, x2 = 175, y2 = 230, w1 = 22, w2 = 30, h1 = 40;

    BufferedImage pict = dk.loadPicture("image/crystalBall.jpg");
    dk.drawPicture(pict, x1, y1);

    Random r = new Random();
    // magicNumber gets a random integer value of 0, 1, 2 or 3.
    int magicNumber = r.nextInt(4);
```

```
// set the font type and size
Font myfont = new Font("ARIAL", Font.ITALIC, 18);
dk.setPaint(Color.gray);
dk.setFont(myfont);

// Based on the value of magicNumber, one of the
// strings shown below is displayed on the screen.
switch(magicNumber) {
    case 0: dk.drawString("Something surprising", x2, y2);
            dk.drawString("will happen", x2 + w2, y2 + h1);
            break;
    case 1: dk.drawString("An exceptional event", x2, y2);
            dk.drawString("has occurred", x2 + w1, y2 + h1);
            break;
    case 2: dk.drawString("Shake the ball", x2 + w2, y2);
            dk.drawString("and focus harder", x2 + w1, y2 + h1);
            break;
    default: dk.drawString("Good fortune", x2 + w2, y2);
             dk.drawString("comes your way", x2 + w1, y2 + h1);
             break;
    }
  }
}
```

A possible output is shown in Figure 4–6. So, how does this program work? First, the image of a crystal ball is loaded from a file crystalBall.jpg and drawn on the screen using the loadPicture and drawPicture methods of class DrawingKit. Then, a pseudorandom integer number (0, 1, 2, or 3) is assigned to the variable magicNumber:

```
Random rand = new Random();
int magicNumber = rand.nextInt(4);
```

In the switch statement, this value of magicNumber is compared with the case constants 0, 1, and 2. If there is a match with any of these, the string in the corresponding case block is displayed on the screen; otherwise, the string in the default statement is displayed.

Modify this program by including more case statements inside the switch block and varying the strings displayed.

A limitation of switch is that you can only use integers such as int, byte, and char as *var* and as case constants, and not objects, strings, or doubles; otherwise, there will be a compilation error. An exception to this is that instances

Figure 4–6

An output of program
CrystalBall.

crystalBall.jpg © Richard Griffin, 123RF.com

of certain classes such as Integer and Character, and enums—to be discussed in Chapter 7—are permitted. Also, range checks (such as *var > value1*) are not possible using switch. Despite these limitations, switch statements are easier to read than other types of conditional constructs and you should use them whenever it is possible to do so.

4.5   Scope of Variables

We stated earlier that variable names should be unique in a program. It would be more accurate to say that variable names should be unique in their *scope*. The **scope** of a variable refers to that portion of the program where the variable can be accessed, and it depends upon where the variable has been declared. A variable can only be accessed in the block where it is declared. For example, a variable declared at the start of a method can be accessed everywhere in that method, whereas a variable declared within a block in that method can be accessed only in that block. Obviously, a variable cannot be accessed until it has been declared. Therefore, a variable's scope starts from the statement where it has been declared in the program.

Figure 4–7 shows the scope of various variables used in a program. The ceo and department variables can be accessed anywhere in the rest of the main method following their declaration, whereas manager can only be used

```
public static void main(String[] args) {
    String ceo;
    int department = 0;
    // other statements
    if (department == 1) {
        String manager;                    Scope of
        // other statements                manager
    } else if (department == 2) {
        String manager;                    Scope of
        // other statements                manager
    }
}
```

Scope of ceo

Figure 4–7
**The scope of variables
depends on where they
are declared in the
program.**

inside the block in which it is declared. The manager variables have been used twice in the program because their scopes do not overlap. On the other hand, declaring ceo or department again anywhere else in main would cause a compilation error.

4.6   Loops

A **loop** is used when an action has to be repeated many times. There are three types of loops: while, do-while, and for. In this section, we will discuss each of these structures in detail. An important point to keep in mind as you read this section pertains to the scope of variables declared inside a loop block: Any variables declared inside a loop block have a scope that is restricted to that loop block.

4.6.1   The while Loop

A while loop executes statements repeatedly until the loop condition becomes false. It has the following format:

```
while (condition) {
    // statements inside loop
}
// statements outside loop
```

Suppose that a pedestrian is crossing at a traffic signal that displays either "*WALK*" or "*DON'T WALK*." The pedestrian should not cross the road while the "*DON'T WALK*" sign is lighted. Let us write this using an if-else statement with the condition "*DON'T WALK* is lighted":

if "*DON'T WALK is lighted*"

   Do not cross the road

else

   Cross the road

The if-else statement does not work correctly here because the condition "*DON'T WALK* is lighted" is checked only *once* instead of repeatedly. Therefore, the pedestrian will never cross if the condition is true at the time he or she checks it. If we rewrite this using a while statement, the sign will be checked repeatedly, and the pedestrian will cross the road after it is no longer lighted (that is, when the condition becomes false):

while "*DON'T WALK is lighted*" {

   Do not cross the road

}

   Cross the road

A flowchart for the while loop is shown in Figure 4–8. First, the condition in the while clause is checked. If the condition is true, then the statements inside the loop are executed. This is repeated *continuously* for as long as the

Figure 4–8

Flowchart for a while **loop.**

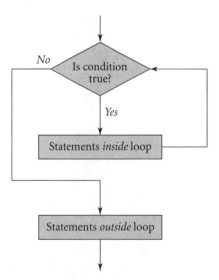

condition is true. The loop exits when the condition becomes false. You can draw a flowchart similar to the one in Figure 4–8 when you have to write code that contains a while loop.

You should indent statements in the while block by a few spaces so that the code is easier to read. Follow this style convention for other loops, such as do-while and for, as well.

Example 3

Draw four blue squares with sides of length 30, at points (100, 150), (150, 150), (200, 150), and (250, 150). Use a while loop in your solution.

Solution: First, it is helpful to draw a flowchart to solve the problem. An example is shown in Figure 4–9. The variable numberOfSquares keeps track of the number of squares that have been drawn on the screen. The first square is drawn at coordinates (100, 150), and the second at (150, 150). You can

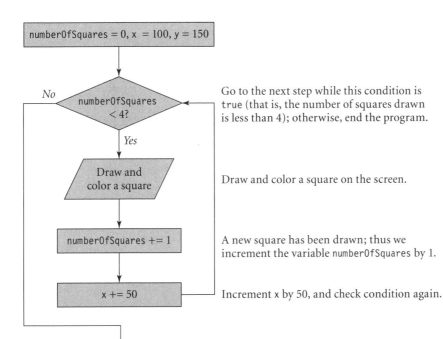

Figure 4–9
Flowchart for program Squares.

numberOfSquares = 0, x = 100, y = 150

numberOfSquares < 4?

Go to the next step while this condition is true (that is, the number of squares drawn is less than 4); otherwise, end the program.

Draw and color a square

Draw and color a square on the screen.

numberOfSquares += 1

A new square has been drawn; thus we increment the variable numberOfSquares by 1.

x += 50

Increment x by 50, and check condition again.

see that the x-coordinate increases by 50, but the y-coordinate does not change. We use this information inside the `while` loop, as shown in the flowchart in Figure 4–9.

Check to ensure that the statements inside the loop are executed four times, as indicated in Figure 4–9. Using this flowchart, we can write the code for this problem:

```java
import java.awt.*;
import java.awt.geom.*;
import com.programwithjava.basic.DrawingKit;

public class Squares {
  public static void main(String[] args) {
    DrawingKit dk = new DrawingKit("Squares");
    int numberOfSquares = 0, x = 100, y = 150, width = 30, height = 30;

    while (numberOfSquares < 4) {
      // draw and color a square
      Rectangle2D.Float rect_same = new Rectangle2D.Float (x, y, width,
height);
      dk.setPaint(Color.blue);
      dk.fill(rect_same);

      // increment number of squares drawn by 1
      numberOfSquares += 1;
      System.out.println(numberOfSquares);

      // increment the x coordinate of the next square by 50.
      x += 50;
    }
  }
}
```

The output from the program is shown in Figure 4–10.

The console output shows the value of `numberOfSquares` in each loop iteration:

```
1
2
3
4
```

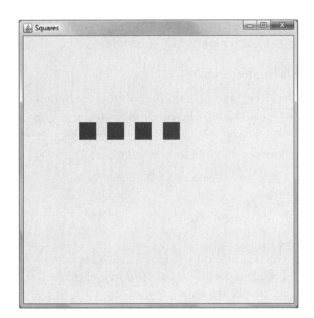

Figure 4–10
Output of the program
Squares.

As an exercise, modify the program to add two more squares at positions (300, 150) and (350, 150).

Example 4

What is the problem in the following loop?

```
int x = 10, y = 5;
while (x < 50) {
    y -= 1;
    x -= 10;
    System.out.println(x);
}
y += 2;
```

Solution: The value of x is decremented inside the loop; thus the values of x are 0, −10, −20, −30, and so on. The condition x < 50 is always true, which results in an **infinite** loop. These types of programs are usually terminated automatically by the system after a certain amount of time has elapsed. A user can also force the program to terminate by typing in special characters on the keyboard, such as pressing the *Ctrl* key and the character *c* key together (called Control-C).   ∎

4.6.2   The do-while Loop

The do-while loop is similar to the while loop with one major difference: In the do-while loop, the condition is tested at the *end* of the loop, whereas in the while loop it is tested at the *beginning* of the loop. So, for the same condition, the do-while loop will execute at least *once*, even if the condition is false at the start. A do-while loop has the following format:

```
do {
  // statements inside loop
} while (condition);
// statements outside loop
```

A flowchart for the do-while loop is shown in Figure 4–11. First, the statements inside the loop are executed. Then the condition in the while clause is checked. If the condition is true, the statements inside the loop are executed again. This is repeated continuously for as long as the condition is true. When the condition becomes false, the statements outside the loop are executed.

Figure 4–11

Flowchart for a do-while loop.

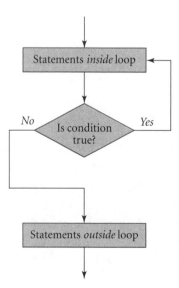

Example 5

Rewrite the while loop in program Squares to draw four squares using a do-while loop.

Solution: The while loop is replaced with the following do-while loop:

```
do {
  // draw and color a square
  Rectangle2D.Float rect_same = new Rectangle2D.Float (x, y, width,
height);
  dk.setPaint(Color.blue);
  dk.fill(rect_same);

  // increment number of squares drawn by 1
  numberOfSquares += 1;
  System.out.println(numberOfSquares);

  // increment the x coordinate of the next square by 50.
   x += 50;
  } while(numberOfSquares < 4);
```

4.6.3 The for Loop

A for loop can be used if we know the number of times that a loop should be executed. The *loop variable* initialization and modification, as well as the *loop condition*, are specified in the for clause itself. The statements inside the loop are executed only while the loop condition is true. A for loop has the following format:

for (*loop variable initialization*; *loop condition*; *loop variable modification*)
{
    // statements inside loop
}
// statements *outside* loop

Figure 4–12(a) shows a flowchart for a generic for loop.

Figure 4–12(b) shows the flowchart for the following for loop:

```
for (int i = 1; i <= 3; i += 1) {
  // Statements inside loop
}
// Statements outside loop
```

Figure 4–12

(a) Flowchart for a `for` loop. (b) A loop that executes three times.

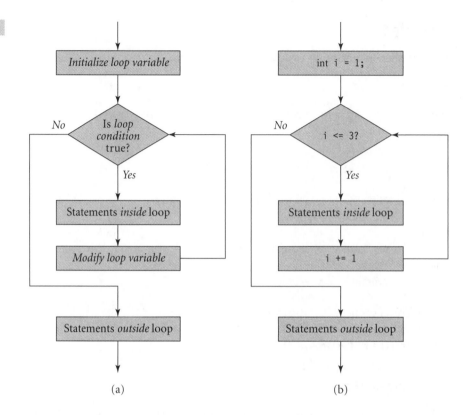

(a)   (b)

The loop variable `i` is first declared and initialized to the value 1. Then the loop condition `i <= 3` is checked. It is `true`; thus the statements inside the loop are executed. At the end of the iteration, the value of `i` is incremented by 1 and the loop condition checked again. This procedure continues and the statements inside the loop are executed until the loop condition becomes `false`. (Note that the loop condition is checked each time after the loop variable is modified.)

Example 6

Use a `for` loop to draw five concentric circles with center at (225, 225). (Concentric circles are circles with the same center.) The radii of the circles are 100, 80, 60, 40, and 20.

Solution: Figure 4–13 shows two circles with radii 100 and 80. The two circles have a center C with coordinates (225, 225). The radius of the outer

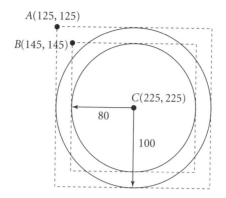

Figure 4–13

Two concentric circles with center at (225, 225) and radii of 100 and 80.

circle is 100 and so, using simple geometry, we get the x- and y-coordinates of point A as $x = 225 - 100 = 125$ and $y = 225 - 100 = 125$. The radius of the inner circles is 80; thus point B has coordinates (145, 145).

We can draw a circle by using the Ellipse2D.Float method and setting the width equal to the height. Therefore, to draw the outer circle, we have to give the coordinates of point A and set the height and width equal to 2 * 100:

```
Ellipse2D.Float circle = new Ellipse2D.Float (125, 125, 2*100, 2*100);
```

In order to draw the inner circle, we have to specify point B's coordinates and set the width and height equal to 2 * 80:

```
Ellipse2D.Float circle = new Ellipse2D.Float (125+20, 125+20, 2*(100-20), 2*(100-20));
```

We can extend this to draw the other circles similarly. For example, the circle with radius 60 is drawn as:

```
Ellipse2D.Float circle = new Ellipse2D.Float (125+40, 125+40, 2*(100-40), 2*(100-40));
```

Do you see the pattern in the statements that draw the circles? The pattern is:

```
Ellipse2D.Float circle = new Ellipse2D.Float (125+i, 125+i, 2*(100-i), 2*(100-i));
```

Here i is a variable that has values 0, 20, 40, 60, and 80, and substituting each of these values in the preceding statement draws the five concentric circles. The value of i is initialized to 0, and it is incremented by 20 at the end of the iteration. This can be written using a for loop, as follows:

```
for (int i = 0; i <= 100; i = i+20) {
  Ellipse2D.Float circle = new Ellipse2D.Float (125+i, 125+i, 2*(100-i),
2*(100-i));
}
```

The complete code for the problem is given here:

```
import java.awt.geom.*;
import com.programwithjava.basic.DrawingKit;

public class ConcentricCircles {
  public static void main(String[] args) {
    DrawingKit dk = new DrawingKit("Concentric Circles");
    float x = 125, y = 125, r = 100;
    int step = 20;

    for (int i = 0; i <= r; i = i+step) {
     // draw a circle with diameter 2*(r-i)
      Ellipse2D.Float circle = new Ellipse2D.Float (x+i, y+i, 2*(r-i),
2*(r-i));
      dk.draw(circle);
    }
  }
}
```

The output is shown in Figure 4–14.

As an exercise, modify this program to draw 10 concentric circles having a center at (250, 250) and radii of 20, 40, 60, and so on.   ∎

4.7   Conditions Using Logical Operators

In addition to the relational operator, there are three other operators, known as **logical operators**, that are used in conditions:

Logical Operator	What the Symbol Means
&&	AND
||	OR
!	NOT

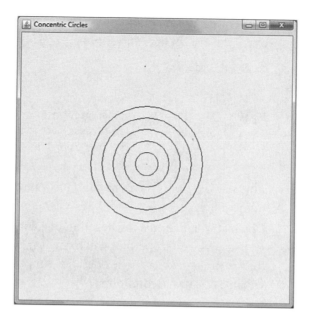

Figure 4–14
Output of program
ConcentricCircles.

Logical operators combine two or more conditions into a single true-or-false value. Unlike relational operators, logical operators have operands that are conditions (that is, boolean expressions). For example, the AND operator is used here to create a new condition:

```
a > 3 && a < 10
```

This condition is true only if a is greater than 3 *and* a is less than 10. It is valid as both operands on either side of the && operator are conditions. Thus, the following expression would be incorrect if c and d were not of type boolean:

```
c && d
```

> **&& operator**: produces the boolean result of true only if *both* cond1 and cond2 are true in the expression:
>
> ```
> cond1 && cond2
> ```

These examples show how this operator is used:

```
7 > 5 && 3 < 10      // true because both conditions are true
a >= 5 && a <= 10    // true if variable a takes values from 5 to 10
x < 5 && x > 10      // false
```

The last expression is false because the variable x cannot be both less than 5 and greater than 10.

|| **operator**: produces the `boolean` result of `true` if *either* one of `cond1` or `cond2` is `true` in the expression:

`cond1 || cond2`

For example:

```
7 > 5 || 11 < 10    // true because 7 > 5
3 > 5 || 11 < 10    // false because both conditions are false
a < 5 || a > 10     // false only if a lies in the range 5 to 10.
a >= 5 || a <= 10   // true
```

This last condition is `true` because this range encompasses all real numbers.

! **operator**: represents the negation of a condition. If a condition is `true`, applying this operator will make it `false`. This is a unary operator because it takes a single operand. Suppose that we have a `boolean` variable `bool` and a condition `E`:

```
!bool // this condition is true only if bool is false
!E // true only if E is false
```

If `E` is a condition that is `true` (such as `20 > 5`), then `!E` is `false`.

4.7.1   Operator Precedence

Previously, we had discussed the operator precedence order for the arithmetic, unary, and assignment operators. Now, we have introduced two more types of operators—relational and logical. The mnemonic PUMAS changes to PUMA LEAPS to help you remember the precedence order for all of these operators:

P for Parentheses (), Postfix   `a++`   `a--`

U for Unary operators (except postfix)   `+`   `-`   `++a`   `--a`   `!`

M for Multiplication & division, Modulus   `*`   `/`   `%`

A for Addition and subtraction   `+` `-`

L for Less than   `<`   `<=`   `>`   `>=`

E for Equality   `==`   `!=`

A for AND   `&&`

P for Parallel lines   `||`

S for Special assignments   `=`   `+=`   `-=`   `*=`   `/=`   `%=`

You can use the mnemonic PUMA LEAPS (instead of PUMAS) to help you remember the order in which to parenthesize the condition or arithmetic expression.

After the expression has been parenthesized, evaluate its value starting from the innermost parentheses and moving toward the outermost parentheses. For example, consider this condition:

```
a > b && c < d || e > f-4
```

This is equivalent to:

```
((a > b) && (c < d)) || (e > (f-4))
```

As we discussed earlier, if there are two or more operators with the *same* priority or importance, evaluate them from left to right. An exception is that the *unary* and *assignment* operators should be evaluated from right to left.

4.8   break and continue Statements

Loops may also contain the break and continue statements. These are a type of control flow statement known as **branching statements**. The most common use of break statements is inside the switch statement. However, you may occasionally also encounter them inside loops. The break statement is used in a loop to *quit* the loop immediately:

```
while (condition1) {
  // statements inside loop
  if (condition2)
      break;
}
// statements outside loop
```

If condition2 is true, exit loop immediately and start executing statements outside loop.

In addition to while loops, break can also be used inside for and do-while loops.

Similar to break, the **continue** statement terminates the *current* iteration of the loop; however, it then starts the next one:

```
while (condition1) {
  // statements inside loop
  if (condition2)
          continue;
    // statements after continue
}
// statements outside loop
```

If condition2 is true, skip statements after continue and start next loop iteration.

When the `continue` statement is executed, the statements that follow will be skipped, and the next loop iteration will be started.

This usage of a `break` statement or a `continue` statement inside a loop should be avoided as much as possible because it makes code difficult to read, and therefore can lead to errors.

Example 7

Write a program to generate 50 random numbers in the range 0 to 10. However, if the number 5 is generated, the program should terminate.

Solution: The random numbers are generated inside a `for` loop. A `break` statement is used to terminate the iteration when the number 5 is generated.

```java
import java.util.*;

public class BreakDemo {
  public static void main(String[] args) {
    int number, x = 10, y = 50;
    for (int i = 0; i < 50; i++) {
      Random r = new Random();
      number = r.nextInt(11);
      System.out.println(number);
      if (number == 5)
        break;
    }
  }
}
```

The output is different each time you run the program. A sample output is shown here:

```
6
4
5
```

The program will terminate if the number 5 is generated. Otherwise, it will terminate after generating 50 numbers because the `for` loop index `i` takes values 0, 1, 2, ..., 49.

As an exercise, write another program to solve this problem without using a break statement.   ∎

4.9 Nested for Loops

A **nested for** loop consists of two for loops with one loop placed inside the other. The outer and inner loops use different loop variables. Each time the outer loop executes once, the inner loop executes with all values of its loop variable. This is an example of a nested for loop:

```
for (i = 0; i < 5; i++) {
    for (j = 0; j < 3; j++) {
      // statements inside loop
      }
}
```

The outer loop executes 5 times. Each time the outer loop executes once, the inner loop executes 3 times. Therefore, the inner loop will execute a total of 15 times.

The nested for loop is useful for iterating through the elements of a two-dimensional array. Consider the pixels in a digital image stored in a two-dimensional array with two rows and three columns, as shown in Figure 4–15. Recall that the rows and columns of an array are numbered starting from 0 instead of 1.

This nested for loop prints out the row and column numbers of each pixel in the image:

```
for (int column = 0; column < 3; column++) {
  for (int row = 0; row < 2; row++) {
    System.out.println(column+"," +row);
  }
}
```

This will print out the following column–row pairs:

```
0,0
0,1
1,0
```

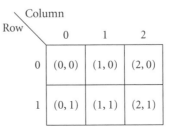

Figure 4–15

Coordinates of pixels in an array with two rows and three columns.

```
1,1
2,0
2,1
```

The coordinates of the pixels in each column are printed out, starting with column 0.

4.10   Modifying Pictures

We will use nested for loops to manipulate a picture, such as changing its colors, transparency, and brightness. It is simple to change the color of a particular pixel. For example, the red, green, and blue components of a pixel at coordinates (1000, 1200) can be changed to the values 55, 10, and 100, respectively, as follows. First, we must create a new color using these values in the Color constructor:

```
Color pixelColor = new Color(55, 10, 100);
```

Next, we convert this Color object into an encoded value using the method getRGB (similar to that in BufferedImage) of class Color:

```
int rgbvalue = pixelColor.getRGB();
```

Finally, we use the setRGB method of BufferedImage to modify the pixel color to rgbvalue at the given location (1000, 1200) in a BufferedImage object (say, picture):

```
picture.setRGB(1000, 1200, rgbvalue);
```

The next example shows how you can change the colors in a photograph.

Example 8

This example shows how to manipulate selectively the colors in a photograph. We change the color of the white background and yellow petals in daffodils.jpg and leave the rest of the picture unchanged. This is done by using conditional statements inside nested for loops. The code is as follows:

```java
import java.awt.*;
import java.awt.image.BufferedImage;
import com.programwithjava.basic.DrawingKit;

public class ChangeImageColors {
  public static void main(String[] args) {
    DrawingKit dk = new DrawingKit("Change colors", 1680, 700);
    BufferedImage picture = dk.loadPicture("image/daffodils.jpg");
```

```
      // draw the original picture
      dk.drawPicture(picture, 0, 50);

      // modify the pixels in the picture
      for (int x = 0; x < picture.getWidth(); x++) {
        for (int y = 0; y < picture.getHeight(); y++) {
          // get the red, green and blue components of pixel at (x, y)
          int colorValue = picture.getRGB(x, y);
          Color pixelColor = new Color(colorValue);
          int red = pixelColor.getRed();
          int green = pixelColor.getGreen();
          int blue = pixelColor.getBlue();

          if (red > 245 && green > 245 && blue > 245) {
            //change a white or nearly white pixel to blue
            red = 100;
            green = 150;
            blue = 255;
          } else if (red >= 2 * green) {
            // leave an orange pixel unchanged
            ;
          } else if (red >= green) {
            // change a yellow pixel to pale pink
            blue = green;
          }
          // update the pixel color in picture
          Color newPixelColor = new Color(red, green, blue);
          int newRgbvalue = newPixelColor.getRGB();
          picture.setRGB(x, y, newRgbvalue);
        } // end inner for loop
      } // end outer for loop

      // draw the modified picture
      dk.drawPicture(picture, 800, 50);
    }
  }
```

Figure 4–16 shows the program output with the modified picture to the right of the original. Using the nested for loops, we can iterate over all the pixels in the picture and modify them selectively. As you already know, pure white has the highest intensity (255) for its red, green, and blue components. This conditional statement selects pixels having component values in the range 246 (nearly white) to 255 (pure white):

```
if (red > 245 && green > 245 && blue > 245)
```

Figure 4–16

The colors of the image on the left are modified to those on the right.

daffodils.jpg © Monika Adamczyk, 123RF.com

The pixels selected by this statement are set to a particular shade of blue. You can change the values inside this if block to change the background to another color.

Orange is created by mixing two parts of green with one part of red. The proportion can vary slightly since various shades of orange are present, and so this statement uses the >= operator instead of ==:

`else if` (red >= 2 * green)

We would like to leave the orange hue unchanged. Therefore, the preceding statement is followed by an empty statement consisting of a single semi-colon.

Yellow is created by mixing red and green in equal proportions with little or no blue. This statement checks for yellow pixels:

`else if` (red >= green)

As the amount of blue is increased, the yellow hue becomes lighter. When the amount of blue becomes equal to green, it results in pink:

`blue = green;`

As an exercise, change the colors used in this program to create a different picture.   ■

Example 9

This program shows how you can change the transparency of a picture by modifying the alpha channel. As the values of alpha are changed from 255 to 0, the picture goes from opaque to fully transparent. In this example, we use a value of 0 for alpha to make a portion of a picture fully transparent.

```java
import java.awt.*;
import java.awt.image.BufferedImage;
import com.programwithjava.basic.DrawingKit;

public class ChangeImageTransparency {
  public static void main(String[] args) {
    DrawingKit dk = new DrawingKit("Change transparency", 850, 700);
    BufferedImage picture1 = dk.loadPicture("image/daffodils.jpg");
    // draw first picture
    dk.drawPicture(picture1, 0, 50);

    // load second picture
    BufferedImage picture2 = dk.loadPicture("image/butterflies.png");

    // check if picture has transparent pixels
    System.out.println(picture2.getColorModel().hasAlpha());

    // modify the pixels in the second picture
    for (int x = 0; x < picture2.getWidth(); x++) {
      for (int y = 0; y < picture2.getHeight(); y++) {
      // get the red, green and blue components of pixel at (x, y)
        int colorValue = picture2.getRGB(x, y);
        Color pixelColor = new Color(colorValue);
        int red = pixelColor.getRed();
        int green = pixelColor.getGreen();
        int blue = pixelColor.getBlue();

        // check if pixel is in the white background
        if (red > 240 && green > 240 && blue > 240) {
          // make this pixel transparent by setting alpha to 0
          int alpha = 0;
          Color newPixelColor = new Color(red, green, blue, alpha);
          int newRgbvalue = newPixelColor.getRGB();
          picture2.setRGB(x, y, newRgbvalue);
        }
      } // end inner for loop
    } // end outer for loop

    // draw the modified second picture
    dk.drawPicture(picture2, 250, 280);
  }
}
```

(a)

(b)

Figure 4–17

(a) Picture of butterflies with an opaque white background. (b) The background is made fully transparent.

butterflies.png courtesy of iclipart.com; daffodils.jpg © Monika Adamczyk, 123RF.com.

The output is shown in Figure 4–17. Figure 4–17(a) shows two butterflies on an opaque (alpha = 255) white background that is partially obscuring the flowers. This output is obtained by commenting out the code in the `for` loops in class `ChangeImageTransparency` so that the alpha values are not changed in `picture2`. In Figure 4–17(b), the pixels in the white background have been made completely transparent by changing their alpha value to 0. This is done by creating a new color in which the red, green, and blue components have the same values as before but alpha is 0:

```
int alpha = 0;
Color newPixelColor = new Color(red, green, blue, alpha);
```

The pixels in the white background of `picture2` are then set to this new color using these two statements:

```
int newRgbvalue = newPixelColor.getRGB();
picture2.setRGB(x, y, newRgbvalue);
```

As discussed earlier, pictures stored in the PNG file format may have an alpha channel that supports transparency. JPEG pictures do not have an alpha channel, and thus they cannot be made transparent. This statement checks whether or not `picture2` has an alpha channel:

```
picture2.getColorModel().hasAlpha();
```

This method returns true for picture2; thus we can modify the alpha channel of this picture, as shown in this program.   ∎

The **ternary operator ?:** provides a succinct way of expressing a special type of if-else statement. It evaluates a condition, and assigns one of two values to a variable depending upon whether the condition is true or false. Consider this if-else statement:

```
if (condition)
    var = value1;
else
    var = value2;
```

This can be written in a single line by using the ?: operator:

```
var = condition? value1 : value2;
```

If *condition* is true, the variable *var* is assigned *value1*; otherwise, it is assigned *value2*. We use this operator in the next example.

Example 10

This program shows how the brightness of a picture can be changed by multiplying the red, green, and blue samples of each pixel in a picture by 1.75. The sample values should not exceed 255; thus, any scaled values that exceed this limit are set to 255.

```
import java.awt.*;
import java.awt.image.BufferedImage;
import com.programwithjava.basic.DrawingKit;

public class ChangeImageBrightness {
  public static void main(String[] args) {
    DrawingKit dk = new DrawingKit("Change brightness", 1680, 700);
    BufferedImage picture = dk.loadPicture("image/yosemite.jpg");
    // draw the original picture
    dk.drawPicture(picture, 0, 50);

    // modify the pixels in the picture
    for (int x = 0; x < picture.getWidth(); x++) {
      for (int y = 0; y < picture.getHeight(); y++) {
        // get the red, green and blue components of pixel at (x, y)
        int colorValue = picture.getRGB(x, y);
        Color pixelColor = new Color(colorValue);
        int red = pixelColor.getRed();
```

```
        int green = pixelColor.getGreen();
        int blue = pixelColor.getBlue();

        // multiply the red, green and blue samples by 1.75
        red = red <= 145? (int)(red * 1.75f): 255;
        green = green <= 145? (int)(green * 1.75f) : 255;
        blue = blue <= 145? (int)(blue * 1.75f) : 255;

        // update the pixel color in picture
        Color newPixelColor = new Color(red, green, blue);
        int newRgbvalue = newPixelColor.getRGB();
        picture.setRGB(x, y, newRgbvalue);
      } // end inner for loop
    } // end outer for loop

    // draw the modified picture
    dk.drawPicture(picture, 860, 50);
  }
}
```

Figure 4–18 shows the result. The following statement scales the value of the red sample by a factor of 1.75 only if it is less than or equal to 145; otherwise, it sets the value to 255.

```
red = red <= 145? (int)(red * 1.75f): 255;
```

This process is repeated for the other two components. The previous statement has the same meaning as the following:

```
if (red <= 145)
  red = (int)(red * 1.75f);
else
  red = 255;
```

Figure 4–18

The image on the right is made brighter than the original on the left.

yosemite.jpg © Ming Huang, 123RF.com

If you multiply the pixels by a value in the range 0 to 1, it will darken the image. Experiment with different factors and note how the brightness varies. You can also use a different factor for each component to produce other interesting visual effects. ∎

4.11 Summary

In this chapter, we discussed how you can describe conditions using `boolean` expressions and use them in conditional statements and loops. Conditional statements are used to select one of many operations depending on whether a `boolean` expression evaluates to `true` or `false`. Loops are useful when an operation must be performed multiple times. Branching statements allow you to perform certain operations selectively inside a loop or terminate the loop. We also introduced image manipulation techniques, which show you how to change the colors and brightness of a picture, and how to combine pictures together. In the next chapter, you will learn other interesting techniques to manipulate images. So keep reading!

Class Summary

`Random()`—a constructor in class `Random` in the `java.util` package that is used to create a random number generator.

`int nextInt(int n)`—a method in class `Random` that returns a pseudorandom integer number in the range 0 to $n-1$.

`int getRGB()`—a method in class `Color` that returns the encoded color value of this `Color` object.

Exercises

1. Draw a flowchart for each of the following problems. Also, find the values of x, y, and z after all the statements in each problem are executed, assuming the following initial values for these variables:

   ```
   int x = 100, y = 5, z = 100;
   ```

   a. ```
       if (x > 50) {
               y *= 5;
               z--;
       }
       x += 5;
       ```
       ```

b.
```
if (x <= 30)
        y -= 10;
    else {
            y += 2;
            z *= 5;
    }
    y++;
```

c.
```
switch(x) {
        case 100: y +=  20;
                    break;
        case 200: z *=  10;
                    break;
        case 300: z +=  y;
                    break;
        default: x = 0;
                    break;
    }
```

d.
```
while (x <= 100) {
        y -= 5;
        x += 10;
    }
    z += 2;
```

e.
```
for (int i = 0; i < 4; i++) {
        x += i;
        y -= i;
    }
```

2. Find the syntax errors in the following code segments. Assume that the variables have been declared as integers.

a.
```
If (x = y)
    System.out.println(x)
```

b.
```
if (x == 10)
        x = x + 3.5f;
    else (x < 10)
        x--;
```

c.
```
for (int 1 = 0, 1 <= 5, 1++)
    sum += 1;
    }
```

d.
```
do {
    sum = sum + 10;
    } while (x < 5)
```

3. Find the error in the following code segment:

```
int x = 50;
while (x < 100) {
    y -= 1;
    x -= 10;
}
y += 2;
```

4. Determine if there is an error in the following nested `for` loop:

```
for (int j = 0; j < 5; j++)
    for (j = 0; j < 10; j++)
        // do something here
```

5. Determine the value of the `boolean` variable `bool` in each of the following problems. Assume that the variables a, b, c, and d are declared as follows:

```
int a = 1, b = 2, c = 3, d = 4;
```

a. `bool = a > b && c < d;`

b. `bool = a > d++ || c <= d;`

c. `bool = !(a---== d);`

d. `bool = (a > b && c + d * 0.5 == 5);`

6. Parenthesize the following boolean/arithmetic expressions and determine their values:

a. `4 > 3 && -7 < 6`

b. `4 + 3 * 5 - 6 / 2`

c. `11 < 13 && 17 > 23 || 5 != 6`

d. `23 % 3 * 5 + 8`

e. `!(5 < 23)`

7. Write a program to print numbers from 1 to 5000.

8. Write a program to print all numbers from 1 to 100 except those that end in 7 or are a multiple of 7. For instance, the program should not print the numbers 7, 14, 17, 21, 27, and so on.

Graphics Problems

9. Write a code segment using `else if` statements to produce graphical output that depends on the value of a variable x. Draw a rectangle,

circle, or ellipse if x is 0, 1, or 2, respectively. For all other values of x, draw a line. You can select any position and size for each shape.

10. The following code segment should draw five squares, each with a side of length 25, at different positions in a window. Complete the code marked with "?".

```
int x = 0, y = 100;
DrawingKit dk = new DrawingKit();
while(?) {
    x = x + 1;
    Rectangle2D.Float r = new Rectangle2D.Float(x * 50, y, 25, 25);
    dk.draw(r);
}
```

11. Using a while loop, write a program that creates six ellipses each of width 100 and height 50, as shown in Figure 4–19. The x and y coordinates of the first ellipse are at 50 and 100, respectively.

Figure 4–19

A set of ellipses.

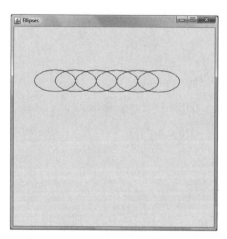

12. Repeat the previous problem using a do-while loop.

13. Complete the following for loop to create nine squares of side 20 arranged in a single column:

```
for (int x = 1; ?; ?) {
    Rectangle2D.Float r = new Rectangle2D.Float(10, x*30, 20, 20);
    dk.draw(r);
}
```

14. Complete the following statements to create five squares of side 10 arranged in a single row:

```
for (int y = 0; ?; ?) {
  Rectangle2D.Float r = new Rectangle2D.Float(?, 50, 10, 10);
  dk.draw(r);
}
```

15. Write a program to create a row of 20 shapes consisting of alternating squares and circles using a for loop. Every square has a side of length 20 and each circle has diameter 20. The distance from the center of a square to the center of its neighboring circle is 20. A row should start with a square.

16. Modify the preceding program so that every third shape is red, and the remaining shapes are blue.

17. Modify the program ConcentricCircles (see Example 6) to draw a set of circles such that they have the same center and the radii of consecutive circles differ by 10. Assume that the outermost circle has radius R. The program draws all of the circles until the diameter of the innermost circle becomes less than 20. The program should then print out on the console the number of circles that have been drawn and the diameter of the innermost circle. Test your program for various values of R. Use a while loop.

18. Repeat the preceding problem using a for loop.

19. Write a program using nested for loops to create a grid of 81 squares, each of side 20, as shown in Figure 4–20. The x- and y-coordinates of

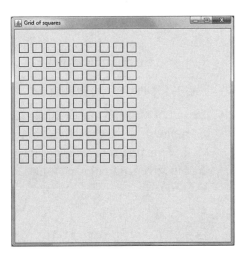

Figure 4–20

A grid of squares.

the square in the first column and first row are (10, 30), and the sides of any two neighboring squares are separated by a distance of 10.

Image Manipulation Problems

20. Modify the program ChangeImageColors (see Example 8) so that the pixels in the white background are set to the following color: red = 100, green = 15, blue = 35.

21. An interesting effect is to create an *inverted-color* image, in which the original colors in the image are replaced with their complementary values. This is done by subtracting each of the red, green, and blue pixel values from 255. Modify the program ChangeImageColors (see Example 8) so that the pixels in the new image are set to the following color: red = 255 – red, green = 255 – green, blue = 255 – blue.

22. Modify the program ChangeImageColors (see Example 8) to display only the *red* channel of the image.

23. Modify the program ChangeImageColors (see Example 8) to display only the *blue* channel of the image.

24. Repeat the preceding problem for the *green* channel.

25. Modify the program ChangeImageTransparency (see Example 9) so that all the pixels in the butterflies.png picture are semitransparent, with an alpha value of 100.

26. Modify the program ChangeImageTransparency (see Example 9) so that the white background in the butterflies.png picture is opaque and the butterflies are fully transparent.

27. Modify the program ChangeImageBrightness (see Example 10) so that all the pixels are multiplied by 1.5.

28. Repeat the preceding problem with a factor of 0.75.

29. Instead of multiplying all three channels by the same factor, use a different factor for each channel to produce interesting visual effects. Modify the program ChangeImageBrightness (see Example 10) so that the red, green, and blue channels are multiplied by 0.5, 1.75, and 1.5, respectively.

Further Reading

You can get more information about the different ways in which images can be manipulated in [2, 3]. To learn about tools used to transform images, refer to [2].

References

1. "The Java™ Tutorials." Web. <http://download.oracle.com/javase/tutorial/>.

2. Brinkmann, Ron. *The Art and Science of Digital Compositing: Techniques for Visual Effects, Animation and Motion Graphics, Second Edition.* Burlington, MA: Morgan Kaufmann/Elsevier, 2008. Print.

3. Guzdial, Mark, and Barbara Ericson. *Introduction to Computing and Programming in Java: A Multimedia Approach.* Upper Saddle River, NJ: Pearson Prentice Hall, 2007. Print.

4. *Java™ Platform, Standard Edition 6, API Specification.* Web. <http://download.oracle.com/javase/6/docs/api/>.

5. Eckel, Bruce. *Thinking in Java.* Upper Saddle River, NJ: Prentice Hall, 2006. Print.

6. Anderson, Julie, and Herve Franceschi. *Java 6 Illuminated: An Active Learning Approach.* Sudbury, MA: Jones and Bartlett, 2008. Print.

7. Sierra, Kathy, and Bert Bates. *Head First Java.* Sebastopol, CA: O'Reilly, 2005. Print.

8. Knudsen, Jonathan. *Java 2D Graphics.* Beijing: O'Reilly, 1999. Print.

CHAPTER 5

User-Defined Classes

CHAPTER CONTENTS

In previous chapters, we used existing classes and methods to create objects in our programs. In this chapter, you will learn how to write your own classes and methods. A class called Lamp is developed incrementally through the chapter to explain various concepts as we go along. By the end of the chapter, it will include graphics to turn a Lamp object on and off inside a window. You will also learn about *compositing*, a technique to combine images together to produce a new image.

5.1   Parts of a Class

Recall from our earlier discussion that a class contains fields and methods. For example, consider the Lamp class shown in Figure 5–1.

Figure 5–1

The Lamp class.

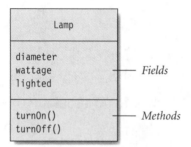

The fields specify the diameter of the bulb globe in inches, its wattage, and whether it is lighted. The lamp is turned on and off using the methods turnOn and turnOff, respectively. The class is declared as follows:

```
class Lamp {
  // body of this class will be written here
}
```

The code for class Lamp is placed within the braces. A class has four important parts: **fields**, **methods**, **constructors**, and **access modifiers**. In the following sections, we discuss each of these parts in detail.

5.2   Fields

The **fields** of the class are placed in the class body at the very beginning of the class definition. The data type of each field must be placed before the field name. Add the fields diameter, wattage, and lighted to the Lamp class as follows:

```
class Lamp {
  // fields
  double diameter;
```

```
  int wattage;
  boolean lighted;
}
```

Each field declaration should be placed on a separate line so that you can add comments to explain the purpose of each field. You can create an instance of this class and assign values to its fields. The following code, which creates a Lamp object called lamp, would go in a different class or a main method:

```
Lamp lamp = new Lamp();
```

This statement assigns a value of 3.0 to lamp's diameter field:

```
lamp.diameter = 3.0;
```

The left side of the assignment contains the object name followed by the field name, with a dot placed between the names. Other fields can be assigned values similarly:

```
lamp.wattage = 50;
lamp.lighted = true;
```

5.3 Methods

Methods are added below the field declarations. A method definition is comprised of two parts: *declaration* and *body*. The **method declaration** consists of the *return type* followed by the method name. For example, this method, named doSomething, has a return type of int:

```
int doSomething() {
  /* body of the method */
}
```

There are two methods (turnOn and turnOff) in the lamp specifications, which are added as follows:

```
class Lamp {
  // fields
  double diameter;
  int wattage;
  boolean lighted;

  // methods
  void turnOn() {
    // do something here
  }
```

```
  void turnOff() {
    // do something here
  }
}
```

Recall that if a method does not return a value, its return type is void. Hence, methods turnOn and turnOff have a return type of void because they do not return a value.

An object's fields are called **instance variables** or **instance fields**, and its methods are called **instance methods**. Therefore, diameter, wattage, and lighted are instance fields, and turnOn and turnOff are instance methods of any object of class Lamp.

5.3.1   The Method Body

The **body** of a method describes the actions that a method undertakes. The body contains statements that might change the fields, compute new results, or perform other operations such as drawing graphics. There are no statements in the turnOn method; thus this method does not do anything yet. Add a statement to method turnOn to change the value of the field lighted to true:

```
void turnOn() {
  lighted = true;
}
```

Similarly, add a statement to the turnOff method to change the field lighted to false.

A method can return data to the calling method. This process is done using the keyword return followed by the name of the variable containing data to be returned. This method returns the value of field diameter in Lamp:

```
double getDiameter() {
  return diameter;
}
```

> A method can return only *one* value and the return type of the method must match the data type of the variable being returned.

Thus the return type of the getDiameter method is double because this method returns the value of diameter, which has the data type double. We add additional methods to return the values of other fields (wattage and lighted) in Lamp. This method returns the value of field lighted:

```
boolean isLighted() {
  return lighted;
}
```

The return type of this method is boolean because lighted is a boolean variable. A similar method can be written to return the value of wattage.

The methods turnOn and turnOff change the value of the field lighted in Lamp. These methods are called **setter** or **mutator methods** because they mutate or change field values. On the other hand, methods that return the values of an object's fields without changing them (such as getDiameter and isLighted) are called **getter** or **accessor methods**.

The Lamp Class   We have now added several methods to Lamp. The modified class follows:

```
class Lamp {
  // fields
  double diameter;
  int wattage;
  boolean lighted;

  // method to turn the lamp on
  void turnOn() {
    lighted = true;
  }
// method to turn the lamp off
  void turnOff() {
    lighted = false;
  }
// method to get lamp diameter
  double getDiameter() {
    return diameter;
  }
// method to find out if lamp is lighted
  boolean isLighted() {
    return lighted;
  }
// method to get lamp wattage
  int getWattage() {
```

```
    return wattage;
  }
}
```

This program shows how the methods in the Lamp class can be used. Add this main method to Lamp:

```
public static void main(String[] args) {
    Lamp lamp1 = new Lamp();
    Lamp lamp2 = new Lamp();
    lamp1.turnOn();
    lamp2.turnOff();
    System.out.println("lamp1 is lighted: " +lamp1.isLighted());
    System.out.println("lamp2 is lighted: " +lamp2.isLighted());
}
```

The program output is:

```
lamp1 is lighted: true
lamp2 is lighted: false
```

The first two statements in main create two instances, lamp1 and lamp2, of class Lamp. Next, the instance lamp1 invokes its turnOn method, which sets its lighted field to true. The next statement is then executed, which sets the lighted field of lamp2 to false. The isLighted method of lamp1 returns true, and this value is printed out by the first println statement. The isLighted method of lamp2 returns false, which is then printed out by the next statement. Figure 5–2 shows the fields and methods that we have added to class Lamp.

The methods written thus far do not have any parameters. Next, we discuss how to write methods that have parameters.

Figure 5–2

Some fields and methods in class Lamp.

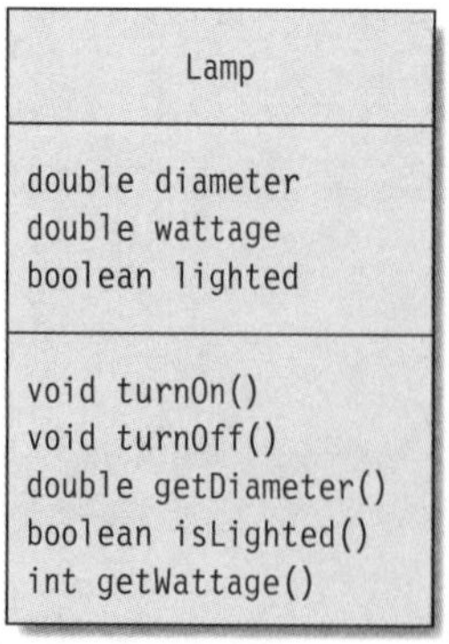

```
              Lamp

double diameter
double wattage
boolean lighted

void turnOn()
void turnOff()
double getDiameter()
boolean isLighted()
int getWattage()
```

5.4   Methods with Parameters

An example of a method declared with three parameters is shown here:

```
int doSomething(int x, double y, float z) {
// body of the method
}
```

This method is called doSomething and it takes three parameters: x, y, and z. A method's parameters are used inside its body to perform a computation or operation. A method can have parameters of both primitive and reference data types. The doSomething method contains parameters of primitive types int, double, and float. You can choose any valid identifier for a parameter.

The scope of a parameter is the entire method in which it is used. Therefore, the parameter names should be unique in a method, and doSomething should not declare another parameter or *local variable* named x, y, or z. A **local variable** is a variable that is declared and used only within a method. The following method contains errors because two parameters have the same name x, and the local variable z has the same name as a parameter:

```
// error, duplicate x and z
int doSomething(int x, double x, float z) {
  int z;
}
```

The name of a method, along with the data types of its parameters, is called the **method signature**. Note that the method signature does not include the return type. The method doSomething has the following signature:

```
doSomething(int, double, float)
```

We now add two mutator methods called setDiameter and setWattage to Lamp to change the values of fields diameter and wattage. This method changes the value of diameter to dia:

```
void setDiameter(double dia) {
  diameter = dia;
}
```

Here, the parameter dia is declared as a double because it will be assigned to diameter, which is of type double. Similarly, we can write a method to change the wattage:

```
void setWattage(int watt) {
  wattage = watt;
}
```

The return type of these two methods is void because they do not return a value.

Add the setDiameter and setWattage methods to Lamp, and modify the main method in Lamp as follows:

```
public static void main(String[] args) {
   Lamp lamp = new Lamp();
   lamp.setWattage(100);
   System.out.println("lamp wattage = " +lamp.getWattage());
}
```

This program produces the following output:

```
lamp wattage = 100
```

In main, the object lamp calls its setWattage method with an argument of 100. When the program is run, this argument is copied into the parameter watt of setWattage, and then is assigned to the wattage field of the object lamp inside this method. Therefore, when lamp calls its getWattage method, the latter will return the value 100, which is then printed out by the println method.

It is important to understand that the scope of parameter watt in setWattage is restricted to this method; that is, watt can be accessed only inside this method. This parameter watt does not exist before method setWattage is called, and it is removed from memory when setWattage completes execution. If we replaced the println statement in the main method with the following statement, a compilation error would result because the variable watt is unknown in main:

```
System.out.println("lamp wattage = " +watt);
```

A class can have several methods with the *same* name, but with different parameter data types and/or a different number of parameters. These methods are known as **overloaded methods**, and they perform similar operations, but with different types of arguments. For example, the println method is declared in all the following ways:

> **void println(boolean x)**—a method that prints the boolean variable x.
>
> **void println(char x)**—a method that prints the char variable x.
>
> **void println(String x)**—a method that prints the String x.

The println method is also defined to take arguments of type float, double, and long, among others. We will discuss overloaded methods in more detail in the next chapter.

5.4.1 Primitive Data Type Arguments

Java passes primitive type arguments to a method using a mechanism known as **pass-by-value**. This means that Java *copies* the arguments into the corresponding parameters. Only the parameters, and not the arguments, can change inside the method. Hence, the arguments will have the same values after the method executes as they did at the start of the method. The following example explains this concept in more detail.

Example 1

What is the value of original that will be printed out in the following program: 1 or 1000?

```java
public class PrimitiveArgumentDemo {
  void modifyVariable(int photocopy) {
    photocopy = 1000;
  }

  public static void main(String[] args) {
    PrimitiveArgumentDemo obj = new PrimitiveArgumentDemo();
    int original = 1;
    obj.modifyVariable(original);
    System.out.println("original = " +original);
  }
}
```

Solution: When you run the program, it produces the following output:

```
original = 1
```

The argument original cannot be changed inside the method modifyVariable. Figure 5–3 explains in more detail how the arguments are passed using a diagram of memory (RAM). Java reserves a separate memory location for the parameters and local variables of every method that is being executed. Initially, the method main is executing and it assigns the value 1 to original, as shown in Figure 5–3(a). Next, the method modifyVariable is called, and it will copy the value of original into its parameter photocopy, as shown in Figure 5–3(b). In method modifyVariable, the value of photocopy is changed to 1000, as shown in Figure 5–3(c). This action does not change the value of original, and so the value 1 is printed out after method main resumes execution. ∎

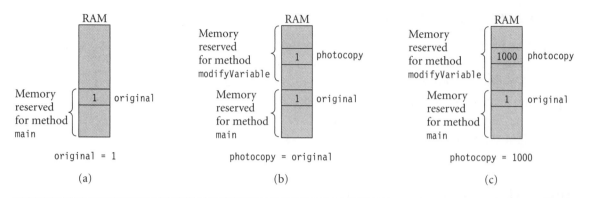

Figure 5–3

Memory diagram to explain how the argument original is passed to the modifyVariable method in class PrimitiveArgumentDemo.

You can think of parameter photocopy as being a photocopy of the argument original. If you modify a photocopy, it will not affect the original. In the same way, original is not changed in the preceding program when photocopy is modified.

5.4.2   Reference Data Type Arguments

Java also uses the **pass-by-value** mechanism for reference data type arguments. For example, consider the reference variable key that references an object of MyClass:

```
MyClass key = new MyClass();
```

This statement copies the value in key into duplicateKey:

```
MyClass duplicateKey = key;
```

As a result, both key and duplicateKey reference the same object, as shown in Figure 5–4. (Recall that a reference variable is not an object itself; instead, it contains information to determine the location of an object, such as the address of the object.)

Figure 5–4

key and duplicateKey reference the same object.

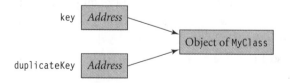

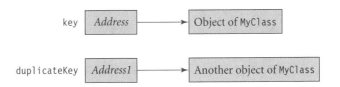

Figure 5–5
key **and** duplicateKey
**reference different
objects.**

On the other hand, after the following statement is executed, duplicateKey references a different object from key, as shown in Figure 5–5:

```
duplicateKey = new MyClass();
```

> You can think of the *reference type argument* as a key, and the corresponding *reference type parameter* (into which this argument is copied) as its duplicate. Both a key and its duplicate can be used to open and close the same lock. Similarly, both the *reference type argument* and the *reference type parameter* can be used to access and modify the fields of the same object.

Even if you alter the *duplicate* key, the *original* key can still be used for the same lock. In the same way, the *reference type argument* continues to reference the same object, even if the *reference type parameter* is changed.

The next example explains pass-by-value for reference types in more detail.

Example 2

What is the value of the field x of object key that will be printed out in main: 10, 100, or 200?

```
class MyClass {
  int x;
}

class ReferenceArgumentDemo {
  // this method takes a reference type argument
  void modifyField(MyClass duplicateKey) {
    duplicateKey.x = 100;
    duplicateKey = new MyClass();
    duplicateKey.x = 200;
  }

  public static void main(String[] args) {
    ReferenceArgumentDemo demo = new ReferenceArgumentDemo();
    MyClass key = new MyClass();
    key.x = 10;
```

```
    demo.modifyField(key);
    System.out.println("key.x = " +key.x);
  }
}
```

Solution: The program output is shown here:

```
key.x = 100
```

In method `modifyField`, `duplicateKey` initially references the same object as `key`. Therefore, this statement in method `modifyField` changes the value of `key`'s x to 100:

```
duplicateKey.x = 100;
```

The next statement changes the object that is referenced by `duplicateKey`:

```
duplicateKey = new MyClass();
```

As a result, the statement that follows cannot change the instance variable x to 200 in the object referenced by `key`.   ■

In the next example, we write a class with methods that take reference type arguments.

Example 3

Write a class called `BoundedCircles` to randomly draw 15 colored circles, each with a radius of 36, on a window. The window contains a square with its top-left corner at (150, 150), and a height and width of 200. All circles that are *completely* inside the square and do not touch any of its sides are filled with red; otherwise, they are outlined in blue. The class should have the following methods:

> **boolean checkIfCircleIsInsideSquare(int x, int y)**—a method that returns `true` if a circle drawn with radius 36 fits perfectly in a square with its top-left corner at (*x, y*); otherwise, it returns `false`.
>
> **void drawCircle(DrawingKit)**—a method that generates a circle with radius 36 at a random location in a window. It draws and colors the circle red if it is completely within the given square; otherwise, the circle is outlined in blue. This method takes a reference argument of type `DrawingKit`.

void generate(DrawingKit)—a method that draws a square with coordinates (150, 150), and a height and width of 200. It calls the drawCircle method to draw 15 circles. This method also takes a reference argument of type DrawingKit.

Solution: Create a class called BoundedCircles and add the following fields to the class:

```
int low_x = 150;     // smallest x-coordinate of the square
int low_y = 150;     // smallest y-coordinate of the square
int width = 200;     // square width
int height = 200;    // square height
int radius = 36;     // circle radius
```

The checkIfCircleIsInsideSquare method determines whether the circle lies completely within the given square by checking whether the points x, y, $(x+72)$, and $(y+72)$ lie inside this square. Here, (x, y) and $(x+72, y+72)$ are the coordinates of the top-left and bottom-right corners of an imaginary square, into which the circle fits perfectly:

```
// Returns true if the circle lies completely within the rectangle.
boolean checkIfCircleIsInsideSquare(int x, int y) {
  boolean result = false;
   int high_x = low_x + width, high_y = low_y + height;
     if ((x > low_x) && ((x + 2 * radius) < high_x) && (y > low_y) && ((y +
2 * radius) < high_y))
     result = true;

  return result;
  }
```

The drawCircle method creates a circle at a random location inside the window. It calls checkIfCircleIsInsideSquare to check if this circle is within the square, and colors it accordingly:

```
  // draw a circle at a random point and color it red if within square
void drawCircle(DrawingKit dk) {
  Random r = new Random();
  int x = r.nextInt(400);
  int y = r.nextInt(400);

  Ellipse2D.Float el = new Ellipse2D.Float(x, y, 2 * radius, 2 * radius);
  boolean insideSquare = checkIfCircleIsInsideSquare(x, y);

// fill circle with red color if it is inside square
```

```
  if(insideSquare) {
    dk.setPaint(Color.RED);
    dk.fill(e1);
  } else {
    dk.setPaint(Color.BLUE);
    dk.draw(e1);
  }
}
```

The method generate draws a square. It then calls the method drawCircle 15 times, using a loop, to draw 15 circles:

```
// draw a square and 15 circles
void generate(DrawingKit dk) {
  int numCircles = 15;
  // draw square at (150, 150) with a height and width of 200

  Rectangle2D.Double r1 = new Rectangle2D.Double(low_x, low_y, width,
height);
  dk.draw(r1);

  // draw 15 circles
  for(int i = 0; i < numCircles; i++) {
    drawCircle(dk);
  }
}
```

Add these methods to BoundedCircles. Inside main, create an instance of this class called circles that invokes the generate method:

```
public static void main(String[] args) {
  DrawingKit myDrawingKit = new DrawingKit("Bounded Circles");
  BoundedCircles circles = new BoundedCircles();
  circles.generate(myDrawingKit);
}
```

The drawCircle and generate methods draw the circles and square inside the same window. This is done by passing the same DrawingKit instance as an argument to these two methods.

Before running your program, add the following four lines at the top of your code:

```
import java.awt.*;
import java.awt.geom.*;
import java.util.Random;
import com.programwithjava.basic.DrawingKit;
```

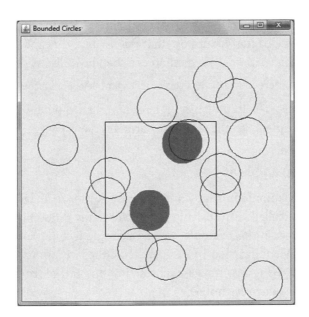

Figure 5–6
Circles that lie completely within the square are filled with red.

A sample output is shown in Figure 5–6. The output will be different each time the program is run. ■

5.4.3　Returning a Reference Type from a Method

Like primitive types, reference types are also returned using the keyword return. The return type in the method declaration should be the same as the data type of the object reference being returned. For example, the following code shows the outline of a method to change the brightness of an image and return a reference to the modified image:

```
BufferedImage changeBrightness(BufferedImage inputImage, double
brightnessValue) {
  BufferedImage outputImage;
  // Create outputImage, which is of type BufferedImage.
  // Then multiply each pixel of inputImage by brightnessValue
  // and store it in outputImage.

  return outputImage;
}
```

The code in this method is similar to that in the ChangeImageBrightness class in Chapter 4. Suppose that changer is an instance of the class that contains this method. The method can then be called as shown here:

```
BufferedImage newPicture = changer.changeBrightness(picture, 1.5f);
```

As a result, the object reference returned by the changeBrightness method is copied into the reference variable newPicture.

Example 4

Manipulating and combining two or more images to produce a new image is called **compositing**. There are many different techniques for compositing; in this example, we use a simple technique that combines two images by adding their pixels together. Other variations are possible, such as multiplying two images, subtracting one image from another, or placing one image over another.

We will write a class called Compositor that contains a method named add. This method takes two input images of type BufferedImage as arguments and returns a new image of the same type BufferedImage. The pixels in the returned image are the sum of the pixels in the input images. Suppose that (r_1, g_1, b_1) and (r_2, g_2, b_2) are the red, green, and blue components of a pixel with coordinates (x, y) in the two input images. After the program is executed, a pixel in the output image at the same location (x, y) has component values $(r_1 + r_2, g_1 + g_2, b_1 + b_2)$. Any component values that exceed 255 are truncated to 255 in the output image.

The output image is created using this BufferedImage constructor:

BufferedImage(int width, int height, int type)—a constructor that creates a BufferedImage having the specified width, height, and type.

There are many constants defined in class BufferedImage to specify different types of images. We will set the type to the constant TYPE_INT_ARGB, which represents an image in the RGB color space with an alpha channel.

The code for this class is shown here:

```
import java.awt.*;
import java.awt.image.BufferedImage;
import com.programwithjava.basic.DrawingKit;

public class Compositor {
  // maximum value of a sample
  static final int MAX_VALUE = 255;
```

```java
// this method returns a new image created by adding
// the source images image1 and image2
BufferedImage add(BufferedImage image1, BufferedImage image2) {
  int width = Math.min(image1.getWidth(), image2.getWidth());
  int height = Math.min(image1.getHeight(), image2.getHeight());

  // create a new BufferedImage called image3
  BufferedImage image3 = new BufferedImage(width, height,
BufferedImage.TYPE_INT_ARGB);

  for (int x = 0; x < width; x++) {
    for (int y = 0; y < height; y++) {
      // get the samples of the pixel at (x, y) in image1
      int colorValue1 = image1.getRGB(x, y);
      Color pixelColor1 = new Color(colorValue1);
      int red1 = pixelColor1.getRed();
      int green1 = pixelColor1.getGreen();
      int blue1 = pixelColor1.getBlue();

      // get the samples of the pixel at (x, y) in image2
      int colorValue2 = image2.getRGB(x, y);
      Color pixelColor2 = new Color(colorValue2);
      int red2 = pixelColor2.getRed();
      int green2 = pixelColor2.getGreen();
      int blue2 = pixelColor2.getBlue();

      // add the samples to create a new color
      int red3 = Math.min(red1 + red2, MAX_VALUE);
      int green3 = Math.min(green1 + green2, MAX_VALUE);
      int blue3 = Math.min(blue1 + blue2, MAX_VALUE);

      // set the color of a pixel in image3
      Color newPixelColor = new Color(red3, green3, blue3);
      int newRgbvalue = newPixelColor.getRGB();
      image3.setRGB(x, y, newRgbvalue);
    }
  }
  // returns a reference to the new image
  return image3;
}

public static void main(String[] args) {
  DrawingKit dk = new DrawingKit("Compositor", 1000, 1000);
  BufferedImage p1 = dk.loadPicture("image/pattern1.jpg");
```

```
            BufferedImage p2 = dk.loadPicture("image/pattern2.jpg");
            Compositor c = new Compositor();
            BufferedImage p3 = c.add(p1, p2);
            dk.drawPicture(p3, 0, 100);
        }
    }
```

The height and width of the output image is set to the smaller of the heights and widths of the input images. This statement in the add method sums the samples of the red components of image1 and image2 together:

```
int red3 = Math.min(red1 + red2, MAX_VALUE);
```

The min method of the Math class returns the smaller of the arguments. It is used here so that the value of red3 does not exceed the largest value a sample can have (255). A description of some of the methods in this class is provided later in this chapter.

Copy the source pictures pattern1.jpg and pattern2.jpg from the JavaBook/image directory on the CD-ROM into the JavaBook/image directory on your computer. Copy the Compositor program into the JavaBook/src directory, and compile and run the program. Figure 5–7(a) and Figure 5–7(b) show the source pictures. Figure 5–8 shows the program output. ∎

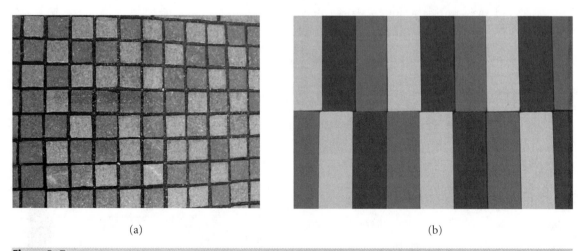

(a)   (b)

Figure 5–7

Source images used in the Compositor program.

pattern1.jpg © Bjorn Erlandsson, 123RF.com; pattern2.jpg © Richard Nelson, 123RF.com

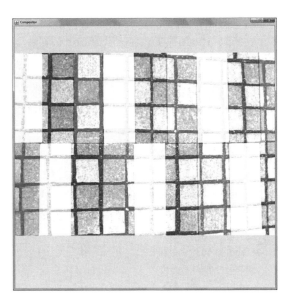

Figure 5–8
Output of the `Compositor` program.

As an exercise, rewrite the `ChangeImageBrightness` class discussed in Chapter 4 so that it uses the method `changeBrightness` that is declared as described in this section.

5.5   Constructors

A **constructor** is used to create an object from a class. It has the *same* name as the class. There are three types of constructors:

1. Constructors without parameters
2. Constructors with parameters
3. Default constructors

Each of these constructors is used in a different way to create an object.

5.5.1   Constructors without Parameters

A constructor without a parameter is the simplest type of constructor. An example of a constructor without a parameter for class `Lamp` is shown here:

```
Lamp() {
  // insert statements here
}
```

Recall that a return type is not specified for constructors because they do not return a value. This constructor is used to initialize the fields at the time the object is created. All objects are created with the same field values when this type of constructor is used.

Suppose that we want to create objects with the following instance field values:

```
diameter = 6.0;
wattage = 60;
lighted = false;
```

Add these statements to the Lamp constructor:

```
Lamp() {
  diameter = 6.0;
  wattage = 60;
  lighted = false;
}
```

Add this constructor to the Lamp class. Although constructors can be put anywhere in a class, by convention they are placed after the field declarations and before the method definitions. This statement in main creates a Lamp object called lamp1 using the preceding constructor:

```
Lamp lamp1 = new Lamp();
```

The fields of the Lamp object we have created are initialized to the values given in the constructor, as shown in Figure 5–9. The top rectangle contains the title *object name* : *class name*, and it is underlined. lamp1 is an object of the Lamp class; thus the title is <u>lamp1 : Lamp</u>. The lower rectangle shows the values of lamp1's fields at a particular instant of time. We borrow this notation from **Unified Modeling Language** (**UML**), which is a language used to describe object-oriented software.

Figure 5–9

The Lamp object called lamp1.

```
     lamp1 : Lamp

  diameter = 6.0
  wattage = 60
  lighted = false
```

5.5.2 Constructors with Parameters

When the programmer wants to create multiple objects with differing field values, a constructor with parameters must be used. There can be any number of parameters and the data type of each parameter should be specified. For example, consider this constructor with parameters for Lamp:

```
Lamp(double dia, int watt, boolean light) {
  diameter = dia;
  wattage = watt;
  lighted = light;
}
```

It has three parameters: dia, watt, and light. Any valid identifier can be used for the parameter name. The assignment statements store the values of dia, watt, and light into the fields diameter, wattage, and lighted, respectively.

The programmer calls this constructor with suitable arguments so that the object's fields are initialized to specific values. Say we want to create a Lamp object with diameter = 6.2, wattage = 40, and lighted = false. The following statement creates an object called lamp2 with these field values:

```
Lamp lamp2 = new Lamp(6.2, 40, false);
```

The values *6.2, 40,* and *false* are this constructor's arguments. The first argument, 6.2, is copied into the first parameter dia. dia is assigned to field diameter inside the constructor; thus diameter gets the value 6.2. Similarly, wattage and lighted are assigned the values 40 and false, respectively. Figure 5–10 shows a Lamp object called lamp2 that is created using this constructor.

The data type and order of arguments should match those of the parameters in the constructor. A call to the following constructor of Lamp gives an error:

```
Lamp(5, 20.0, false)    // error!
```

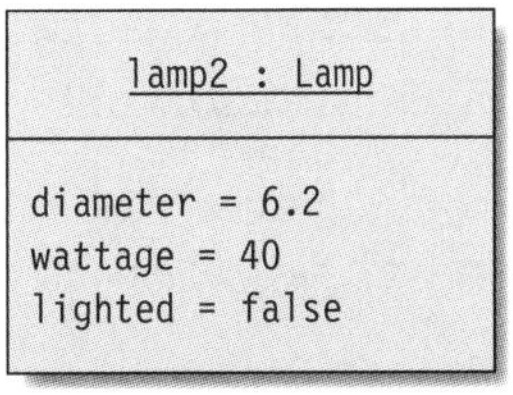

```
          lamp2 : Lamp

   diameter = 6.2
   wattage = 40
   lighted = false
```

Figure 5–10

A Lamp **object created using the constructor with parameters.**

This error results because the second argument should be of type `int`. Recall the conversion rules we discussed earlier: A floating-point number (20.0) cannot be passed to an integer parameter (`watt`) without casting. However, the integer argument (5) is converted automatically to a floating-point value, and thus it can be passed to `dia` without a problem.

5.5.3   Default Constructors

When a class does not contain a constructor, the compiler creates one. This type of constructor is called a **default constructor**. The constructor initializes the object's fields in the following manner:

- Numeric types such as `int`, `float`, and others are set to 0.

- Variables of type `boolean` are set to `false`.

- Object references are set to `null`.

Even when a class has constructors, instance fields and *static fields* (discussed in Section 5.9) are automatically initialized to these default values if they are not explicitly initialized within the class. Recall that local variables, on the other hand, must be explicitly initialized before they are used.

How would an object be created if a constructor were not provided? If we did not provide any constructors in class `Lamp`, we could still create an object of `Lamp` (say, `lamp3`) in the following manner:

```
Lamp lamp3 = new Lamp();
```

This calls the default constructor, and the fields of `lamp3` are initialized to the preceding default values.

5.5.4   Overloaded Constructors

A class can have only *one* constructor without arguments, but it can contain *multiple* constructors with arguments. For example, we can use these two constructors in `Lamp` to initialize different fields:

```
Lamp(double dia, int watt) { }
Lamp(int watt, boolean light) { }
```

When there are many constructors in a class, Java determines which constructor is being called based on its *signature*. The **signature** of the constructor comprises its name and the data types of its parameters. The constructors in a class with different signatures are called **overloaded constructors**.

All constructors in a class must have different signatures. If a class called SomeClass contained the following two constructors, it would cause a compiler error because the data types of the parameters are identical in both:

```
SomeClass(int s1, int s2, float s3) {}
SomeClass(int s4, int s5, float s6) {} // error!
```

Although the following two constructors both contain one float and two ints, the order is different, and thus these declarations are allowed:

```
SomeClass(int s1, int s2, float s3) {}
SomeClass(float s1, int s2, int s3) {}  // okay
```

Example 5

The Rectangle2D.Double class in Java 2D is used to construct rectangles. This is similar to the Rectangle2D.Float class, except that the arguments are of type double instead of float. This class contains two overloaded constructors:

> **Rectangle2D.Double()**—a constructor that creates a rectangle at the point $(0, 0)$ with a width and height of 0.
>
> **Rectangle2D.Double(double x, double y, double width, double height)**— a constructor that creates a rectangle at the point (x, y) of the given width and height.

Describe how you can create an instance using each constructor.

Solution: This statement creates an instance called rect1, using the first constructor:

```
Rectangle2D.Double rect1 = new Rectangle2D.Double();
```

This creates an instance called rect2, using the second constructor:

```
Rectangle2D.Double rect2 = new Rectangle2D.Double(10.0, 100.0, 50.0, 20.0);
```

Likewise, the Ellipse2D.Double and Line2D.Double classes are similar to Ellipse2D.Float and Line2D.Float, respectively, the difference being that the first two take arguments of type double instead of float in their constructors and methods.   ■

Example 6

Java 2D contains a `Color` class, which is used to create different colors. There are several overloaded constructors in this class, one of which is shown here:

> `public Color(int red, int green, int blue)`—a constructor that creates a new color. The values of red, green, and blue should lie in the range (0–255).

a.   Create an instance of this class called `newColor` in which red = 127, green = 25, and blue = 50.

b.   Color a rectangle using `newColor`, and display it in a window.

Solution:

a.   The following statement creates the instance called `newColor`:

```
Color newColor = new Color(127, 25, 50);
```

b.   The following program shows how a rectangle can be colored with this color `newColor`:

```java
import java.awt.*;
import java.awt.geom.*;
import com.programwithjava.basic.DrawingKit;

public class TestColor {
  public static void main(String[] args) {
    DrawingKit dk = new DrawingKit("New Color");
    Rectangle2D.Double r = new Rectangle2D.Double(100.0, 100.0,
        250.0, 120.0);
    Color newColor = new Color(127, 25, 50);
    dk.setPaint(newColor);
    dk.fill(r);
  }
}
```

The rectangle r is colored with `newColor` and is drawn in a window, as shown in Figure 5–11. Use the `Color` class whenever you want to create a custom color.   ■

5.6   The this keyword

The keyword `this` is used within a method or constructor to refer to the object that has invoked that method or constructor. One use for `this` comes when a method parameter **shadows** a field; that is, the parameter has the

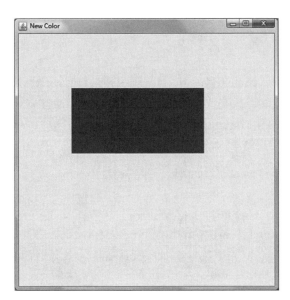

Figure 5–11
Creating custom colors using the Color class.

same name as the field. For example, suppose that the method setDiameter uses the parameter diameter:

```
void setDiameter(double diameter) {
  diameter = diameter; // logical error
}
```

The parameter identifier diameter is identical to the field identifier diameter. Therefore, the field diameter is not visible inside the class, and it is not changed inside the method. This leads to a logical error in the program because it is not flagged at compilation or run time even though the field assignment is not made. This error can be corrected by writing the method as follows:

```
void setDiameter(double diameter) {
  this.diameter = diameter;
}
```

The keyword this is used here to reference the instance field diameter of the class so that it is updated correctly. In general, however, keep parameter names different from field names in a class to avoid inadvertent mistakes.

The preceding discussion applies to constructor parameters as well. Consider the following Lamp constructor:

```
Lamp(double dia, int watt, boolean light) {
  diameter = dia;
```

```
  wattage = watt;
  lighted = light;
}
```

We change the identifiers of the parameters so that they are identical to those of the fields. The fields will not be updated if this constructor is used:

```
Lamp(double diameter, int wattage, boolean lighted) {
  diameter = diameter;   // logical error
  wattage = wattage;     // logical error
  lighted = lighted;     // logical error
}
```

To correct the logical errors, prefix this before the instance field names, as you did earlier in the method setDiameter:

```
Lamp(double diameter, int wattage, boolean lighted) {
  this.diameter = diameter;      // okay!
  this.wattage = wattage;        // okay!
  this.lighted = lighted;        // okay!
}
```

Another use for this is to invoke another constructor in the same class from within a constructor. In this case, this resembles a call to a method with parameters:

```
Lamp() {
 // calls the Lamp(double, int, boolean) constructor
  this(10, 100, false);
}
```

The constructor whose parameter types match the types of the arguments to the this statement will be called. Therefore, the Lamp(double, int, boolean) constructor is called with arguments 10, 100, and false. This produces the same result as if we had written the constructor without parameters as follows:

```
Lamp() {
  diameter = 10;
  wattage = 100;
  lighted = false;
}
```

5.7   Organizing .java Files in Packages

You may have noticed that the JavaBook/src directory is getting crowded. Instead of putting all the files in the same directory, a better option is to

Figure 5–12
A package called "pkg".

organize them in subdirectories created inside src. These subdirectories are called packages. In this section, we discuss how you can create and name packages, and how you can compile and run the .java files in a package.

Figure 5–12 shows the diagram for a package named pkg. The package name is specified in the smaller box on the top.

5.7.1 Creating Packages

A **package** is a subdirectory of src, which contains the .java files. To create a package called userdefinedclasses, create a subdirectory called userdefined-classes in src. Figure 5–13 shows the packages userdefinedclasses, com, and programwithjava.

When you put a class in a package, you have to add the **package statement** to the class. This statement comprises the keyword package followed by the

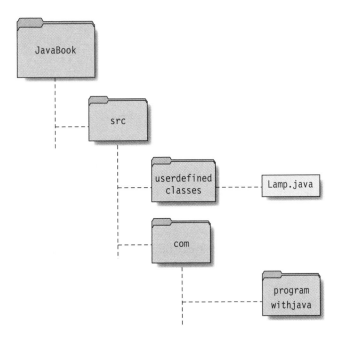

Figure 5–13
The subdirectories of src (for example, user-definedclasses, com, and programwithjava) are called packages.

name of the package, and it is placed at the start of the code for that class. For example, move the `Lamp.java` file into the `userdefinedclasses` directory and add the following as the first statement in its code:

```
package userdefinedclasses;
```

There can only be *one* `package` statement in a file because a class can belong to only a single package. Note that the `package` statement must be the *first* statement in a file. In addition, if there are any `import` statements, they should be placed right after the `package` statement.

When a package contains another package, the latter is called the **subpackage** of the former. Thus, in Figure 5–13, `programwithjava` is a subpackage of `com`. When a .java file is in a subpackage, the `package` statement should contain the names of all packages in the hierarchy separated by a dot. `DrawingKit.java` is placed in the hierarchy comprised of the package `com` and its subpackages `programwithjava` and `basic`. If you examine this file, you will see that the `package` statement is the following:

```
package com.programwithjava.basic;
```

The .java files placed in the `src` folder do not need a `package` statement and are said to be in the **default package**. We have been using this approach up until this point; however, it is preferable to avoid using the default package, and place classes in named packages instead. This helps us organize code better because related classes can be placed in the same package. Another reason to use packages is to restrict access; we discuss this in Section 5.8, *Access Modifiers*. In the following chapters, we will put each chapter's code in a different package.

5.7.2 Naming Packages

Although classes in the same package must have distinct names, it is possible for two classes in different packages to have the same name. By prefixing the package name before the class name, collisions of class names can be prevented in a program. However, package names must also be unique in order to prevent collisions. One way to ensure this is by using the Internet domain name. For example, suppose that a company with the Internet domain `xyz.com` has provided a package called `graphics`. The package name becomes `com.xyz.graphics`, because the package name is prefixed with `com.xyz`. If another company with domain `abc.net` also develops a package called graphics, this package name becomes net.abc.graphics. This naming scheme avoids collision of package names, because domain names are always unique. The programwithjava.com domain name has been reserved for this purpose. When it is reversed, it provides a unique package name com.programwithjava for the classes provided with this book.

Class names and package names must be distinct. By convention, package names should not contain any uppercase characters. This also avoids conflict with class names in a package because class names begin with an uppercase character.

5.7.3 Compiling .java Files in Packages

When you compile a file that is in a package, you should provide the complete pathname for the file starting from the src directory. Apart from that difference, compiling a program is the same as for files not in any package.

We have moved Lamp.java to the src\userdefinedclasses directory; thus we will give this pathname when compiling the program. Also, provide the names of both files DrawingKit.java and Lamp.java when you compile the program because we will add graphics to class Lamp:

```
C:\JavaBook> javac -d bin src\com\programwithjava\basic\DrawingKit.java
src\userdefinedclasses\Lamp.java
```

The class file is automatically placed inside the bin directory in a package hierarchy that is identical to that of the source code file. Therefore, compiling Lamp.java creates the class file Lamp.class inside the userdefinedclasses package in the bin directory, as shown in Figure 5–14. Examine the contents of the bin directory to verify that the Lamp.class file has been created in the bin\userdefinedclasses directory.

To run this program, prefix the package name before the class filename using a dot as a separator, as shown in this statement:

```
C:\JavaBook> java -classpath bin userdefinedclasses.Lamp
```

The program output is as follows:

```
lamp1 is lighted: true
lamp2 is lighted: false
```

Figure 5–14

The class file `Lamp.class` is placed automatically in the `bin` directory in a package hierarchy that is identical to that of the source file `Lamp.java`.

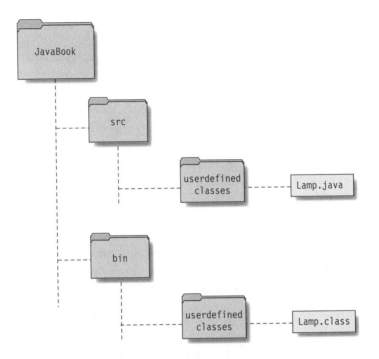

5.8 Access Modifiers

Access modifiers are used for defining whether a field, method, or constructor in a class is hidden or visible to other classes. There are four types of access identifiers:

1. `private`
2. `public`
3. *Package-private* (also called *default*)
4. `protected`

A **top-level class** (that is, a class not inside another class) is declared using the `public` or default access modifiers only. The **members** (fields and methods) and constructors in a class can be declared using any of the four modifiers. We discuss modifiers next.

5.8.1 `private` Access Modifier

When a field, method or constructor in a class is declared as `private`, it can only be accessed within that class and not by any other class. This modifier is used to hide the implementation details of a class, such as its fields and methods that should not be accessed by other classes. The private members of a class can be modified later if necessary, without affecting other classes that use this class.

Suppose that we declare the diameter field in Lamp as private:

```
private double diameter;
```

As a result, this private field cannot be modified or accessed by a Lamp object in another class:

```
public class Temp {
  public static void main(String [] args) {
    Lamp lamp = new Lamp(6.2, 15, false);
    lamp.diameter = 3.2;                 // error, cannot modify diameter
    System.out.println(lamp.diameter); // error, cannot access diameter
  }
}
```

The field diameter of class Lamp is not visible to Temp because diameter is a private data member of Lamp; thus a compilation error occurs. Instead, we can use Lamp's getDiameter method to retrieve the value of diameter. Do not make this method private, because we want to be able to call it in another class, as discussed next.

5.8.2   public **Access Modifier**

When a field, method, or constructor is declared as public, it can be accessed by all classes. If we declare diameter as public inside Lamp, then we can modify it or access it in Temp:

```
public double diameter;
```

As a result, a Lamp instance can access and modify its diameter field in class Temp:

```
public class Temp {
  public static void main(String [] args) {
    Lamp lamp = new Lamp(6.2, 15, false);
    lamp.diameter = 3.2;                 // okay
    System.out.println(lamp.diameter); // okay
  }
}
```

However, it is good programming practice to declare an object's fields as private, because doing so prevents accidental or unwanted changes to the fields and keeps them secure. Instead of accessing an object's field directly, use an accessor method to retrieve the value. Do not declare accessor and mutator methods as private; leave them as public so that they can be called outside the class in which they are declared. For example, declare the getDiameter method in Lamp as public:

```
public double getDiameter() {
  return diameter;
}
```

Make all the fields in Lamp private:

```
private double diameter;
private int wattage;
private boolean lighted;
```

Although the diameter field is private, the getDiameter method can be used in another class to get its value:

```
public class Temp {
  public static void main(String [] args) {
    Lamp lamp = new Lamp(6.2, 15, false);
    // works fine because getDiameter() is declared as public
    System.out.println(lamp.getDiameter());
  }
}
```

Similarly, declare the other accessor and mutator methods in the Lamp class to be public.

A class that is declared as public is visible to all other classes. For example, the following statement declares Lamp as public:

```
public class Lamp {
  // code for this class
}
```

On the other hand, declaring this class as private would not allow it to be used at all. In fact, if you tried to declare a class as private, the compiler would flag it as an error.

If the constructors in a class are declared private, they cannot be accessed by other classes. This statement makes the Lamp constructor public, so that a Lamp object can be instantiated in any other class:

```
public Lamp(double dia, int watt, boolean light) {
  // rest of the code in the constructor
}
```

5.8.3   Package-private Access Modifier (Default)

When no access modifier is specified, a class can be accessed only by classes that are in the *same* package as this class. This type of modifier is also called a **package-private** or **default access modifer**. For example, this method printDiameter in Lamp has a default access modifier, because none of the keywords private, public, or protected is added before the return type in the method declaration:

```
// method uses the default access modifier
void printDiameter() {
  // some code
}
```

This printDiameter method can be called in any class that is in the *same* package as Lamp; however, it cannot be called in a class that is in a *different* package from Lamp.

Suppose that we declare Lamp with no modifier:

```
class Lamp {
  // code for this class
}
```

As a result, the entire class Lamp is not visible to a class in a different package.

Earlier, we said that you should organize your classes into packages. By placing your class in a package and using the package-private access modifiers, you can selectively allow other classes to use this class (or parts of it).

5.8.4   protected Access Modifier

The protected modifier is similar to the package-private access modifier. When the **protected access modifier** is used, the **members** (fields and methods) and constructors of a class can be accessed only by classes that are in the *same* package as this class. However, there is an exception to this rule as the protected keyword has a special significance when classes are related using *inheritance*. We discuss this modifier in more detail when we introduce inheritance in Chapter 6.

Figure 5–15

Using access modifier symbols.

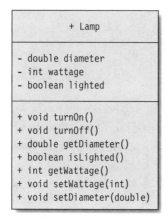

5.8.5   Access Modifier Symbols

Access modifiers for fields and methods can be depicted using the symbols
+, -, #, and ~:

+   public

-   private

protected

~   default

The updated diagram for class Lamp with access modifiers is shown in Figure 5–15. Add the constructors of Lamp, along with their access modifiers, to Figure 5–15.

Example 7

Write a class called Ball that contains the following fields:

x, y: Describes the current position of the ball

width: The ball's diameter

speedX, speedY: Describes the speed of the ball (in pixels per second) along the x and y axes, respectively.

direction: The current direction of the ball, which is either 0 (for UP) or 1 (for DOWN).

Write the code for the following method in `Ball`:

> `public void step(float timeInterval)`—a method that updates the current position of the ball, based on its speed and the distance traveled in the specified time interval.

Also, add a constructor without parameters to this class to initialize `x` and `y` to 0, `width` to 40, `speedX` and `speedY` to 100 and 200, respectively, and `direction` to 1.

Solution: The code for class `Ball` is shown here:

```
public class Ball {
  private float x;         // x-coordinate of ball's position
  private float y;         // y-coordinate of ball's position
  private float speedX;    // speed of ball in pixels/second along x-axis
  private float speedY;    // speed of ball in pixels/second along y-axis
  private int direction;   // direction = 0 (UP) or 1 (DOWN)
  private float width;     // ball's width

  // constructor without parameters
  public Ball() {
    setWidth(40);          // mutator method for width field
    x = y = 0;
    speedX = 100;
    speedY = 200;
    direction = 1;
  }

  public void step(float timeInterval) {
    x += speedX * timeInterval;
    y += speedY * timeInterval;
  }
}
```

As an exercise, add accessor and mutator methods for each field, as well as a `main` method, and test the class. We will use a modified version of this `Ball` class to develop an animated game later in the book. ◾

5.9   Static Fields and Methods

A **static field** (also called a **class variable**) is a field that does not belong to any particular instance of a class; instead, it is shared among all instances of that class. Therefore, if an instance changes the value of a static field, all instances of that class see the same updated value. The static keyword is used to declare a static field. To understand how static and instance fields differ, consider the class StaticDemo:

```
public class StaticDemo {
  static int staticField;      // static field
  int instanceField;           // instance field
}
```

Two instances sd1 and sd2 of StaticDemo are created in the following main method, and sd1 modifies the value of both fields in the class. What is the output?

```
public static void main(String [] args ){
  StaticDemo sd1 = new StaticDemo();
  StaticDemo sd2 = new StaticDemo();
  sd1.staticField = 102;           // sd1 modifies staticField
  sd1.instanceField = 103;         // sd1 modifies instanceField
  System.out.println("sd2.staticField = "+sd2.staticField);
  System.out.println("sd2.instanceField = "+sd2.instanceField);
}
```

The program output is as follows:

```
sd2.staticField = 102
sd2.instanceField = 0
```

Static fields are shared between the instances of a class; as a result, sd2 prints out the updated value 102 of staticField. On the other hand, sd1 modifies only its copy of instanceField, and thus sd2's instanceField that was initialized to 0 remains unchanged.

Static fields are not associated with any particular instance, and thus they should be invoked using the *class* name instead of an instance name. Therefore, staticField should be called using StaticDemo.staticField instead of sd2.staticField.

A common use for static fields is to keep track of the number of instances of a class. Add this static field called numberOfObjects to class Lamp:

static int numberOfObjects;

This field keeps count of how many Lamp objects have been created. Add a statement to increment this value in each Lamp constructor:

```
Lamp(double dia, int watt, boolean light) {
  diameter = dia;
```

```
  wattage = watt;
  lighted = light;
  ++numberOfObjects;
}
```

For example, if two Lamp objects are created, numberOfObjects will have the value 2.

All of the methods that we have seen so far are **instance methods**, because they must be invoked by an object of the class that contains this method. **Static methods** or **class methods** are different in that they are not called by an object of the class. These methods are declared by prefixing the static keyword before the return type in the method declaration:

```
static int someMethod () {
  // code
}
```

A static method can be used to get the value of static fields. Add this static method to Lamp to get the value of the static field numberOfObjects in Lamp:

```
static int getNumberOfObjects () {
  return numberOfObjects;
}
```

Like static fields, static methods are also invoked using the *class* name and not the instance name. Therefore, the static method getNumberOfObjects is called as follows:

```
Lamp.getNumberOfObjects();
```

A static method is not associated with any instance. As a result, it cannot be used to modify instance fields or call other instance methods in that class, because a compilation error will result:

```
static void reset() {
  wattage = 0; // error as wattage is an instance field
}
```

5.9.1   A Useful Static Method: String.format

The format method is defined as a static method in the String class and is used for **formatting data**. It can have any number of arguments, but the first argument is always a **format string** containing **format specifiers** and (optionally) text. A format specifier, in its simplest form, starts with the symbol % and is followed by a **conversion character** such as d (for decimal numbers), f (for floating-point numbers), c (for character data), or s (for strings).

```
double val1 = 10.5678; int val2 = 15;
```

```
                                    format specifier
String s = String.format("Value is = %f", val1);
                          format string
```

The format specifier %f acts as a placeholder in the format string for the second argument val1. When the program is run, the value of val1 is substituted in the place of %f. The formatted string s can be printed out as usual:

```
System.out.println(s);
```

Its output is:

```
Value is = 10.567800
```

We used the conversion character f here because val1 is a floating-point number. To print out multiple arguments you have to use multiple format specifiers in the format string, one for each argument. For example, this format string has two specifiers, %f and %d for val1 and val2, respectively.

```
String s1 = String.format("Val 1 = %f, Val 2 = %d", val1, val2);
System.out.println(s1);
```

Its output is:

```
Val 1 = 10.567800, Val 2 = 15
```

The format specifiers must have the correct conversion character, or a runtime error will result. val1 is of type double; thus you cannot use the %d specifier for it:

```
String.format("val1 = %d, val2 = %f", val1, val2); //error
```

A runtime error also occurs if you have extra format specifiers. The following statement has three format specifiers, but only two arguments, val1 and val2, follow the format string:

```
String.format("val1 = %f, val2 = %d  %c", val1, val2); // error
```

On the other hand, this next statement does not substitute the values of val1 and val2 in the format string, because it is missing the format specifiers:

```
String.format("val1 = , val2 = ", val1, val2); // logical error
```

If you print out the string returned, the result will be:

```
val1 = , val2 =
```

We next examine some special formatting capabilities of this method. For a floating-point number, you can specify the **field width** and **precision** by using a format specifier of %n.mf. The value n represents the minimum number of characters reserved to display the number (field width), and m represents the number of decimal spaces (precision) in the number. (The value of n cannot be 0; otherwise, a runtime error will occur.) The number will be right-aligned in its field. For example, the format specifier %10.2f means that the number will be placed in a minimum of 10 spaces and will be rounded to 2 digits after its decimal point:

```
String s2 = String.format("val1 = %10.2f", val1);
System.out.println(s2);    // Output is: val1 =      10.57
```

The rounded value 10.57 takes 5 characters, and because the field width is 10, there are 5 spaces inserted before the number. Other examples are shown here:

```
String s3 = String.format("val1 = %5.2f", val1);
System.out.println(s3);    // Output is: val1 = 10.57
```

The following example specifies a precision of 3, but not the field width:

```
String s4 = String.format("val1 = %.3f", val1);
```

Therefore, the number is displayed rounded to 3 decimal places:

```
System.out.println(s4);    // Output is: val1 = 10.568
```

For decimal numbers, use the specifier %nd, where n is the field width. (The precision value m is not provided here.) Some examples follow:

```
String s5 = String.format("val2 = %10d", val2);
System.out.println(s5);  // Output is: val2 =          15
```

The field width is ignored if the number has more characters than the field width:

```
String s6 = String.format("val2 = %1d", val2);
System.out.println(s6);  // Output is: val2 = 15
```

Strings can be formatted similarly. The string "there" is substituted in the place of the format specifier %10s in this next example:

```
String s7 = String.format("Hello%10s", "there");
System.out.println(s7);  // Output is: Hello     there
```

In the next subsection, we explore more examples of the `String.format`
method.

5.9.2   The Math Class

The `Math` class contains only static fields and methods. Therefore, you do
not have to create an instance of `Math` in your programs to use these methods. In fact, you *cannot* create an instance because this class contains only
private constructors. Two fields and several methods in this class are shown
in Figure 5–16.

Figure 5–16

A partial list of fields and methods in the `Math` class.

Math	
`static final double E`	Constant field representing the value of the base of the natural logarithm.
`static final double PI`	Constant field representing the value of pi.
`static double max(double num1, double num2)`	Returns the *larger* of num1 and num2. Overloaded methods take arguments of type `int`, `long`, and `float`.
`static double min(double num1, double num2)`	Returns the *smaller* of num1 and num2. Overloaded methods take arguments of type `int`, `long`, and `float`.
`static double pow(double x, double y)`	Returns x raised to the power of y; that is, x^y.
`static double random()`	Returns a pseudorandom number from 0.0 (inclusive) to 1.0 (exclusive).
`static double abs(double num)`	Returns the absolute value of num. Overloaded methods take arguments of type `int`, `float`, and `long`.
`static double floor(double num)`	Returns the largest integer that is less than or equal to num.
`static double ceil(double num)`	Returns the smallest integer that is greater than or equal to num.
`static double round(double num)`	Returns the result of rounding num.
`static double sin(double a)`	Returns the sine of an angle a (specified in radians).
`static double cos(double a)`	Returns the cosine of an angle a (specified in radians).
`static double tan(double a)`	Returns the tangent of an angle a (specified in radians).

Example 8

The following example shows how you can use some of the Math class methods.

```java
package userdefinedclasses;

public class MathClassDemo {
  public static void main(String[] args) {
    double n1 = -85.6, n2 = 70.4;
    int angle = 45;     // in degrees

  System.out.println(String.format("The larger of %.2f and %.2f is %.2f ",
n1, n2, +Math.max(n1, n2)));

  System.out.println(String.format("The smaller of %.2f and %.2f is %.2f ",
n1, n2, +Math.min(n1, n2)));

  System.out.println(String.format("The value of %.2f raised to the power
of 5 is %.2f ", n2, +Math.pow(n2, 5)));

  System.out.println(String.format("abs(%.2f) = %.2f ", n1,
+Math.abs(n1)));

  System.out.println(String.format("floor(%.2f) = %.2f ", n1,
+Math.floor(n1)));

  System.out.println(String.format("floor(%.2f) = %.2f ", n2,
+Math.floor(n2)));

  System.out.println(String.format("ceil(%.2f) = %.2f ", n1,
+Math.ceil(n1)));

  System.out.println(String.format("ceil(%.2f) = %.2f ", n2,
+Math.ceil(n2)));

  System.out.println(String.format ("round(%.2f) = %d ", n1,
+Math.round(n1)));

  System.out.println(String.format("round(%.2f) = %d ", n2,
+Math.round(n2)));

    // For trigonometric functions, angle should be specified in radians
    double rad = (angle * Math.PI)/ 180;
    System.out.println(String.format ("sin(%d) = %.2f ", angle,
+Math.sin(rad)));
```

```
System.out.println(String.format ("cos(%d) = %.2f ", angle,
+Math.cos(rad)));
    System.out.println(String.format ("tan(%d) = %.2f ", angle,
+Math.tan(rad)));
  }
}
```

Create the file `MathClassDemo.java` in the `src\userdefinedclasses` directory (that is, in the package `userdefinedclasses`), and compile and run the program as follows:

```
C:\JavaBook> javac -d bin src\userdefinedclasses\MathClassDemo.java
```

```
C:\JavaBook> java -classpath bin userdefinedclasses.MathClassDemo
```

The program output is shown here:

```
The larger of -85.60 and 70.40 is 70.40
The smaller of -85.60 and 70.40 is -85.60
The value of 70.40 raised to the power of 5 is 1729271944.97
abs(-85.60) = 85.60
floor(-85.60) = -86.00
floor(70.40) = 70.00
ceil(-85.60) = -85.00
ceil(70.40) = 71.00
round(-85.60) = -86
round(70.40) = 70
sin(45) = 0.71
cos(45) = 0.71
tan(45) = 1.0
```

5.10   The DrawingKit Class

We have been using `DrawingKit` to create windows and draw graphical shapes in the examples described so far. `DrawingKit` uses a Java 2D class (`Graphics2D`), and two Swing classes (`JFrame` and `JPanel`). Next, we will briefly explain each of these classes.

5.10.1   The Graphics2D Class

The `Graphics2D` class in the `java.awt` package is *the* most important class in Java 2D. It contains methods to draw and color shapes in a window. In fact, each time you invoke a `DrawingKit` method to draw and color an image, `Graphics2D` does the actual work. The `DrawingKit` class is used like a wrapper around the `Graphics2D` class to hide some of the complexity associated with

+ Graphics2D	
+ void draw(Shape s)	Draw object s.
+ void setPaint(Paint p)	Set the color to p.
+ void fill(Shape s)	Color the object s.
+ void setStroke(Stroke st)	Set the line thickness to st.
+ void setFont(Font f)	Set the font to f.
+ void drawString(String str, int x, int y)	Write text str at coordinates (x, y).
+ abstract void rotate (double r, double x, double y)	Add a rotation of r radians about the point (x, y).
+ abstract void scale (double s1, double s2)	Scale an image by value s1 in the x direction, and value s2 in the y direction.
+ abstract void shear(double s1, double s2)	Shear an image by value s1 in the x direction, and value s2 in the y direction.

Figure 5–17
A partial list of methods in class Graphics2D.

using the Graphics2D class. Figure 5–17 lists some of the methods in this class. These methods will be familiar to you, because most of them are used in the same way with DrawingKit.

The setPaint method is slightly different. It takes an argument of type Paint instead of Color. Although you can also pass in a Color reference type as an argument, as you did with DrawingKit's setPaint method, the Paint type lets you apply textures and color gradients to a color. Graphics2D also contains many of the methods not available in DrawingKit, such as drawPolygon (to draw a polygon), draw3DRect (to draw a three-dimensional rectangle), rotate (to rotate an image), and scale (to increase or decrease the size of an image), among others.

Unlike other classes, you *cannot* create an instance of Graphics2D using a constructor:

```
Graphics2D myGraphics = new Graphics2D(); // error
```

You might want to think about why this would not work: A graphics object (also called **graphics context**) must be associated with a window in order to draw on it. Therefore, we have to create a window first, and then obtain its graphics context. A window is drawn using the JFrame and JPanel classes. We discuss this next.

5.10.2   The JFrame Class

The JFrame class in the javax.swing package is used to create a window with a title on the screen. Other methods in this class include those used to resize and close windows. The following statement creates a JFrame called window with the title Lamp:

```
JFrame window = new JFrame("Lamp");
```

Before we can draw graphics in this window, though, an instance of the JPanel class must be added to it. The JPanel class is described next.

5.10.3   The JPanel Class

All of the drawing is done on a panel inside the window. This panel is created using the JPanel class. An instance of this class is created as follows:

```
JPanel drawingSheet = new JPanel() {
  public void paintComponent(Graphics g) {
    Graphics2D myGraphics = (Graphics2D) g;
  }
};
```

(Note that the syntax used here to create the instance drawingSheet is somewhat unusual. Do not worry about it for now; we will cover it in a later chapter.)

The actual drawing is done inside the paintComponent method. This method takes an argument that is an instance of a Graphics class. The Graphics class contains methods for drawing graphics, and the Graphics2D class is a special type of Graphics class with more features. A portion of the paintComponent() method is explained here:

```
public void paintComponent(Graphics g) {
  Graphics2D myGraphics = (Graphics2D) g;
}
```

The Graphics object g does not have to be created explicitly; instead, it is passed *automatically* into this method. The following statement converts the Graphics object g into a Graphics2D object called myGraphics:

```
Graphics2D myGraphics = (Graphics2D) g;
```

A Graphics2D constructor is not used here. Instead, **casting** is used, which is specified using the class name Graphics2D within parentheses. Recall that with primitive types, casting converts a wider type into a narrower type. Casting reference types is similar in that their type is converted from a "superclass" to a "subclass." (You will learn about superclasses and subclasses in Chapter 6, *Inheritance*.) Now, myGraphics can call its methods draw, fill, and so forth, to create the graphics inside the window.

The JPanel instance (called drawingSheet here) must be added to a window before the graphics can be seen. The following statement accomplishes this task of adding it to window:

```
window.setContentPane(drawingSheet);
```

Figure 5–18 explains how the instances myGraphics, drawingSheet, and window are related. Here, myGraphics is the graphics context that does the drawing. You can think of it as an imaginary crayon. The JPanel instance called drawingSheet is the object on which the drawing is done. The JFrame instance is called window.

The DrawingKit class provides a method called getGraphics that returns a Graphics2D object associated with the window created using DrawingKit. It is declared as follows:

```
public Graphics2D getGraphics();
```

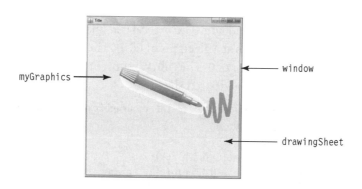

Figure 5–18
A conceptual view of the window, drawingSheet, and myGraphics objects.

In the following chapters, we will use the Graphics2D class directly so that we can access the full set of methods available in this class instead of the limited subset available in DrawingKit.

Adding Graphics to Class Lamp   In this section, we will show how to brighten things up by adding graphics to our Lamp class to draw and light up the lamp. We will draw a Lamp object and turn it on or off. A Graphics2D graphics context is used in the methods of this class. First, we add a new instance field called circle of type Ellipse2D.Double to class Lamp:

```
private Ellipse2D.Double circle;
```

This represents the circular shape of the lamp. The Ellipse2D.Double constructor is similar to that of Ellipse2D.Float, except that the former takes arguments of type double instead of float. Next, we add a new method called drawOutline, and modify the turnOn and turnOff methods in class Lamp:

> **public void drawOutline(int x, int y, Graphics2D myGraphics)**—a method that draws the outline of a lamp in the shape of a circle at the point (x, y) using the graphics context myGraphics.
>
> **public void turnOn(Graphics2D myGraphics)**—a method that colors the field circle yellow to show that the lamp is turned on.
>
> **public void turnOff(Graphics2D myGraphics)**—a method that colors circle gray to show that the lamp is turned off.

We also add the field visible to this class:

```
private boolean visible = false;
```

The drawOutline method sets the value of this field to true. The turnOn and turnOff methods display graphics only if the lamp outline has been drawn; that is, visible is set to true.

The drawOutline Method   The drawOutline method draws a lamp globe in the shape of a circle at a given point (x, y). The diameter of this circle will be set equal to diameter X 20. The third argument to this method is a Graphics2D instance to draw the desired shapes:

```
public void drawOutline(int x, int y, Graphics2D myGraphics) {
  int w = 20, z = 50;
  visible = true;
  myGraphics.setPaint(Color.black);
  circle = new Ellipse2D.Double(x, y, diameter * w, diameter * w);
```

```
myGraphics.draw(circle);
Line2D line = new Line2D.Double(x + diameter * w/2, y, x + diameter *
w/2, y - z);
myGraphics.draw(line);
}
```

The turnOn Method   This method takes a Graphics2D instance as an argument. The instance calls the fill method to color the circle instance field yellow:

```
public void turnOn(Graphics2D myGraphics) {
  lighted = true;
  if (visible) {
    myGraphics.setPaint(Color.yellow);
    myGraphics.fill(circle);
  }
}
```

The turnOff Method   This method also takes a Graphics2D instance as an argument. The instance calls the fill method to color the circle instance field gray:

```
public void turnOff(Graphics2D myGraphics) {
  lighted = false;
  if (visible) {
    myGraphics.setPaint(Color.gray);
    myGraphics.fill(circle);
  }
}
```

The main Method   A new main method is written for Lamp. A Lamp object called lamp1 is created with diameter = 6.2, wattage = 20, and lighted = false:

```
public static void main(String[] args) {
  DrawingKit dk = new DrawingKit("Lamp");
  Graphics2D myGraphics = dk.getGraphics();
  Lamp lamp1 = new Lamp(6.2, 20, false);
  lamp1.drawOutline(180, 180, myGraphics);
  lamp1.turnOn(myGraphics);
}
```

The Graphics2D context is obtained from DrawingKit using the getGraphics method:

```
Graphics2D myGraphics = dk.getGraphics();
```

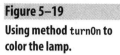

Figure 5–19
Using method `turnOn` to color the lamp.

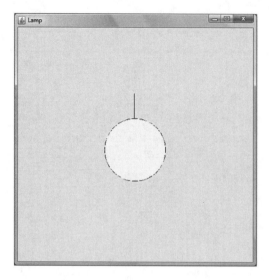

The context is passed to the `drawOutline` and `turnOn` methods as an argument. This step is necessary so that all the drawing is done inside the *same* window in all of these methods.

Compile and run this program after adding these `import` statements:

```
import java.awt.*;
import java.awt.geom.*;
import com.programwithjava.basic.DrawingKit;
```

The output is shown in Figure 5–19. Modify the program to use the `turnOff` method instead, and see how the display changes.

5.11   Documenting Programs

The documentation for a class describes the purpose of the class, and how its constructors and methods can be used. Java has a special syntax that can be used to create comments in a class. These comments can then be extracted automatically from the source file by a tool called **Javadoc** to create the documentation for that class. Javadoc stores the comments in an HTML file that can be viewed in a web browser. This is a convenient method of generating documentation because it relieves the programmer from having to maintain documentation separately from the code.

Javadoc comments start with /** and end with the usual */. These comments are inserted before a class, field, or method definition. You can also insert special tags that start with "@" to provide specific information about the class or method. The various comments and tags are explained next.

5.11.1 Class Comments

Class comments summarize the purpose of the class, and are inserted right before the class definition. They can contain one or more **author tags** labeled @author to provide information about the author of the code. These tags are used as follows:

@author *author information*

The @author tag is followed by the name, email address, or some other information about the author. Each author tag starts on a new line. The following example shows a class comment for Lamp that contains two author tags:

```
/** The Lamp class defines a lamp object that can be drawn in a window,
* and lighted or turned off. The wattage of the bulb and the diameter
* of the lamp globe can also be specified.
*
* @author Radhika Grover
* @author programwithjava.com
*/
public class Lamp {
  // rest of the code
}
```

The comments can be continued over several lines. If you forget to start a comment with /** and start it with a /* instead, Javadoc will ignore that comment and not generate any documentation for it.

5.11.2 Constructor Comments

Constructor comments explain what the constructor does, and are placed before each constructor definition. These comments can include **parameter tags** labeled @param and are used as shown here:

@param *parameter-name description*

The @param tag is followed by the name of the parameter and a description of how the parameter is used. There is a separate @param tag for each parameter in the method. The parameter tags are omitted if the constructor does not have any parameters. Their use is shown in this constructor comment in Lamp:

```
/** Constructor to create a lamp with the specified shade diameter,
* wattage and turned on or off.
*
* @param dia the shade diameter.
* @param watt the bulb wattage.
```

```
* @param light true if the lamp is turned on, otherwise false.
*/
public Lamp(double dia, int watt, boolean light) {
   diameter = dia;
   wattage = watt;
   lighted = light;
   ++numberOfObjects;
}
```

5.11.3   Method Comments

Method comments describe what a method does, and are placed right before a method definition. Like constructors, they contain parameter tags if the method has one or more parameters. In addition, method comments can also contain a **return tag** called @return that describes the value returned by the method:

@return *description*

The @return tag is followed by a description of the primitive or reference type that is returned by the method. The following example shows a method comment with a @return tag for the getWattage method in Lamp:

```
/** Method to get lamp wattage.
*
* @return the wattage of the bulb.
*/
 public int getWattage() {
   return wattage;
 }
```

There can be only one return tag in a method; it is omitted if the method has a return type of void.

5.11.4   Field Comments

Field comments can also be specified for the fields in a class. An example of a field comment in Lamp is shown here:

```
/** diameter of lamp globe */
   private double diameter;
```

However, because this field is private, Javadoc ignores this comment. By default, Javadoc only generates comments for the protected and public members of a class.

5.11.5   The `javadoc` **Command**

When you execute the `javadoc` command at the command prompt, it generates the documentation for the specified files as HTML files. The name of the HTML file is the same as the source file, but the extension is .html. You can specify the destination directory for the HTML file using the -d flag. Specify the pathnames for the source files for which you want to create the documentation starting from the `src` directory. For example, the following command will store the documentation for `Lamp.java` in the `Lamp.html` file in the `doc.userdefinedclasses` package:

```
C:\JavaBook> javadoc -d doc src\userdefinedclasses\Lamp.java
```

The subdirectory `doc\userdefinedclasses` is generated automatically inside JavaBook. Figure 5–20 shows the contents of the `Lamp.html` file viewed in a web browser.

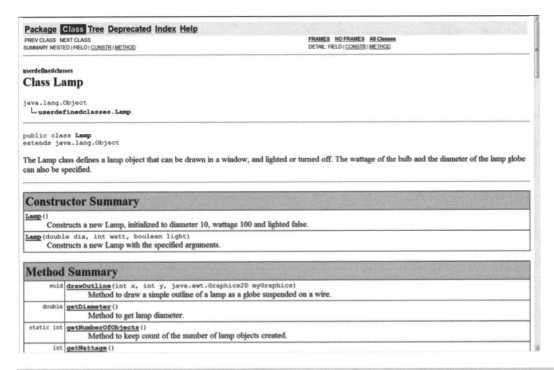

Figure 5–20

Documentation created for `Lamp.java` using the Javadoc tool.

5.12   The Java API

The documentation for the Java language is referred to as the Java API. It is available online and is in a format similar to the format shown in Figure 5–20. The Java API is a part of the Java Standard Edition documentation, which also provides tutorials, user guides, and other information about the language. You can either download this documentation to your computer or browse it online. (The entire API is very extensive; as a result, we have limited ourselves to describing only a small subset of it in this book. Anytime we introduce a new class, you should refer to the API.)

Figure 5–21 shows some of the fields in the BufferedImage class in the java.awt.image package. The listing for this class includes a summary as well as a detailed explanation of its fields, constructors, and methods.

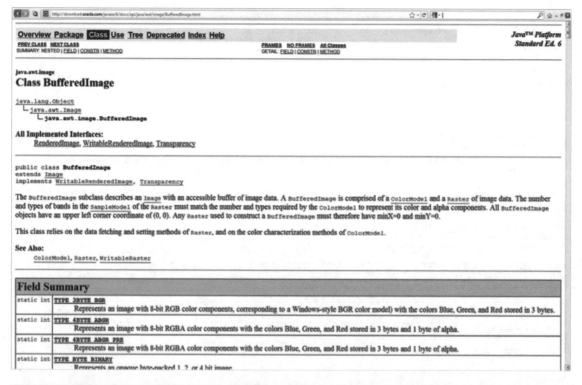

Figure 5–21

The BufferedImage class.

5.13 Summary

This chapter detailed how to create classes, and how to write constructors and methods. Other topics covered included the use of the keyword `this`; organizing .java files in packages, access modifiers, static variables and methods; and a brief explanation of some of the graphics classes that we have been using. Read further; in Chapter 6 you will learn how to create animations and, in Chapter 7, we will develop a board game called Crystals.

`BufferedImage` Class Summary

`BufferedImage(int width, int height, int type)`—a constructor that creates a `BufferedImage` having the specified width, height, and type. The type is a constant such as `TYPE_INT_ARGB`, which represents an image in the RGB color space with an alpha channel.

`int getHeight()`—a method that returns the number of pixels in a column of the image.

`int getWidth()`—a method that returns the number of pixels in a row of the image.

`int getRGB(int x, int y)`—a method that returns the encoded color value of a pixel at location (x, y).

`void setRGB(int x, int y, int rgbvalue)`—a method that sets the color of a pixel at location (x, y) to an encoded color value `rgbvalue`.

`Graphics2D` Class Summary

`void draw(Shape s)`—a method that is used to draw an object s.

`void setPaint(Paint p)`—a method that is used to set the color to p.

`void fill(Shape s)`—a method that is used to color the object s.

`void setStroke(Stroke st)`—a method that is used to set the line thickness to st.

`void setFont(Font f)`—a method that is used to set the font to f.

`void drawString(String str, int x, int y)`—a method that is used to write the text str at the coordinates (x, y).

Exercises

1. Explain the following terms:

   a. Method signature

   b. Local variable

    c. Access modifiers

    d. `return` keyword

    e. Overloaded constructors

    f. Compositing

2. Explain the differences between the following items:

    a. Instance field and static field

    b. Instance method and class method

    c. `public` and `private` access modifiers

    d. Default constructor and constructor without parameters

    e. Accessor methods and mutator methods

3. State whether the following statements are true or false.

    a. Constructors have a return type.

    b. The default constructor can be invoked by an instance of a class that contains a constructor with parameters.

    c. A method can return only one value.

    d. A class can be declared using any of the four access modifiers.

    e. The signature of a method contains its name, return type, and the data types of its parameters.

    f. By convention, the name of a class should begin with an uppercase letter.

    g. By convention, a package name can contain uppercase letters.

    h. A `private` constructor can be called in another class.

4. Write the states and behaviors of any object in your room. Write a class using these specifications.

5. Correct the compilation errors in this class:

```
Class HasErrors {
  int a;

  void getA(){
    return a;
  }

  int getA(float val){
    a = val;
  }
}
```

6. Correct the access modifiers used in the following program so that it compiles correctly. Consider each of these cases separately:

   a. The classes CheckAccess and Test are in the same package.

   b. The classes CheckAccess and Test are in different packages.

   ```
   private class CheckAccess {
     private int code;

     private int getCode() {
         return code;
     }
   }

   public class Test {
     public static void main(String[] args) {
         CheckAccess c = new CheckAccess();
         System.out.println(c.getCode());
     }
   }
   ```

7. Create a class called Country with these fields: name, population, and capital. Write the accessor and mutator methods for all of its fields. Make the fields private and the methods public.

8. Add comments to the class in Problem 7. Create documentation for it using Javadoc.

9. Give the output of the following program without running it first, and then run the program to verify your answer.

   ```
   public class PredictOutput {
     int x = -5;
     static int y = -5;

     public PredictOutput() {
       x++;
       y++;
     }

     public static void main(String[] args) {
       PredictOutput p = new PredictOutput();
       for (int i = 0; i < 10; i++) {
         p = new PredictOutput();
       }
   ```

```
        System.out.println("The value of x is " +p.x);
        System.out.println("The value of y is " +PredictOutput.y);
    }
}
```

10. Write the following equations using Java statements. Assume that the variables used in the equations have been declared and initialized. (Use the methods in the Math class).

    a. Area of sector of circle $= \dfrac{r^2\theta}{2}$

    where r is the radius of the circle, and θ is the angle in radians.

    b. Range for a projectile $= \dfrac{v^2\sin 2\theta}{g}$

    where, v is the initial speed, θ is the angle of elevation, and g is the acceleration of gravity.

    c. Electrostatic force $= k_e \dfrac{c_1 c_2}{d^2}$

    where, k_e is the Coulomb constant; c_1 and c_2 are electrostatic charges; and d is the distance between the charges. This is known as Coulomb's law.

    d. Curve $y = \sqrt{2\pi e}^{\;-\frac{x^2}{2}}$

11. Create a class called IDCard that contains a person's name, ID number, and the name of a file containing the person's photograph. Write accessor and mutator methods for each of these fields. Add the following two overloaded constructors to the class:

```
public IDCard()
public IDCard(String n, int ID, String filename)
```

    Test your program by creating different objects using these two constructors and printing out their values on the console using the accessor and mutator methods.

12. Add comments to the class in Problem 11 and create documentation for it using Javadoc.

Graphics Problems

13. Java 2D contains an `Ellipse2D.Double` class, which can be used to construct ellipses. This class contains two overloaded constructors:

    `Ellipse2D.Double()`—a constructor that creates an ellipse at the point (0.0, 0.0) with size (0.0, 0.0).

    `Ellipse2D.Double(double x, double y, double width, double height)`—a constructor that creates an ellipse at the point (x, y) of the given `width` and `height`.

    Give the statements needed to create an object using each constructor.

14. Using the following constructor and method of Java 2D's `Polygon` class, write a program to create and display a polygon with four vertices:

    `Polygon()`—a constructor to create a polygon with no sides.

    `void addPoint(int x, int y)`—a method that adds a vertex at the point (x, y) to the polygon.

15. Create an instance of the `Color` class called `myColor`, where red = 255, green = 15, and blue = 15. Write a program to display an ellipse that is colored using the color `myColor` inside a window.

16. Modify the class `BoundedCircles` (Example 3) so that the programmer can specify the position of the square instead of using the default location (150, 150). The program should run correctly regardless of where the square is positioned.

17. Modify the `BoundedCircles` class (Example 3) so that a circle that is completely outside the square is colored yellow.

18. Write a class called `Bat` that contains the (x, y) coordinates of the bat (or racket) in a window, and the width and length of the bat. Write accessor and mutator methods for each of these fields. Specify the access modifiers that must be used for this class and all of its fields and methods.

    a. Write the body of a method called `drawShape` to draw a bat of any shape having the following width and length:

    ```java
    public void drawShape(Graphics2D myGraphics)
    ```

b. Add a main method to test this class. Create an instance of Bat using the default constructor and invoke the drawShape method to display it in a window.

c. Modify the instance fields using the mutator methods in main. Print out the instance field values using the accessor methods and verify that they are correct.

d. Add two constructors to the class. One constructor takes no arguments, and the second constructor takes four arguments of type float. Create instances of Bat using both constructors and display them in the window.

Image Manipulation Problems

19. Add a subtract method to the Compositor class described in this chapter. This method takes two input images of type BufferedImage as arguments and returns a new image, which is also of type BufferedImage. The pixels in the returned image are the *difference* of the pixels in the input images. Suppose that (r_1, g_1, b_1) and (r_2, g_2, b_2) are the red, green, and blue components of a pixel with coordinates (x, y) in the input images. Then a pixel in the output image at the same location (x, y) has component values $(r_1 - r_2, g_1 - g_2, b_1 - b_2)$. Any negative component values should be set to 0. Write a program to test this method. Is the result of subtracting the first image from the second the same as subtracting the second from the first?

20. Add a multiply method to the Compositor class. This method takes two input images of type BufferedImage as arguments and returns a new image, which is also of type BufferedImage. This method is similar to the subtract method of the preceding problem, except that the pixels in the returned image are the *product* of the pixels in the input images. Write a program to test this method.

21. Add a method called weightedAdd to the Compositor class. This method creates and returns a new image formed by adding together the input images using different weights. Suppose that (r_1, g_1, b_1) and (r_2, g_2, b_2) are the red, green, and blue components of a pixel with coordinates (x, y) in the input images. If a weight of 0.20 is used, then 20% of the first image is combined with 80% of the second. Therefore, a pixel in the output image at (x, y) has component values $(0.20 * r_1 + 0.80 * r_2, 0.20 * g_1 + 0.80 * g_2, 0.20 * b_1 + 0.80 * b_2)$. The method should also

have a parameter called `weight` of type `double`. Write a program to test this method using different weights.

22. Add a method called `randomAdd` to the `Compositor` class. This creates an output image by randomly selecting pixels from either of the two input images. Write a program to test this method.

Further Reading

In Unified Modeling Language (UML), diagrams of classes and objects are called class diagrams and object diagrams, respectively. To learn more about how UML is used to model object-oriented software, see [8].

References

1. "The Java™ Tutorials." Web. <http://download.oracle.com/javase/tutorial/>.

2. Brinkmann, Ron. *The Art and Science of Digital Compositing: Techniques for Visual Effects, Animation and Motion Graphics, Second Edition*. Burlington, MA: Morgan Kaufmann/Elsevier, 2008. Print.

3. Guzdial, Mark, and Barbara Ericson. *Introduction to Computing and Programming in Java: A Multimedia Approach*. Upper Saddle River, NJ: Pearson Prentice Hall, 2007. Print.

4. Eckel, Bruce. *Thinking in Java*. Upper Saddle River, NJ: Prentice Hall, 2006. Print.

5. Anderson, Julie, and Herve Franceschi. *Java 6 Illuminated: An Active Learning Approach*. Sudbury, MA: Jones and Bartlett, 2008. Print.

6. Sierra, Kathy, and Bert Bates. *Head First Java*. Sebastopol, CA: O'Reilly, 2005. Print.

7. Knudsen, Jonathan. *Java 2D Graphics*. Beijing: O'Reilly, 1999. Print.

8. "Unified Modeling Language." *Object Management Group—UML*. Web. <http://www.uml.org/>.

9. *Java™ Platform, Standard Edition 6, API Specification*. Web. <http://download.oracle.com/javase/6/docs/api/>.

CHAPTER 6

Inheritance

CHAPTER CONTENTS

Java gets richer through inheritance! Inheritance means that a class gets some fields and methods from another class. The advantage is that a new class can reuse code from existing classes, which saves time and effort for the programmer. In this chapter, we will discuss how a class can inherit from another class. In addition, we will use several code examples to illustrate how to include animation in programs—we will make cars move, airplanes fly, and other fun stuff!

6.1   What Is Inheritance?

Consider a class Animal with two methods: eat and move. Suppose that we would like to create a class Skunk with the same methods as in Animal, and an additional method emitScent. With inheritance, Skunk can acquire the methods in Animal, removing the need to rewrite these methods in Skunk. Additionally, Skunk can be specialized with a new method emitScent, which highlights a well-known trait of skunks. Skunk is called the **child class** or **subclass**, and Animal is called the **parent class** or **superclass**. This inheritance relationship between Animal and Skunk is depicted in Figure 6–1 by using an arrowhead that is not filled in. The arrow means that Skunk reuses code in Animal. In other words, Skunk is *derived* from Animal.

6.2   When Is Inheritance Used?

A class X can inherit the fields and methods of another class Y when there is a special type of **is-a** relationship between these two classes. The "is-a" rela-

Figure 6–1

Class Skunk inherits from the Animal class.

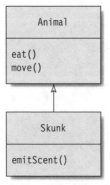

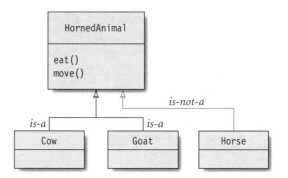

tionship means that X is a specialization of Y. For example, Skunk is-a Animal is true.

Assume that we have written a class called Vehicle and another called Car. Class Car can inherit from Vehicle because Car is-a Vehicle. Note that the reverse is not true, because not all vehicles are cars. Therefore, Vehicle cannot inherit from Car. In addition, if a third class called Door exists, it may seem plausible that Car should inherit from Door. However, Car is-a Door and Door is-a Car are both not true, so neither should inherit from the other. The derived class is a specialized form of the parent class. Therefore, it is important that this "is-a" relationship holds true whenever you write a derived class.

Figure 6–2 shows that the Cow and Goat classes can inherit from the HornedAnimal class. Next, we want to write a class Horse that also has two methods: eat and move. You may want to make Horse a subclass of HornedAnimal merely to reuse the methods available in the latter, but this is a bad idea—Horse is not a HornedAnimal, and so it should not inherit from HornedAnimal.

6.3 The extends Keyword

The keyword extends is used to denote that one class inherits from another class. The code for class Skunk that inherits from Animal is shown here:

```
public class Skunk extends Animal {
  public void emitScent() {
    System.out.println("Emit scent");
  }
}
```

The `Animal` class implements the methods `eat` and `move`, which are inherited by `Skunk`:

```java
public class Animal {
  public void eat() {
    System.out.println("Eat");
  }
  public void move() {
    System.out.println("Move");
  }
}
```

As discussed previously, the advantage of using inheritance is that `Skunk` can reuse the code in `Animal`. Otherwise, `Skunk` would need to define explicitly all the fields and methods, as shown in the `NotSoSmartSkunk` class (see Figure 6–3):

```java
//Class NotSoSmartSkunk does not use inheritance
public class NotSoSmartSkunk {
  public void eat() {
    System.out.println("Eat");
  }
  public void move() {
    System.out.println("Move");
  }
  public void emitScent() {
    System.out.println("Emit scent");
  }
}
```

The `Skunk` class is the same as the `NotSoSmartSkunk` class. However, less code (and effort) is required to write the `Skunk` class using inheritance. Inheritance is especially useful when the superclass is large and complex, or when there are many classes that share a portion of code.

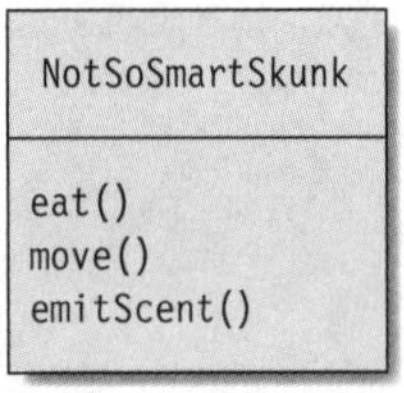

Figure 6–3

The `NotSoSmartSkunk` class must implement all three methods because it does not use inheritance.

```
NotSoSmartSkunk

eat()
move()
emitScent()
```

6.4   Types of Inheritance

Single-level inheritance is a simple form of inheritance in which there are only two classes involved: one superclass and a subclass. Its form is shown in Figure 6–4. Here, class BoardGame inherits from class Game. Therefore, Game is a superclass and BoardGame is a subclass of Game.

In **multilevel inheritance,** a class that acts as both a superclass and a subclass is present. For example, let us add a third class Chess that inherits from BoardGame, as shown in Figure 6–5. Here, BoardGame is a superclass of Chess and a subclass of Game. Now, Chess inherits the fields and methods of both classes Game and BoardGame. There can be any number of classes in the multilevel inheritance path; for example, class V inherits from class U, class W inherits from V, and so on.

Hierarchical inheritance is a form of inheritance in which many classes inherit from the same superclass. An example is shown in Figure 6–6. In the figure, BoardGame, TableGame, and CourtGame inherit fields and methods from the same superclass Game. However, some of the other fields and methods in these three subclasses will differ.

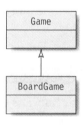

Figure 6–4
Single-level inheritance.

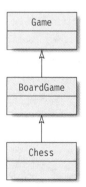

Figure 6–5
Multilevel inheritance.

Figure 6–6
Hierarchical inheritance.

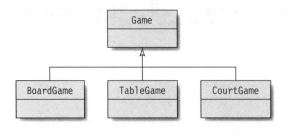

Figure 6–7
Multiple inheritance is not supported in Java.

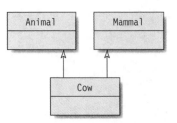

In **multiple inheritance**, a class can have more than one superclass. This form of inheritance is not supported in Java, although it is supported in other languages, such as C++ and Python. Figure 6–7 shows an example of multiple inheritance in which class Cow has two superclasses, Animal and Mammal.

6.5   Access Modifiers

The subclass can access the methods and fields of a superclass just as it would access its own methods and fields. Note that constructors are not inherited. In addition, some restrictions are imposed by the access modifiers used. In Chapter 5, we discussed the four types of access identifiers: private, public, *default*, and protected. We also described how these modifiers affect the ability of a class to access the fields and methods in another (unrelated) class. Now, we extend this discussion to the case when the classes are related; that is, one class is a subclass of another. These access modifiers decide which fields and methods can be inherited by a subclass:

- public: All public fields and methods of the parent class are inherited by its child class. For example, the Skunk class inherits all of the public methods in Animal.

- private: Fields and methods that are declared private cannot be inherited by a subclass. This structure is shown in Figure 6–8.

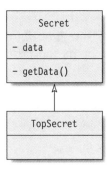

```
//code segment
TopSecret t = new Top Secret();
t.getData();        // error!
int v = t.data;     // error!
```

Figure 6–8
Private fields and methods of Secret cannot be accessed by TopSecret.

- *Package-private* or *default* access modifier: Fields and methods that have a package-private access modifier are inherited by a subclass *only* if it is in the same package as the superclass. This structure is shown in Figure 6–9. Both Bird and Iguana are subclasses of Pet; however, only Pet and Bird are in the same package myHouse. Therefore, only Bird (and not Iguana) can access the package-private method eatWorm in Pet.

- protected: Fields and methods declared as protected are inherited by a subclass even if it is in a different package from its superclass. Therefore, if the eatWorm method in Pet were instead declared as protected, Iguana would be able to access it.

When a class is designed, a different access modifier can be selected for each of its fields and methods, depending upon the amount of visibility required

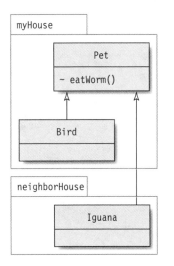

```
//code segment
Bird earlyBird = new Bird();
earlyBird.eatWorm(); // okay

Iguana lizard = new Iguana();
lizard.eatWorm();    // error!
```

Figure 6–9
Bird can access the package-private method eat-Worm, but Iguana cannot.

for that field or method. If a field or method is to be used only within the class, it should be declared as private. On the other hand, if a field or method is to be used within the class and by its subclasses, it should be declared as protected.

The Vehicle Class   We are going to create a new class called Vehicle, and we will build upon it through the rest of the chapter to explain new concepts:

```
package inheritance;
import java.awt.*;

public class Vehicle {
   // method to draw shape of Vehicle
   protected void drawShape(Graphics2D myGraphics) {
   }
}
```

This class contains a single empty method called drawShape. For convenience, we put this and all of the other classes in this chapter in a package called inheritance in the src directory. You should add this statement to all the classes in this chapter:

package inheritance;

Next, we create two subclasses of Vehicle, called Car and Airplane. Car and Airplane are types of Vehicle; that is, they have an "is-a" relationship with Vehicle, and so they can inherit the code in Vehicle. In addition, these classes will be developed further by adding new methods to them. This arrangement is a form of hierarchical inheritance and is shown in Figure 6–10.

The class declaration for Car, which is a subclass of Vehicle, is shown here:

```
package inheritance;

public class Car extends Vehicle {
}
```

Figure 6–10

Class Vehicle and its subclasses, Car and Airplane.

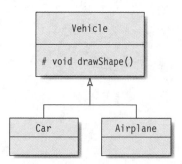

The class declaration for Airplane, which is also a subclass of Vehicle, is shown here:

```
package inheritance;

public class Airplane extends Vehicle {
}
```

We will develop these two classes further later in this chapter.

6.6   Overriding Methods

A subclass can contain a method with the same *signature* and *return type* as in its superclass. In this case, the method in the superclass is not inherited. The method of the subclass is said to **override** the method of the superclass.

An **overriding** method has:

- the same signature (method name, number of parameters, and parameter types) as a method M in the superclass, and

- the same return type as M, and

- a different body from M.

Consider a Cat class with subclasses HouseCat and Lion. The Cat class contains the method vocalize:

```
// vocalize method in Cat
public void vocalize() {
  System.out.println("Meow");
}
```

With method overriding, the Lion class can define its own vocalize method instead of inheriting it from Cat:

```
// vocalize method in Lion
public void vocalize() {
  System.out.println("ROAR!");
}
```

The signature and return type of the overriding method in the subclass should match those of the overridden method in the superclass exactly. Let us add a main method to this class:

```
public static void main(String[] args) {
  Lion lion = new Lion();
  lion.vocalize();
  HouseCat housecat = new HouseCat();
  housecat.vocalize();
}
```

The program output is shown here:

```
ROAR!
Meow
```

The vocalize method of class Lion, and not class Cat, is called. On the other hand, the HouseCat class inherits the vocalize method of Cat because it does not have an overriding method. Method overriding is shown in Figure 6–11.

Fields that are inherited from the superclass do not have to be overridden because instances can select different values for the same field. The type field of Cat is inherited by Lion and HouseCat, and instances of both classes can assign different values to this field. However, if the subclass contains a field with the same *name* as a field inherited from the superclass, the super-class field is not visible to the subclass even if the types of the two fields are different. In this case, the superclass field is said to be **hidden** by the sub-class field.

It is not a good idea to add the field type to Lion and HouseCat because this would hide the field inherited from Cat.

> Fields should not be hidden because doing so makes the code confusing.

6.6.1   Polymorphism

Polymorphism refers to an object's ability to select a particular behavior based on its type while the program is executing. To understand how poly-morphism works, consider the following statement:

```
Cat cat = new Lion();
```

Figure 6–11

The vocalize **method in the** Lion **class overrides the** vocalize **method in** Cat.

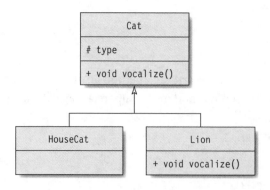

An object of type Lion is assigned to the reference variable cat of type Cat. This is different from the way in which we have been constructing objects up until now, where the reference variable and the object belong to the same class, as in the following example:

```
Lion cat1 = new Lion();
```

However, by inheritance, Lion is-a Cat, and so we can assign an object of type Lion to a reference variable of type Cat. In other words, *an object can be assigned to a reference variable of its superclass.* This process is known as **upcasting**. Similarly, we can also write the following:

```
Cat cat2 = new HouseCat();
```

The reverse assignment cannot be made; that is, we cannot assign an object of Cat to a reference variable of type HouseCat:

```
HouseCat cat3 = new Cat(); // error!
```

In the following assignment, an explicit cast must be used:

```
HouseCat cat3 = (HouseCat) cat2; // okay because cat2 references a HouseCat
```

The cast consists of a class type within parentheses that is placed in front of the object being cast. This is similar to casting primitive types, in which a larger type is converted to a narrower type using a cast. However, a cast cannot be used with two unrelated classes:

```
Vehicle v = (Vehicle) new Animal();  // error
```

It simply does not make sense to cast an object of type Animal to type Vehicle, because these classes are not related. Doing so will cause a compiler to issue an error message that the cast from Animal to Vehicle is not allowed.

Furthermore, suppose that the method vocalize is called as follows:

```
Cat cat = new Lion();
cat.vocalize();
```

Which vocalize method is called now—that of Cat or Lion? To find out, add this main method to the Lion or HouseCat class:

```
public static void main(String[] args) {
  Cat lion = new Lion();
  lion.vocalize();
  Cat housecat = new HouseCat();
  housecat.vocalize();
}
```

The program output is:

```
ROAR!
Meow
```

The correct vocalize method of a particular object is called, even though the reference variable is of type Cat in both cases. lion references an object of type Lion; as a result, it calls the vocalize method of Lion, and not Cat. Thus, the method called by an object depends on its type determined at run time—a process known as **polymorphism**. Polymorphism is achieved via *method overriding* in this example.

6.6.2　Access Modifiers for Overriding Methods

The access modifier of the superclass method decides what the access modifier of the overriding subclass method can be. Table 6–1 shows the relationship between the access modifier of a superclass method and the corresponding overriding method in the subclass. If the access modifier of the superclass method is protected, the overriding method in the subclass can only be protected or public—it cannot be private. The reason for this is that an overriding method in the subclass cannot be *less* visible than the corresponding method in the superclass. The relationships for the package-private and public access modifiers are also shown in the table. If the access modifier of the superclass method is private, the method is not inherited by the subclass, and thus it cannot be overridden in the subclass.

The following example explains, in more detail, how the modifiers can be used.

TABLE 6–1　Access Modifiers for Overriding Methods

Access Modifier of a Superclass Method	Access Modifier of an Overriding Subclass Method
protected	protected or public
package-private	package-private, protected, or public
public	public

Example 1

Consider two classes `Bank` and `OnlineBank`, where `OnlineBank` is a subclass of `Bank`. Only the method declarations in these two classes are shown here:

```
class Bank {
      public void deposit(float amount) { }
      protected void withdraw(float amount) { }
      void name() { };
      private void update() { };
}

class OnlineBank extends Bank {
      private void deposit(float amount) { }
      private void withdraw(float amount) { }
      protected void name() { }
      private void update() { }
}
```

Pick out the overriding methods in `OnlineBank`. Using Table 6–1, explain which access modifiers in `OnlineBank` are incorrect and result in an error.

Solution:

```
class OnlineBank extends Bank {
   private void deposit(float amount); // error!
   private void withdraw(float amount); // error!
   protected void name(); // overrides method name in Bank
   private void update(); // does not override method update in Bank
}
```

The method `deposit` cannot have an access modifier of `private`. The reason is that, according to Table 6–1, if a method is declared as `public` in a superclass, the overriding method should also be `public` in the subclass. Therefore, `deposit` should be made `public`. Similarly, `withdraw` also has an incorrect access modifier of `private`. This method is declared as `protected` in `Bank`, and thus it can have access modifiers of `protected` or `public` only. The method `update` is declared as `private` in `Bank`, and it is not visible to `OnlineBank`. Therefore, `update` in `OnlineBank` does not override `update` in `Bank`.   ■

6.6.3   Covariant Return Types

Recall that an overriding method has the same return type as the method in its superclass. However, an exception exists when the return types are different. These return types are called **covariant return types** and they differ in that the return type of the overriding method can be a *subclass* of the return type of its superclass method. We explain this with an example.

Consider four classes Animal, Goat, Zoo, and PettingZoo, where Goat is derived from Animal, and PettingZoo is derived from Zoo. The class Zoo has a method called getAnimal with the return type Animal:

```
public class Zoo {
  private Animal myAnimal;

  public Animal getAnimal() {
    return myAnimal;
  }
}
```

The getAnimal method in PettingZoo has a return type of Goat:

```
public class PettingZoo extends Zoo{
  private Goat billy;
  public PettingZoo() {
    billy = new Goat();
  }
  // A return type of Goat is allowed
  // since Goat is a subclass of Animal.
  public Goat getAnimal() {
    return billy;
  }
}
```

The return type of getAnimal is Goat, which does not match the return type of Animal in the superclass method. However, no error exists, because Goat is a subclass of Animal. Therefore, the getAnimal method of PettingZoo overrides that of Zoo correctly. On the other hand, if the return type of the subclass method were different and not a subclass of the return type of the superclass method, it would be flagged as a compilation error.

Adding an Overriding Method to Car   Here, we will add a method called drawShape to the Car class to draw the shape of a car. This method overrides the empty method drawShape in Vehicle.

It is important to note that all drawing is done relative to a point on the vehicles. Any point on the object can be chosen as this **reference point**. For the car, we select the upper-left corner of the trunk as the reference point (x, y). Recall that the reason for using this reference point is so that we can draw this object at another position in the frame by merely changing the values of *x* and *y*, which will make it easy to animate the objects. Thus, the position of all graphics objects, such as ellipses, lines, and rectangles, that we will use to draw our vehicles, will be specified relative to point (*x*, *y*).

```
// Method in class Car to draw the shape of a car.
public void drawShape(Graphics2D myGraphics) {
  int w1 = 250, h1 = 90, w2 = 143, h2 = 75, w4 = 50, h4 = 45, w5 = 35;
  float e1 = 62.5f, e2 = 22.5f, e3 = 125, e4 = 45, w3 = 16.67f, h3 = 30;
  // draw the lower body
  RoundRectangle2D.Float lower = new RoundRectangle2D.Float(x, y, w1,
h1, e1, e2);
  myGraphics.setPaint(Color.white);
  myGraphics.fill(lower);
  myGraphics.setPaint(Color.blue);
  myGraphics.draw(lower);

  // draw the upper body
  RoundRectangle2D.Float mid = new RoundRectangle2D.Float(x+50, y-63, w2,
h2, e1, e2);
  myGraphics.setPaint(Color.white);
  myGraphics.fill(mid);
  myGraphics.setPaint(Color.blue);
  myGraphics.draw(mid);
  Rectangle2D.Float top = new Rectangle2D.Float(x+50, y, w2, w4/2);
  myGraphics.setPaint(Color.white);
  myGraphics.fill(top);

  // color a yellow headlight
  Ellipse2D.Float light = new Ellipse2D.Float(x+238, y+18, w3, h3);
  myGraphics.setPaint(Color.yellow);
  myGraphics.fill(light);
  myGraphics.setPaint(Color.black);
  myGraphics.draw(light);

  // color a red taillight
  Ellipse2D.Float taillight= new Ellipse2D.Float(x-10, y+18, w3, h3);
  myGraphics.setPaint(Color.red);
  myGraphics.fill(taillight);

  // color windows
  RoundRectangle2D.Float window1 = new RoundRectangle2D.Float(x+62.5f, y-
45, w4, h4, e1/2, e2/2);
  myGraphics.setPaint(Color.lightGray);
  myGraphics.fill(window1);
```

```
    RoundRectangle2D.Float window2 = new RoundRectangle2D.Float(x+125, y-45,
w4, h4, e1/2, e2/2);
  myGraphics.fill(window2);

  // color the bumpers
  RoundRectangle2D.Float b1 = new RoundRectangle2D.Float(x+225, y+65, e1/2,
e2, e3, e4);
  myGraphics.setPaint(Color.gray);
  myGraphics.fill(b1);

  RoundRectangle2D.Float b2 = new RoundRectangle2D.Float(x-5, y+65, w5,
e2, e3, e4);
  myGraphics.fill(b2);

  // draw the wheels
  Ellipse2D.Float wh1 = new Ellipse2D.Float(x+37.5f, y+63, w4, w4);
  Ellipse2D.Float wh2 = new Ellipse2D.Float(x+167.5f, y+63, w4, w4);
  myGraphics.setPaint(Color.white);
  myGraphics.fill(wh1);
  myGraphics.fill(wh2);
  myGraphics.setPaint(Color.darkGray);
  myGraphics.draw(wh1);
  myGraphics.draw(wh2);
}
```

In addition, we add two fields x and y to Vehicle, to represent the *x*- and *y*-coordinates of the vehicle's position in the window.

```
public class Vehicle {
  // vehicle's position
  protected float x = 30, y = 300;
  // method to draw shape of Vehicle
  protected void drawShape(Graphics2D myGraphics) {
  }
}
```

Add these import statements to Car:

```
import java.awt.*;
import java.awt.geom.*;
import com.programwithjava.basic.DrawingKit;
```

Finally, add this main method to Car, and then run the program:

```
public static void main(String[] args) {
  DrawingKit dk = new DrawingKit("Car");
```

```
Graphics2D myGraphics = dk.getGraphics();
Vehicle myVehicle = new Car();
myVehicle.drawShape(myGraphics);
}
```

Place the classes Vehicle.java, Car.java, and Airplane.java in the inheritance package inside the JavaBook\src directory. To compile and run this program, type the following at the command prompt:

```
C:\JavaBook> javac -d bin src\com\programwithjava\basic\DrawingKit.java
src\inheritance\Vehicle.java src\inheritance\Car.java
```

```
C:\JavaBook> java -classpath bin inheritance.Car
```

The overriding method drawShape of Car will be called and the shape will be drawn as shown in Figure 6–12.

6.6.4   The Advantage of Overriding Methods

So, what is the advantage of overriding methods? The advantage is that the decision of which of these methods should be used can be put off until run time. Therefore, we can simply write the following:

```
v.drawShape(myGraphics);
```

Figure 6–12
Drawing a car using the overriding method drawShape **of class** Car.

At run time, depending on whether v is an object of type Car or Airplane, the corresponding drawShape method of that class is invoked. We clarify this with an example. Let us add a third class called Traffic, as shown here:

```java
package inheritance;
import java.awt.*;
import com.programwithjava.basic.DrawingKit;

public class Traffic {
  Traffic(Vehicle v) {
    DrawingKit dk = new DrawingKit("Traffic");
    Graphics2D myGraphics = dk.getGraphics();
    v.drawShape(myGraphics);
  }
}
```

The constructor for Traffic has a parameter of type Vehicle. The Car and Airplane classes are subclasses of Vehicle; as a result, objects of these classes can also be passed as an argument to this constructor. Add the following main method to the Traffic class:

```java
public static void main(String[] args) {
  Car c = new Car();
  Traffic t = new Traffic(c); // Call to Traffic constructor
}
```

The Traffic constructor is called and the object is passed in as an argument to this constructor is of type Car. Therefore, the statement v.drawShape calls the drawShape method of Car.

If method overriding were not allowed, how could the Traffic class be written to accomplish the same effect? For one, there could be multiple constructors, each with a different type of parameter:

```java
public class Traffic {
  Traffic(Vehicle v) {
    // some code
    v.drawShape(myGraphics);
  }

  Traffic(Car v) {
    // some code
    v.drawShape(myGraphics);
  }

  Traffic(Airplane v) {
```

```
      // some code
      v.drawShape(myGraphics);
   }
}
```

Although this alternative works, it makes the code both lengthy and diffi-cult to maintain because each time a new subclass of Vehicle is added, the code for Traffic must be updated. Of course, the ability to override methods removes the need to do any of this, which makes the technique very useful.

6.6.5   The super Keyword

The subclass can call the overridden method in its superclass by using a special keyword called super. The next example shows why this keyword is useful, and how it can be used.

Suppose that we have a class called PieRecipe that contains a method called getDirections. This method describes how to make the crust of a pie:

```
package inheritance;

public class PieRecipe {
  public void getDirections() {
    System.out.println("To prepare crust, roll out dough and chill in
pie pan.");
  }
}
```

The class BlueberryPieRecipe extends the class PieRecipe. It contains an over-riding method called getDirections that describes how to make the filling for the pie:

```
package inheritance;

public class BlueberryPieRecipe extends PieRecipe {
  // overriding method in BlueberryPieRecipe
  public void getDirections() {
    System.out.println("To prepare filling, combine blueberries, flour,
lemon juice and sugar and put in pie pan, then cover with extra dough
and bake.");
  }
}
```

There is a problem with BlueberryPieRecipe—its getDirections method only describes how to make the filling and not the crust. The getDirections method in `PieRecipe` describes how to make the crust, but this method is overridden and therefore is not inherited by `BlueberryPieRecipe`. This problem can be easily resolved by using the keyword `super`. The overridden method in `PieRecipe` can be accessed in the subclass using the following method:

```
super.getDirections();
```

The `getDirections` method in `BlueberryPieRecipe` is modified as shown here:

```
// modified method in BlueberryPieRecipe
public void getDirections() {
      super.getDirections();
      System.out.println("To prepare filling, combine blueberries,
flour, lemon juice and sugar and put in pie pan, then cover with extra
dough and bake.");
}
```

Write a `main` method to test the `getDirections` method in `BlueberryPieRecipe`:

```
public static void main(String[] args) {
  PieRecipe r = new BlueberryPieRecipe();
  r.getDirections();
}
```

The directions for both the crust and the filling are printed out when the program is run:

```
To prepare crust, roll out dough and chill in pie pan.
To prepare filling, combine blueberries, flour, lemon juice and sugar and
put in pie pan, then cover with extra dough and bake.
```

Hidden fields can also be accessed in the subclass by using `super`. Suppose that `BlueberryPieRecipe` contains a field called `ingredients` that hides this field in `PieRecipe`. Then the hidden field can be accessed in `BlueberryPieRecipe` using `super.ingredients`. Remember, though, that in general, fields should not be hidden.

6.7   Overloaded Methods

As with constructors, methods can also be overloaded. Overloaded methods are methods with the same name but different parameter lists. (It is important not to confuse *overloaded* methods with the *overriding* methods we discussed earlier.)

An **overloaded method** meets the following requirements:

- It has the same name as another method M within the class or in a superclass.

- It has a *different* parameter list from M.

The return types and access modifiers of overloaded methods do not have to be the same. However, the data types of the parameters in the method declaration should be different in these methods.

For example, consider a class Geom with two methods called intersects:

```
class Geom {
  public static boolean intersects(Line2D.Float line1, Line2D.Float line2)
{
    /* code to check if line1 intersects with line2 */
  }

  public static boolean intersects(Rectangle2D.Float r, Line2D.Float line1)
{
    /* code to check if line1 intersects the rectangle r */
  }
}
```

The intersects methods are said to be *overloaded* because they have the same name, but a different parameter list. Although the bodies of over-loaded methods are different, the goal is to provide the same functionality. For example, both methods check whether the given shapes intersect or not. Nevertheless, which of these methods will be called? This depends on the data type of the arguments passed to intersects. If both arguments are of type Line2D.Float, the first method will be called. Alternately, if the first argument is of type Rectangle2D.Float and the second is of type Line2D.Float, the second method is called. In general, the overloaded method to be invoked is the one whose parameter types match those of the arguments in the method call.

You are already familiar with the println method. This method is also over-loaded, and for this reason, we can use it to print out arguments that are of different types, such as int, float, and String. This is more convenient than having to call a method with a different name for each data type.

Java 2D contains many classes with overloaded methods. One example is the `Rectangle` class. The `Rectangle` class has four overloaded methods called `contains`, each of which checks whether a given point or shape lies inside the `Rectangle` object and returns `true` or `false` accordingly:

`public boolean contains(int x, int y)`—a method that checks whether the point (x, y) is inside the `Rectangle` object that calls this method.

`public boolean contains(int x, int y, int w, int h)`—a method that checks whether the rectangle formed at coordinates (x, y) with width w and height h is completely inside the `Rectangle` object that calls this method.

`public boolean contains(Point p)`—a method that checks whether the object p of type `Point` is inside the `Rectangle` object that calls this method. (`Point` is another class in Java 2D.)

`public boolean contains(Rectangle r)`—a method that checks whether the `Rectangle` object r is entirely within the `Rectangle` object that calls this method.

Example 2

Which of the following are valid declarations of the overloaded method compute in class Abacus?

```
class Abacus {
  public int compute(int a, double b, int c) {
    /* some code */
}
  private long compute(double a, long b) {
    /* some code */
  }
  public float compute(double b, int a, int c) {
    /* some code */
  }
  public double compute(double a1, long b1) {
    /* some code */
  }
}
```

Solution: Overloaded methods must not have the same signature. The second and fourth methods have the same signature, shown here, which causes a compilation error:

```
compute(double, long)
```

Note that although the first and third methods both contain two ints and one double in the method signature, they are valid because the order of these parameters is different.   ∎

6.8   Constructor Chaining

As you already know, an object of a class is created using a constructor of that class. In Chapter 5, we discussed the three different types of constructors: default, constructor without parameters, and constructor with parameters. In this section, we are going to see how the object is created when inheritance is used, because there are multiple constructors involved. It is important to understand these two key points:

1. **A class does not inherit the constructors from its superclass:** Whereas methods and fields can be inherited by a subclass, constructors are *not* inherited.

2. **The first line of any constructor is a call to another constructor:** Either a superclass constructor or another constructor within the same class is called. This happens in one of the following two ways:

   a. Java automatically calls the superclass constructor.

   b. The programmer explicitly calls a superclass constructor or another constructor in the same class.

We will examine these in more detail next.

6.8.1   Java Automatically Calls the Superclass Constructor

To create an object of a class Y, all of the objects in the inheritance hierarchy of Y, starting at the parent class, must be created. Java calls the superclass constructor by inserting the following statement automatically in the first line of the constructor body:

```
super();
```

The super keyword was used earlier to call the superclass methods. Here we use it to call the superclass *constructor*. If the superclass does not have any constructors, the *default constructor* of the superclass will be executed. Otherwise, the *constructor without parameters* in the superclass is executed. We clarify this with an example. Figure 6–13(a) shows two classes, Structure and House, where Structure is a superclass of House.

Structure contains a constructor without parameters:

```
package inheritance;

public class Structure {
  // constructor without parameters
  public Structure() {
    System.out.println("Build foundation.");
  }
}
```

House also has a constructor without parameters. In main, create an object of House:

```
package inheritance;

public class House extends Structure {
  // constructor without parameters
  public House() {
    System.out.println("Set up floor, walls and roof.");
  }

  public static void main(String[] args) {
    // create a house
    House myHouse = new House();
  }
}
```

Figure 6–13

(a) The classes Structure **and** House. **(b) Java inserts the** super **statement automatically to call** Structure's **constructor.**

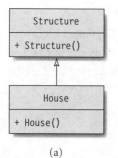

```
public House() {
    super();  // Java inserts this
    System.out.println("Set up floor, walls and roof.");
}
```

(a)   (b)

When you run this program, it produces the following output:

```
Build foundation.
Set up floor, walls and roof.
```

The first line of the output shows that the constructor in Structure has been invoked. But who calls this constructor? This is what happens: *Java inserts a call to the superclass constructor inside* House's *constructor using the* super *keyword*, as shown in Figure 6–13(b). This calls Structure's constructor to create an object of this class first, and then House's constructor will execute. The reason for this is that the parent must be created before the child, which is logical.

House calls Structure's constructor; thus this constructor must be declared as protected or public. Otherwise, it is not visible to House, which will result in an error because an object of Structure cannot be created.

> Superclass constructors should not be made private.

The observant reader will note that a super statement is inserted automatically in Structure's constructor. However, given that Structure does not extend another class, which constructor is called? We explain this next.

6.8.2   Object: **The Granddaddy of All Classes**

Java contains a class called Object from which *all* classes are derived. Object does not have a superclass. Even if a class does not declare that it is derived from another class, it is implicitly derived from Object.

Thus, Object is the *parent* of Structure and the *grandparent* of House. We could have also written:

```
public class Structure extends Object {
   // code for Structure goes here
}
```

There can be any number of intermediate classes between Object and another class.

Object contains a constructor without parameters. The super statement in Structure's constructor calls this constructor of Object. (There is no super statement in Object's constructor.) The sequence of calls needed to create an object of House is shown in Figure 6–14. First, House's constructor is called. The super statement is executed here, and the constructor in its superclass Structure is called. Similarly, after the super statement in Structure's

Figure 6–14
Sequence in which constructors are called to create an instance of House.

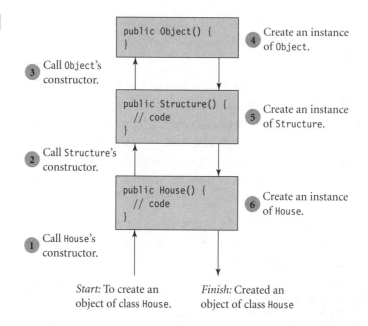

Call Object's constructor. ③

public Object() {
}
④ Create an instance of Object.

public Structure() {
    // code
}
⑤ Create an instance of Structure.

Call Structure's constructor. ②

public House() {
    // code
}
⑥ Create an instance of House.

Call House's constructor. ①

Start: To create an object of class House.

Finish: Created an object of class House

constructor is executed, Object's constructor is called. After this, there are no more constructors to call. The objects are now created in the order Object, Structure, and finally House.

To create an object of a class (say, House), all superclass constructors are called, up to the topmost class Object. Then the constructors are executed in reverse order, from top to bottom; that is, starting from the constructor Object down to the constructor House. This process is known as **constructor chaining**. Figure 6–14 shows an example of constructor chaining.

6.8.3   A Program with an Error

The super statement *cannot* call a constructor with parameters. Additionally, it *can* call the default constructor of the superclass *only* if there is no other constructor in the superclass. To see why this might create an error, let us write a class AnotherStructure with a constructor that takes an argument:

```
package inheritance;

public class AnotherStructure {
  // constructor with parameters
  public AnotherStructure(String type) {
    System.out.println("Build foundation of type " +type);
  }
}
```

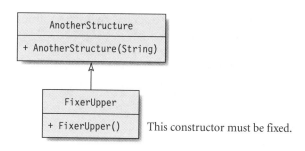

This constructor must be fixed.

Figure 6–15
The implicit super **statement in** FixerUpper's
**constructor cannot call
the** AnotherStructure
constructor.

Next, we will write a class called FixerUpper (see Figure 6–15) that has an
error in its constructor:

```
package inheritance;

public class FixerUpper extends AnotherStructure {
  // this constructor needs to be fixed!
  public FixerUpper() {
    System.out.println("Set up floor, walls and roof.");
  }
}
```

The program will not compile if you add this main method to create an
instance of FixerUpper:

```
public static void main(String[] args) {
  FixerUpper fixerupper = new FixerUpper();
}
```

So, what goes wrong when an object of FixerUpper is to be created? The
(implicit) super statement in FixerUpper's constructor cannot call the constructor with parameters in the superclass AnotherStructure. It cannot call
the default constructor because there is already a constructor present in
AnotherStructure. In this case, to create an object of FixerUpper, the programmer must call the constructor of AnotherStructure *explicitly*, as explained
next.

6.8.4 The Programmer Explicitly Calls a Constructor

The programmer can call a superclass constructor directly, or can call
another constructor within the class itself. If the programmer wants to call
a superclass constructor with parameters, the programmer must make this
call explicitly. This call is made by supplying arguments to the super statement:

```
super(argument 1, argument 2, ..., argument n);
```

The constructor in the superclass whose parameter list matches these arguments is then invoked.

Modify FixerUpper's constructor to call explicitly the superclass constructor AnotherStructure(String) in AnotherStructure, as shown here:

```
// FixerUpper fixed!
public FixerUpper() {
  super("Slab"); // calls the superclass constructor correctly
  System.out.println("Set up floor, walls and roof.");
}
```

super has a String argument; as a result, it calls the matching constructor in AnotherStructure with a String parameter. The program compiles and runs correctly now.

> If the superclass does not have a constructor without parameters, but contains constructors with parameters, the programmer should explicitly call the superclass constructor.

Instead of calling a superclass constructor, the programmer can call another constructor in the same class by using the keyword this. We saw examples of using this in constructors in Chapter 5. Here, we will briefly review the process again.

The keyword this takes arguments and calls a constructor in the class whose parameters match the data type and order of these arguments. Let us add a new constructor to FixerUpper that takes a String parameter:

```
FixerUpper(String value) {
  super(value); // calls the AnotherStructure(String) constructor
  System.out.println("Set up floor, walls and roof.");
}
```

The constructor without arguments in FixerUpper can be modified to call the preceding constructor using this:

```
FixerUpper() {
  this("Slab"); // calls the FixerUpper(String) constructor
}
```

Next, we will build the Vehicle and Car classes further by adding overloaded constructors to these classes.

Adding Constructors to `Vehicle`   Let us add two overloaded constructors to the `Vehicle` class. The first constructor without parameters sets the fields x and y (representing the *x*- and *y*-coordinates of the `Vehicle` in the window) to 0. The second constructor updates x and y to values passed in as arguments. The updated code for `Vehicle` is shown here:

```
public class Vehicle {
  // vehicle's position
  protected float x, y;

  // constructor updates x and y to specific values
  public Vehicle() {
    this(0, 0);
  }

  // constructor updates x and y to values passed in as arguments
  public Vehicle(float xValue, float yValue) {
    x = xValue;
    y = yValue;
  }

  // method to draw shape of Vehicle
  protected void drawShape(Graphics2D myGraphics) {
  }
}
```

A constructor is also added to `Car`. Objects of this class will be positioned at the specified coordinates in the window:

```
// constructor updates x and y to specific values
public Car() {
  super(30, 300);
}
```

Similarly, the constructor for `Airplane` is:

```
// constructor updates x and y to specific values
public Airplane() {
  super(100, 400);
}
```

Note that the programmer explicitly calls `Vehicle`'s constructor here using the super keyword with arguments.

In the next section, we discuss abstract classes and their use.

6.9   Abstract Classes

Consider the class Vehicle described earlier in this chapter. Should we create an object of this class? The answer is no, because a vehicle has no particular shape or size; it is simply a generic term specifying a mode of transport. Let us write a new class called Subject (see Figure 6–16) with two subclasses, Science and English. Does it make sense to create an object of class Subject?

A class that should not be instantiated can be made **abstract**. We do this by prefixing the keyword abstract before the class declaration. Let us make Subject an abstract class:

```
public abstract class Subject {
}
```

This means an object of this class cannot be created:

```
Subject subject = new Subject(); // error! Subject is an abstract class
```

What is the purpose, then, of an abstract class if it cannot be instantiated? *An abstract class is used primarily to create subclasses.* An object of Science can be created as follows:

```
public class Science extends Subject {
  public static void main(String[] args) {
    Science sci = new Science(); // okay
  }
}
```

Like any parent class, the abstract class contains methods that can be inherited by these subclasses depending on the access modifiers used for these methods. However, an abstract class *can* also contain special methods called **abstract methods**. Abstract methods do not have a body. They are declared using the keyword abstract. The subclass can **implement** an

Figure 6–16

It is pointless to make an object of class Subject.

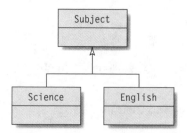

abstract method by providing a body for it. For example, let us add an abstract method called getSyllabus to Subject:

```
public abstract class Subject {
  public abstract void getSyllabus(); // abstract method
}
```

In an abstract method, only the declaration is provided; there is no body. Thus, the following declaration of getSyllabus would be incorrect because a body is specified by including braces:

```
public abstract void getSyllabus() {}; // error!
```

Now, the subclasses Science and English can provide a body for this method getSyllabus:

```
public class Science extends Subject{
  public void getSyllabus() {
    /* some code */
  }
}
```

A subclass must **implement** *all* abstract methods in its parent class; otherwise, it must be declared as abstract. This is another reason for creating an abstract class—*to force its subclasses to implement the abstract methods*. For example, if the class Science did not implement the method getSyllabus, it would have to be declared abstract, or a compilation error occurs.

Earlier in the chapter, we discussed how polymorphism can be achieved through *method overriding*. Polymorphism can be achieved using *abstract methods* as well. Suppose that we have declared a reference variable subject of type Subject. Then, the following statements call the getSyllabus method of the subclass object that subject references at the time the program is run:

```
Subject subject;
subject = new Science();
// gets the Science syllabus
subject.getSyllabus();

subject = new English();
// gets the syllabus of the subject English
subject.getSyllabus();
```

A method declared as abstract should not be made private because subclasses cannot implement the private methods of a superclass. Another restriction is that the implemented method cannot be less visible than the corresponding superclass method (see Table 6–1).

Example 3

In this example, you will learn how to create a star shape by extending the java.awt.Polygon class. Java 2D's Polygon class is used to construct polygons. A constructor and method in this class are shown in Figure 6–17.

Recall that a *vertex* is a point where two sides meet. For example, the following code draws a line joining points (10, 20) and (30, 40) of a polygon called p:

```
p.addPoint(10, 20);
p.addPoint(30, 40);
```

This example is broken into three parts.

a.   Using this class, create a polygon that connects the vertices *A, B, C,* and *D,* where *A* = (100, 200), *B* = (50, 300), *C* = (75, 400), and *D* = (200, 150). Display the polygon in a window.

Solution:

```
package inheritance;

import java.awt.*;
import com.programwithjava.basic.DrawingKit;

public class PolygonDemo {
  public static void main(String[] args) {
    // store x- and y-coordinates of points A, B, C and D
    int xA = 100, yA = 200, xB = 50, yB = 300, xC = 75, yC = 400,
    xD = 200, yD = 150;

    DrawingKit dk = new DrawingKit("Polygon");
    Polygon p = new Polygon();
    p.addPoint(xA, yA);    // add point A
    p.addPoint(xB, yB);    // add point B
    p.addPoint(xC, yC);    // add point C
    p.addPoint(xD, yD);    // add point D
```

Figure 6–17

A constructor and method in the Polygon class.

Polygon	
Polygon()	Constructor to create a polygon with no sides.
addPoint(int x, int y)	Method adds a vertex at the point (x, y) to the polygon.

```
    dk.draw(p);
  }
}
```

The polygon is displayed in the window shown in Figure 6–18.

b.   Write an abstract class called `Star` that is derived from the `Polygon` class. `Star` contains three integer fields x, y, and s that represent the *x*- and *y*-coordinates and length of a *side*, respectively. It also contains the following constructor and method:

`public Star(int xstart, int ystart, int length)`—a constructor that initializes the values of fields x, y, and s to the given arguments.

`public abstract void drawShape(Graphics2D g)`—an abstract method to draw a star shape.

Solution:

```
package inheritance;
import java.awt.*;

public abstract class Star extends Polygon {
  protected int x;  // x-coordinate
  protected int y;  // y-coordinate
  protected int s;  // length of a side
```

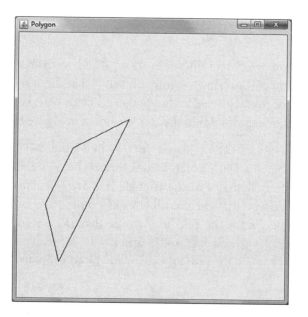

Figure 6–18

Drawing a polygon using the addPoint **method in** class Polygon.

```
public Star(int xstart, int ystart, int length) {
  x = xstart;
  y = ystart;
  s = length;
}
public abstract void drawShape(Graphics2D myGraphics);
}
```

c. Write a class called FivePointStar to create a five-pointed star. This class is derived from class Star. It implements the method drawShape to create the desired shape. The programmer gives the star's position and the length of a side as arguments to its constructor. Add a main method to test the class.

Solution: First, we review some results from trigonometry. In a right triangle, the sine of an angle is equal to the opposite side divided by the hypotenuse. The cosine of an angle in a right triangle is equal to the adjacent side divided by the hypotenuse. For example, consider a right triangle *ABC* with a right angle at angle *C*:

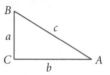

$$\sin A = a/c$$
$$\cos A = b/c$$

You can obtain the values of sin *B* and cos *B* similarly, so that sin *B* = cos *A* and cos *B* = sin *A*. Another result is that the sum of the interior angles in a polygon with *n* sides is equal to 180 * (*n* − 2). We can use this result to calculate the angles in the star, as shown in Figure 6–19.

Consider the pentagon *JBDFH* in Figure 6–19. The sum of its interior angles is 540°, which means that each angle is 108°. Using this result, the internal angles of the triangle *AJB* are calculated to be 36°, 72°, and 72°. Suppose that the coordinates of point *A* are (*x, y*). Drop a perpendicular line *AK* on the side *JB*. Assume that *JK* = *a* and *AK* = *b*. Applying these results gives *a* = *s* * *sin* 18 and *b* = *s* * *cos* 18. The coordinates of point *J* are (*x* − *a, y* + *b*). Similarly, calculate the coordinates of the other points.

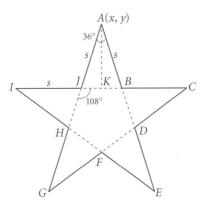

Figure 6–19
Calculating the coordinates of the vertices of a five-pointed star.

The Math class contains the cos and sin methods to calculate the cosine and sine values of the angles. Note that the arguments to these methods should be specified in radians. There are pi (also denoted as π) radians in 180°, so we can convert an angle into radians from degrees by multiplying it with pi/180. The Math class contains the constant PI to define the value of pi (which is approximately 3.14159):

```
static final double PI;
```

To use this value in your program, you write it as Math.PI. The following program uses the addPoint method in Polygon to create the star shape:

```
package inheritance;
import java.awt.*;
import com.programwithjava.basic.DrawingKit;

public class FivePointStar extends Star {

  private static final double RADIANS_PER_DEGREE = Math.PI/180;


  public FivePointStar(int xstart, int ystart, int length) {
    // call the superclass constructor explicitly
    super(xstart, ystart, length);
  }

  // this method implements the abstract drawShape method of Star
  public void drawShape(Graphics2D myGraphics) {
    int angle = 18;        // internal angle of 18 degrees
```

```
    int a = (int) (s * Math.sin(angle * RADIANS_PER_DEGREE));
    int b = (int) (s * Math.cos(angle * RADIANS_PER_DEGREE));
    int c = (int) ((s + 2 * a) * Math.sin(angle * RADIANS_PER_DEGREE));
    int d = (int) ((s + 2 * a) * Math.cos(angle * RADIANS_PER_DEGREE));
    int e = (int) (2 * (s + a) * Math.sin(angle * RADIANS_PER_DEGREE));
    int f = (int) (2 * (s + a) * Math.cos(angle * RADIANS_PER_DEGREE));
    int g = (int) (s * Math.sin(2 * angle * RADIANS_PER_DEGREE));
    addPoint(x, y);                         // Point A
    addPoint(x + a, y + b);                 // Point B
    addPoint(x + s + a, y + b);             // Point C
    addPoint(x + c , y + d);                // Point D
    addPoint(x + e, y + f);                 // Point E
    addPoint(x, y + f - g);                 // Point F
    addPoint(x - e, y + f);                 // Point G
    addPoint(x - c , y + d);                // Point H
    addPoint(x - s - a, y + b);             // Point I
    addPoint(x - a, y + b);                 // Point J
    myGraphics.draw(this);
  }

  public static void main(String[] args) {
    // draw the star at location (230, 180) with side of length 20
    int x = 230, y = 180, length = 20;

    DrawingKit dk = new DrawingKit("Five Point Star");
    Graphics2D myGraphics = dk.getGraphics();
    Star s = new FivePointStar(x, y, length);
    s.drawShape(myGraphics);
  }
}
```

Compile and run this program to see a star shape appear in the window at the specified location, as shown in Figure 6–20.

Note another use of the keyword this in the following statement:

```
myGraphics.draw(this);
```

The keyword this refers to the object that invokes this method, which is of type Star. The Star class extends Polygon, which is of type Shape, and therefore an instance of Star is of type Shape as well. (You will learn about Shape in Chapter 8, *Interfaces and Nested Classes*.) For this reason, an instance of Star can be passed as an argument to myGraphics's draw method, which takes an argument of type Shape.

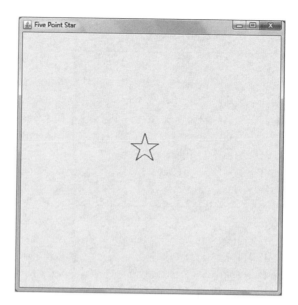

Figure 6–20
A five-pointed star.

Experiment with the program by creating stars of different sizes at various positions.

6.9.1 The Calendar Class

The Java API contains the abstract class Calendar, which contains several methods for working with dates and times. The class GregorianCalendar extends the Calendar class. Although many different types of calendars are followed around the world, such as Chinese, Indian, and Japanese, the one most commonly used is the Gregorian calendar, and it is the only calendar implementation provided in the Java API. Note that because Calendar is an abstract class, you cannot instantiate it.

A few fields and methods in the GregorianCalendar class are shown in Figure 6–21. The GregorianCalendar class inherits the constant fields shown in this figure from the Calendar class. These fields are used as arguments to the methods in this class. Other constant fields inherited from Calendar include those representing the months of a year (JANUARY, FEBRUARY, ..., DECEMBER), and the days of the week (MONDAY, TUESDAY, ..., SUNDAY). The methods add and get-Maximum, declared as abstract in Calendar, are implemented in this class.

Figure 6–21
Some fields and
methods in the
GregorianCalendar
class.

GregorianCalendar	
static final int YEAR	Constant field representing a year.
static final int MONTH	Constant field representing a month.
static final int DATE (or DAY_OF_MONTH)	Both fields represent the day of the month.
static final int DAY_OF_WEEK	This constant represents a day of the week.
static final int HOUR	This constant represents the 12-hour time.
static final int MINUTE	Constant representing minutes in time.
static final int SECOND	Constant representing seconds.
static final int AM_PM	Constant representing AM/PM.
GregorianCalendar()	Constructor.
void add(int field, int amount)	Adds the specified amount to the given field.
int get(int field)	Returns the value of the given field.
int set(int field, int value)	Sets a field to the given value.
int set(int year, int month, int date)	Sets the values of the YEAR, MONTH, and DATE fields.
int getMaximum(int field)	Maximum possible value of a field; for example, number of days in a month is 31.
int getActualMaximum(int field)	Actual maximum value of a field; for example, number of days in February 2009 is 28.

Examine the complete API for GregorianCalendar, and identify the inherited, overriding, and implemented methods in this class. Also, determine which new fields and methods (that is, those not inherited from Calendar) have been added to it.

Example 4

This example shows how to use the GregorianCalendar class.

```
package inheritance;
import java.util.*;
```

```
public class CalendarDemo {
  public static void main(String[] args) {
    // create a new GregorianCalendar
    Calendar calendar = new GregorianCalendar();

    // set the date to July 16, 2008;
    // note that January = 0, February = 1,..., December = 11
    calendar.set(2008, 06, 16);

    // add one to the month and print it out
    calendar.add(Calendar.MONTH, 1);
    System.out.println("Month = " +calendar.get(Calendar.MONTH));

    // subtract 10 from the date and print it out
    calendar.add(Calendar.DATE, -10);
    System.out.println("Day = " +calendar.get(Calendar.DATE));

    // print maximum number of days in any month
    System.out.println("Maximum days in a month = "
+calendar.getMaximum(Calendar.DAY_OF_MONTH));

    // change the year to 2009, and month to February
    // then print out maximum number of days in February 2009
    calendar.set(Calendar.YEAR, 2009);
    calendar.set(Calendar.MONTH, Calendar.FEBRUARY);
    System.out.println("Maximum days in February 2009 is "
+calendar.getActualMaximum(Calendar.DAY_OF_MONTH));
  }
}
```

The program output is:

```
Month = 7
Day = 6
Maximum days in a month = 31
Maximum days in February 2009 is 28
```

The set method sets the YEAR, MONTH, and DATE fields to 2008, 6, and 16, respectively. The first call to the add method increments MONTH by 1, and the second call to add decrements DATE by 10.

Note the the getMaximum method takes the constant field Calendar.DAY_OF_MONTH to print out the maximum number of days in any month. On the other hand, the getActualMaximum method uses the month and year that is currently set on the calendar, so that it returns the number of days in February 2009 in this example. As an exercise, use other fields as arguments to these methods and observe how the outputs change.   ■

Vehicle as an abstract Class   We have created objects of the Car and Airplane classes, but not of the Vehicle class. The reason is that this class represents a generic vehicle without a specific form or shape. Therefore, this class can be made abstract:

```
public abstract class Vehicle {
  // rest of the code is unchanged
}
```

There is no code in method drawShape of Vehicle. By making this method abstract, we can force all subclasses of Vehicle to implement it. Thus, the updated code for Vehicle is:

```
package inheritance;
import java.awt.*;

public abstract class Vehicle {
  protected float x = 30, y = 300; // vehicle's position

  // constructor updates x and y to specific values
  public Vehicle() {
    this(0, 0);
  }

  // constructor updates x and y to values passed in as arguments
  public Vehicle(float xValue, float yValue) {
    x = xValue;
    y = yValue;
  }

  // method to draw shape of Vehicle
  protected abstract void drawShape(Graphics2D myGraphics);
}
```

The class Car already implements the drawShape method, but Airplane does not because it is not necessary for a subclass to override a method in the superclass. However, now that drawShape has been made abstract in the superclass, we must either implement this method in Airplane or declare it as an abstract class. The following drawShape method is added to the Airplane class:

```
// method in class Airplane to draw the shape of an airplane
public void drawShape(Graphics2D myGraphics) {
    // body of the airplane
    Line2D line1 = new Line2D.Float(x, y, x-4, y-10);
    myGraphics.draw(line1);
    Line2D line2 = new Line2D.Float(x-4, y-10, x+120, y-95);
    myGraphics.draw(line2);
    QuadCurve2D curve1 = new QuadCurve2D.Float();
    curve1.setCurve(x+120, y-95, x+190, y-115, x+130, y-65);
    myGraphics.draw(curve1);
    Line2D line3 = new Line2D.Float(x+130, y-65, x+115, y-55);
    myGraphics.draw(line3);
    Line2D line4 = new Line2D.Float(x+81, y-36, x+14, y-3);
    myGraphics.draw(line4);
    Line2D line5 = new Line2D.Float(x, y, x+4, y);
    myGraphics.draw(line5);

    // left wing
    Line2D wing1 = new Line2D.Float(x+89, y-75, x, y-80);
    myGraphics.draw(wing1);
    Line2D wing2 = new Line2D.Float(x, y-80, x-10, y-70);
    myGraphics.draw(wing2);
    Line2D wing3 = new Line2D.Float(x-10, y-70, x+58, y-52);
    myGraphics.draw(wing3);

    // right wing
    Line2D wing4 = new Line2D.Float(x+110, y-60, x+165, y);
    myGraphics.draw(wing4);
    Line2D wing5 = new Line2D.Float(x+165, y, x+150, y+5);
    myGraphics.draw(wing5);
    Line2D wing6 = new Line2D.Float(x+150, y+5, x+76, y-40);
    myGraphics.draw(wing6);
    Line2D wing7 = new Line2D.Float(x+110, y-60, x+76, y-40);
    myGraphics.draw(wing7);

    // tail
    Line2D tail1 = new Line2D.Float(x+16, y-10, x+10, y+15);
    myGraphics.draw(tail1);
    Line2D tail2 = new Line2D.Float(x+10, y+15, x+5, y+18);
    myGraphics.draw(tail2);
    Line2D tail3 = new Line2D.Float(x+5, y+18, x+5, y-1);
    myGraphics.draw(tail3);
```

```
Line2D tail4 = new Line2D.Float(x+5, y-1, x+16, y-10);
myGraphics.draw(tail4);
Line2D tail5 = new Line2D.Float(x+15, y-25, x-10, y-40);
myGraphics.draw(tail5);
Line2D tail6 = new Line2D.Float(x-10, y-40, x-20, y-35);
myGraphics.draw(tail6);
Line2D tail7 = new Line2D.Float(x-20, y-35, x, y-14);
myGraphics.draw(tail7);
Line2D tail8 = new Line2D.Float(x, y-14, x-15, y-14);
myGraphics.draw(tail8);
Line2D tail9 = new Line2D.Float(x-15, y-14, x-18, y-10);
myGraphics.draw(tail9);
Line2D tail10 = new Line2D.Float(x-18, y-10, x-2, y-6);
myGraphics.draw(tail10);

//cockpit
QuadCurve2D cockpit= new QuadCurve2D.Float();
cockpit.setCurve(x+120, y-95, x+125, y-75, x+140, y-100);
myGraphics.draw(cockpit);

// logo
Ellipse2D logo = new Ellipse2D.Float(x-10, y-34, 10, 10);
myGraphics.setPaint(Color.red);
myGraphics.fill(logo);
Line2D line6 = new Line2D.Float(x-1, y-8, x+145, y-80);
myGraphics.draw(line6);
Line2D line7 = new Line2D.Float(x+60, y-65, x+7, y-73);
myGraphics.draw(line7);
Line2D line8 = new Line2D.Float(x+110, y-35, x+150, y-6);
myGraphics.draw(line8);
}
```

Observe that we are using *upcasting* in the drawShape method of class Airplane. The Line2D class in the java.awt.geom package is the abstract superclass of the Line2D.Float and Line2D.Double classes. For this reason, using upcasting, we can write:

Line2D line1 = new **Line2D.Float**(x, y, x-4, y-10);

The object of type Line2D.Float is assigned to a reference variable of type Line2D instead of Line2D.Float. The Ellipse2D and QuadCurve2D classes are the abstract superclasses of Ellipse2D.Float and QuadCurve2D.Float, respectively, and you can use them similarly.

Now we are ready to test the drawShape method. Add a main method to Airplane. Inside this main, we randomly create a Car or Airplane object and assign it to a `myVehicle` variable of type `Vehicle`. Then the following statement calls the corresponding `drawShape` method of that object:

```
myVehicle.drawShape();
```

The `main` method is shown here:

```
public static void main(String[] args) {
  DrawingKit dk = new DrawingKit("Vehicle");
  Graphics2D myGraphics = dk.getGraphics();
  Vehicle myVehicle;
  // assign vehicleType a random number equal to 0 or 1
  Random rand = new Random();
  int vehicleType = rand.nextInt(2);
  // if vehicleType is 0, create an object of type Car
  if(vehicleType == 0)
    myVehicle = new Car();
  else
    myVehicle = new Airplane();
  // This will draw the corresponding shape of the
  // object based on its type determined at run time.
  myVehicle.drawShape(myGraphics);
}
```

Add these `import` statements to `Airplane`:

```
import java.awt.*;
import java.awt.geom.*;
import java.util.Random;
import com.programwithjava.basic.DrawingKit;
```

Compile and run the program as follows:

```
C:\JavaBook> javac -d bin src\com\programwithjava\basic\DrawingKit.java
src\inheritance\Vehicle.java src\inheritance\Car.java
src\inheritance\Airplane.java

C:\JavaBook> java -classpath bin inheritance.Airplane
```

Each time the program runs, a car or airplane is drawn in the window. The decision of whether a car or airplane will appear depends on the value of the random variable `rand`. If `rand` is 0, an instance of `Car` is created and assigned to the variable `myVehicle`; however, if `rand` is 1, an instance of `Airplane` is created and assigned to `myVehicle`. The `drawShape` method of the `Car` class is called if `myVehicle` references a car object, and it draws a car shape in the window; otherwise, the `drawShape` method of the `Airplane` class is called.

Figure 6–22
Implementing the
drawShape method in
Airplane to draw an
airplane in the window.

This is an example of polymorphism. Here, polymorphism is achieved by *implementing* an *abstract* method. For example, if the object is of type Car, a car shape will be drawn when the method drawShape is called; otherwise, if the object has type Airplane, an airplane shape will be drawn.

Run the program several times. Either an airplane or a car is drawn inside the window. A result is shown in Figure 6–22.

6.10   The final Keyword

Java has a special keyword called final that can be used for creating **final methods**, **final classes**, and **final variables**. Each of these is explained in more detail next.

6.10.1   Final Methods

Final methods are methods whose implementations cannot be changed. When a method is declared as final, it cannot be overridden by a subclass method. For example, consider a class E that contains a final method called computeSquare that computes the square of its argument:

```
public class E {
  public final int computeSquare(int x) {
    return x*x;
  }
}
```

By declaring computeSquare as final, we ensure that it will not be overridden in a subclass. Thus, if subclass F attempts to override computeSquare, it causes a compilation error:

```
public class F extends E {
 // error: cannot override the final method computeSquare in E
  public int computeSquare(int x) {
    // some code goes here
  }
}
```

6.10.2   Final Classes

When a class is declared as final, it cannot be used to create subclasses. This also ensures that none of the methods in this class can be overridden; that is, all of its methods are final. For example, let us declare a new final class G:

```
public final class G {
  // some code
}
```

Then, an attempt to create a subclass of G results in an error:

```
// error: G cannot be subclassed
public class H extends G {
}
```

A class can be declared as final for either of the following two reasons:

1. *None of the methods in the class should be overridden.*

2. *The class should not be extended further.*

Examples of final classes in the Java API are Float, Double, Integer, Boolean, and String. The Float class, for example, is a specialized class for manipulating floating-point numbers, and its methods should not be changed.

6.10.3   Final Variables

Final variables are declared using the final keyword. A final variable can be assigned a value only *once*. This declares a variable called ANGLE:

```
final int ANGLE = 10;
```

Reassigning to ANGLE again results in an error:

```
ANGLE = 20; // error, ANGLE has been already assigned.
```

Final variables are useful in local and anonymous classes, which are discussed in Chapter 8, *Interfaces and Nested Classes.*

How do final variables differ from constants? Constants are *class* variables, because they are declared with the static modifier. This means that a single copy of this variable is shared among all instances of a class. Final variables, on the other hand, are *instance* variables.

6.11   Animation

Animation is the art of making things appear to change with time. Thus, in animation, objects can appear to move or change shape. There are many different techniques and tools to do animation, but all of them use the same basic principle of displaying a sequence of pictures with incremental changes over a short time to produce an impression of continuous movement. For example, to make a ball appear to move, show a sequence of pictures of the ball with each at a location that is slightly different from the previous one, as shown in Figure 6–23.

When these pictures are shown quickly, one after another, the viewer perceives the ball as moving in one smooth, continuous motion. On the ball, the (x, y) coordinates of a point are shown. You can see that the x-coordinate is increasing gradually, which gives the impression that the ball is moving to the viewer's right.

The smoothness of motion depends on how quickly the pictures are shown. Thus, if very few pictures (say, 5) are shown in one second, the movement can appear jerky. On the other hand, if too many pictures are shown, the motion can look blurry. The rate at which pictures are shown is known as frame rate and is abbreviated as **fps (frames per second)**. For example, 24 fps means that 24 pictures are shown in one second. In theaters, movies are displayed at 24 fps.

Figure 6–23

This sequence of pictures, shown one after another quickly, gives the impression that the ball is moving to the right.

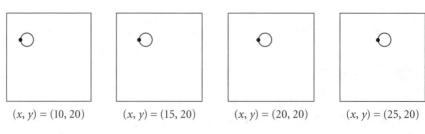

$(x, y) = (10, 20)$ $(x, y) = (15, 20)$ $(x, y) = (20, 20)$ $(x, y) = (25, 20)$

→ *time*

To give an impression of a moving object, you must follow these steps:

1. Clear the window.

2. Draw an image in the window at location (x, y).

3. Change the position (x, y).

4. Repeat Steps 1–3.

In the following sections, we will develop the code needed to animate the Car and Airplane objects. We will add a method called step to Vehicle and its subclasses. Inside step, the vehicle's position, represented by the coordinates (x, y), is changed. This method is abstract in Vehicle, and its implementation is provided in Car and Airplane.

Adding Animation to Class Vehicle   The step method added to Vehicle is shown here:

```
// change the (x, y) position by a small amount
protected abstract void step();
```

The step method in Car is:

```
protected void step() {
  x += 2.5f;
}
```

The step method increases the value of x slightly to give the impression that the car is moving to the right. The step method of Airplane can be written similarly. Both the x and y coordinates are changed here:

```
// change the (x,y) position of the airplane
protected void step() {
  y = y - 1.5f;
  x = x + 2.5f;
}
```

Two classes, called Controller and View, are provided in the package com.programwithjava.animation on the CD-ROM. The Controller class controls the animation, and the View class displays the animation. These classes are explained in more detail in the next section, *Model View Controller Architecture.*

Create a directory called `animation` inside the `src\com\programwithjava` directory on your computer. Copy the `Controller.java`, `View.java`, and
`Vehicle.java` files from the CD-ROM into the `animation` directory.

Replace the `main` method in the `Airplane` class with this method:

```
public static void main(String[] args) {
  Airplane topGun = new Airplane();
  View v = new View(topGun);
  Controller ct = new Controller(topGun, v);
  v.setVisible(true);
}
```

We will not use `DrawingKit` here, so you should remove this statement from
`Airplane`:

```
import com.programwithjava.basic.DrawingKit;
```

Also, add this `import` statement to `Airplane`:

```
import com.programwithjava.animation.*;
```

Note that the `Vehicle` class written earlier is also present in the `animation`
subpackage. Therefore, while compiling the program, only use the `Vehicle`
class from the `animation` subpackage:

```
C:\JavaBook> javac -d bin src\inheritance\Airplane.java
src\com\programwithjava\animation\*
```

```
C:\JavaBook> java -classpath bin inheritance.Airplane
```

An instance of `Airplane` is created, and it is passed to the `View` and `Controller`
classes. Compile and run the program with the `View` and `Controller` classes,
which are briefly described in the next section. Now run your program to
see the animation. You can press the "start" and "stop" buttons on the window at any time to start and pause the animation.

Run the program to see the plane fly. The output is shown in Figure 6–24.

Model View Controller (MVC) Architecture   The *Model View Controller*
architecture is used to separate an object's design (the **model**) from its
display (the **view**). The advantage is that by decoupling the model from the
view, we can change the code for the model without affecting the view, and
vice versa. Consider the code in `Airplane` or `Car`. This code describes the
design of these objects, and it represents the model in the MVC
architecture. However, this code does not specify *how* the object will be
displayed. We could choose to display the information about these objects

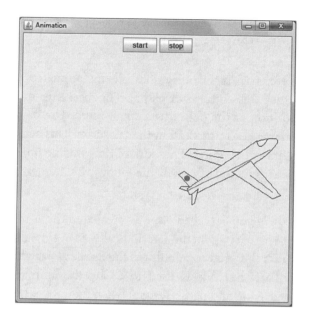

Figure 6–24
Animating an instance of
class Airplane.

in different ways, such as by using text, or graphics, or both—these details are part of the view. The code in View creates the window, buttons, and so on, and represents the view in MVC. There could be many different views for the same model. The **controller** links the model to a view. The code in Controller passes the user actions (such as mouse clicks) from the view to the model, and the results are sent back to the view from the model. Both of these classes are in the com.programwithjava.animation package.

Controller and View Classes   Here, the Controller and View classes contain code that can be used for animating instances of subclasses of Vehicle. In fact, you can write a new Vehicle subclass, and use the same Controller and View classes provided here to do the animation for this new subclass. However, it is not necessary to understand the code in these two classes for now. Therefore, if you want, you can skip the discussion that follows, and proceed directly to using the code given for Controller and View by adding the package com.programwithjava.animation to your code. You should, however, revisit this section after reading Chapter 9, *GUI Programming*.

Next, we briefly discuss two important methods in these classes. The class Controller contains one method called actionPerformed:

```
public void actionPerformed(ActionEvent e) {
  // move the model by one step
  model.step();
```

```
// call the paintComponent method in view
view.repaint();
}
```

Here, model is the object that is being animated, and view is the window in which this object is displayed. The model.step method changes the current position of the object by a small value. The view.repaint method calls the paintComponent method in the View class. This action clears the window and redraws the object. The work of drawing the object is done in the paintComponent method of View by the following statement:

```
model.drawShape(myGraphics);
```

A *swing timer* (called timer) is created in the Controller class and it calls the actionPerformed method periodically. Each time that it is called, this method clears the window and draws the image at a slightly different position. The rest of the code is used to create the animation for the two buttons (start/stop and pause/restart) when they are clicked.

The code for the Controller class is:

```
package com.programwithjava.animation;
import java.awt.event.*;
import javax.swing.*;

public class Controller implements ActionListener {
  // List the models and views that the controller interacts with
  private Vehicle model; // object being animated
  private View view;
  private Timer timer; // create a swing timer to run periodically

  public Controller(Vehicle m, View v) {
    model = m;
    view = v;
    timer = new Timer(30, this);

    // add listeners to view
    view.addStartListener(new ActionListener() {
      public void actionPerformed(ActionEvent e) {
      // when the start button is pressed timer starts running
        timer.start();
      }
    });

    // add listeners to view
    view.addStopListener(new ActionListener() {
      public void actionPerformed(ActionEvent e) {
```

```
      // when the stop button is pressed timer stops running
      timer.stop();
    }
  });
  }

  // action performed by timer
  public void actionPerformed(ActionEvent e) {
    // move the model by one step
    model.step();
    // call the paintComponent method in view
    view.repaint();
  }
}
```

The code for the View class is:

```
package com.programwithjava.animation;
import java.awt.*;
import java.awt.event.*;
import javax.swing.*;

public class View extends JFrame {
  // Components
  private JButton startButton;  // button to start the animation
  private JButton stopButton;   // button to stop the animation

  // Model
  private Vehicle model;

  public View(Vehicle m) {
    model = m;
    // Lay the components
    JPanel panel = new JPanel() {
      public void paintComponent(Graphics g) {
      super.paintComponent(g);
      Graphics2D myGraphics = (Graphics2D) g;
      model.drawShape(myGraphics);
     }
    };
    // create the buttons
    startButton = new JButton("start");
    stopButton = new JButton("stop");

    // add the buttons to the panel
    panel.add(startButton);
    panel.add(stopButton);
```

```
    // add the panel to this window
    setContentPane(panel);
    panel.setOpaque(true);
    setDefaultCloseOperation(JFrame.EXIT_ON_CLOSE);
    setSize(500, 500);
    setTitle("Animation");
  }

  // add a listener to the start button
  public void addStartListener(ActionListener listener) {
    startButton.addActionListener(listener);
  }

  // add a listener to the stop button
  public void addStopListener(ActionListener listener) {
    stopButton.addActionListener(listener);
  }
}
```

Example 5

Write a main method to animate an object of Car.

Solution: An instance of Car called roadster is created, and is passed to View and Controller. Add this import statement to Car.java:

```
import com.programwithjava.animation.*;
```

Again, because DrawingKit is not used in this example either, you must comment out this line:

```
import com.programwithjava.basic.DrawingKit;
```

Replace the main method in Car with the following:

```
public static void main(String[] args) {
  Car roadster = new Car();
  View v = new View(roadster);
  Controller ct = new Controller(roadster, v);
  v.setVisible(true);
}
```

Now run your program to see the animation.

You can use this technique to animate other types of vehicles. To do so, you create a subclass of Vehicle, and then define the drawShape and step methods in this class. Then, use a main method that is similar to the one previously described to run the animation. The Controller and View classes do not have to be changed.

6.12   Advanced Graphics (Optional)

In this section, we briefly discuss two useful features of Java 2D: the General-Path class and how to perform transformations using Graphics 2D. As an example, we show how to create rotating wheels for the Car object.

The GeneralPath class in the java.awt.geom package allows the programmer to build any kind of shape. Using the methods in this class, lines and curves can be joined together to form a regular or irregular shape. There are several overloaded constructors in this class. The constructor without parameters can be used to create a path called myPath as follows:

```
GeneralPath myPath = new GeneralPath();
```

The position at which the path should start is given by the moveTo method of GeneralPath:

> **public void moveTo(float x, float y)**—a method to add the point (x, y) to a path.

For example, the following statement starts myPath at the point (20, 30):

```
myPath.moveTo(20, 30);
```

Now, lines, curves, and other shapes can be added to this path by using the append method:

> **public void append(Shape s, boolean connect)**—a method to connect s to the path if connect is true.

Shape is an interface, and classes that draw lines and regular shapes (such as Line2D.Float, Rectangle2D.Float, and Ellipse2D.Float) implement this interface. Objects of all classes that implement this interface can be passed as arguments to this method. If the parameter connect is true, this shape is connected to the current position of the path with a line segment. For example, add line1 to myPath:

```
Line2D.Float line1 = new Line2D.Float(100, 200, 300, 400);
myPath.append(line1, true);
```

This step adds line1 to myPath. In addition, it also draws a line segment connecting the current position (20, 30) with the starting position of line1 (100, 200).

If you want a curved line, you can draw a quadratic curve using the quadTo method to join points ($x1$, $y1$) and ($x2$, $y2$):

> **public void quadTo(float x1, float y1, float x2, float y2)**—a method that draws a quadratic curve joining points (x1, y1) and (x2, y2).

Another method to draw a curved line is the curveTo method, which draws a cubic curve connecting points ($x1$, $y1$) and ($x3$, $y3$) that passes through ($x2$, $y2$):

> **public void curveTo(float x1, float y1, float x2, float y2, float x3, float y3)**—a method that draws a cubic curve connecting points (x1, y1) and (x3, y3) and passing through (x2, y2).

The Wheel Class   We next write a class called Wheel that contains a method called createShape. The constructor has four parameters: *x*- and *y*-coordinates of a reference point on the wheel, *diameter* and *thickness*. The createShape method draws a circular shape of the given diameter.

The constructor and createShape method for Wheel follow. The createShape method has a return type of Shape. The class GeneralPath implements the Shape interface. Therefore, the instance path in the createShape method is also of type Shape. We will discuss this interface in Chapter 8, *Interfaces and Nested Classes*.

```
package inheritance;

import java.awt.*;
import java.awt.geom.*;

public class Wheel {
    float x, y, width, height, angle, thickness;
```

```
public Wheel(float x1, float y1, float diameter, int thick) {
  x = x1;
  y = y1;
  height = diameter;
  width = diameter;
  angle = 0;
  thickness = thick;
}

// creates circular shape with two spokes representing a wheel
  protected Shape createShape(Graphics2D g2) {
    GeneralPath path = new GeneralPath();
    g2.setPaint(Color.black);
    Stroke s = new BasicStroke(thickness);
    g2.setStroke(s);
    Ellipse2D e1 = new Ellipse2D.Float(x, y, height, width);
    g2.draw(e1);
    path.append(e1, false);
    g2.setPaint(Color.white);
    g2.fill(e1);
    g2.setPaint(Color.black);
    Line2D l1 = new Line2D.Float(x, y+width/2, x+width, y+width/2);
    path.append(l1, false);
    Line2D l2 = new Line2D.Float(x+width/2, y, x+width/2, y+ width);
    path.append(l2,false);
    return path;
    }
  }
```

Next, we will show how the wheel can be rotated by using Graphics2D transformations.

6.12.1 Graphics2D **Transformations**

Some simple transformations can be performed on a Graphics2D object. These basic transformations are:

- *Rotate:* Rotate the object about a given point
- *Translation:* Move the object to a new point

- *Scale:* Make the object smaller or bigger

- *Shear:* Stretch the object in a nonuniform manner

For example, to rotate a Graphics2D object g2, the rotate method can be used:

```
g2.rotate(angle, x, y);
```

This produces a rotation by the specified angle with (x, y) as the center of the object, and where angle must be specified in radians. (Recall that 360 degrees = 2 * PI radians.) When successive transformations are applied to a Graphics2D object, their effect is additive. For example, suppose that the Graphics2D object g2 is rotated by PI radians with a call to the following method:

```
g2.rotate(PI, x, y);
```

The next call to this method will rotate by 2 * PI radians instead of PI. To prevent this from occurring, the original Graphics2D context should be saved and restored after the transformation. You can do this by using a class called AffineTransform, as follows:

```
AffineTransform t = g2.getTransform();
// perform rotate, translate and other transformations
g2.setTransform(t);
```

The original graphics context is saved using getTransform, and it is restored using setTransform. The next section describes how to use this transformation in the rotateWheel method of the Wheel class.

Adding Rotating Wheels to the Car   We will add two more methods to Wheel: drawShape and step. The method drawShape draws the Wheel instance after rotating it about its center by the specified angle:

```
public void drawShape(Graphics2D g2) {
  AffineTransform t = g2.getTransform();
  Shape shape = createShape(g2);

  // rotate the shape by the specified angle around its center.
  g2.rotate(angle, x + width/2, y + height/2);
  g2.draw(shape);
  g2.setTransform(t);
}
```

The step method takes the displacement in the wheel position as an argument and modifies its position and angle accordingly:

```java
public void step(float displacement) {
  x += displacement;
  angle += displacement/width;
}
```

Some methods in Car will need to be changed to add the Wheel objects to Car. Add the following field to Car:

```java
private Wheel wheel1, wheel2;
```

In the constructor for Car, create two new wheels using Wheel, in the same position as the previous ones:

```java
public Car() {
  super(30, 300);
  wheel1 = new Wheel(x+37.5f, y+63, 50, 5);
  wheel2 = new Wheel(x+167.5f, y+63, 50, 5);
}
```

Modify the drawShape method of Car so that the wheels are drawn as well. Insert the following statements into this method:

```java
// draw the wheels
wheel1.drawShape(myGraphics);
wheel2.drawShape(myGraphics);
```

The wheels must be moved forward by the same distance as the car. Modify the step method in Car to call the step method of Wheel:

```java
protected void step() {
  float displacement = 2.5f;
  x += displacement;
  wheel1.step(displacement);
  wheel2.step(displacement);
}
```

Check to ensure that you have added the main method and made the other changes described in Example 5. Then, run the program as follows:

```
C:\JavaBook> javac -d bin src\inheritance\Car.java
src\inheritance\Wheel.java src\com\programwithjava\animation\*

C:\JavaBook> java -classpath bin inheritance.Car
```

Figure 6–25

Animating an instance of class Car with rotating wheels.

You can now see the wheels rotate as the car moves. The animation is shown in Figure 6–25.

6.13   Computers in Business: Credit Card Finance Charge Calculator

Computers programs are used for processes in accounting, the stock market, and personal finance, among others. Accounting software is used by businesses to keep track of inventory, purchases and sales, and billing. Stock market software programs help investors manage investments. Personal finance software uses include tax calculations and money management. Statistical software can analyze large amounts of data to discern patterns (such as which items are most or least popular among shoppers), and also can predict future outcomes based on both current and historical data. In this section, we will discuss how credit card companies calculate consumer credit. We will write a program to calculate the finance charges for a given card **balance** based on its **APR** (**Annual Percentage Rate**), and the time needed to pay off the balance of the card.

First, we discuss some terminology and the basics needed to understand how finance charges are calculated. Whenever you make a purchase using a credit card, you put a **balance** on the card. Credit card companies charge interest—called a **finance charge**—on this balance. The finance charge is added to the existing balance, which continues to grow unless you pay it off. Finance charges are determined by two factors: the APR of the card and the calculation method used by the company. The APR is a numeric value provided by the company. Many different methods are used to calculate finance charges, but most credit card companies use what is called the **average daily balance method**. In this method, the finance charges are calculated for each day on the **average daily balance**, which is the sum of the charges made on the card during a billing period divided by the number of days in that billing period. The **daily periodic rate** (**DPR**) is used to calculate the daily finance charge, and is given by the (APR/100) divided by the number of days in a year:

$$DPR = \frac{APR}{100 \times 365}$$

The finance charges are calculated during a billing period N (typically one month), as follows:

Finance Charge = Average Daily Balance $\times$ DPR $\times$ N

For example, suppose that you charge $100.00, $305.50, and $50.00 on your credit card on the 1st, 7th, and 25th of January, respectively. What is the average daily balance? There is a balance of $100 for the first 6 days, followed by a balance of $405.50 for the next 18 days, and a balance of $455.50 for the remaining 7 days. Use these figures to calculate the average daily balance:

$$\text{Average Daily Balance} = \frac{100 \times 6 + 405.50 \times 18 + 455.50 \times 7}{31} = \$357.66$$

The finance charge on this balance is calculated next. Suppose that the card has an APR of 15%. Plugging these values into the equation for finance charge gives the following:

$$\text{Finance Charge} = 357.66 \times \frac{15}{(100 \times 365)} \times 31 = \$4.56$$

The finance charge of $4.56 is added to the balance of $455.50, and so the new balance for February is $460.06. The finance charge for February will be calculated similarly. Suppose that you made a payment of $100 on February 1st. (For simplicity, assume that this payment is recorded immediately.) Then the finance charge would be calculated on the reduced balance of $360.06.

6.13.1   The `BigDecimal` Class

Before writing the program, we discuss the `BigDecimal` class in the `java.math` package. This class is useful for high-precision operations, especially in financial calculations. You should not use the `double` or `float` types to store currency values in programs, because these numbers might not be stored accurately internally. For example, the value of `num` printed out here is 0.45999999999999996 instead of 0.46:

```
double num = 0.02 + 0.14 + 0.3;
System.out.println(num); // prints out 0.45999999999999996
double num1 = 0.101 + 0.001 + 0.201;
System.out.println(num1==0.303); // prints out false instead of true
```

Using a `float` can result in increasingly pronounced errors:

```
float val = 0.65f * 0.3f;
System.out.println(val); // prints out 0.19500001
```

This type of inaccuracy is unacceptable in financial calculations. The `BigDecimal` class stores values accurately with the **precision** (number of digits after the decimal point) that you specify. A field in this class, as well as some constructors and methods, are shown in Figure 6–26.

Let us recompute the previous result using `BigDecimal`. The following statement creates a `BigDecimal` object storing the number 0.02. Note that the number should be specified as a string:

```
BigDecimal num1 = new BigDecimal("0.02");
```

These two statements create two more `BigDecimal`s, storing values 0.14 and 0.3:

```
BigDecimal num2 = new BigDecimal("0.14");
BigDecimal num3 = new BigDecimal("0.3");
```

The `add` method is used to add the numbers in these three objects together:

```
num1 = num1.add(num2).add(num3); // num1 = num1 + num2 + num3
```

BigDecimal	
static BigDecimal ZERO	A constant representing a BigDecimal object storing the value 0.
BigDecimal(String num)	Creates a BigDecimal object that stores the string num as a number.
BigDecimal(int num)	Creates a BigDecimal object that stores the int num.
BigDecimal add(BigDecimal obj)	Returns a BigDecimal object that stores the sum of the numbers in this object and obj.
BigDecimal subtract(BigDecimal obj)	Returns a BigDecimal object that stores the difference of the numbers in this object and obj.
BigDecimal multiply(BigDecimal obj)	Returns a BigDecimal object that stores the product of the numbers in this object and obj.
BigDecimal divide(BigDecimal obj, int precision, int roundingMode)	Returns a BigDecimal object that stores the result (with the specified precision and rounding mode) of dividing the number in this object by the number in obj.
BigDecimal setScale (int precision, int roundingMode)	Sets the number of digits after the decimal point (precision) and the rounding mode.
String toString()	Displays the number stored in this object.
int compareTo(BigDecimal obj)	Compares the number stored in this object with that in obj. Returns 1, 0, or –1, depending on whether the BigDecimal value is greater than, equal to, or less than that of obj.

Figure 6–26

Some constructors and methods in the BigDecimal class.

The resulting value in num1 can be printed out using the toString method. This will print out the correct value of 0.46:

```
System.out.println(num1.toString());
```

We can use the methods subtract and multiply similarly. Like the add method, each of these methods also takes an argument of type BigDecimal.

The compareTo method compares the numbers stored in two objects of type BigDecimal. The following code segment shows how to check whether the BigDecimal num1 is equal to 0:

```
if (num1.compareTo(BigDecimal.ZERO) == 0)
  System.out.println("The two numbers are equal");
else if (num1.compareTo(BigDecimal.ZERO) < 0)
  System.out.println("num1 is less than 0");
```

```
else if (num1.compareTo(BigDecimal.ZERO) > 0)
  System.out.println("num1 is greater than 0");
```

The constant field `ZERO` in `BigDecimal` represents a `BigDecimal` object storing the value 0. This answer will print out:

```
num1 is greater than 0
```

`BigDecimal` also contains constant fields `TEN` and `ONE` to represent the values 10 and 1, respectively.

You can specify the number of digits after the decimal point and the rounding mode using the `setScale` method. To display a number with two decimal places that are rounded up, use the following:

```
BigDecimal num4 = new BigDecimal("1234.56789");
num4 = num4.setScale(2, RoundingMode.HALF_UP);
System.out.println(num4.toString()); // prints out 1234.57
```

Other rounding modes include `ROUND_UP` (rounds upward toward 0) and `ROUND_DOWN` (round downward, away from 0).

Nonterminating numbers (with an infinite number of digits) cannot be represented exactly as `BigDecimal` numbers. For example, dividing 1 by 3 results in a nonterminating decimal and causes a run-time error:

```
BigDecimal one = new BigDecimal("1");
BigDecimal three = new BigDecimal("3");
BigDecimal nonterm = one.divide(three); // 0.3333...
```

Upon running the program, the following error message is issued:

```
Exception in thread "main" java.lang.ArithmeticException: Non-terminating
decimal expansion; no exact representable decimal result.
        at java.math.BigDecimal.divide(BigDecimal.java:1594)
```

In the divide operation, specify the scale and the rounding mode of the result. For example, the following statement will set the number of decimal places in the result to 20 and the rounding mode to `HALF_UP`:

```
BigDecimal term = one.divide(three, 20, RoundingMode.HALF_UP);
```

The result shows that the number stored in `term` has a precision of 20:

```
System.out.println(term.toString()); // displays 0.33333333333333333333
```

6.13.2   Program to Calculate Time to Pay Off Balance

In this section, we write a program to calculate the total time needed to pay off the balance on a credit card by making fixed monthly payments. We also calculate the total finance charges incurred over this period. Let us work out an example to explain the steps needed. Suppose that you have a credit card with an APR of 15% and a balance of $1000. You would like to make a payment of $500 on the first day of each month and put no new charges on the card, starting January 1, 2008 (a leap year), until the balance is fully paid off.

Step 1: Starting balance = $1000

Payment on January 1 = $500

New balance on January 1 = $500

No new charges are made to the card; thus the average daily balance is $500.

$$\text{Finance Charge} = 500 \times \frac{15}{(100 \times 366)} \times 31 = \$6.35$$

Step 2: Add the finance charge to the previous balance. The balance on February 1 = $506.35.

Payment on February 1 = $500

New balance on February 1 = $6.35

$$\text{Finance Charge} = 6.35 \times \frac{15}{(100 \times 366)} \times 29 = \$0.08$$

Step 3: The balance on March 1 = $6.43.

Payment on March 1 = $6.43

New balance on March 1 = $0.0

The total payment made in 3 months is $1006.43, of which the net finance charges were $6.43.

The algorithm and program for this problem are discussed next.

```
while balance > 0 {
    Calculate average daily balance after monthly payment is made at start of month
    Calculate DPR
    Calculate finance charge
    Print out the balance and finance charge for this month
    Update running totals of finance charges and monthly payments
    Increment month to next
    Add finance charge to balance to obtain new balance at start of this month
}
```

The class `CreditCardInterestCalculator` is declared as follows:

```java
package inheritance;
import java.util.*;
import java.math.*;

public class CreditCardInterestCalculator extends FinancialCalculator {
  // monthly credit card payment
  private BigDecimal monthlyPayment;

  // starting month from which to calculate interest
  private int startMonth;

  // starting year from which to calculate interest
  private int startYear;

  // annual percentage rate
  private BigDecimal apr;

  // current balance
  private BigDecimal balance;

  // number of months taken to pay off balance
  private int numMonths;

  // monthly finance charge
  private BigDecimal financeCharge;

  // total finance charges until balance is paid
  private BigDecimal totalFinanceCharge;

  // total payments made until balance is paid off
  private BigDecimal totalPayment;

  // precision
  private int precision = 100;

  public CreditCardInterestCalculator() {
    calendar = new GregorianCalendar();
    totalFinanceCharge = new BigDecimal("0");
    totalPayment = new BigDecimal("0");
  }
  // methods for this class will be added here
}
```

This class extends the class FinancialCalculator, which is the superclass representing all types of calculators, such as mortgage and tax calculators. It contains a field of type Calendar and two methods to determine the number of days in a specific month and the number of days in a particular year (365 or 366). Both of these methods, and the Calendar field, will be inherited by the subclasses of this class. The CreditCardInterestCalculator class must implement the abstract methods getUserInput and compute:

```java
package inheritance;
import java.util.*;

public abstract class FinancialCalculator {
  // calendar
  protected Calendar calendar;

  // returns the number of days for the current month set on calendar
  protected int getDaysInMonth() {
    return calendar.getActualMaximum(Calendar.DAY_OF_MONTH);
  }

  // returns the number of days in the current year set on calendar
  protected int getDaysInYear() {
    return calendar.getActualMaximum(Calendar.DAY_OF_YEAR);
  }

  protected abstract void getUserInput();
  protected abstract void compute();
}
```

The methods in class CreditCardInterestCalculator are described next. The following method calculates the average daily balance. It assumes that a payment is recorded at the start of the month and that no other purchases are made during that month. In the last month, the balance might fall below the monthly payment, in which case only the remainder is paid.

```java
private BigDecimal calculateAverageDailyBalance() {
  // check if balance is less than monthlyPayment
  if (balance.compareTo(monthlyPayment) < 0)
    monthlyPayment = balance;
```

```
// average daily balance is balance remaining after monthly payment
// is made
balance = balance.subtract(monthlyPayment);
return balance;
}
```

This method calculates the daily periodic rate:

```
// Daily periodic rate (dpr) = APR/(100 * number of days in year)
private BigDecimal calculateDailyPeriodicRate() {
  BigDecimal percent = new BigDecimal("100");
  BigDecimal numDaysInYear = new BigDecimal(getDaysInYear());
  BigDecimal dpr = apr.divide(percent).divide(numDaysInYear, precision,
RoundingMode.HALF_UP);
  return dpr;
 }
```

This method calculates the finance charge on the balance for one month:

```
// finance charge = average daily balance * dpr * num days in month
private BigDecimal calculateMonthlyFinanceCharge(){
  BigDecimal averageDailyBalance = calculateAverageDailyBalance();
  BigDecimal dpr = calculateDailyPeriodicRate();
  BigDecimal numDaysInMonth = new BigDecimal(getDaysInMonth());
  financeCharge =
averageDailyBalance.multiply(dpr).multiply(numDaysInMonth);
  return financeCharge;
}
```

The following code implements the abstract getUserInput method in the FinancialCalculator class. It prompts the user to enter the card balance, the card APR, and the month and year when payments will begin:

```
public void getUserInput() {
  Scanner scanner = new Scanner(System.in);
  System.out.print("Enter balance on credit card (in dollars):");
  balance = new BigDecimal(scanner.next());
  System.out.print("Enter credit card APR (%):");
  apr = new BigDecimal(scanner.next());
  System.out.print("Enter your monthly payment (in dollars):");
  monthlyPayment = new BigDecimal(scanner.next());
  System.out.print("Enter the starting month and year[Example, 1 2009 for
January 2009]:");
  startMonth = scanner.nextInt();
  startYear = scanner.nextInt();
}
```

The following code implements the abstract compute method in the superclass. It calculates the total finance charges and the time to pay off the balance using the algorithm we discussed previously:

```java
public void compute() {
  // initialize calendar
  calendar.set(startYear, startMonth - 1, 1);

  // print out table header
  System.out.println("Month      Year" +"      Balance ($)      "
+"Interest ($)");

  BigDecimal monthlyFinanceCharge;

  while(balance.compareTo(BigDecimal.ZERO) > 0){
    // calculate finance charges for each month
    monthlyFinanceCharge = calculateMonthlyFinanceCharge();

    // round monthlyFinanceCharge and balance up to two decimal places
    monthlyFinanceCharge = monthlyFinanceCharge.setScale(2,
RoundingMode.HALF_UP);
    balance = balance.setScale(2, RoundingMode.HALF_UP);

    // print out monthly finance charge and balance
    System.out.println(String.format("%3d      %5d   %10s    %10s ",
calendar.get(Calendar.MONTH)+1, calendar.get(Calendar.YEAR),
balance.toString(), monthlyFinanceCharge.toString()));

    // running total of credit card finance charges
    totalFinanceCharge = totalFinanceCharge.add(monthlyFinanceCharge);

    // running total of credit card payments
    totalPayment = totalPayment.add(monthlyPayment);

    // increment month by 1
    calendar.add(Calendar.MONTH, 1);
    numMonths++;

    // calculate new balance at the start of next month
    balance = balance.add(monthlyFinanceCharge);
  }
  // round up to two decimal places and print
  totalFinanceCharge = totalFinanceCharge.setScale(2,
RoundingMode.HALF_UP);
  totalPayment = totalPayment.setScale(2, RoundingMode.HALF_UP);
```

```
System.out.println("Total payment in " +numMonths +" months: $"
+totalPayment.toString() + "   Total Finance Charges paid: $"
+totalFinanceCharge.toString());
}
```

We have specified a precision of 2, and the HALF_UP rounding mode in the setScale method. A different precision and rounding mode could be used, depending upon the application requirements.

Add the preceding methods to CreditCardInterestCalculator. Test the class using this main method:

```
public static void main(String[] args) {
    FinancialCalculator calc = new CreditCardInterestCalculator();
    calc.getUserInput(); // polymorphism
    calc.compute();      // polymorphism
}
```

A sample run of the program is shown here:

```
Enter balance on credit card (in dollars):1000
Enter credit card APR (%):15
Enter your monthly payment (in dollars):500
Enter the starting month and year[Example, 1 2009 for January 2009]:1 2008
Month   Year    Balance ($)    Interest ($)
  1     2008       500.00          6.35
  2     2008         6.35          0.08
  3     2008         0.00          0.00
Total payment in 3 months: $1006.43   Total Finance Charges paid: $6.43
```

The output matches the hand calculation. Run the program for other values of input to verify that it works correctly.

6.14   Summary

In this chapter, we discussed what inheritance is and how it can be used. Some important points to remember are:

- Inheritance allows a class to reuse code from its superclass and enables method overriding.

- There are many types of inheritance—single-level, multilevel, and hierarchical. Java does not support multiple inheritance.

- Access modifiers determine which fields and methods are inherited by a subclass.

- The keyword super can be used to call a superclass method or constructor.

- Polymorphism means that the behavior of an object is based on its type that is determined during run time. Polymorphism is achieved by overriding methods or implementing abstract methods.

- Constructors are not inherited. The first line of a constructor must be a call to another constructor. This can be done automatically by Java, or explicitly by the programmer, using the keywords super or this.

- Classes declared abstract cannot be instantiated.

- Abstract classes can contain abstract methods that do not have a body. A subclass must implement all abstract methods of its superclass; otherwise, it must be made abstract.

- Final methods cannot be overridden.

- Final classes cannot be subclassed.

Exercises

1. Identify which of the following examples of inheritance are correct by determining whether the *is-a* relationship of each is true or false:

   a. Class Dog inherits from class Animal

   b. Class Flower inherits from class Seed

   c. Class Sun inherits from class Star

   d. Class Planet inherits from class Earth

   e. Class Rectangle inherits from class GeometricalShapes

   f. Class Customer inherits from class Bank

2. Explain each of the following:

   a. Single-level, multilevel, and hierarchical inheritance

   b. super keyword

   c. Upcasting

   d. Overridden method

   e. Hidden field

3. Explain briefly:

   a. Why is inheritance useful?

b. What is polymorphism?

c. Why are methods overloaded?

d. When should a class be made abstract?

e. Why are abstract classes useful?

f. What is an abstract method?

4. Which of the following statements are true?

a. Overloaded methods have different signatures.

b. Overloaded methods can have the same signature if they have different return types.

c. The super keyword can be used only in constructors, and not methods of a class.

d. A class that contains an abstract method should be declared abstract.

e. A class cannot be made abstract unless it contains an abstract method.

f. A class cannot be both abstract and final.

g. The methods in a final class can be overridden.

h. Private methods in a class cannot be overridden.

i. The super statement must always be the first statement in a constructor.

5. Predict the output of the following program without running it:

```java
public class ClassA {
  protected int x = 10;
  public void printA() {
    System.out.println("x = " +x);
  }
}

public class ClassB extends ClassA {
  ClassB() {
    x = 20;
  }
}

public class ClassC extends ClassB {
  ClassC() {
    x = 30;
  }
```

```
public void printC() {
  System.out.println("x = " +x);
}

public static void main(String[] args) {
  ClassC c = new ClassC();
  c.printA();
  c.printC();
  }
}
```

Run the program to check your answer.

6. a. Write a class called Arachnid that contains a constructor without parameters. In the body of this constructor, add a statement to print the words "Executing Arachnid constructor." Next, create a class called Spider that extends Arachnid. Similarly, add a constructor to this class with a statement that prints out "Executing Spider constructor." Lastly, create a class called GardenSpider that extends Spider and has a constructor with a print statement. In a main method, create an object of GardenSpider. In which order are the constructors called?

   b. Add a protected field called numberOfLegs to Arachnid, and initialize it to 8 in its constructor. Add a method to GarderSpider called print-NumberOfLegs that displays the value of this field. Call this method in main. What is the output?

   c. Explain what happens if the numberOfLegs field in Arachnid is made:

      –private

      –package-private

7. Create a class called Account with the following fields: number, name, balance, and interestRate. Add acessor methods to display the value of each field in this class. Create another class called SavingsAccount that inherits from Account. Add three fields called day, month, and year. Add overloaded constructors to initialize the fields. Add three methods called deposit, withdraw, and computeInterest to this class, which are declared as follows:

```
public void deposit(BigDecimal amount);

public boolean withdraw(BigDecimal amount);
public BigDecimal computeInterest();
```

The computeInterest() method calculates the monthly interest using the formula:

$$\text{Monthly interest} = \frac{\text{balance} \times \text{interestRate}}{12}$$

Add at least two overloaded constructors to both SavingsAccount and Account. Create two instances of SavingsAccount in the main method and determine the interest on a given balance at the end of a year.

8. a. Create a class called Book with two private fields: name and cost of type String and float, respectively. Write a constructor in this class that takes two arguments and uses them to initialize these two fields. Add two accessor methods, getName and getCost, to Book to return the name and cost of the book.

   b. Create a class called Textbook that inherits from Book. Add a constructor to this class that takes a parameter of type String and another of type float. Use the arguments passed to this constructor to initialize the name and cost fields of Book.

   c. Write a main method to test the two classes. Create an instance of Textbook using the following statement:

   ```
   Textbook myBook = new Textbook("Java Programming", 100);
   ```

Print out the name and cost of this book in the main method as follows:

```
System.out.println(myBook.getName());
System.out.println(myBook.getCost());
```

9. Create a class called CourtGame. Add a method to this class called playGame that prints out the class name along with a message. Create two subclasses of CourtGame called Tennis and Badminton.

   a. Override the playGame method in the Tennis class, but not in Badminton. Create an instance of Tennis and Badminton in the main method, and invoke the playGame method for each instance. Which playGame method is called for each instance?

   b. Now override the playGame method in the Badminton class. Rerun the program, and check which playGame method is called for the Badminton instance.

10. Create an abstract class called Bird. Write a method called chirp in this class that prints out the word "chirp." Create two classes, Goose and Mallard, which extend Bird, and override the chirp method in both

classes. In the Goose class, this method should print out the word "Honk," and in the Mallard class, it should print out "Quack." Write a main method to demonstrate polymorphism. In main, create a reference variable of type Bird as follows:

```
Bird bird;
```

Prompt the user to enter a number that is either 1 or 2. If the user enters a 1, this statement should call the chirp method of the Goose class; otherwise, it should call the method of the Mallard class:

```
bird.chirp();
```

a. Create a new class that extends Bird called Crow, but do not add an overriding method. Modify the main program so that if the user enters the number 3, the chirp method in Crow is called. What is the output of the program?

b. Make the chirp method in Bird abstract. Which changes must be made to the class Crow? Make the necessary changes and rerun the program. How does the output change?

11. Create a final class called MyFinalClass. Write a program to show that this class cannot be extended.

12. Write a class called MortgageCalculator that extends the FinancialCalculator class discussed in this chapter. The compute method of this class prints out the total interest paid on a mortgage. The monthly payment is computed using this formula:

$$\text{Monthly payment} = \frac{A \times r/n}{1 - [1/(1 + r/n)^{nT}]}$$

where A is the mortage amount, r is the interest rate, n is the number of payments in a year, and T is the term of the mortgage in years. The total interest paid is calculated by taking the product of the monthly payment, the number of payments in a year n, and the term T. Write a program to test this class.

Graphical Programs

13. The following questions refer to the Vehicle, Car, and Airplane classes that were described in this chapter.

a. Create a new subclass of Vehicle called Ship. Add a constructor to this class. Also, add a method called drawShape, with the following declarations:

```
public void drawShape(Graphics2D myGraphics);
```

The method drawShape draws the shape of a ship. Use your imagination to decide what the ship should look like. Write a main method to test your class.

b. Add animation to the Ship class. To do so, include a new method called step:

```
protected void step(Graphics2D g2) {
    // your code to change the (x, y) coordinates of ship
}
```

Implement this step method so that the ship will move right to left across the window.

c. Write a main method in which you create an instance of Ship, Controller, and View classes. Pass this instance of Ship to the Controller and View classes. Run your program along with the classes in the src\com\programwithjava\animation package.

d. Which methods of Vehicle should not be made final? Explain your reasoning.

e. Add a new constructor to the Ship class. The constructor updates the x and y position of the ship to specific values that are passed as arguments to the constructor.

14. Write an abstract class called Fish that contains the following two abstract methods:

```
abstract void displayInformation();
abstract void drawShape(Graphics2D g);
```

Select any two fishes (say, shark and clownfish) that you want to use in your program, and create a class for each of them as a subclass of Fish. Add any fields and methods that are needed to store and modify information (such as type, size, weight, and interesting facts) about each fish. In each class, override the displayInformation method of Fish to print out this information on the console. Also, implement the abstract drawShape method in the subclasses to draw a fish of a particular type in a window. For example, suppose that you write classes `Shark` and `ClownFish`. Write a `main` method to test your program and verify polymorphic behavior as follows:

```
public static void main(String[] args) {
  DrawingKit dk = new DrawingKit();
  Graphics2D myGraphics = dk.getGraphics();
  Fish f;
  f = new Shark();
  f.drawShape(myGraphics); // shark shape should be displayed
  f = new ClownFish();
  f.displayInformation(); // print information about clown fish
}
```

Move the subclasses to a different package from the parent class. What should the access modifiers of the `getInformation` and `drawShape` methods in `Fish` be?

15. a. Write a class called `FourPointStar` that is derived from the `Star` class described in this chapter. Implement the abstract `drawShape` method of `Star` in this class to draw a four-pointed star shape.

 b. Repeat part (a) to create a six-pointed star instead. Write a class called `SixPointStar` that extends the `Star` class and implements the `drawShape` method of `Star`.

 c. Write a program to demonstrate polymorphism. In the `main` method, prompt the user to enter a number from 1 to 3. A four-, five-, or six-pointed star shape is then drawn on the screen depending on whether a 1, 2, or 3 is entered, respectively. An outline of this method is shown here:

```
public static void main(String[] args) {
// insert code to draw a window and get its graphics context
// prompt user to enter a number from 1 to 3 and store it in a
// variable called input
  Star s;
  if (input == 1)
    s = new FourPointStar();
else if (input == 2)
    s = new FivePointStar();
else if (input == 3)
    s = new SixPointStar();
```

```
else
  // print out an error message and exit
  s.drawShape(myGraphics);
}
```

16. Write a class called `Pentagon` to create regular polygons with 5 sides. (A regular polygon is a polygon whose sides are equal.) This class is derived from the `Polygon` class. The constructor for this class takes one argument of type `int` that represents the length of the side. Write a `main` method in this class to create and display three pentagons having sides of length 25, 50, and 100.

17. Write a class called `Octagon` to create regular polygons with 8 sides. This class is derived from the `Polygon` class. The constructor for this class takes one argument of type `int` that represents the length of the side. Write a `main` method in this class to create and display two octagons having sides of length 15 and 50. Write a program showing polymorphic behavior using the `Pentagon` and `Octagon` classes.

Further Reading

We used the *average daily balance* method to calculate the finance charges. Creditors also use other methods such as the *unpaid balance method*. You can find more information about these methods in [3] as well as on the websites of various credit card companies.

References

1. "The Java™ Tutorials." Web. <http://download.oracle.com/javase/tutorial/>.

2. Brinkmann, Ron. *The Art and Science of Digital Compositing: Techniques for Visual Effects, Animation and Motion Graphics, Second Edition*. Burlington, MA: Morgan Kaufmann/Elsevier, 2008. Print.

3. Bluman, Allan G. *Business Math Demystified*. New York: McGraw-Hill, 2006. Print.

4. Eckstein, Robert. "Java SE Application Design With MVC." *Oracle Technology Network*. March 2007. Web. <http://www.oracle.com/technetwork/articles/javase/index-142890.html>.

5. Eckel, Bruce. *Thinking in Java.* Upper Saddle River, NJ: Prentice Hall, 2006. Print.

6. Anderson, Julie, and Herve Franceschi. *Java 6 Illuminated: An Active Learning Approach.* Sudbury, MA: Jones and Bartlett, 2008. Print.

7. Sierra, Kathy, and Bert Bates. *Head First Java.* Sebastopol, CA: O'Reilly, 2005. Print.

8. Knudsen, Jonathan. *Java 2D Graphics.* Beijing: O'Reilly, 1999. Print.

9. *Java ™ Platform, Standard Edition 6, API Specification.* Web. <http://download.oracle.com/javase/6/docs/api/>.

CHAPTER 7

Arrays and Strings

CHAPTER CONTENTS

An array is a data structure commonly used in programs to make it easier to work with large groups of data. In this chapter, we discuss how you can create and use single- and multidimensional arrays. We also discuss the Enum and ArrayList classes that are used to create special types of arrays. Another topic covered is strings. You already know how to create strings using the String class. You will learn about some of the methods in the String class and another related class called StringBuilder. We will develop a two-player grid game called Crystals throughout this chapter. This game shows how to use arrays, enums, array lists, and strings in a larger program.

7.1   What Is an Array?

An array is a data structure used to store related data in a program. The data can consist of numbers, characters, strings, or objects. The advantage of using an array is that we can use a single name to reference all of the data in the array. This makes it easy to read and modify the data values stored in the array. Figure 7–1 shows three arrays that contain the names, IDs, and marks of students in a class.

An array has a *fixed* size that is decided when the array is created. The data values stored in the array are called its **elements**. Each element of the array is at a specific position referred to as its **index** or **subscript**. The first index is always 0. For example, in the array named ID, the element 1083 is at index 0, element 2001 is at index 1, and so on. The last element of the array is therefore at index 4, because the array contains five elements. For an array containing n elements, the indices range from 0 to $n - 1$. An element can

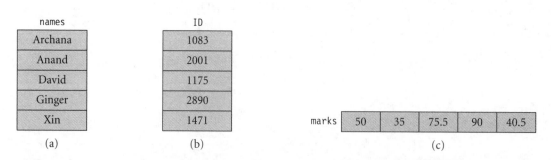

(a)   (b)   (c)

Figure 7–1

Examples of arrays: (a) a string array, (b) an array of integers, and (c) an array of floating-point numbers.

be accessed by specifying the name of the array and the index of the element within square brackets. Thus, marks[0] refers to the first element of the marks array, marks[1] refers to its second element, and so on.

7.2   Creating Arrays

An array of the specified type and size is declared and created as shown here:

```
type[] newArray;          // declare the array
newArray = new type[size]; // create the array of the given size
```

Here, type represents a primitive or reference type. Square brackets are placed after the type to indicate that an array is being created. The first statement *declares* an array called newArray that can store elements of the given type but does not specify its size. The second statement *creates* the array of the given size. Both of these statements can be combined into a single one if the array size is known when it is declared:

```
type[] newArray = new type[size]; // declare and create the array
```

An important point to note is that the size of the array cannot be changed after it has been created.

These two statements declare and create an integer array called array of size 3:

```
int[] array;
array = new int[3];
```

Another valid format for declaring an array is to place the square brackets *after* the identifier instead of before it:

```
int array1[];
```

You can declare and create an array using a *single* statement as follows:

```
int[] array2 = new int[3];   // declare and create array2
int array3[] = new int[5];   // declare and create array3
```

Specifying the size when the array is declared results in a compile-time error:

```
int[100] array4;       // error
```

However, it is necessary to specify the size when the new operator is used; otherwise, a compile-time error results:

```
int[] array4 = new int[]; // error, array size not specified
```

Other examples of array declarations are shown here:

```
char[] vowels;            // a character array
int[] ages;               // an integer array
double[] averageRainfallPerMonth;   // an array of doubles
String[] colors;          // an array of strings
Ball[] balls;             // an array to hold objects of type Ball
```

As an exercise, write statements to create arrays of the preceding primitive and reference types.

7.3   Initializing Arrays

After the array has been created, we can populate it with some data. This is done by assigning values to the array elements. Suppose that we want to store the numbers 100, 200, and 300 in array1, created as follows:

```
int array1 = new int[3];
```

The array is of type int; thus its elements will have a default value of 0.

Arrays are initialized automatically to default values when they are created. Arrays of type int, float, and double have default values of 0, 0.0f, and 0.0 respectively. Arrays of type char have a default value of \u0000, which represents a special type of character called the **null character**. Arrays of reference types are initialized to null. Arrays of type boolean have a default value of false.

The following statement sets the first element of array1, which is at index 0, to 100:

```
array1[0] = 100;
```

These statements set its second and third elements to 200 and 300, respectively:

```
array1[1] = 200;
array1[2] = 300;
```

Figure 7–2 shows the resulting array.

An array can be initialized using an **initializer list** when it is created:

```
int[] array2 = {200, -30, -400, 50};
```

Figure 7–2

An array with three elements.

array1[0]	100
array1[1]	200
array1[2]	300

The elements in the list should be separated using commas and placed within braces. The array size depends upon the number of elements in the list.

The elements of a `char` array should be placed within *single* quotation marks. The arrays `vowels` and `letters` hold a single character at each index:

```
char[] vowels = {'a', 'e', 'i', 'o', 'u'};
char[] letters = new char[10];
```

The following statement sets the first element of array `letters` to b:

```
letters[0] = 'b';
```

The remaining elements of `letters` have a default value of \u0000.

The elements of a `String` array should be placed within *double* quotation marks. Examples of creating and initializing `String` arrays are given here:

```
String[] daysOfWeek = {"Sunday", "Monday", "Tuesday", "Wednesday",
"Thursday", "Friday", "Saturday"};
String[] months = new String[12];
months[0] = "January";
months[1] = "February";
```

The remaining elements of the `months` array have a default value of `null` because they are objects, not primitives.

Arrays are usually modified using loops. Suppose that we want to populate an array of size 100 with the values 0, 1, 2, 3, ..., 99. It would be tedious to write out 100 assignment statements. The values can be assigned easily using a `for` loop, as shown here:

```
// declare and create array arr
int[] arr = new int[100];

// initialize array arr to 100 values
for (int i = 0; i < 100; i++)
    arr[i] = i;
```

The array index i takes the values 0, 1, ..., 99. Therefore, arr[0] gets the value 0, arr[1] gets the value 1, and so on.

> It is important to remember that for an array of size n, the last element of that array is at index $n - 1$, and not n.

A run-time error will result if you try to assign a value to an index that lies outside the bounds of the array. For example, if you try to assign a value to arr[100], the program will fail while executing because the last element of arr is at index 99.

Example 1

Give the contents of both arrays after these statements are executed:

a.   ```
double[] arr1 = new double[2];

arr1[0] = 3.0;

arr1[1] = 2.2;
```

b.    ```
int[] arr2 = new int[10];

for (int i = 0; i < 10; i++)

  arr2[i] = i * 10 + 3;
```

Solution:

a.   The first element of arr1 is 3.0, and the second element is 2.2.

b.   The array arr2 has 10 elements. An element at index i has value $i \times 10 + 3$. Thus, the last element of the array at index 9 has value 93. The other values can be calculated similarly. The array contents are shown in Figure 7–3.   ■

Figure 7–3

The contents of array arr2.

arr2

3
13
23
33
43
53
63
73
83
93

7.4   Using Arrays

By using loops, you can read and modify some or all of the elements in an array with just a few statements. Suppose that an instructor has stored the marks of 50 students in an array called test1 and wants to compute the average marks. The total marks received by all the students are calculated by first summing all the elements in test1. Then, the average is calculated by dividing this sum by the number of students. The following code segment shows how a for loop is used to sum the elements in the array test1:

```
int sum = 0;                    // initialize sum to 0
int numStudents = 50;           // number of students
for (int i = 0; i < numStudents; i++)
  sum += test1[i];              // add the marks

int average = sum/numStudents; // calculate the average
```

Suppose that the instructor wants to increment the marks of all students by 2 points. The code for this is shown next:

```
for (int i = 0; i < numStudents; i++)
   test1[i] += 2;
```

7.4.1   The length Field

Every array contains an *instance field* called length that stores the array size:

```
System.out.println(test1.length); // prints out test1's length
```

This for loop shows how you can use the length field to iterate over all the array elements:

```
for (int i = 0; i < test1.length; i++)
   // do something here
```

Note that the last element of test1 has index test1.length − 1.

7.4.2   Enhanced for Statement

There is a variant of the for loop that is especially suited for iterating through array elements. It loops through each element of an array and stores the element into a given variable. Its form is shown here:

```
for (type data : myArray) {
  // do something here
}
```

Here, data is a variable used to store an element of the array called myArray of the specified type. This enhanced for loop stores the first element of myArray into data, processes it in the loop block, stores the second element into data, and so on. The advantage of using this structure is that it removes the possibility that the programmer may incorrectly specify a loop index that lies outside the bounds of the array. For example, to display the contents of test1, use:

```
for (int element : test1)
  System.out.println(element);
```

This will print out all the elements in test1 without having to specify the index of each element. Consider another array called vowels:

```
char[] vowels = {'a', 'e', 'i', 'o', 'u'};
```

The elements of this array are of type char. Therefore, to iterate over this array, use:

```
for (char value : vowels)
  // use the element stored in the variable value
```

Note that you cannot modify the contents of a primitive type array using an enhanced for loop.

7.4.3   Arrays of Objects

Arrays of reference types are declared and created similarly as arrays of primitive types:

```
Book[] books;          // declares an array to hold objects of type Book
books = new Book[10]; // creates an array to hold 10 Book objects
```

This statement stores an instance of Book at index 0 in the books array:

```
books[0] = new Book();
```

Each object in the array can contain multiple fields; thus the value of these fields can be obtained using either the field name or an accessor method. Suppose that Book contains a public field called name. This gives the name of the first element books[0] stored in the array books:

```
books[0].name
```

If name is a private field of Book, an accessor method could be used instead, assuming the class provides one:

```
books[0].getName()
```

This next example illustrates how arrays of objects are created and used. An art museum wants to create an online catalog of its paintings. The catalog will be stored in an array of type Painting, where the Painting class contains information relevant to each painting. This class is outlined here:

```java
package arraysandstrings;

public class Painting {
  private String name;
  private String artist;
  private int year;

  // constructor
  public Painting(String name, String artist, int year) {
    this.name = name;
    this.artist = artist;
    this.year = year;
  }

  // accessor method to get the name of the painting
  public String getName() {
    return name;
  }

  // returns the name of the artist
  public String getArtist() {
    return artist;
  }

  // returns the year when completed
  public int getYear() {
    return year;
  }
}
```

This statement creates an array called catalog to store information about three paintings:

```java
Painting[] catalog = new Painting[3];
```

Each element of the array references a new instance of Painting after the following statements are executed:

```java
catalog[0] = new Painting("Impression, Sunrise", "Claude Monet", 1873);
catalog[1] = new Painting("Mona Lisa", "Leonardo da Vinci", 1505);
catalog[2] = new Painting("Three Musicians", "Pablo Picasso", 1921);
```

	name	artist	year
catalog[0]	Impression, Sunrise	Claude Monet	1873
catalog[1]	Mona Lisa	Leonardo da Vinci	1505
catalog[2]	Three Musicians	Pablo Picasso	1921

Figure 7–4 shows how the data is stored in this array.

The first element of `catalog` is at index 0 and is referenced as `catalog[0]`. The fields of this object are `private`; thus they can only be accessed using the accessor methods in this class:

```
catalog[0].getName();     // get name of first painting
catalog[0].getArtist();   // get artist name of first painting
```

The objects stored in the array `catalog` can also be accessed using an enhanced `for` loop. This enhanced `for` loop prints out the name and artist of every `Painting` object stored in the array:

```
for (Painting p : catalog)
  System.out.println("Painting name = " +p.getName() +" Artist = "
+p.getArtist());
```

The array entries can be modified using mutator methods. As an exercise, add the method `setYear` to the `Painting` class, and use it to modify the `year` field of the objects in the `catalog` array.

7.5   Multidimensional Arrays

A single-dimensional array is a single row or column of values. A multidimensional array contains several rows and columns. Figure 7–5 shows a two-dimensional array with four rows and three columns. Every element in this array has two indices, where the first index is the *row* number and the second is the *column* number. Thus, the element in row 1 and column 2 has indices [1, 2].

A two-dimensional array is declared using two pairs of square brackets after the data type, followed by the name of the array. This declares a two-dimensional array named `a`:

```
int[][] a;
```

To create this array, specify the number of rows and columns in the array:

```
a = new int[10][3]; // a has 10 rows and 3 columns
```

	Column 0	Column 1	Column 2
Row 0	a[0][0]	a[0][1]	a[0][2]
Row 1	a[1][0]	a[1][1]	a[1][2]
Row 2	a[2][0]	a[2][1]	a[2][2]
Row 3	a[3][0]	a[3][1]	a[3][2]

Figure 7–5

A two-dimensional array with four rows and three columns.

It is not necessary to provide the number of columns, but not specifying the number of rows causes a compilation error:

```
a = new int[5][]; // okay, array has 5 rows
a = new int[][3]; // error, the number of rows is not specified
a = new int[][]; // error, the number of rows is not specified
```

A multidimensional array can be initialized when it is created. The size of the array depends on the number of elements in the initializer list:

```
int[][] numArray = { {0, 1, 2},
                     {3, 4, 5},
                     {6, 7, 8},
                     {9, 10, 11}
                   };
```

This creates an array with four rows and three columns. The elements of the array are laid out as shown in Figure 7–6.

Array elements can be initialized or modified using nested `for` loops. These statements increment the values of all the elements in numArray by 5:

```
for (int row = 0; row < 4; row++)
  for (int column = 0; column < 3; column++)
    numArray[row][column] += 5;
```

The outer and inner loops iterate over all of the rows and columns, respectively. The `length` field can be used to obtain the number of rows and columns. For example, the number of rows in numArray is given by num-Array.length, and the number of columns in row r is given by numArray[r].length. These nested for loops print out the array elements in all of its rows and columns:

```
for (int row = 0; row < numArray.length; row++)
  for (int column = 0; column < numArray[row].length; column++)
    System.out.println(numArray[row][column]);
```

Assuming that each element in the array shown in Figure 7–6 has been incremented by 5, the output is shown here:

```
5
6
7
8
9
10
11
12
13
14
15
16
```

As an exercise, try to predict the output of the code segment shown here:

```
for (int column = 0; column < 3; column++)
  for (int row = 0; row < 4; row++)
    System.out.println(numArray[row][column]);
```

This discussion of two-dimensional arrays can be extended to arrays of dimension greater than 2. An n-dimensional array has n indices per element.

7.6 The Crystals Game

In the Crystals game [6], players create patterns on a grid of squares by taking turns coloring individual squares on the grid. Each colored square is called an **atom**. A crystal consists of a group of atoms such that each atom is joined to at least one other atom along one *side*. A **perfect** crystal must have the following properties:

- It contains at least four atoms.
- It is symmetrical.
- It does not contain any holes.

The size of a crystal is limited only by the size of the grid and the number of available squares. A player can prevent another player from creating or growing crystals by placing atoms strategically inside the other player's crystals. The winner is the player with the largest number of atoms in all of his or her *perfect* crystals. We will develop the algorithm and code for this game in two classes named `Crystals` and `Crystal` later in this chapter. The `Crystal` class will contain code to determine whether a crystal is perfect. The `Crystals` class will contain the GUI for the game and determine each player's score.

How can you determine that a crystal is symmetrical? First, imagine that horizontal, vertical, and diagonal lines are drawn through its center. As a result, each half of the crystal on either side of these lines (called **lines of symmetry**) should be a mirror image of the other half. Therefore, if you fold the crystal at a line of symmetry, the colored squares in each half should coincide. Figure 7–7(a) depicts a perfect crystal with five atoms that

(a)

(b)

(c)

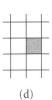
(d)

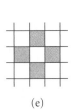
(e)

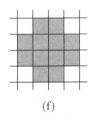
(f)

Figure 7–7

(a) A perfect crystal. (b) Not a perfect crystal, because it is not symmetrical about the dotted line. (c) A perfect crystal. (d) Not a perfect crystal, because it contains fewer than four atoms. (e) Not a crystal, because the atoms are joined only at the corners. (f) A perfect crystal.

is symmetrical about the dotted lines passing through its center. Figure 7–7(b) is not a perfect crystal, because the pattern is not symmetrical about the horizontal dotted line: If you fold it over at the dotted line, a colored square in the lower half does not coincide with a colored square in the top half. Look at the other examples in Figure 7–7.

The Crystals class contains a two-dimensional array called playerGrid to store the moves of each player. For a two-player game, the grid size is 20 × 20. The turn field keeps track of who the current player is, RED or YELLOW. RED starts the game. Some fields in this class are shown here:

```
package arraysandstrings;

public class Crystals {

    // Constants
    public static final int WIDTH = 20;  // grid width
    public static final int HEIGHT = 20; // grid height
    public static final int INITIAL = 0;
    public static final int RED = 1;
    public static final int YELLOW = 3;
    private int turn = RED;       // current player
    private int[][] playerGrid; // grid to record each player's move
    private int row, column;     // position of most recently added atom
    private int player1Score = 0;    // RED's score
    private int player2Score = 0;    // YELLOW's score
}
```

We explain how these fields are used as we develop the code for the game.

7.6.1   The Crystals Game: Checking for Symmetric Crystals

This section describes how to check whether a crystal is symmetrical about the horizontal, vertical, and two diagonal axes. For simplicity, we will use a 5 × 5 grid in our discussion. Each colored square in the grid represents an atom. Figure 7–8(a) shows a crystal with nine atoms. The lines of symme-

Figure 7–8

(a) A crystal in a grid. (b) A two-dimensional array that stores this crystal.

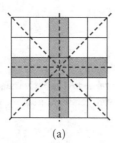

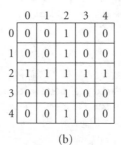

(a)   (b)

try are shown as dotted lines. This crystal can be stored in a two-dimensional array, as shown in Figure 7–8(b). If an atom is present in the grid, it is stored as a 1 in the corresponding position in the array; otherwise, a 0 is stored in that array location.

Let us call the array in Figure 7–8(b) grid. The pattern stored in this array is symmetrical about the *vertical* line passing through its center if the following pairs of array values are equal: grid[0][0] and grid[0][4], grid[0][1] and grid[0][3], grid[1][0] and grid[1][4], grid[1][1] and grid[1][3], etc. So, to check for vertical symmetry in an array with five columns, simply check that the following is true for all elements:

```
grid[row][column] == grid[row][4-column]
```

You can generalize this result to an array with a different number of columns. Note that the number of rows and columns are equal in a symmetric crystal (this is checked in another procedure). The following code checks that the crystal stored in the two-dimensional array called grid with width+1 columns and rows is symmetrical about the vertical line passing through its center:

```
for (int row = 0; row <= width; row++)
  for (int column = 0; column <= width; column++)
    if (grid[row][column] != grid[row][width - column])
      return false;
```

In the same way, you can write code to check whether a pattern is symmetrical about the horizontal line through its center as well as the two diagonal lines through its center. The method isSymmetrical shown next returns true if a crystal is symmetrical about all of these lines of symmetry. Assume that this crystal is stored in a two-dimensional static array called grid with width+1 rows and columns:

```
// checks whether a crystal stored in the 2D array called grid is
// symmetrical
public static boolean isSymmetrical() {
  boolean horizontalSym, verticalSym, diagonal1Sym, diagonal2Sym;

  for (int row = 0; row <= width; row++) {
    for (int column = 0; column <= width; column++) {
      // symmetrical about horizontal axis?
      horizontalSym = (grid[row][column] == grid[width - row][column]);

      // symmetrical about vertical axis?
      verticalSym = (grid[row][column] == grid[row][width - column]);
```

```
      // symmetric about first diagonal?
      diagonal1Sym = (grid[row][column] == grid[column][row]);

      // symmetric about second diagonal?
      diagonal2Sym = (grid[row][column] == grid[column][width - row]);

      // return false if not symmetrical about any of the above axes
      if (!horizontalSym || !verticalSym || !diagonal1Sym || !diagonal2Sym)
        return false;
      }
  }
  // is symmetrical
  return true;
}
```

Later in this chapter, we will add this method to a class called Crystal. We will also add other methods to this class to determine whether a crystal is perfect.

7.7   Passing Arrays as Arguments to Methods

Array instances can be passed as arguments to a method. Like other objects, arrays are also passed by reference. Consider the class TestArray in the next example, with two methods print and increment that take an array as an argument. Note that increment actually modifies the data in the array that is passed as an argument to this method.

Example 2

This program shows how arrays are passed to methods:

```
package arraysandstrings;

public class TestArray {
  public static void print(int[] array) {
    for (int value : array)
      System.out.println(value);
  }
  public static void increment(int[] array) {
    for (int i = 0; i < array.length; i++)
      array[i]++; // add 1 to data value at index i
  }
}
```

A test array called newArray is created in main and passed as an argument to the increment method. Then the print method is called to print out its elements:

```java
public static void main(String[] args) {
  int[] newArray = {10, -9, 8, -7, 6};
  TestArray.increment(newArray);
  TestArray.print(newArray);
}
```

As the following output shows, the increment method modifies the elements of newArray passed in as an argument. The program output is:

```
11
-8
9
-6
7
```

7.8 The Arrays Class

The Arrays class, defined in the java.util package, contains static methods for use with arrays. Some of these methods are shown in Figure 7–9. In addition, the class contains overloaded versions of these methods that take arguments of type char, float, long, double, and others.

Arrays	
static boolean equals(int[] array1, int[] array2)	Returns true if array1 and array2 have the same size and their elements are the same.
static void sort(int[] array)	Sorts array in *ascending* order.
static void sort(int[] array, int startIndex, int endIndex)	Sorts a portion of array, from the index startIndex up to (and including) the index endIndex.
static void fill(int[] array, int value)	Populates all indices of array with value.
static void fill(int[] array, int startIndex, int endIndex, int value)	Populates only the indices from startIndex to endIndex with value.

Figure 7–9

Some methods in the Arrays class.

Example 3

In main, create an integer array and use the sort method of the Arrays class to sort its elements in ascending order. Print out the resulting array.

Solution: The program to sort an array's elements is shown here:

```
package arrays and strings;
import java.util.Arrays;

public class TestArray {
  public static void main(String[] args) {
    int[] arr = {10, -9, 8, -7, 6};
    Arrays.sort(arr);
    for (int value : arr)
      System.out.println(value);
  }
}
```

The program output is:

```
-9
-7
6
8
10
```

Arrays of both primitive and reference types can be sorted using the sort method.   ∎

7.9   Enums

Like classes and interfaces, an **enum** creates a new reference type. An enum can contain fields and methods, just like a class. There are two important differences from classes, however:

1. An enum contains a fixed *array* of **enum objects**.

2. An enum implicitly extends the Enum class in the java.lang package.

In the simplest form, an enum contains only enum objects (usually called **enum constants**), and no fields or methods. The following shows an enum called EnumColor, defined using the enum keyword:

```
public enum EnumColor {
  RED,
  CYAN,
  MAGENTA;
}
```

There are three enum objects of type `EnumColor` called `RED`, `CYAN`, and `MAGENTA` in this enum. Objects cannot be created outside the enum using the `new` operator as follows:

```
EnumColor e = new EnumColor();  // error
```

By convention, these objects are specified in uppercase characters because they are used as constants. We have created a new reference type called `EnumColor`, and can create a variable of this type as follows:

```
EnumColor color;
```

The variable `color` can reference any of the enum objects in `EnumColor`:

```
color = RED;  // okay, because RED is in EnumColor
color = BLUE;  // error, because BLUE is not in EnumColor
```

7.9.1 The `Enum` Class

An enum implicitly extends the `Enum` class; thus it inherits the methods of this class. Two methods in `Enum` are shown in Figure 7–10.

The ordinal is the position of an enum object. The first enum object in an enum is at ordinal 0. For example, RED, CYAN, and MAGENTA in Enum-Color have ordinals of 0, 1, and 2, respectively. The following code shows how the `name` and `ordinal` methods can be used:

```
package arraysandstrings;

public enum EnumColor {
  RED,
  CYAN,
  MAGENTA;

  public static void main(String[] args) {
    EnumColor color = CYAN;
    System.out.println(color.name() +" has ordinal "+color.ordinal());
  }
}
```

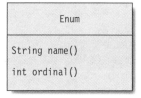

Enum	
String name()	Returns the name of the enum object.
int ordinal()	Returns the position of this enum object in the array.

Figure 7–10
Two methods in the Enum class.

The program output is:

```
CYAN has ordinal 1
```

7.9.2   The `values()` Method

All enums have a static method called `values` that returns an array of the objects in the enum. The following call returns an enum object with ordinal 0 in enum `e`:

```
e.values()[0]
```

The ordinal 0 must be placed inside square brackets, as shown. Thus, calling method `values` indexed by the ordinal returns the object with that ordinal. The number of objects in the enum array can be printed out using the `length` field of an array:

```
e.values().length
```

This is shown in the following program:

```java
package arrays and strings;

public enum EnumColor {
  RED,
  CYAN,
  MAGENTA;

  public static void main(String[] args) {
   for (int i = 0; i < EnumColor.values().length; i++)
    System.out.println(EnumColor.values()[i]);
  }
}
```

The program output is:

```
RED
CYAN
MAGENTA
```

Alternately, the following enhanced for loop can be used to print out the values:

```java
for (EnumColor  obj : EnumColor.values())
  System.out.println(obj);
```

7.9.3   Adding Methods to an Enum

You can add methods to an enum just as you would to a class. All enum objects inherit these methods. If you declare a method abstract, it is necessary for each enum object to implement that method. An enum object can also have other methods of its own that are not present in other enum objects. However, an enum object cannot define static methods of its own.

The following example shows that EnumColor contains an abstract method called getColor, which is overridden in the enum objects. Can you figure out the output of this program?

```java
package arraysandstrings;
import java.awt.*;

public enum EnumColor {
  RED {
    public Color getColor() {
      return Color.RED;
    }
  },
  CYAN {
    public Color getColor() {
      return Color.CYAN;
    }
  },
  MAGENTA {
    public Color getColor() {
      return Color.MAGENTA;
    }
  };

  public abstract Color getColor();

  public static void main(String[] args) {
    System.out.println(EnumColor.values()[0].getColor());
  }
}
```

By passing an argument of EnumColor.values()[0].getColor() to println, the getColor method of the instance RED with ordinal 0 is invoked. Therefore, the values of the red, green, and blue components of Color.RED are printed out:

```
java.awt.Color[r=255,g=0,b=0]
```

7.9.4   Adding Fields and Constructors to an Enum

Fields and constructors can be added to an enum just as you would to a class. The constructors generate the enum objects automatically, and cannot be invoked by the programmer. Consider the enum called EnumShape that contains objects representing shapes:

```
public enum EnumShape {
  RECTANGLE,
  ELLIPSE,
  CIRCLE,
  SQUARE;
}
```

Suppose that we want to create each shape with a fixed width and height. We can add these two fields and this constructor:

```
int width, height;

EnumShape(int w, int h) {
  width = w;
  height = h;
}
```

The enum constructor must be declared as private or package-private; it cannot be made public or protected. Add an abstract method called createShape to this enum. We also add overriding methods called createShape to each enum instance to create a specific shape. For example, the RECTANGLE object has the following createShape method, where width and height are its fields:

```
Shape createShape() {
  return (Shape) ( new Rectangle2D.Float(50, 100, width, height) );
}
```

We discussed earlier that Shape is the parameter type in the Graphics2D draw method. You can think of it as the supertype of a number of other graphics types, such as Rectangle2D.Float, Ellipse2D.Float, and Line2D.Float. For this reason, it is possible to cast all instances of these classes to type Shape. Shape is actually an interface; you will learn about interfaces in more detail in the next chapter. Now, the RECTANGLE instance is created by specifying arguments as:

```
RECTANGLE(100, 200)
```

This passes the arguments 100 and 200 to the width and height fields of RECTANGLE using the EnumShape constructor. (If an enum contains multiple constructors, the matching constructor is called.) The complete code for EnumShape is shown here:

```java
package arraysandstrings;

import java.awt.*;
import java.awt.geom.*;

public enum EnumShape {
  RECTANGLE(200, 100) {
    Shape createShape() {
      return (Shape) ( new Rectangle2D.Float(50, 100, width, height) );
    }
  },
  ELLIPSE(200, 300) {
    Shape createShape() {
      return (Shape) ( new Ellipse2D.Float(50, 100, width, height) );
    }
  },
  CIRCLE(300, 300) {
    Shape createShape() {
      return (Shape) ( new Ellipse2D.Float(50, 100, width, height) );
    }
  },
  SQUARE(350, 350) {
    Shape createShape() {
      return (Shape) ( new Rectangle2D.Float(50, 100, width, height) );
    }
  };    // note the semicolon here

  int width, height;
  EnumShape(int w, int h) {
    width = w;
    height = h;
  }
  abstract Shape createShape();
}
```

The next example shows how EnumColor and EnumShape can be used in a program.

Example 4

Rewrite the MagicShapes program (Example 1 in Chapter 4) to use enums. Recall that in this program, two random numbers called magicColor and magicShape were generated. Then, based on the values of these numbers and using a sequence of if-else statements, a colored shape was drawn. The interesting point to note here is that by using enums, we can rewrite the same program *without* using any if-else statements!

Solution:

```
package arraysandstrings;

import java.awt.*;
import java.awt.geom.*;
import java.util.Random;
import com.programwithjava.basic.DrawingKit;

public class MagicShapes {
  public static void main(String[] args) {
    DrawingKit dk = new DrawingKit("Magic Shapes");
    Graphics2D myGraphics = dk.getGraphics();
    Random r = new Random();

    // magicShape gets a random integer value of 0, 1, 2 or 3.
    int magicShape = r.nextInt(EnumShape.values().length);

    // magicColor gets a random integer value of 0, 1 or 2
    int magicColor =  r.nextInt(EnumColor.values().length);

    // set the color
    myGraphics.setPaint(EnumColor.values()[magicColor].getColor());

    // create the shape
    Shape s =  EnumShape.values()[magicShape].createShape();

    // draw and fill all shapes except squares, which are not filled.
    myGraphics.draw(s);
    if (magicShape != EnumShape.SQUARE.ordinal())
      myGraphics.fill(s);
  }
}
```

Compile and run this program:

```
C:\JavaBook> javac -d bin src\com\programwithjava\basic\DrawingKit.java
src\arraysandstrings\EnumColor.java src\arraysandstrings\EnumShape.java
src\arraysandstrings\MagicShapes.java

C:\JavaBook> java -classpath bin arraysandstrings.MagicShapes
```

The output is the same as for the program in Chapter 4. First, the values of `magicShape` and `magicColor` are generated randomly. For example, `EnumShape.values().length` has the value 4, because there are four objects in `EnumShape`. Therefore, `magicShape` is assigned a random value from 0 to 3. Similarly, `magicColor` is assigned 0, 1, or 2, randomly. This calls the `getColor` method of the enum object with ordinal `magicColor`:

```
EnumColor.values()[magicColor].getColor()
```

The `setPaint` method then sets the color to `Color.RED`, `Color.CYAN`, or `Color.MAGENTA`, depending on which `getColor` method is executed. The next statement creates a graphics shape and assigns it to the reference variable s of type `Shape`:

```
Shape s = EnumShape.values()[magicShape].createShape();
```

Note that the preceding statement calls the `createShape` method of the object with ordinal `magicShape`. Finally, in the remaining statements, the shape s is drawn and colored.   ∎

7.9.5   The Crystals Game: The Enum `Direction`

Here we will create an enum called `Direction` that gives the coordinates of the squares that are to the north, south, east, and west of a particular square on the grid. For example, suppose that we want to find the neighbors of the square at row 10 and column 0, represented as (10, 0). The north, south, east, and west neighbors are (9, 0), (11, 0), (10, 1), and null, respectively. (There is no neighbor to the west of this square because it is in the leftmost column in the grid; thus the coordinates of the west neighbor are null.) It is convenient to represent the coordinates of a point using the `java.awt.Point` class. This class has two integer fields, namely x and y. Two constructors and accessor methods for this class are shown in Figure 7–11.

Point	
`Point()`	Constructor creates a point that is initialized to (0, 0).
`Point(int x, int y)`	Constructor creates a point initialized to (x, y).
`double getX()`	Returns the value of x.
`double getY()`	Returns the value of y.

Figure 7–11

Some constructors and methods in the `Point` class.

The `Direction` enum contains four objects: NORTH, SOUTH, EAST, and WEST. Each of these objects implements the abstract method index to return the coordinates of the north, south, east, or west neighbor. Each index method takes the coordinates of a square at row r and column c as its parameters. Therefore, the index method of NORTH returns the coordinates of the neighboring square to the north of the square at (r, c). If a square is adjacent to a grid edge, it will have fewer than four neighbors. For example, squares in row 0 do not have a neighbor to the north, and so the index method of NORTH returns null for these squares. The other methods are similar. The constants HEIGHT and WIDTH defined in class Crystals are the number of rows and columns in the grid, respectively. The code for this enum is shown here:

```
package arraysandstrings;
import java.awt.Point;

public enum Direction {
  NORTH {
    Point index(int r, int c) {
      if (r > 0)
        return new Point(r-1, c);
      else
        return null;
    }
  },
  SOUTH {
    Point index(int r, int c) {
      if (r < Crystals.HEIGHT - 1)
        return new Point(r+1, c);
      else
        return null;
    }
  },
  EAST {
    Point index(int r, int c) {
      if (c < Crystals.WIDTH - 1)
        return new Point(r, c+1);
      else
        return null;
    }
  },
  WEST {
    Point index(int r, int c) {
```

```
      if (c > 0)
        return new Point(r, c-1);
      else
        return null;
    }
  };

  abstract Point index(int r, int c);
}
```

7.10   The ArrayList Class

The ArrayList class in the java.util package is used when we want an array whose size changes while the program executes. You know that arrays have a fixed size that must be specified when the array is created. How can an element be added to an array that is filled to capacity? One way to do this is for the programmer to create a larger array and copy all of the elements from the smaller array into the larger one, with the remaining space for new elements. An alternative is to use the ArrayList class for arrays whose sizes change frequently. An instance of this class contains an array that grows and shrinks *automatically* as elements are added or removed, so that it relieves the programmer from the burden of doing this. Figure 7–12 shows some of the constructors and methods in this class.

ArrayList	
ArrayList()	Constructor creates an empty array of size ten.
ArrayList(int n)	Constructor creates an empty array of size n.
boolean add(Object obj)	Adds the object obj to the end of the array and returns true.
Object remove(int index)	Removes and returns the object at the given index.
int size()	Returns the number of elements in this array.
boolean isEmpty()	Returns true if this array does not have any elements; otherwise, returns false.
Object get(int i)	Returns (without removing) the element at index i from the array.
Object set(int i, Object obj)	Changes the element at index i to obj and returns the previous element at this index.

Figure 7–12

Some constructors and methods in the ArrayList class.

The following statements show how to use the add method:

```
ArrayList list = new ArrayList();
list.add(100);
list.add(200);
list.add(300);
```

This prints out the size of list:

```
System.out.println(list.size());
```

The size is 3 because list has three elements: 100, 200, and 300. Note that the length *field* is used to obtain the array size for a regular array, whereas the size *method* is used for an instance of the ArrayList class.

This removes the element at index 1:

```
list.remove(1);
```

The list now contains the elements 100 and 300, and has size 2.

We will use an ArrayList in the isHoley method in the Crystals game to check whether a crystal contains a hole. This is explained next.

7.10.1   The Crystals Game: Checking for Holes

One requirement of a perfect crystal is that it not have any holes. The algorithm to find a hole in a crystal is based on the observation that an empty square *along the edge of the grid* (called a **space**) cannot be a hole. Any empty square that is connected to a space along a *side* will also be a space, and the spaces are thus grown by connecting them together. Any empty squares left unconnected are holes. In this section, we explain the algorithm used to determine whether the crystal contains a hole by using an example. Figure 7–13(a) shows a symmetrical crystal that has a hole in its center. Figure 7–13(b) shows the same crystal stored in a two-dimensional array, with the empty squares and atoms represented by elements with the values 0 and 1, respectively.

The algorithm used to find holes follows:

1. Find all squares that are not atoms along the *edges* of the grid and mark them as SPACE in the array. (A space is represented by an ele-

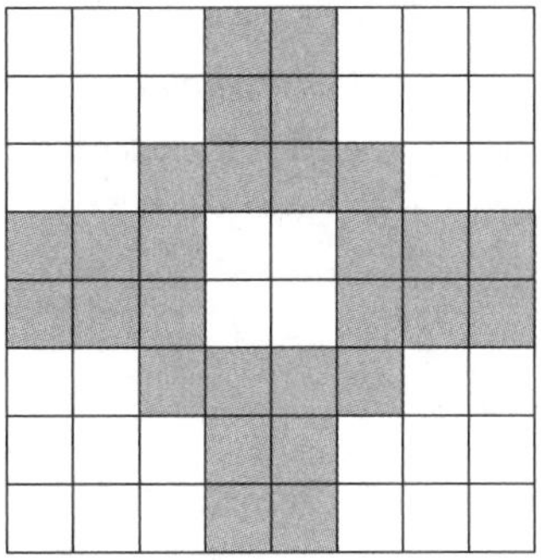

(a)

0	0	0	1	1	0	0	0
0	0	0	1	1	0	0	0
0	0	1	1	1	1	0	0
1	1	1	0	0	1	1	1
1	1	1	0	0	1	1	1
0	0	1	1	1	1	0	0
0	0	0	1	1	0	0	0
0	0	0	1	1	0	0	0

(b)

Figure 7–13

(a) A crystal with a hole in its center. (b) The crystal stored in a two-dimensional array.

ment that has the value 2.) Create an `ArrayList` called `spacesArray` and store the coordinates of each space as a `Point` object in `spacesArray`. For example, `Point(2, 3)` represents the space at row 2 and column 3. Figure 7–14 shows the spaces along the four edges of the grid. After all of these spaces have been stored in it, `spacesArray` contains these `Point` objects: `Point(0, 0)`, `Point(0, 1)`, `Point(0, 2)`, `Point(0, 5)`, `Point(0, 6)`, `Point(0, 7)`, `Point(1, 0)`, `Point(1, 7)`, `Point(2, 0)`, `Point(2, 7)`, `Point(5, 0)`, `Point(5, 7)`, `Point(6, 0)`, `Point(6, 7)`, `Point(7, 0)`, `Point(7, 1)`, `Point(7,2)`, `Point(7, 5)`, `Point(7, 6)`, and `Point(7, 7)`.

2. We now try to "grow" the spaces by marking all empty squares connected to a space along a side as a space. If `spacesArray` is not empty,

2	2	2	1	1	2	2	2
2	0	0	1	1	0	0	2
2	0	1	1	1	1	0	2
1	1	1	0	0	1	1	1
1	1	1	0	0	1	1	1
2	0	1	1	1	1	0	2
2	0	0	1	1	0	0	2
2	2	2	1	1	2	2	2

Figure 7–14

Identifying the spaces (marked with 2) along the edges of the grid.

remove its first element. Find the squares that are not atoms or marked as SPACE to the north, south, east, and west of this element in the grid. Mark each empty square as SPACE and add it to spacesArray. The first element removed from spacesArray is Point(0, 0), which corresponds to the space at (0, 0). It has a square to the east and a square to the south, but both are already marked as SPACE, and so nothing is inserted into spacesArray.

3. Repeat step 2 until spacesArray is empty. For example, Point(0, 1) is removed next, which corresponds to the space at (0, 1). This has an empty square to the south with coordinates (1, 1). Mark this square as SPACE and insert it into spacesArray. This procedure is continued until spacesArray becomes empty, at which point all of the spaces have been found. Figure 7–15 shows all the spaces that have been found in the crystal using this method.

4. Any squares left that are not atoms and not marked as SPACE are holes. Figure 7–15 shows that the four squares in the center are still marked as 0, and therefore are holes.

This algorithm is used in the method isHoley in the Crystal class to determine whether a crystal has a hole. The method returns false after the first hole is found. The crystal being checked is stored in the two-dimensional array called grid with width+1 rows and columns. The following statement checks whether the given square is an atom, because turn specifies which player played in that square (either RED or YELLOW):

```
if (grid[row][column] == turn)
```

Figure 7–15

All the spaces (marked with 2) have been identified. The squares that contain the value 0 are holes.

2	2	2	1	1	2	2	2
2	2	2	1	1	2	2	2
2	2	1	1	1	1	2	2
1	1	1	0	0	1	1	1
1	1	1	0	0	1	1	1
2	2	1	1	1	1	2	2
2	2	2	1	1	2	2	2
2	2	2	1	1	2	2	2

The code for this method follows:

```
// This method in the Crystal class returns true if the crystal
// contains a hole.
public static boolean isHoley() {
  ArrayList spacesArray = new ArrayList();

  // check for spaces along the four edges of the grid
  // and mark each space as "SPACE"
  for (int row = 0; row <= width; row++)
    for (int column = 0; column <= width; column++)
      if (row == 0 || row == width || column == 0 || column == width) {
        if (grid[row][column] != turn) {
          grid[row][column] = SPACE;
          spacesArray.add(new Point(row, column));
        }
      }

  // find all spaces adjacent to the spaces found above
  while (!spacesArray.isEmpty()) {
    Point neighbor;
    Point p = (Point) spacesArray.remove(0);

    // get the row and column number of Point p
    int row = (int) p.getX();
    int column = (int) p.getY();

    // add spaces to the north, south, east and west of p to spacesArray
    for (Direction dir : Direction.values())
      if ( (neighbor = dir.index(row, column)) != null)
        addSpace((int) neighbor.getX(), (int) neighbor.getY(),
spacesArray);
  }

    // any cell that is not an atom or not marked as SPACE is a hole
    for (int row = 0; row <= width; row++)
      for (int column = 0; column <= width; column++)
        if (grid[row][column] != turn && grid[row][column] != SPACE)
          return true; // found a hole

  return false; // no holes found
}

// mark cell at (row, column) as SPACE if it is not an atom
// or already marked as SPACE, and add it to spacesArray
```

```
public static void addSpace(int row, int column, ArrayList spacesArray) {
  if (grid[row][column] != turn && grid[row][column] != SPACE) {
    grid[row][column] = SPACE;
    spacesArray.add(new Point(row, column));
  }
}
```

The enhanced for and if statements are used to iterate over the objects in the Direction enum to find the north, south, east, and west nonnull neighbors of the square with the given row and column numbers:

```
for (Direction dir : Direction.values())
  if ( (neighbor = dir.index(row, column)) != null)
```

The addSpace method adds each neighbor found to spacesArray if it is not an atom and not already marked as a space (to prevent an infinite loop).

7.10.2   The Crystals Game: Finding a Perfect Crystal

The isPerfect method in the Crystal class determines whether the given crystal is perfect. The crystal is stored in the two-dimensional array crystal-Grid and has width w and height h. Besides calling the isSymmetrical and isHoley methods written earlier in this chapter, the isPerfect method also checks that the crystal's height is equal to its width and that it has four or more atoms. The remaining code for the Crystal class is shown here:

```
package arraysandstrings;

import java.util.*;
import java.awt.*;

public class Crystal {
  private static int[][] grid;
  private static int width, height;
  private static int turn;
  private static int numberOfAtoms;
  public static final int SPACE = 4;

  // checks if crystal is perfect
  public static boolean isPerfect(int[][] crystalGrid, int w, int h,
  int player) {
    grid = crystalGrid;
    width = w;
    height = h;
    turn = player;

    // check if crystal is square; otherwise, it cannot be perfect
```

```
    if (width != height) {
      return false; // not a perfect crystal
    }

    // check that number of atoms is 4 or greater
    if (getNumberOfAtoms() < 4) {
      return false;
    }

    // check if symmetrical
    if (!isSymmetrical()) {
      return false;
    }

    // check for holes
    if (isHoley()) {
      return false;
    }

    // perfect crystal
    return true;
  }

// method returns the number of atoms in the crystal
  public static int getNumberOfAtoms() {
    numberOfAtoms = 0;
    for (int row = 0; row <= width; row++)
      for (int column = 0; column <= width; column++)
        if (grid[row][column] == turn)
          numberOfAtoms++;

    return numberOfAtoms;
  }
// insert the other methods isSymmetrical, isHoley, and addSpace here
}
```

The rest of the code in this game is in the Crystals class, which is described in Section 7.16, *The Crystals Game Revisited.* The methods in this class create a GUI, find each player's crystals, and compute the scores.

7.11 Strings

Previously, we defined a string literal to be a set of characters on a single line enclosed within double quotes. A string is an instance of the String class defined in the java.lang package. There are two ways to create a string:

using a string literal and using a constructor. This statement creates a string called s1 by using a string literal:

```
String s1 = "This is a string literal";
```

Another way to create a string is by using a constructor. Figure 7–16 shows two constructors in class String.

This constructor is used to create the string s2:

```
String s2 = new String("This is another string");
```

However, it is preferable that you create a string using the first approach (that is, a string literal), instead of a constructor. To see why, consider this next example. In it, s1 and s2 are created using a string literal, and s3 is created using a String constructor:

```
String s1 = "A string";
String s2 = "A string";
String s3 = new String("A string");
```

The following print statements show that the reference variables s1 and s2 are equal, whereas s1 and s3 are different:

```
System.out.println(s1 == s2);     // displays true
System.out.println(s1 == s3);     // displays false
```

The reference variables s1 and s2 are assigned to the same object in memory when the string literals are the same. Therefore, the condition s1 == s2 is true. On the other hand, when the constructor is used, a different object is created. Thus, s3 is assigned to a different object from s1 and s2 even though the string literal is the same. This results in the condition s1 == s3 being false. Using string literals to create strings conserves memory when the literals are identical, and is therefore preferred over using constructors. Note that it works this way only with strings and not other objects.

A string can also be created from a character array. This creates the string "July" using the elements of charArray:

```
char[] charArray = {'J', 'u', 'l', 'y'};
String s4 = new String(charArray);
```

Figure 7–16

Two constructors in class String.

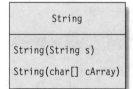

String
String(String s)
String(char[] cArray)

Constructor creates a new string that is a copy of string s.

Constructor creates a string using the array cArray that contains elements of type char.

An important point to remember is that an object of the String class cannot be changed after it has been created. For example, let us modify s2 as shown here:

```
s2 = s2 + " that has been modified";
```

s1 and s2 referenced the same object previously, so let us check whether s1 has changed:

```
System.out.println(s1);     // prints out "A string"
```

The reference variable s1 is still assigned to the same object as it was before s2 was modified. However, s2 is now assigned to a new object, as shown by the output of this statement:

```
System.out.println(s2); // prints out "A string that has been modified"
```

Therefore, anytime you modify an existing string—whether by using the concatenation operator or methods in the String class—Java creates a new string, leaving the original string unchanged in memory. If the original string is not used anywhere in the program, it will be removed automatically by the garbage collector.

7.12   Methods in the String Class

The String class contains methods to retrieve information about a string, search for a substring, and modify strings, such as by concatenating two strings or changing case. Some of these methods are shown in Figure 7–17 and described in detail next.

7.12.1   Length of a String

The length *method* is used to determine the length of a string. Note that this is different from the length *field* used to determine the length of an array. For example, the length of the string city can be printed out as follows:

```
String city = "New York";
System.out.println(city.length());
```

This prints out the value 8, because the single blank space between the two words is counted as one character.

Figure 7–17

Some methods in the String class.

String	
`int length()`	Returns the number of characters in this string.
`boolean equals(Object s)`	Returns `true` if this string is identical to the string object s passed in as an argument; otherwise, returns `false`.
`char charAt(int i)`	Returns the character at index i in this string.
`int indexOf(int ch)`	Returns the index at which character ch first occurs in this string.
`int indexOf(int ch, int startIndex)`	Searches this string from index `startIndex` and returns the index at which character ch first occurs.
`int lastIndexOf(int ch)`	Returns the index at which character ch first occurs when the string is searched backward.
`int lastIndexOf(int ch, int startIndex)`	Returns the index at which character ch first occurs when the string is searched backward starting from `startIndex`.
`int indexOf(String s)`	Returns the index at which substring s first occurs within this string.

7.12.2   Comparing Strings

Use the `equals` method to determine whether two strings are identical. The equals sign should not be used to compare strings. Consider this example:

```
String str1 = new String("How now brown cow?");
String str2 = new String("How now brown cow?");
```

The string literals are identical; thus the `equals` method returns `true`:

```
str1.equals(str2);    // returns true
```

However, this condition that tests for equality returns `false`:

```
str1 == str2          // condition is false
```

In this case, the values of the reference variables are compared, and because they refer to different objects in memory, the condition is false.

Note that the `equals` method will return `false` if the argument passed to it is not of type `String`.

7.12.3   Methods That Use/Retrieve an Index

Suppose that you want to find out which character occurs at a particular index in a string. The `charAt` method can be used as follows:

```
String city = "New York";
char ch = city.charAt(2); // ch is assigned the value "w"
```

This assigns w to ch because it is at index 2 in the string "New York."

The indexOf and lastIndexOf methods determine the index of the specified character in a string by searching the string forward and backward, respectively. If a character occurs multiple times, only the index of the first occurrence is returned. If the character cannot be found, the methods return −1. The following examples show how to use these methods:

```
String ocean = "Atlantic Ocean";
int index1 = ocean.indexOf('a');        // index1 = 3
int index2 = ocean.lastIndexOf('a');    // index2 = 12
int index3 = ocean.indexOf('a', 4);     // index3 = 12
int index4 = ocean.lastIndexOf('a', 0); // index 4 = -1
```

Overloaded versions of the indexOf and lastIndexOf methods whose first parameter is of type String are also provided in this class. A group of consecutive characters within a string is called a **substring**. The indexOf(String) method finds the index of a given substring. This method is similar to those described earlier, except that a substring s is specified as an argument instead of a single character ch. For example, the substring "re" occurs at indices 0 and 8 in "repertoire":

```
String r = "repertoire";
System.out.println(r.indexOf("re"));
```

This prints out the index 0, which is the first occurrence of the specified substring.

Example 5

Suppose that you are writing the code for a Hangman game in Java. The objective of the game is for the player to guess all of the letters of a hidden word. A letter might occur multiple times in a word. Write a method to determine all the indices of the specified letter in the hidden word.

Solution: Assume that the hidden word is "anagram," and the player has specified the letter "a." The method should display the indices 0, 2, and 5. We use the indexOf method in our solution:

```
public void indexesOf(int c, String hiddenWord) {
  int index = 0;
  while ((index != -1)) {
    index = hiddenWord.indexOf(c, index);
    if (index != -1) {
```

```
      System.out.println(index);
      index++;
    }
  }
}
```

The first call to indexOf returns 0, which is the index of the first occurrence of a in anagram. Then index is incremented by 1 in the if block, and the next call to indexOf searches anagram starting from index 1, which returns 2. Subsequent calls to indexOf return 5 and −1. As an exercise, trace the indexesOf method for different arguments and verify that its output is correct. ∎

7.12.4 Methods to Retrieve a Substring or Its Index

Earlier in this chapter, we discussed the indexOf(String) method that retrieves the index at which a substring occurs. Figure 7–18 shows some other methods for working with substrings.

The startsWith and endsWith methods determine whether a string contains the specified prefix and suffix, respectively. These examples show how you can use these methods:

```
String city = "San Francisco";
city.startsWith("San F");            // returns true
city.startsWith("Francisco");        // returns false
city.endsWith("sco");                // returns true
city.endsWith("esco");               // returns false
city.startsWith("San Francisco");    // returns true
city.endsWith("San Francisco");      // returns true
```

Figure 7–18

Methods in class String that retrieve a substring or its index.

String	
boolean startsWith(String s)	Returns true if this string *starts* with the specified substring s; otherwise, it returns false.
boolean endsWith(String s)	Returns true if this string *ends* with the specified substring s; otherwise, it returns false.
String substring(int startIndex)	Returns a substring that contains all the characters from index startIndex to the end of this string.
String substring(int startIndex, int endIndex)	Returns a substring that contains all the characters from index startIndex to index endIndex − 1 of this string.

You can extract a set of consecutive characters from a string using these methods:

```
String word = "meteorological";
word.substring(7);          // returns "logical"
word.substring(0, 6);       // returns "meteor"
word.substring(5, 0);       // error
```

The last statement results in a run-time error, because startIndex should not be greater than endIndex.

The methods we discuss in the remainder of this section create a new string using an existing string, and are shown in Figure 7–19. It is important to note that the original string is left unchanged.

7.12.5   Concatenating Strings

In addition to the "+" operator, strings can also be combined using the concat method:

```
String s1 = "Par";
String s2 = s1.concat("is");
System.out.println(s2);     // prints out "Paris"
```

The preceding statements create and print out the string "Paris". The original string s1 is unchanged:

```
System.out.println(s1);     // prints out "Par"
```

String	
String concat(String s)	Returns the new string created by appending the string s to the end of this string. A string is not created if the argument string s is empty.
String replace(char old, char new)	Returns a new string in which all occurrences of the character old are replaced by the character new.
String trim()	Returns a new string created by removing all the spaces at the beginning and end of this string.
String toLowerCase()	Returns a new string in which all the characters are lowercase.
String toUpperCase()	Returns a new string in which all the characters are uppercase.

Figure 7–19
String methods that create a new modified string from an existing string.

Another example is shown here:

```
String s3 = " is the capital of France.";
String s4 = s2.concat(s3);
System.out.println(s4);
```

The last statement prints out the phrase "Paris is the capital of France."

7.12.6   Replacing/Removing Characters

The `replace` and `trim` methods substitute and remove particular characters, respectively, from the string. Consider this example:

```
String word1 = "banyan".replace('a', 'i');
String word2 = word1.replace('b', 'p');
```

Now, word1 references the new string "binyin," and word2 references "pinyin."

This shows how the `trim` method can be used:

```
String pie = " apple pie  ".trim();
```

The spaces at the beginning and the end are removed, which creates the new string "apple pie."

7.12.7   Converting to Uppercase/Lowercase

The `toLowerCase` and `toUpperCase` methods change the case of a given string. For example:

```
"frieNd".toLowerCase();    // returns the string "friend"
"frieNd".toUpperCase();    // returns the string "FRIEND"
```

7.13   The StringBuilder Class

The methods in the `String` class do not modify the original string, but instead create a new string with the desired changes. This approach can create many temporary strings that take up space in the computer's memory before the final string is obtained. An alternative is to use the `StringBuilder` class, which creates string objects that can be modified. This class resides in the `java.lang` package, along with `String`, `Math`, and other classes. Some constructors and methods in this class are shown in Figure 7–20. The `insert` and `append` methods are overloaded for arguments of type `int`, `boolean`, `float`, `double`, `String`, and `Object`.

Here is an example:

```
StringBuilder sb = new StringBuilder("warts");
sb.reverse();                    // sb contains "straw"
```

Figure 7–20
A partial list of the constructors and methods in
class StringBuilder.

StringBuilder	
StringBuilder()	Constructor creates an empty object that can hold up to 16 characters initially.
StringBuilder(String str)	Constructor creates an object initialized with the contents of str and having space for 16 more characters initially.
String toString()	Converts this StringBuilder object to a string.
int length()	Returns the number of characters in this object.
char charAt(int i)	Returns the character at index i in this object.
StringBuilder delete(int start, int end)	Removes the characters from index start to index end–1 in this object.
StringBuilder append(char ch)	Adds the character ch to the end of this object.
StringBuilder insert(int index, char ch)	Inserts the character ch at the specified index of this object.
StringBuilder reverse()	Reverses the sequence of characters.
int indexOf(String str)	Returns the index of the first occurrence of the string str.

```
sb.length();            // returns 5
sb.charAt(3);           // returns 'a'
sb.insert(0, 'l');      // sb contains "lstraw"
sb.insert(1, 'a');      // sb contains "lastraw"
sb.insert(2, 's');      // sb contains "lasstraw"
sb.insert(3, 't');      // sb contains "laststraw"
sb.insert(4, ' ');      // sb contains "last straw"
sb.indexOf("raw");      // returns 7
sb.delete(1, 8);        // sb contains "law"
```

Example 6

Write a method called extractKeywords that takes a String argument and prints out all the individual words in this string. The words can be separated by any number of spaces, tabs, commas, or semicolons. We will use this method to extract keywords that the user uses to tag photographs in the *PhotoFinder* application, which is developed in Chapter 12.

```
package arraysandstrings;

public class StringBuilderDemo {
  public void extractKeywords(String s) {
```

```
        int index = 0;
        StringBuilder sb = new StringBuilder();

        while (index != s.length()) {
          // skip leading blanks, tabs, semicolons and commas, if any
          char ch = s.charAt(index);
          while (ch == ' ' || ch == '\t' || ch == ',' || ch == ';') {
            if (++index == s.length())
             break;
            // read the next character in String s
            ch = s.charAt(index);
          }

          // read all characters in a word until a blank, comma, tab
          // or semicolon is encountered
          while (ch != ' ' && ch != '\t' && ch != ',' && ch != ';') {
            // add the character ch to sb
            sb.append(ch);
            if (++index == s.length())
             break;
            // read the next character in String s
            ch = s.charAt(index);
          }
          // print out the word in sb
          System.out.println(sb);

          // erase contents of sb to store the next word in s
          sb.delete(0, sb.length());
        }
      }

    public static void main(String[] args) {
      StringBuilderDemo sd = new StringBuilderDemo();
      sd.extractKeywords(" yellow, boat; blue         sky, mountain;");
    }
  }
```

The program output is:

```
yellow
boat
blue
sky
mountain
```

The outer `while` loop in the `extractKeywords` method executes until all the words in the argument `s` have been found. The first inner `while` loop skips all of the blanks, tabs, semicolons, and commas tht precede a word in `s`. The second inner `while` loop finds the next word in `s` and stores it in the `String-Builder` instance `sb`. After this word in `sb` is displayed, the contents of `sb` are erased and the process repeated to find the next word in `s`.

This statement from the proceding program prints out the string stored in the `StringBuilder` object `sb`:

```
System.out.println(sb);
```

The `toString` method of the `StringBuilder` object `sb` is called implicitly inside the `println` method, which prints out the string stored in this object. ∎

7.14   Primitive Wrapper Classes

As you already know, a `char` is a primitive type. Java has a class called `Character` to represent a primitive type as an object. The reason for doing so is that classes in some packages (such as the `java.util.Collection` classes that we discuss later) require objects to be passed in as arguments to their methods. `Character` is also called a "wrapper class" because it encloses a `char` primitive type. There are eight wrapper classes defined in the `java.lang` package, one for each of the primitives. They are shown in Table 7–1.

TABLE 7–1   Wrapper Classes

Primitive Type	Wrapper Class
char	Character
int	Integer
short	Short
long	Long
byte	Byte
float	Float
double	Double
boolean	Boolean

The following statements show how to use these classes:

```
Character charA = new Character('A');
Integer int10 = new Integer(10);     // int10 is of type Integer
double d1 = 3.8;
Double dvalue = new Double(d1);     // dvalue is of type Double
```

With the exception of Character and Boolean, all of these classes are sub-classes of Number.

The compiler can automatically put the primitive inside its wrapper class, in a process called **boxing**.

```
Character ch;
Integer val1, val2;
ch = 'b';          // boxing
val1 = 20;         // boxing
val2 = 30;         // boxing
```

Similarly, the compiler can extract the primitive from its wrapper—a process known as **unboxing**. In the statement that follows, the compiler extracts the integer values of val1 and val2 and multiplies them together:

```
int mult = val1 * val2;      // unboxing
```

Figure 7–21 shows some methods in the Integer class. These methods are defined similarly in the other wrapper classes.

These classes contain a static method called toString that converts a primitive type to a string. For example, the toString method in Integer takes an

Figure 7–21

Some methods in the Integer class.

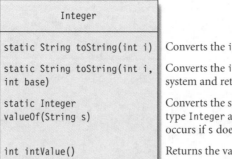

Integer	
static String toString(int i)	Converts the int value to a string and returns it.
static String toString(int i, int base)	Converts the int i to a value in the specified base system and returns it as a string.
static Integer valueOf(String s)	Converts the string s that holds an integer value into type Integer and returns it. A run-time exception occurs if s does not contain a value of type int.
int intValue()	Returns the value in this Integer as an int.

integer argument and returns this number as a string. These examples show how to use this method:

```
Integer.toString(10);      // returns a string representation of 10
Double.toString(3.5);      // returns 3.5 as a string
Float.toString(1.5f);      // returns 1.5 as a string
```

One reason it might be necessary to convert the numeric values into strings is to display them on a Graphical User Interface (GUI). GUI components such as text fields can input and display only strings. For example, the Integer.toString method is used in the Crystals class to display the player scores on the GUI.

The toString method takes a number in the decimal (or base-10) system as an argument. This method has an overloaded version in the Integer and Long classes to return a value in a different base, such as base-2 (also called binary), base-4, base-16, or any other base. These two statements return the value of 10 in base-2 and base-8 systems:

```
String str1 = Integer.toString(10, 2);    // str1 = "1010"
String str2 = Integer.toString(10, 8);    // str2 = "12"
```

Whereas the toString method converts a numeric value to a string, the method valueOf converts a string into a wrapper class object:

```
float valf = 10.5f;
String strf = Float.toString(valf);  // strf = "10.5f"
Float objf = Float.valueOf(strf);    // objf object holds 10.5
System.out.println(objf);            // prints out 10.5
```

strf contains a floating-point value; thus trying to convert it to an Integer would cause a run-time error:

```
Integer obji = Integer.valueOf(strf); // error
```

7.14.1 The BigDecimal and BigInteger Classes

Besides the primitive wrapper classes mentioned previously, Number has two other subclasses in the java.math package: BigDecimal and BigInteger. These two classes are used when the numbers are larger than can be represented in a double or a long, and a high precision of the output result is desired. You saw how to use BigDecimal in the business application that we developed in Chapter 6. The BigInteger class is similar to BigDecimal, except that it can

Figure 7–22

Some methods in the BigInteger class.

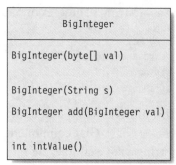

Figure 7–22

Some methods in the BigInteger class.

BigInteger	
BigInteger(byte[] val)	Constructor converts binary values stored in an array into a BigInteger.
BigInteger(String s)	Constructor converts the string s into a BigInteger.
BigInteger add(BigInteger val)	Adds this BigInteger to the argument val and returns the result.
int intValue()	Converts this BigInteger to an int and returns it.

store an integer (instead of a decimal) number of any size. Figure 7–22 shows some constructors and methods in this class.

For example, the following number is larger than can be held in a variable of type long, which results in a compilation error:

```
long n1 = 92233720368547758081L;    // error
```

However, a BigInteger can be used to store this value by passing it as a string argument to its constructor:

```
BigInteger bigInt = new BigInteger("92233720368547758081"); // okay
```

There are several methods in this class to perform arithmetic operations such as add, subtract, multiply, and divide. Here is an example of add:

```
BigInteger bigInt1 = new BigInteger("5000");
BigInteger result1 = bigInt.add(bigInt1); // result1 = 92233720368547763081
```

Like the wrapper classes, BigInteger has an intValue method that returns the value stored in the BigInteger as an int. This is a narrowing conversion, in which information will be lost if the BigInteger holds a numeric value that is larger than can be stored in an int. The following statement converts the BigInteger to an int correctly because bigInt1 stores 5000:

```
int num3 = bigInt1.intValue();
```

7.15 Command-Line Arguments

The main method is declared as shown here:

```
public static void main(String[] args) {
  // your program goes here
}
```

This method is declared as void because it does not return a value. When you run the program, you can supply data values on the command line that are known as **command-line** arguments and are read into the program during execution. These arguments are stored in the String array (called args) of the main method. Any number of command-line arguments can be given to a program. The number of arguments can be obtained using the length field of the array. For example, the following command shows how to run a program called DrawImage that takes three command-line arguments—the name of the file (space.jpg) and the *x*- and *y*-coordinates of its position in the window.

```
C:> java –classpath bin DrawImage space.jpg 5 5
```

The next example shows how these arguments can be used within the program.

Example 7

We will modify the program DisplayPicture from Chapter 3 to display any picture whose name is passed in using command-line arguments:

```java
package arraysandstrings;
import java.awt.image.*;
import com.programwithjava.basic.DrawingKit;

public class DisplayPicture {
  public static void main(String[] args) {
    if (args.length < 3) {
      System.out.println("Error: Too few arguments");
      System.out.println("Enter filename followed by x and y
coordinates");
      System.exit(1);
    }

    DrawingKit dk = new DrawingKit(1000, 1000);

    // the filename is stored in args[0]
    BufferedImage pict = dk.loadPicture(args[0]);

    // draw pict on the screen at the coordinates in args[1] and args[2]
    dk.drawPicture(pict,Integer.valueOf(args[1]),Integer.valueOf(args[2]));
  }
}
```

The program is compiled as described previously:

```
C:\JavaBook> javac -d bin src\com\programwithjava\basic\DrawingKit.java
src\arraysandstrings\DisplayPicture.java
```

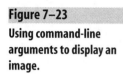

Figure 7–23

Using command-line arguments to display an image.

space.jpg © Adrian Niederhäuser, 123RF.com

The command-line arguments are provided when the program is run, and they must be specified after the class name:

```
C:\JavaBook> java -classpath bin arraysandstrings.DisplayPicture
image/space.jpg 100 100
```

The first command-line argument is image/space.jpg and it is stored in args[0]. The next two command-line arguments are the numeric values 100 and 100, and they are stored in args[1] and args[2]. Note how the valueOf method in the Integer class is used to convert the String argument arg[1] into an int.

The output is shown in Figure 7–23. Run the program with different command-line arguments each time, and observe how the output changes.   ■

7.16   The Crystals Game Revisited

The Crystals game contains two classes: Crystal and Crystals. We have developed the Crystal class throughout this chapter to test for a perfect crystal. The Crystals class is described briefly in this section. Copy the code for this class from the JavaBook\src\arraysandstrings directory on the CD-ROM into the arraysandstrings directory on your computer, and run the game.

The Crystals class contains the createGUIAndPlay method, which creates a GUI and updates the score after each player's move. (You can revisit this

method after reading Chapter 9, *GUI Programming*.) The score is calculated
by counting the total number of atoms in each player's perfect crystals. The
findCrystal method finds a player's crystal that contains the atom at a given
row r and column c and puts it in crystalGrid. This is done by "growing" the
crystal by finding all neighboring atoms that are attached to this atom at
location (r, c), and continuing this procedure for each neighbor until all of
the atoms in the crystal are found. This method is similar to how the spaces
were grown in the method to find a hole in the crystal. The shadowGrid field
keeps track of which crystals have already been found for this player. The
isPerfect method of class Crystal is used to determine whether a crystal is
perfect, and the player's score is incremented if it is found to be perfect.

To compile the source files, use:

```
C:\JavaBook> javac -d bin src\arraysandstrings\Crystals.java
src\arraysandstrings\Crystal.java src\arraysandstrings\Direction.java
```

The program is then run as follows:

```
C:\JavaBook> java -classpath bin arraysandstrings.Crystals
```

Figure 7–24 shows the GUI and a game in progress.

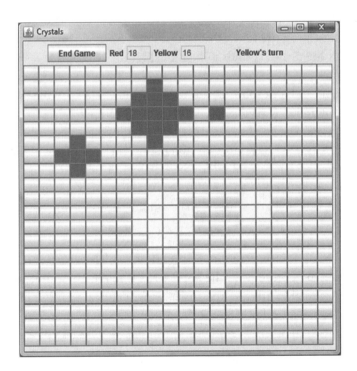

Figure 7–24
The Crystals GUI.

7.17   Computers in Science: Human DNA

In 2003, the Human Genome Project, a global initiative to determine the structure of the human DNA, was completed. As a result, human DNA has been mapped using an alphabet of four letters (A, C, G, and T), and it takes over 3 billion letters to describe in its entirety! Supercomputers played an important role in helping to determine this sequence by combining smaller sequences of DNA fragments into a single sequence. Computers will continue to play a vital role in this field in the future as scientists study and analyze this tremendous amount of information to better understand the intricate cellular machinery within our bodies that makes us what we are. In this section, we will discuss the role DNA plays to generate **proteins**, and will write a program to determine proteins generated for a given DNA sequence.

Different types of proteins are responsible for different functions in our body, such as for muscular motion, providing support to tissues, and fighting germs. The process to generate proteins is complex; as a result, we will provide only a very simplified explanation here and refer the reader to the references at the end of the chapter for more details.

Human DNA forms the building block for each cell in the human body. In 1953, J. D. Watson and F. H. C. Crick published their seminal paper proposing a structure for DNA in the journal *Nature*. They described DNA as consisting of *two* strands joined together in the shape of a spiral staircase. The rungs of this staircase are formed by combining oxygen, nitrogen, hydrogen, and phosphorus atoms into four types of **bases**: **A** (adenine), **T** (thymine), **C** (cytosine), and **G** (guanine). Each DNA strand is described by combinations of these bases, and 3 billion bases describe each strand completely. DNA is double-stranded; thus *each* cell in the human body contains *6 billion* bases (or 3 billion base pairs, because each base pair contains two bases bonded together to form one rung of the staircase). For example, a portion of a DNA strand may contain the following bases:

   T A C G A T A A G A A A T T C C C A A T T

DNA is responsible for creating **RNA**, which in turn is responsible for synthesizing proteins in the body. RNA is made up of four bases: **A**, **C**, **G**, and **U** (uracil), with the first three being identical to those in DNA. Unlike the double-stranded DNA, RNA contains a single strand. A protein is created in two steps: *transcription* and *translation*. These steps are described next.

TABLE 7–2 RNA Base Synthesized from a Given DNA Base	
DNA Base	**RNA Base**
A	U
C	G
G	C
T	A

Transcription   This process creates RNA from DNA. First, two DNA strands separate partially from each other, exposing their bases. Then, the RNA strand is created by pairing the RNA bases with exposed bases of one of the two DNA strands, as shown in Table 7–2. For example, if the DNA base is A, the corresponding RNA base will be U.

An example will help to clarify the process: Suppose that the DNA strand being used to create the RNA has the same sequence as shown previously:

(DNA sequence) **T A C G A T A A G A A A T T C C C A A T T**

Using Table 7–2, the first and second bases T and A in this DNA sequence will create the RNA bases A and U, respectively. The other RNA bases can be derived similarly, and so the RNA sequence that is synthesized from this DNA sequence is:

(RNA sequence) **A U G C U A U U C U U U A A G G G U U A A**

After the transcription is completed, the next step is to generate the proteins using translation.

Translation   In this step, proteins are generated from the RNA sequence. A **codon** is a set of three RNA bases that code a particular type of amino acid. Long chains comprising thousands of amino acids make up a specific protein. For example, the codon UUU codes the amino acid phenylalanine. Distinct sets of codons can code the same amino acid. Therefore, the codons UUU and UUC both code the amino acid phenylalanine. There are only 20 different amino acids, but by combining these in different orders, thousands of different types of proteins can be created. Table 7–3 shows the codons and the corresponding amino acids. In the table, the symbol * represents any one of these four RNA bases: U, G, C, or A. For example, the codon UC* is

TABLE 7–3   A Table of Codons, and the Amino Acids Coded by Each Codon (A * represents any one of the four RNA bases: A, C, U, or G)

Codons	Amino Acid	Codons	Amino Acid
UUU, UUC	Phenylalanine	AUU, AUC, AUA	Isoleucine
UC*, AGU, AGC	Serine	AUG	**(Start)** Methionine
UAU, UAC	Tyrosine	AC*	Threonine
UGU, UGC	Cysteine	AAU, AAC	Asparagine
UGG	Tryptophan	AAA, AAG	Lysine
UAA, UAG, UGA	**Stop**	GU*	Valine
CU*, UUA, UUG	Leucine	GC*	Alanine
CC*	Proline	GAU, GAC	Aspartate
CAU, CAC	Histidine	GAA, GAG	Glutamate
CAA, CAG	Glutamine	GG*	Glyscine
CG*, AGA, AGG	Arginine		

merely an abbreviation for the four codons UCU, UCG, UCC, and UCA. Table 7–3 also shows that UC* codes the amino acid serine—this means that all four codons (UCU, UCG, UCC, and UCA) code for serine. Some codons have special meanings. For instance, the codon AUG signals the start of the protein, and the codons UAA, UAG, and UGA signal the completion of the protein synthesis. We will use the previous RNA sequence:

(RNA sequence) **A U G C U A U U C U U U A A G G G U U A A**

The first codon in this RNA sequence is the start codon AUG. Examining Table 7–3 tells us that it codes the amino acid methionine. The next codon in this sequence is CUA, which codes the amino acid leucine. Using this procedure, we can determine that the protein is composed of the following amino acids:

(protein) **methionine - leucine - phenylalanine - phenylalanine - lysine - glyscine**

The last codon in the sequence is UAA, which is a stop codon that signals the completion of the protein synthesis.

Let us work out another example to illustrate the process. Suppose that the DNA strand is composed of the following bases:

(DNA strand) **TTTACTTTGTTGCAAGTACCATCGG**

Using Table 7–2, the RNA bases synthesized from this sequence are:

(RNA strand) **AAAUGAAACAACGUUCAUGGUAGCC**

The start codon AUG occurs at index 2 in the RNA strand, and so the first two letters (AA) are skipped. Table 7–3 is used to determine the amino acid that is coded by each codon. The protein created has these amino acids:

(protein) **methionine – lysine – glutamine – arginine – serine – tryptophan**

The class ProteinSynthesisDemo displays the protein synthesized for a given DNA sequence. It contains a two-dimensional static array named codon-ToAminoAcid. This array stores the codons and the corresponding amino acids as shown in Table 7–3. A scanner reads in the input DNA sequence. The transcribe method determines the corresponding RNA sequence from this DNA sequence and stores it in the field rnaStrand. The translate method determines the amino acids that make up a protein and stores it in the field protein. The code for this class follows:

```
package arraysandstrings;
import java.util.*;

public class ProteinSynthesisDemo {
    Scanner scanner;
    String dnaStrand;        // DNA strand entered by the user
    StringBuilder rnaStrand; // corresponding RNA strand
    StringBuilder protein;   // amino acids in the protein

    static String[][] codonToAminoAcid = { {"GC", "alanine"}, {"UUU",
"phenylalanine"}, {"UUC", "phenylalanine"}, {"UUA", "leucine"}, {"UUG",
"leucine"}, {"CU", "leucine"}, {"CC", "proline"}, {"AC", "threonine"},
{"GG", "glycine"}, {"UC", "serine"}, {"UAU", "tyrosine"}, {"UAC",
"tyrosine"}, {"UAA", "stop"}, {"UAG", "stop"}, {"UGU", "cysteine"}, {"UGC",
"cysteine"}, {"UGA", "stop"}, {"UGG", "tryptophan"}, {"CAU", "histidine"},
{"CAC", "histidine"}, {"CAA", "glutamine"}, {"CAG", "glutamine"}, {"CG",
"arginine"}, {"AUU", "isoleucine"}, {"AUC", "isoleucine"}, {"AUA",
"isoleucine"}, {"AUG", "methionine"}, {"AAU", "asparagine"}, {"AAC",
"asparagine"}, {"AAA", "lysine"}, {"AAG", "lysine"}, {"AGU", "serine"},
{"AGC", "serine"}, {"AGA", "arginine"}, {"AGG", "arginine"}, {"GU",
"valine"}, {"GAU", "aspartate"}, {"GAC", "aspartate"}, {"GAA",
"glutamate"}, {"GAG", "glutamate"}
    };
```

```
ProteinSynthesisDemo () {
  scanner = new Scanner(System.in);
  rnaStrand = new StringBuilder();
  protein = new StringBuilder();
}
// add the methods getUserInput, transcribe, getAminoAcid, and
// translate here
}
```

Only the fields are shown in the preceding class definition; however, we will discuss the methods in more detail next. After you have completed reading the remainder of this section, add the following methods to this class, and compile and run the program.

The `getUserInput` method reads the bases in the DNA strand entered by the user:

```
// prompts the user to enter the bases in a DNA strand and reads it
public void getUserInput() {
System.out.print("Enter the bases (A, C, G, T) in a DNA strand: ");
  dnaStrand = scanner.next();
}
```

The `transcribe` method builds the corresponding RNA sequence from the DNA sequence by replacing all occurrences of 'A' with 'U', 'C' with 'G', 'G' with 'C', and 'T' with 'A'. The `charAt` method is used to retrieve a character in `dnaStrand` at the current `index`. The `append` method is used to build the new sequence in `rnaStrand`.

```
// builds the RNA from the DNA
public void transcribe() {
  int index = 0;
  char ch;

  // clear the previous contents of StringBuilder rnaStrand
  rnaStrand.delete(0, rnaStrand.length());

  while (index < dnaStrand.length()) {
    ch = dnaStrand.charAt(index);
      switch(ch) {
        case 'A' : rnaStrand.append('U');
                   break;
        case 'C' : rnaStrand.append('G');
                   break;
        case 'G' : rnaStrand.append('C');
                   break;
```

```
        case 'T' : rnaStrand.append('A');
                   break;
        default  : System.out.println("Invalid base. Only A, C, G and T
are allowed.");
                   System.exit(1);
                   break;
      }
    index++;
  }

  System.out.println("The corresponding RNA strand is:" +rnaStrand);
  }
```

The getAminoAcid method searches through the codonToAminoAcid array to find the matching codon and returns the corresponding amino acid. For example, suppose that the codon GCC is given as an argument to this method. The startsWith method of String checks whether this codon is present and has a matching prefix in the array. The array element in row 0 and column 0 is "GC," thus this method returns the array element in row 0 and column 1, which is the amino acid alanine.

```
// returns the protein coded by the given codon
public String getAminoAcid(String codon) {
  for (int i = 0; i < codonToAminoAcid.length; i++) {
    if (codon.startsWith(codonToAminoAcid[i][0]))
      return codonToAminoAcid[i][1];
  }
  System.out.println("Error: Amino acid not found for codon" +codon);
  return null;
}
```

The translate method determines the structure of the protein that will be synthesized using the RNA sequence stored in rnaStrand. The method finds the first occurrence of the start codon AUG, and then finds all the remaining codons until a stop codon is encountered. It calls the getAminoAcid method to find the amino acid coded by each codon.

```
// finds all the amino acids that make up the protein
// starting from the start codon AUG to a stop codon.
public void translate() {
  int codonLength = 3; // a codon has 3 characters
  boolean stopCodonFound = false;

  // clear the previous contents of StringBuilder proteins
  protein.delete(0, protein.length());
```

```
// find the index where the starting codon "AUG" occurs
int index = rnaStrand.indexOf("AUG");
if (index != -1) {
  // get protein for this codon "AUG"
  protein.append(getAminoAcid("AUG"));
  protein.append(" ");
} else {
  System.out.println("Starting codon AUG not found");
  System.exit(1);
}

    // find the remaining codons until a stop codon is reached
  do {
      // get index of next codon
      index += codonLength;

      if (index + codonLength <= rnaStrand.length()) {
        // get next codon and determine if it is stop codon
        String codon = rnaStrand.substring(index, index + codonLength);
        stopCodonFound = ( codon.equals("UAA") || codon.equals("UAG") ||
codon.equals("UGA") );

          // get amino acid coded by this codon and add it to
          // StringBuilder protein
          if (!stopCodonFound) {
            protein.append(getAminoAcid(codon));
            protein.append(" ");
          }
      } else {
        System.out.println("Stop codon UAA, UAG or UGA not found");
        System.exit(1);
      }
  } while (!stopCodonFound);

  System.out.println("The protein is: " +protein);
 }
```

This main method is used to test the preceding class:

```
public static void main(String[] args) {
  ProteinSynthesisDemo demo = new ProteinSynthesisDemo();
  demo.getUserInput();
  demo.transcribe();
  demo.translate();
}
```

Add the preceding methods to the ProteinSynthesisDemo class, and then compile and run it. A sample output is shown here:

```
Enter the bases (A, C, G, T) in a DNA strand: TACTTTGTTGCAAGTACCATCCGG
The corresponding RNA strand is:AUGAAACAACGUUCAUGGUAGGCC
The protein is: methionine lysine glutamine arginine serine tryptophan
```

7.18 Summary

In this chapter, we discussed how to create and use arrays and strings. We also discussed how to create an enum and add constructors and methods to it. The Arrays class contains static methods to sort the contents of an array, determine whether two arrays are equal, and so forth. The ArrayList class is used to create arrays whose size changes dynamically as the program executes. The String class contains methods to get the length of a string and manipulate substrings, among others. However, the strings created using this class cannot be modified, and so we must use the StringBuilder class to create a string that can be modified. We developed the Crystals game throughout the chapter to underscore how many of these classes and methods can be used in a larger program.

In the next chapter, we introduce another important topic: interfaces and nested classes.

Exercises

1. Explain these terms:

   a. array elements

   b. array index

   c. multidimensional array

   d. enum

   e. array list

2. Find the compilation errors in each of these code segments:

   a. `int[100] a1;`

   b. `float b1 = new float[50];`

   c. `int [][] c1;`

   `c1 = new int[][30];`

   d. `float[] array1 = [ 10.5f, 3.5f, -5, -1 ];`

e. Assume that `ballArray` contains elements of type `Ball`:

```
for (int ball : ballArray)
    System.out.println(ball);
```

3. Create an array of type `String` and initialize it to the days of the week using a single statement.

4. Predict the output of this code segment:

```
double[] array1 = { 1.3, 2.5, 3.5, 4.5 };
double[] array2 = array1;
for (double element : array2)
    System.out.println(element);
```

5. What is the value in `sum` after the following statements are executed?

```
int[] data = { 1, 3, 5, 7, 9 };
int sum = 0;
for (int i = 0; i < data.length - 1 ; i++)
    sum += data[i] + data[i+1];
```

6. Write a program that prompts a user to enter 10 integers on the console. The program should read in the values from the console and store them in an array. Before the program exits, it should display the contents of the array on the console.

7. The *n*th triangular number, t_n, is the sum of the first *n* numbers:

    $$t_n = 1 + 2 + 3 + \dots + n$$

    A sequence of triangular numbers is 1, 3, 6, 10, 15, 21, 28, …

    a. Write a program to generate and display the first 10 triangular numbers.

    b. Write a method to generate the first *n* triangular numbers and return them in an array. Assume that the method is declared as shown here:

    ```
    public static int[] computeTriangularNumbers(int n);
    ```

    c. Write a program that prompts the user to enter the value of *n* and uses the given method to compute the first *n* triangular numbers. The program should display these triangular numbers.

8. Write a program that uses the `sort` method in the `Arrays` class to sort these values in the array `numberArray` in ascending order:

```
int [] numberArray = { -10, 20, 0, 5, -20, 50, -7, 19, 51, 2 };
```

9. Write a method to reverse the contents of an array passed in as an argument. The method is declared as shown here:

```
public void reverse(double[] array);
```

10. Find the compilation errors in this enum:

```
public enum EnumWithErrors {
    SOCCERBALL (27.0f),
    TENNISBALL (2.25f),
    PINGPONGBALL (0.75f)

    public float radius;  // radius in inches

    public EnumWithErrors(float r) {
        radius = r;
    }

    public float getRadius() {
    return radius;
    }
}
```

11. Create an enum called CarBodyStyle that contains these instances: COUPE, CONVERTIBLE, HATCHBACK, and LIMOUSINE. Write a class called Car that contains a field of type CarBodyStyle. Add a constructor to this class and create four instances of this class in which each has a different body style.

12. Create an enum called Taste containing these instances: SWEET, BITTER, SOUR, and SALTY.

    a. Write a program to show how you can use the static method values.

    b. Write a program to display the *ordinal* of each enum object.

    c. Add a method called getStrength to this enum. Implement this method so that it takes an integer argument called *rating* in the range 1 to 10 and returns one of the following strings:

       "mildly" if rating is in the range 1–4

       "moderately" if rating is in the range 5–7

       "strongly" if rating is in the range 8–10

    d. Write a class called Food that contains a field of type Taste and another of type int that is the rating. Add accessor and mutator methods to this class. Create instances of Food with different tastes and ratings. Show how you can use the name method in class Enum to print out the taste of each food as a string. In addition, print out each food's rating using the getStrength method of Taste.

A sample output is shown here:

```
ice cream is strongly SWEET
pretzel is moderately SALTY
```

13. The Direction enum described in this chapter provides the coordinates of a point to the north, south, east, and west of a given point (r, c). Modify this enum so that the coordinates of points to the northeast, northwest, southeast, and southwest of point (r, c) can also be obtained.

14. Find the errors, if any, in these statements:

```
String s1 = "alpha";
String s2 = new String(s1);
String[] s3 = new String[10]();
String[] s4 = new String()[20];
String[] s5 = new String[20];
String s6 = "orange" + "ade";
```

15. This problem uses the methods in the String class. The strings s, s1, and s2 are declared as shown here:

```
String s = "alpha";
String s1 = s.concat("betic");
String s2 = s1.substring(4);
```

What is the output of each of these statements?

```
System.out.println(s);
System.out.println(s2);
System.out.println(s1.startsWith("alp"));
System.out.println(s1.endsWith("pha"));
System.out.println(s1.equals(s2));
System.out.println(s1.toUpperCase());
```

16. Write a method to determine whether a particular word is in the dictionary. The method is declared as follows:

```
boolean isValidWord(String word, String[] dictionary);
```

Assume that `dictionary` is a string array that contains all the words in the dictionary. The method should search through the array and return `true` only if a match is found.

17. Write a method to determine the number of positions that two strings differ by. For example, "peace" and "piece" differ in two positions. The method is declared as follows:

```
int compare(String word1, String word2);
```

If the strings are identical, the method returns 0. It returns −1 if the two strings have different lengths.

18. Write a program that reads in words from the console and stores them in an array. Each word is entered on a new line on the console, and the last word is always "END." Assume that the number of words that can be input varies each time the program is run and is not known until the program starts execution. The program should display all of the words that have been entered and a count of the total number of words read by the program.

19. Assume that a two-dimensional array stores data representing a game of tic-tac-toe and a move has just been completed. The array has three rows and three columns. Write a method to determine whether there is a winner. A set of three noughts or crosses along any of the rows, columns or diagonals represents a win. Assume that a nought is stored in the array as a 1, a cross is stored as a 2, and an empty square is a 0.

20. Repeat the previous problem assuming that a nought is stored in the array using the character '0', a cross is stored using the character 'X', and an empty square is a blank.

21. Write a program to create a game called "Seven-Word Morph," in which the player must modify a word in seven steps. In each step, exactly one letter of the previous word is changed. The new word should be a valid word that can be found in a dictionary, and it should not repeat a word created in any of the previous steps. The player who successfully modifies the word in the seventh step wins the game. Only the starting word in the first step is provided. Assume that an array containing all the words in the dictionary has been provided. For example, the word "clink" is transformed to "plans," and "drink" is changed to "plant":

clink	drink
blink	brink
blank	blink
plank	blank
plane	plank
plant	plane
plans	plant

Other sequences with the same starting word are possible, but some of these may terminate before the seventh step.

22. Show how a wrapper class can be used to store each of the following literals:

    a. 100

    b. 10.5

    c. A

    Use the `toString` method in the wrapper class to return a string representation of each of the preceding values.

23. Modify the `DisplayPicture` class given in this chapter so that the window size can also be specified using command-line arguments.

24. Write a program to convert a given amino acid sequence into the corresponding DNA base sequence.

25. Write a program that reads a DNA base sequence entered by the user on the keyboard. The program should compute the frequency with which each codon appears in this sequence.

26. Modify the code in the Crystals game developed in this chapter so that the size of the grid can be provided using command-line arguments.

Image Manipulation Problems

27. Write a program to read the pixels in an image and store them in two-dimensional arrays. Each channel is stored in a separate array, and so three arrays are used to store the red, green, and blue channels. Display the contents of each array.

28. *Convolution* is an important operation in image processing that modifies a pixel in an image based on the values of neighboring pixels.

Using convolution, you can perform a variety of operations on an image, including blurring and sharpening it, detecting its edges, and embossing it for a 3D effect. Each pixel in the image is modified by adding its weighted value to the weighted values of the neighboring pixels. The weighted value of a pixel is obtained by multiplying each pixel with a floating-point number called a *weight*.

Figure 7–25 explains how convolution works. The same weight of 0.25 is used for all the pixels here. The pixel in the center then gets the new value 152, which is obtained by multiplying it and the neighboring pixels with this weight and adding them together:

$200 * 0.25 + 110 * 0.25 + 63 * 0.25 + 71 * 0.25 + 91 * 0.25 + 15 * 0.25 + 10 * 0.25 + 20 * 0.25 + 31 * 0.25 = 152.75.$

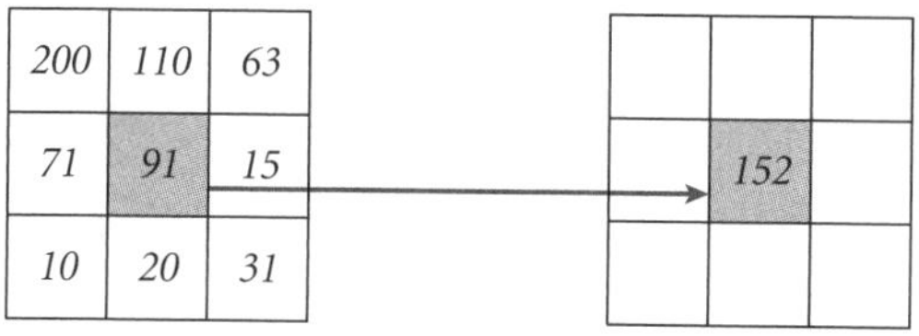

Figure 7–25

An example of a convolution. The new pixel value of 152 is obtained by multiplying this pixel and its eight neighbors with a weight of 0.25 and then adding them together.

In general, different weights are used for the neighboring pixels and are stored in a two-dimensional array called a **kernel**. For example, Figure 7–26 shows a kernel that stores the weights $w0, w1, w2, \ldots, w8$, each of which is a floating-point number.

Figure 7–26

A kernel is a two-dimensional matrix that stores weights.

The new pixel value is obtained by multiplying each pixel by its corresponding weight:

$200 * w0 + 110 * w1 + 63 * w2 + 71 * w3 + 91 * w4 + 15 * w5 + 10 * w6 + 20 * w7 + 31 * w8$

This procedure is repeated for *each* pixel in the image. Any values below 0 or above 255 are truncated. If the image has red, green, and blue channels, the convolution is performed separately for each channel. Note that the pixels along the edges have fewer than eight neighbors contributing to the new pixel value.

a. Write a method to perform the convolution of an image. Declare the method as shown here:

```
public BufferedImage convolve(int[][] kernel, BufferedImage
inputImage);
```

The method should process inputImage by applying the convolution operator stored in kernel and return the resulting image of type BufferedImage. Assume that kernel has size 3 × 3.

b. Write a program to test this method using different kernels. The kernels shown in Figures 7–27(a)–(c) are described in [5]:

Figure 7–27

(a) Sharpening kernel.
(b) Blurring kernel.
(c) Edge-detecting kernel.
(d) Embossing kernel.

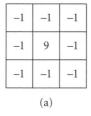

	(a)			(b)			(c)			(d)	
−1	−1	−1	$\frac{1}{9}$	$\frac{1}{9}$	$\frac{1}{9}$	−1	−1	−1	−2	−2	−2
−1	9	−1	$\frac{1}{9}$	$\frac{1}{9}$	$\frac{1}{9}$	−1	8	−1	−1	1	1
−1	−1	−1	$\frac{1}{9}$	$\frac{1}{9}$	$\frac{1}{9}$	−1	−1	−1	2	2	2

The sharpening kernel will make the picture appear sharper, whereas the blurring kernel will make it appear slightly blurred. The edge-detecting kernel highlights the edges of the picture. Another interesting effect is to make the picture appear embossed. A kernel that you can use for this effect is given in Figure 7–27(d).

Further Reading

You can find a lot of information about the Human Genome Project in [3]. This website also contains animations and videos on genetics and related topics. The Crystals game is described in [6].

References

1. "Java™ Platform, Standard Edition 6, API Specification". Web. <http://download.oracle.com/javase/6/docs/api/>.

2. "The Java™ Tutorials." Web. <http://download.oracle.com/javase/tutorial/>.

3. "Human Genome Project Information." *U.S. Department of Energy Genome Programs.* Web. <http://www.ornl.gov/sci/techresources/ Human_Genome/home.shtml>.

4. *BSCS Biology: An Ecological Approach.* Dubuque, IA: Kendall/Hunt, 2006. 207-214. Print.

5. Brinkmann, Ron. *The Art and Science of Digital Compositing: Techniques for Visual Effects, Animation and Motion Graphics, Second Edition.* Burlington, MA: Morgan Kaufmann/Elsevier, 2008. Print.

6. Wise, Debra, and Sandra Forrest. *Great Big Book of Children's Games: Over 450 Indoor and Outdoor Games for Kids.* New York: Reader's Digest Association, 1999. 105-106. Print.

7. Eckel, Bruce. *Thinking in Java.* Upper Saddle River, NJ: Prentice Hall, 2006. Print.

8. Anderson, Julie, and Herve Franceschi. *Java 6 Illuminated: An Active Learning Approach.* Sudbury, MA: Jones and Bartlett, 2008. Print.

9. Sierra, Kathy, and Bert Bates. *Head First Java.* Sebastopol, CA: O'Reilly, 2005. Print.

10. Knudsen, Jonathan. *Java 2D Graphics.* Beijing: O'Reilly, 1999. Print.

CHAPTER 8

Interfaces and Nested Classes

CHAPTER CONTENTS

An interface defines some behavior. Classes that are not directly related can implement these behaviors. Recall that we discussed earlier that a class cannot inherit from multiple classes because Java does not support multiple inheritance. However, this limitation does not extend to interfaces, and so a class can implement any number of interfaces. Two additional topics that we will discuss in this chapter are nested interfaces and nested classes. A nested interface is an interface that is defined inside another class. Likewise, a nested class is a class defined inside another class. Nested classes are widely used, especially in graphics and graphical user interface programming. A graphical example called *Palette* will be developed throughout this chapter to illustrate how interfaces and nested classes are used.

8.1   What Are Interfaces?

An interface is a collection of methods that describe a certain behavior. Consider a "smart" home and car. In the smart home, lights and heaters are turned on or off automatically when someone enters or leaves a room. A smart car can be driven automatically without a driver. Both this home and car have a special behavior that we will call "Smartness." The *Smart Home* **is-a** *Home* that **implements** *Smartness*. Similarly, the *Smart Car* **is-a** *Car* that **implements** *Smartness*. Recall that the "is-a" relation implies inheritance. However, we cannot say that the *Smart Home* is-a *Smartness* or that the *Smart Car* is-a *Smartness*. Instead, we can say that the *Smart Home* **has-a** *Smartness* or **implements** *Smartness*. *Smartness* is an abstract behavior or functionality. This behavior can be put in an **interface**, as shown here:

```
public interface Smartness {
    public abstract void doSomethingSmart();
}
```

You can create an interface by using the interface keyword followed by the interface name. The body can contain one or more *abstract* methods, which are methods that do not have a body. The *Smartness* interface does not specify what the method doSomethingSmart should do, and so *Smart Home* and *Smart Car* can provide their own implementations of this method.

A class uses an interface by using the keyword implements followed by the interface name. For example, we can write the classes SmartHome and SmartCar as follows:

```
public SmartHome extends Home implements Smartness {
    public void doSomethingSmart() {
```

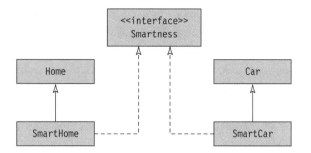

Figure 8–1
The Smartness **interface**
is implemented by the
classes SmartHome **and**
SmartCar.

```
    // code to turn on light and room heater when person enters room
    // code to turn off light and heater when person leaves room
  }
}

public SmartCar extends Car implements Smartness {
  public void doSomethingSmart() {
    // code to drive after person presses a drive button
  }
}
```

The interface Smartness contains an abstract method doSomethingSmart. Both
SmartHome and SmartCar implement doSomethingSmart, but they do different
things in this method.

The relationships between classes and interfaces can be described as shown
in Figure 8–1. The word "<<interface>>" is included in the box to indicate
that Smartness is an interface. Whereas inheritance is depicted using a solid
line, the *implements* relation is shown with a dotted line. Thus, SmartHome
inherits from class Home and implements the interface Smartness.

8.2   Defining an Interface

An **interface** is a group of *abstract methods* and *constant fields*. For example,
an interface called Rotatable is shown here:

```
public interface Rotatable {
  int SECONDS_PER_MINUTE = 60;    // constant field

  // abstract methods
  double angularSpeed();
  void rotate(double angularSpeed);
}
```

The keyword interface is used to declare Rotatable. By convention, the first letter of the interface name should be capitalized. Constants in an interface are *implicitly* declared as public, static, and final. Therefore, it is not necessary to use these modifiers when declaring a constant (such as SECONDS_PER_MINUTE) in an interface. Rotatable also contains two abstract methods, angularSpeed and rotate. All methods in an interface are implicitly public and abstract, and so these modifiers can be omitted. The modifiers protected and private cannot be used for constants and methods in an interface. In addition, static methods and instance fields are not allowed in interfaces. Interfaces cannot be instantiated because they are abstract.

An interface must be declared with a public or *default* access modifier only. When the public modifier is used, the interface can be accessed by all classes. When the default modifier is used, the interface can be accessed only by the classes that are in its package.

8.2.1   Palette: The ColorMixable Interface

We will create an interface called ColorMixable here. This interface is a behavior that we call "color mixable," which is the ability to mix colors to make new colors. You already know that combining two colors produces a new color. For example, mixing the colors red and blue gives purple, mixing blue and yellow gives green, and so on. A class that implements this interface will have the ability to mix colors.

The following code shows the ColorMixable interface:

```
package interfaces;
import java.awt.*;

public interface ColorMixable {
  void setColor(Color c);
  void mixColor(Color c);
  Color getColor();
}
```

This interface specifies three methods: setColor, mixColor, and getColor, which are explained here:

> **void setColor(Color c)**—a method to set a color to c.
>
> **void mixColor(Color c)**—a method to mix two colors.
>
> **Color getColor()**—a method to retrieve a color.

The method mixColor is abstract; thus a class can define its own way to mix colors, so that combining red with blue produces a color other than purple!

It is necessary to specify the parameter identifiers in interface methods; otherwise, a compilation error results. For example, the setColor method in ColorMixable cannot be declared as void setColor(Color).

Example 1

Find the errors in the following interface declaration:

```
interface NewInterface {
  public static final float ALPHA = 5.5f;
  private float BETA = 1.2f;

  // methods
  private void method1(int i);
  void method2(int);
  public static int method3(float j);
  int method4(float k);
  public abstract method5();
}
```

Solution: The errors are explained here:

```
private float BETA = 1.2f;       // error: constants cannot be private
private void method1(int i);     // error: methods cannot be private
void method2(int);               // error: parameter identifier missing
public static int method3(float j); // error: methods cannot be static
public abstract method5();       // error: method return type is missing
```

The remaining statements are correct.

8.3 Using an Interface

A class that implements an interface must provide the body for *all* the methods in that interface; otherwise, the class must be declared abstract. The class can use the constant fields in this interface as if they were defined in the class itself. Rotatable contains the methods angularSpeed and rotate; therefore, class Wheel must define these methods:

```
public class Wheel implements Rotatable {
  private int revolutionsPerMinute = 10;
```

```
public double angularSpeed() {
  double speed = (revolutionsPerMinute * 2 * Math.PI)/SECONDS_PER_MINUTE;
  return speed;
}

public void rotate(double angularSpeed) {
 // code to move wheel by the angular speed
 }

 // other methods
}
```

The method angularSpeed determines the angular speed of a wheel based on the number of revolutions it must make in a minute. Angular speed is measured in radians per second, and one complete revolution equals 2 × PI radians. Hence, a wheel that has 10 revolutions per minute (rpm) will rotate 10 × 2 × PI radians per minute, or PI/3 radians per second. The angular speed of this wheel is therefore PI/3 radians per second. The rotate method contains code to move the wheel by the desired angular speed.

Recall that a class that contains an abstract method must be declared abstract. Assume that a class called RotatingToy implements Rotatable, but does not define one or both of the methods in this interface:

```
public abstract class RotatingToy implements Rotatable {
}
```

In this case, class RotatingToy must be made abstract because it inherits the abstract methods of Rotatable.

As an example, two classes called ColoredEllipse and ColoredRectangle that implement the ColorMixable interface are developed next.

8.3.1   Palette: The ColoredEllipse Class

You have been using Java 2D's Ellipse2D.Float class to create ellipses. The class ColoredEllipse inherits from Ellipse2D.Float and creates ellipses that are colored. This class has two constructors that are shown in the following code:

```
package interfaces;
import java.awt.*;
import java.awt.geom.*;
```

```
public class ColoredEllipse extends Ellipse2D.Float {
  protected Color ellipseColor;

  public ColoredEllipse() {
    this(0, 0, 0, 0);
  }
  public ColoredEllipse(float x, float y, float width, float height) {
    super(x, y, width, height);
    // set initial color to white
    ellipseColor = new Color(255, 255, 255);
  }
}
```

The second constructor calls the constructor of the parent class
Ellipse2D.Float, using the super keyword, to create an ellipse of the desired
size. Recall that Java 2D's Color class is used to represent colors. The field
ellipseColor is of type Color and it stores the color of the ellipse. We have
used the methods getRed, getGreen, and getBlue, and the following constructor of this class, in previous chapters:

> **public Color(int red, int green, int blue)**—a constructor that cre-
> ates a new color. The values of the components red, green, and
> blue should fall in the range (0, 255).

Next, we modify the ColoredEllipse class to implement the interface ColorMixable. We must define the interface methods getColor, setColor, and mix-
Color in this class:

```
package interfaces;
import java.awt.*;
import java.awt.geom.*;

public class ColoredEllipse extends Ellipse2D.Float implements
ColorMixable {
  protected Color ellipseColor;

  public ColoredEllipse() {
    this(0, 0, 0, 0);
  }

  public ColoredEllipse(float x, float y, float width, float height) {
    super(x, y, width, height);
```

```
    // set initial color to white
    ellipseColor = new Color(255, 255, 255);
  }

  // accessor method for field ellipseColor
  public Color getColor() {
    return ellipseColor;
  }

  // mutator method sets field ellipseColor to c
  public void setColor(Color c) {
    ellipseColor = c;
  }

  // method to add ellipseColor with color c to create a new color
  public void mixColor(Color c) {
    // create a new color
    int red = (ellipseColor.getRed() + c.getRed())/2;
    int green = (ellipseColor.getGreen() + c.getGreen())/2;
    int blue = (ellipseColor.getBlue() + c.getBlue())/2;
    ellipseColor = new Color(red, green, blue);
  }
}
```

In the mixColor method, the red, blue, and green components of the color c and the current color ellipseColor are added together to create a new color. For example, the red component is modified as follows:

```
int red = (ellipseColor.getRed() + c.getRed())/2;
```

The sum of the red components of c and ellipseColor is divided by 2 so that the result does not exceed 255. However, a class is free to implement the interface methods in *any* way it likes. Therefore, a different class might choose to implement mixColor differently. We will describe another class, ColoredRectangle, next, with a different mixColor method.

Add this main method to the ColoredEllipse class:

```
public static void main(String[] args) {
  DrawingKit dk = new DrawingKit("ColoredEllipse");
  Graphics2D g2 = dk.getGraphics();
  ColoredEllipse ce = new ColoredEllipse(150, 125, 200, 250);
  ce.setColor(Color.red);      // set the color to red
  ce.mixColor(Color.yellow);   // add yellow
  ce.mixColor(Color.blue);     // add blue
  g2.setPaint(ce.getColor());  // set the new color
```

```
  g2.fill(ce);        // color the ellipse with the new color
}
```

An instance of ColoredEllipse is created in main. It mixes different colors together to create an ellipse with a new color. Add this statement to the preceding class to import DrawingKit:

```
import com.programwithjava.basic.DrawingKit;
```

Compile and run ColoredEllipse along with the interface ColorMixable as follows:

```
C:\JavaBook> javac -d bin src\com\programwithjava\basic\DrawingKit.java
src\interfaces\ColorMixable.java src\interfaces\ColoredEllipse.java

C:\JavaBook> java -classpath bin interfaces.ColoredEllipse
```

An ellipse with a new color is displayed, as shown in Figure 8–2. Experiment with different sets of colors to see how the colors change.

8.3.2   Palette: The ColoredRectangle Class

Although the ColoredRectangle class is similar to ColoredEllipse, it has two differences. The first difference is that ColoredRectangle is derived from Rectangle2D.Float instead of Ellipse2D.Float. The second is that ColoredRectangle

Figure 8–2

Using the Colored-
Ellipse class to create
ellipses of different
colors.

has a different `mixColor` method that creates a new color by subtracting, instead of adding, colors. The code for this class follows:

```java
package interfaces;
import java.awt.*;
import java.awt.geom.*;
import com.programwithjava.basic.DrawingKit;

public class ColoredRectangle extends Rectangle2D.Float implements
ColorMixable {
  protected Color rectangleColor;

  public ColoredRectangle() {
    this(0, 0, 0, 0);
  }

  public ColoredRectangle(float x, float y, float width, float height) {
    super(x, y, width, height);
    // set initial color to white
    rectangleColor = new Color(255, 255, 255);
  }

  public Color getColor() {
    return rectangleColor;
  }

  public void setColor(Color c) {
    rectangleColor = c;
  }

  // This method is different from the mixColor method
  // in ColoredEllipse
  public void mixColor(Color c) {
    // create a new color
    int red = (Math.abs(rectangleColor.getRed() - c.getRed()))/2;
    int green = (Math.abs(rectangleColor.getGreen() - c.getGreen()))/2;
    int blue = (Math.abs(rectangleColor.getBlue() - c.getBlue()))/2;
    rectangleColor = new Color(red, green, blue);
  }
}
```

Write a `main` method in which an instance of `ColoredRectangle` and `Colored-Ellipse` is created. Explore how the colors of these two instances change by mixing a set of randomly chosen colors using the `mixColor` method. Figure 8–3 shows the relationships between the various classes and interfaces developed in this chapter.

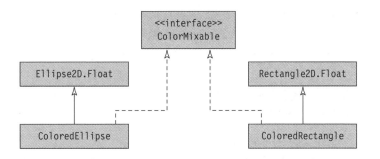

Figure 8–3

Classes ColoredEllipse and ColoredRectangle extend classes Ellipse2D.Float and Rectangle2D.Float, respectively, and implement the interface ColorMixable.

8.4   Differences Between Interfaces and Abstract Classes

Both interfaces and abstract classes represent a type and cannot be instantiated. However, there are important differences between these two:

- Unlike an abstract class, an interface cannot contain any constructors.

- It is not necessary for an abstract class to have any abstract methods; however, an interface contains only abstract methods.

- An abstract class can contain instance, static, and constant fields, whereas an interface contains only constant fields.

- The methods in an abstract class can be declared using any of the access modifiers; all methods of an interface *must* be public.

- An abstract class can contain static methods, but an interface cannot.

This raises an important question: Should you declare a group of abstract methods as an interface or as an abstract class? In general, it is better to create an interface when the methods describe the behaviors of objects that are not in the same inheritance hierarchy; otherwise, you can create an abstract class. If it is necessary to define instance fields and provide definitions (that is, bodies) for at least some of the methods, then you must use an abstract class instead of an interface.

8.5   Implementing Multiple Interfaces

Java does not allow multiple inheritance. However, a class can implement any number of interfaces. The names of all of the interfaces must be specified after the implements keyword. For example, consider this new interface called Whistler:

```
public interface Whistler {
  void whistle();
}
```

We now create a class SpinningTop that implements both Rotatable and Whistler. In this case, SpinningTop must provide the definitions of *all* the methods in *both* interfaces; otherwise, it needs to be declared as an abstract class:

```
public class SpinningTop implements Rotatable, Whistler {
  private int revolutionsPerMinute = 100;

  public double angularSpeed() {
    double speed = (revolutionsPerMinute * 2 * Math.PI)/SECONDS_PER_MINUTE;
    return speed;
  }

  public void rotate(double angularSpeed) {
    System.out.println("Rotating with angular speed " +angularSpeed);
  }

  public void whistle() {
    System.out.println("Whistling");
  }
}
```

8.6   An Interface as a Data Type

Like a class name, the name of an interface also represents a data type. Therefore, ColorMixable is a data type, and you can create variables of this type:

```
ColorMixable cm;
```

The variable cm can be assigned to an instance of *any* class that implements this interface. For example, both ColoredEllipse and ColoredRectangle implement the interface ColorMixable. Therefore, cm can be assigned to an instance of either class:

```
cm = new ColoredEllipse(10, 10, 50, 70);
```

cm is assigned to an instance of ColoredEllipse; thus it can invoke the methods getColor, setColor, and mixColor in this class.

As another example, consider two interfaces, Bounce and Roll:

```
public interface Bounce {
  void bounce();
}
```

```
public interface Roll {
  void roll();
}
```

Suppose that we define a class called Ball that implements these interfaces:

```
public class Ball implements Bounce, Roll {
  public void bounce() {
    System.out.println("Bouncing ball");
  }
  public void roll() {
    System.out.println("Rolling ball");
  }
  public void inflate() {
    System.out.println("Inflate ball");
  }
  public void deflate() {
    System.out.println("Deflate ball");
  }
}
```

The variable r of type Roll can be assigned to an instance of Ball:

```
Roll r = new Ball();
```

This statement calls the roll method of the Ball class:

```
r.roll();
```

The following two statements cause a compilation error because the bounce and inflate methods are not declared in the Roll interface:

```
r.bounce();      // error
r.inflate();     // error
```

r is of type Roll; thus it can only call method roll, and not methods bounce or inflate, even though these methods are defined in class Ball. To call the other two methods, **casting** must be used. You have used casting with primitive data types; it can be used similarly with interface types. Casting is needed to convert a reference variable of a parent data type to a child data type. The reference variable r can be cast to type Ball by inserting the class name Ball in parentheses in front of this variable:

(Ball) r

Now, the bounce and inflate methods in Ball can be called as follows:

```
((Ball) r).bounce();
((Ball) r).inflate();
```

Note that it would be incorrect to write this in the following way:

```
(Ball) r.bounce();  // error
```

Doing so will cast the value returned by the method bounce (and not the reference variable r) to type Ball.

Using an interface as a parameter type can be particularly useful in methods, as the next example shows.

Example 2

Write a class that contains a static method to compare colors of two objects that implement the ColorMixable interface. The method returns true if the colors are the same.

Solution: The class InterfaceDemo contains the compare method to compare the colors of two ColorMixable types passed in as arguments:

```
package interfaces;
import java.awt.*;

public class InterfaceDemo {
  public static boolean compare(ColorMixable m1, ColorMixable m2) {
    Color c1 = m1.getColor();
    Color c2 = m2.getColor();

    // return true if the red, green and blue components are equal,
    // otherwise, return false.
    if ( (c1.getRed() == c2.getRed()) && (c1.getGreen() == c2.getGreen())
&& (c1.getBlue() == c2.getBlue()) )
      return true;
    else
      return false;
  }
}
```

The method compare can take any instance of a class that implements ColorMixable as an argument:

```
public static void main(String[] args) {
  ColoredEllipse ce = new ColoredEllipse(20, 20, 30, 20);
  ce.setColor(Color.red);
```

```
ColoredRectangle cr = new ColoredRectangle(20, 20, 30, 20);
cr.setColor(Color.red);
System.out.println(InterfaceDemo.compare(ce, cr));
}
```

The advantage of using an interface type as an argument in the compare method should be evident now. This method can compare colors of two unrelated objects if their classes implement ColorMixable. Otherwise, you might have to write overloaded methods, such as:

```
public static boolean compare(ColoredEllipse m1, ColoredRectangle m2);
```

```
public static boolean compare(ColoredEllipse m1, ColoredEllipse m2);
```

```
public static boolean compare(ColoredRectangle m1, ColoredRectangle m2);
```

This step is not needed now, because the interface name ColorMixable is a data type that can be assigned to instances of both ColoredEllipse and ColoredRectangle classes.   ∎

8.6.1   The instanceof Keyword

As you have seen, casting lets you convert a reference variable of a parent type to a child type. There are situations, however, when casting can lead to a run-time error in a program. Let us look at an example when this can happen. Suppose that another class Dice also implements the Roll interface:

```
public class Dice implements Roll {
  public void roll()  {
   System.out.println("Rolling dice");
  }
}
```

You can create a reference variable of type Roll and assign it to an instance of Dice:

```
Roll dice = new Dice();
```

The Ball class also implements the Roll interface, but it would be an error to cast dice to type Ball, as shown in these two statements:

```
Ball b = (Ball) dice;      // error!
((Ball) dice).roll();      // error!
```

The reason is that the classes Ball and Dice are unrelated as they are not in the same inheritance hierarchy. Therefore, dice should not be cast to type

Ball because it does not reference an instance of Ball. The compiler will *not* flag the previous statements as an error, but a run-time error will occur.

The following rule should be followed when casting is done.

> A reference variable ref should be cast to type T only if:
> - ref references an instance of class T, or
> - ref references an instance of a class that implements the interface T.

Java contains a keyword instanceof that can be used to determine whether an object is of a given type. This statement returns true if object obj is of type T; otherwise, it returns false:

```
if (obj instanceof T)
```

The following statement prevents a run-time error by checking whether dice references an object of type Ball before it is cast to Ball:

```
if (dice instanceof Ball)
  ((Ball) dice).roll();
```

This if statement returns false because dice references an object of class Dice, which is not an instance of class Ball. The roll method will not be called as a result. Before you do casting, use the instanceof keyword to check whether the reference variable can be cast safely.

Example 3

Two classes and an interface are defined as follows:

```
// interface Recorder
public interface Recorder {
  void record();
}

// class AudioRecorder
public class AudioRecorder implements Recorder {
  public void record() {
    System.out.println("Recording audio");
  }
  public void playAudio() {
    System.out.println("Playing audio");
  }
}
```

```
// class AudioVideoRecorder
public class AudioVideoRecorder extends AudioRecorder {
  public void record() {
    System.out.println("Recording audio and video");
  }
  public void playVideo() {
    System.out.println("Playing video");
  }
}
```

There are no compilation errors in this code. Explain why the following method test might not run correctly:

```
public class Tester {
  public void test(Recorder r) {
    r.record();
    ((AudioRecorder) r).playAudio();
    ((AudioVideoRecorder) r).playVideo();
  }
}
```

Solution: A run-time error occurs if an instance of AudioRecorder class is passed as an argument to the test method, because the instance cannot be cast to type AudioVideoRecorder.

This error can be corrected by using instanceof, as shown here, in method test:

```
if (r instanceof AudioRecorder)
  ((AudioRecorder) r).playAudio();
if (r instanceof AudioVideoRecorder)
  ((AudioVideoRecorder) r).playVideo();
```

8.7 Extending an Interface

If we add some new methods to an existing interface I, *all* of the classes that use I must be changed as well. Therefore, it is not a good idea to change an existing interface. Instead, it is better to create a new interface J that contains all the constants and abstract methods of I and defines new ones of its own. This can be done by extending interface I. Like classes, interfaces are extended using the extends keyword:

```
public interface J extends I {
  // new abstract methods and constants
}
```

I is called the **superinterface** of J, and J is the **subinterface** of I. Only the new methods and constants must be defined in J because it inherits all the abstract methods and constants of I.

Unlike a class, an interface can extend multiple interfaces:

```
public interface M extends J, K, L {  // J, K and L are interfaces
  // new abstract methods and constants
}
```

A class that implements M must provide the body for all of the methods in interfaces J, K, L, and M. For example, here is an interface that extends the ColorMixable interface:

```
public interface NewColorMixable extends ColorMixable {
  Color getComplementaryColor();
}
```

Any class that implements NewColorMixable must also implement the methods in ColorMixable.

8.8   Predefined Interfaces

Some important interfaces that are part of the language are described briefly next.

8.8.1   The Shape Interface

All classes that create geometrical shapes—such as Rectangle2D.Float, Rectangle2D.Double, Line2D.Float, Line2D.Double, and Polygon—implement Java 2D's Shape interface. Therefore, all instances of these classes are also of type Shape. The draw and fill methods of the Graphics2D class are defined as follows:

```
public abstract void draw(Shape s)
```

```
public abstract void fill(Shape s)
```

These two methods take an instance of type Shape as an argument. For this reason, we can pass instances of Rectangle2D.Float, Rectangle2D.Double, Line2D.Float, and the other classes that implement Shape as arguments to this method.

8.8.2   The Collection Interface

Java specifies an interface called Collection that declares methods to manipulate a group of objects. Some methods in this interface are shown in Figure 8–4.

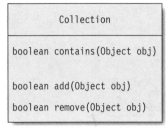

Figure 8–4
Some methods in the
Collection **interface.**

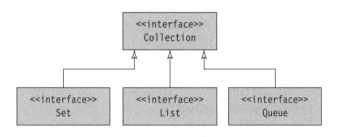

The Set, List, and Queue interfaces extend Collection, as shown in Figure 8–5. A Set is a special type of group with the property that duplicate objects cannot be present. The Set interface extends the Collection interface to include this "no duplicates allowed" type of behavior. The List is another collection where objects are placed at a certain position or index, and duplicates are allowed. The List interface specifies methods to find and modify elements based on their position. Objects also have a given order in a Queue, but the ordering scheme is different from that in List.

The Collection interface and its subinterfaces are a part of the **Java Collections Framework**. This framework consists of classes and interfaces that simplify working with groups of objects. There are many classes in this framework, such as ArrayList, LinkedList, HashMap, and TreeMap, and interfaces such as SortedSet, Map, and SortedMap. We discuss this topic in detail in Chapter 12, *Generics and Collections*.

8.8.3   The EventListener **Interface**

The EventListener interface defined in the java.util package does not have any methods or constants:

```
public interface EventListener {
}
```

What, then, is the purpose of this empty interface? This interface is the superinterface of several other *listener* interfaces. A listener interface

Figure 8–6

The `WindowListener`, `MouseListener`, and `KeyListener` **interfaces extend the** `Event-Listener` **interface.**

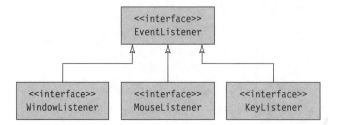

defines the behavior of an object that reacts to actions such as clicking a mouse, pressing a key on the keyboard, or closing a window on the screen. Figure 8–6 shows the listener interfaces `WindowListener`, `MouseListener`, and `KeyListener` that extend `EventListener`.

The `MouseListener` interface declares methods that are invoked when a mouse is pressed, released, or moved:

```
public interface MouseListener extends EventListener {
  public abstract void mouseClicked(MouseEvent e);
  public abstract void mousePressed(MouseEvent e);
  public abstract void mouseReleased(MouseEvent e);
  public abstract void mouseEntered(MouseEvent e);
  public abstract void mouseExited(MouseEvent e);
}
```

Any class that implements `MouseListener` must implement all the methods in this interface. An instance of this class is automatically notified whenever a *mouse action* occurs (such as when the user clicks, presses, or releases a mouse button) via a `MouseEvent` object. The `MouseEvent` class contains methods to obtain information about a mouse action.

The `WindowListener` interface declares methods that are invoked when a window is opened, closed, or changed. The `KeyListener` interface declares methods that are invoked when a key is pressed or released on the keyboard. The `MouseListener`, `WindowListener`, and `KeyListener` interfaces are in the `java.awt.event` package. We discuss these and other listener interfaces in more detail in Chapter 13, *More on GUI Programming.*

8.8.4   The `Runnable` **Interface**

The `Runnable` interface in the `java.lang` package contains a `run` method:

```
public interface Runnable {
  public abstract void run();
}
```

Any class that implements this interface must provide the implementation for the method run. This method can then be used as the body of *threads* in a multithreaded program. A **multithreaded** program consists of many threads executing code in parallel. We discuss what threads are and how they work in Chapter 14, *Multithreaded Programming*.

8.9 Nested Interfaces and Nested Classes

You can define an interface within another class. These interfaces are known as **nested interfaces**. Similarly, a **nested class** is a class defined within another class.

A nested interface should be declared using the static modifier, because it is associated with the class itself and not the instances of the class. The class Bulb contains a nested interface called Glow:

```
public class Bulb {
  public static interface Glow {
  }
}
```

A nested interface that is declared private can be used only within its enclosing class; however, a public nested interface can be accessed outside the class in which it is defined. You must make a nested interface private when it will be used only within the class where it is defined.

For example, the class Filament in Bulb implements the nested interface Glow. Filament is a nested class, because it is defined within the class Bulb:

```
public class Bulb {
  public static interface Glow {
  }
  public class Filament implements Glow {
  }
}
```

Bulb is known as a **top-level class** because it is not within another class. There can be two or more levels of nested classes (for example, a nested class within Filament, and so on), although it is rare to do so.

Recall that top-level classes and interfaces must be declared with the public or default modifiers only. However, nested classes and nested interfaces can be declared using any access modifier (private, protected, default, or public). Nested classes can also be made abstract or final by declaring them with the abstract or final modifiers.

In case you are wondering whether a class or an interface can be defined inside another interface, the answer is yes—this is permitted in Java. In fact, you *can* nest interfaces and classes inside each other, within an interface, to an arbitrary depth. However, it is not a good idea to nest classes and interfaces in this manner because it makes code difficult to read and use; therefore, we will not discuss it further.

Until now, we have used top-level classes and interfaces only. Nested classes are also very useful, and in the following sections, we explore the different types of nested classes and their usage. These classes are of two types:

- **Static nested** classes, and

- **Non-static nested** classes (also known as **inner classes**).

8.10   Static Nested Classes

A static nested class is defined as a *static* member of the top-level class that encloses it:

```
public class TopLevel {
  // code for TopLevel

  private static class StaticNested {
    // code for class StaticNested
  }
}
```

Recall that all instances of a class share a static field. In the same way, all instances of a top-level class share a *single* instance of a static nested class. A static nested class can access even the private *static* fields of its top-level class.

As an example, we will write a class called Ticket that can be used to generate tickets. Ticket contains a static nested class called Counter, which generates a new ticket number for each ticket so that successive tickets are numbered consecutively.

```
package interfaces;

public class Ticket {
  private int number;
  private static int count;
```

```
// assign a new number to this ticket
Ticket() {
  number = Counter.getNextNumber();
}

// Counter is a static nested class
private static class Counter {
  // increments count
  private static int getNextNumber() {
    count++;
    return count;
  }
}

public int getNumber() {
  return number;
}
}
```

The task of generating ticket numbers is relegated to the nested class Counter. Counter is a static class; thus it is shared by all instances of Ticket. This ensures that all ticket numbers are unique, regardless of how many instances of Ticket exist. This class is declared as private because it is needed only within Ticket.

A static class can access the static fields and methods of its enclosing class. Thus, class Counter can access the static field count of Ticket even though count is declared as private. However, Counter cannot access the instance fields and methods (number and getNumber) of Ticket.

The enclosing class can access all of the fields and methods of the static nested class using the latter's class name. Thus, Ticket can access the private method getNextNumber in Counter as Counter.getNextNumber().

A static nested class is created automatically using the default constructor when an instance of its enclosing class is created. It can also be created by calling a constructor explicitly. The following statement creates an instance of Counter as well:

Ticket t1 = new Ticket(); // creates Ticket with a Counter object

Ticket objects that are created subsequently share this Counter object:

Ticket t2 = new Ticket(); // creates a Ticket only

The following main, added to class Ticket, demonstrates that tickets are generated with consecutive numbers:

```
public static void main(String[] args) {
  Ticket t1 = new Ticket();
  System.out.println("Ticket t1 has id: " +t1.getNumber());
  Ticket t2 = new Ticket();
  System.out.println("Ticket t2 has id: " +t2.getNumber());
}
```

The program output is:

```
Ticket t1 has id: 1
Ticket t2 has id: 2
```

A private static nested class is useful because it provides added functionality for the enclosing class. A nested class should be made private when it is of interest only within the class that uses it.

Nested classes can be made public as well. For example, Java 2D defines Float as a public nested class inside class Rectangle2D:

```
public abstract class Rectangle2D {
  // fields and methods in Rectangle2D
  public static class Float extends Rectangle2D {
    // fields and methods of Float
  }
  public static class Double extends Rectangle2D {
    // fields and methods of Double
  }
}
```

Double is another nested class in Rectangle2D. The Float and Double classes define fields of type float and double, respectively. Public nested classes are referenced by prefixing the top-level class name to the nested class name with a dot separating the two, such as Rectangle2D.Float and Rectangle2D.Double. (You will recognize Rectangle2D.Float to be the class that you have been using to draw rectangular shapes.) The advantage of nesting these classes inside Rectangle2D is that they can be referenced using the class names Rectangle2D.Float and Rectangle2D.Double, which are more descriptive than merely using Float and Double.

8.11   Inner Classes

An inner class is a class defined inside another class and declared *without* using the static modifier. It is best to declare a class as an inner class when it will be used only within another class and its code is short. For example, Camera contains an inner class called CameraBody:

```
public class Camera {
  private class CameraBody {
    // fields and methods of inner class
  }
}
```

Recall that a static nested class is shared by all instances of its enclosing class. Inner classes are different in that every instance of the enclosing class contains a *separate* instance of the inner class. CameraBody is not declared as static because each camera has a separate body. An inner class can be declared using the private, public, protected, or default access modifiers.

All fields and methods of the inner class can be accessed by the enclosing class, and vice versa. Let us add some code to Camera to illustrate this:

```
package interfaces;

public class Camera {
  private int size;

  public Camera() {
  }

  public Camera(int s) {
    // create an instance of the inner class
    CameraBody body = new CameraBody(s);
  }

  // inner class
  private class CameraBody {
    // assign argument v to Camera's field size
    private CameraBody(int v) {
      size = v;
    }
  } // end inner class CameraBody
```

```
  public void printSize() {
    System.out.println("The size is " +size +" cubic inches");
  }

  public static void main(String[] args) {
    // create an instance of class Camera
    Camera c1 = new Camera(10);
    c1.printSize();

    // create another instance of Camera
    Camera c2 = new Camera(20);
    c2.printSize();
  }
}
```

The program output is:

```
The size is 10 cubic inches
The size is 20 cubic inches
```

Two instances of this class, called c1 and c2, are created in main. Each time the constructor for Camera is called, an instance of CameraBody is created in that object. Although size is a private field of Camera, it can be accessed inside CameraBody. Similarly, the enclosing class can access all the fields and methods of the inner class.

An instance of the inner class can also be created explicitly. Suppose we have created an instance of Camera called c3 by calling the constructor without arguments:

```
Camera c3 = new Camera();
```

The constructor for CameraBody is not called inside this constructor. The following statement can be used to create an instance of CameraBody in c3:

Camera.CameraBody in = **c3.new** CameraBody(15);

The visibility rules dictate where this instance of the inner class can be created. If the inner class is private, the preceding statement can only be used inside the enclosing class. On the other hand, if the inner class is public, this statement can be used in any other class.

An inner class *cannot* contain static fields, static methods, or interfaces, but can contain constants:

```
public class Outside {
  private class Inside {
    public static final int i = 10; // okay
    public interface i {            // error
```

```
      }
   public static int x;          // error
   public static int setX() {    // error
      }
   }
}
```

8.11.1   Palette: The Palette Class

We will develop a class called Palette to illustrate how interfaces and inner
classes are used. This class is used to create a palette that contains paints of
different colors. In the center is a mixing area where different colors can be
mixed. We will use the ColoredEllipse or ColoredRectangle class to create the
mixing area. In addition, we will develop an inner class called ColorButton to
create the paints. A ColorButton object is an ellipse of a given size that can
store one color. The Palette class is described here:

```
package interfaces;
import java.awt.geom.*;
import java.awt.*;

public class Palette {
  // mixing area
  private ColorMixable mixingArea;

 // colored ellipses represent paint swatches
  private ColorButton red;
  private ColorButton blue;
  private ColorButton yellow;
  private ColorButton green;

  public Palette(ColorMixable cm) {
    red = new ColorButton(Color.red, 170, 145, 20, 20);
    blue = new ColorButton(Color.blue, 210, 135, 23, 23);
    yellow = new ColorButton(Color.yellow, 250, 135, 26, 26);
    green = new ColorButton(Color.green, 290, 140, 28, 28);
    mixingArea = cm;
  }

  // start inner class ColorButton
  private class ColorButton extends Ellipse2D.Float  {
    private Color color;

    private ColorButton(Color cl, float x, float y, float w, float h) {
      super(x, y, w, h);
      color = cl;
    }
```

```
    private Color getColor() {
      return color;
    }
  } // end inner class ColorButton

  private void changeColor(Color newColor) {
    mixingArea.mixColor(newColor);
  }
}
```

It is important to note that we have declared `mixingArea` as type `ColorMixable` instead of `ColoredEllipse` or `ColoredRectangle`. What is the advantage of doing this? Doing so allows us to use an instance of either class (or even a different class that will be developed in the future) to create the mixing area of the palette without changing any code in class `Palette`. The only restriction is that the instance used must be of a class that implements `ColorMixable`.

The class `ColorButton` is an inner class that inherits from `Ellipse2D.Float`. The constructor for `Palette` uses this class to create four small colored circles on the palette called `red`, `blue`, `yellow`, and `green`.

Inner classes are especially useful in GUI programming. We will enhance the `ColorButton` class so that when the mouse is clicked on a `ColorButton` object (which represents a paint swatch), its color will be added to the mixing area in the palette. To do so, the `ColorButton` class must implement the `MouseListener` interface. Whenever the mouse is clicked, a mouse event is created and sent to all instances of this class. We will add some code to the `mouseClicked` method to change the color of the mixing area, depending on which paint swatch was clicked. The modified code for `ColorButton` is shown next. (Feel free to skip this part if it seems to be more than you can grasp at this time, and revisit it after you have read Chapter 9, *GUI Programming*.)

To see how the program works, modify the code for `ColorButton` inside `Palette` to match what is shown here:

```
// modified code for the ColorButton class in class Palette
private class ColorButton extends Ellipse2D.Float implements
MouseListener {
  private Color color;

  private ColorButton(Color cl, float x, float y, float w, float h) {
```

```
    super(x, y, w, h);
    color = cl;
  }
  private Color getColor() {
    return color;
  }
  // checks whether the mouse was clicked inside this object
  // and updates the color of mixingArea
  public void mouseClicked(MouseEvent e) {
    // get the coordinates of the point where mouse is clicked
    int x = e.getX();
    int y = e.getY();

    // check if this object was clicked
    // update the color of mixingArea accordingly
    if (this.contains(x, y))
      changeColor(color);
  }
  // no action is taken for other types of mouse motion
  public void mousePressed(MouseEvent e) {}
  public void mouseReleased(MouseEvent e) {}
  public void mouseEntered(MouseEvent e) {}
  public void mouseExited(MouseEvent e) {}
} // end inner class ColorButton
```

Add this `import` statement to `Palette` to import the `MouseListener` and `MouseEvent` interfaces in the `java.awt.event` package:

```
import java.awt.event.*;
```

The code in the `mouseClicked` method describes what must be done each time the mouse button is clicked. First, the coordinates of the point clicked are obtained and stored in (x and y):

```
int x = e.getX();
int y = e.getY();
```

The next two lines check to determine whether the mouse was clicked inside a `ColorButton` object:

```
if (this.contains(x, y))
  changeColor(color);
```

It uses the method `contains` that is inherited from `Ellipse2D.Float`:

> **contains(x, y)**—a method that returns `true` if the coordinates x, y are inside the boundary of the object calling this method; otherwise, it returns `false`.

If the `contains` method returns `true`, then the `changeColor` method in `Palette` is called. Thus, if the `ColorButton` called `red` calls `changeColor`, red is added to the mixing area `mixingArea`; if `yellow` calls `changeColor`, yellow is added to `mixingArea`; and so on. Note that `changeColor` can be accessed from `ColorButton` even though it is a `private` method in `Palette`.

The complete code for `Palette` is shown in Section 8.13. This code adds a graphical user interface to `Palette`. Run this program and click on the red, blue, yellow, and green circles on the palette shown in the window. See how the colors in the mixing area change each time you click on a colored circle!

8.12   Anonymous Classes

An **anonymous class** is an *inner class* without a name, and it must be defined inside a method or a constructor. An anonymous class is created by extending an *existing* class or implementing an *existing* interface. Only the default access modifier can be used to declare an anonymous class. It is convenient to use this type of inner class because an instance is created at the same time that the class is defined.

8.12.1   Extending an Existing Class

Let us see how an anonymous class can be created by extending another class. Suppose that class `DigitalBook` has been defined as follows:

```
public class DigitalBook {
  public void displayMenu() {
    System.out.println("In method displayMenu of DigitalBook");
  }
}
```

An anonymous class can be created by extending this `DigitalBook` class as shown here:

```
new DigitalBook() {
  public void displayMenu() {
    System.out.println("In method displayMenu of anonymous class");
  }
}; // note the semi-colon
```

Although the keyword `extends` is not used here, this anonymous class *implicitly* inherits from the `DigitalBook` class that was defined earlier. In addition, an instance of this class is also created at the same time by using the new keyword. The displayMenu method in this anonymous class overrides the displayMenu method in DigitalBook. The syntax is different in that the class keyword is not used to declare this new class, and the class body is terminated by a semicolon. Another important point to note is that the preceding definition of the anonymous class must be placed inside a method or constructor.

You can assign this instance of the anonymous class that has been created to a reference variable:

```
DigitalBook book = new DigitalBook () {
  public void displayMenu() {
    System.out.println("In method displayMenu of anonymous class");
  }
};
```

Here, the object created is referenced by variable book. Can you predict which displayMenu method is invoked by the following statement (that of the anonymous class or its parent class DigitalBook)?

```
book.displayMenu();
```

The displayMenu method of the anonymous class is called because it overrides that of its parent class. Therefore, it prints out:

```
In method displayMenu of anonymous class
```

If a class contains any abstract methods, then an anonymous class that extends this class must implement all of its abstract methods. Suppose that we modify DigitalBook so that it contains an abstract method nextPage:

```
public abstract class DigitalBook {
  public void displayMenu() {
    System.out.println("Method displayMenu of DigitalBook");
  }

  public abstract void nextPage();
}
```

The anonymous class that extends DigitalBook *must* implement the abstract method nextPage:

```
DigitalBook book = new DigitalBook () {
  public void displayMenu() {
    System.out.println("In method displayMenu of anonymous class");
  }
```

```
  public void nextPage() {
    // code to display the next page of book
  }
};
```

An anonymous class has no name; thus it is not possible to define constructors in this class. An instance of an anonymous class is created using its superclass constructor. If no constructors are defined in the superclass, the anonymous class instances are created using the default constructor of the superclass. However, a superclass constructor can also be explicitly called, as we show next. Let us add two constructors to DigitalBook:

```
public abstract class DigitalBook {
  // size of memory to hold data in Mega Bytes
  int memorySize;

  DigitalBook() {
    this(256);
  }

  DigitalBook(int size) {
    memorySize = size;
  }

  public void displayMenu() {
    System.out.println("In method displayMenu of DigitalBook");
  }

  public abstract void nextPage();
}
```

Now, it is okay to create the anonymous class as shown here, because the constructor DigitalBook(int) gets called:

```
DigitalBook book = new DigitalBook(1024) {
  public void nextPage(){
    // code to display the next page of book
  }
};
```

8.12.2   Implementing an Existing Interface

Another way to create an anonymous class is by implementing an existing interface. In this case, it is necessary for the anonymous class to implement all the methods in the interface. For example, consider the interface Bounce that was defined earlier in the chapter. The following code defines an anonymous class that implements Bounce, as well as creates an instance of this class at the same time:

```
new Bounce() {
  public void bounce() {
    System.out.println("Jump up and down");
  }
};
```

This anonymous class implements the abstract method bounce of interface Bounce. A reference variable called trampoline is assigned to the object that is created:

```
Bounce trampoline = new Bounce() {
  public void bounce() {
    System.out.println("Jump up and down");
  }
};
```

An anonymous class is allowed to implement only a single interface, and not multiple interfaces. It can access fields and methods of its enclosing class, and those inherited from its superclass. An anonymous class can also access local final variables and final parameters of the method in which it is defined.

8.13   Palette: A Preview of GUI Programming

The complete code for the Palette class follows. (In the next chapter, we will explain how you can create different types of GUIs using the Swing toolkit.) Run this program and click on the red, blue, yellow, and green circles on the palette with the mouse. You will see that when a particular color is clicked, it is added to the mixing area in the palette:

```
package interfaces;
import java.awt.geom.*;
import java.awt.*;
import java.awt.event.*;
import javax.swing.*;

public class Palette extends JPanel {
  // mixing area
  private ColorMixable mixingArea;

  // colored ellipses represent paint swatches
  private ColorButton red;
```

```
    private ColorButton blue;
    private ColorButton yellow;
    private ColorButton green;

    public Palette(ColorMixable cm) {
      red = new ColorButton(Color.red, 170, 145, 20, 20);
      blue = new ColorButton(Color.blue, 210, 135, 23, 23);
      yellow = new ColorButton(Color.yellow, 250, 135, 26, 26);
      green = new ColorButton(Color.green, 290, 140, 28, 28);
      mixingArea = cm;

      // GUI programming - these ColorButtons respond to mouse clicks
      addMouseListener(red);
      addMouseListener(blue);
      addMouseListener(yellow);
      addMouseListener(green);
    }

    // start inner class ColorButton
    private class ColorButton extends Ellipse2D.Float implements
MouseListener {
    private Color color;

    private ColorButton(Color cl, float x, float y, float w, float h) {
      super(x, y, w, h);
      color = cl;
    }
    private Color getColor() {
      return color;
    }
    // adds this color to mixingArea upon mouse click
    public void mouseClicked(MouseEvent e) {
      // get the coordinates of the point where mouse is clicked
      int x = e.getX();
      int y = e.getY();

      // check if this object was clicked
      // update the color of mixingArea accordingly
      if (this.contains(x, y))
        changeColor(color);
        repaintWindow();
      }
      // no action is taken for other types of mouse motion
      public void mousePressed(MouseEvent e) {}
      public void mouseReleased(MouseEvent e) {}
```

```java
    public void mouseEntered(MouseEvent e) {}
    public void mouseExited(MouseEvent e) {}
} // end inner class ColorButton

  private void changeColor(Color c) {
    mixingArea.mixColor(c);
  }

  //GUI programming
  private void repaintWindow() {
  // this will call the paintComponent method to update
  // the color in the area mixingArea occupies in the window
    repaint();
  }

  // GUI programming
  protected void paintComponent(Graphics g) {
    super.paintComponent(g);
    Graphics2D g2 = (Graphics2D) g;
    // draw the palette shape
    drawPaletteShape(g2);

    // update mixingArea's color in the window
    g2.setPaint(mixingArea.getColor());

    // note how instanceof is used here
    if (mixingArea instanceof Shape)
      g2.fill((Shape) mixingArea);
  }

  // draw the palette shape and four color buttons
  protected void drawPaletteShape(Graphics2D g2) {
    Ellipse2D outline = new Ellipse2D.Float(125, 125, 250, 150);
    g2.draw(outline);
    Ellipse2D hole = new Ellipse2D.Float(145, 190, 20, 20);
    g2.draw(hole);
    g2.setPaint(Color.white);
    Ellipse2D hide = new Ellipse2D.Float(150, 225, 80, 60);
    g2.fill(hide);
    g2.setPaint(Color.black);
    QuadCurve2D notch = new QuadCurve2D.Float();
    notch.setCurve(170, 240, 205, 200, 210, 260);
    g2.draw(notch);
    notch.setCurve(170, 240, 160, 255, 153, 246);
    g2.draw(notch);
```

```
    notch.setCurve(210, 260, 205, 270, 223, 272);
    g2.draw(notch);

    // draw the red, blue, yellow and green buttons
    g2.setPaint(red.getColor());
    g2.fill(red);
    g2.setPaint(blue.getColor());
    g2.fill(blue);
    g2.setPaint(yellow.getColor());
    g2.fill(yellow);
    g2.setPaint(green.getColor());
    g2.fill(green);
  }
}
```

Add this main to the preceding class to test it. We are using the classes in the Swing toolkit to draw the window, instead of DrawingKit:

```
public static void main(String[] args) {
  // GUI program to set up the window
  int x = 220, y = 180, w = 100, h = 70;
  JFrame f = new JFrame("Palette");

  ColorMixable mixingArea = new ColoredEllipse(x, y, w, h);
  Palette palette = new Palette(mixingArea);

  palette.setBackground(Color.white);
  palette.setOpaque(true);
  f.setContentPane(palette);
  f.setDefaultCloseOperation(JFrame.EXIT_ON_CLOSE);
  f.setSize(500, 500);
  f.setVisible(true);
}
```

Compile and run the program as follows:

```
C:\JavaBook> javac -d bin src\interfaces\ColorMixable.java
src\interfaces\ColoredEllipse.java src\interfaces\ColoredRectangle.java
src\com\programwithjava\basic\DrawingKit.java
src\interfaces\Palette.java

C:\JavaBook> java -classpath bin interfaces.Palette
```

The program output is shown in Figure 8–7. As an exercise, modify main so that mixingArea references an instance of ColoredRectangle instead of Colored-Ellipse. Run the program again and see how the output changes. What happens if mixingArea references an instance that is not of type Shape?

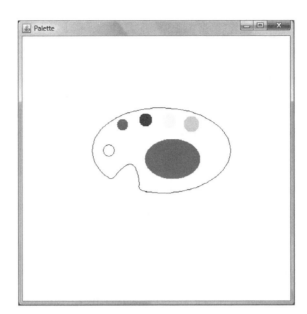

Figure 8–7
Clicking with the mouse on a paint swatch in the palette adds its color to the mixing area.

Before we conclude our discussion, we briefly discuss the class Palette. You must include the javax.swing package to use Swing. All the drawing work is done in the paintComponent method of Palette. Whenever the mouse is clicked, the mouseClicked method of ColorButton is executed automatically. Note that this method has been changed slightly to include a call to the repaintWindow method of Palette. Therefore, the repaintWindow method is called when the mouse is clicked inside a colored circle:

```
private void repaintWindow() {
// this will call the paintComponent method to make
// the changes in the area mixingArea occupies in the window
     repaint();
}
```

The repaint method, in turn, clears the window and calls paintComponent automatically, and the latter redraws the window with the new color in the mixing area.

The method drawPaletteShape creates the palette outline with the colored circles. Palette inherits from Swing's JPanel class to create a drawing surface. In the main method, Swing's JFrame class is used to create a window.

In the following chapters, we will discuss this in more detail. You will get a better understanding of the graphics that we have been using, and will learn how to create GUIs and interactive applications.

8.14   Summary

In this chapter, we discussed how you can create and use interfaces. A class can implement an interface by defining all the methods in that interface. An existing interface can be extended to create a new one. An interface also represents a data type, and it can be used for the type of parameters in methods. Nested classes are of two types, static and inner. Only a single instance of a static nested class can be created, and it is shared by all of the instances of the enclosing class. An inner class is different in that each instance of the enclosing class contains a separate instance of the inner class. We developed a program called *Palette* in this chapter to show how you can use interfaces and nested classes in a program.

Summary of Static Nested Classes   The key points to remember about a static nested class are:

- It is declared inside a class using the `static` keyword and any of the four access modifiers.

- It can access *all* static fields and methods of the enclosing class (even those that are `private`), but it cannot access any instance fields and methods of the enclosing class.

- The enclosing class can access all of its fields and methods.

Summary of Anonymous Classes   An anonymous class has the following characteristics:

- It is declared inside a method or constructor in a class using the default access modifier only, and does not have a name.

- It cannot contain a constructor.

- It must either extend a class or implement an interface but cannot do both.

- It cannot implement multiple interfaces.

Exercises

1. State whether each of the following statements is true or false:

   a.   An interface cannot define any methods.

   b.   A class can implement multiple interfaces.

   c.   An interface can contain constructors.

d. An interface can extend multiple interfaces.

e. Nested classes can be declared as `abstract` or `final`.

f. A nested class can implement an interface.

g. The default constructor for a static nested class is called automatically when an instance of the enclosing class is created.

h. The default constructor for an inner class is called automatically when an instance of the enclosing class is created.

i. A static nested class can access the instance fields and methods of the enclosing class.

j. It is not necessary to declare an interface defined inside a class with the `static` modifier.

k. An interface can be defined inside an inner class.

l. An anonymous class must either extend another class or implement an interface.

m. An anonymous class can be made static.

n. An anonymous class can be declared using the `private` modifier.

2. Define and give an example for each of the following:

a. Interface

b. Static nested class

c. Inner class

d. Anonymous class

3. Explain how the following are different:

a. Interfaces and abstract classes

b. Superinterfaces and subinterfaces

c. Static nested and inner classes

4. Create an interface called `Excavator`. Declare a method called `dig` in this interface. Create three classes called `Archaeologist`, `Mole`, and `BackHoe` that implement this interface. Each class should implement the method `dig` of `Excavator`. Include any other fields and methods in these classes that you think are needed. In `main`, create instances of each of these classes, and invoke the `dig` method for each instance.

5. Create an interface called `Tuner` with a method `tune`. Create two classes called `Radio` and `Guitar` that implement this interface. In `main`, create instances of each of these classes, and invoke the `tune` method for each instance.

6. Give an example showing why it is useful to use an interface as the data type of a parameter in a method.

7. Write a program showing how a static nested class is created. Also, show how the fields and methods of the enclosing class can be accessed in the static nested class.

8. Correct the errors (if any) in the following segments of code containing static nested classes and interfaces:

a.
```java
public class Top {
    private int a;
    public static class Nested {
      public void incrementA {
        a++;
      }
    }
}
```

b.
```java
public class Top {
    private static int b;
    private static class Nested {
      public void incrementB {
        b++;
      }
    }
}
public class TopDemo {
    public static void main(String[] args) {
      Top.Nested.incrementB();
    }
}
```

c.
```java
public class Top {
    private static class Nested {
    }
    public static void main(String[] args) {
      Top.Nested n1 = new Top.Nested();
    }
}
```

d.
```java
public class Top {
    public static class Nested1 {
      public static int getD() {
        return Nested2.d;
      }
    }
```

```
      private static class Nested2 {
        private static int d;
      }
    }
```

9. Correct the errors in the following main methods of these classes:

   a.
```
   public class Out {
     public class In {
     }
     public static void main(String[] args) {
       Out e = new Out();
       In i = e.new Out.In();
     }
   }
```

   b.
```
   public class Out {

     public static interface I {

       void method1(int a);

     }


     public class In implements I {

       public void method1(int a) {

         System.out.println("In method1 of class In a=" +a);

       }

     }


     public static void main(String[] args) {

       Out o = new Out();

       I i = new In();

       i.method1(10);

     }

   }
```

10. Write a main method in which an instance of the inner class B is created using its constructor:

```
public class A {
  public class B {
    int value1, value2;
    public B(int a, int b) {
```

```
        value1 = a;
        value2 = b;
      }
    }
  }
```

11. Show how you can create an instance of the inner class D using the method createD in C:

```
public class C {
  public D createD(int a, int b) {
    return new D(a, b);
  }
  private class D {
    int value1, value2;
    private D(int a, int b) {
      value1 = a;
      value2 = b;
    }
  }
}
```

12. Create a class called Data that contains two private fields, a and b. Create an inner class called Display in Data. Write a print method in Display to display the values of Data's fields. Write a program to test the print method.

13. Create an anonymous class that implements the MouseListener interface. Implement the MouseClicked method so that it displays a "Mouse clicked" message on the console each time the mouse is clicked.

14. Create an anonymous class called MyThread that implements the Runnable interface. Display the message "Running..." in the run method of this class.

Graphics and Image Manipulation Problems

15. Modify the Palette class in the following ways:

  a. Add a new color swatch to the palette. Test your program.
  b. Change the ColoredEllipse in Palette to a ColoredRectangle. Run the program and note how the colors are mixed differently.

16. Examine the API for the interface Transparency, which represents the type of transparency an image can have, in the java.awt package. This

interface has three constants (`OPAQUE`, `BITMASK`, and `TRANSLUCENT`) and the following method declaration:

`int getTransparency()` method returns one of the following values:

- The value 1 (`OPAQUE`) is returned if the image is fully opaque and cannot be made transparent.

- The value 2 (`BITMASK`) is returned if the image can only be either fully opaque or fully transparent.

- The value 3 (`TRANSLUCENT`) is returned if the image can be partially transparent.

The `BufferedImage` class implements this interface. Write a program to load images from files of different types, such as JPEG, GIF, and PNG, into the computer's memory (you can use `DrawingKit`), and determine their transparency. For example, JPEG images are fully opaque and cannot be made transparent, and so these are of type `OPAQUE`. Check whether it is possible to modify the transparency of an image for which the `getTransparency` method returns the value 1.

Further Reading

By now, you should be making extensive use of the Java API[1]. Whenever you come across a new interface or class, check its API for a complete listing.

References

1. *Java™ Platform, Standard Edition 6, API Specification.* Web. <http://download.oracle.com/javase/6/docs/api/>.

2. "The Java™ Tutorials." Web. <http://download.oracle.com/javase/tutorial/>.

3. Knudsen, Jonathan. *Java 2D Graphics.* Beijing: O'Reilly, 1999. Print.

4. Eckel, Bruce. *Thinking in Java.* Upper Saddle River, NJ: Prentice Hall, 2006. Print.

5. Anderson, Julie, and Herve Franceschi. *Java 6 Illuminated: An Active Learning Approach.* Sudbury, MA: Jones and Bartlett, 2008. Print.

6. Sierra, Kathy, and Bert Bates. *Head First Java.* Sebastopol, CA: O'Reilly, 2005. Print.

CHAPTER 9

GUI Programming

CHAPTER CONTENTS

A graphical user interface, or GUI (pronounced "gooey"), enables a user to interact with a program using graphics instead of text. A GUI consists of a window with elements such as buttons on it that you can click on to perform tasks (think of an online pizza ordering form as an example). The user can click or type on the GUI using a mouse or keyboard to input some data to the program. The program can display graphical and text output on the GUI. In this chapter, you will learn how to use Swing to create GUIs for your programs. In addition to Swing, other libraries that are used to create GUIs are Abstract Window Toolkit (AWT), Microsoft's Application Foundation Classes (AFC), Standard Widget Toolkit (SWT), and XML User Interface (XUI), among others. We will develop a photo-editing program in this chapter that lets you perform operations such as rotating, enlarging, and shrinking pictures. After reading this chapter, you will understand the code in the DrawingKit class that you have used in previous chapters to draw graphics.

9.1   Creating a Window

To create a window, use the JFrame class in the javax.swing package. Although the Swing API contains many packages, the javax.swing package is the one most commonly used. The programmer can specify the size, title, and other attributes for a window, and then display the window on the screen. Figure 9–1 shows some constructors and methods for JFrame.

After the window is created (using a constructor), we can add panels, buttons, labels, and other objects to make it interactive. For example, when the user clicks a button, the program might compute some values and display the results on the window. A **component** is a type of object in a window with which the user can interact. Figure 9–2 shows some components, including buttons, labels, text fields, check boxes, scroll panes, sliders, and radio buttons. A **container** is an object, such as a window or a panel, that can hold these components. Unlike panels, a window cannot be added to another container, and so it is known as a **top-level container**.

By default, a window is not visible. A window must be made visible, using the setVisible method, only after all of its components have been created and added to it. The setSize method takes the width and height of the window to be created as arguments. Alternatively, you can call the pack method,

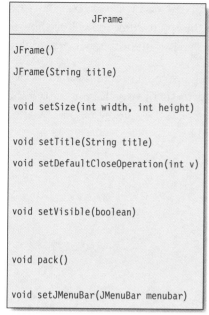

JFrame
JFrame()
JFrame(String title)
void setSize(int width, int height)
void setTitle(String title)
void setDefaultCloseOperation(int v)
void setVisible(boolean)
void pack()
void setJMenuBar(JMenuBar menubar)

Constructor creates an invisible window.

Constructor creates an invisible window with the given title.

Sets the width and height of this window to the specified values.

Sets the title of this window.

Specifies what should happen when the user closes this window. v is usually set to JFrame.EXIT_ON_CLOSE.

Makes this window visible on the screen if the boolean argument is true; otherwise, the window is hidden.

Sets this window's size automatically so that its various components can be displayed.

Adds the given menu bar to this window.

Figure 9–1
Some methods in class JFrame.

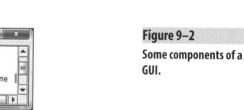

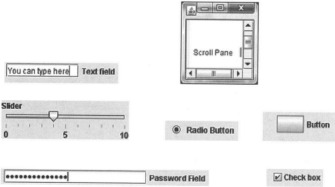

Figure 9–2
Some components of a GUI.

which sets the window size automatically depending on the sizes of the components in that window.

The argument to the method setDefaultCloseOperation determines the action taken when the user closes a window. The default value of the argument is WindowConstants.HIDE_ON_CLOSE, which hides the window. (WindowConstants is an interface in the javax.swing package that is implemented by

JFrame.) A commonly used argument to this method is JFrame.EXIT_ON_CLOSE, which closes the window and terminates the application. You will see how to use these and other methods, such as setJMenuBar, in the following examples.

The PhotoOp Class   In this chapter, we will develop a program called PhotoOp to modify photographs. This program consists of two classes: PhotoOp and PhotoOpDrawingPanel. The following code creates a window of the specified size with the given title and makes it visible:

```java
package guiprogramming;
import javax.swing.*;
import java.awt.*;

public class PhotoOp {
  private JFrame window;

  public PhotoOp() {
    // create the window
    window = new JFrame();

    // when window is closed, terminate the program as well
    window.setDefaultCloseOperation(JFrame.EXIT_ON_CLOSE);

    // set window size
    window.setSize(600, 600);

    // set window title
    window.setTitle("Photo Op");

    // make window visible
    window.setVisible(true);
  }

  public static void main(String[] args) {
    new PhotoOp();
  }
}
```

The argument of JFrame.EXIT_ON_CLOSE to method setDefaultCloseOperation closes this window and terminates the program when the user closes the window. When you run this program, it brings up the window shown in Figure 9–3. We will further develop this class in this chapter.

Figure 9–3
A window with the title "Photo Op."

9.2   The Swing Inheritance Tree

The inheritance tree of some important Swing classes is shown in Figure 9–4. The classes that you will use most often are JFrame, JPanel, and subclasses of JComponent, which we will cover later in this chapter. All classes whose names begin with J are part of Swing, whereas others, such as Window and Frame, are part of AWT (Java's older GUI toolkit). These classes reside in the javax.swing and java.awt packages.

The Component class is an abstract base class from which all of these other classes are derived. The Container class, derived from Component, defines several add methods to add a component to a container, two of which are shown in Figure 9–5.

The Window and JComponent classes are derived from Container. The Window class contains methods to create a window and generate events when the window is opened or closed. (We will discuss events and event handling later in this chapter.) The class Frame, which extends class Window, is used to create a window that contains a title and a border. Class JFrame further extends Frame and has some additional features, such as letting the programmer specify which action must be taken when a window is closed.

Figure 9–4

Inheritance tree of various Swing classes.

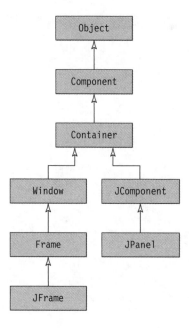

Figure 9–5

Methods to add a component to a container.

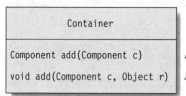

Container	
Component add(Component c)	Adds component c to the end of this container.
void add(Component c, Object r)	Adds component c to the region r.

The JComponent class is an abstract base class for all Swing components, such as panels, labels, text fields, and other components that are not top-level containers. We discuss the JPanel class that is derived from JComponent next.

9.3   The JPanel Class

As noted previously, a panel is a *container* that can hold components such as buttons, labels, text fields, and even other panels. As we will see later, graphics can be drawn on panels. A panel must be added to a window in order to be displayed; thus a panel is also a *component*, because it can be added to another container. To create a panel, use the JPanel class in the javax.swing package. Figure 9–6 shows some constructors and methods in this class.

JPanel	
JPanel()	Constructor creates a panel.
JPanel(LayoutManager manager)	Constructor creates a panel using the specified layout manager manager.
void setBorder(Border b)	Adds the border b to this panel.
void setLayout(LayoutManager manager)	Sets the layout to the specified layout manager manager.
void repaint()	Clears the contents of this panel and calls its paintComponent method.
void setPreferredSize(Dimension size)	Sets the size of this panel.
protected void paintComponent(Graphics g)	Paints on this panel using the graphics context g.

Figure 9–6
A few constructors and methods in class JPanel.

Note that a constructor and the setLayout method have a parameter of type LayoutManager. A layout manager is an instance of a class that implements the interface LayoutManager. Using a layout manager makes it easy to place components inside a panel. We will discuss this in detail in Section 9.4, Layout Managers. These statements create two panels named newPanel and topPanel:

```
JPanel newPanel = new JPanel();
JPanel topPanel = new JPanel();
```

We are now ready to see the different ways in which a panel can be used.

9.3.1 Adding Panels to Another Panel

You can add one or more panels to another panel using the add method defined in Container. For example, to add the panel newPanel to the panel topPanel, use the following statement:

```
topPanel.add(newPanel);
```

9.3.2 Setting the Content Pane of a Window

Every window contains a built-in **content pane**. All components must be added to the content pane of a window so that they can be seen inside a window. You cannot add components directly to a window. The content pane is obtained using the method getContentPane, and is changed using the setContentPane method of JFrame. Figure 9–7 shows these two methods.

Figure 9–7

**Methods to retrieve and
set the content pane of a
window.**

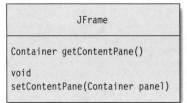

JFrame
Container getContentPane()

void
setContentPane(Container panel) |

Returns the content pane for this window.

Sets panel as the content pane of the window.

There are two ways to add components to a window. One way is to acquire the built-in content pane of the window with the getContentPane method, and then add a panel (that contains other components) to it. These statements add the panel topPanel to the content pane of a window:

```
Container contentPane = window.getContentPane();
contentPane.add(topPanel);
```

The second way is to set a panel as the content pane of a window by using method setContentPane. This statement sets the panel topPanel as the content pane of a window:

```
window.setContentPane(topPanel);
```

Let us create a new class called PanelsDemo to see how panels are used:

```
// class PanelsDemo – version 1
package guiprogramming;
import javax.swing.*;

public class PanelsDemo {
  public static void main(String[] args) {
    JFrame window = new JFrame();

    // create four panels
    JPanel topPanel = new JPanel();
    JPanel panel1 = new JPanel();
    JPanel panel2 = new JPanel();
    JPanel drawingPanel = new JPanel();

    // add panel1, panel2, drawingPanel to topPanel
    topPanel.add(panel1);
    topPanel.add(panel2);
    topPanel.add(drawingPanel);

    // set topPanel as content pane for this window
    window.setContentPane(topPanel);
```

```
    window.setSize(500, 500);
    window.setTitle("Panels Demo");
    window.setDefaultCloseOperation(JFrame.EXIT_ON_CLOSE);
    window.setVisible(true);
  }
}
```

When you run this program, a window appears. But, where are the panels that we added? The panels themselves are not visible, but we can view their outlines by adding a border to them. We do this next.

9.3.3   Adding Borders to the Panels

We can delegate the task of creating borders to the class BorderFactory in the javax.swing package. This class contains methods to create borders of different types (such as line, titled, matte, and others) for Swing components. The border is then added to a component using the method setBorder in JComponent. We will confine ourselves to the line border for now, and then briefly explore other types of borders later in this chapter.

To create a line border, invoke the createLineBorder method of BorderFactory. The color and (optionally) the thickness of the border can be specified:

```
public static Border createLineBorder(Color color);
```

```
public static Border createLineBorder(Color color, int thickness);
```

These methods return a variable of type Border, which is an interface in the javax.swing.border package.

Next we add the following code segment, which creates three borders of different widths and colors, to the PanelsDemo class (before the window.setVisible statement):

```
Border red = BorderFactory.createLineBorder(Color.red, 5);
Border blue = BorderFactory.createLineBorder(Color.blue, 3);
Border black = BorderFactory.createLineBorder(Color.black);
```

Use the setBorder method (inherited from JComponent) to add the borders to the panels in class PanelsDemo, as shown here:

```
panel1.setBorder(red);
panel2.setBorder(blue);
drawingPanel.setBorder(black);
```

We also add these statements to class PanelsDemo to import the class Color in the java.awt package and the interface Border in the javax.swing.border package:

```
import java.awt.*;
import javax.swing.border.*;
```

Compile and run the program PanelsDemo. This brings up a window with three empty panels outlined by their borders, as shown in Figure 9–8. The panel topPanel, which was set as the content pane of this window, occupies the entire window. As an exercise, add a border to this panel and rerun the program.

9.3.4   Adding Components to a Panel

Components can be added to a panel by using the add method of the Container class. There are many different types of components in Swing, such as buttons, labels, check boxes, radio buttons, dialog boxes, and scroll bars, to name just a few! Let us start by adding some buttons to the panels in the PanelsDemo class.

A button is created using the JButton class in the javax.swing package. Two constructors for creating a button are shown in Figure 9–9.

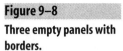

Figure 9–8

Three empty panels with borders.

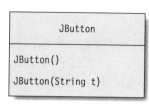

Figure 9–9
Two constructors for creating buttons.

JButton	
JButton()	Constructor creates a button.
JButton(String t)	Constructor creates a button with the text t displayed in it.

Create two buttons, called button1 and button2, and add them to panel1:

```
JButton button1 = new JButton("Rectangle");
panel1.add(button1);
JButton button2 = new JButton("Circle");
panel1.add(button2);
```

Add these statements to the PanelsDemo class, after panel1 is created but before the window is made visible, and then compile and run the program. The output is shown in Figure 9–10. Note that panel1 (outlined by the thickest border) is resized automatically as the two buttons are added to it. Clicking on the buttons does nothing at present, but we will change this in Section 9.6, *The Event Model.*

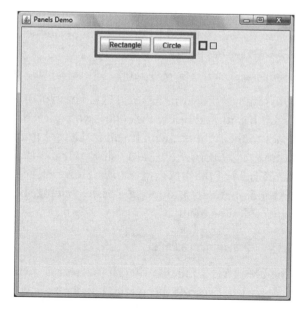

Figure 9–10
Two buttons added to a panel.

9.3.5   Managing the Layout of Components in a Panel

In Figure 9–10, the two buttons we created are arranged in a row. The reason for this is that, by default, panels use a layout scheme called FlowLayout, which arranges components in a row from left to right. For the same reason, the three panels that were added to topPanel were also placed in a row. Other layout schemes, such as BoxLayout, GridLayout, and BorderLayout, are discussed in Section 9.4, *Layout Managers.*

9.3.6   Changing Panel Size

So far, we have seen that a panel's size is set automatically. Panel size depends on many factors, such as window size, the number of panels and components in a window, and the layout scheme used. JComponent includes a method called setPreferredSize that you can use to explicitly specify the size of a panel (or some other component). However, using this method will not necessarily produce the desired change in the size of a component, because doing so depends on the various factors described previously.

The Dimension class, in the java.awt package, is used to specify the width and height of an object. Thus, to set a panel's width to 200 and its height to 500, we can create an instance of this class that contains this information and pass it as an argument to method setPreferredSize:

```
panel.setPreferredSize(new Dimension(200, 500));
```

For example, we might want to make drawingPanel larger to draw graphics inside it. We could add the following statement to class PanelsDemo after drawingPanel has been created:

```
drawingPanel.setPreferredSize(new Dimension(400, 400));
```

The result is shown in Figure 9–11. The size of drawingPanel has increased and it has moved below the other two panels because there is insufficient space to the right of them. If you make the window larger by dragging the bottom right corner outward using your mouse, the panel will move back to the right of the other two panels. However, keep in mind that calling this method might not produce the desired change because the layout manager supercedes the method.

9.3.7   Drawing on a Panel

The JPanel class inherits the paintComponent method from JComponent. It is necessary to override this method to draw on a panel:

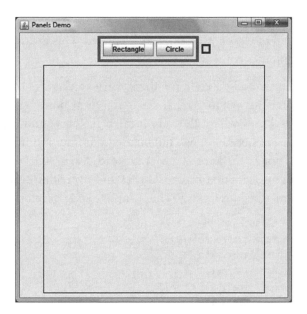

Figure 9–11

The panel drawingPanel is made larger using the setPreferredSize method.

```
protected void paintComponent(Graphics g) {
  super.paintComponent(g);
  // add some code here to draw graphics
}
```

The Graphics object g for this panel is obtained automatically through paint-Component, and it can be used to draw on the panel. Recall that the Graphics class is an abstract base class in the java.awt package, and that it contains methods to draw graphics on components. The first statement in paintComponent is a call to the super.paintComponent method. This calls the paintComponent method of the superclass to paint the background of this component before drawing other graphics on it. (We discuss this in more detail in Section 9.3.9, *Painting a Panel's Background.*)

Add the following statements to method paintComponent to draw a circle:

```
public void paintComponent(Graphics g) {
  super.paintComponent(g);
  Graphics2D myGraphics = (Graphics2D) g;
  Ellipse2D circle = new Ellipse2D.Float(100, 100, 200, 200);
  myGraphics.draw(circle);
}
```

Although the methods in the Graphics class can be used to draw the graphics, it is better to use its subclass, Graphics2D, instead. Therefore, we have cast the Graphics object g to a Graphics2D instance called myGraphics, and use the latter to do all the drawing in paintComponent. Next, an instance (called circle) of class Ellipse2D.Float is created. This is drawn on the panel using the graphics context myGraphics.

The modified code for the PanelsDemo class follows. One change from the previous version is that we do not draw borders around the panels because we know where they are located in the window. In addition, we remove panel2, because it will not be used. Another modification is that drawingPanel is not an instance of JPanel. Instead, drawingPanel is an instance of an anonymous class that extends JPanel and overrides its paintComponent method, as described previously. The complete code developed so far is shown here:

```
// class PanelsDemo – version 2
package guiprogramming;
import javax.swing.*;
import java.awt.*;
import javax.swing.border.*;
import java.awt.geom.*;

public class PanelsDemo {
  public static void main(String[] args) {
    JFrame window = new JFrame();

    // create three panels named topPanel, panel1 and drawingPanel
    JPanel topPanel = new JPanel();
    JPanel panel1 = new JPanel();

    // draw graphics on drawingPanel
    JPanel drawingPanel = new JPanel() {
      public void paintComponent(Graphics g) {
        super.paintComponent(g);
        Graphics2D myGraphics = (Graphics2D) g;
        Ellipse2D circle = new Ellipse2D.Float(100, 100, 200, 200);
        myGraphics.draw(circle);
      }
    };

    // add panel1 and drawingPanel to topPanel
    topPanel.add(panel1);
    topPanel.add(drawingPanel);

    // set topPanel as content pane for this window
    window.setContentPane(topPanel);
```

```
    // add two buttons to panel1
    JButton button1 = new JButton("Rectangle");
    panel1.add(button1);
    JButton button2 = new JButton("Circle");
    panel1.add(button2);

    // set the size of drawingPanel
    drawingPanel.setPreferredSize(new Dimension(400, 400));

    window.setSize(500, 500);
    window.setTitle("Panels Demo");
    window.setDefaultCloseOperation(JFrame.EXIT_ON_CLOSE);
    window.setVisible(true);
  }
}
```

The output of this program is shown in Figure 9–12. An ellipse is drawn on drawingPanel at the position specified in the paintComponent method. After working out this example, try drawing other types of graphics on panels.

An important point to remember is that the paintComponent method should not be called directly.

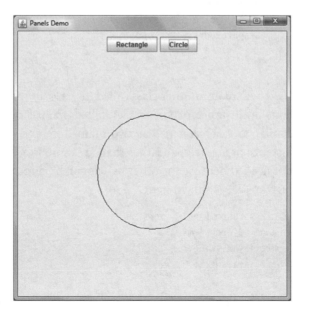

Figure 9–12
Drawing on a panel.

It would be incorrect to write:

```
drawingPanel.paintComponent(g);   // error
```

Instead, this method is called automatically when the panel is *created*. The paintComponent method can also be called explicitly by the repaint method defined in Component. You can change the graphics displayed on a panel using repaint; we will see examples of how to do this later in Section 9.6.

9.3.8   Creating Custom Panels

In the class PanelsDemo, we created all of the panels in the main program itself. An alternate approach is to create a separate class for the panels that extends JPanel. All of the code related to the panels goes into this class. As an example, we move the code for drawingPanel into a new class called SimplePanel:

```
// class SimplePanel - version 1
package guiprogramming;
import java.awt.*;
import java.awt.geom.*;
import javax.swing.*;

public class SimplePanel extends JPanel {
  public void paintComponent(Graphics g) {
    super.paintComponent(g);
    Graphics2D myGraphics = (Graphics2D) g;
    Ellipse2D circle = new Ellipse2D.Float(100, 100, 200, 200);
    myGraphics.draw(circle);
  }
}
```

Next, we create another class called CustomPanel that extends JPanel and contains an instance of SimplePanel called drawingPanel. Although this class is similar to PanelsDemo, it has two main differences: First, drawingPanel is an instance of SimplePanel rather than an anonymous class. Second, topPanel is not needed because the other panels can be directly added to an instance of CustomPanel, as shown here:

```
// class CustomPanel - version 1
package guiprogramming;
import javax.swing.*;
import java.awt.*;

public class CustomPanel extends JPanel {
```

```
  private JPanel panel1;
  private SimplePanel drawingPanel;
  private JButton button1;
  private JButton button2;

  public CustomPanel() {
    panel1 = new JPanel();
    drawingPanel = new SimplePanel();

    // create two buttons and add to panel1
    button1 = new JButton("Rectangle");
    panel1.add(button1);
    button2 = new JButton("Circle");
    panel1.add(button2);

    drawingPanel.setPreferredSize(new Dimension(400, 400));

    // add panel1 and drawingPanel to this panel
    add(panel1);
    add(drawingPanel);
  }
}
```

The class CustomPanel is a special type of panel because it extends JPanel. Therefore, we can add the panels panel1 and drawingPanel directly to an instance of this class using either add(panel1) or this.add(panel1).

Add the following main method to the CustomPanel class. In this main, an instance of CustomPanel is set as the content pane for the window. Note that the main shown here is shorter than in PanelsDemo:

```
public static void main(String[] args) {
  JFrame window = new JFrame();

  // create a custom panel
  CustomPanel mainPanel = new CustomPanel();

  // set mainPanel as content pane for this window
  window.setContentPane(mainPanel);

  window.setSize(500, 500);
  window.setTitle("Custom Panel");
  window.setDefaultCloseOperation(JFrame.EXIT_ON_CLOSE);
  window.setVisible(true);
}
```

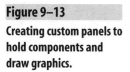

Figure 9–13

Creating custom panels to hold components and draw graphics.

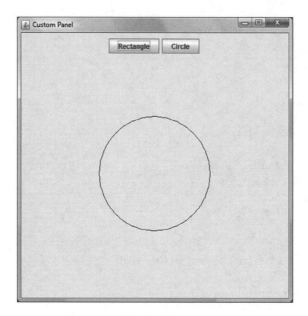

Compile and run classes SimplePanel (version 1) and CustomPanel (version 1). The output of this program is shown in Figure 9–13. In Section 9.6.3, we will add code to activate the buttons.

It is better to create a separate class for drawing panels, especially if the code to do the drawing is complicated and lengthy. We will use this approach in the PhotoOp class.

9.3.9   Painting a Panel's Background

Every component has an opaque property that can be set to true or false. If the property is false, the component's background is not painted; if true, it is. This property can be changed by using the setOpaque method from the class JComponent.

Add the following statement to the constructor of CustomPanel:

```
drawingPanel.setBackground(Color.red);
```

The default setting of the opaque property for panels is usually true, but this is not necessary, depending on the particular Swing implementation that you are using. When you run the program, the background of drawing-Panel will be painted red because this panel is opaque by default. If you change its opacity to false using the setOpaque method, the background will not be painted.

Suppose that you also add the following statement to the constructor in CustomPanel:

drawingPanel.setOpaque(false);

Run the program and note that the background of the drawingPanel is not painted now. You can try this out with the other panels, as well as with the buttons that you have added to panel1.

To paint its background, a component must also call the method super.paintComponent in its paintComponent method. If you comment out the call to this method, that component's background will not be drawn when it calls the method setBackground, regardless of its opacity setting. As an exercise, comment out the call to super.paintComponent in the paintComponent method of drawingPanel, and then check whether this panel's background is drawn.

9.4 Layout Managers

When you create a GUI, you can use a layout manager to position and size the components automatically. This makes it much easier to create the GUI because you do not have to specify the position and size of every component (which can be tricky). Swing provides several classes, such as FlowLayout, BoxLayout, BorderLayout, and GridLayout, for specifying different types of layout. A **layout manager** is an instance of any one of these classes. All components are placed in panels and/or content panes; thus you must provide a layout manager for these containers only.

9.4.1 The FlowLayout Class

The FlowLayout class is used to create a layout in which all components are placed in a single row within the container. (Multiple rows are used if the container size is too small to fit all components in one row.) This is the default layout for all instances of class JPanel.

Two constructors are shown in Figure 9–14. The first argument of the second constructor lets you specify how the values should be aligned in their fields. Some values for this argument are FlowLayout.LEFT (left justified), FlowLayout.RIGHT (right justified), and FlowLayout.CENTER (centered). Note that you can only align horizontally, not vertically. This constructor also allows you to indicate the horizontal and vertical spacing between components.

Figure 9–14

Two constructors in class FlowLayout.

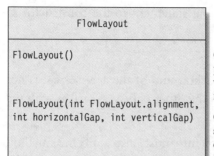

FlowLayout
FlowLayout()
FlowLayout(int FlowLayout.alignment, int horizontalGap, int verticalGap)

Constructor creates a FlowLayout that provides default 5-unit horizontal and vertical gaps between components and is center aligned.

Constructor creates a FlowLayout with the specified alignment and gaps between components. Some values of alignment are LEFT, RIGHT, and CENTER.

Example 1

The following code shows how to add five buttons to a panel using FlowLayout:

```java
package guiprogramming;
import java.awt.*;
import javax.swing.*;

public class FlowLayoutDemo {
  public static void main(String[] args) {
    JFrame window = new JFrame("FlowLayout Demo");

    // create a panel with the FlowLayout layout manager
    JPanel panel = new JPanel(new FlowLayout(FlowLayout.LEFT, 20, 50));
    window.setContentPane(panel);

    // create five buttons
    JButton button1 = new JButton("Button 1");
    JButton button2 = new JButton("Button 2");
    JButton button3 = new JButton("Button 3");
    JButton button4 = new JButton("Button 4");
    JButton button5 = new JButton("Button 5");

    //  add the buttons to panel using FlowLayout
    panel.add(button1);
    panel.add(button2);
    panel.add(button3);
    panel.add(button4);
    panel.add(button5);

    window.pack();
    window.setVisible(true);
  }
}
```

Figure 9–15
**Placing components
using class FlowLayout.**

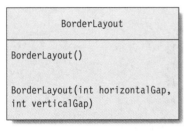

Figure 9–16
**Constructors to create a
BorderLayout.**

BorderLayout	
BorderLayout()	Constructor creates a border layout with no gaps between components.
BorderLayout(int horizontalGap, int verticalGap)	Constructor creates a border layout with the specified horizontal and vertical gaps between components.

In this class, the JPanel(LayoutManager) constructor is used to create the panel. Also, note that the window size is set using the pack method instead of setSize so that the window size is set automatically to display the components. The output is shown in Figure 9–15. Experiment with different vertical gaps, horizontal gaps, and alignments, as well as with changing the window size using your mouse, and see how the layout changes. ∎

9.4.2 The BorderLayout Class

The BorderLayout class can be used to create a layout that places one component in the center and arranges four components to the north, south, east, and west of it. It has the two constructors shown in Figure 9–16.

Use the add(Component c, Object r) method (shown earlier, in Figure 9–5) to add components with this layout. The region r can take one of the string constants BorderLayout.NORTH, BorderLayout.EAST, BorderLayout.CENTER, Border-Layout.WEST, or BorderLayout.SOUTH, which represent the north, east, center, west, and south regions of the window, respectively.

Example 2

The BorderLayoutDemo class shows how to use this layout manager:

```
package guiprogramming;
import java.awt.*;
import javax.swing.*;
```

```
public class BorderLayoutDemo {
  public static void main(String[] args) {
    JFrame window = new JFrame();

    // create a panel that uses BorderLayout
    JPanel panel = new JPanel(new BorderLayout());
    window.setContentPane(panel);

    // create the buttons
    JButton button1 = new JButton("Button 1");
    JButton button2 = new JButton("Button 2");
    JButton button3 = new JButton("Button 3");
    JButton button4 = new JButton("Button 4");
    JButton button5 = new JButton("Button 5");

    // add the buttons to the panel using BorderLayout
    panel.add(button1, BorderLayout.NORTH);
    panel.add(button2, BorderLayout.SOUTH);
    panel.add(button3, BorderLayout.WEST);
    panel.add(button4, BorderLayout.EAST);
    panel.add(button5, BorderLayout.CENTER);

    window.pack();
    window.setTitle("BorderLayout Demo");
    window.setVisible(true);
  }
}
```

The output is shown in Figure 9–17. If you increase the window size, the sizes of the buttons increase, with the center button occupying the largest area. As an exercise, change the size of the window using the setSize method, and note how the component sizes change.   ∎

The PhotoOp Class: Drawing an Image   In this section, we create a drawing panel for PhotoOp called PhotoOpDrawingPanel and draw an image on it. We will

Figure 9–17

Placing components using class BorderLayout.

also see how BorderLayout is used to arrange the layout of the different panels. Before doing so, we discuss how to read an image from a file and store it in the computer's memory using the getImage method in classes ImageIcon and Toolkit.

The interface javax.swing.Icon contains methods to get an image's height and width. The class ImageIcon that implements this interface is used to create pictures (known as icons). Some constructors and a method in this class are shown in Figure 9–18.

The getImage method of class ImageIcon returns an image of type java.awt.Image, which is the parent class of the BufferedImage class. This statement assigns the reference variable backgroundImage to the image that is loaded from the file bricks.jpg into the computer's memory:

```
Image backgroundImage = new
javax.swing.ImageIcon("image/bricks.jpg").getImage();
```

Another way to read an image is to use the Toolkit class:

```
Image backgroundImage =
Toolkit.getDefaultToolkit().getImage("image/bricks.jpg");
```

This also reads the image in file bricks.jpg and stores it in backgroundImage.

After the image has been read from a file, the next step is to draw it on the screen. The image can be drawn on a panel or some other component using the drawImage methods in the Graphics class (see Figure 9–19).

It takes a small amount of time to load an image from a file into the computer's memory. The getImage method in the Toolkit class returns immediately without waiting for an image to be completely read from the file. If a

ImageIcon	
ImageIcon(String file)	Constructor creates an icon from the image in the specified file.
ImageIcon(Image i)	Constructor creates an icon from the Image object i.
ImageIcon(URL u)	Constructor creates an icon from the image at URL u.
Image getImage()	Returns this icon's image as an object of type Image.

Figure 9–18
Some constructors and a method in class ImageIcon.

Figure 9–19

Methods in the Graphics class to draw an image in the computer's memory on the screen.

Graphics	
abstract boolean drawImage(Image image, int x, int y, ImageObserver o)	Draws image at the position (x, y). If no image observer is used, it is specified to be null.
abstract boolean drawImage(Image image, int x, int y, int width, int height, ImageObserver o)	Scales image to the specified width and height, and then draws it at position (x, y).

large number of photographs are loading, it is likely that they will not load in time, and therefore they will not display correctly. This can be rectified by specifying an *image observer* in the drawImage method, as explained next.

An **image observer** is an instance of a class that implements the interface ImageObserver, and it is automatically notified when an image has finished loading from a file. The ImageObserver interface resides in the java.awt.image package. Classes that implement this interface must define its abstract imageUpdate method. The observer's imageUpdate method is executed when the notification is received. This method decides what should be done next. The default behavior of the method is to redraw the image on some component. All components are of type ImageObserver because the Component class implements this interface. Therefore, you can use any component (on which the image must be drawn) as an image observer by passing it to draw-Image with the keyword this:

```
g2.drawImage(bimage, 0, 0, this);
```

After the image has finished loading from the file, it is drawn automatically on that component. An image observer does not have to be used when the image is read using the getImage method in ImageIcon.

We now develop the PhotoOpDrawingPanel class to create a custom panel and draw the image in the file squirrelMonkey.jpg on it. Copy squirrelMonkey.jpg from the JavaBook/image directory on the CD-ROM into the JavaBook/image directory on your computer. The code for PhotoOpDrawingPanel is similar to that of SimplePanel, except that it draws an image instead of a circle on the panel:

```
// class PhotoOpDrawingPanel
package guiprogramming;
import java.awt.*;
```

```
import javax.swing.*;

public class PhotoOpDrawingPanel extends JPanel {
  private Image bimage;

  public PhotoOpDrawingPanel() {
    bimage = new
javax.swing.ImageIcon("image/squirrelMonkey.jpg").getImage();
  }

  public void paintComponent(Graphics g) {
    super.paintComponent(g);
    Graphics2D g2 = (Graphics2D) g;
    g2.drawImage(bimage, 0, 0, null);
  }
}
```

The getImage and drawImage methods have been used to read and draw the image, respectively. An instance of PhotoOpDrawingPanel is added to the window created earlier. You will need to make some changes to the PhotoOp class, as described next.

First, add these fields to PhotoOp:

```
private JPanel topPanel, groupPanel;
private PhotoOpDrawingPanel drawingPanel;
```

We will add buttons, check boxes, and other components to groupPanel later to modify the picture. Next, we add the method createPanels to PhotoOp to create these panels:

```
public void createPanels() {
  topPanel = new JPanel(new BorderLayout());
  drawingPanel = new PhotoOpDrawingPanel();
  groupPanel = new JPanel();

  // add drawingPanel to topPanel
  topPanel.add(drawingPanel, BorderLayout.CENTER);
  topPanel.add(groupPanel, BorderLayout.EAST);
}
```

Finally, we add these two lines to the constructor in PhotoOp after the statement to create a window:

```
createPanels();
window.setContentPane(topPanel);
```

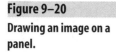

Figure 9–20

Drawing an image on a panel.

squirrelMonkey.jpg © Simone Van Den Berg, 123RF.com

The preceding statement sets `topPanel`, which contains `drawingPanel` and `groupPanel`, as the content pane of the window. Compile and run the program as follows:

```
C:\JavaBook> javac -d bin src\guiprogramming\PhotoOp.java
src\guiprogramming\PhotoOpDrawingPanel.java
```

```
C:\JavaBook> java -classpath bin guiprogramming.PhotoOp
```

The output is shown in Figure 9–20. A squirrel monkey appears on the window, ready for its photo op! The image is drawn on `drawingPanel`, and `groupPanel` is the narrow, empty box to its right; `topPanel` occupies the entire window. In the following sections, you will learn how to add a title and border to this picture, as well as add components such as buttons and check boxes to modify its orientation, size, and shape.

9.4.3   The `GridLayout` Class

The `GridLayout` class is used when components need to be placed in a grid-like structure with a certain number of columns and rows within a container. All components have the same size in this type of layout. There are three constructors in this class, as described in Figure 9–21. In the second and third constructors, the number of rows (or columns) can be set to 0. This creates a layout with the smallest number of rows (or columns) neces-

GridLayout
GridLayout()
GridLayout(int rows, int columns)
GridLayout(int rows, int columns, int horizontalGap, int verticalGap)

Constructor places components in a single row.

Constructor creates a layout with the specified number of rows and columns.

Constructor creates a layout with the given number of rows and columns, and the specified horizontal and vertical gaps between components.

Figure 9–21
Constructors to create a
GridLayout.

sary to hold all of the components in the container. (Note that the values of rows and columns cannot both be 0.)

Example 3

This example shows how GridLayout lays out five buttons in a grid of 0 rows and 3 columns with horizontal and vertical gaps between components of 40 and 20, respectively.

```
package guiprogramming;
import java.awt.*;
import javax.swing.*;

public class GridLayoutDemo {
  public static void main(String[] args) {
    JFrame window = new JFrame("GridLayout Demo");

    // panel will arrange components in 3 columns with the given spacing
    JPanel panel = new JPanel(new GridLayout(0, 3, 40, 20));

    window.setContentPane(panel);

    // create five buttons
    JButton button1 = new JButton("Button 1");
    JButton button2 = new JButton("Button 2");
    JButton button3 = new JButton("Button 3");
    JButton button4 = new JButton("Button 4");
    JButton button5 = new JButton("Button 5");

    // add the buttons to panel
    panel.add(button1);
    panel.add(button2);
```

```
        panel.add(button3);
        panel.add(button4);
        panel.add(button5);

        window.pack();
        window.setVisible(true);
    }
}
```

The output is shown in Figure 9–22. Two rows are needed to hold the five buttons in three columns. Try changing the number of rows and columns, and the spacing between components, to see how the layout is affected. ■

9.4.4   The BoxLayout Class

The BoxLayout class (see Figure 9–23) is used to create a layout that places components in a single row or column within a container. This class can be used in conjunction with the class javax.swing.Box to provide better control over how the components are placed.

You can use the Box class to create *struts* and *glue* to control the spacing and sizes of the components. A **strut** is a space of fixed width or height between components. **Glue** is used to create variable spacing between components. Figure 9–24 shows some methods in this class. To create a strut, two static methods, createHorizontalStrut and createVerticalStrut, are provided. The static methods createHorizontalGlue and createVerticalGlue create glue.

Figure 9–22
Placing components using a GridLayout.

Figure 9–23
A constructor in class BoxLayout.

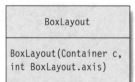

BoxLayout(Container c, int BoxLayout.axis)   Constructor to create a box layout for container c. Set axis to X_AXIS or Y_AXIS to arrange components in a row or a column, respectively.

Box	
static Component createHorizontalStrut(int width)	Returns a component with a *fixed* width.
static Component createVerticalStrut(int height)	Returns a component with a *fixed* height.
static Component createHorizontalGlue()	Returns a component that creates *variable* spacing in the horizontal direction.
static Component createVerticalGlue()	Returns a component that creates *variable* spacing in the vertical direction.

Figure 9–24

Methods in the Box class to create struts and glue.

Example 4

This program shows how BoxLayout is used:

```
package guiprogramming;
import java.awt.*;
import javax.swing.*;

public class BoxLayoutDemo {
  public static void main(String[] args) {
    JFrame window = new JFrame();
    JPanel panel = new JPanel();

    // panel will arrange components in a single row
    panel.setLayout(new BoxLayout(panel, BoxLayout.X_AXIS));

    window.setContentPane(panel);
    JButton button1 = new JButton("Button 1");
    JButton button2 = new JButton("Button 2");
    JButton button3 = new JButton("Button 3");
    JButton button4 = new JButton("Button 4");
    JButton button5 = new JButton("Button 5");
    panel.add(button1);
    panel.add(button2);

    // create a horizontal strut between buttons 2 and 3
    panel.add(Box.createHorizontalStrut(10));

    panel.add(button3);

    // create horizontal glue between buttons 3 and 4
```

```
        panel.add(Box.createHorizontalGlue());

        panel.add(button4);
        panel.add(button5);
        window.pack();
        window.setTitle("BoxLayout Demo");
        window.setVisible(true);
    }
}
```

A horizontal strut and horizontal glue have been added after buttons 2 and 3, respectively. Compile and run this code. The output is shown in Figure 9–25.

To see the difference between the glue and the strut, make the window larger, as shown in Figure 9–26. Note that the strut between buttons 2 and 3 has the same width as before, but the width of the glue between buttons 3 and 4 has increased.   ∎

9.4.5   Insets

Although the preferred (and easier) approach for layout is to use the various layout managers that are provided in Swing, it is also possible to create a layout without them using **absolute positioning**. In this case, the container's layout manager is set to null, and each component's setBounds method is called to position and size it. The setBounds method is described in Component and can be used as follows:

> **public void setBounds(float x, float y, float w, float h)**—a method that is used for absolute positioning so that the component is positioned at (x, y) and has width w and height h.

Figure 9–25

Placing buttons using BoxLayout.

Figure 9–26

The horizontal strut between buttons 2 and 3 does not change, whereas the width of the horizontal glue between buttons 3 and 4 increases.

Spaces or borders around the edges of a container are called **insets**. In absolute positioning, the components should not overlap this space. You can get information about the insets using the getInsets method in class JFrame:

> **Insets getInsets()**—a method that returns an instance of class Insets containing information about the borders of this component.

An example is shown here:

```
JFrame window = new JFrame();
Insets inset = window.getInsets();
```

The Insets class which resides in the java.awt package, has four fields named bottom, top, left, and right that give the widths of the border at the bottom, top, left, and right of the container, respectively. The next example shows how to use insets.

Example 5

Two buttons are created and placed in a window using absolute positioning. The sizes and positions of the buttons do not change if the window is resized. In addition, the first button is positioned incorrectly on top of the panel's border, whereas the second button is positioned correctly using the insets:

```
package guiprogramming;
import java.awt.*;
import javax.swing.*;
import javax.swing.border.*;

public class AbsolutePositioningLayoutDemo {
  public static void main(String[] args) {
    JFrame window = new JFrame();
    JPanel panel = new JPanel();

    // a layout manager is not used
    panel.setLayout(null);

    window.setContentPane(panel);
    JButton button1 = new JButton("Button 1");
    JButton button2 = new JButton("Button 2");
    panel.add(button1);
    panel.add(button2);
```

```
    // create a gray-colored border of width 8 around panel
    Border border = BorderFactory.createLineBorder(Color.gray, 8);
    panel.setBorder(border);

    // this button is positioned incorrectly on top of the border
    button1.setBounds(400, 0, 100, 50);

    // get information about the panel's borders
    Insets inset = panel.getInsets();

    // this button is positioned inside the border
    button2.setBounds(inset.left, inset.top, 100, 50);

    // prints out 8, which is the border width
    System.out.println(inset.left);
    System.out.println(inset.top);

    window.setSize(500, 500);
    window.setTitle("AbsolutePositioning Demo");
    window.setVisible(true);
  }
}
```

The println statements print out the width of the panel's border to the left and top. The output is shown in Figure 9–27. ∎

Figure 9–27

Two buttons placed using absolute positioning; button 2 is positioned correctly inside the gray border using insets.

9.5   Borders

The class BorderFactory makes it easy to create borders of different types, such as beveled, etched, compound, matte, line, and titled. These borders are defined in the classes BevelBorder, EtchedBorder, and so forth in the java.awt.border package. To create these borders, BorderFactory provides the static methods shown in Figure 9–28.

The createBevelBorder method creates a border that is raised or lowered. A raised beveled border makes the component appear to be raised toward the viewer, whereas a lowered border gives the component a slight sunken look. After the border has been created, a component can set the border using

Figure 9–28
Methods to create different types of borders.

BorderFactory	
static Border createBevelBorder(int type)	Creates a beveled border where type is BevelBorder.LOWERED or BevelBorder.RAISED.
static Border createEtchedBorder()	Creates an etched border in the component's background color.
static Border createEtchedBorder(int type)	Creates an etched border of type EtchedBorder.RAISED or EtchedBorder.LOWERED.
static Border createEmptyBorder()	Creates a border where the width of its sides is 0.
static CompoundBorder createCompoundBorder(Border outerBorder, Border innerBorder)	Creates two nested borders innerBorder and outerBorder, where innerBorder is placed inside outerBorder.
static createLineBorder(Color color, int width)	Creates a line border of the specified color and width.
static MatteBorder createMatteBorder(int top, int left, int bottom, int right, Color color)	Similar to method createLineBorder, except that the width of each side can be specified separately.
static MatteBorder createMatteBorder(int top, int left, int bottom, int right, Icon icon)	Creates a matte border with the specified widths using the image icon.
static TitledBorder createTitledBorder(String t)	Creates a border with the title t.
static TitledBorder createTitledBorder(Border b, String t)	Adds the title t to an existing border b.

the setBorder method. The following statement gives an example of how to draw a beveled border around a JPanel instance called panel:

panel.**setBorder**(**BorderFactory.createBevelBorder**(BevelBorder.LOWERED));

To create a raised border, use the argument BevelBorder.RAISED in method createBevelBorder.

Similar to beveled borders, a raised etched border makes the border appear to be raised toward the user, and a lowered etched border has a sunken look:

panel.setBorder(**BorderFactory.createEtchedBorder**(EtchedBorder.LOWERED));

The different types of borders are shown in Figure 9–29. The following statements show how to create these borders.

This statement creates a transparent border:

panel.setBorder(**BorderFactory.createEmptyBorder**());

You can create a border with a title (using default settings for its type, font, and other properties) as follows:

panel.setBorder(**BorderFactory.createTitledBorder**("Title"));

This statement creates a beveled border with the title "Title" around panel:

panel.setBorder(**BorderFactory.createTitledBorder**(BorderFactory.createBevelB
order(BevelBorder.LOWERED), "Title"));

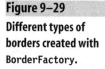

Figure 9–29

Different types of borders created with BorderFactory.

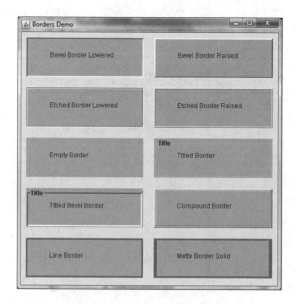

The following call to the `createCompoundBorder` method creates a beveled raised border around an etched lowered border:

```
panel.setBorder(BorderFactory.createCompoundBorder(BorderFactory.createBevel
Border(BevelBorder.RAISED), BorderFactory.createEtchedBorder(EtchedBorder
.LOWERED)));
```

This statement creates a gray line border of width 3 around `panel`:

```
panel.setBorder(BorderFactory.createLineBorder(Color.gray, 3));
```

This statement creates a gray matte border with width 3 at the top and bottom and width 6 to the left and right of `panel`:

```
panel.setBorder(BorderFactory.createMatteBorder(3, 6, 3, 6, Color.gray));
```

The `createMatteBorder` method that takes an argument of type `Icon` can be used to set an icon as the border. `BorderFactory` also contains other methods (not discussed here) for setting other parameters, such as highlights and shadows, around borders.

The `PhotoOp` Class: Adding Panels and Borders We develop our `PhotoOp` class further by adding a panel to display the name of the photograph. Add this field to class `PhotoOp`:

```
private JPanel titlePanel;
```

Add the method `createTitlePanel` to `PhotoOp`. This method creates a light gray panel at the top of the window to label the picture:

```
public JPanel createTitlePanel() {
  JPanel titlePanel = new JPanel();
  topPanel.add(titlePanel, BorderLayout.NORTH);
  titlePanel.setBorder(BorderFactory.createEtchedBorder(EtchedBorder
.RAISED));
  titlePanel.setBackground(Color.lightGray);
  return titlePanel;
}
```

Recall that `topPanel` is the content pane of the window. Call this method in the `createPanels` method in `PhotoOp`:

```
// panel to hold photo's title
titlePanel = createTitlePanel();
```

Figure 9–30
Adding a panel at the top of the window.

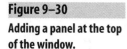

Figure 9–30

Adding a panel at the top of the window.

squirrelMonkey.jpg © Simone Van Den Berg, 123RF.com

Add these statements to the createPanels method in PhotoOp to add borders and backgrounds to the other panels:

```
groupPanel.setLayout(new BoxLayout(groupPanel, BoxLayout.Y_AXIS));
groupPanel.setBorder(BorderFactory.createEtchedBorder(EtchedBorder.RAISED));
groupPanel.setBackground(Color.lightGray);
topPanel.setBackground(Color.lightGray);
```

This will set the layout of groupPanel to a BoxLayout and add components to it in a single column. We have now added backgrounds and a border to these panels.

In addition, add this import statement to PhotoOp, and then compile and run the program:

```
import javax.swing.border.*;
```

The output is shown in Figure 9–30. The panel titlePanel appears in gray above the picture. We will add a label to this panel, in Section 9.7.1, to display the name of the photograph.

9.6   The Event Model

In computer games, a player can interact with the game by clicking the mouse or pressing keys. This interactivity is what makes the game exciting.

In this section, you will learn how to make GUIs respond to user actions using the Swing *event model*.

The **event model** is composed of three types of objects: *event source, event object*, and *event handler*. An **event** occurs when the user performs an action on a GUI, such as clicking the mouse, moving the mouse, or pressing keys on the keyboard. The **event source** is the object that generated the event. Components of a GUI, such as buttons and panels, are examples of event sources. For example, a button generates an event object when the user presses on it. The **event object** contains information about the event, such as what type of event occurred, which component generated this event, and so forth. Swing then automatically sends a message to one or more event handlers using the event object. The **event handler** (also called **event listener**) performs some action to respond to the event. The action could be drawing graphics on the GUI, computing data and displaying it to the user, or a similar action.

Consider this analogy to understand the sequence of operations: Suppose that a friend calls you on your phone. When you hear the phone ring, you pick it up and answer it. Can you identify the event source, event object, and event handler here? The event source is the phone, the event object is the message on your phone identifying the caller, and you are the event handler.

The same event handler might be listening for events generated by different event sources, just as you can respond to both the sound of knocking at the door and the ringing of a phone at your home. There can also be multiple event handlers listening for events generated by a particular component, and each one may respond to the component differently.

9.6.1   Creating Event Sources

Event sources are components such as buttons, labels, check boxes, and radio buttons. To create an event source, you must add these components to your GUI. Top-level components, such as windows, also generate events. In the CustomPanel class, the event sources are panel1 and drawingPanel, and buttons button1 and button2. When you click on a button or another component, Java *automatically* creates an event object.

9.6.2   Event Objects

Different GUI components generate ("fire off") different types of events. Buttons, for example, fire off an event of type ActionEvent. A radio button

TABLE 9–1 Types of Event Objects Created by Different Types of Event Sources	
Event Source	**Event Object**
Button, text field	ActionEvent
Check box, radio button, menu item	ActionEvent, ItemEvent
Slider	ChangeEvent

can fire off different types of events, such as ActionEvent or ItemEvent. An event object encapsulates important information about the event, such as the event source and the time at which the event occurred. Event objects for some different types of event sources are described in Table 9–1.

The class EventObject is the superclass of ActionEvent, ItemEvent, ChangeEvent, and other types of event objects. The following method (defined in class EventObject) is used to identify the event source:

> **public Object getSource()**—a method that returns a *reference* to the source of the event.

If a button or text field generated an event, you can use the following method in ActionEvent to identify the source:

> **public String getActionCommand()**—a method that returns a *string* containing information about the source of the event.

In the examples that follow, you will see how to use this method to determine which component was clicked by the user.

Other events, such as MouseEvent and KeyEvent, will be discussed later in Chapter 13, *More on GUI Programming*.

9.6.3   Creating Event Handlers

An event handler performs some action to respond to an event, and is an instance of a class that implements a *listener interface*. A **listener interface** declares methods that the event-handling class must implement. The **event-handling** code is written in the body of these methods. We explain this in more depth in the examples that follow.

Swing provides a listener interface called EventListener that has several subinterfaces, such as ActionListener, ChangeListener, ItemListener, and

`ListListener`, among others. (All of these interfaces are defined in the `java.awt.event` package.) The simplest of these interfaces is `ActionListener`:

```
public interface ActionListener extends EventListener {
  public void actionPerformed(ActionEvent e);
}
```

We can use `ActionListener` to create an event handler that responds to button clicks. For example, we can modify the class `SimplePanel` so that whenever the user clicks the Rectangle or Circle button, a rectangle or circle is drawn. We will write a new event-handling class called `EventHandler` to handle these button-clicking events. At a very minimum, this class must declare it implements the `ActionListener` interface and provide the body for the `actionPerformed` method. The outline of this class is shown here:

```
public class EventHandler implements ActionListener {
  public void actionPerformed(ActionEvent e) {
    // do something here to draw the shapes on the GUI
  }
}
```

As noted previously, whenever a button is clicked, Java automatically creates an event object. This event object can be accessed inside the `actionPerformed` method to get more information about the event. In the `actionPerformed` method of this class, the event object e (of type `ActionEvent`) contains information about the button-click event. To find out whether the Rectangle or Circle button was clicked, use the `getActionCommand` method:

```
public void actionPerformed(ActionEvent e) {
  if (e.getActionCommand().equals("Rectangle")) {
    // draw a rectangle on drawingPanel of panel
  else if (e.getActionCommand().equals("Circle")) {
    // draw a circle on drawingPanel of panel
}
```

The `getActionCommand` method returns the text on the button that was clicked—in this case, either "Rectangle" or "Circle". We next modify the code in `SimplePanel` to draw a rectangle or circle.

Recall that the drawing is done in the `paintComponent` method of a panel. The graphic is drawn on `drawingPanel`, which is an instance of `SimplePanel`; thus we will modify the `paintComponent` method of this class. A field called `shape` and a method called `changeShape` are added to `SimplePanel`. By using the changeShape method, the value of shape can be set to 1 or 2 to draw a rectangle or a circle, respectively. The modified code for SimplePanel follows:

```
// SimplePanel - version 2
package guiprogramming;
import java.awt.*;
import java.awt.geom.*;
import javax.swing.*;

public class SimplePanel extends JPanel {
  int shape = 0; // shape = 1 for rectangle, 2 for circle

  // draws a rectangle or circle depending on the value of shape
  public void paintComponent(Graphics g) {
    super.paintComponent(g);
    Graphics2D myGraphics = (Graphics2D) g;
    Shape obj;
    if (shape == 1) {
      obj = new Rectangle2D.Float(125, 125, 200, 100);
      myGraphics.draw(obj);
    } else if (shape == 2) {
      obj = new Ellipse2D.Float(175, 125, 100, 100);
      myGraphics.draw(obj);
    }
  }

  // sets shape to the argument, and calls paintComponent
  public void changeShape(int value) {
    shape = value;
    repaint();
  }
}
```

The changeShape method performs two actions. First, it sets the value of shape to the argument value, which is 1 or 2. Second, it calls the repaint method (defined in class Component). The effect of calling repaint is that Swing automatically clears the graphic on the panel and executes the paintComponent method to redraw the graphic on this panel. (As noted earlier, the paintComponent method should only be called using method repaint and not directly.)

Add a field called drawingPanel that references the panel on which the graphic should be drawn to the EventHandler class. The event-handling code checks to see which button was clicked, and then calls method changeShape with the appropriate argument of 1 or 2 to draw a rectangle or circle on drawingPanel. Modify the actionPerformed method of this class as follows:

```
// event handler method
public void actionPerformed(ActionEvent e) {
  if (e.getActionCommand().equals("Rectangle")) {
    // draw a rectangle, if "Rectangle" button was clicked
    drawingPanel.changeShape(1);
  } else if (e.getActionCommand().equals("Circle")) {
    // draw a circle, if "Circle" button was clicked
    drawingPanel.changeShape(2);
  }
}
```

We add a method called getDrawingPanel to the CustomPanel class. This method returns a reference to the private instance drawingPanel:

```
// method in CustomPanel returns drawingPanel
public SimplePanel getDrawingPanel() {
  return drawingPanel;
}
```

The code for creating the GUI (SimplePanel and CustomPanel classes) has been separated from the event-handling code (written in the EventHandler class). The last step is to connect the event handler to the buttons on the GUI. After this step is completed, the event handler can receive the event objects from the buttons. We discuss this step next.

9.6.4 Registering Event Handlers

The GUI must provide some "hooks" so that event handlers can be attached. These hooks are simply methods that attach event handler(s) to the various components in the GUI. To attach an event handler that is of type ActionListener to a button, use the addActionListener method in class Button:

> **public void addActionListener(ActionListener listener)**—a method that adds the event handler listener to this button.

For example, this statement adds the event handler e1 to button button1 so that e1 is notified automatically whenever button1 is clicked:

```
button1.addActionListener(e1);
```

The reason for declaring an event handler as type ActionListener is to use the addActionListener method to register the event handler with the button.

We add the following method called `registerEventHandler` to the `CustomPanel` class so that an event handler can be attached to the buttons in the GUI:

```
public void registerEventHandler(ActionListener eventhandler) {
  button1.addActionListener(eventhandler);
  button2.addActionListener(eventhandler);
}
```

Here, the same event handler is attached to both buttons. However, different components of a GUI can have different event handlers attached to them.

The complete code for `EventHandler` follows. In the constructor, `drawingPanel` is initialized to the instance of `SimplePanel`, on which the graphics will be drawn in the window:

```
// class EventHandler
package guiprogramming;
import javax.swing.*;
import java.awt.event.*;

public class EventHandler implements ActionListener {
  private SimplePanel drawingPanel;

  public EventHandler (SimplePanel p) {
    drawingPanel = p;
  }

  public void actionPerformed(ActionEvent e) {
    if (e.getActionCommand().equals("Rectangle")) {
      // draw rectangle, if Rectangle button was clicked
      drawingPanel.changeShape(1);
    } else if (e.getActionCommand().equals("Circle")) {
      // draw circle, if Circle button was clicked
      drawingPanel.changeShape(2);
    }
  }
}
```

The complete code for the `CustomPanel` class is provided here:

```
// class CustomPanel – version 2
package guiprogramming;
import java.awt.*;
import javax.swing.*;
import java.awt.event.*;

public class CustomPanel extends JPanel {
  private JPanel panel1;
```

```
  private SimplePanel drawingPanel;
  private JButton button1;
  private JButton button2;

  public CustomPanel() {
    setLayout(new BorderLayout());
    panel1 = new JPanel();
    drawingPanel = new SimplePanel();

    // create two buttons and add them to panel1
    button1 = new JButton("Rectangle");
    panel1.add(button1);
    button2 = new JButton("Circle");
    panel1.add(button2);

    // add panel1 and drawingPanel to this CustomPanel
    add(panel1, BorderLayout.NORTH);
    add(drawingPanel, BorderLayout.CENTER);
  }

  public SimplePanel getDrawingPanel() {
    return drawingPanel;
  }

  public void registerEventHandler(ActionListener eventhandler) {
    button1.addActionListener(eventhandler);
    button2.addActionListener(eventhandler);
  }
}
```

Let us replace the main method in CustomPanel with this one to test the GUI:

```
public static void main(String[] args) {
  JFrame window = new JFrame();
  CustomPanel mainPanel = new CustomPanel();

  // create the event handler
  EventHandler handler = new EventHandler(mainPanel.getDrawingPanel());

  // register the event handler
  mainPanel.registerEventHandler(handler);

  // set mainPanel as content pane for this window
  window.setContentPane(mainPanel);

  window.setSize(500, 500);
  window.setTitle("Event Handler Demo");
```

```
window.setDefaultCloseOperation(JFrame.EXIT_ON_CLOSE);
window.setVisible(true);
}
```

Compile EventHandler.java, SimplePanel.java (version 2), and CustomPanel .java (version 2). Run the program CustomPanel. The window is shown in Figure 9–31. Click on the Rectangle and Circle buttons to see the shape change in the GUI.

The sequence of actions taken when the user clicks on the Rectangle button is shown in Figure 9–32. First, an ActionEvent message is created automatically by Swing. This message is then sent to the event handler that is registered on this button. If several event handlers are registered on a button (or another component), Swing sends the message to all of them. When the event handler receives the message, it executes its actionPerformed method. In the actionPerformed method of the EventHandler class, first a check is made to determine whether the Rectangle button initiated the event by checking if the following condition is true:

```
e.getActionCommand().equals("Rectangle")
```

Figure 9–31

Adding event handlers to the buttons.

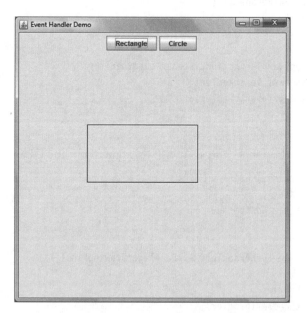

Figure 9–32

Sequence of operations after a button is clicked.

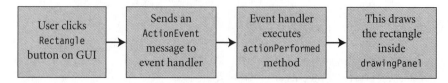

The condition is true; thus the next statement is executed:

```
drawingPanel.changeShape(1);
```

This statement executes the changeShape method of class SimplePanel, which in turn sets the field shape to 1 and calls repaint. The effect of repaint is to first clear the current contents of drawingPanel and then execute its paintComponent method, which draws the rectangle in drawingPanel.

Try to work out, similarly, the sequence of steps taken to display a circle on the window when the Circle button is clicked. The steps to set up a GUI with event handling are summarized here:

1. Create a custom panel by extending JPanel. Add panels and other components such as buttons, labels, and so forth to this custom panel. Set the custom panel as the content pane of a window.

2. Create event handlers for the various components of the GUI. An event handler should implement a listener interface, such as ActionListener, and implement all the methods in that interface.

3. Register the event handlers with the GUI components. For example, to add an event handler of type ActionListener, use the addActionListener method.

A component can have multiple event handlers attached to it. Components can also share an event handler, as the Rectangle and Circle buttons do in the CustomPanel class.

9.6.5   Creating Event Handlers Using Anonymous Classes

Another common approach to creating event handlers is to use anonymous classes. There is no need to create a separate class for the event handler in this case. An anonymous event handler is created in the following way:

```
new ActionListener() {
  public void actionPerformed(ActionEvent e) {
    // do something
  }
}
```

This anonymous event handler is added the usual way, using the addActionListener method:

```
componentName.addActionListener(new ActionListener() {
  public void actionPerformed(ActionEvent e) {
    // do something
  }
});
```

For example, we add an event handler to button1 that calls changeShape with an argument of 1 as follows:

```
button1.addActionListener(new ActionListener() {
  public void actionPerformed(ActionEvent e) {
    drawingPanel.changeShape(1);
  }
});
```

The event handler is attached to a single button button1 in this case; thus it is not necessary to test which button initiated the ActionEvent e. This makes the event-handling code easier to read.

An anonymous event handler for button button2 can be written similarly. We will rewrite the CustomPanel class so that the event handlers are created using anonymous classes. The resulting CustomPanelAnonHandler class is shown here:

```
// class CustomPanelAnonHandler
package guiprogramming;
import java.awt.*;
import javax.swing.*;
import javax.swing.border.*;
import java.awt.event.*;

public class CustomPanelAnonHandler extends JPanel {
  private JPanel panel1;
  private SimplePanel drawingPanel;
  JButton button1, button2;

  public CustomPanelAnonHandler() {
    setLayout(new BorderLayout());
    panel1 = new JPanel();
    drawingPanel = new SimplePanel();

    // create two buttons and add to panel1
    button1 = new JButton("Rectangle");
    panel1.add(button1);
    button2 = new JButton("Circle");
    panel1.add(button2);

    // adding panel1, drawingPanel to CustomPanel
    this.add(panel1, BorderLayout.NORTH);
```

```
      this.add(drawingPanel, BorderLayout.CENTER);

      // add an event handler to both buttons
      button1.addActionListener(new ActionListener() {
        public void actionPerformed(ActionEvent e) {
          drawingPanel.changeShape(1);
        }
      });

      button2.addActionListener(new ActionListener() {
        public void actionPerformed(ActionEvent e) {
          drawingPanel.changeShape(2);
        }
      });
    }
}
```

As an exercise, write a main to test this class. Compile it with the SimplePanel class and run the program.

Once you understand the basics of the event-handling mechanism, you are ready to see how components other than buttons can be added to a GUI.

9.7 GUI Components

The JComponent class is the abstract base class for all Swing components, such as JButton, JLabel, JPanel, and others. This class defines methods to paint a component and set its font, border, background, size, tool tips, and more. JComponent and all classes *descended* from it (that is, direct or indirect subclasses of JComponent) reside in the javax.swing package.

Figure 9–33 shows some methods for setting or retrieving the border and background of a component. The opacity of a component can be tested or set using the isOpaque or setOpaque methods, respectively, in JComponent. The setForeground method is used for changing the foreground color, such as the color of the text, on a component.

Figure 9–34 shows some methods to get or set the component size. The getWidth and getHeight methods return the actual size of the component. These two methods should be called only after the component's size has been set by a layout manager. A component's size is represented by three fields: minimumSize, maximumSize, and preferredSize. The fields minimumSize and

Figure 9–33
Methods to get or set the borders, background and foreground colors, and opacity of a component.

JComponent	
`Border getBorder()`	Returns a component's border or `null` if there is no border.
`void setBorder(Border border)`	Sets the specified border on the component.
`Insets getInsets()`	Returns the insets for this component.
`void setForeground(Color c)`	Sets the foreground color for this component.
`void setBackground(Color c)`	Sets the background color for this component.
`Color getForeground()`	Gets the foreground color for this component.
`Color getBackground()`	Gets the background color for this component.
`void setOpaque(boolean b)`	Sets the opaque property to `true` or `false`, depending on the argument to this method.
`boolean isOpaque()`	Returns `true` if this component is opaque.

Figure 9–34
Methods to set or retrieve the size of a component.

JComponent	
`int getWidth()`	Returns the width of this component.
`int getHeight()`	Returns the height of this component.
`Dimension getPreferredSize()`	Returns the preferred size of this component.
`void setPreferredSize(Dimension preferredSize)`	Requests the layout manager to set this component to the size specified by this method.
`Dimension getMaximumSize()`	Returns the maximum size of this component.
`Dimension getMinimumSize()`	Returns the minimum size of this component.
`void setMaximumSize(Dimension maximumSize)`	Sets the maximum size of this component.
`void setMinimumSize(Dimension minimumSize)`	Sets the minimum size of this component.

maximumSize are the smallest and largest sizes of this component when it is placed in a container, whereas preferredSize is the favored size for this component. Each method takes an argument of type Dimension, which contains the component's width and height. For example, the following method sets the minimum height and width of the component panel to 500:

```
panel.setMinimumSize(new Dimension(500, 500));
```

The setPreferredSize, setMinimumSize, and setMaximumSize methods allow the programmer to request a specific size for a component, as well as its minimum and maximum sizes. Note, however, that the layout manager will not necessarily size the component accordingly.

Figure 9–35 shows other methods in this class. The setVisible method makes a component visible or invisible depending on the argument. By default, all components except windows are visible when they are created. The setFont method lets you change the style and size of the text displayed on a component. For example, to set the component comp's font to Lucida Sans, italicized, with size 25, use:

```
comp.setFont(new Font("Lucida Sans", Font.ITALIC, 25));
```

A tool tip is the information box that appears when you position the cursor over some component on the GUI. You can use the setToolTipText method to display some information about a particular component. We will discuss this and other methods in the following sections.

JComponent	
protected void paintComponent(Graphics g)	Paints on the component using the graphics context g.
void setVisible(boolean flag)	Makes this component visible if flag is true.
void setEnabled(boolean b)	Enables this component (if the argument is true) so it can respond to user actions.
void setFont(Font f)	Sets the font to f for this component.
void setToolTipText(String t)	Sets a tool tip with the text t for this component.
void setFocusable(boolean b)	Gives the component the focus when the argument is true so that it can receive mouse and key events.

Figure 9–35

Miscellaneous methods, such as to draw on a component and to make it visible.

9.7.1 The JLabel Class

The JLabel class is used to add a label to a user interface. The label can be used to name a component or display some information. Figure 9–36 shows a partial list of constructors and methods in this class. In addition, JLabel inherits the methods in its superclass JComponent.

This statement creates a label with text "Score":

```
JLabel label = new JLabel("Score");
```

Unlike other components, a label does not generate event objects, and it cannot have an event handler attached to it.

The PhotoOp Class: Displaying the Name of the Photograph   We now show how you can display the photograph's name using a label. Add this field to PhotoOp:

```
private JLabel titleLabel;
```

Add these two statements to the constructor in PhotoOp (after the call to method createPanels):

```
// create a label
   titleLabel = new JLabel("squirrelMonkey.jpg");
   titlePanel.add(titleLabel);
```

Compile and run the program. The name of the photograph is displayed as shown in Figure 9–37.

9.7.2 The JButton Class

Buttons are created using the JButton class, which extends JComponent. Some constructors and a method are shown in Figure 9–38.

When the user clicks a button, an event is fired. As shown earlier in Table 9–1, buttons create events of type ActionEvent. This button-click event is

Figure 9–36

Some constructors and methods in class JLabel.

JLabel	
JLabel()	Constructor creates a label without an image or a name.
JLabel(Icon image)	Constructor creates a label with a small image displayed on it.
JLabel(String t)	Constructor creates a label with the text t displayed on it.
String getText()	Returns the text displayed on this label.
void setText(String t)	Sets the text displayed on this label to t.

squirrelMonkey.jpg © Simone Van Den Berg, 123RF.com

Figure 9–37
Displaying a title using a
label.

Figure 9–38
Constructors and a
method in class JButton.

JButton	
JButton()	Constructor creates a button without an image or text on it.
JButton(Icon image)	Constructor creates a button with a small image displayed on it.
JButton(String t)	Constructor creates a button with the text t displayed on it.
String getActionCommand()	Returns the text displayed on this button.

sent to all event handlers that are attached to the button (see Figure 9–32). The event handler should be of type ActionListener to respond to an event of type ActionEvent. The method addActionListener is used to attach an event handler to a button. When the event handler receives an event, it executes its actionPerformed method. The programmer can get more information about the event using the method getActionCommand. This is useful when the same event handler handles events from several buttons. For example, the text "Rectangle" is returned when this button b invokes its getActionCommand method:

```
JButton b = new JButton("Rectangle");
```

Alternately, you can create another action command associated with button b using the setActionCommand method in JButton:

```
b.setActionCommand("Blue");
```

Figure 9–39

Inserting a tool tip.

You can add a tool tip "Click on me" to a button b as follows:

```
b.setToolTipText("Click on me");
```

Figure 9–39 shows the tool tip for the button b. You can add a tool tip in a similar manner to any of the other components as well.

The PhotoOp Class: Rotating the Picture   Next we add two buttons to the GUI to rotate the picture. Add the following createRotatePanel method to PhotoOp. In this method, two buttons called rotateButton1 and rotateButton2 are created and added to a panel. We have attached event handlers to these buttons to call the rotateImage method of drawingPanel whenever a button is clicked. Tool tips are also added to the two buttons to let the user know what they do.

```
// method in class PhotoOp to rotate the picture
public JPanel createRotatePanel() {
  JPanel rotatePanel = new JPanel();

  // create two buttons to rotate image
  JButton rotateButton1 = new JButton(new
ImageIcon("image/leftButton.jpg"));
  JButton rotateButton2 = new JButton(new
ImageIcon("image/rightButton.jpg"));

  rotatePanel.add(rotateButton1);
  rotatePanel.add(rotateButton2);

// add an event handler to rotateButton1
  rotateButton1.addActionListener(new ActionListener() {
    public void actionPerformed(ActionEvent e) {
      // rotate image to the left by 45 degrees
      drawingPanel.rotateImage(-Math.PI/4);
    }
  });
```

```
// add an event handler to rotateButton2
  rotateButton2.addActionListener(new ActionListener() {
    public void actionPerformed(ActionEvent e) {
      // rotate image to the right by 45 degrees
      drawingPanel.rotateImage(Math.PI/4);
    }
  });

  rotateButton1.setToolTipText("Rotate left by 45 degrees");
  rotateButton2.setToolTipText("Rotate right by 45 degrees");
  rotatePanel.setMaximumSize(new Dimension(200, 60));
  rotatePanel.setBackground(Color.lightGray);
  return rotatePanel;
}
```

The two buttons are created with icons using the image files leftButton.jpg and rightButton.jpg. Copy these two files from the JavaBook/image directory on the CD-ROM into the JavaBook/image directory on your computer.

Add this import statement to PhotoOp:

```
import java.awt.event.*;
```

Add rotatePanel to groupPanel by calling the createRotatePanel method in PhotoOp's constructor (after the createPanels method):

```
// create rotate panel
groupPanel.add(createRotatePanel());
```

Some changes are needed in PhotoOpDrawingPanel before the image can be rotated. Add an angle field to this class:

```
private double angle = 0.0; // rotate image by this angle
```

Add this rotateImage method to PhotoOpDrawingPanel:

```
public void rotateImage(double a) {
  angle += a;
  repaint();
}
```

This method stores the angle by which the original image should be rotated, and calls the method repaint to clear the contents of the drawing panel and redraw the rotated image on it.

The rotation is performed using the rotate method in Graphics2D:

> **abstract void rotate (double r, double x, double y)**—a method
> that adds a rotation of r radians about the point (x, y).

Figure 9–40

Rotating the photograph using buttons.

squirrelMonkey.jpg © Simone Van Den Berg, 123RF.com

The `paintComponent` method of `PhotoOpDrawingPanel` is modified as shown here:

```
public void paintComponent(Graphics g) {
  super.paintComponent(g);
  Graphics2D g2 = (Graphics2D) g;
  // rotate
  g2.rotate(angle, 250, 250);

  // draw image
  g2.drawImage(bimage, 0, 0, null);
}
```

The image will be rotated by the specified angle about the point (250, 250) when a button is clicked. You can change this point's coordinates if you like. The program output is shown in Figure 9–40.

9.7.3   The `JTextField` Class

The `JTextField` component is used to read or display a *single* line of text. This component fires an `ActionEvent` when the user presses Enter after entering a line of text. Therefore, an event handler of type `ActionListener` can be attached to an instance of `JTextField`. Figure 9–41 shows some methods and constructors in this class, which is *descended* from `JComponent`. (In

JTextField	
JTextField(int c)	Constructor creates a text field that is c columns wide.
JTextField(String t, int c)	Constructor creates a text field with c columns that is initialized with the text t.
String getSelectedText()	Returns the text that has been selected inside this field.
String getText()	Returns all the text in this text field.
void setText(String t)	Sets all the text in this text field to t.
void setEditable(boolean)	Allows the user to write in this text field if the argument is true. By default, a text field is editable.
void setHorizontalAlignment(int JTextField.align)	Aligns text to the center, left, or right by setting align to CENTER, LEFT, or RIGHT, respectively.

Figure 9–41

A partial list of constructors and methods in class JTextfield.

other words, it is in the inheritance tree where JComponent is the highest superclass.)

The two constructors take the desired number of columns in the text field as an argument. They are used to create text fields with a fixed width that does not change even if the window is resized. Nevertheless, the user can enter *any* number of characters in the text field, regardless of its width. The number of columns specified in the constructors cannot be negative; otherwise, a run-time error occurs. A text field can also be created with a string initially displayed within it. For example, the following statement creates a text field with a width of 10 columns displaying the text "Type here":

```
JTextField inputField = new JTextField("Type here", 10);
```

Example 6

The following program shows how you can create two text fields, one for user input and the other to echo this input. The text field inputField is made editable using the setEditable method. It has an event handler to read the data entered by the user and display it on the second text field named displayField.

```
package guiprogramming;
import javax.swing.*;
import java.awt.event.*;

public class JTextFieldDemo {
  private JTextField inputField;
  private JTextField displayField;

  public JTextFieldDemo() {
    // create text fields with 10 columns
    inputField = new JTextField("Type here", 10);
    displayField = new JTextField(10);

    // make displayField non-writable
    displayField.setEditable(false);

    // attach an event handler to inputField
    inputField.addActionListener(new ActionListener() {
      public void actionPerformed(ActionEvent e) {
        //get the text entered in inputField and put it in displayField
        displayField.setText(inputField.getText());
      }
    });

    JFrame window = new JFrame();
    JPanel topPanel = new JPanel();

    // add the text fields to topPanel
    topPanel.add(inputField);
    topPanel.add(displayField);

    window.setContentPane(topPanel);
    window.pack();
    window.setTitle("JTextField Demo");
    window.setDefaultCloseOperation(JFrame.EXIT_ON_CLOSE);
    window.setVisible(true);
  }

  public static void main(String[] args) {
    new JTextFieldDemo();
  }
}
```

In class JTextFieldDemo, two text fields named inputField and displayField are created. An event handler is created using an anonymous class, and

Figure 9–42

The user can enter text in the field on the left.

Figure 9–43

The field on the right displays the same text after the Enter key is pressed.

attached to inputField using the addActionListener method. In the event-handling code, data entered by the user in inputField is read using the get-Text method, and it is displayed on displayField using the method setText. Figures 9–42 and 9–43 show how the text fields work. The text field on the left (called inputField in the program) allows the user to enter some text (Figure 9–42), and the text field on the right (displayField) displays this text after the user presses the Enter key (Figure 9–43). ▪

9.7.4 The JFormattedTextField Class

Although the JTextField works well with string input, the JFormatted-TextField is better for other data types, such as int and float. If the user incorrectly enters a string when a number is expected in a JFormatted-TextField, the value entered will be ignored and the program will not crash. JFormattedTextField extends the class JTextField. Figure 9–44 shows a constructor and some methods of this class.

We use a formatted text field to scale the image size in class PhotoOp, as described next.

JFormattedTextField	
JFormattedTextField()	Constructor to create a formatted text field.
JFormattedTextField(Object obj)	Constructor to create a formatted text field that is initialized with the value in obj.
Object getValue()	Returns the value in this formatted text field.
void setValue(Object obj)	Sets the value in this formatted text field to the value in obj.

Figure 9–44

A constructor and some methods for formatted text fields.

The PhotoOp Class: Changing the Picture Size   This example shows you how our picture can be enlarged or shrunk. The user can enter a scaling value (as a percentage) in a text field on the GUI. A value greater than 100 will enlarge the picture size, whereas a value less than 100 will reduce the size correspondingly. We use the scale method in Graphics2D to change the image size.

Add the following formatted text field called scaleField to PhotoOp:

```
private JFormattedTextField scaleField;
```

The user can enter the amount by which the picture should be scaled in this field.

Add the createScalePanel method shown next, to PhotoOp. In this method, the formatted text field called scaleField is created with an initial value of 100. The event handler reads the value entered by the user in this field and passes it to the scaleImage method of drawingPanel:

```
// method in class PhotoOp to scale image
public JPanel createScalePanel() {
  JPanel scalePanel = new JPanel();
  JLabel scaleLabel = new JLabel("Scale:");

  // create a formatted text field called scaleField
  scaleField = new JFormattedTextField(new Float(100));
  scaleField.setColumns(3);
  // add a label to scaleField
  JLabel percentLabel = new JLabel("%");
  scalePanel.add(scaleLabel);
  scalePanel.add(scaleField);
  scalePanel.add(percentLabel);

  // actionListener for scaleField
  scaleField.addActionListener(new ActionListener() {
    public void actionPerformed(ActionEvent e) {
      // scale the image by the value in scaleField
      float scale = (Float) scaleField.getValue()/100.0f;
      drawingPanel.scaleImage(scale);
    }
  });

  scalePanel.setMaximumSize(new Dimension(200, 40));
  scalePanel.setBackground(Color.lightGray);
  return scalePanel;
}
```

Call this method in PhotoOp's constructor after the createRotatePanel method:

```
// create scale panel
groupPanel.add(createScalePanel());
```

Make the following changes in PhotoOpDrawingPanel. Add the scaleValue field and scaleImage method to the class:

```
private float scaleValue = 1.0f; // resize image by this amount

public void scaleImage(float s) {
  scaleValue *= s;
  repaint();
}
```

Add this statement to paintComponent after the g2.rotate statement in class PhotoOpDrawingPanel:

```
// scale image
g2.scale(scaleValue, scaleValue);
```

This will call the scale method of Graphics2D to resize the image:

> **abstract void scale (double s1, double s2)**—a method to scale an image by value s1 in the *x* direction and value s2 in the *y* direction.

Now compile and run the program. The image is scaled by the value that is entered in the text field, as shown in Figure 9–45. As an exercise, add a separate text field to scale the image by different amounts in the *x* and *y* directions. In addition, add tool tips to these fields.

9.7.5 The JPasswordField Class

The JPasswordField class extends JTextField to provide a text field for entering passwords. There are two main differences between JPasswordField and JTextField. First, the user input is displayed as "*" in the JPasswordField. Second, the getPassword method is used instead of getText to read data from JPasswordField. A constructor and method in this class are shown in Figure 9–46.

This code fragment shows how to create a password field and attach a listener to it:

```
// create a password field that is 20 columns wide
final JPasswordField passwordField = new JPasswordField(20);

// attach an event handler to passwordField
passwordField.addActionListener(new ActionListener() {
```

Figure 9–45

Using the scale field to change the image size.

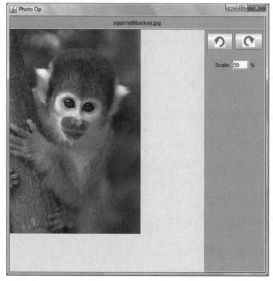

squirrelMonkey.jpg © Simone Van Den Berg, 123RF.com

Figure 9–46

A constructor and method in class JPasswordField.

JPasswordField	
JPasswordField(int c)	Constructor creates an empty password field with c columns.
char[] getPassword()	Returns the password contained in this field.

```
public void actionPerformed(ActionEvent e) {
  // read the password using passwordField.getPassword()
  // do something
  }
});
```

Recall that an anonymous class can only access final local variables of the method in which it is declared. Therefore, to access passwordField in the actionPerformed method of the anonymous class, we must declare password-Field as final. Figure 9–47 shows a JPasswordField that has some data entered in it.

Figure 9–47
A password field.

9.7.6 The JTextArea Class

The JTextArea component is useful for entering, editing, and displaying *multiple* lines of text. Some constructors and methods are shown in Figure 9–48. The insert and append methods add new text to the existing text in the text area. The insert method inserts the given text at position p in the document, where p is the offset in characters from the start of the document. The first character is at position 0, and a blank space and *newline* count as one character each. (The **newline** character is the special character "\n" that is inserted when the user presses the Enter key on the keyboard.) The append method adds text to the end of the existing text in the document. By default, lines are not wrapped around. Hence, if a string is longer than the width of the window, a portion of it will not be visible in the text area. The setLineWrap method can be used to wrap this string to the next line; that is, continue it on the next line in the window.

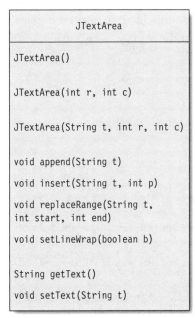

JTextArea	
JTextArea()	Constructor creates a text area with no rows or columns.
JTextArea(int r, int c)	Constructor creates a text area with r rows and c columns.
JTextArea(String t, int r, int c)	Constructor creates a text area that displays the text t and has r rows and c columns.
void append(String t)	Adds the text t to the end of this text area.
void insert(String t, int p)	Inserts the text t at position p in this text area.
void replaceRange(String t, int start, int end)	Replaces all text between positions start and end with the text t.
void setLineWrap(boolean b)	Continues a line on the next line if it is too long to fit in the current width when the argument is true.
String getText()	Returns all the text in this text area.
void setText(String t)	Changes all the text in this text area to t.

Figure 9–48

Some constructors and methods in class
JTextArea.

Can you determine the final contents of textArea in the following code segment?

```
JTextArea textArea = new JTextArea();
textArea.setText("Hello");
textArea.setText("You  it out.\n");
textArea.append("Good job!\n");
textArea.insert("figured", 4);
```

Figure 9–49 shows the solution.

9.7.7   The JCheckBox Class

The JCheckBox component is a small box in which a check mark can be placed by the user to indicate that this box has been selected. Check boxes can be used when the user is allowed to select all or some of a given set of choices. Figure 9–50 shows some constructors and a method in JCheckBox. This class is descended from JComponent.

By default, check boxes do not initially contain a check mark. The JCheck-Box(String, boolean) method is used to create a check box with a check mark if the boolean argument is true.

Each time a check box is selected or deselected, it fires two types of events: ActionEvent and ItemEvent. As you have seen in previous examples, an Action-Event is handled similarly for check boxes by attaching an event handler of type ActionListener to the check box. To handle an ItemEvent, create a class

Figure 9–49

A text area containing two lines.

Figure 9–50

Some constructors and a method in class JCheckBox.

JCheckBox	
JCheckBox()	Constructor for a check box that is initially unselected and contains no text.
JCheckBox(String t)	Constructor for a check box that is initially unselected and contains the given text t.
JCheckBox(String t, boolean selected)	Constructor to create a check box that contains the given text t, and a check mark if selected is true.
boolean isSelected()	Returns true if the check box contains a check mark.

that implements the `ItemListener` interface. The `ItemListener` interface is defined in the `java.awt.event` package as follows:

```
public interface ItemListener extends EventListener  {
  public void itemStateChanged(ItemEvent e);
}
```

For example, you can create an event handler of type `ItemListener` using an anonymous class, and add it to check box `checkbox1` using the `addItemListener` method, as shown here:

```
checkbox1.addItemListener(new ItemListener() {
  public void itemStateChanged(ItemEvent e) {
    // do something
});
```

You can choose to handle either type of event, `ActionEvent` or `ItemEvent`, for a check box.

Example 7

Create two check boxes and a text area and add them to the content pane of a window. Add item listeners to the check boxes so that whenever either one is selected or deselected by the user, a message is printed in the text area identifying the check box and its state.

Solution: Two check boxes, `checkbox1` and `checkbox2`, are created and added to `checkboxPanel`. A text area called `textArea` is created for displaying messages. Then, `checkboxPanel` and `textArea` are added to `topPanel`, which is set as the content pane. In the `addItemListener` method, the state of the check box is determined, and the appropriate message is displayed:

```
package guiprogramming;
import javax.swing.*;
import java.awt.*;
import java.awt.event.*;

public class JCheckBoxDemo  {
  private JTextArea textArea;
  private JCheckBox checkbox1;
  private JCheckBox checkbox2;

  public JCheckBoxDemo() {
    JFrame window = new JFrame();
    JPanel topPanel = new JPanel(new BorderLayout());
    JPanel checkboxPanel = new JPanel();
```

```
      textArea = new JTextArea(10, 25);
      checkbox1 = new JCheckBox("Check box 1", false);
      checkbox2 = new JCheckBox("Check box 2", false);

      // create and add the event handler to checkbox1
      checkbox1.addItemListener(new ItemListener() {
        public void itemStateChanged(ItemEvent e) {
          if(checkbox1.isSelected())
            textArea.append("Check box 1 is selected\n");
          else
            textArea.append("Check box 1 is deselected\n");
        }
      });

      // create and add the event handler to checkbox2
      checkbox2.addItemListener(new ItemListener() {
        public void itemStateChanged(ItemEvent e) {
          if(checkbox2.isSelected())
            textArea.append("Check box 2 is selected\n");
          else
            textArea.append("Check box 2 is deselected\n");
        }
      });

      // add the checkboxes to checkboxPanel
      checkboxPanel.add(checkbox1);
      checkboxPanel.add(checkbox2);

      // use border layout for topPanel
      topPanel.add(checkboxPanel, BorderLayout.NORTH);
      topPanel.add(textArea, BorderLayout.CENTER);

      window.setContentPane(topPanel);
      window.pack();
      window.setTitle("JCheckBox Demo");
      window.setDefaultCloseOperation(JFrame.EXIT_ON_CLOSE);
      window.setVisible(true);
    }

    public static void main(String[] args) {
      new JCheckBoxDemo();
    }
  }
```

The program output is shown in Figure 9–51.   ∎

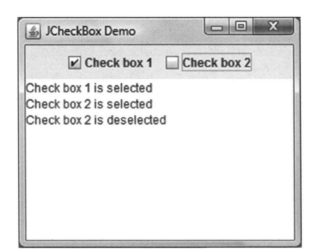

Figure 9–51
Output of program
JCheckBoxDemo.

The PhotoOp Class: Shearing the Picture   Imagine that you are holding the image along one corner and pulling it at the opposite corner while turning the image sideways—this is called **shearing**. In this section, we show how you can use the shear method in class Graphics to achieve this effect.

We will add check boxes to the PhotoOp class so that whenever a check box is selected, the picture will be sheared by a random amount in the *x* or *y* directions. This is shown in the following method, createShearPanel. In this method, two check boxes are created and event handlers are attached to them. The event handlers execute the shearAction method when a check box is selected or deselected. Add this method to PhotoOp:

```
// method in class PhotoOp to create a panel with check boxes
public JPanel createShearPanel() {
  JPanel shearPanel = new JPanel();
  shearPanel.setLayout(new BoxLayout(shearPanel, BoxLayout.Y_AXIS));

  // create two panels for holding each check box
  JPanel shearPanel1 = new JPanel(new FlowLayout(FlowLayout.LEFT, 6, 6));
  JPanel shearPanel2 = new JPanel(new FlowLayout(FlowLayout.LEFT, 6, 6));
  shearPanel.add(shearPanel1);
  shearPanel.add(shearPanel2);
  JLabel shearLabel = new JLabel("Shear:");

  // create check box for horizontal shear
  shearBox1 = new JCheckBox("Horizontal");
  shearPanel1.add(shearLabel);
  shearPanel1.add(shearBox1);
```

```
// create check box for vertical shear
shearBox2 = new JCheckBox("Vertical");
shearPanel2.add(Box.createHorizontalStrut(37));
shearPanel2.add(shearBox2);

// add event handlers to the check boxes
shearBox1.addItemListener(new ItemListener() {
  public void itemStateChanged(ItemEvent e) {
    shearAction();
  }
});
shearBox2.addItemListener(new ItemListener() {
  public void itemStateChanged(ItemEvent e) {
    shearAction();
  }
});

shearPanel.setBackground(Color.lightGray);
shearBox1.setBackground(Color.lightGray);
shearBox2.setBackground(Color.lightGray);
shearPanel1.setBackground(Color.lightGray);
shearPanel.setBackground(Color.lightGray);
shearPanel2.setBackground(Color.lightGray);
shearPanel.setMaximumSize(new Dimension(200, 60));
return shearPanel;
}
```

The shearAction method shears the image by a random amount in the horizontal and/or vertical directions, depending on which check boxes are selected. Add this method to PhotoOp:

```
// method in class PhotoOp to shear image
public void shearAction() {
  Random r = new Random();
  int value = r.nextInt(100);

  // shears the image by a random value
  if (shearBox1.isSelected() && shearBox2.isSelected())
    drawingPanel.shearImage(value/100.0f, value/100.0f);
  else if (shearBox1.isSelected())
    drawingPanel.shearImage(value/100.0f, 0);
  else if (shearBox2.isSelected())
    drawingPanel.shearImage(0, value/100.0f);
  else
    drawingPanel.shearImage(0, 0);
}
```

Add these fields to PhotoOp:

```
private JCheckBox shearBox1;
private JCheckBox shearBox2;
```

In PhotoOp's constructor, invoke the createShearPanel method (after the createScalePanel method is called):

```
// create shear panel
groupPanel.add(createShearPanel());
```

The PhotoOpDrawingPanel class is modified as described next. Add these fields and the shearImage method to this class:

```
// fields representing horizontal and vertical shear
private float horizontalShear = 0.0f;
private float verticalShear = 0.0f;

// method in PhotoOpDrawingPanel to shear an image by the given amounts
public void shearImage(float hshear, float vshear) {
  horizontalShear = hshear;
  verticalShear = vshear;
  repaint(); // calls the paintComponent method of this class
}
```

Add this statement to the paintComponent method of this class after the call to the scale method:

```
// shear image
g2.shear(horizontalShear, verticalShear);
```

The shear method in Graphics2D takes two arguments that represent the shear in the x and y directions. The paintComponent method in PhotoOpDrawingPanel should look like this now:

```
public void paintComponent(Graphics g) {
  super.paintComponent(g);
  Graphics2D g2 = (Graphics2D) g;

  // rotate image
  g2.rotate(angle, 250, 250);

  // scale image
  g2.scale(scaleValue, scaleValue);

  // shear image
  g2.shear(horizontalShear, verticalShear);

  g2.drawImage(bimage, 0, 0, null);
}
```

Figure 9–52

Shearing an image by a random amount in horizontal and/or vertical directions.

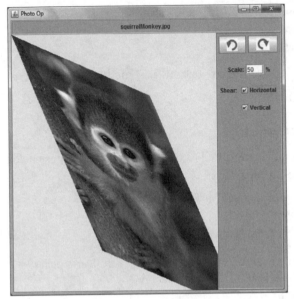

squirrelMonkey.jpg © Simone Van Den Berg, 123RF.com

Add this statement to import the class Random in PhotoOp:

```
import java.util.Random;
```

Compile and run the program. Figure 9–52 shows the sheared image in the *x* and *y* directions. As an exercise, add a tool tip to each check box to inform the user that these shear the image by a random amount in the horizontal and vertical directions.

9.7.8   The JRadioButton and ButtonGroup Classes

Like check boxes, radio buttons can also be selected or deselected by the user. However, unlike check boxes, radio buttons are used when the user must select only *one* choice from among a given set of choices. A group of radio buttons can be grouped together into a *button group*. A **button group** has the intrinsic property that only one button in the group can be selected at a time. Every time a new button is selected, the previously selected button is deselected automatically. The JRadioButton and ButtonGroup classes are used to create a radio button and a button group, respectively. Some constructors of JRadioButton are shown in Figure 9–53. The ButtonGroup class contains only a single constructor without arguments. Class JRadioButton is

JRadioButton	
JRadioButton()	Constructor creates an unselected radio button with no text.
JRadioButton(String t)	Constructor creates an unselected radio button with the text t.
JRadioButton(String t, boolean state)	Constructor creates a radio button with text t and selection setting specified by state.
boolean isSelected()	Returns true if this radio button is selected; otherwise, returns false.

Figure 9–53
Some constructors and a method in class JRadioButton.

descended from JComponent, whereas ButtonGroup extends Object. Both classes reside in the javax.swing package.

The following code segment shows how you can create two radio buttons and add them to a button group:

```
JRadioButton rbutton1 = new JRadioButton("true");
JRadioButton rbutton2 = new JRadioButton("false");

// add these buttons to a button group
ButtonGroup group = new ButtonGroup();
group.add(rbutton1);
group.add(rbutton2);
```

A JRadioButton component fires both ActionEvent and ItemEvent. You can add an event handler of type ActionListener and/or ItemListener to a radio button. An example using radio buttons is provided in the JScrollPane class, which is discussed next.

9.7.9   The JScrollPane Class

You might have noticed in the JCheckBoxDemo example that when the check boxes are repeatedly clicked, the text area eventually runs out of space, and we are unable to view any further changes. This can be rectified by adding scroll bars to the window. The JScrollPane class (see Figure 9–54) is used to

JScrollPane	
JScrollPane(Component c)	Constructor creates a JScrollPane that displays horizontal and vertical scroll bars for the component c.

Figure 9–54
Constructor to add horizontal and vertical scroll bars to a component.

add horizontal and vertical scroll bars to any component. The scroll bars disappear if the window is enlarged enough to make all the data on it visible, and they appear automatically whenever some data is obscured in the window. This class extends JComponent.

You can add scroll bars to a component comp as follows:

```
JScrollPane scrollpane = new JScrollPane(comp);
```

Example 8

Create two radio buttons that can be used to answer a true/false question. Add a text field to give the user feedback on whether the answer was correct. Add scroll bars to the window.

Solution: The program JScrollPaneDemo provides a solution:

```
package guiprogramming;
import java.awt.*;
import javax.swing.*;
import java.awt.event.*;

public class JScrollPaneDemo {
  private JTextField textField;
  private JFrame window;
  private JPanel topPanel;
  private JRadioButton rbutton1;
  private JRadioButton rbutton2;

  public JScrollPaneDemo() {
    window = new JFrame();
    topPanel = new JPanel(new BorderLayout());
    textField = new JTextField();

    // create the radio buttons and put them in a group
    rbutton1 = new JRadioButton("true");
    rbutton2 = new JRadioButton("false");
    ButtonGroup group = new ButtonGroup();
    group.add(rbutton1);
    group.add(rbutton2);

    // item listeners for the radio buttons
    rbutton1.addItemListener(new ItemListener() {
      public void itemStateChanged(ItemEvent e) {
```

```
      if( ((JRadioButton) e.getSource()).isSelected())
        textField.setText("That is correct!");
    }
  });

  rbutton2.addItemListener(new ItemListener() {
    public void itemStateChanged(ItemEvent e) {
      if( ((JRadioButton) e.getSource()).isSelected())
        textField.setText("That is incorrect!");
    }
  });

  // add radioButtonPanel and textField using border layout
  JPanel radioButtonPanel = new JPanel();
  radioButtonPanel.add(new JLabel("Java is a programming language and the
name of an island"));
  radioButtonPanel.add(rbutton1);
  radioButtonPanel.add(rbutton2);
  topPanel.add(radioButtonPanel, BorderLayout.CENTER);
  topPanel.add(textField, BorderLayout.SOUTH);

  // create the scroll pane and add topPanel to it
  JScrollPane scrollPane = new JScrollPane(topPanel);

  // add the scroll pane to the content pane
  window.getContentPane().add(scrollPane, BorderLayout.CENTER);

  window.setSize(100, 100);
  window.setTitle("JScrollPane Demo");
  window.setDefaultCloseOperation(JFrame.EXIT_ON_CLOSE);
  window.setVisible(true);
  }

  public static void main(String[] args) {
    new JScrollPaneDemo();
  }
}
```

Figure 9–55 shows the horizontal and vertical scroll bars.

When the window is enlarged so that all the text within it is visible, as shown in Figure 9–56, the scroll bars disappear. If the radio button with the label *true* is selected, the words "That is correct!" are printed out on the text area. An ItemEvent is generated whenever the state of *any* radio button changes. For example, suppose that the radio button labeled *false* is selected

Figure 9–55

A window with horizontal and vertical scroll bars.

Figure 9–56

The scroll bars disappear automatically when the window is made sufficiently large to display all the text inside it.

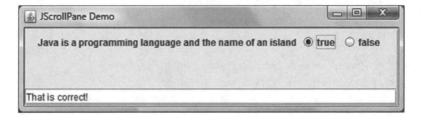

next. An ItemEvent is generated by both radio buttons, because the radio button labeled *true* gets deselected simultaneously. The event handlers for both radio buttons execute the itemStateChanged method. This statement checks whether the radio button that generated the event is selected:

```
if ( ((JRadioButton) e.getSource()).isSelected())
```

The getSource method returns a reference to the event source as type Object. This is cast back to type JRadioButton, and then the isSelected method of JRadioButton is used to determine whether the radio button is selected.   ▪

9.7.10   The JSlider Class

A slider lets the programmer enter integer input within a given range. The JSlider class, shown in Figure 9–57, extends JComponent and is used to create sliders.

A slider contains minor and major tick marks, and these values can be set and displayed with the methods in this class. Suppose that the argument to the method setMajorTickSpacing is 5; then the major tick marks are 0, 5, 10, 15, and so forth. If the argument to the setMinorTickSpacing method is 2, the minor tick marks are 0, 2, 4, 6, and so forth.

The JSlider component fires a ChangeEvent. The event handler attached to this component should be of type ChangeListener and have its stateChanged method implemented. Note that the interface ChangeListener and event ChangeEvent are defined in the javax.swing.event package.

Figure 9–57

A constructor and some
methods in class JSlider.

JSlider	
JSlider(int align, int min, int max, int init)	Constructor creates a horizontal slider (if align has value JSlider.HORIZONTAL) or vertical slider (if align is JSlider.VERTICAL), with a range from min to max and an initial setting of init.
void setMajorTickSpacing(int units)	Sets the number of units between major tick marks.
void setMinorTickSpacing(int units)	Sets the number of units between minor tick marks.
int getValue()	Returns the current value of this slider.
void setPaintLabels(boolean)	Displays the values of the tick marks if the argument to this method is true.
void setPaintTicks(boolean)	Draws the tick marks on the slider if the argument to this method is true.

Example 9

Create a slider that can be used to rate a particular ice cream. Add the text "Rate the ice cream on a scale of 0–10" above the slider. Display the value selected by the user below the slider. Set the initial value on the slider to 4, and the minor and major tick spacing to 1 and 5, respectively.

Solution: A label is used to display the text "Rate the ice cream...", and the slider's value is displayed in a text field. The complete program is shown in class JSliderDemo.

```
package guiprogramming;
import java.awt.*;
import javax.swing.*;
import javax.swing.event.*;

public class JSliderDemo {
  public static void main(String[] args) {
    JFrame window = new JFrame();
    JPanel topPanel = new JPanel(new BorderLayout());
    final JTextField textField = new JTextField();

    // create a slider
    JSlider slider = new JSlider(JSlider.HORIZONTAL, 0, 10, 4);
    slider.setMinorTickSpacing(1);
    slider.setMajorTickSpacing(5);
```

```
    slider.setPaintLabels(true);
    slider.setPaintTicks(true);

    // add event handler to display slider's value
    slider.addChangeListener(new ChangeListener() {
      public void stateChanged(ChangeEvent e) {
        int value = ((JSlider) e.getSource()).getValue();
        textField.setText("Your rating is " + value);
      }
    });

    topPanel.add(slider, BorderLayout.CENTER);
    topPanel.add(new JLabel("Rate the ice cream on a scale of 0-10"),
BorderLayout.NORTH);
    topPanel.add(textField, BorderLayout.SOUTH);
    window.setContentPane(topPanel);
    window.pack();
    window.setTitle("JSlider Demo");
    window.setDefaultCloseOperation(JFrame.EXIT_ON_CLOSE);
    window.setVisible(true);
  }
}
```

Figure 9–58 shows the slider with the initial value of 4. As an exercise, change this value on the slider and rerun the program.

9.7.11   The JOptionPane Class

The JOptionPane class, which extends JComponent, is used to create pop-up dialog boxes. There are four types of dialogs: confirm, input, message, and option. **Message dialogs** display some information about the program. **Confirm dialogs** ask a question, to which the user can respond with yes,

Figure 9–58
Output of program
JSliderDemo.

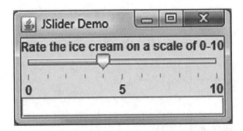

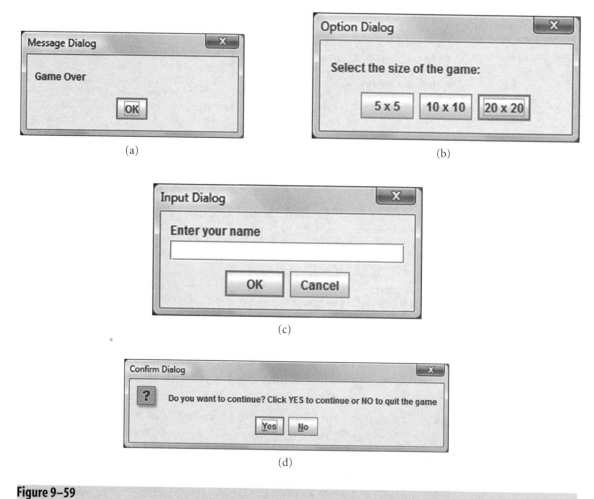

Figure 9–59

Four types of dialog boxes: (a) message, (b) option, (c) input, and (d) confirm.

no, or cancel. **Input dialogs** prompt the user to enter some data. **Option dialogs** are a combination of the preceding three dialogs.

Figure 9–59 shows the various types of dialog boxes. The methods in JOptionPane, shown in Figure 9–60, are used to create these dialog boxes.

Figure 9–60

Creating dialog boxes using class JOptionPane.

JOptionPane	
static void showMessageDialog(Component frame, Object message, String title, int **JOptionPane.type**)	Creates a dialog box with a message on it (type is INFORMATION_MESSAGE, ERROR_MESSAGE, WARNING_MESSAGE, QUESTION_MESSAGE, or PLAIN_MESSAGE) attached to the window called frame and with the given title.
static int showConfirmDialog(Component frame, Object message, String title, int **JOptionPane.optionType**, int JOptionPane.type)	Similar to showMessageDialog, except that the user can also select from a given set of options (optionType is YES_NO_OPTION, OK_CANCEL_OPTION, or YES_NO_CANCEL_OPTION).
static String showInputDialog(Component frame, Object message, String title, int JOptionPane.type)	Similar to showMessageDialog, except it returns the data entered by the user in the dialog box when the user presses OK; otherwise, a null value is returned.
static int showOptionDialog(Component frame, Object message, String title, int JOptionPane.optionType, int JOptionPane.type, Icon icon, **Object[] options**, Object initialValue)	Similar to showConfirmDialog, except that the user can also specify the options on the dialog box by passing them in an array of type Object to this method.

The showMessageDialog method creates a simple dialog box with a message. By selecting different options for type, you can create a message with a different icon. For example, the following code will display a "Game Over" message in the dialog box (see Figure 9–59(a)) in the specified window:

```
JOptionPane.showMessageDialog(window, "Game Over", "Message Dialog",
JOptionPane.PLAIN_MESSAGE);
```

The showConfirmDialog method displays a message, as well as allows the user to select one of the options displayed on the dialog box. The programmer can set the options to yes/no, ok/cancel, or yes/no/cancel. The option selected by the user is returned by this method. Figure 9–59(d) shows a dialog box with a yes/no option, created as follows:

```
JOptionPane.showConfirmDialog(window, "Do you want to continue? Click YES
to continue or NO to quit the game", "Confirm Dialog",
JOptionPane.YES_NO_OPTION, JOptionPane.QUESTION_MESSAGE);
```

The message type is given as QUESTION_MESSAGE; thus an icon of a question mark is displayed on the dialog box. The constant JOptionPane.YES_OPTION or JOptionPane.NO_OPTION is returned by this method, depending on whether the first button (with the text "Yes") or the second (with the text "No") is clicked by the user.

The showInputDialog method creates a dialog box with a text box in which the user can type some data, and returns this data back to the program. For example, this creates a dialog box that prompts the user to enter his or her name (see Figure 9–59(c)):

```
JOptionPane.showInputDialog(window, "Enter your name", "Input Dialog",
JOptionPane.PLAIN_MESSAGE);
```

The showOptionDialog method prompts the user to select one of many available options. For example, the dialog box in Figure 9–59(b) prompts a user to select the size of the grid on which a game will be played, and is created as follows:

```
Object[] options = {"5 x 5", "10 x 10", "20 x 20"};

JOptionPane.showOptionDialog(window, "Select the size of the game: ",
"Option Dialog", JOptionPane.YES_NO_CANCEL_OPTION,
JOptionPane.PLAIN_MESSAGE, null, options, options[2]);
```

You can specify an icon to be displayed on this type of dialog box. The last argument to method showOptionDialog is the value that will be shown as selected initially on the dialog box. This method returns the index of the selected option in the array options. For example, if the user clicked on the button labeled "5 x 5" on this dialog box, a value of 0 will be returned.

Several overloaded versions of these methods are also defined in this class.

9.7.12   The JMenuBar, JMenu, and JMenuItem Classes

A **menu bar** contains a set of headers such as "File", "View," and "Help" that appear at the top of applications such as word processors and browsers. The JMenuBar class can be used to create a menu bar to hold these headers called **menus**. A menu can contain several **menu items**, which specify operations. For example, the File menu may contain menu items Open, Save, and so forth. The menu and menu items can be created using the JMenu and JMenuItem classes, respectively. An action listener can be attached to a menu item to perform the desired operation when the item is selected. Some constructors and methods in these classes are shown in Figure 9–61. All three classes are descended from JComponent.

A menu bar is added to a window using the setJMenuBar method in class JFrame.

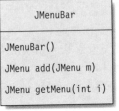

Constructor to create a menu bar.

Adds the menu m to the end of this menu bar.

Returns the menu at index i, where the first menu is at index 0.

(a)

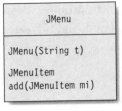

Constructor to create a menu labeled with the text t.

Adds the menu item mi to the end of this menu, and returns it.

(b)

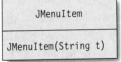

Constructor to create a menu item labeled with the text t.

(c)

Figure 9–61

Some constructors and methods in classes (a) JMenuBar, (b) JMenu, and (c) JMenuItem.

The PhotoOp Class: Adding a Menu Bar   We now add a menu bar to PhotoOp so that we can load different pictures for editing. The menu bar contains a menu called File and a menu item called Open Image. An event handler is attached to this menu item and it calls the selectFile method when this item is selected. The selectFile method is described in Section 9.7.13, *The JFileChooser and File Classes*. Add this method to PhotoOp to create a menu bar:

```
// method in class PhotoOp to create a menu bar
public JMenuBar createMenuBar() {
  // create a menuBar
  JMenuBar menuBar = new JMenuBar();
```

```
// add a menu called File to menuBar
JMenu menu = new JMenu("File");
menuBar.add(menu);

// add a menu item called Open Image to File
JMenuItem menuItem = new JMenuItem("Open Image");
menu.add(menuItem);

menuItem.addActionListener(new ActionListener() {
  public void actionPerformed(ActionEvent e) {
    selectFile();
  }
});

menuBar.setBackground(Color.lightGray);
return menuBar;
}
```

Add the following statement to the constructor in PhotoOp:

```
// create menu bar
window.setJMenuBar(createMenuBar());
```

9.7.13   The JFileChooser and File Classes

The JFileChooser class, which extends JComponent, is used to create a dialog box that makes it easy to select files. A file filter can be attached so that only files of the specified type can be opened by the user. See Figure 9–62 for a constructor and some methods in this class.

The showOpenDialog method returns the constant JFileChooser.APPROVE_OPTION or JFileChooser.CANCEL_OPTION, depending upon whether the user selects a file.

JFileChooser	
JFileChooser()	Constructor creates a file chooser.
int showOpenDialog(Component c)	Creates a dialog box (associated with the given component) that shows the contents of a drive or directory.
File getSelectedFile()	Returns an instance of the File class that contains information about the file selected by the user.

Figure 9–62
A constructor and some methods in class JFileChooser.

Figure 9–63

A constructor and some methods in the File class.

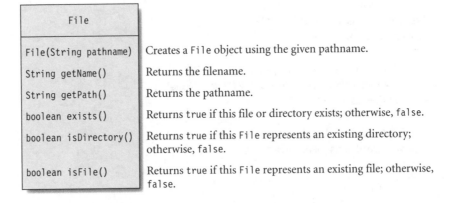

File	
File(String pathname)	Creates a File object using the given pathname.
String getName()	Returns the filename.
String getPath()	Returns the pathname.
boolean exists()	Returns true if this file or directory exists; otherwise, false.
boolean isDirectory()	Returns true if this File represents an existing directory; otherwise, false.
boolean isFile()	Returns true if this File represents an existing file; otherwise, false.

The java.io.File class (see Figure 9–63) contains methods to retrieve information about file and directory attributes, such as their names and pathnames. In addition, you can determine whether an object is a file or directory, among other tasks. Therefore, it is better to use the File class, instead of class String, to represent files and directories. Note that you cannot get any information about the *contents* of a file using these methods.

We will use these methods in the PhotoOp class to let the user select different photographs for modification.

The PhotoOp Class: Using a File Chooser to Select a Different Picture   We add a method called selectFile that lets the user select a JPEG file from the disk and display it in the window. A file chooser is created and a file filter is attached to this chooser so that only JPEG files can be opened. The filter is an instance of the class FileNameExtensionFilter and is created using the following constructor:

> **FileNameExtensionFilter(String description, String... extensions)**— a constructor that creates a filter to select files with the given extensions.

Note that there are three dots following the type String of the second parameter. This indicates that the preceding constructor is a *variadic* constructor. A **variadic** method or constructor is one that takes a *variable* number of arguments. Therefore, you can pass in *any* number of String arguments corresponding to the second parameter of this constructor.

Add this field to class PhotoOp:

```
private JFileChooser chooser;
```

Add this `selectFile` method to class `PhotoOp`:

```
// method in class PhotoOp to select image file from disk
public void selectFile() {
  // create a file chooser
  chooser = new JFileChooser();

  // This file filter allows the user to select JPEG files only
  FileNameExtensionFilter filter = new FileNameExtensionFilter("JPEG
files", "JPG", "JPEG");
  chooser.setFileFilter(filter);

  int returnVal = chooser.showOpenDialog(window);

  if (returnVal == JFileChooser.APPROVE_OPTION) {
    // open a dialog box to select files
    File file = chooser.getSelectedFile();
    System.out.println(file.getPath());

    // load the image from the file and display it in drawing panel
    Image image = new javax.swing.ImageIcon(file.getPath()).getImage();
    drawingPanel.loadImage(image);

    // update the title of the image
    titleLabel.setText(file.getName());
    titlePanel.repaint();
  }
}
```

Import these two classes in `PhotoOp`:

```
import javax.swing.filechooser.FileNameExtensionFilter;
import java.io.File;
```

Finally, add this method to `PhotoOpDrawingPanel` to load and redraw the new image:

```
public void loadImage(Image i) {
  bimage = i;
  repaint();
}
```

Figure 9–64 shows the dialog box that comes up when the Open Image menu item is selected in the File menu.

Figure 9–64

Dialog box to select a JPEG file from any directory on the disk and display it in the window.

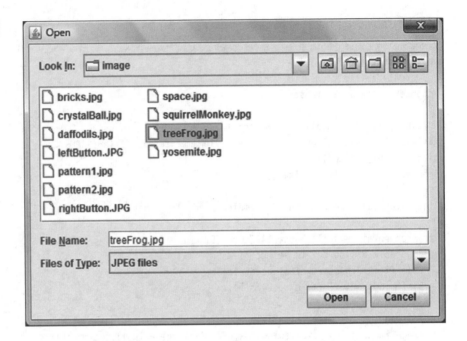

You can now load different photographs from the disk and transform them in PhotoOp.

As an exercise, modify the loadImage method in PhotoOpDrawingPanel so that fields angle, horizontalShear, and verticalShear are reset to 0, and scaleValue is reset to 1 when the new image is loaded. Also, make the necessary changes in PhotoOp so that the two check boxes are unchecked and the text in the text field is reset to 100.

9.8   Look and Feel Architecture

Swing uses a **look and feel** (**L&F**) architecture for its GUIs. Here, "look" refers to the general appearance of the GUI such as colors, fonts, sizes, shapes, and so forth, and "feel" refers to the behavior of the GUI. The programmer can choose from a set of available L&Fs, such as GTK, Motif, Windows, and Metal, modify them, or even develop a custom L&F for an application.

Consider, for example, that when you create a GUI, you do not have to define the sizes and positions of its components. So, how are these values calculated? This work is done by **UI delegates** (also called **look and feel delegates**). Every component contains a UI delegate, which decides not only the size, but also the color, font, opaqueness, and other properties for this component. A particular L&F implementation has its own UI delegate for every component. Therefore, if the user does not explicitly set the position using the setPreferredSize method of the component, the layout manager queries that component's UI delegate for this information.

The abstract class ComponentUI in javax.swing.plaf is the parent class for all UI delegates. A UI delegate provides its own implementation of all methods in this class for a particular L&F. The programmer does not call any method of ComponentUI or its subclasses directly. Instead, to set a specific L&F, the programmer uses the setLookAndFeel method of class UIManager in javax.swing:

```
static void setLookAndFeel(LookAndFeel newLookAndFeel)
```

There are other ways to change the L&F as well, which are not discussed here. If the programmer does not specify the L&F, the default L&F will be used.

9.9 Summary

In this chapter, we discussed how to create windows, add components to windows, and handle events using Swing. We covered various Swing classes to create containers and components, such as JFrame, JPanel, JButton, JLabel, JTextField, JFormattedTextField, JTextArea, JCheckBox, JRadioButton, JScrollPane, and JSlider. Layout managers, such as FlowLayout, BoxLayout, GridLayout, and BorderLayout, make it easy to place components within containers. A menu bar with menus and menu items is created using the JMenuBar, JMenu, and JMenuItem classes. Dialog boxes are created using the class JOptionPane. The Swing event model uses event sources, event objects, and event handlers. The programmer must write an event handler and attach it to an event source. We created the PhotoOp application in this chapter, which lets you load a JPEG image from the disk and apply various transformations to it such as rotation, scaling, and shearing.

Exercises

1. Name the Swing class that is used to create each of the following: window, panel, button, check box, slider, text field, scroll bars, button group, and menu bar.

2. What are the two ways to set the content pane of a window?

3. What is an event source? Give two examples.

4. What is an event object? How is it created?

5. What is an event handler? Why is it necessary for the event-handling class to implement an event listener interface?

6. Why is a layout manager useful? Briefly describe each of the following layouts:

    a.   Box layout

    b.   Flow layout

    c.   Border layout

    d.   Grid layout

7. Explain each of the following terms:

    a.   Content pane

    b.   Absolute positioning

    c.   Insets

    d.   Tool tip

8. Explain how the message, confirm, input, and option dialog boxes differ from each other.

9. Create and display a window of width 500 and height 400. The window should have a title and contain a label that displays your name.

10. Create a window that contains a single panel. Set this panel as the content pane of the window.

11. Create a window with four panels added to its content pane. Each panel has two buttons. Create a border around each panel. Show how the panels are arranged when the following layouts are used:

    a.   Flow layout

    b.   Border layout

    c.   Grid layout with one column

12. Create two text fields in a window. The first text field is editable, whereas the second text field is not. When the user presses the Enter key in the first text field, the program should display the count of the number of characters in this text field in the second text field.

13. Create an editable text area with 10 rows and 50 columns with line wrapping. Add scroll bars to the text area.

14. Write a program to create a text field and a text area in a window. The text field is editable, whereas the text area is not. Each time the user

presses the Enter key in the text field, the text area should display the sum of all numbers entered so far in the text field.

15. Create three check boxes with the text "Name," "Address," and "Phone number." The check boxes should be placed in a single row. When all three check boxes are selected, a person's name, address, and phone number should be displayed in a text area. Otherwise, a subset of this information should be displayed, depending on which check boxes are selected.

16. Create a window with six radio buttons and the text "Green," "Red," "Orange," "Blue," "Yellow," and "Black." Add the radio buttons to a button group. The radio buttons should be placed in three rows. Add a text area to display which radio button is selected.

17. Create a slider that displays values in the range 0–100 with major ticks at intervals of 10 and minor ticks at intervals of 5.

18. Explain what the following statement does in the `HelloWorld` program written in Chapter 1:

```
window.getContentPane().add(new JLabel(new ImageIcon("blimp.png")));
```

Image and Graphics Manipulation

19. Write a program to create a window with four radio buttons with text "Rectangle," "Circle," "Red," and "Green." The first two radio buttons are in one button group and the other two radio buttons are in another button group. Draw graphics in the window, depending on which radio buttons have been selected. For example, if "Rectangle" and "Red" are selected, a red rectangle should be drawn in the window.

20. Write a program to create a window with three radio buttons with text "Scenery," "Space," and "Tree Frog." Selecting a particular radio button displays the corresponding picture in the window.

21. Write a program that lets a user display and modify pictures. Add four buttons so that clicking a particular button will shift the image by a small amount in the north, south, east, or west direction inside the window. Also, add a menu bar with two menus: File and Image. The File menu should contain an Open menu item that the user can select to display JPEG and PNG files from the disk in the window. The Image menu should contain these menu items: Rotate, Shear, and Scale. When the user selects any one of these items, an input dialog box should display, in which the user can specify the rotation angle,

horizontal, and vertical shear values, or the scale amount. The modified image should then be displayed in the window. Add tool tips to all components on the GUI.

22. Examine the GUI for the Crystals game developed in Chapter 7, *Arrays and Strings*. Modify this game so that the size of the grid can be varied using command-line arguments.

23. Write a program to play a game of tic-tac-toe. The game is to be played on a 3 × 3 grid that is composed of 9 buttons. The player "x" goes first, and an "x" or "0" appears on each button alternately when a button is clicked. If a button is clicked more than once, the letter displayed on it should not change. The first player to get three in a row (vertically, horizontally, or diagonally) wins the game.

24. Write a program to play a two-player game of hangman. The first player enters a secret word using a dialog box. This word should be represented as a row of dashes (or spaces) in the window. The second player has to guess all the letters in the word to win the game. Each time a letter is guessed correctly, it is displayed in the correct positions over the dashes where it appears in the word. The game is over when the second player either guesses the complete word correctly or makes six incorrect guesses. Optionally, include a picture or stick figure in the window that changes each time the player makes a wrong guess.

Further Reading

We have only covered a small subset of the classes and interfaces in the Swing toolkit. This toolkit is covered in more detail in [3, 4].

References

1. "Java™ Platform, Standard Edition 6, API Specification." Web. <http://download.oracle.com/javase/6/docs/api/>.

2. "The Java™ Tutorials." Web. <http://download.oracle.com/javase/tutorial/>.

3. "Trail: Creating a GUI With JFC/Swing (The Java™ Tutorials)." Web. <http://download.oracle.com/javase/tutorial/uiswing/>.

4. Loy, Marc, and Robert Eckstein. *Java Swing*. Sebastopol, CA: O'Reilly, 2003. Print.

5. Knudsen, Jonathan. *Java 2D Graphics*. Beijing: O'Reilly, 1999. Print.

6. Brinkmann, Ron. *The Art and Science of Digital Compositing: Techniques for Visual Effects, Animation and Motion Graphics, Second Edition*. Burlington, MA: Morgan Kaufmann/Elsevier, 2008. Print.

7. Eckel, Bruce. *Thinking in Java*. Upper Saddle River, NJ: Prentice Hall, 2006. Print.

CHAPTER 10

Exception Handling

An exception refers to an error that occurs while a program is running. This type of error does not appear while a program is being compiled. For example, suppose that a program needs to read the contents of a file that does not exist. This program will compile fine, but it will result in an exception when the program is executed because the file cannot be found. Java has an exception-handling mechanism built into the language. This mechanism lets the programmer specify the action that should be taken when an exception occurs, such as printing an error message and terminating the program, prompting the user for additional input, or some other action.

The idea behind the exception-handling mechanism is simple, but the syntax can be confusing at first. In this chapter, we discuss the constructs used to handle exceptions and illustrate them with various examples.

10.1   The try and catch Blocks

This first example makes it easier to understand the syntax and use of exception handlers. The class BakeACake is a program that bakes a cake. It contains four methods: mixIngredients, setOvenTimer, putCakeInOven, and turnOvenOff.

```java
// BakeACake program – first version
public class BakeACake {
  public void mixIngredients() {
    System.out.println("Mix cake batter");
  }

  public void putCakeInOven() {
    System.out.println("Put cake in oven");
  }

  public void setOvenTimer(int time) {
    System.out.println("Oven will be turned on for " +time +" minutes");
  }

  public void turnOvenOff() {
    System.out.println("Oven turned off");
  }

  public static void main(String[] args) {
    BakeACake eChef = new BakeACake();
```

```
    eChef.mixIngredients();
    eChef.putCakeInOven();
    eChef.setOvenTimer(45);
  }
}
```

Suppose that the timer is broken and does not turn off the oven when the bake time is over. This situation can cause a fire! To prevent the fire, as well as other problems, we rewrite main in BakeACake using exception handling. This uses a try block followed by the catch block, as shown here:

```
try {
  // program code
} catch (Exception identifier) {
  // exception handling code
}
```

The program code is placed within the try block. An exception occurs if something goes wrong while the code in this block is being executed. The catch block specifies the action that must be taken to handle the exception when it occurs, and is called the **exception handler**. You can think of it as a method named catch that takes an argument of type Exception. (We discuss the Exception class later in this chapter.) The code inside this block is called the **exception-handling code**. The identifier must always be specified in the catch clause, and it can be used to get more information about the exception inside the catch block. The modified main is shown here:

```
public static void main(String[] args) {
  BakeACake eChef = new BakeACake();
  try {
    eChef.mixIngredients();
    eChef.putCakeInOven();
    eChef.setOvenTimer(45);
  } catch (Exception brokenTimer) {
    eChef.turnOvenOff();
  }
}
```

Note that the code in main is enclosed within a try block. We have also added exception-handling code in the catch block to turn off the oven. Assume that if the oven timer is broken, an exception is created while the program is executing. If this exception occurs, the exception handler will be invoked, which will turn off the oven. This can prevent a fire if the oven timer is broken.

Although we have not described in this simplified example how the *broken-Timer* exception is generated (we will revisit this issue later in the chapter), it must be specified in a program. Exception objects are created by one or more of the methods in the try block. Examine the HelloWorld program that we wrote in Section 1.6 of the first chapter. This program displays the image stored in the blimp.png file inside a window on the screen. The program runs even when the file is missing, although it will display an empty window in this case. We would like to modify this program so that it exits with an error message when the image file cannot be found. The following program shows how to do this using exception handling:

```java
// HelloWorld program - second version
package exceptionhandling;
import javax.swing.*;
import java.io.File;

public class HelloWorld {
  public static void main(String[] args) {
    try {
      File image = new File("blimp.png");

      if (!image.exists())
        throw new Exception("Image not found");

      JFrame frame = new JFrame("My First Program");
      frame.getContentPane().add(new JLabel(new ImageIcon("blimp.png")));
      frame.pack();
      frame.setVisible(true);
    } catch (Exception error) {
      System.out.println(error.getMessage());
    }
  }
}
```

The if statement checks whether the file exists:

```java
if (!image.exists())
```

If the file does not exist, this statement creates a new exception object carrying the message "Image not found," and sends it to the JVM using the throw keyword (this is called **throwing an exception**):

```java
throw new Exception("Image not found");
```

The JVM passes this exception to the exception handler, and the exception-handling code in the catch block is executed (this is called **catching an exception**):

```
System.out.println(error.getMessage());
```

This statement prints out the "Image not found" message carried by the exception object. The identifier of this object, error, is only visible inside this catch block. *It is important to note that the rest of the code following the throw statement in the try block is not executed after the exception is thrown.* Therefore, the window frame is not created and displayed on the screen if the exception occurs. Instead, the program terminates after the exception handler has executed. Remove the blimp.png file and rerun the HelloWorld program to see how the exception-handling mechanism works.

On the other hand, if the exception is not thrown, the rest of the statements following the throw statement in the try block are executed. In our HelloWorld program, this creates the window and displays it on the screen with the image. In this case, the catch block is not executed.

Programming languages that provide support for exception handling implement one of two models—*termination model* and *resumption model*. In the **termination model**, the program terminates after the exception handler has executed. In the **resumption model**, the exception handler attempts to correct the problem that caused the exception, and then the program resumes execution from where it had left off. Java supports the termination model, and so the rest of the code following the throw statement in the try block is not executed after the exception occurs.

The Exception class is defined in the java.lang package. An exception object is an instance of this class or its subclasses. The constructors and methods in this class are discussed next.

10.2 The Exception Class

The class Exception and its subclasses are used to create different types of exceptions. An exception is an instance of any one of these classes. The Exception class provides methods to obtain information about the type of error that has occurred in the program. Figure 10–1 shows the inheritance tree for a few of the exception classes. You can also write your own exception class by extending Exception or its subclasses, which may be necessary

Figure 10–1

A portion of the inheritance tree for the Exception class.

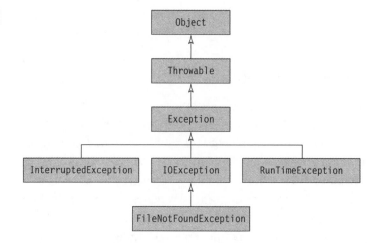

Figure 10–2

Some constructors and methods in class Exception.

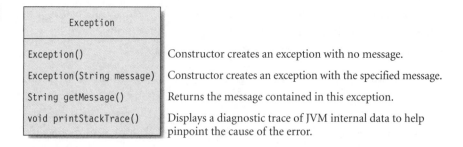

Exception	
Exception()	Constructor creates an exception with no message.
Exception(String message)	Constructor creates an exception with the specified message.
String getMessage()	Returns the message contained in this exception.
void printStackTrace()	Displays a diagnostic trace of JVM internal data to help pinpoint the cause of the error.

when the exception cannot be created using any of the existing classes. User-defined exceptions are discussed a little later, in Section 10.4.

Figure 10–2 shows some constructors and methods in Exception. The getMessage and printStackTrace methods are inherited from class Throwable. These methods provide information about the exception to the exception handler. The printStackTrace method is called within the catch block as follows:

```
catch (Exception error) {
    error.printStackTrace();
}
```

If you use printStackTrace instead of getMessage in the HelloWorld class, it displays the following message on the console if the given file cannot be found:

```
java.lang.Exception: Image not found
        at exceptionhandling.HelloWorld.main(HelloWorld.java:13)
```

10.3 Methods That Throw Exceptions

The HelloWorld program shows how an exception can be thrown inside a method (main in this case) using the throw keyword. An exception handler is also provided inside this method. However, it is not necessary to handle an exception inside a method. Instead, a method may simply declare that it throws an exception and leave it to the calling method to handle it in any way that it chooses. For example, let us move the first three statements in the HelloWorld program into a method called checkIfImageExists:

```
// does not compile
public void checkIfImageExists(){
  File image = new File("blimp.png");
  if (!image.exists())
    throw new Exception("Image not found");
}
```

This method will not compile because an exception handler has not been provided within the method. Therefore, this method must declare that it throws an exception using the throws keyword followed by the type of the exception in the method declaration:

```
public void checkIfImageExists() throws Exception {
  File image = new File("blimp.png");
  if (!image.exists())
    throw new Exception("Image not found");
}
```

It is important to note here that the keyword throw is used in the method body, whereas the keyword throws is used in the method declaration.

> Suppose that method *X* declares that it throws an exception. A method *Y* that calls *X* must either handle this exception OR declare that it also throws this exception. If the exception is thrown by the main method, then the program crashes with a run-time error.

The calling method *might* or *might not* provide a suitable exception handler, depending on its needs. If an exception handler is provided, different methods might choose to handle the exception differently. For example, one method might print out the message carried by the exception, whereas another method might print out the stack trace in its exception-handling code. The displayImageInWindow method in the following HelloWorldAgain program calls the checkIfImageExists method and provides a different exception handler from the one in the `HelloWorld` program to handle the exception thrown by this method:

```
package exceptionhandling;
import javax.swing.*;
import java.io.File;

public class HelloWorldAgain {
  public void checkIfImageExists() throws Exception {
    File image = new File("blimp.png");
    if (!image.exists())
      throw new Exception("Image not found");
  }

  // This method handles the exception thrown by checkIfImageExists.
  public void displayImageInWindow()  {
    try {
      checkIfImageExists();
      JFrame frame = new JFrame("My First Program");
      frame.getContentPane().add(new JLabel(new ImageIcon("blimp.png")));
      frame.pack();
      frame.setVisible(true);
    } catch (Exception error) {
      error.printStackTrace();
    }
  }

  public static void main(String[] args) {
    HelloWorldAgain hw = new HelloWorldAgain();
    hw.displayImageInWindow();
  }
}
```

If the calling method does not provide an exception handler, it must declare that it throws the exception. Therefore, if the `displayImageInWindow` method in the `HelloWorldAgain` program did not provide an exception handler, we would have written it as shown here using the `throws` clause in the method signature:

```
// This method does not handle the exception thrown by
// checkIfImageExists.
public void displayImageInWindow()throws Exception {
  checkIfImageExists();
  JFrame frame = new JFrame("My First Program");
  frame.getContentPane().add(new JLabel(new ImageIcon("blimp.png")));
  frame.pack();
  frame.setVisible(true);
}
```

The exception thrown by this method should now be handled in the method that calls it. Suppose that main calls displayImageInWindow. If main also does not provide an exception handler, it should throw this exception:

```
// The exception is sent to the console.
public static void main(String[] args) throws Exception {
  HelloWorldAgain hw = new HelloWorldAgain();
  hw.displayImageInWindow();
}
```

We have used the throws exception clause in main's declaration because the exception is not caught and handled inside this method. If an exception occurs now, the exception is sent to the console and the JVM terminates. This type of an exception is known as an **unhandled exception** because it is not caught by the program when it occurs.

Examine the code in the BakeACake program that uses exception handling. The main method catches and handles a brokenTimer exception. How is this exception created? It should be created and thrown by at least one of the methods in the try block. To complete this program, let us add a diagnostic method to class BakeACake to determine whether the timer is broken and return true if it is:

```
public boolean timerIsBroken() {
  // code returns true if timer is broken
  // otherwise it returns false
}
```

The setOvenTimer method is modified so that it calls the timerIsBroken method and throws an exception if the timer is broken:

```
public void setOvenTimer(int time) throws Exception {
  if (timerIsBroken() == true)
    throw new Exception("Timer is broken");
  System.out.println("Oven will be turned on for " +time +" minutes");
}
```

The following program output is obtained if the timerIsBroken method returns true:

```
Mix cake batter
Put cake in oven
Oven turned off
```

The exception thrown by the setOvenTimer method is caught by the exception handler in main, which executes the turnOvenOff method. Therefore, the statement "Oven will be turned on…" in setOvenTimer will not be executed.

Figure 10–3

A call stack with three methods.

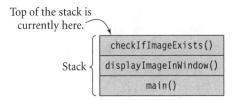

Top of the stack is currently here.

Stack {
checkIfImageExists()
displayImageInWindow()
main()

A method can throw more than one exception. We discuss this in more detail in Section 10.4.

10.3.1   The Call Stack

As you have seen, the responsibility of handling an exception is passed to the calling method if the method that throws the exception does not provide the handler for it. How does the JVM keep track of the calling methods? It does so by using a data structure called the **call stack**. Each time a new method is called, it is stored on the top of the call stack. As more methods are added, the top of the call stack moves upward. For example, in the HelloWorldAgain program, main calls the displayImageInWindow method, which in turn calls the checkIfImageExists method. Figure 10–3 shows how the three methods are stored on the call stack, with main at the bottom of the call stack and checkIfImageExists at the top.

The method currently executing is at the top of the stack. If this method throws an exception, the JVM checks to see whether it provides an exception handler. If the method does not provide a handler, the JVM removes it from the call stack and checks the next method, which is now on the top of the call stack. The JVM continues to do this for all the methods in the call stack until an appropriate handler is found for the exception. If main also does not handle the exception, the exception is sent to the console and the JVM terminates.

10.4   A try Block with Multiple catch Blocks

When the methods in the try block throw different types of exceptions, you can provide a different exception handler for each type of exception. To do so, you should write a different catch block for each exception type:

```
try {
  // different types of exceptions are thrown here
} catch (ExceptionType1 e1) {
  // exception handler for ExceptionType1
```

```
} catch (ExceptionType2 e2) {
  // exception handler for ExceptionType2
} catch (ExceptionType3 e3) {
  // exception handler for ExceptionType3
}
//...continue adding as many catch blocks as needed
```

This is the more general form of the try-catch block. Each catch clause has a parameter with a different type. This type may be Exception, any of its existing subclasses, or a user-defined class that extends Exception. For example, the parameter e1 in the first catch clause has type ExceptionType1. A try block can have as many catch blocks as needed.

A method can throw multiple exceptions. It can provide exception handlers for these exceptions by using multiple catch blocks with its try block. Alternately, if the method does not provide handlers, it must declare that it throws the exceptions by using the throws keyword followed by the names of all of the exceptions. For example, the following method throws two user-defined exceptions Exception1 and Exception2:

```
void someMethod() throws Exception1, Exception2 {
  // statements
  throw new Exception1();

  // other statements
  throw new Exception2();
}
```

The next example explains the finer points of using multiple catch blocks as well as how user-defined exceptions can be created.

A program inside a copy machine raises exceptions when various problems occur, such as the toner has run out (OutOfTonerException), the machine is out of paper (OutOfPaperException), a paper jam has occurred (PaperJamException), or some other maintenance (MaintenanceException) is required. Figure 10–4 shows the inheritance tree for these exceptions.

You can provide constructors inside an exception class, as shown in CopyMachineException:

```
class CopyMachineException extends Exception {
  public CopyMachineException() {
    this("Copy Machine Exception");
  }
```

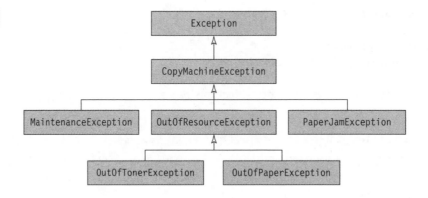

```
public CopyMachineException(String message) {
  super(message);
 }
}
```

Alternately, the default constructor can be used, as shown here for OutOf-
ResourceException:

```
class OutOfResourceException extends CopyMachineException {}
```

The other exception classes can also be created in one of these two ways.

The CopyMachine class is written next. The makeCopies method in this class
throws multiple exceptions but does not provide any handlers for them.
Note how all of these exceptions must be specified in the throws clause with
commas separating them:

```
public class CopyMachine {
  public void makeCopies() throws OutOfTonerException, OutOfPaperException,
PaperJamException {
  // Code for this method
  }
}
```

The main method for this class calls the makeCopies method in the try block
and uses multiple catch blocks to handle all the exceptions thrown by this
method:

```
public static void main(String[] args) {
  try {
    CopyMachine copier = new CopyMachine();
    copier.makeCopies();
  } catch (OutOfTonerException ex1) {
    System.out.println(ex1.getMessage());
```

```
  } catch (OutOfPaperException ex2) {
    System.out.println(ex2.getMessage());
  } catch (PaperJamException ex3) {
    System.out.println(ex3.getMessage());
  }
}
```

The JVM checks each of the catch clauses, beginning with the first one, to determine whether the type of its parameter matches the type of the exception that has occurred. For example, method makeCopies throws a Paper-JamException if a paper jam has occurred in the machine. When a PaperJamException occurs, the JVM stops executing the try block. It then checks to see if an exception handler is provided in the makeCopies method. There is no handler provided here, and so it checks the next method in the call stack. This is the main method and it contains an exception handler. The JVM checks each of the catch blocks in main to find a match, starting with the first block. The third catch clause catches the PaperJamException, and so its exception-handling code is executed. The order in which the catch blocks are placed does not matter here, but you will see an example later in this section where it does.

An exception type in the catch block can be replaced with its super type. Thus, the two catch blocks that catch OutOfTonerException and outOfPaperException can be replaced with a single catch block that catches the OutOfResourceException:

```
try {
  CopyMachine copier = new CopyMachine();
  copier.makeCopies();
} catch (OutOfResourceException ex1) {
  ex1.printStackTrace();
} catch (PaperJamException ex2) {
  ex2.printStackTrace();
}
```

The order of the catch blocks can be changed here as well.

If we were only interested in providing a separate exception handler for OutOfPaperException, we could write:

```
  try {
    CopyMachine copier = new CopyMachine();
    copier.makeCopies();
  } catch (OutOfPaperException ex1) {
```

```
    ex1.printStackTrace();
  } catch (CopyMachineException ex2) {
    ex2.printStackTrace();
  }
```

The catch block with exception type `CopyMachineException` will catch all the remaining exceptions thrown in the try block. The order of the catch blocks is important here. If we move the `CopyMachineException` block *before* the `OutOfPaperException` block, the latter will never be executed. This is because `OutOfPaperException` is a subtype of `CopyMachineException`, and so the catch block with exception type `CopyMachineException` catches `OutOfPaperException` as well. The following results in a compilation error:

```
// don't put CopyMachineException before OutOfPaperException
try {
  CopyMachine copier = new CopyMachine();
  copier.makeCopies();
} catch (CopyMachineException ex1) {
  ex1.printStackTrace();
} catch (OutOfPaperException ex2) {      // error
  // this code is never executed
  ex2.printStackTrace();
}
```

As an exercise, modify the code in the subclasses of `CopyMachineException` so that the message displayed describes the specific type of exception that has occurred. For example, if a paper jam occurs, the message should display "Paper Jam Exception."

10.5   Run-Time Exceptions

The exceptions that we have discussed thus far are caused by errors that are outside the programmer's control. The image file needed in the `HelloWorld` program might be missing because someone deleted it or put it in an incorrect directory, and not due to an error in the program itself. Similarly, a paper jam in the copier is not caused by an error in the program running the copier.

A run-time exception is different from these exceptions in that it is caused by errors *within* the program. An example of this is using an invalid index to access an array element. This program does not give a compilation error but causes an exception when run:

```
package exceptionhandling;

public class ExceptionDemo {
  public static void main(String[] args) {
    char[] array = {'a', 'e', 'i', 'o', 'u'};
    String s = new String(array, 0, 6);
    System.out.println(s);
  }
}
```

The run-time exception is `ArrayIndexOutOfBoundsException`, and it is caused by trying to access the array element at index 6:

```
Exception in thread "main" java.lang.StringIndexOutOfBoundsException:
String index out of range: 6
        at java.lang.String.<init>(Unknown Source)
        at exceptionhandling.ExceptionDemo.main(ExceptionDemo.java:6)
```

The second and third arguments to the `String` constructor in `ExceptionDemo` should be valid indices of some elements in the array. This exception is caused by an error in the program as the last element "u" of the array is at index 4 and there is no element at index 6.

A run-time exception occurs if you remove the square brackets that follow `String` when declaring `main`. These exceptions are instances of the class `RuntimeException` or its subclasses. You could write an exception handler to catch and handle run-time exceptions, but this is not a good idea. The main reason for this is that these types of errors should not be present in your code to begin with. Another reason is that trying to handle all types of run-time exceptions that might occur (and these could be numerous) can clutter your code considerably. You must check your code thoroughly to remove errors instead of relying on run-time exceptions to notify you when something goes wrong. The compiler will *not* flag it as an error if an exception handler is not provided to handle this type of exception. Run-time exceptions are also called **unchecked exceptions** because they are not checked by the compiler, whereas all other types of exceptions are known as **checked exceptions**.

10.6   The finally Block

The finally block is used to hold code that must be executed at the end of the program regardless of whether an exception has occurred. This is usually used for cleanup code, such as releasing resources that are no longer needed. There can be only one finally block associated with a try-catch block, and its use is optional. The general syntax is shown here:

```
try {
  // different types of exceptions are thrown here
} catch (ExceptionType1 e1) {
  // exception handler for ExceptionType1
} catch (ExceptionType2 e2) {
  // exception handler for ExceptionType2
} catch (ExceptionType3 e3) {
  // exception handler for ExceptionType3
} finally {
  // cleanup code
}
```

Let us revisit the second version of the BakeACake program to see how the finally block can be used in it. Suppose that the cake pan must always be cleaned at the end, even if a brokenTimer exception occurred and the cake was not baked. Let us add this method to BakeACake:

```
public void cleanCakePan() {
    System.out.println("Cleaned cake pan");
}
```

This method can be called inside the try block as follows, but there is a problem with it. Can you spot it?

```
try {
  eChef.mixIngredients();
  eChef.putCakeInOven();
  eChef.setOvenTimer(45);
  eChef.cleanCakePan();
} catch (Exception brokenTimer) {
  eChef.turnOvenOff();
}
```

The problem is that if an exception occurs, the cleanCakePan method will not be executed. This is because the exception is thrown in setOvenTimer and so all the code following the throw statement in the try block is skipped. We can also call the cleanCakePan method inside the catch block, but this duplicates code.

The solution to this problem is to call the `cleanCakePan` method inside the `finally` block:

```
try {
  eChef.mixIngredients();
  eChef.putCakeInOven();
  eChef.setOvenTimer(45);
} catch (Exception brokenTimer) {
  eChef.turnOvenOff();
} finally {
  eChef.cleanCakePan();
}
```

The `finally` block is always executed; thus the `cleanCakePan` method is called regardless of whether the exception occurs.

In the following chapters, you will see how to handle other types of exceptions, such as `IOException` and `InterruptedException`. An `IOException` occurs when the program tries unsuccessfully to read or write data from the computer screen or a file. The `finally` block is used here to close a file at the end of a program and thereby release system resources.

10.7 Summary

In this chapter, we discussed how exceptions are thrown and caught in a program using the `try-catch` block. An exception does not have to be handled in the method in which it is thrown. Instead, an exception handler can be provided in the calling method. Java keeps track of calling methods using the call stack. We also discussed some constructors and methods in class `Exception` and its related classes. You can extend `Exception` to create a custom exception class to meet the needs of a specific application. A runtime exception is caused by an error in the program. These exceptions are not checked by the compiler and need not be handled by the programmer.

Exercises

1. What is the syntax of the `try-catch` block?

2. Explain the following terms:
   a. Exception handler
   b. Unhandled exception
   c. Call stack

3. How are the following different?

   a. Checked exceptions vs. unchecked exceptions

   b. `throws` vs. `throw`

4. Describe the two ways in which an exception can be generated.

5. What is the `finally` block? When should it be used?

6. What is class `Throwable`?

7. What are unchecked exceptions? Why is it better that the programmer not handle these types of exceptions?

8. State whether each of the following statements is true or false:

   a. An exception can occur due to some system resources that are needed by a program but are not available, as well as errors in a program.

   b. A `try` block must be followed by at least one `catch` block or a `finally` block.

   c. A `try` block can contain methods that do not throw an exception.

   d. A method can contain multiple `try-catch` blocks.

   e. The method `foo` is required to handle all exceptions that are thrown by the method that `foo` calls.

   f. The statements following the `throw` keyword are always executed.

   g. A checked exception occurs due to an error in the code.

   h. Unchecked exceptions do not have to be handled.

   i. The JVM passes an unhandled exception to the console.

   j. A `finally` block must be present in every `try-catch` block.

   k. A `catch` block that catches an exception of type `Exception` must be placed before the other `catch` blocks when multiple `catch` blocks are present.

9. Find the errors in the following code segments (a) through (e), where `methodA` and `methodB` are defined as follows:

```
public void methodA() {
    // code
}
public void methodB() throws Exception {
    // code
}
```

a.
```
try {
    methodA();
} catch (Exception e) {
    // code
}
```

b.
```
try {
    methodB();
}
System.out.println("outside try block");
catch(Exception e) {
    e.printStackTrace();
}
```

c.
```
public void methodG() throws Exception {
    methodA();
}
```

d.
```
public void methodH() {
    methodB();
}
```

e.
```
try {
    methodB();
} catch {
    methodB();
}
```

10. When is the order of the catch blocks important? Give an example.

11. Write a program to show that the finally block is always executed.

12. This constructor in FileInputStream class throws a FileNotFoundException:

    `public FileInputStream(String name) throws FileNotFoundException`

    Write a method to create an instance of FileInputStream using this constructor. This method should also provide an exception handler to catch the exception FileNotFoundException.

13. Write a custom exception class that extends Exception. Add constructors to this class. Write a method that throws this exception. Also, write a program that calls this method and contains an exception handler. The exception-handling code should display an error message on the console.

14. An automobile manufacturer is developing a diagnostic system for a car. This system can determine whether the lights or brakes are faulty, and whether there are problems in the ignition or battery that do not allow a car to be started up. Create the following types of exception classes: NoStartException with subclasses BadIgnitionException and DeadBatteryException; LightsException with subclasses HeadLightException, BrakeLightException, and TailLightException; and BrakeException with subclasses FootBrakeException and ParkingBrakeException. Write a method called diagnostics that occasionally throws any one of these exceptions, depending on the values generated by a random-number generator.

    a. Write a method called display that calls diagnostics and provides exception handlers to display an appropriate message if an exception occurs. Otherwise, if an exception does not occur, method display should print out "Diagnostic test completed—no problems found."

    b. Suppose that display contains three catch clauses with parameter types FootBrakeException, BrakeException, and Exception. Explain which orders of the catch blocks would prevent the execution of an exception handler.

15. A class named Foo contains three methods: bar1, bar2, and bar3, where bar1 throws CustomException1 and bar2 throws CustomException2. The method bar3 calls both of these methods. Furthermore, assume that both bar1 and bar2 throw an exception when the following main method is executed. Which of these two exceptions will be caught and handled by the exception handler in main—CustomException1 or CustomException2? What is a potential problem here?

```
public void bar3() throws CustomException1, CustomException2 {
  try {
    bar1();
  } finally {
    bar2();
  }
}

public static void main(String[] args) {
  Foo f = new Foo();
```

```
    try {
      f.bar3();
    } catch(Exception e) {
        e.printStackTrace();
    }
  }
```

16. Write a program that causes a run-time exception to occur.

References

1. "Java™ Platform, Standard Edition 6, API Specification." Web.
   <http://download.oracle.com/javase/6/docs/api/>.

2. "The Java™ Tutorials." Web.
   <http://download.oracle.com/javase/tutorial/>.

3. Eckel, Bruce. *Thinking in Java.* Upper Saddle River, NJ: Prentice Hall,
   2006. Print.

4. Anderson, Julie, and Herve Franceschi. *Java 6 Illuminated: An Active
   Learning Approach.* Sudbury, MA: Jones and Bartlett, 2008. Print.

5. Sierra, Kathy, and Bert Bates. *Head First Java.* Sebastopol, CA: O'Reilly,
   2005. Print.

CHAPTER 11

File I/O

CHAPTER CONTENTS

In the previous chapters, you wrote programs that read from and wrote to the console. Java also contains classes for reading from or writing to *files*. In this chapter, we will discuss the various classes to do file input and output (called **file I/O** for short). As an example, we will describe the format of a file (known as a WAV file) used to store audio data, and develop an audio-mixing program to combine audio tracks stored in WAV files and to reverse an audio track, among other tasks.

11.1   Overview of I/O Classes

One program might read data that is typed in from a keyboard or that comes from a file stored on a disk, whereas another might display information on a console or write data to a disk. These are all examples of I/O. Java provides several classes to ease the task of performing I/O. You have already used the Scanner class to read data from the console; this class can also be used to read text files. In addition, there are other I/O classes in the java.io package, including Reader, Writer, InputStream, OutputStream, and RandomAccessFile.

A **stream** is a flow of data in one direction, from a device (such as a keyboard, disk, or network device) to a program, or vice versa. This data can be binary, or composed of primitive data types or even objects. Java's I/O classes provide methods for reading or writing streams. Reader and Writer are abstract classes, with subclasses FileReader and FileWriter to read and write **character streams**. The abstract classes InputStream and OutputStream contain many subclasses for reading and writing **binary streams**. All of these classes, with the exception of RandomAccessFile, read or write data *sequentially*. The RandomAccessFile class provides methods to read data from and write data to any *random* location in a file.

In the following sections, we will discuss how you can use these classes.

11.2   Reading and Writing Text Files

You can read from and write to text files using the FileReader and FileWriter classes, respectively. A constructor and some methods of FileReader are shown in Figure 11–1. The constructor creates a FileReader for the file that is passed in as an argument to it. The read methods read data sequentially

FileReader	
FileReader(File f)throws FileNotFoundException	Constructor creates a reader to read from the given file f.
int read() throws IOException	Reads and returns a single character or −1 if the end of the file is reached.
int read(char[] array) throws IOException	Reads up to *n* characters into array of size *n*. It returns the number of characters read or −1 if the end of the file is reached.
void close() throws IOException	Closes this file reader.

Figure 11–1

The FileReader class.

from this file and return the special value −1 (called **end-of-file** or **EOF**) to indicate that the end of the file has been reached; that is, there is no more data left to read in the file.

Figure 11–2 shows some constructors and methods in class FileWriter. The FileWriter(File) constructor creates a writer object for writing to the given file. The file is created if it does not exist already. If the file already exists, its contents are erased. To *append* data to the existing contents of a file, you can use the second constructor FileWriter(File, boolean) with a boolean argument of true.

FileWriter	
FileWriter(File f)	Constructor creates a writer for writing to the given file f.
FileWriter(File f, boolean b) throws IOException	Constructor creates a writer to append data to the end of the file f if the second argument is true.
void write(int c) throws IOException	Writes a single character c to the file.
void write(String s) throws IOException	Writes the string s to the file.
void write(char[] array) throws IOException	Writes the array of characters stored in the given array to the file.
void close() throws IOException	Closes this file writer.

Figure 11–2

The FileWriter class.

We have only shown constructors for these classes that take an argument of type File. Recall that a file or directory name can be represented using the java.io.File class. This class contains methods to get information about the attributes of that file or directory, such as its pathname, length, whether it exists, and so forth. Overloaded versions of these constructors that take other types of arguments, such as String, are also present in FileReader and FileWriter.

After a file has been read or written to, it is important to close it using the close method. This will free up system resources that are associated with that file. The steps to read a file are shown in the flowchart in Figure 11–3.

Example 1

Using a text editor, create a text file called info.txt in the JavaBook/text directory containing the following text: "Audio files can be stored in a variety of formats such as wav, wma, mp3, aiff, au and many others." Then, write a program that will:

   a.   Print out each character of info.txt on the console.

   b.   Copy the contents of info.txt to a new file called copyOfInfo.txt.

Solution:

   a.   The read method reads each character ch sequentially from info.txt and returns it. When all of the data has been read, it returns −1, which indicates that the end of the file has been reached. The System.out.print statement prints out each character ch read from the file on the console. The cast to char is needed here because the read method returns each character as type int. We use a try-catch block to catch and handle the exceptions that are thrown inside main.

Figure 11–3

Flowchart showing how data is read from a file.

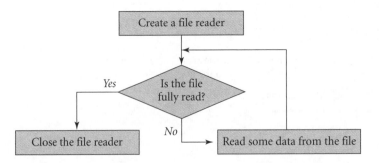

```
package fileio;
import java.io.*;

public class FileReaderWriterDemo {
  public static void main(String[] args) {
    FileReader reader = null;

    try {
      // create a file reader
      reader = new FileReader(new File("text/info.txt"));

      int ch;

      // read all characters in file until -1 is received
      while ( (ch =  reader.read()) != -1) {
        // Cast ch to type char and print it out
        System.out.print((char)ch);
      }

      reader.close();     // close the file reader
    } catch (FileNotFoundException e) {
      System.err.println("File could not be found" +e.getMessage());
    } catch (IOException e) {
      System.err.println("IOException" +e.getMessage());
    }
  }
}
```

As an exercise, create an array of type char with size 5, and use the read(char[]) method to read data from info.txt.

b. To copy the contents of a file into another file, modify this program as follows: Declare a FileWriter and add it to the preceding code in main:

```
FileWriter writer = null;
```

Inside the try block, create a FileWriter:

```
writer = new FileWriter(new File("text/copyOfInfo.txt"));
```

To write to the new file, replace the call to System.out.print with the following statement:

```
writer.write(ch);
```

Finally, close the new file with this call:

```
writer.close();
```

Run the program and, using a text editor, check that the desired text has been copied from info.txt into the file copyOfInfo.txt. Note that any error messages will be displayed on **standard error** using the System.err.println statement. Standard error, defined in the System class, is typically the console. However, you can change this using the setErr method in System so that error messages are sent to another destination, such as a log file, instead of the console.   ■

11.2.1   Improving Read/Write Efficiency with BufferedReader/ BufferedWriter

A program that wants to read from or write to a file must of course have access to the disk. Reading from a disk takes a lot more time than reading from a computer's memory (RAM). To address this, Java provides Buffered-Reader and BufferedWriter classes to optimize reading from, and writing to a stream of type Reader.

Let us first examine how FileReader's read() method reads data from a file. Each time read is called, one character is read from disk. This is an inefficient way of reading a file—especially a large one—because it takes longer to access the disk than to actually read the data from the RAM. Instead of getting a single character at a time from the disk, a BufferedReader gets a fixed number of characters from the disk and puts them in a buffer in the RAM. The program can then read data from this buffer instead of from disk. When all the data in the buffer has been read, the buffer is again filled with data by accessing the file on disk. This procedure reduces the total number of times the disk is accessed to read the same amount of data. The number of characters that are read at a time from the disk by BufferedReader depends on its buffer size. The programmer can either specify the size explicitly in the constructor or use the default size. The BufferedWriter's write(int) method writes each character to a buffer in the RAM, and then transfers all the data from the buffer to the disk in one batch when the buffer is *full*—a much more efficient system than writing one character at a time to the disk.

Although this discussion is in the context of file I/O, it applies to I/O with other types of streams (such as console) as well. A BufferedReader and BufferedWriter can be wrapped around any stream of type Reader to optimize the read/write operation.

Figure 11–4
The `BufferedReader`
class.

BufferedReader	
`BufferedReader(Reader r)`	Constructor to create a `BufferedReader` with a default buffer size.
`BufferedReader(Reader r, int bufferSize)`	Constructor to create a `BufferedReader` with the given buffer size.
`int read() throws IOException`	Reads and returns a single character or −1 if the end of the stream is reached.
`int read(char[] array) throws IOException`	Reads characters into `array` and returns a count of the number of the characters read. Returns −1 if the end of the stream is reached.
`long skip(long num) throws IOException`	Skips over the next `num` characters without reading them.
`void close() throws IOException`	Closes this stream.

Some methods in `BufferedReader` are shown in Figure 11–4. The `read` methods return −1 if the end of the file is reached. The `skip` method skips over the specified number of characters; however, no characters are skipped if the argument to this method is negative.

`BufferedWriter` contains the methods shown in Figure 11–5. Before a `BufferedWriter` closes the stream, it must call its `flush` method so that any data remaining in the buffer is written to that stream.

Figure 11–5
The `BufferedWriter`
class.

BufferedWriter	
`BufferedWriter(Writer w)`	Constructor to create a `BufferedWriter` with a default buffer size.
`BufferedWriter(Writer w, int bufferSize)`	Constructor to create a `BufferedWriter` with the given buffer size.
`void write(int ch) throws IOException`	Writes the character `ch`.
`void write(String s) throws IOException`	Writes the string `s`.
`void write(char[]) throws IOException`	Writes an array of characters.
`void flush() throws IOException`	Writes the data remaining in the buffer to the stream.
`void close() throws IOException`	Closes this stream.

When a BufferedReader (or BufferedWriter) is closed, the corresponding file reader (writer) streams that it wraps are automatically closed. Therefore, it is not necessary to close these streams explicitly.

> Closing a buffered reader or buffered writer also closes the underlying streams.

You can also implement your own buffered reader (writer) by using the methods that take an argument of type char[] in class FileReader (FileWriter) to read (write) an array of characters at a time.

Example 2

Modify the FileReaderWriterDemo program so that it uses a BufferedReader for reading from the file info.txt and a BufferedWriter for writing to the file copyOfInfo.txt. Starting with the first character, only alternate characters should be written to the file.

Solution: A BufferedReader and a BufferedWriter wrap a reader and writer as shown here:

```
bufferedReader = new BufferedReader(reader);
bufferedWriter = new BufferedWriter(writer);
```

Alternate characters are skipped using this statement:

```
bufferedReader.skip(1);
```

It is also necessary to flush the buffer before closing any of the writers in case any data that has not yet been written to the disk remains in the buffer. The following statement causes any remaining data in the buffer to be written to the file:

```
bufferedWriter.flush();
```

The program is shown here:

```
package fileio;
import java.io.*;

public class BufferedReaderWriterDemo {
  public static void main(String[] args) {
    FileReader reader = null;
    FileWriter writer = null;
    BufferedReader bufferedReader = null;
    BufferedWriter bufferedWriter = null;
```

```
    try {
      // create a file reader and writer
      reader = new FileReader(new File("text/info.txt"));
      writer = new FileWriter(new File("text/CopyOfInfo.txt"));

      // create a buffered reader and buffered writer
      bufferedReader = new BufferedReader(reader);
      bufferedWriter = new BufferedWriter(writer);

      int ch;

      // read all characters in file until end-of-file
      while ( (ch = bufferedReader.read()) != -1) {
        bufferedWriter.write(ch);
        // skip the next character
        bufferedReader.skip(1);
      }

      // close buffered reader
      bufferedReader.close();      // also closes reader

      // flush and close buffered writer
      bufferedWriter.flush();
      bufferedWriter.close();      // also closes writer
    } catch (FileNotFoundException e) {
      System.err.println("File could not be found" +e.getMessage());
    } catch (IOException e) {
      System.err.println("IOException " +e.getMessage());
    }
  }
}
```

The contents of the file CopyOfInfo.txt are shown below:

```
Adoflscnb trdi  ait ffrassc swv m,m3 if uadmn tes
```

Note that we have placed the statements that close the readers and writers inside the try block. This is not good practice because these statements will not be executed if an exception occurs. It is important to close the file readers and writers when they are not needed because they take up space in the computer's memory. Therefore, it is better to place the close statements in the finally block instead of the try block because the former is always executed, even when an exception occurs:

```
// close the readers and writers in the finally block
finally {
  try {
```

```
    // close buffered reader
    bufferedReader.close();

    // flush and close buffered writer
    bufferedWriter.flush();
    bufferedWriter.close();
  } catch (IOException e) {
    System.err.println("IOException" +e.getMessage());
  }
}
```

■

Close the readers and writers in the `finally` block.

11.2.2   Using Class Scanner to Read from a File

You have used the Scanner class previously to read data from the console. This class is commonly used to read from files as well because it is simpler and more versatile than the FileReader and BufferedReader classes. Figure 11–6 shows the constructors and methods in this class for reading data from the console or a text file. Methods such as hasNext and hasNextLine determine whether the input has more data available to read.

Figure 11–6

Some constructors and methods in the Scanner class.

Scanner	
`Scanner(File f)throws FileNotFoundException`	Constructor creates a scanner for reading from the given file f.
`Scanner(InputStream source)`	Constructor creates a scanner for reading from the stream source.
`boolean hasNextInt()`	Returns true if the next value in the input is an int.
`boolean hasNextDouble()`	Returns true if the next value in the input is a double.
`boolean hasNext()`	Returns true if the next value in the input is a token.
`boolean hasNextLine()`	Returns true if the next value in the input is a line of data.
`int nextInt()`	Reads an int from the input.
`double nextDouble()`	Reads a double from the input.
`String nextLine()`	Reads a line from the input.
`String next()`	Reads a token from the input.
`void close()`	Closes this scanner.
`Scanner useDelimiter(String s)`	Sets the delimiter to the specified string s.

A scanner reads data in the form of *tokens*. A **token** consists of a set of consecutive characters that by default are separated by *whitespace*. (Whitespace is generated when you press the space bar, as well as the Tab and Enter keys on the keyboard.) The next method reads one token from the input each time it is called. You can use the hasNext method to determine whether a token is available before calling next.

This next example shows how to use a scanner to read data from a file.

Example 3

We use a scanner for reading the contents of the text file info.txt and printing them out on the console:

```
package fileoi;
import java.util.*;
import java.io.*;

public class ScannerDemo1 {
  public static void main(String [] args) {
    try {
      Scanner scanner = new Scanner(new File("text/info.txt"));

      while(scanner.hasNext())
        System.out.print(scanner.next());

      scanner.close();
    } catch(FileNotFoundException e) {
        e.printStackTrace();
    }
  }
}
```

The next method returns one word from the file info.txt each time that it is called because tokens are, by default, separated from each other by whitespace. However, next does not return the separator, which is a space in this program. Therefore, the program prints out these words without any spaces between them, as shown in the following output:

```
Audiofilescanbestoredinavarietyofformatssuchaswav,wma,mp3,aiff,auandmany
others.
```

Use the nextLine and hasNextLine methods instead of next and hasNext:

```
while(scanner.hasNextLine())
  System.out.print(scanner.nextLine());
```

If the program is rerun using these two methods, it displays the following:

```
Audio files can be stored in a variety of formats such as wav, wma, mp3,
aiff, au and many others.
```
■

You can specify a separator other than whitespace for the tokens in the input by using the useDelimiter method of Scanner. For example, if you set the delimiter to "s," the first call to the next method retrieves all the data up to the first "s" in info.txt as a single token:

```
Audio file
```

The next example shows the output when a comma is set as the delimiter.

Example 4

This program uses a comma as the delimiter in the file info.txt, and displays each token returned by the next method on a separate line:

```
package fileio;
import java.util.*;
import java.io.*;

public class ScannerDemo2 {
  public static void main(String [] args) {
    try {
      Scanner scanner = new Scanner(new File("text/info.txt"));

      // set a comma as the delimiter instead of a whitespace
      scanner.useDelimiter(",");

        while(scanner.hasNext())
          // print out each token on a new line
          System.out.println(scanner.next());

        scanner.close();
    } catch(FileNotFoundException e) {
        e.printStackTrace();
    }
  }
}
```

Each group of words until the next comma is treated as a token and returned by the next method. The program output is shown here:

```
Audio files can be stored in a variety of formats such as wav
 wma
```

```
mp3
aiff
au and many others.
```

11.3   Reading and Writing Binary Files

Some files, such as image and audio files, contain binary data instead of text. **Binary data** is composed of ones and zeroes. You cannot view the contents of these binary files using a text editor. The subclasses of InputStream and OutputStream are used to read and write the data in binary streams. Two of these classes are FileInputStream and FileOutputStream (shown in Figure 11–7), which contain methods for reading and writing **bytes** (not character data) from binary files. (Recall that a **byte** is a group of 8 bits, where each bit is a 1 or a 0.) Apart from this difference, these methods are similar to those in FileReader and FileWriter. The read methods in FileInputStream return −1 when the end of the file is reached. Note, also, that the bytes read are returned as type int.

11.3.1   Improving Read/Write Efficiency with BufferedInputStream/

BufferedOutputStream

You can use BufferedInputStream and BufferedOutputStream to optimize reading from, and writing to, a stream. These classes are similar to Buffered-Reader and BufferedWriter, except they are used for binary data. A BufferedInputStream reader fills its buffer in the computer's memory with a

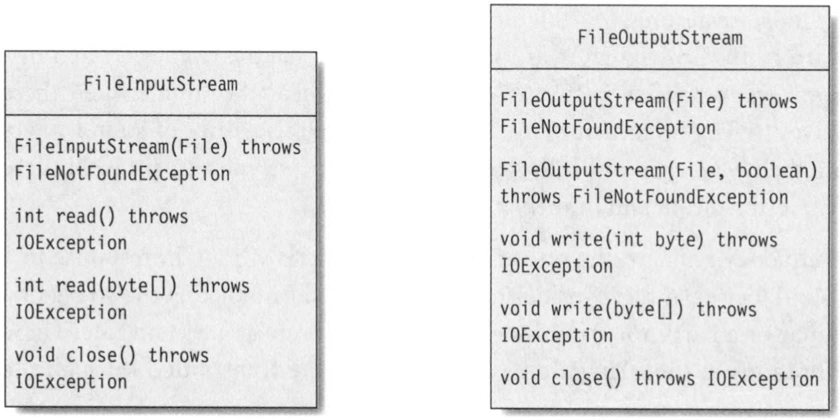

```
FileInputStream

FileInputStream(File) throws
FileNotFoundException

int read() throws
IOException

int read(byte[]) throws
IOException

void close() throws
IOException
```

(a)

```
FileOutputStream

FileOutputStream(File) throws
FileNotFoundException

FileOutputStream(File, boolean)
throws FileNotFoundException

void write(int byte) throws
IOException

void write(byte[]) throws
IOException

void close() throws IOException
```

(b)

Figure 11–7

(a) Class FileInput-Stream and (b) class FileOutputStream.

fixed number of bytes by reading data from the file on the disk. After this, all calls to read get data from this buffer and do not need to access the disk. Once all of the bytes from this buffer have been read, the next call to read fills it up again from the disk. This strategy makes the program run faster by reducing the number of times the program has to access the file on disk. The read and write methods are the same as for FileInputStream and FileOutputStream described earlier. To avoid reading a certain number of bytes in the buffer, the skip method in BufferedInputStream can be used:

> public long skip(long b) throws IOException—a method that skips over the next b bytes in the buffer. If b is negative, no bytes are skipped. The number of bytes that can be skipped is limited to those in the buffer. Thus, if there are 8000 bytes in the buffer, and the programmer writes skip(10000), only 8000 bytes will be skipped.

Section 11.4 contains examples that use these classes.

11.4   Reading and Manipulating WAV Files

Music files that store audio tracks are binary files. In this section, we provide a brief overview of how digital audio is captured and stored, and then describe WAV, a commonly used file format for storing audio. Once you have this background, you will learn how to write the AudioMixer class to read and manipulate music files.

11.4.1   Sound Waves

Sounds create pressure fluctuations in air. These fluctuations travel outward from the originator of the sound (much like the ripples created in a pond when a stone is thrown in it). We can hear the sound when these waves strike our eardrums. Two important characteristics of sound waves are their *frequency* and *intensity*. In this section, we will explain what these two terms mean, and how they can be measured.

Frequency refers to the rate at which air particles vibrate in response to a sound. For example, consider the sound created by plucking the string of a guitar or a harp. You can observe the string vibrate at a certain rate. These vibrations in the string are its frequency and are transmitted through the air at the same rate. The frequency indicates the **pitch** of the sound. If the frequency is high, the sound has a higher pitch, whereas if the frequency is low, the pitch is lower. So, what exactly *is* pitch? When you run your fingers over the keys of a piano from left to right, the notes on the left have a lower, deeper quality (a lower pitch), whereas those on the right have a higher, bell-like tone (a higher pitch). Each piano key has lower frequency than the key to its right, and so the pitch increases from left to right on a piano.

Intensity describes the loudness of a sound. If you pluck the string of the guitar or harp harder, the sound would be louder than if you pluck it gently. Another way to look at intensity is to consider your proximity to the source of a sound. A sound wave has more "energy" near the source of the sound, and this energy drops with distance. Therefore, a sound gets fainter as you move farther away from the source. The volume of sound is measured in **decibels**, or **dB** for short. A whisper has an intensity of about 15–20 dB, whereas normal conversation is around 60 dB. The **decibel scale** is a logarithmic scale where every increase of 10 dB means a sound is 10 times louder. On this scale, normal conversation is about 10^4 times louder than a whisper!

A sound wave can be plotted on a graph as a sinusoidal curve (see Figure 11–8) to show how its frequency and intensity varies with time. The horizontal line in Figure 11–8 shows the position of an air particle at rest. The curve shows the various positions of the particle as it vibrates over some time interval. The **amplitude** of the wave shows the largest distance that the particle is displaced from its position of rest. More loosely, the term amplitude can also be used to refer to any displacement from the position of rest.

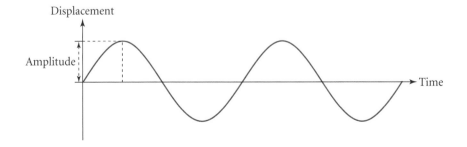

Figure 11–8

A sound wave.

Figure 11–9

Period of a wave.

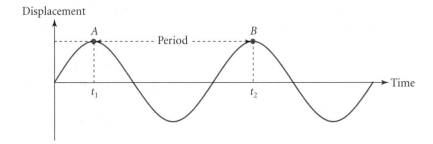

Figure 11–9 shows the shortest time it takes for an air particle to return to its previous position. For example, suppose that the particle has displacement A at time t_1. It has the same displacement at time t_2 (labeled B). This pattern of motion in the interval (t_1, t_2) is repeated in the following intervals of the same length. The **period** of the wave is the length of any of these intervals. Thus, the period can be written as:

$$Period = t_2 - t_1$$

The *frequency* of the wave is the number of times a wave repeats (or cycles) in 1 second. You can think of it as the number of times a particle returns to its starting position in 1 second. Frequency can be related to the period using this equation:

$$Frequency = 1/period$$

The unit of measurement for frequency is **Hertz** (abbreviated as **Hz**). Thus, if a particle has a period of 0.1 seconds, it has a frequency of 10 cycles per second, or 10 Hz. (In other words, it comes back to its starting position 10 times in 1 second.) Humans can hear frequencies in the range 20 Hz to 20,000 Hz. Different species of animals have varying frequency ranges for hearing. For example, dogs can hear frequencies to about 45,000 Hz, cows and horses to about 35,000 Hz, and frogs to only about 3000 Hz.

11.4.2   Digitizing Sound

The sound wave shown in Figure 11-9 is analog and needs to be converted to a digital form in order to be stored in a computer. Sound is digitized via two steps: *sampling* and *quantization*.

To begin the process, the amplitudes of the points on the sound wave must be measured and stored. The analog wave contains an infinite number of points, but when it is digitized, the amplitudes of a finite number of points are recorded. This process of recording amplitudes is called **sampling**, and the values recorded are called **samples**. The **sample rate** is the total number of samples recorded in one second. The frequency itself is not directly recorded in the samples. However, during playback, when the samples are played back at the same rate they were recorded in, the original frequency is produced.

At the very minimum, at least two points must be chosen every period to approximate the shape of a sine curve, as shown in Figure 11–10. For example, if the wave has frequency 4 Hz, a minimum of eight samples should be selected. A sound wave can be composed of individual waves with different frequencies. Therefore, the sampling rate should be at least twice the maximum frequency contained in the wave. This rate is known as the **Nyquist rate**.

The unit for a sample rate is also **Hz**, which is the number of *samples per second*. The human ear can hear frequencies up to 20,000 Hz. What should the sampling rate for audio be? The value should be at least 40,000 samples per second, or 40,000 Hz. In fact, the sampling rate for CDs is 44.1 kHz.

Of course, the original sound wave is approximated more closely by taking more samples (that is, more than two) per period, as shown in Figure 11–11. A higher sampling rate means that the sound is closer to the original, but the tradeoff is that more storage space is needed for the samples.

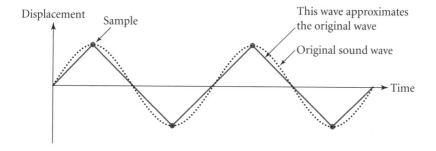

Figure 11–10
Sampling a sound wave.

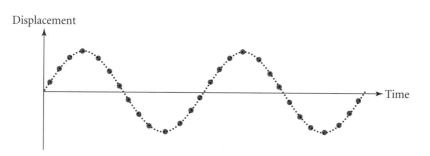

Figure 11–11
Taking several samples per period.

The samples are stored in a computer as binary numbers. Recall from our previous discussion that a sample represents the intensity, or loudness, of sound. The number of bits in each sample determines how many sound levels are available. Each sound level is represented by an integer. If a single bit is used in a sample, there will be only two distinct sound levels: 0 and 1. If 2 bits are used, there will be four sound levels, with values 00, 01, 10, and 11. Thus, the number of sound levels increases with each additional bit in a sample. With 8 bits, there are 256 levels. CD-quality sound uses 16 bits, which provides 65,536 sound levels. This process of converting real-valued amplitudes in a sound signal into integer-valued samples is called **quantization**. Although the digital signal throws away some information present in its analog counterpart, the difference is not detectable by the human ear when a sufficiently large number of samples are taken and the number of bits per sample is large (16 bits or more). With fewer bits per sample (such as 8 or less), though, a hissing noise might be heard in the audio.

In a computer, sound can be digitized using a **sound card**. The sound is input through the microphone to the sound card. The sound card contains an analog-to-digital converter (ADC) and a digital-to-analog converter (DAC). The sampling and quantization is performed by the ADC, and the binary values are stored in a file. To play back the file, the process is reversed. The digital values are converted back to analog using the DAC, and the sound is played through the speakers.

11.4.3   Audio File Formats

Audio files have different formats in various platforms: **WAV** on a Windows platform, **AIFF** on a Macintosh platform, and **au** on a Unix platform. Other formats include **MP3**, **Ogg Vorbis**, and **Windows Meta File** (**WMA**), which are *compressed*. In **compressed** formats, some information stored in the file is discarded (with the goal of preserving the best possible quality of audio). Compression reduces the size of an audio file, which is useful for PDAs and other devices with limited storage because a single uncompressed audio file can take up to several gigabytes of storage. Although WAV (also known as WAVE) files can be compressed, they usually are not.

In the following sections, we will discuss the WAV file format, and how you can write code to read WAV files and create special effects such as mixing, reversing, and changing the volume. We will use the files `blues.wav` and `groovy.wav`, provided in the `JavaBook/audio` directory on the CD-ROM, in the examples.

11.4.4   The WAV File Format

Before you start using WAV files, it is necessary to understand how data is stored in this type of format. A WAV file contains two main parts: a *header* and *audio samples*. The **header** contains important information about the file, such as its audio format, sample rate, and byte rate. The **audio samples** are the binary data values representing an audio track.

Figure 11–12 shows the header of a WAV file. It consists of an array of *bytes*, and each index in the array stores 1 byte (8 bits) of data. The audio format is always stored at indices 20 and 21 in the array. If this data represents the decimal number 1, it means that the audio data is stored in the file in an uncompressed form; otherwise, it is in a compressed form. The data at indices 22 and 23 contains the number of channels. A single channel means that the audio is mono, whereas two channels mean that the audio is stereo. There are three IDs, which are constants of 4 bytes each. The first ID (RIFF Chunk ID) is stored in bytes 0–3 and indicates the start of the audio file. The second ID (Format Chunk ID), stored in bytes 12–15, tells us that the formatting information (the number of bytes of format data, audio format, number of channels, and so forth) follows in bytes 16–35. The third ID

Indices	Data	Explanation
0–3	RIFF Chunk ID	Constant value indicating start of file
4–7	File Size	Total number of bytes in file − 8 (excludes the first 8 bytes)
8–11	Type: WAV	Constant value indicating the file format is WAV
12–15	Format Chunk ID	Constant value indicating that format information follows
16–19	Format Chunk Size	Total bytes of format information
20–21	Audio Format	Uncompressed format has value 1
22–23	Number of Channels	Mono = 1, Stereo = 2
24–27	Sample Rate	Sample rate
28–31	Byte Rate	Total bytes transferred in 1 second for all channels
32–33	Channel Rate	Total bytes transferred at a given time for all channels
34–35	Bits per Sample	8, 16, 24, or 32 bits
36–39	Data Chunk ID	Constant value indicating that audio samples will follow the next field
40–43	Data Chunk Size	Total number of bytes of audio samples stored from index 44 to the end of the file

Figure 11–12
A WAV file header.

(Data Chunk ID) tells us that the audio information (number of bytes of audio data and audio samples) is in the remainder of the file. The header shown here has a size of 44 bytes. In the examples that follow, we will only use audio files that have a header of this size. (The header can be larger in files that use an extended version of this format.)

The audio samples are stored in the file starting from index 44. If there is a single channel, the audio samples are placed one after another, as shown in Figure 11–13(a) (assuming that each sample has 16 bits). Otherwise, if there are two channels, samples for both (left and right) channels, which will be played simultaneously, are placed at successive indices, as shown in Figure 11–13(b). If the sample size is 8 bits and there is a single channel, each sample is stored at a single index; hence, sample 0 is stored at index 44, sample 1 at index 45, and so on.

11.4.5   The AudioMixer Class: Displaying a WAV File Header

Here, we will write a method called printHeader in the class AudioMixer to display a WAV file header. This method is similar to Example 2, in which we read a text file. In this case, though, we will use subclasses of InputStream instead of Reader, and will read bytes instead of characters from the file. For simplicity, in the examples shown we will write code only for *uncompressed* WAV files with a *single* channel and a sample size of *8 bits*. The FileInput-Stream instance called fileIn is wrapped inside a BufferedInputStream called bufferedIn to avoid reading each byte directly from the disk:

```
bufferedIn = new BufferedInputStream(fileIn);
```

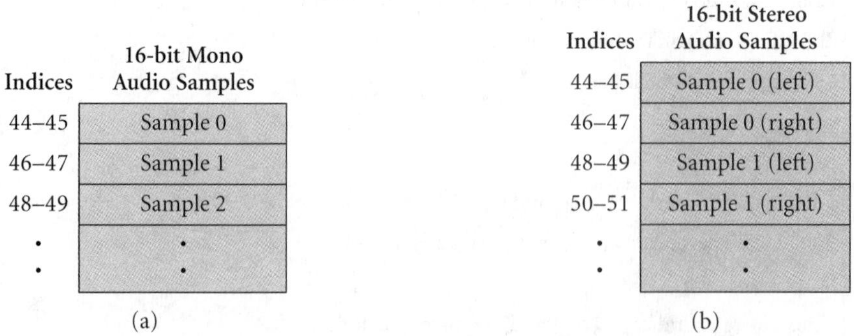

	16-bit Mono Audio Samples
Indices	
44–45	Sample 0
46–47	Sample 1
48–49	Sample 2
⋮	⋮

(a)

	16-bit Stereo Audio Samples
Indices	
44–45	Sample 0 (left)
46–47	Sample 0 (right)
48–49	Sample 1 (left)
50–51	Sample 1 (right)
⋮	⋮

(b)

Figure 11–13

How 16-bit audio samples are stored in a WAV file, where the number of channels is (a) one (mono), or (b) two (stereo).

WAV files have a header size of 44 bytes, and a complete header of 44 bytes will be present unless the file is corrupted. The following program reads and prints out the header that is contained in the first 44 bytes:

```java
package fileio;
import java.io.*;

public class AudioMixer {
  public static final int HEADER_SIZE = 44;

  // prints out the header of an uncompressed WAVE
  public void printHeader(File s) {
    FileInputStream fileIn = null;
    BufferedInputStream bufferedIn = null;

    try {
      // create a buffered reader
      fileIn = new FileInputStream(s);
      bufferedIn = new BufferedInputStream(fileIn);

      int data = 0;
      int bytesRead = 0;

      // read until header is read fully and end-of-file is not reached
      while ( bytesRead < HEADER_SIZE && (data = bufferedIn.read()) != -1 )
{
        String binaryData = Integer.toString(data, 2);
        System.out.println(String.format("Byte at index %d: %08d\n",
bytesRead, Integer.valueOf(binaryData)));
        ++bytesRead;
      }
    } catch (FileNotFoundException e) {
      System.err.println("File could not be found" +e.getMessage());
    } catch (IOException e) {
      System.err.println("IOException" +e.getMessage());
    } finally {
      try {
        bufferedIn.close();
      } catch (IOException e) {
        System.err.println("IOException" +e.getMessage());
      }
    }
  }
}
```

```
public static void main(String[] args) {
  AudioMixer mixer = new AudioMixer();
  File musicFile = new File("audio/blues.wav");
  mixer.printHeader(musicFile);
}
}
```

The `while` loop executes until the header is fully read or the end of the file is reached. The `read` method reads 1 byte of data at a time from the file and returns it as an `int`. To convert it back to binary, use the `toString` method in `Integer` with a radix of 2:

```
String binaryData = Integer.toString(data, 2);
```

The problem with this conversion is that it discards any leading zeroes. Hence, if `data` has the binary value `00000010`, the resulting `binaryData` is simply 10. Some formatting is needed when `binaryData` is printed to display all 8 bits of each byte. This is done by using the `String.format` method and the placeholder `%08d`, which will add the missing zeroes so that each byte is printed out with 8 bits:

```
String.format("Byte at index %d: %08d\n", bytesRead,
Integer.valueOf(binaryData))
```

Run the program and examine the output. The first 4 bytes (in binary) are 01010010, 01001001, 01000110, and 01000110. The corresponding decimal values are 82, 73, 70, and 70. These bytes represent the *RIFF Chunk ID* and their value will be the same for all WAV files. The bytes at indices 8–11 have the decimal values 87, 65, 86, and 69. These 8 bytes identify an audio file's type as WAV. As an exercise, modify method `printHeader` to verify that the file passed in as an argument is a WAV file by checking the values of these bytes.

Can you find the 4 bytes that represent the sample rate? These values are stored at indices 24–27: 01000100, 10101100, 00000000, and 00000000. What are the bytes for the number of channels, sample rate, byte rate, and data chunk size? These will differ for different WAV files. Check the program output and determine these values.

11.4.6   The `AudioMixer` Class: Getting the Decimal Value of a Byte Array

In the file `blues.wav`, the sample rate is stored in 4 bytes in indices 24–27. After these 4 bytes are read from the file, they must be combined into a single value because the sample rate is a single 32-bit number. Bytes can be stored in a file or the computer's memory in two different ways: *little-endian* and *big-endian.*

In **little-endian** ordering, the *leftmost* byte of a multibyte number is stored at the largest index, whereas in **big-endian** ordering, the *rightmost* byte of a multibyte number is stored at the largest index. In the WAV file, for example, the 4 bytes for sample rate are stored in little-endian order. These bytes, shown in Figure 11–14(a), are read from *bottom* to *top.* They are combined to form a 32-bit value, as shown in Figure 11–14(b), in which the byte at the largest index (27) is placed leftmost, and the byte at the smallest index (24) is placed rightmost. The decimal value of this 32-bit binary number is 44100, which is the sampling rate for CDs.

Although the *Sample Rate* is stored in little-endian order, the *RIFF Chunk ID* is stored in big-endian order (in which the *rightmost* byte is stored at the largest index). Here, the bytes shown in Figure 11–15(a) are read from *top* to *bottom.* The corresponding 32-bit binary number is shown in Figure 11–15(b).

In Figure 11–12, the fields *RIFF Chunk ID, Type, Format Chunk ID,* and *Data Chunk ID* are stored in big-endian order, whereas the remaining fields are stored in little-endian order. We will write a method to convert a set of bytes stored in the WAV file to a decimal number. This conversion can be

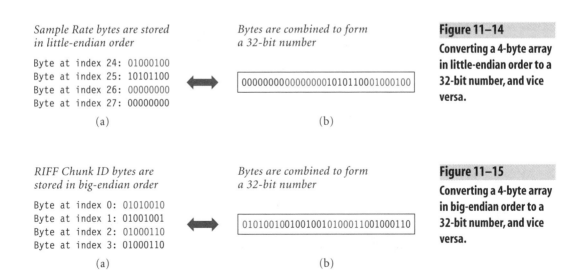

Sample Rate bytes are stored in little-endian order

```
Byte at index 24: 01000100
Byte at index 25: 10101100
Byte at index 26: 00000000
Byte at index 27: 00000000
```
(a)

Bytes are combined to form a 32-bit number

`00000000000000001010110001000100`

(b)

Figure 11–14

Converting a 4-byte array in little-endian order to a 32-bit number, and vice versa.

RIFF Chunk ID bytes are stored in big-endian order

```
Byte at index 0: 01010010
Byte at index 1: 01001001
Byte at index 2: 01000110
Byte at index 3: 01000110
```
(a)

Bytes are combined to form a 32-bit number

`01010010010010010100011001000110`

(b)

Figure 11–15

Converting a 4-byte array in big-endian order to a 32-bit number, and vice versa.

done quite easily using the `BigInteger` class. The constructor for this class takes an array of bytes that is in big-endian order and combines the bytes into a single number:

> `public BigInteger(byte[] val)`—a constructor that converts a byte array in big-endian order to a `BigInteger`.

Suppose that the 4 bytes of *Sample Rate* in Figure 11–14(a) are stored in an array of type `byte` called `sampleRateArray`:

```
sampleRateArray [0] = 00000000
sampleRateArray [1] = 00000000
sampleRateArray [2] = 10101100
sampleRateArray [3] = 01000100
```

The decimal value of this byte array can be obtained with this statement:

```
BigInteger sampleRate = new BigInteger(sampleRateArray);
```

The value of the sample rate can be printed out as follows:

```
System.out.println("Sample Rate=" +sampleRate);
```

This prints out:

```
Sample Rate=44100
```

To view the binary number stored in `sampleRate`, use the `toString` method with a radix of 2:

```
System.out.println(sampleRate.toString(2));
```

This prints out the value shown in Figure 11–14(b) (after dropping the leading zeroes):

```
1010110001000100
```

Note that the array passed to the `BigInteger` constructor must be in big-endian order. If the array is in little-endian order, it must be reversed to change its order to big-endian. You can use the `intValue` method in `BigInteger` to convert a `BigInteger` to an `int`. This conversion is correct (that is, information is not lost) as long as the `BigInteger` does not have more than 4 bytes. The fields in a WAV file have a size of 4 bytes or less; thus the `intValue` method can be used without loss of information. This process is shown next in the method `getDecimalValueOfByteArray`. Add this method to `AudioMixer`, along with these two constant fields:

```
private static final int LITTLE_ENDIAN = 0;
private static final int BIG_ENDIAN = 1;
```

```
// method in class AudioMixer to return the integer value of a byte array
private int getDecimalValueOfByteArray(byte[] array, int order) {
  if (order == BIG_ENDIAN) {
    BigInteger number = new BigInteger(array);
    return number.intValue();
  } else {
    // order is LITTLE_ENDIAN
    int length = array.length;

    // create a new array called array1
    byte[] array1 = new byte[length];

    // reverse the contents of array and put in array1
    int up = 0, down = length - 1;
    while (up <= down) {
      array1[up] = array[down];
      array1[down] = array[up];
      up++;
      down--;
    }
    BigInteger number = new BigInteger(array1);
    return number.intValue();
  }
}
```

Next, we use this method to print out the header fields in decimal instead of binary.

11.4.7   The AudioMixer Class: Printing a WAV Header Summary

The method printSummary prints out the decimal values of the audio format, number of channels, sample rate, byte rate, bytes per sample for all channels, bits per sample, and the audio data size. Data is read sequentially; thus all bytes in the header must be read, but the method only prints out those values that are of interest to us and skips the rest. Two arrays of type byte, called array2 and array4 of size 2 and 4, respectively, are created. Fields that contain 4 bytes (such as *Sample Rate* and *Byte Rate*) are read into array4, and those that contain 2 bytes (such as *Number of Channels*) are read into array2. The getDecimalValueOfByteArray method is called to get the decimal value of each header field. This program also shows how you can use the read method that takes an argument of type byte[] to read multiple bytes at a time from the file:

```java
// method in class AudioMixer to print header summary
private void printSummary(File s) {
  FileInputStream fileIn = null;
  BufferedInputStream bufferedIn = null;
  byte[] array2 = new byte[2];   // stores 2 bytes
  byte[] array4 = new byte[4];   // stores 4 bytes

  try {
    // create a buffered file reader
    fileIn = new FileInputStream(s);
    bufferedIn = new BufferedInputStream(fileIn);

    // verify this is a WAV file (RIFF chunk id must be 82, 73, 70, and 70)
    bufferedIn.read(array4);
    if ((array4[0] != 82) || (array4[1] != 73) || (array4[2] != 70) ||
(array4[3] != 70))
        throw new IOException(" Not a WAV file ");

    // verify this is a WAV file (Type field must be 87, 65, 86, and 69)
    bufferedIn.skip(4);
    bufferedIn.read(array4);
    if ((array4[0] != 87) || (array4[1] != 65) || (array4[2] != 86) ||
(array4[3] != 69))
        throw new IOException(" Not a WAV file ");

    // check that the complete header is present
    if (s.length() < HEADER_SIZE)
      throw new IOException(" Incorrect header size ");

    // skip the next 8 bytes of header
    bufferedIn.skip(8);

    // read audio format
    bufferedIn.read(array2);
    System.out.println("Audio Format = "
+getDecimalValueOfByteArray(array2, LITTLE_ENDIAN));

    // read number of channels
    bufferedIn.read(array2);
    System.out.println("Number of Channels = "
+getDecimalValueOfByteArray(array2, LITTLE_ENDIAN));
```

```
    // read sample rate
    bufferedIn.read(array4);
    System.out.println("Sample Rate = " +getDecimalValueOfByteArray(array4,
LITTLE_ENDIAN));

    // read byte rate
    bufferedIn.read(array4);
    System.out.println("Byte Rate = " +getDecimalValueOfByteArray(array4,
LITTLE_ENDIAN));

    // read bytes in each sample for all channels
    bufferedIn.read(array2);
    System.out.println("Bytes per sample = "
+getDecimalValueOfByteArray(array2, LITTLE_ENDIAN));

    // read bits per sample
    bufferedIn.read(array2);
    System.out.println("Bits per sample for all channels = "
+getDecimalValueOfByteArray(array2, LITTLE_ENDIAN));

    // skip data chunk id, don't print it out
    bufferedIn.skip(4);

    // read audio data size
    bufferedIn.read(array4);
    System.out.println("Total bytes of audio data  = "
+getDecimalValueOfByteArray(array4, LITTLE_ENDIAN));
  } catch (FileNotFoundException e) {
    System.err.println("File could not be found" +e.getMessage());
  } catch (IOException e) {
    System.err.println("IOException" +e.getMessage());
  } finally {
    try {
      bufferedIn.close();
    } catch (IOException e) {
      System.err.println("IOException" +e.getMessage());
    }
  }
}
```

Add the printSummary method to AudioMixer and call it by adding the following statement to main:

```
mixer.printSummary(musicFile);
```

Add this import statement to AudioMixer:

```
import java.math.BigInteger;
```

Compile and run the program. The output tells us that this file is uncompressed (because the audio format is 1) with a single channel, and stores each sample in 8 bits:

```
Audio Format = 1
Number of Channels = 1
Sample Rate = 44100
Byte Rate = 44100
Bytes per sample = 1
Bits per sample for all channels = 8
Total bytes of audio data = 1320290
```

11.4.8   The AudioMixer Class: Mixing Two WAV Files

In this section, we will write a method to combine the audio samples in two WAV files. This example also shows how you can use BufferedOutputStream to write bytes into a file. Note that (for simplicity) the method will only mix files that store uncompressed audio, have a single channel, and measure 8 bits per sample. The sample rate must also be the same in both files.

The idea behind merging the files is simple: Combine the samples in two source files and write them to a destination file, until the end of the smaller source file is reached. Then copy the remaining samples from the other source file into the destination file. The method merge implements this idea by combining the audio in two source files called source1 and source2 into a single file called destination. The main steps are described briefly here:

1. The sizes (that is, the number of bytes of audio samples) of the two source files are determined, and the header of the larger source file is copied into destination.

2. Using a while loop, the audio samples from source1 and source2 are combined and written to destination. The samples are added using the following statement:

   ```
   data3 = data1 + data2 - 128;
   ```

Here, data1 is a sample from source1, and data2 is a sample from source2. The value 128 represents silence for 8-bit audio. Subtracting this value from the sum of data1 and data2 ensures that when data1 and data2 are both 128, data3 is also 128. Additionally, because the samples can have values only from 0 to 255 for 8-bit audio, data3 is constrained to lie within this range with these two statements:

```
if (data3 > 255)
  data3 = 255;
else if(data3 < 0)
  data3 = 0;
```

(16-bit samples have values ranging from $-32,768$ to $32,767$.) The loop is exited from when the end of either file is reached.

3. Any samples that have not been read yet from source1 (or source2, depending on which file is longer) are copied to destination in the second (or third) while loops.

4. It is necessary to flush the BufferedOutputStream before closing it using the following statement:

```
bufferedOut.flush();
```

This will write any bytes remaining in the buffer in RAM to the file on disk.

The merge method combines the samples in files source1 and source2 and writes them to the file named destination. Add this method to AudioMixer:

```
// method in class AudioMixer to mix two WAV files
public void merge(File source1, File source2, File destination) {
  FileInputStream fileIn1 = null, fileIn2 = null;
  BufferedInputStream bufferedIn1 = null, bufferedIn2 = null;
  FileOutputStream fileOut = null;
  BufferedOutputStream bufferedOut = null;
  int size1, size2;
  int data1 = 0, data2 = 0, data3;

  try {
    // create two buffered readers and a buffered writer
    fileIn1 = new FileInputStream(source1);
    bufferedIn1 = new BufferedInputStream(fileIn1);
    fileIn2 = new FileInputStream(source2);
    bufferedIn2 = new BufferedInputStream(fileIn2);
    fileOut = new FileOutputStream(destination);
    bufferedOut = new BufferedOutputStream(fileOut);

    int bytesRead = 0;
```

```
byte[] buffer = new byte[HEADER_SIZE];

// get audio data size of source files
size1 = getDataChunkSize(source1);
size2 = getDataChunkSize(source2);
int minSize = Math.min(size1, size2);

// copy header of larger source file into destination
if (size1 >= size2) {
  bufferedIn1.read(buffer);
  bufferedOut.write(buffer);
  bufferedIn2.skip(HEADER_SIZE);
} else {
  bufferedIn2.read(buffer);
  bufferedOut.write(buffer);
  bufferedIn1.skip(HEADER_SIZE);
}

// merge the audio samples in two files
while (bytesRead < minSize) {
  data1 = bufferedIn1.read();
  data2 = bufferedIn2.read();
  data3 = data1 + data2 - 128;
  if (data3 > 255)
    data3 = 255;
  else if(data3 < 0)
    data3 = 0;

// write the merged data to destination file
bufferedOut.write(data3);
  bytesRead++;
}

// copy any remaining bytes in source1 to destination file
while (bytesRead < size1) {
  data1 = bufferedIn1.read();
  bufferedOut.write(data1);
  bytesRead++;
}

// copy any remaining bytes in source2 to destination file
while (bytesRead < size2) {
  data2 = bufferedIn2.read();
  bufferedOut.write(data2);
```

```
      bytesRead++;
    }
  } catch (FileNotFoundException e) {
    System.err.println("File could not be found" +e.getMessage());
  } catch (IOException e) {
    System.err.println("IOException" +e.getMessage());
  } finally {
    try {
      bufferedIn1.close();
      bufferedIn2.close();
      // flush bufferedOut
      bufferedOut.flush();
      bufferedOut.close();
    } catch (IOException e) {
      System.err.println("IOException" +e.getMessage());
    }
  }
}
```

The merge method uses the getDataChunkSize method to obtain the number of bytes of audio samples. Add this method to AudioMixer:

```
// method in class AudioMixer to read the Data Chunk Size field
public int getDataChunkSize(File filename) {
  int size = 0;  // decimal value of Data Chunk Size file
  FileInputStream fileIn = null;
  BufferedInputStream bufferedIn = null;
  byte[] array = new byte[4];

  try {
    // create two file readers
    fileIn = new FileInputStream(filename);
    bufferedIn = new BufferedInputStream(fileIn);

    // verify this is a WAV file (first four bytes must be 82, 73, 70 and
70)
    bufferedIn.read(array);
    if ( (array[0] != 82) || (array[1] != 73) || (array[2] != 70) ||
(array[3] != 70) )
      throw new IOException(" "+filename +" is not a WAV file ");

    // verify this is a WAV file (Type field must be 87, 65, 86, and 69)
    bufferedIn.skip(4);
    bufferedIn.read(array);
    if ( (array[0] != 87) || (array[1] != 65) || (array[2] != 86) ||
(array[3] != 69) )
```

```
        throw new IOException(" Not a WAV file");

    // skip next 28 bytes in header
    bufferedIn.skip(28);

    // get number of audio samples in this file stored in bytes 40-43
    bufferedIn.read(array);
    size = getDecimalValueOfByteArray(array, LITTLE_ENDIAN);

    // check that size + header size is equal to actual file size
    if ( (size + HEADER_SIZE) != filename.length() )
      throw new IOException(" Incorrect data chunk size field in header of "
+filename);

  } catch (FileNotFoundException e) {
    System.err.println("File could not be found" +e.getMessage());
  } catch (IOException e) {
    System.err.println("IOException" +e.getMessage());
  } finally {
    try {
      bufferedIn.close();
    } catch (IOException e) {
      System.err.println("IOException" +e.getMessage());
    }
  }

  return size;
}
```

Add these lines to `main` to combine the tracks of files `blues.wav` and `groovy.wav`:

```
File musicFile1 = new File("audio/groovy.wav");
File mergedMusicFile = new File("audio/groovyblues.wav");
mixer.merge(musicFile, musicFile1, mergedMusicFile);
```

Run the program, and note that a file called `groovyblues.wav` has been created in the `JavaBook/audio` directory. Play this file in an audio player. You will be able to hear the merged tracks of both source files.

11.5   Accessing Files Randomly

In all of the I/O classes that we have seen so far, reading is done sequentially. The `RandomAccessFile` class can be used to read from or write to any arbitrary location within a file. Additionally, you can read both textual and

Figure 11–16
Some methods in class
RandomAccessFile.

RandomAccessFile	
RandomAccessFile(File name, String mode) throws FileNotFoundException	Creates a random access file reader, using mode "r" for reading only and mode "rw" for both reading and writing.
void seek(long b) throws IOException	Moves the file pointer forward by the given number of *bytes* b from the *beginning* of the file (regardless of its current position).
int read() throws IOException	Reads a single byte starting from the current position of the file pointer and returns it as an int.
int read(byte[] array) throws IOException	Reads up to array.length bytes from the current position of the file pointer into array. Returns the number of bytes read or –1 if the end of the file is reached.
int read(byte[] array, int index, int len) throws IOException	Reads up to len bytes into consecutive indices in array with the first byte placed at the specified index. Returns the number of bytes read or –1 if the end of the file is reached.
final String readLine() throws IOException	Returns text from the current position of the file pointer until a terminating character, such as newline ("\n") or carriage return ("\r"), is reached. Returns null if the end of the file is reached.
void write(int b) throws IOException	Writes the byte b into a file at the current position of the file pointer.
void write(byte[] array) throws IOException	Writes the entire contents of the byte array array into the file at the current position of the file pointer.
void write(byte[] array, int index, int len) throws IOException	Writes len bytes (starting from the specified array index) of array to this file.
long length() throws IOException	Returns the total number of bytes in the file.
void setLength(long length) throws IOException	Sets the total number of bytes in the file to length, truncating the file if necessary.

binary data using this class. Figure 11–16 shows a portion of the API for this class. The constructor for RandomAccessFile takes the filename and mode as arguments. An instance of this class contains a **file pointer**, which can be moved forward or backward by the programmer inside a file. Initially, the file pointer is at the beginning of the file. Reading or writing is done starting from the location where this file pointer is positioned. The seek method is used to move the file pointer to a new location. This method will throw an IOException if the argument passed to it is negative.

The following code fragment shows how to create a RandomAccessFile instance called rafile to read and write the file info.txt and then move the file pointer ahead by 4 bytes:

```
RandomAccessFile rafile = new RandomAccessFile("info.txt", "rw");
rafile.seek(4);
```

Before we discuss how to read or write to this text file, you must understand how text is stored in a computer. A text file can be stored using *ASCII*, *ANSI*, or *Unicode* formats. These formats have a fixed binary number for each character. **ASCII** uses a 7-bit code to represent a character. For example, the lowercase letter "a" has the ASCII code "1100001" (or decimal value 97), and the uppercase letter "A" has the ASCII code "1000001" (or decimal value 65). In the WAV header, bytes 0–3 and 4–7 are the ASCII codes for "RIFF" and "WAVE," respectively. The ASCII code is limited to letters in the English alphabet and some special symbols (such as + and −) that can be seen on a keyboard. The **ANSI** format extended this to 8-bit codes to include more symbols and letters from some European languages. **Unicode** stores characters as 16-bit values. A larger number of bits can be used in Unicode; thus it can represent a wider range of characters, which includes all of the symbols represented in ANSI and more (such as characters from Asian alphabets).

Different editors available on various platforms allow you to store a text file in any of these formats. The file info.txt is stored in an ANSI format, and so each character takes up 1 byte. Therefore, moving the file pointer in info.txt forward by 4 bytes moves it ahead by four characters in the file. The new position of the file pointer is shown here marked with an arrow:

> Audio files can be stored in a variety of formats such as wav, wma, mp3, aiff, au and
> ⇑
> many others.

Adding the next statement to the code fragment moves the pointer ahead by 10 characters from the *start* of the file:

```
rafile.seek(10);
```

Remember that each blank space is also a character, and thus takes 1 byte. The new position of the pointer is shown here:

Audio files can be stored in a variety of formats such as wav, wma, mp3, aiff, au and
⇑
many others.

Several methods are provided in this class for reading and writing to a file. The `read` and `write` methods are used to read **binary** data, and are similar to those discussed previously for the other I/O classes. To read other types of data, this class also contains `readChar`, `readBoolean`, `readInt`, `readFloat`, `read-Double`, `readLong`, and others. There are several methods available to write other types of data such as `writeChars`, `writeBoolean`, `writeInt`, `writeFloat`, `writeDouble`, and `writeLong`. The `readChar` and `writeChars` method read and write characters in the Unicode method, respectively. The methods `writeInt`, `writeChars`, `writeFloat`, `writeDouble`, and `writeLong` write data into the file in *big-endian* order.

The `setLength` method sets the length of the file. If the current length of the file is larger than `length`, data at the end of the file is removed so that the file has the desired length.

A `RandomAccessFile` instance *cannot* be wrapped inside a buffered stream. This means that the programmer is responsible for optimizing file accesses by using buffers of appropriate sizes inside his or her program, and trying to reduce the number of disk accesses.

Example 5

Using a text editor, create the file `rand.txt` in ANSI format (where each character takes 1 byte) in the `JavaBook/text` directory. It should contain the following text:

"Audio files can be stored in a variety of formats such as wav, wma, mp3, aiff, au and many others."

Predict the output of this program:

```java
package fileio;
import java.io.*;

public class RandomAccessFileDemo {
  public static void main(String[] args) {
    try {
      RandomAccessFile rafile = new RandomAccessFile(new
File("text/rand.txt"), "rw");

      rafile.seek(6);
      System.out.println((char)rafile.read());
      System.out.println((char)rafile.read());

      rafile.seek(82);

      int ch = 'e';
      rafile.write(ch);

      ch = 't';
      rafile.write(ch);

      ch = 'c';
      rafile.write(ch);

      ch = '.';
      rafile.write(ch);

      rafile.seek(0);
      System.out.println(rafile.readLine());
      rafile.setLength(86);
    }
    catch (FileNotFoundException e) {
      System.err.println("File could not be found" +e.getMessage());
    }
    catch (IOException e) {
      System.err.println("IOException" +e.getMessage());
    }
  }
}
```

Solution: The file pointer skips the first six characters and prints out the character "f". Reading continues from the current position of the pointer, so the character "i" in the word "files" is read and printed out next. The write statements *replace* the word "and" with "etc." The file pointer is then sent back to the start of the file using a seek offset of 0. The readLine statement prints out the contents of the line following the current position of the file pointer:

```
Audio files can be stored in a variety of formats such as wav, wma, mp3,
aiff, au etc.many others.
```

The extraneous characters ("many others.") at the end of the file are truncated using the setLength method. Open rand.txt using a text editor. The final contents of the file are:

```
Audio files can be stored in a variety of formats such as wav, wma, mp3,
aiff, au etc.
```

When the "rw" mode is specified, the file will be created if it does not already exist. In this case, the FileNotFoundException is thrown if the file already exists but cannot be read for some reason (if it is a directory, for example). Another important point to note is that all methods that write to a file *replace* the contents of the file at the specified position so that the file size does not increase. If you write to the *end* of a file, however, it will *append* the new data to the file and increase the file size.

11.5.1 The AudioMixer Class: Playing Audio in Reverse

We will add a method to AudioMixer to reverse the audio samples in the WAV file. The idea is simple: Copy the header (without making any changes) to a new file, and then write the audio samples to the new file in **reverse** order. Let us examine two ways in which we can do this.

Suppose that we want to use BufferedOutputStream to read the audio samples and reverse them. This type of stream reads data sequentially; thus we would have to read all the audio samples in the file into an array in the computer's memory, reverse the array, and then write the array contents to the new file. However, WAV files can be large because they usually do not compress the audio information, which would require a large array to store the samples. The second solution shows how you can do this using a smaller array.

We instead can use RandomAccessFile to reverse the audio samples. A simple algorithm would be to read one sample at a time, starting from the end of the file, and write it to the new file. Thus, the samples would be read in reverse order from the original file. For example, suppose that a file contains three samples at offsets 45, 46, and 47 bytes. The procedure would be to read the sample at offset 47 and write it to the new file, then read the previous sample at offset 46 and write it, and so on. The problem with this approach is that it uses one disk access for each sample. Remember that every disk access is expensive, and a program should attempt to reduce the number of accesses. To address this, we modify the algorithm. Instead of reading a single sample at a time from the original file, we read a fixed number of samples (starting near the end of the file) into an array. Then, we reverse the contents of the array and write it to the new file. Repeat this procedure until all the samples have been read.

The code for method reverse follows. The size of the array (BUFFER_SIZE) is arbitrarily selected to be 10,000 bytes in this example. The contents of file source are reversed and written into file destination. This method only works for WAV files that store uncompressed audio in a single channel with 8 bits per sample. You can modify it to work with other types of files as an exercise. Add this method to AudioMixer:

```
// method in class AudioMixer to reverse audio samples
public void reverse(File source, File destination) {
  RandomAccessFile fileIn = null;
  RandomAccessFile fileOut = null;

  int BUFFER_SIZE = 10000;
  byte[] header = new byte[HEADER_SIZE];  // stores the header
  byte[] buffer = new byte[BUFFER_SIZE];  // stores the samples

  try {
    // create a random access file reader
    fileIn = new RandomAccessFile(source, "r");

    // create a random access file writer
    fileOut = new RandomAccessFile(destination, "rw");

    // copy the header of source to destination file
    int numBytes = fileIn.read(header);
    fileOut.write(header, 0, numBytes);
```

```
  // read & write audio samples in blocks of size BUFFER_SIZE
  // starting from the end of the source
  long seekDistance = fileIn.length();
  int bytesToRead = BUFFER_SIZE;   // bytes read at a time
  long totalBytesRead = 0;         // total bytes read so far

do {
  seekDistance -= BUFFER_SIZE;

  if (seekDistance >= 0)
    bytesToRead = BUFFER_SIZE;
  else if (seekDistance < 0) {
    // fewer than BUFFER_SIZE bytes left to read in file
    seekDistance = 0;
    bytesToRead = (int) (fileIn.length() - totalBytesRead);
  }

  // move file pointer forward by seekDistance bytes from start
  fileIn.seek(seekDistance);

  // read a block of audio samples from the file into buffer
  int numBytesRead = fileIn.read(buffer, 0, bytesToRead);
  totalBytesRead += numBytesRead;

  // reverse contents of buffer
  int up = 0;
  int down = numBytesRead-1;
  byte temp;
  while (up < down) {
    temp = buffer[up];
    buffer[up] = buffer[down];
    buffer[down] = temp;
    up++;
    down--;
  }

  // write buffer to destination
  fileOut.write(buffer, 0, numBytesRead);
} while (totalBytesRead < fileIn.length());

// remove the header that was copied to the end of destination
fileOut.setLength(fileIn.length());
} catch (FileNotFoundException e) {
```

```
    System.err.println("File could not be found" +e.getMessage());
  } catch (IOException e) {
    System.err.println("IOException" +e.getMessage());
  } finally {
    try {
      fileIn.close();
      fileOut.close();
    } catch (IOException e) {
      System.err.println("IOException" +e.getMessage());
    }
  }
}
```

These three statements position the file pointer at the beginning of the last BUFFER_SIZE bytes in the file:

```
long seekDistance = fileIn.length();
seekDistance -= BUFFER_SIZE;
fileIn.seek(seekDistance);
```

This statement reads the bytes into the array called buffer:

```
fileIn.read(buffer, 0, bytesToRead);
```

After the array contents have been reversed, they are written to the destination file using:

```
fileOut.write(buffer, 0, numBytesRead);
```

The file pointer is then moved backward by another BUFFER_SIZE bytes by decrementing seekDistance again. The steps described previously are repeated to read the bytes into the array, reverse them, and then write them into the destination file. These two statements ensure that the offset does not become negative if fewer than BUFFER_SIZE bytes are left to be read from the file:

```
else if (seekDistance < 0) {
  seekDistance = 0;
```

The header also is copied at the end of the file; thus it is removed using the setLength method. To test the program, add these two statements to the main method in class AudioMixer:

```
File reversedMusicFile = new File("audio/revgroovy.wav");
mixer.reverse(musicFile1, reversedMusicFile);
```

After you compile and run this program, check that the file revgroovy.wav has been created. Play this file in a media player for WAV files; the music is played in reverse. As an exercise, modify method reverse to verify that the file source is a valid WAV file. In addition, check that the sum of the value in the Data Chunk Size field and the header size is equal to the size of the file source.

11.6   Serialization

The objects in our programs exist only while the program is executing. When the program is closed, these objects cease to exist. How can we save an object in our program and restore it when the program is run again? For example, suppose that we are playing a computer chess game. We close the game before it is finished. When we restart the game, it should resume from where we had left it, instead of from the beginning. One way to accomplish this would be to save information about the game (such as the locations of various game pieces, scores, and so forth) to a file, and then read this information back from the file to restore the game to the state where we had left it when it is run next. This is the idea behind *serialization*. **Serialization** is saving an object's state as a binary stream (that is, as a sequence of bytes). When an object is serialized, it is said to be **flattened** or **deflated**. The reverse process of constructing an object from the binary data is known as **deserialization**. Thus, a deserialized (or **inflated**) object is one whose state has been restored.

Java provides two classes to implement serialization: ObjectOutputStream and ObjectInputStream. The ObjectOutputStream class is used to convert the instance fields of an object into a stream of bytes. This byte stream can then be sent to a FileOutputStream, which writes it to a file. The binary data can then be read back from the file using a FileInputStream and sent to an ObjectInputStream class to restore the object.

Figure 11–17 shows the readObject and writeObject methods of these two classes that are used to read and write objects, respectively. A class whose objects will be serialized must implement the java.io.Serializable interface. Otherwise, a NotSerializableException will be thrown at run time.

Although the state of objects can be saved to a file using the classes discussed earlier in this chapter, it is much simpler to do so using these object stream classes. Additionally, these classes reduce the chances of introducing errors in your program—for example, by reading back the fields in a different order than they were written in. If the object being saved contains references to other objects, the latter are also saved along with the former.

Figure 11–17

(a) The writeObject method of Object-OutputStream serializes an object. (b) The read-Object method of ObjectInputStream deserializes an object.

```
ObjectOutputStream

ObjectOutputStream(OutputStream)
throws IOException

final void writeObject(Object)
throws IOException

void close() throws IOException
```

```
ObjectInputStream

ObjectInputStream(InputStream)
throws IOException

final Object readObject() throws
IOException, ClassNotFoundException

void close() throws IOException
```

(a)   (b)

This next example shows how objects can be serialized. Consider a class called AudioPlayer with a field called audioFile and a play method to play the contents of audioFile. Let us write a program in which we create an instance of this class called player that is playing some audio file. When we close the program and then rerun it again later, we would like to have it replay the file that was played last. This can be done by saving the value of player's audioFile field in some file, and then reading it back from this file when the program is run again. The AudioPlayer class must implement the Serializable interface:

```java
public class AudioPlayer implements Serializable {
  public File audioFile;

  public void setAudioFile(File f) {
    audioFile = f;
  }

  public void play() throws Exception {
    // code to play audioFile
  }
}
```

You will see how to write the code in method play to play an audio file a little later. Create an instance of AudioPlayer called player:

```java
AudioPlayer player = new AudioPlayer();
player.setAudioFile(new File("audio/groovy.wav"));
```

Next, we discuss how to serialize this object player.

11.6.1   Object Serialization

An object is serialized using the following steps:

1. Create a `FileOutputStream` to write to a file (say, `object.dat`) and wrap it inside an `ObjectOutputStream`.

2. Invoke the object stream's `writeObject` method to save the object's state to `object.dat`.

For example, this shows how to serialize the instance `player` by saving its state in the file `player.dat`:

```
// wrap a FileOutputStream inside an ObjectOutputStream
FileOutputStream fileOut = new FileOutputStream("text/player.dat");
ObjectOutputStream objectOut = new ObjectOutputStream(fileOut);

// save the contents of field audioFile in player into file player.dat
objectOut.writeObject(player);
objectOut.close();
```

In this example, `player` contains only one field, but if there are multiple fields, all of their values will be saved by the `writeObject` method. Multiple objects (say, `object1`, `object2`, and `object3`) can also be saved to the same file by calling the `writeObject` method successively for each object:

```
objectOut.writeObject(object1);
objectOut.writeObject(object2);
objectOut.writeObject(object3);
```

11.6.2   Object Deserialization

An object is deserialized using the following steps:

1. Create a `FileInputStream` to read from a file (say, `object.dat`) and wrap it inside an `ObjectInputStream`.

2. Invoke the object stream's `readObject` method to restore the object's state from the file `object.dat`.

Suppose that the `AudioPlayer` program is rerun again, and a new instance of `AudioPlayer` called `player` is created. When the `player` object is deserialized, the `audioFile` field of `player` will be initialized to the file played last using the data in the file `player.dat`:

```
FileInputStream fileIn = new FileInputStream("text/player.dat");
ObjectInputStream objectIn = new ObjectInputStream(fileIn);
```

```
// restore player's audioFile field by reading it from player.dat
player = (AudioPlayer) objectIn.readObject();
objectIn.close();
```

When the object is read using method readObject, it is necessary to cast it back to its original type, as previously shown.

If the object being deserialized has several fields, all of the fields are restored when the readObject method is invoked. Multiple objects can be restored similarly via successive calls to readObject:

```
object1 = (type) objectIn.readObject();
object2 = (type) objectIn.readObject();
object3 = (type) objectIn.readObject();
```

The instance player is serialized, as shown in Figure 11–18(a), and then deserialized, as shown in Figure 11–18(b).

String and array objects can be serialized similarly. However, static fields cannot be serialized. Java contains a keyword called transient that the programmer can use to specify fields that are not to be serialized. Suppose that

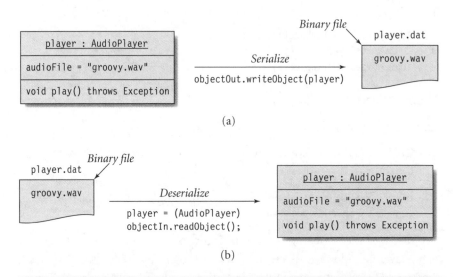

(a)

(b)

Figure 11–18

(a) Serialization: Save the instance field audioFile of player to a binary file called player.dat. (b) Deserialization: Restore the instance field audioFile of player by reading it back from the player.dat file.

AudioPlayer has a field called isPlaying that is set to true while player is playing audio:

```
transient boolean isPlaying;
```

This field will not be saved when the instance player is serialized because it is declared as transient. When an object is deserialized, the transient fields of this object will be reinitialized to default values (null for objects). For example, the isPlaying field will be reinitialized to false.

The AudioMixer Class: Serialization This section shows how serialization works using the AudioMixer class. The example used here is similar to the AudioPlayer example, except that we will implement the play method in AudioMixer so that it can play audio files. Java contains many classes and interfaces to support playing and recording audio in the javax.sound.sampled package. These are discussed briefly next.

The main class in Java's sound API is the AudioSystem class. The AudioSystem class contains various static methods that provide information about audio files and resources on your computer for playing sound. Some of these methods are shown in Figure 11–19. You can obtain the format of some audio file—say, groovy.wav—by using the getAudioFileFormat method:

```
File audioFile = new File("audio/groovy.wav ");
AudioSystem.getAudioFileFormat(audioFile);
```

AudioSystem	
static AudioFileFormat getAudioFileFormat(File file) throws UnsupportedAudioFileException, IOException	Returns the file format of the specified audio file.
static AudioInputStream getAudioInputStream(File file) throws UnsupportedAudioFileException, IOException	Returns an audio input stream for the specified file.
static AudioInputStream getAudioInputStream(InputStream stream) throws UnsupportedAudioFileException, IOException	Returns an audio input stream for the specified stream.
public static Clip getClip() throws LineUnavailableException	Returns a clip for playing an audio file or audio stream.

Figure 11–19
Some methods in the AudioSystem class.

The output is similar to the `printSummary` method of `AudioMixer`.

To read the contents of an audio file, convert it to an **audio stream** using the `getAudioInputStream` method of `AudioSystem`:

```
AudioInputStream stream = AudioSystem.getAudioInputStream(audioFile);
```

Figure 11–20 shows some methods in class `AudioInputStream`. The audio samples can then be read one at a time using the `read()` method of `AudioInputStream`:

```
stream.read();
```

Alternately, several samples can be read into an array using the `read(byte[])` method:

```
byte[] sampleArray = new byte[100];
stream.read(b);
```

An audio stream can be played by using either a *clip* or a *source data line*. A **clip** is used when the audio data is fully available before playback starts and is not too large. An example of this is a song file stored on a CD. A **source data line** is used when the data is not fully available before playback starts or when the audio file is too large to be stored in the computer's memory. An example of this is a concert being broadcast live. We explain how to use a clip.

You can obtain a clip using the `getClip` method in `AudioSystem`. The `Clip` interface declares several methods (see Figure 11–21) to open and play a clip. After the clip is obtained, it can open an audio stream and play it. To open a stream, use an `AudioInputStream` as an argument to a clip's open

Figure 11–20

Some methods in the AudioInputStream class.

AudioInputStream	
`int read() throws IOException`	Returns the next byte from this audio input stream or −1 if the end of the stream is reached.
`int read(byte[] b) throws IOException`	Returns up to `b.length` bytes from this audio input stream or −1 if the end of the stream is reached.
`void close()throws IOException`	Closes this stream.

Figure 11–21
Some methods in the Clip interface.

```
<<interface>>
       Clip

void open(AudioInputStream stream)
throws LineUnavailableException,
IOException

void start()

void loop(int count)
```

Opens the specified audio stream.

Starts playing the audio.

Repeats the audio count number of times.

method. The playback is started by invoking the start method in Clip, as shown here:

```
Clip clip = (Clip) AudioSystem.getClip();
clip.open(stream);      // open the audio stream
clip.start();           // start playing the audio
```

After the audio has been played fully, a special type of event called LineEvent.Type.STOP is generated. The clip can add an event handler of type LineListener to listen for this event using the addLineListener method in Clip. The interface LineListener contains an update method, which must be implemented by the event handler:

```
void update(LineEvent event)
```

The LineEvent class contains the method getType to obtain the type of the event that has occurred (such as START or STOP, among others).

With this background, we are now ready to modify AudioMixer so that it can play audio files. Add the field audioFile and the methods play and set-AudioFile to AudioMixer. Also, declare the class to implement the Serializable interface to see how serialization works:

```
public class AudioMixer implements Serializable {
  private File audioFile;

  public void setAudioFile(File f) {
    audioFile = f;
  }

  public void play() throws Exception {
    AudioInputStream stream =   AudioSystem.getAudioInputStream(audioFile);
    Clip clip = (Clip) AudioSystem.getClip();
```

```
    // line listener causes program to exit after play is completed
    clip.addLineListener(new LineListener() {
        public void update(LineEvent evt) {
            if (evt.getType() == LineEvent.Type.STOP) {
                System.exit(0);
            }
        }
    });
    // open the audio stream and start playing the clip
    clip.open(stream);
    clip.start();
    // program waits here while the music is played
    Thread.sleep(1800*1000);
  }
    // remaining methods written earlier in this chapter
}
```

This statement might appear somewhat strange because we have not yet discussed multithreading (we cover it in Chapter 14, *Multithreaded Programming*):

```
Thread.sleep(1800*1000);
```

If you comment out this line, the audio will not be played because the program will exit prematurely. This statement simply says that our program should wait for a specified time interval (1800 seconds in this case), which ensures that the audio is played by the player. If the audio ends before 1800 seconds, a STOP line event is generated, and the line listener attached to the clip handles this event by terminating the program. If you need to play audio files longer than 30 minutes, you must make the time interval larger. (We will discuss the sleep method of class Thread in Chapter 14.)

Update the main method in AudioMixer as follows to see how serialization works. This example shows how an audio player can be made to restart playing the same audio file that it was playing before it was closed. The code in this method is almost identical to that discussed earlier in class AudioPlayer:

```
public static void main(String[] args) {
  try {
    AudioMixer player = new AudioMixer();
    System.out.print("Enter name of file to play:");
    Scanner s = new Scanner(System.in);
```

```
      String input = s.next();
      player.setAudioFile(new File(input));
      FileOutputStream fileOut = new FileOutputStream("text/player.dat");
      ObjectOutputStream objectOut = new ObjectOutputStream(fileOut);
      objectOut.writeObject(player);    // serialize
      objectOut.close();
      System.out.println("Written AudioMixer object called player to file
player.dat");

      System.out.println("Create new AudioMixer object called player1");
      AudioMixer player1 = new AudioMixer();
      System.out.println("Initialize player1 fields from file player.dat");
      FileInputStream fileIn = new FileInputStream("text/player.dat");
      ObjectInputStream objectIn = new ObjectInputStream(fileIn);
      player1 = (AudioMixer) objectIn.readObject();        // deserialize
      objectIn.close();
      player1.play(); // play the audio
    } catch (Exception e) {
      e.printStackTrace();
    }
}
```

You will also need to add these statements to AudioMixer:

```
import javax.sound.sampled.*;
import java.util.Scanner;
```

In main, an AudioMixer instance called player is created and its audioFile field
is set to the filename entered by the user on the console. This player is then
serialized to the file player.dat by using the writeObject method of objectOut.
After this, player is assigned to a new AudioMixer instance so that its audioFile
field becomes null. Then, player1 is deserialized from the file player.dat by
calling the readObject method of objectIn, and so audioFile is set to the filename that was previously entered by the user. Finally, player1 plays the
audio by calling its play method. When you compile and run the program,
you will get the following output:

```
Enter name of file to play:audio/groovy.wav
Written AudioMixer object called player to file player.dat
Create new AudioMixer object called player1
Initialize player1 fields from file player.dat
```

The new player named player1 also starts playing the same file groovy.wav.

11.7   Summary

In this chapter, we discussed the various classes for binary and text I/O. The classes FileReader and FileWriter are for reading and writing text files, whereas FileInputStream and FileOutputStream are for reading and writing binary files. The BufferedReader, BufferedWriter, BufferedInputStream, and BufferedOutputStream classes should be wrapped around these classes to optimize I/O. In addition to reading from the console, the Scanner class can also read data from files. When random access to a file is required, class RandomAccessFile provides many useful methods to write to both text and binary files. Serialization writes the instance fields of objects to a stream, whereas deserialization is the reverse process of reconstructing the objects from this stream. The classes ObjectOutputStream and ObjectInputStream provide methods to serialize and deserialize objects respectively.

Exercises

1. Explain each of the following briefly.

   a. What is a stream?

   b. Why are buffered readers/buffered writers useful?

   c. Which classes are used to read text files? Which classes are used for binary files?

   d. What information does a WAV file header provide?

   e. What are some audio file formats?

2. Define or explain the following terms.

   a. Audio sample

   b. Frequency of sound

   c. Intensity of sound

   d. Hertz

   e. Decibel

   f. Quantization

   g. Sampling rate

3. State whether the following statements are true or false.

   a. The buffer size used by BufferedReader and BufferedWriter is fixed for a given system and cannot be changed by the programmer.

b. All classes except RandomAccessFile contain methods to access data sequentially in a file.

c. A class must implement the Serializable interface in order to be serialized.

d. Static and transient fields cannot be serialized.

e. Each call to writeObject saves only a single field of an object.

4. Rearrange the order of statements in the following program so that it runs correctly:

```java
public class Exercise_rearrange {
  public static void main(String[] args) {
    FileReader reader = null;
    BufferedReader bufferedReader = null;
    try {
      int ch;
      while ( (ch = bufferedReader.read()) != -1) {
        System.out.print((char)ch);
      }
      bufferedReader = new BufferedReader(reader);
      reader = new FileReader("C:/data.txt");
    } catch (FileNotFoundException e) {
      System.err.println("File could not be found" +e.getMessage());
    } catch (IOException e) {
      System.err.println("IOException " +e.getMessage());
    } finally {
      try {
        bufferedReader.close();
      } catch (IOException e) {
        System.err.println("IOException" +e.getMessage());
      }
    }
  }
}
```

5. Write a program to count the number of characters in a text file.

6. Using class Scanner, write a program to count the number of lines in a text file.

7. Write a program to count the number of occurrences (frequency) of characters in a text file. The program should print out the name of each character along with its frequency. (Use a BufferedReader in your program.)

8. Write a program that reverses the contents of a text file and writes it to a new file using the following:

   a.   Classes of type `Reader`

   b.   `RandomAccessFile` class

9. Write a serializable class called `Thermometer` that contains these two fields:

   ```
   private String type; // type = mercury or digital
   private int temperature;
   ```

   Write a `main` program in which an instance of `Thermometer` is created. Initialize the fields of this instance using data entered by the user on the console. Serialize this instance using `ObjectOutputStream` and write data into the file `thermometer.dat`. Verify that the instance was serialized correctly by reading the data back from `thermometer.dat` and displaying it.

10. Write a class called `TemperatureMonitoringSystem` that contains two fields of type `Thermometer`. (Use the `Thermometer` class developed in Exercise 9.) Create an object called `temperatureMonitor` of this class and serialize it. Write a program that verifies that the `Thermometer` instances in `temperatureMonitor` were serialized correctly.

11. Determine whether any classes in the Swing library can be serialized.

Audio Programs

12. Write a method called `changeVolume` so that you can modify how loud a sound is (without using the volume knob of your computer's speakers). The method takes a floating-point argument called `scale` and scales (multiplies) all the samples in a WAV file up or down by this value.

    ```
    public void changeVolume(String source, String dest, float scale);
    ```

    Test your program with different values of `scale`.

13. Write a method called `createEcho` to create an echo effect when a WAV file is played. (This is done by adding the current sample at index i to a previous sample at index i − n.) Experiment with different values of n, such as 500, 1000, and 1500.

14. Write a method to merge two WAV files with a single channel and a sample size of 16 bits.

15. Write a method to merge two WAV files with two channels and a sample size of 16 bits.

16. Write a method to reverse a WAV file in which each sample has 16 bits.

17. Repeat Exercise 16 using a method that takes an integer argument specifying the sample size (16, 24, or 32).

18. Repeat Exercise 16 for WAV files with two channels.

19. Write a method called `convertIntToByteArray`. This takes an integer argument, converts it to a 4-byte binary number, and writes each byte to an array in little-endian order.

20. Write a method to change the sample rate of a WAV file so that it can be played at a different frequency. Use the method `convertIntToByteArray` to convert the new frequency to a binary value before writing it to the WAV file at indices 24–27.

Further Reading

The WAV file format is based on the Resource Interchange File Format (RIFF), which was developed by Microsoft Corporation and IBM Corporation. You can find more information on these formats in [3, 4].

References

1. "Java™ Platform, Standard Edition 6, API Specification." Web. <http://download.oracle.com/javase/6/docs/api/>.

2. "The Java™ Tutorials." Web. <http://download.oracle.com/javase/tutorial/>.

3. Rumsey, Francis. *Desktop Audio Technology: Digital Audio and MIDI Principles.* Boston: Focal Press, 2003. 173-175. Print.

4. "Multimedia Programming Interface and Data Specifications 1.0." IBM Corporation and Microsoft Corporation. August 1991. Web.

5. Eckel, Bruce. *Thinking in Java.* Upper Saddle River, NJ: Prentice Hall, 2006. Print.

6. Anderson, Julie, and Herve Franceschi. *Java 6 Illuminated: An Active Learning Approach.* Sudbury, MA: Jones and Bartlett, 2008. Print.

CHAPTER 12

Generics and Collections

CHAPTER CONTENTS

A **collection** is a group of objects that are related to each other in some way. Examples of collections include pictures from a photo album, action videos, comic books, trading cards, and sports cars. Each of these is a collection of objects of a specific category, such as photographs, videos, books, cards, and cars. In this chapter, we will discuss the various interfaces and classes that are used to store and manipulate collections. As an example, we will develop an application called *PhotoFinder* to tag photos stored on your computer's hard drive, and then search for and retrieve them.

12.1   The Collections Framework

The **collections framework** consists of several *interfaces* and *classes* (in the `java.util` package) that define data structures to store data, search for and retrieve data, and perform other operations on a collection efficiently. An example is the `ArrayList` class used previously in Section 7.10. This class implements the `List` interface in the collections framework. There are two main interfaces in the collections framework from which all other interfaces are derived: `Collection` and `Map`. The `Collection` interface is extended by the `Set` and `List` interfaces. These interfaces are shown in Figure 12–1.

The `List`, `Set`, and `Map` interfaces are described as follows:

- The `List` interface: A *list* is a specific arrangement of elements in a collection. The elements in a list can be accessed via their indices. This interface defines methods to read, add, and remove elements from the specified indices. The `ArrayList` and `LinkedList` classes implement this interface.

- The `Set` interface: The main feature of a *set* is that it cannot have any duplicate elements. This distinguishes it from a list in which duplicates are allowed. For example, consider a *set* of fingerprints

Figure 12–1

The `Collection`, `Set`, `List`, **and** `Map` **interfaces in the collections framework.**

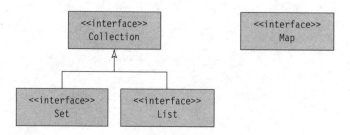

in which each fingerprint is unique. The Set interface declares methods to check whether an element is present in a set, and also to add and remove a specified element from a set. The HashSet, TreeSet, and LinkedHashSet classes implement this interface.

- The Map interface: A *map* associates a **key** with a **value**. This makes it possible to find and retrieve objects efficiently from a collection. For example, consider a world map. The *key* is the coordinates of the place on a map, and the *value* is the place's name. Once you know the coordinates, you can locate the place easily on the map. (This will be elaborated on in more detail in Section 12.4 on the Map interface.) The classes that implement the Map interface are TreeMap, HashMap, and LinkedHashMap.

The framework also contains other interfaces, such as Queue, SortedSet, and SortedMap, as well as other classes, such as PriorityQueue.

12.2   Generics

Before we discuss the interfaces and classes in the collections framework, it is important to understand generics. **Generics** is used to enforce *type-safety* in a program. A **type-safe** program will not have compilation and run-time errors that can result from using incorrect data types. The following example explains this concept in more detail.

Recall from our earlier discussion that the ArrayList class is used to create an array to store elements. The size of the array changes automatically as elements are added or removed from it. First, we describe a potential problem with using ArrayList without generics. Let us create an array list as shown here:

```
ArrayList todoList = new ArrayList();
```

Suppose that we would like to use this list to keep track of the weekly chores associated with caring for a pet cat. We can add elements to this list using the add method in ArrayList:

```
todoList.add("Buy gourmet cat food");
todoList.add("See funny cat pictures online");
todoList.add("Walk the cat");
```

All of the elements added to the list are of type String. If you put the preceding code in a main method and run it, it would run correctly without any errors. Recall, however, that the add method is defined as shown here:

> **public boolean add(Object obj)**—a method that adds the object obj to the end of the list.

Therefore, you will be able to add an object of *any* type (say, Box) to todoList using this method:

```
todoList.add(new Box());
```

There are two problems with this approach. First, it is odd that a to-do list contains an element that is not of type String. Second—and worse—is that it can cause an error at run time. This is explained next in more detail.

Suppose that we would like to display the items in the to-do list. This can be done with ArrayList's get method:

> **public Object get(int index)**—a method that returns the element at the given index.

The element returned is of type Object; thus it must be cast back to its original type. A programmer has written this statement to read the fourth item in todoList, expecting it to be of type String:

```
String s = (String) todoList.get(3);
System.out.println(s);
```

Running the program now results in the following ClassCastException:

```
Exception in thread "main" java.lang.ClassCastException:
genericsandcollections.Box cannot be cast to java.lang.String at
genericsandcollections.ListDemo.main(ListDemo.java:14)
```

The problem is that the fourth element at index 3 is an instance of Box, and it cannot be cast to type String after it is retrieved using the get method. To prevent this error, we will create a list that can only hold elements of type String. This is done as follows:

```
ArrayList<String> newList = new ArrayList<String>();
```

Note that we have inserted the type String within angle brackets (<, >). This declaration tells the compiler that newList can only store elements of type String. The advantage of doing this is that if the programmer tried to insert an element of a different type in this list, it would be caught during compilation and thus prevent a run-time error. Generics makes this type of declaration possible. With generics, we can specify the type of elements that will be stored in a particular collection before it is created.

Let us examine the documentation for the ArrayList class with generics. This class is defined to be generic by adding the letter E within angle brackets:

```
public class ArrayList<E> extends AbstractList<E> implements List<E>,
RandomAccess, Cloneable, Serializable {
  // code ..
}
```

The letter E is a placeholder for the actual element type that will be defined by the programmer. E is known as the **type parameter** of the ArrayList class. By convention, the type parameter is a single uppercase letter, and is defined to be E for the collection classes. For example, this declares an ArrayList called myPictures that can hold elements of type Picture:

```
ArrayList<Picture> myPictures;
```

The type parameter E is replaced by Picture in ArrayList. Here, Picture is called the **type argument** to the ArrayList class. When you create myPictures, you must again specify that it store elements of type Picture:

```
myPictures = new ArrayList<Picture>();
```

The type argument Picture is inserted within angle brackets between ArrayList and the parentheses. Now, myPictures can only hold elements of class Picture (and its subclasses). Note that you cannot create an object of type parameter E because it is not an actual data type.

The type argument can be a class type or interface type, but it cannot be a primitive type. This statement results in a compilation error because it creates an ArrayList with a primitive type argument of int:

```
ArrayList<int> newList = new ArrayList<int>(); // error!
```

However, you can use a wrapper class, such as Integer, in place of the primitive type.

Generic methods are declared using *type parameters*. In ArrayList, methods add and get are defined to be generic using the type parameter E:

> **public boolean add(E e)**—a method that adds the element e to the end of the list.
>
> **public E get(int index)**—a method that returns the element at the specified index in the list.

The methods add and get have a type parameter E instead of Object. After the ArrayList instance has been created, you can use these methods just as you would use any other method in a class. Note that you do not need to cast the value returned by the get method because it is of the data type represented by E and not Object.

To see how the generic methods are called, let us create todoList using generics:

```
ArrayList<String> todoList = new ArrayList<String>();
```

This replaces the type parameter E with String in todoList's methods. Therefore, this call to add works correctly:

```
todoList.add("Buy gourmet cat food");
```

However, the following statement results in a compilation error because add can take only a String argument:

```
todoList.add(new Box());    // error
```

The get method retrieves the objects as type String instead of Object:

```
String s = todoList.get(2);
```

Note that a cast to String is not needed now because the object retrieved is of type String.

12.3   The Set Interface and Its Implementations

Previously, we described a set as a collection in which duplicate elements are not present. In this section, we will discuss three classes that implement the Set interface: HashSet, TreeSet, and LinkedHashSet. These three data structures do not allow duplicates, and TreeSet and LinkedHashSet have the additional property that they store the elements in some order. TreeSet sorts the elements according to a specified order, such as, for example, a set of strings in alphabetical order. LinkedHashSet maintains the order in which the elements were added to the set. Thus, if we add the String "Second" before the String "First" to a LinkedHashSet, "Second" will be printed out before "First" when the elements of this set are displayed, which is not necessarily the case if a HashSet or TreeSet is used.

This next example shows how to use these classes. Suppose that a video rental store wants to determine which videos are not being rented by customers. A list of these unused video rentals is available, but it contains many duplicate titles. We will write a program to remove the duplicates from the list so that each title appears exactly once. This can be done easily using a HashSet. Create a HashSet that can hold elements of type String:

```
HashSet<String> videoSet = new HashSet<String>();
```

Next, add the video titles from the list to videoSet. Note that duplicates of some titles are also added.

```
videoSet.add("Ex-terminator");
videoSet.add("The Dark Night");
videoSet.add("Mission Possible");
videoSet.add("The Dark Night");
videoSet.add("The Zzzz Movie");
videoSet.add("Ex-terminator");
```

Now, print out all the elements in videoSet:

```
System.out.println(videoSet);
```

Insert the preceding code into a main method in a class and run the program. Remember to import the necessary classes in the java.util package. The output is shown here:

```
[The Zzzz Movie, The Dark Night, Ex-terminator, Mission Possible]
```

The add method of a Set does not add an element if it is already present in that set. Therefore, the preceding output does not contain any duplicates.

Although there are no duplicates, the output is not in any specific order. If we want to print out this list of titles in alphabetical order, a TreeSet should be used instead. Change videoSet to be of type TreeSet:

```
TreeSet<String> videoSet = new TreeSet<String>();
```

Rerun the program, and note that the titles are now arranged in alphabetical order:

```
[Ex-terminator, Mission Possible, The Dark Night, The Zzzz Movie]
```

A variation to this would be to print the titles out in exactly the same order in which they were added to the data structure. A LinkedHashSet is used for this. Rerun the same program after changing the type of videoSet to Linked-HashSet. The output is shown here:

```
[Ex-terminator, The Dark Night, Mission Possible, The Zzzz Movie]
```

You can check that the video titles appear in the same order in which they were added to the list, the difference being that duplicates have been removed.

You can use an enhanced for loop or an iterator to access the individual elements of a collection. We will discuss iterators a little later in the chapter. This loop prints out all the elements of videoSet:

```
for (String s : videoSet)
  System.out.println(s);
```

So far, we have seen how the add method works. Figure 12–2 shows some of the methods in the Collection interface that are inherited by Set. All of these methods are implemented by the three classes discussed previously. The size method gives the number of elements in the set:

```
System.out.println(videoSet.size());
```

This prints out the value 4. For practice, use the other methods in the preceding program and note how the program output changes.

The Set interface also has special methods (inherited from Collection) to perform operations such as finding the intersection and union of the elements of two sets, which will be discussed later in Section 12.8. All methods that *modify* the contents of a collection (such as add and remove in the Set interface) are **optional methods**. A class that extends an interface must implement all the methods in that interface; however, it is *not* necessary for a class to implement optional methods. If an instance of a class invokes a method that is not implemented in that class, an UnsupportedOperationException is thrown.

Figure 12–2

Some of the methods in the Collection interface. These methods are inherited by the Set and List interfaces.

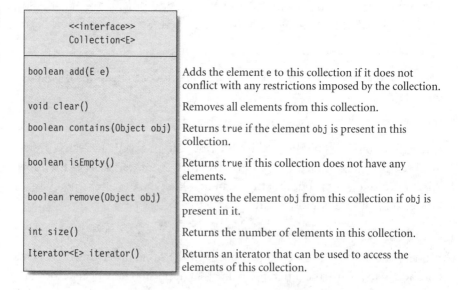

`<<interface>>` `Collection<E>`	
`boolean add(E e)`	Adds the element e to this collection if it does not conflict with any restrictions imposed by the collection.
`void clear()`	Removes all elements from this collection.
`boolean contains(Object obj)`	Returns true if the element obj is present in this collection.
`boolean isEmpty()`	Returns true if this collection does not have any elements.
`boolean remove(Object obj)`	Removes the element obj from this collection if obj is present in it.
`int size()`	Returns the number of elements in this collection.
`Iterator<E> iterator()`	Returns an iterator that can be used to access the elements of this collection.

The `PhotoFinder` Class: Extracting Photo Tags   We will develop a program called `PhotoFinder`, in which you can create tags for the photos that are stored on your computer's disk, and then retrieve and display the photos that contain a given tag.[1] To begin with, we will write a method called `extractTags` that returns unique tags from the text entered by a user. The user should be able to enter the tags separated by any number of blanks, tabs, semicolons, or commas. The code for the method is shown next, and it is similar to the `extractKeywords` method we wrote in Chapter 7. Separators such as blanks and tabs are skipped inside this `while` loop:

```
while (ch == ' ' || ch == '\t' || ch == ',' || ch == ';')
```

All consecutive characters of a word are then read into a `StringBuilder` object called sb. After a complete word has been read, it is added to a `Linked-HashSet` called tags, using the add method, as follows:

```
tags.add(sb.toString());
```

The advantage of adding the word to a `LinkedHashSet` is that duplicates are removed and the tags are stored in the same order in which they were entered. The method `extractTags` is shown here:

```
package genericsandcollections;
import java.util.*;

public class PhotoFinder {

  // extract the tags (removing duplicates) from user input
  public LinkedHashSet<String> extractTags(String s) {
    int index = 0;
    StringBuilder sb = new StringBuilder();
    LinkedHashSet<String> tags = new LinkedHashSet<String>();

    while (index != s.length()) {
      // skip leading blanks, tabs, semicolons and commas, if any
      char ch = s.charAt(index);
      while (ch == ' ' || ch == '\t' || ch == ',' || ch == ';') {
        if (++index == s.length())
          break;
        ch = s.charAt(index);
      }
```

---

[1]This program uses the method of inverted indices. For more information, see [3].

```
// read all characters in a word until a blank, comma, tab
// or semicolon is reached
while (ch != ' ' && ch != '\t' && ch != ',' && ch != ';') {
  // add the character ch to sb
  sb.append(ch);
  if (++index == s.length())
    break;
  // read the next character
  ch = s.charAt(index);
}

// don't add an empty string
if (sb.length() > 0)
  tags.add(sb.toString());

// erase contents of sb to store next word
sb.delete(0, sb.length());
    }
    return tags;
  }
}
```

You can test the extractTags method by adding this main to PhotoFinder:

```
public static void main(String[] args) {
  PhotoFinder pf = new PhotoFinder();
  System.out.println( pf.extractTags("blue sky sky boat;;  mountain, boat
camera"));
}
```

The program output is shown here:

```
[blue, sky, boat, mountain, camera]
```

Later, we will create a GUI for PhotoFinder that contains a text field where the user can enter the tags for a photograph.

12.4   The Map Interface and Its Implementations

As described earlier, maps use **key-value pairs** to store and retrieve data efficiently. The *key* is used to retrieve the corresponding *value*. A **hash map** is a type of map that stores the values in an array and uses a *hash function* to convert the key into an index that is the location of the value in the array. To understand why maps are useful, consider a library catalog system. When you need to find a book in a library, you can enter its title on a computer terminal in the library and retrieve its call number. Then, using this call number, you can locate the book without having to search through all of the books. In this example, think of the book's title as the *key*, its call number as the *hash function* that gives the location of the book in the library, and the book itself as the *value*. Similarly, the hash function of a hash map directly gives the location of the value in the array so that the entire array does not have to be searched.

Figure 12–3 shows a hash map that stores the places on a treasure map and their coordinates. The key is the name of a place on the map (such as Gold mine), and the value is its location (1° N 15° E). Assume that the hash function maps the key "Treasure" to index 5, "Murky river" to index 6, "Gold mine" to index 1, and "Fiery volcano" to index 3. Each key-value pair is stored at the specified index, as shown in this hash map.

To retrieve an element in the array, the key must be provided. For example, a treasure hunter can use the key "Treasure" to retrieve the corresponding value from the map. Inside the hash map, the key is first converted to the index 5 by the hash function, and then the value at this index is retrieved. Thus, the value retrieved is "Cross the river, volcano, and mine." The hash function directly gives the index at which the value is stored for the given key; thus it is not necessary to search through the entire array sequentially for the matching key.

The **hash function** uses a two-step process to calculate the index from the key. The first step is to compute the *hash code* from the key. A simple way to do this would be to assign a numeric value to each letter in the key and then add them together. In practice, sophisticated functions are used to calculate this value, but it is not necessary for the programmer to know these details in order to use a hash map. The Object class has a method called hashCode, which returns a hash code value for a given object. The second step is to

Index	Hash Map
0	
1	"Gold mine"– "1° N 15° E"
2	
3	"Fiery volcano"– "2° N 15° E"
4	
5	"Treasure"—"Cross the river, volcano, and mine"
6	"Murky river"—"1°10′N 15° E

Figure 12–3

A hash map storing key-value pairs where the key is the name of a place on a map and the value is the coordinates of the place.

convert this hash code to an index. One way to do this is by using the % (modulo) operator and the size of the hash map. If the array in the hash map has size n, the index can be calculated from the hash code as shown here:

```
index = hashcode % n
```

It is possible that the hash code will be the same for different objects. In this case, the indexes calculated for two different keys are the same—this is called a **collision**. Therefore, there can be multiple key-value pairs at the same index in the array. Hash maps use different strategies for handling collisions; one way is to insert the key-value pairs at the same index into a linked list. (We will look at how linked lists work later in this chapter.) To use a hash map, you only need to understand what a collision is, and do not have to be concerned with how it is resolved.

Besides hash maps, two other types of maps are tree maps and linked hash maps. The corresponding classes HashMap, TreeMap, and LinkedHashMap implement the Map interface. Unlike hash maps, tree maps and linked hash maps impose a specific order on the values stored in the map. A TreeMap class stores key-value pairs in ascending key order, and a LinkedHashMap stores them in the order in which the keys were inserted into the map. Figure 12–4 shows some of the methods in the Map interface.

Figure 12–4

Some methods in the Map interface.

`<<interface>>` `Map<K, V>`	
`void clear()`	Removes all elements from this map.
`boolean containsKey(Object key)`	Returns true if this map contains the specified key.
`V get(Object key)`	Retrieves the value corresponding to the given key.
`boolean isEmpty()`	Returns true if the map does not have any elements.
`V put(K key,V value)`	Adds the specified key-value pair to this map. If the key already exists in the map, the old value is replaced with the new one.
`int size()`	Returns the number of key-value pairs in this map.
`Set <Map.Entry<K, V>> entrySet()`	Returns a set containing all the key-value pairs in the map.
`Set<K> keySet()`	Returns a set containing all the keys in the map.
`Collection<V> values()`	Returns a collection containing all the values in the map.

With this background on hash maps, we are now ready to examine the HashMap class in the java.util package. The class is declared as HashMap<K, V>, where K is the type parameter for the keys and V is the type parameter for the values.

12.4.1   Using Hash Maps

Figure 12–5 shows two constructors in class HashMap. For example, this statement creates a hash map called treasureMap in which both type parameters are strings:

```
HashMap<String, String> treasureMap = new HashMap<String, String>();
```

The various key-value pairs shown in Figure 12–3 are added to treasureMap using the put method:

```
treasureMap.put("Gold mine", "1 degree N 15 degrees E");
treasureMap.put("Treasure", "Cross the river, volcano and mine");
```

Add the other entries similarly to the map. The entries can be placed in different locations from those seen in Figure 12–3, at indexes decided by the hash function used in the hash map.

The get method returns the value for a given key. This statement prints out the value corresponding to the key "Gold mine":

```
System.out.println(treasureMap.get("Gold mine"));
```

The output is:

```
1 degree N 15 degrees E
```

The keySet method returns all the keys in treasureMap:

```
System.out.println(treasureMap.keySet());
```

The output is:

```
[Murky river, Fiery volcano, Treasure, Gold mine]
```

The method entrySet returns all key-value pairs:

```
System.out.println(treasureMap.entrySet());
```

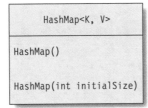

HashMap<K, V>	
HashMap()	Constructor creates a hash map with a default initial size of 16.
HashMap(int initialSize)	Constructor creates a hash map with the specified initial size.

Figure 12–5

Constructors to create a HashMap.

The output is:

```
[Murky river=1 degree 10 minutes N 15 degrees E, Fiery volcano=2 degrees N
15 degrees E, Treasure=Cross the river, volcano and mine, Gold mine=1
degree N 15 degrees E]
```

The `values` method returns all the values in the map.

The `PhotoFinder` Class: Creating a Hash Map to Retrieve a Photo's Tags   Suppose
that you want to retrieve the tags of a photo in a collection using the
filename of the photo. If a list were used as the collection, you would have
to search through all the filenames in the list until you found the one that
you were looking for. With a map, however, the key (filename) is converted
to a number (array index) that takes you directly to the value (the photo).
In this section, we will create a hash map called `nameToTagsMap` that stores
filenames as keys and photos as values.

The package `com.programwithjava.collections` contains a class called `Photo`
with two fields: the filename, and the tags associated with a photo. We will
use this class in `PhotoFinder`:

```java
package com.programwithjava.collections;
import java.util.*;
import java.io.*;

public class Photo implements Serializable {
  private File filename;          // complete filename including path
  private Collection<String> tags;  // tags

  public Photo(File name, Collection<String> t) {
    filename = name;
    tags = t;
  }

  public Collection<String> getTags() {
    return tags;
  }

  public File getFilename() {
    return filename;
  }
}
```

Create a hash map called nameToTagsMap to store the tags for each photo. The filename is the key and a Photo is the value. Add this field to PhotoFinder:

```
private HashMap<String, Photo> nameToTagsMap;
```

Add these import statements and constructor to PhotoFinder:

```
import com.programwithjava.collections.*;
import java.io.File;

public PhotoFinder() {
  nameToTagsMap = new HashMap<String, Photo>();
}
```

The nameToTagsMap maps a filename to tags. For example, suppose that the photo stored in the file JavaBook/image/treeFrog.jpg has the tags "tree, frog, red, feet." The user can use the key "treeFrog.jpg" to retrieve a value of type Photo that contains the corresponding filename and tags. This is implemented in the getPhoto method. Add this method to PhotoFinder:

```
// method in PhotoFinder to return the photo with given filename
public Photo getPhoto(String name) {
  if (nameToTagsMap.containsKey(name)) {
    Photo p = nameToTagsMap.get(name);
    return p;
  } else {
    return null;
  }
}
```

Also add this method to PhotoFinder to store the tags of a newly added picture in nameToTagsMap:

```
// insert a new key-value pair where key is the name of photo
// and the value is the Photo object
public void addPhoto(String name, Photo p) {
  // insert photo in nameToTagsMap
  nameToTagsMap.put(name, p);
}
```

Add the following statements to the main method to test the addPhoto and getPhoto methods of the PhotoFinder instance pf:

```
// create a Photo object
Photo photo1 = new Photo(new File("image/space.jpg"),
pf.extractTags("spaceship; planet"));
```

```
// add photo1 using the name "space.jpg" to PhotoFinder
pf.addPhoto("space.jpg", photo1);

// display the filename and tags of photo with the name "space.jpg"
Photo p = pf.getPhoto("space.jpg");
System.out.println("Filename =" +p.getFilename() +"  Tags=" +p.getTags());
```

Compile and run the program as follows:

```
C:\JavaBook> javac -d bin src\genericsandcollections\PhotoFinder.java
src\com\programwithjava\collections\Photo.java

C:\JavaBook> java -classpath bin genericsandcollections.PhotoFinder
```

This program prints out the following information about the photo:

```
Filename =image\space.jpg  Tags=[spaceship, planet]
```

As an exercise, add more photos and test your program.

12.4.2   Multimap

In the maps discussed so far, each key has exactly one value. You can also create maps, known as **multimaps**, in which a key is associated with multiple values. These values are usually stored as List or Set instances. Consider a map that stores <student name, student ID> pairs. There may be many students with the same name, but each has a unique student ID. Therefore, this map is a multimap because it associates several IDs with a given name. Suppose that we would like to store the IDs in a set of type Integer. To do so, we can declare the multimap (called nameToIDsMap) as follows:

```
HashMap<String, Set<Integer>> nameToIDsMap;
```

The PhotoFinder Class: Creating a Multimap to Retrieve All Photos with a Given Tag   Our picture collection might contain many pictures with the same tag. The user should be able to retrieve all pictures that contain a given tag. For example, suppose that both pictures stored in files bridge.jpg and scenery.jpg contain the tag "bridge." Hence, when the user provides the key "bridge," two values (bridge.jpg and scenery.jpg) should be retrieved from the multimap. This can be done by creating a multimap in which a photo tag is the key and all filenames containing that tag are its values. Let us add a multimap called tagToNamesMap to PhotoFinder. Add this field to PhotoFinder:

```
private HashMap<String, TreeSet<File>> tagToNamesMap;
```

The multimap tagToNamesMap has keys of type String and values of type TreeSet<File>. Thus, when the user supplies a tag, all the filenames associated with that tag should be retrieved. Note that a TreeSet is used to store the values because we want to store the filenames in alphabetical order without any duplicates present.

Create the multimap by adding this statement to PhotoFinder's constructor:

```
tagToNamesMap = new HashMap<String, TreeSet<File>>();
```

When a new photo (say, bridge.jpg) is added, each tag in the photo must be added to tagToNamesMap as a key-value pair, such as (bridge, bridge.jpg), (bay, bridge.jpg), where bridge and bay are the photo's tags. Modify PhotoFinder's addPhoto method as shown here:

```
// insert photo and tags in nameToTagsMap and tagToNamesMap
public void addPhoto(String name, Photo p) {
  // insert photo in nameToTagsMap
  nameToTagsMap.put(name, p);

  // for each tag, insert this filename in tagToNamesMap
  for (String tag : p.getTags()) {
    TreeSet<File> filenameSet = tagToNamesMap.get(tag);
    if (filenameSet == null)
      filenameSet = new TreeSet<File>();

    filenameSet.add(p.getFilename());
    tagToNamesMap.put(tag, filenameSet);
  }
}
```

It is possible that a key (tag) will already contain some values (filenames) in tagToNamesMap. These statements in addPhoto check whether a set of filenames associated with this tag already exists in tagToNamesMap, and create the set if it does not exist:

```
TreeSet<File> filenameSet = tagToNamesMap.get(tag);
if (filenameSet == null)
  filenameSet = new TreeSet<File>();
```

Suppose that the user enters a tag and wants to obtain the names of all photos that contain that tag. This can be done using the get method:

```
tagToNamesMap.get(tag);
```

Add this method to PhotoFinder to display the names of all photos that contain the given tag:

```
// display all photos that contain the given tag
  public void displayPhotosWithTag(String tag) {
    System.out.println(tagToNamesMap.get(tag));
  }
```

Add the following statements to the main in PhotoFinder. These statements create two instances of Photo and add them to the hash maps:

```
Photo p1 = new Photo(new File("bridge.jpg"), pf.extractTags("bridge,
bay"));
Photo p2 = new Photo(new File("scenery.jpg"), pf.extractTags("bridge,
boat"));
pf.addPhoto("bridge.jpg", p1);
pf.addPhoto("scenery.jpg", p2);
pf.displayPhotosWithTag("bridge");
```

The method displayPhotosWithTag is passed the argument bridge and displays all the photos that contain this tag. When you compile and run the program, this method retrieves the values bridge.jpg and scenery.jpg from tagToNamesMap:

```
[blue, sky, boat, mountain, camera]
Filename =image\space.jpg  Tags=[spaceship, planet]
[bridge.jpg, scenery.jpg]
```

12.5   The List Interface and Its Implementations

The ArrayList and LinkedList classes implement the List interface. Like ArrayList, a LinkedList maintains the order in which elements are added to it. Another similarity is that in both types of lists, elements can be accessed via their indices. The difference between the two is that an array list stores its elements in an array, whereas a linked list uses a group of connected **nodes**. Each node stores object data and is linked to the previous and next node. (This configuration is analogous to how the cars in a train are connected.) A linked list is traversed by starting from either end and following the links from one node to the next. Array lists generally offer better performance than linked lists and tend to be used more often. Array lists provide faster random access of elements because in them, an element can be accessed directly using its index, whereas in a linked list the intermediate nodes must be traversed before the required element can be accessed. However, when elements need to be inserted or removed frequently from the middle of the list, a linked list can be faster than an array list.

Figure 12–2 showed the methods in the Collection interface that are inherited by List. Additional methods in List are shown in Figure 12–6. The

Figure 12–6
Additional methods in the List **interface.** List **also inherits the methods shown in Figure 12–2 from the** Collection **interface.**

void add(int index, E e)	Inserts the element e at the specified index.
E get(int index)	Returns the element at the specified index in the list.
E remove(int index)	Removes the element at the specified index in the list.
ListIterator<E> listIterator()	Returns a list iterator for this list.
ListIterator<E> listIterator(int index)	Returns a list iterator that starts at the given index for this list.
E set(int index, E e)	Replaces the element at the given index with the element e.

ArrayList and LinkedList classes implement this interface. Examples of using an ArrayList are shown here:

```
ArrayList<Double> list1 = new ArrayList<Double>();
list1.add(10.5);              // list1 = [10.5]
list1.add(30.5);              // list1 = [10.5, 30.5]
list1.add(1, 20.5);          // list1 = [10.5, 20.5, 30.5]
list1.set(2, 50.5);          // list1 = [10.5, 20.5, 50.5]
list1.remove(0);
System.out.println(list1);  // list1 = [20.5, 50.5]
```

A LinkedList can be used similarly:

```
LinkedList<Double> list2 = new LinkedList<Double>();
list2.add(10.5);              // list2 = [10.5]
list2.add(1, 20.5);          // list2 = [10.5, 20.5]
list2.remove(1);
System.out.println(list2);  // list2 = [10.5]
```

12.6   Iterators

An **iterator** is an object that can be used to move sequentially through the data stored in a collection. You have already seen how the enhanced for loop can be used for the same purpose. An iterator is used when the elements in a collection have to be removed during traversal. Figure 12–7 shows the methods in the interface Iterator. Sets and lists provide an iterator, whereas maps do not.

Figure 12–7

Some methods in the
Iterator **interface.**

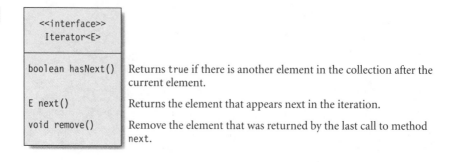

<<interface>> Iterator<E>	
boolean hasNext()	Returns true if there is another element in the collection after the current element.
E next()	Returns the element that appears next in the iteration.
void remove()	Remove the element that was returned by the last call to method next.

The iterator method returns an iterator to access the elements of a set. This code segment shows how to use an iterator to print out and delete each of the elements in the set videoSet:

```
Iterator<String> i = videoSet.iterator();
while (i.hasNext()) {
  // print out the next element
  System.out.println(i.next());

  // delete the element printed out
  i.remove();
}
```

Another type of iterator is defined by the ListIterator interface. With this iterator, a collection can be traversed in both the forward and backward directions. The ListIterator interface extends the Iterator interface and contains several additional methods, some of which are shown in Figure 12–8. The LinkedList class contains an iterator of this type, and it is obtained using the listIterator method.

Figure 12–8

Some methods in the
ListIterator **interface.**

<<interface>> ListIterator<E>	
boolean hasPrevious()	Returns true if there is another element in the collection before the current element.
E previous()	Returns the element that appears before the current one during the iteration.
void remove()	Removes the element that was returned by the last call to method next or previous.

12.7 More on Generics

Wildcards are not just used in card games; Java uses them as well. In this section, we will see why wildcards are needed. The symbol for a Java wildcard is a question mark (?).

As you already know, upcasting occurs when an object is assigned to a reference variable of its superclass. For example, an object of type Integer can be assigned to a reference variable of type Number because the latter is a superclass of the former:

```java
Number num = new Integer(10);
Number[] num = new Integer[5]; // creates an array
```

However, upcasting does not apply to generic type arguments. The following produces a compilation error:

```java
HashSet<Number> set = new HashSet<Integer>(); // error!
```

A set of Integer cannot be assigned to set, which holds a reference to a set of Number. In fact, this type of assignment cannot be made with any generic type. Before we discuss how wildcards can be used for these types of assignments, let us examine generic classes in more depth.

12.7.1 Understanding Generic Classes

You are undoubtedly familiar with Venn diagrams, which are used to find elements that are common between two sets (**intersection**), elements that are present in both of the sets (**union**), and elements that are present in one set but not the other (**difference**). Suppose that there are two sets A = {1, 2, 3, 5} and B = {2, 5, 7, 9}. Their intersection = {2, 5}, union = {1, 2, 3, 5, 7, 9}, and difference = {1, 3}.

Let us write a class to perform the intersection operation on the two sets without using generics:

```java
import java.util.*;

public class SetOperations {
  Set intersection(Set s1, Set s2) {
    Set s3 = new LinkedHashSet();

    for (Object value1 : s1) {
      for (Object value2 : s2) {
        if (value1.equals(value2))
```

```
            s3.add(value1);
         }
      }

   return s3;
   }
}
```

This class contains a method to find the intersection of two sets s1 and s2 using this algorithm:

For each element in set s1, add it to set s3 if the same element is present in s2.

We will digress briefly here to examine the equals method that is used to compare objects in the method intersection. The equals method is defined in class Object, and so it is inherited by all other classes. This method determines whether two objects are equal to each other by checking whether their *references* are equal. Many classes, such as String, Integer, Double, File, and Point, override this method to compare *fields* (instead of references) of objects. For example, consider the two strings s1 and s2:

```
String s1 = new String("Test");
String s2 = new String("Test");
```

The String class overrides equals; hence, the following statement prints out true because both strings contain the same string literal:

```
System.out.println("s1 is equal to s2? " +s1.equals(s2));    // true
```

On the other hand, the StringBuilder class does not override method equals. The following println statement displays false even though the string literals are the same in both s3 and s4:

```
StringBuilder s3 = new StringBuilder("Test");
StringBuilder s4 = new StringBuilder("Test");
System.out.println("s3 is equal to s4? " +s3.equals(s4)); // false
```

If we change s4 to reference the same object as s3, equals will return true:

```
s4 = s3;   // references are equal
System.out.println("s3 is equal to s4? " +s3.equals(s4)); // true
```

Returning to our discussion on generics, to include type-safety at run time, the class SetOperations is made generic, as shown here:

```
import java.util.*;

public class SetOperations<T>  {
  Set<T> intersection(Set<T> s1, Set<T> s2){
    Set<T> s3 = new LinkedHashSet<T>();
```

```
    for (T value1 : s1) {
      for (T value2 : s2) {
        if (value1.equals(value2))
          s3.add(value1);
      }
    }

    return s3;
  }
}
```

The class name is changed to SetOperations<T>, and the method parameters and return type are changed to Set<T>. In the enhanced for loops, the iteration takes place over elements of type T and not Object, and so these are modified accordingly. An instance of this class can be created for any type argument (say, Number) as follows:

```
SetOperations<Number> setOps = new SetOperations<Number>();
```

This will replace the type parameter T with Number in the methods of the class. Therefore, the compiler sees method intersection to be declared as the following:

```
Set<Number> intersection(Set<Number> s1, Set<Number> s2)
```

Create two sets of Number called s1 and s2. We use the intersection method to find the numbers that are common to both sets:

```
HashSet<Number> s1 = new HashSet<Number>();
Set<Number> s2 = new LinkedHashSet<Number>();
s1.add(30.5f);
s1.add(40);
s2.add(50);
s2.add(40);
Set<Number> result = setOps.intersection(s1, s2);
System.out.println(result);
```

As expected, this prints out the number 40, which is present in both s1 and s2.

12.7.2 Using Wildcards

The previous example shows how the intersection method in SetOperations works. Now let us look at another example, in which it does not work as expected. Assume that setOps is a set of Number:

```
SetOperations<Number> setOps = new SetOperations<Number>();
```

Create two sets and pass them to the `intersection` method, as shown here:

```
HashSet<Number> s3 = new HashSet<Number>();
Set<Integer> s4 = new HashSet<Integer>();
System.out.println(setOps.intersection(s3, s4)); // error
```

The last statement results in a compilation error. Only a set of `Number` (such as s3) can be passed in as an argument to `intersection`, and not s4, which is a set of `Integer`. The reason is the same as explained earlier—upcasting does not apply to generic type arguments.

This error can be corrected by making use of the following wildcard:

```
? extends T
```

This wildcard stands for "any type that extends `T`," or in other words, "a descendant of `T`." We redefine method `intersection` in `SetOperations` to use wildcards:

```
Set<T> intersection(Set<? extends T> s1, Set<? extends T> s2){
  Set<T> s3 = new LinkedHashSet<T>();

  for (T value1 : s1) {
    for (T value2 : s2) {
      if (value1.equals(value2))
        s3.add(value1);
    }
  }

  return s3;
}
```

Now, this invocation of `intersection` works correctly because the type argument of s4 is `Integer`, which is a subclass of `Number`:

```
System.out.println(setOps.intersection(s3, s4)); // okay
```

> A **wildcard** is used as a type parameter to allow *upcasting* of generic type arguments.

An important restriction here is that although data can be read from sets s1 and s2, these sets cannot be written to inside the `intersection` method. The reason is that the actual type of the elements stored in these sets is unknown and it might be `T` or some particular descendant of `T`. The compiler will flag it as an error if an attempt is made to add an element to these sets. Therefore, if you add the following statement to `intersection`, it will be flagged as an error:

```
s1.add(value1);      // error
```

A more general wildcard is "?", which stands for "? extends Object". This can be used to represent *any* type. A collection declared with this wildcard as the type argument also has the restriction that it can be read from, but not written to:

```
Set<?> wildCardSet = new HashSet<Integer>();
wildCardSet.add(new Integer(30));// error, cannot write
wildCardSet.remove(new Integer(50)); // okay to read
```

As an exercise, add the methods `union` and `difference` to class `SetOperations`, and verify that they work correctly.

12.8   Performing Set Operations

The `Collection` interface contains methods to perform operations on sets, such as finding the intersection, union, and difference of elements in the set. These methods are shown in Figure 12–9.

Methods `addAll`, `removeAll`, and `retainAll` modify a collection and are optional. The `containsAll` method does not modify a collection, but only

<<interface>> Collection<E>	
boolean addAll(Collection<? extends E> c)	Adds the elements of collection c to the collection that invokes this method (union operation).
boolean removeAll(Collection<?> c)	Removes all the elements from the collection that calls this method that are also present in the collection c (difference operation).
boolean retainAll(Collection<?> c)	Modifies the collection calling this method so that it only contains elements that are also present in c (intersection operation).
boolean containsAll(Collection<?> c)	Returns true if the collection calling this method contains all the elements in c.

Figure 12–9

Methods in the Collection interface for set operations.

checks whether one collection is a subset of another. For example, let us create an array list and hash set as shown here:

```
ArrayList<Number> al = new ArrayList<Number>();
al.add(50);
al.add(10);
al.add(30.5);
al.add(0);
HashSet<Integer> h1 = new HashSet<Integer>();
h1.add(10);
h1.add(25);
h1.add(30);
```

The array list al has type argument Number and contains the elements [50, 10, 30.5, 0]. The hash set h1 has type argument Integer and contains the elements [25, 10, 30]. This statement adds all the elements in h1 to the array list al:

```
al.addAll(h1); // al = [50, 10, 30.5, 0, 25, 10, 30]
```

The addAll method uses the wildcard ? extends E as the type argument of the collection passed as an argument to this method. Therefore, the following statement results in a compilation error because the type argument of al (Number) does not extend the type argument of h1:

```
h1.addAll(al);    // error
```

As an exercise, examine how the elements of al change when it invokes the other methods.

The PhotoFinder Class: Retrieving Photos That Contain a Given Set of Tags   In this section, a method to retrieve all photos that contain a given set of tags is described. For example, assume that tagToNamesMap contains the following key-value pairs:

"bridge"—bridge.jpg, scenery.jpg
"boat"—scenery.jpg

Suppose that a user wants to find all photos that contain both tags "bridge" and "boat." The solution is "scenery.jpg," because it contains both tags. The method getPhotosContainingAllTags takes a set of tags as its argument and returns the photos that contain all of these tags. This method finds the photos for each tag and performs an intersection operation to find common photos. For example, first the photos for the tag "bridge" are found.

This retrieves bridge.jpg and scenery.jpg from tagToNamesMap. Then the photos for the tag "boat" are found. This retrieves scenery.jpg. The intersection of the two retrieval operations gives scenery.jpg. Add this method to PhotoFinder:

```
public TreeSet<File> getPhotosContainingAllTags(Set<String> s) {
  String tag;
  TreeSet<File> photos = new TreeSet<File>();
  Iterator<String> tagIterator = s.iterator();

  // iterate over the tags in set s
  while (tagIterator.hasNext()) {
    tag = tagIterator.next();

    // find the photos that contain this tag
    if (tagToNamesMap.containsKey(tag)) {
      if (photos.isEmpty()) {
        photos = (TreeSet<File>) tagToNamesMap.get(tag).clone();
      } else {
        // perform the intersection operation
        photos.retainAll(tagToNamesMap.get(tag));
      }
    } else {
      // no common photos found for this set of tags
      photos.clear();
      break;
    }
  }

  return photos;
}
```

The first iteration of the while loop in the preceding method retrieves all photos that contain the first tag "bridge." This is done by the following statement:

```
photos = (TreeSet<File>) tagToNamesMap.get(tag).clone();
```

The get method returns an object reference to the TreeSet<File> object containing the values {bridge.jpg, scenery.jpg} that match the key "bridge" in tagToNamesMap. Let us see what the clone method does.

The Object class contains a clone method, which can be used to create a **new object** with the same fields as the object that invokes this method. Any instance of a class that implements the Cloneable interface can invoke this method. If method `clone` is called by an instance of a class that does not implement `Cloneable`, an exception (`CloneNotSupportedException`) is thrown. `TreeSet` implements `Cloneable`, and so `clone` is used to *copy* the values {bridge.jpg, scenery.jpg} in the tree set returned by `get` into `photos`. We can then modify the contents of `photos` without affecting the data in `tagToNamesMap`.

Let us see what goes wrong if we do not use the `clone` method:

```
photos = (TreeSet<File>) tagToNamesMap.get(tag); // error
```

The preceding statement introduces a subtle error because `photos` *references* the `TreeSet<File>` object that contains the filenames {bridge.jpg, scenery.jpg} corresponding to the key "bridge" in `tagToNamesMap` directly, and changing `photos` in any way changes these values in `tagToNamesMap`.

An object being cloned might contain primitives and/or other objects (let us refer to them as inner objects). The `clone` method creates duplicates of all primitives in the new object. However, `clone` only copies *object references* of these inner objects into the new object; that is, it does not create duplicates of the inner objects themselves.

In the second iteration of the `while` loop, the `get` method returns the value scenery.jpg corresponding to the key "boat" from `tagToNamesMap`. An intersection is performed using the `retainAll` method in this statement:

```
photos.retainAll(tagToNamesMap.get(tag));
```

Now, `photos` will contain the filename scenery.jpg. As an exercise, add statements in `main` to test this method in `PhotoFinder`. When you compile the program, you will see this warning:

```
Note: src\genericsandcollections\PhotoFinder.java uses unchecked or unsafe
operations.
Note: Recompile with -Xlint:unchecked for details.
```

The reason is that the `clone` method returns data of type `Object`, and the cast to `TreeSet<File>` causes a warning. An alternative to using method `clone` is to use the following constructor in `TreeSet` to copy the filenames into `photo`:

> **TreeSet(Collection<? extends E> c)**—a constructor that creates a new tree set and copies the elements of the collection `c` into this tree set.

Replace the following statement in method getPhotosContainingAllTags:

```
photos = (TreeSet<File>) tagToNamesMap.get(tag).clone();
```

with this one:

```
photos = new TreeSet<File>(tagToNamesMap.get(tag));
```

The compiler does not generate a warning when you compile the program now. As an exercise, add additional statements to main to test this method.

12.9 Comparing Objects

In the class SetOperations, we used the equals method to check whether the elements of two sets are equal. A problem arises if a set contains elements of a user-defined class. Let us look at what can go wrong. Suppose that we have defined a class called Stamp:

```
class Stamp {
  String name;

  public Stamp() {}

  public Stamp(String n) {
    name = n;
  }
}
```

Create an instance of class SetOperations with type argument Stamp:

```
SetOperations<Stamp> setOps = new SetOperations<Stamp>();
```

Also, create three stamps named either "Dolphin" or "Celebrate," and two stamp collections s1 and s2:

```
Stamp stamp1 = new Stamp("Dolphin");
Stamp stamp2 = new Stamp("Celebrate");
Stamp stamp3 = new Stamp("Dolphin");

HashSet<Stamp> s1 = new HashSet<Stamp>();
HashSet<Stamp> s2 = new HashSet<Stamp>();
s1.add(stamp1);
s1.add(stamp2);
s1.add(stamp3);
s2.add(stamp3);
```

(Remember to import the `java.util` package in your program.) Let us print out the contents of hash set s1 using these two statements:

```
for (Stamp e : s1)
  System.out.println(e.name);
```

The output contains duplicates:

```
Dolphin
Celebrate
Dolphin
```

This is an error because a set should not contain duplicates.

Here is another example that also gives an incorrect result. What will the output be when setOps invokes its `intersection` method?

```
Set<Stamp> result = setOps.intersection(s1, s2);
for (Stamp e : result)
  System.out.println(e.name);
```

You might expect the result to be "Dolphin," because the stamp with this name is present in both s1 and s2; instead, the result is `null`. Let us examine why these errors occur.

For user-defined classes, the default behavior of the `equals` method is to check whether the object references (of the objects being compared) are equal. The references of the Dolphin stamps are `stamp1` and `stamp3`, and because they are different, the `equals` method returns `false`. For user-defined classes, therefore, the programmer must specify how objects of that class can be determined to be equal. This is done by overriding the `equals` method of class `Object`. Add an `equals` method to `Stamp` that compares the names of the `Stamp` objects and returns `true` if the names are the same:

```
// the equals method in Stamp overrides that in Object
public boolean equals(Object s) {
  if (s instanceof Stamp) {
    if (name.equals(((Stamp) s).name))
      return true;
  }
  return false;
}
```

The `equals` method has a parameter of type `Object`. It would be an error to define it with a parameter of type `Stamp`, because it would then not override the corresponding method in class `Object`. The first `if` statement in method `equals` checks whether the argument to this method is an instance of `Stamp`, and the second if statement checks whether the stamp names are the same. The method returns true if the names are the same.

Whenever you override the equals method of Object, it becomes necessary to override the hashCode method of Object as well. The reason for this is that if two objects are determined to be equal using the equals method, they *must* have the same hash code value. However, unequal objects are not required to have different hash code values. Let us check the hash code values of the two Dolphin stamp objects stamp1 and stamp3:

```
stamp1.hashCode();     // returns a hash code of 1671711
stamp3.hashCode();     // returns a hash code of 11394033
```

Although stamp1 and stamp3 are equal, their hash code values are different. This is incorrect, and so we will add an overriding hashCode method in class Stamp to return the same hash code for objects that are equal. The hash code can be generated using one or more of the fields used to determine that the objects are equal. For example, in Stamp, we will generate the hash code using the following name field:

```
// this hashCode method in Stamp overrides that in Object
public int hashCode() {
  return name.hashCode();
}
```

stamp1 and stamp3 now have the same hash code values:

```
stamp1.hashCode();     // returns a hash code of -793243202
stamp3.hashCode();     // returns a hash code of -793243202
```

After you add the overriding equals and hashCode methods to class Stamp, the following code segment prints out "Dolphin," which is correct:

```
Set<Stamp> result = setOps.intersection(s1, s2);
for (Stamp e : result)
  System.out.println(e.name);
```

In addition, the error in the other program—in which the hash set s1 printed out duplicates—does not occur now.

> A key point to glean from our preceding discussion is that the elements (keys) of a HashSet (HashMap) must be instances of a class that overrides the methods equals and hashCode of class Object.

Another way to compare objects is by using the Comparable and Comparator interfaces. These interfaces are described next.

12.9.1   The Comparable **Interface**

The Comparable interface in the java.lang package has a comparison method to *sort* objects of a class:

```
public interface Comparable<T> {
  int compareTo(T obj);
}
```

A class that implements Comparable defines an ordering for its objects based on the values returned by the compareTo method:

> **int compareTo(T obj)**—a method that returns one of these three values: 0 if the instance is equal to obj, a negative integer if the instance is less than obj, or a positive integer if the instance is greater than obj.

Several classes implement Comparable. These include String, File, and the wrapper classes Integer, Float, and Double. The next example shows how user-defined classes can implement Comparable.

Suppose that we would like to display a set of paintings sorted by the artist name. The Painting class is defined as follows:

```
class Painting {
  String name;
  String artist;
  int year;

  // constructor
  public Painting(String name, String artist, int year) {
    this.name = name;
    this.artist = artist;
    this.year = year;
  }
}
```

Let us create four instances of class Painting and add them to a TreeSet:

```
Painting p1 = new Painting("Three Musicians", "Picasso", 1921);
Painting p2 = new Painting("Mona Lisa", "da Vinci", 1505);
Painting p3 = new Painting("Impression, Sunrise", "Monet", 1873);
Painting p4 = new Painting("The Last Supper", "da Vinci", 1498);

TreeSet<Painting> setOfPaintings = new TreeSet<Painting>();
setOfPaintings.add(p1);
setOfPaintings.add(p2);
setOfPaintings.add(p3);
setOfPaintings.add(p4);
setOfPaintings.add(p4);
```

As you have seen earlier, elements in a TreeSet are ordered in alphabetical order. What happens if we try to print out the elements of setOfPaintings?

```
for(Painting p : setOfPaintings)
  System.out.println("name = " +p.name +";  artist = " +p.artist +";  year
= " +p.year);
```

This action results in the following exception when the program is executed:

```
Exception in thread "main" java.lang.ClassCastException:
genericsandcollections.Painting cannot be cast to java.lang.Comparable
        at java.util.TreeMap.put(TreeMap.java:542)
        at java.util.TreeSet.add(TreeSet.java:238)
            at genericsandcollections.Painting.main(Painting.java:23)
```

This error occurs because Painting is a user-defined class, and TreeSet does not know how to sort instances of this class. To correct this, we must either modify class Painting to implement the Comparable interface or provide a Comparator. The following code segment shows how the comparison can be done by implementing Comparable so that the paintings are sorted by the names of both the artist and the painting:

```
class Painting implements Comparable<Painting> {
  String name;
  String artist;
  int year;

  // constructor
  public Painting(String name, String artist, int year) {
    this.name = name;
    this.artist = artist;
    this.year = year;
  }

  public int compareTo(Painting p) {
    // compare paintings by artist name
    int result = artist.compareTo(p.artist);

    // paintings by the same artist are compared by name of painting
    if (result == 0)
      result = name.compareTo(p.name);

    return result;
  }
}
```

The program output is sorted as shown next. The paintings are sorted by the name of the artist, and paintings of each artist are further sorted by the name of the painting:

```
name = Impression, Sunrise;  artist = Monet;  year = 1873
name = Three Musicians;  artist = Picasso;  year = 1921
name = Mona Lisa;  artist = da Vinci;  year = 1505
name = The Last Supper;  artist = da Vinci;  year = 1498
```

Note that the output does not contain any duplicates, and that names beginning with uppercase characters (Monet, Picasso) are printed out before names with lowercase characters (da Vinci).

> One caveat with regard to this program is that the combination of fields on which the comparison is performed must be unique.

Suppose that we wrote the comparison method so that the comparison is done only by the name of the artist:

```java
// a comparison method with an error
public int compareTo(Painting p) {
  // compare paintings by artist name
  return artist.compareTo(p.artist);
}
```

The program output displays only a single painting for each artist:

```
name = Impression, Sunrise;  artist = Monet;  year = 1873
name = Three Musicians;  artist = Picasso;  year = 1921
name = Mona Lisa;  artist = da Vinci;  year = 1505
```

The TreeSet stores only a single painting for each artist when the comparison is done using the artist field. The name and artist fields uniquely identify each painting; thus we used these in the comparison method. However, it would be an error to only use the fields artist and year because these may not uniquely identify each painting (an artist may complete several paintings in a year).

By overriding the equals and hashCode methods of Object, a class can specify how its instances are determined to be *equal*. On the other hand, by implementing Comparable, a class can specify how its instances are to be *sorted*.

Next, we discuss how Comparator can be used.

12.9.2 The Comparator Interface

You might have heard the idiom "you cannot compare apples and oranges," but you can do so in Java! The Comparator interface provides a comparison method that lets you compare objects of *different* classes. This interface is defined in the java.util package:

```
public interface Comparator<T> {
  int compare(T o1, T o2);
  boolean equals(Object o);
}
```

It is not necessary to implement the equals method because it is inherited from Object, but the compare method must be implemented:

> **int compare (T obj1, T obj2)**—a method that returns one of these three values: 0 if obj1 is equal to obj2, a negative integer if obj1 is less than obj2, or a positive integer if obj1 is greater than obj2.

Suppose that we would like to sort the paintings by the name of the painting (instead of artist). The Painting class already implements a different comparison method, and a class cannot have more than one compareTo method. We write a new class that implements Comparator:

```
import java.util.*;

public class ComparePaintings implements Comparator<Painting> {
  public int compare(Painting p1, Painting p2) {
    // compare paintings by name
    int result = p1.name.compareTo(p2.name);

    // paintings with the same name are compared by artist name
    if (result == 0)
      result = p1.artist.compareTo(p2.artist);

    return result;
  }
}
```

The compare method takes arguments of type Painting. Use the following constructor if you want to use a Comparator to sort the elements of a tree set:

> **public TreeSet(Comparator<? super E> comparator)**—a constructor that creates a tree set that sorts its elements based on the values returned by the compare method of comparator.

The wildcard "? super E" is read as "any type that is a supertype of E." This lets us perform sort operations in a collection that contains objects of different classes, but with a common superclass.

Create an instance of ComparePaintings and pass it as an argument to the TreeSet constructor:

```
ComparePaintings comparator = new ComparePaintings();
TreeSet<Painting> setOfPaintings = new TreeSet<Painting>(comparator);
```

Add the instances of Painting created earlier to setOfPaintings, and print out its elements. The elements are displayed in the following order:

```
name = Impression, Sunrise;  artist = Monet;  year = 1873
name = Mona Lisa;  artist = da Vinci;  year = 1505
name = The Last Supper;  artist = da Vinci;  year = 1498
name = Three Musicians;  artist = Picasso;  year = 1921
```

The paintings in the TreeSet are now sorted by field name, and those with the same name are further sorted by field artist. If you need to sort the results differently, you can create another class that implements Comparator, but with a different compare method.

> A key point to remember is that the elements (keys) of a TreeSet (TreeMap) must be instances of a class that implements the Comparable interface. Alternately, the TreeSet (TreeMap) must be constructed using the constructor with parameter of type Comparator.

The next example shows how you can create a comparator to sort elements of different classes.

Example

Write a comparator to sort two lists, containing home and kitchen appliances, in alphabetical order, where the various classes are defined as follows:

```
package genericsandcollections;
import java.util.*;

abstract class Appliance {
  String name;
  String manufacturer;
}

class HomeAppliance extends Appliance {}

class KitchenAppliance extends Appliance {}
```

Solution: The `ApplianceCompare` class implements the `compare` method of the
`Comparator` interface:

```
public class ApplianceCompare implements Comparator<Appliance> {
  public int compare(Appliance o1, Appliance o2) {
      // compare the name fields
      int result = (o1.name).compareTo(o2.name);

      // if names are same, compare the manufacturers
      if (result == 0)
        result = (o1.manufacturer).compareTo(o2.manufacturer);

      return result;
  }
}
```

The `name` and `manufacturer` fields identify each appliance uniquely; as a
result, the sorting is done using both of these fields. The `compare` method
takes arguments of type `Appliance`, each of which could be a `HomeAppliance` or
`KitchenAppliance`. The appliances are sorted by the `name` field, and those with
the same name are sorted by the `manufacturer` field. This `main` method tests
the preceding classes:

```
public static void main(String[] args) {
  // create a comparator to sort appliances
  ApplianceCompare comparator = new ApplianceCompare();

  KitchenAppliance app1 = new KitchenAppliance();
  app1.name = "Oven";
  app1.manufacturer = "Kitchen Corp";

  KitchenAppliance app2 = new KitchenAppliance();
  app2.name = "Oven";
  app2.manufacturer = "App Inc";

  HomeAppliance app3 = new HomeAppliance();
  app3.name = "Heater";
  app3.manufacturer = "App Inc";

  KitchenAppliance app4 = new KitchenAppliance();
  app4.name = "Blender";
  app4.manufacturer = "App Inc";

  KitchenAppliance app5 = new KitchenAppliance();
  app5.name = "Oven";
  app5.manufacturer = "Kitchen Corp";
```

```
// create a tree set with a comparator
TreeSet<Appliance> setOfAppliances = new TreeSet<Appliance>(comparator);
setOfAppliances.add(app1);
setOfAppliances.add(app2);
setOfAppliances.add(app3);
setOfAppliances.add(app4);
setOfAppliances.add(app5);
setOfAppliances.add(app2);

for (Appliance a : setOfAppliances)
   System.out.println("name:" +a.name +"   manufacturer:"
+a.manufacturer);
}
```

The output is sorted and duplicates are removed, as shown here:

```
name:Blender   manufacturer:App Inc
name:Heater    manufacturer:App Inc
name:Oven    manufacturer:App Inc
name:Oven    manufacturer:Kitchen Corp
```

12.10   The Complete PhotoFinder Class

In this section, we will discuss how you can add a GUI to the PhotoFinder class. A GUI makes it easy for the user to display photographs from the disk and add tags to the photographs. Furthermore, because we would like the tags to be persistent across invocations of the program, we will serialize this class.

12.10.1   The PhotoFinder Class: Adding a GUI

The package com.programwithjava.collections contains an interface called ImageSearcher and four classes: Photo, ImageSearcherView, ImageSearcherDrawing-Panel, and ImageSearcherController.

The last three classes are the view and controller for a model that implements the ImageSearcher interface. You can examine the code in these classes, if you like, to get a better understanding of the Model View Controller architecture. The class ImageSearcherView creates a window with a menu bar. The class ImageSearcherDrawingPanel displays the photos, which are returned as the result of a user query, as a set of thumbnails. The Model View Controller architecture is used to retrieve and display the photographs on the GUI. The class ImageSearcherController (the controller) is the glue between PhotoFinder (the model) and ImageSearcherView (the view).

When the user selects a menu item on the window, the controller performs some action by calling a corresponding method in the model and/or view. The ImageSearcher interface is shown here:

```
package com.programwithjava.collections;
import java.io.*;
import java.util.*;

public interface ImageSearcher extends Serializable {
  Collection<String> extractTags(String s); // extract individual tags

  // adds new photo to database
  void addPhoto(String filename, Photo p);

  // get the photo with this filename
  Photo getPhoto(String filename);

  // get all photos that have all of the tags in set s
  Collection<File> getPhotosContainingAllTags(Set<String> s);

  // returns name of file to which object is serialized
  File getSerializationFileName();
}
```

We must modify the class declaration of PhotoFinder as follows so that it implements ImageSearcher, and then we can use the classes in the package to create a GUI for this program:

```
public class PhotoFinder implements ImageSearcher {
  // code for this class
}
```

Note that the PhotoFinder class already implements all the methods in this interface, with the exception of getSerializationFileName; it is added in the next section. After this method is added, we will be able to use the classes ImageSearcherView and ImageSearcherController to create a GUI for PhotoFinder.

12.10.2   The PhotoFinder Class: Serialization

We would like to save the tags that we have entered for the photos, so that they are not lost when the program is closed. The hash maps that contain the tags are stored in the computer's memory, and when you close the program these hash maps will be removed. It is necessary to serialize the hash maps to a file when the program is closed, and then deserialize them when the program is next run. It is easy to do this because the HashMap class implements the Serializable interface. To make PhotoFinder serializable, it must implement the Serializable interface. PhotoFinder implements ImageSearcher, and so it implements Serializable as well because interface ImageSearcher extends Serializable.

Add this field and accessor method to PhotoFinder:

```
private File serialized;
```

```
public File getSerializationFileName() {
  return serialized;
}
```

The serialized field stores the name of the file in which PhotoFinder will be serialized. Also, modify the PhotoFinder constructor so that serialized is initialized with this filename (let us call it photofinder.dat):

```
public PhotoFinder() {
  nameToTagsMap = new HashMap<String, Photo>();
  tagToNamesMap = new HashMap<String, TreeSet<File>>();

  // set up the name of the serialization file
    serialized = new File("text/photofinder.dat");
}
```

The class ImageSearcherController contains two methods called serialize and deserialize to perform serialization and deserialization when the program is closed and started, respectively.

Modify the main in PhotoFinder as shown here:

```
public static void main(String[] args) {
  PhotoFinder pf = new PhotoFinder();
  ImageSearcherView view = new ImageSearcherView(pf);
  new ImageSearcherController(view, pf);
}
```

treeFrog.jpg © Sebastian Duda, 123RF.com

Figure 12–10

The tags for the photo treeFrog.jpg are entered in the text field after the photo is loaded using the Open Photo menu item in the File menu.

Compile and run the PhotoFinder program, along with all the classes in the src.com.programwithjava.collections package:

```
C:\JavaBook> javac -d bin src\genericsandcollections\PhotoFinder.java
src\com\programwithjava\collections\*
```

```
C:\JavaBook> java -classpath bin genericsandcollections.PhotoFinder
```

Figure 12–10 shows PhotoFinder in action.

Now, the tags added to treeFrog.jpg photo will persist even after the PhotoFinder program is closed. Select the Serialize menu item on the File menu. When you display this photo again after closing the program, the tags associated with it will be displayed. Add tags to other photographs that are stored on your computer's hard drive. To find all pictures that contain a given set of tags, choose the With All Given Tags menu item from the Find Photos menu.

12.11 Summary

In this chapter, we discussed the List, Set, and Map collections. A List maintains the order in which elements are added to it, and might contain duplicates. A Set orders its elements and, unlike a List, cannot store duplicates. A

Map stores key-value pairs and is used for fast access to the corresponding value given the key. Unlike a List and a Set, the elements in a Map are not stored in a specific order. Generics is used with collections to provide type-safety. We also discussed how a user-defined class can override the hashCode and equals methods of Object to determine whether two instances of that class are equal in a collection such as a HashSet or HashMap. A user-defined class can implement the interface Comparable or use a Comparator to define how the objects of that class should be sorted in a collection such as TreeSet or TreeMap. Using these data structures, we developed the PhotoFinder program to tag photographs stored on the user's computer, as well as to retrieve photographs with matching tags.

Exercises

1. Explain how the following collection classes are different from each other: List, Map, and Set.

2. Describe the distinguishing features of each of these collections: TreeSet, HashSet, TreeMap, HashMap, ArrayList, and LinkedList.

3. Explain the following terms.

    a. Collection
    b. Type-safety
    c. Type argument
    d. Type parameter

4. What is hash code? How is the index calculated in a map? What is a collision?

5. Describe how generics provides type-safety and provide an example.

6. Which of the following statements cause a compilation error?

    a. `ArrayList<Painting> paintings1 = new ArrayList<Painting> ();`
    b. `Set<Painting> paintings2 = new TreeSet<Painting>();`
    c. `TreeSet<Object> paintings3 = new TreeSet<Painting>();`
    d. `List<Object> paintings4 = new ArrayList<Object>();`

7. State whether the following statements are true or false.

    a. The class of the elements stored in HashSet must override the methods equals and hashCode of class Object.

b. It is necessary for the class of the elements stored in a TreeSet to implement the Comparable interface.

c. If two objects are equal, the compare method of a Comparator must return the same value for these objects.

d. If two objects are not equal, they must have distinct hash codes.

8. You have added the names of these six cities to a HashSet in this order: Hong Kong, Cairo, London, New York, Cairo, and London. What is the output when the elements of the HashSet are displayed? How does the output change if a TreeSet is used? If a LinkedHashSet is used?

9. Write a program to store the names of 10 countries and their capitals in a HashMap, where the name of the country is the key and its capital is the value. Assume that each country has only one capital. Determine how the output changes if

   a. A TreeMap is used.

   b. A LinkedHashMap is used.

10. Some countries, such as Bolivia and South Africa, have more than one capital. Modify the previous program so that a country (key) can have multiple capitals (values). Use a hash map to store the data. Verify that your program runs correctly.

11. We have added a method named equals to class Car that overrides the corresponding method in the Object class. This method returns true if two cars have the same brand and name. Find the errors in this equals method in class Car:

```
public boolean equals(Car c) {
    if (brand.equals(c.brand) && name.equals(c.name))
      return true;
    return false;
}
```

12. Create an ArrayList to store integer numbers. Write a program to add elements to this list, and print out its contents and size. Show that a list can contain duplicates. Repeat this problem using a LinkedList.

13. Write a class called Sculpture with fields name, sculptor, and year. Add constructors and accessor and mutator methods to this class.

   a. Write a program to create six instances (include duplicates) of Sculpture and add them to a HashSet. An example sculpture is the

Gran Cavallo by da Vinci in the year 1495. Display the elements of this HashSet. Check whether the program runs correctly.

b. Add overriding methods equals and hashCode to Sculpture. Verify that the program runs correctly.

14. Write a program to create instances of the Sculpture class (described in Example 13) and add them to a TreeSet. Print out the elements of the TreeSet. Does the program run correctly?

a. Modify the Sculpture class so that it implements the Comparable interface. The sculptures should be sorted by field name, and those with the same name should be further sorted by sculptor. Run the program and check whether the elements are sorted correctly.

b. Suppose we would like to sort the TreeSet differently. This can be done by creating a custom Comparator. Write a class called SculptureCompare that implements Comparator. Implement the compare method in this class to sort by field sculptor, and those with the same sculptor by field name. Use this Comparator to sort the elements in the TreeSet.

Graphics Manipulation

15. Add a method to PhotoFinder called getPhotosContainingSomeTags:

```
public TreeSet<File> getPhotosContainingSomeTags(Set<String> s)
```

The argument to this method is a user-supplied list of tags that is a set of String. It returns all photos that contain at least one tag in this list as a TreeSet of File. For example, suppose the photo zoo.jpg contains the tags "tiger, cheetah, cage," and the photo jungle.jpg contains the tags "swamp, elephant, herd." If the user provides the tags *tiger* and *swamp*, both photos (zoo.jpg and jungle.jpg) should be retrieved by this method.

16. In PhotoFinder, picture tags cannot be changed after the Submit button has been clicked. Modify this program so that the user can change the picture tags. The hash maps will need to be updated so that the tags deleted by the user are removed from both hash maps and the new tags are added to the hash maps. You will also need to make some changes to the classes provided in the com.programwithjava.collections package.

References

1. "Java™ Platform, Standard Edition 6, API Specification." Web. <http://download.oracle.com/javase/6/docs/api/>.

2. "The Java™ Tutorials." Web. <http://download.oracle.com/javase/tutorial/>.

3. Subrahmanian, V. S. *Principles of Multimedia Database Systems.* San Francisco, CA: Morgan Kaufmann, 1998. 173. Print.

4. Eckel, Bruce. *Thinking in Java.* Upper Saddle River, NJ: Prentice Hall, 2006. Print.

5. Anderson, Julie, and Herve Franceschi. *Java 6 Illuminated: An Active Learning Approach.* Sudbury, MA: Jones and Bartlett, 2008. Print.

6. Sierra, Kathy, and Bert Bates. *Head First Java.* Sebastopol, CA: O'Reilly, 2005. Print.

7. Knudsen, Jonathan. *Java 2D Graphics.* Beijing: O'Reilly, 1999. Print.

CHAPTER 13

More on GUI Programming

CHAPTER CONTENTS

Previously, we discussed how the Swing event model works. GUI components fire events of type ActionEvent, ItemEvent, and ChangeEvent. Two other types of events that we have not discussed are MouseEvent and KeyEvent. In this chapter, we will discuss how these two events are generated, as well as how to write listeners to handle these events. In addition, you will also learn about Swing timers and the JDialog class. In Section 13.5, we will develop a simple 2D animation game called *BallGame*, the objective of which is to use a bat to keep a set of balls from reaching the bottom of a window.

13.1   Handling Mouse Events

A MouseEvent is created automatically when the user presses, releases, moves, or drags the mouse in a GUI. The MouseEvent class contains methods to find the *x*- and *y*-coordinates of the mouse position in the window, which mouse button was clicked, and the number of mouse clicks associated with this event. Some of these methods are shown in Figure 13–1.

A MouseEvent is sent to all event handlers that are registered on this component. The event handler should be of type MouseListener or MouseMotionListener, and implement all the methods in these interfaces. The MouseListener interface is defined in the java.awt.event package:

```
public interface MouseListener extends EventListener {
  public void mouseClicked(MouseEvent e);
  public void mousePressed(MouseEvent e);
  public void mouseReleased(MouseEvent e);
  public void mouseEntered(MouseEvent e);
  public void mouseExited(MouseEvent e);
}
```

Figure 13–1

Some methods in class MouseEvent.

MouseEvent	
int getX()	Returns the *x*-coordinate of the mouse in the component.
int getY()	Returns the *y*-coordinate of the mouse in the component.
int getClickCount()	Returns the number of times the mouse button was clicked.

The mouseClicked method is invoked when a mouse button is pressed and released without moving the mouse. The mouseEntered or mouseExited methods are called when the mouse is inside or outside the component on which the event handler is registered.

The MouseMotionListener interface is defined in the java.awt.event package:

```
public interface MouseMotionListener extends EventListener {
  public void mouseDragged(MouseEvent e);
  public void mouseMoved(MouseEvent e);
}
```

The mouseDragged method is called when the mouse is *dragged* (that is, moved with a button pressed) on the component to which the event handler is attached. The mouseMoved method is invoked similarly, except that the mouse must be moved without pressing any of its buttons. The MouseInputListener interface, defined in package javax.swing.event, combines the MouseListener and MouseMotionListener interfaces.

You may wonder why event handlers for MouseEvent were not created for the components discussed earlier, such as button, text field, and others. The reason is that these components convert mouse clicks and key presses into other events such as ActionEvent and ChangeEvent, which are more convenient to handle. Hence, it is not necessary to know whether a button was pressed using a mouse or a key because both types of events are converted into an ActionEvent by the button. However, to draw graphics on a drawing panel or some other component and control it with the mouse or keyboard, you will need to handle a MouseEvent or KeyEvent directly. Use the methods defined in java.awt.Component (see Figure 13–2) to register the mouse listeners with components.

Component
void addMouseListener(MouseListener ml)
void addMouseMotionListener(MouseMotionListener mml)

Adds the specified mouse listener ml to the component.

Adds the specified mouse motion listener mml to the component.

Figure 13–2

Methods in class Component to add a mouse listener to a component.

Example 1

Write a mouse event handler that prints out the appropriate message on the console whenever the mouse is pressed, released, clicked, moved, or dragged inside a window, as well as when it enters or exits the window.

Solution: The following program creates an event handler that listens to mouse events that occur in a window.

```
package moreguiprogramming;
import javax.swing.event.*;
import java.awt.event.*;
import javax.swing.*;

public class MouseEventHandler implements MouseInputListener {

  public void mouseClicked(MouseEvent e) {
    System.out.println("Mouse clicked");
  }

  public void mousePressed(MouseEvent e){
    System.out.println("Mouse pressed");
  }

  public void mouseReleased(MouseEvent e){
    System.out.println("Mouse released");
  }

  public void mouseEntered(MouseEvent e){
    System.out.println("Mouse entered");
  }

  public void mouseExited(MouseEvent e){
    System.out.println("Mouse exited");
  }

  public void mouseDragged(MouseEvent e){
    System.out.println("Mouse dragged");
  }

  public void mouseMoved(MouseEvent e){
    System.out.println("Mouse moved");
  }
```

```
public static void main(String[] args) {
   JFrame window = new JFrame();

   // create the event handler
   MouseEventHandler eventHandler = new MouseEventHandler();

   // add it to the window
   window.addMouseListener(eventHandler);
   window.addMouseMotionListener(eventHandler);

   window.setDefaultCloseOperation(JFrame.EXIT_ON_CLOSE);
   window.setSize(500, 500);
   window.setVisible(true);
 }
}
```

Run this program and observe which messages are printed out on the console for different mouse actions in the window. ▪

13.1.1 The MouseAdapter and MouseMotionAdapter Classes

Suppose that you would like to write an event handler that listens to mouse clicks only. Although you only want to implement the mouseClicked method in MouseListener, you will have to implement the other methods as well because MouseListener is an interface. An alternative is to use the Mouse-Adapter class when only a subset of the methods in MouseListener must be implemented. MouseAdapter is an abstract class in the java.awt.event package, and it implements all the methods in the MouseListener interface using **method stubs**; that is, methods with empty bodies:

```
public abstract class MouseAdapter implements MouseListener {
     public void mouseClicked(MouseEvent e) {}
     public void mousePressed(MouseEvent e) {}
     public void mouseReleased(MouseEvent e) {}
     public void mouseEntered(MouseEvent e) {}
     public void mouseExited(MouseEvent e) {}
}
```

Similarly, MouseMotionAdapter is an abstract class that implements all the methods in the MouseMotionListener interface using method stubs.

You can create an event handler to handle only mouse click events by creating an instance of an anonymous class that overrides the mouseClicked method in MouseAdapter as follows:

```
new MouseAdapter() {
  public void mouseClicked(MouseEvent e) {
    // do something
  }
}
```

To add this handler to a component comp, use the addMouseListener method:

```
comp.addMouseListener(new MouseAdapter() {
  public void mouseClicked(MouseEvent e) {
    // do something
  }
});
```

Example 2

The following program displays the x- and y-coordinates of the point where the mouse is clicked in a window.

```
package moreguiprogramming;
import javax.swing.*;
import java.awt.event.*;

public class MouseAdapterDemo {
  public static void main(String[] args) {
    JFrame window = new JFrame("MouseAdapter Demo");

    // create the event handler and add it to window
    window.addMouseListener( new MouseAdapter() {
      public void mouseClicked(MouseEvent e) {
        // display the position where the mouse was clicked
        System.out.println("(" +e.getX() +"," +e.getY() +")");
      }
    } );

    window.setDefaultCloseOperation(JFrame.EXIT_ON_CLOSE);
    window.setSize(500, 500);
    window.setVisible(true);
  }
}
```

13.2 Handling Key Events

A KeyEvent is created when the user presses or releases a key on the keyboard. A key listener is an event handler that listens for key events and takes the appropriate action when a key is pressed. In this section, we will discuss how you can create key listeners.

The KeyEvent class in the java.awt.event package contains methods to identify the key that generated the KeyEvent. Keys can be identified either by their character or by their key code using methods getKeyChar and getKeyCode, respectively, shown in Figure 13–3.

Class KeyEvent also defines constants that represent key codes identifying all types of keys. For example, the key code for the Enter key on your keyboard is VK_ENTER, and for the Tab key it is VK_TAB. Table 13–1 shows some key codes.

KeyEvent	
char getKeyChar()	Used to identify alphanumeric keys (the letters A–Z and the numbers 0–9), punctuation mark keys (?, ",", and so forth), and special symbol keys (+, !, @, %, and so forth). Returns the character for the key that generated this event.
int getKeyCode()	Returns the key code for the key that generated this event.

Figure 13–3
Some methods in class KeyEvent.

TABLE 13–1 Key Codes

Key	Key Code
Numbers 1–9	VK_0 to VK_9
Letters A–Z	VK_A to VK_Z
Backspace, Tab, Caps Lock, Enter	VK_BACKSPACE, VK_TAB, VK_CAPS_LOCK, VK_ENTER
Arrow keys	VK_UP, VK_DOWN, VK_LEFT, VK_RIGHT
< > { }	VK_LESS, VK_GREATER, VK_BRACELEFT, VK_BRACERIGHT

13.2.1   The KeyListener Interface and KeyAdapter Class

A key listener should implement the KeyListener interface and *all* of its methods. This interface resides in the java.awt.event package:

```
public interface KeyListener extends EventListener {
  public void keyTyped(KeyEvent e);
  public void keyPressed(KeyEvent e);
  public void keyReleased(KeyEvent e);
}
```

Alternately, it might be more convenient to use the KeyAdapter class, in which case you only need to override the methods that will be used. The KeyAdapter class is an abstract class (in package java.awt.event) that implements the methods in KeyListener using method stubs.

The keyPressed (keyReleased) method is executed whenever a key is pressed (released). These two methods are executed for *all* types of keys on the keyboard. The keyTyped method is executed only for certain keys, such as alphanumeric, punctuation, and special symbol keys.

A key listener must be registered on a component so that it can receive the key events from that component. There are two steps involved:

1. A component must have *focus* in order to receive *keyboard* events. Make the component focusable using the setFocusable method. Exactly *one* component can have focus at any given time.

2. Add a key listener to that component using the addKeyListener method.

The following code will add a KeyListener to the JPanel instance called panel:

```
// make the panel focusable
panel.setFocusable(true);

// add a key event handler to the panel
panel.addKeyListener( new KeyAdapter() {
  public void keyPressed(KeyEvent e) {
    // do something
  }
});
```

Run the following example, and determine which of the three methods in KeyEventHandler is called while typing on the keyboard. The program output is displayed on the console.

Example 3

Write a key event handler and add it to a panel so that whenever a key is pressed, released, or typed on the keyboard, the appropriate method is called and a message is displayed on the console. The methods keyPressed and keyReleased should display the key code, and the method keyTyped should print out the key character.

Solution: The class KeyEventHandler implements KeyListener and prints out an appropriate message in each of its methods.

```java
package moreguiprogramming;
import java.awt.event.*;
import javax.swing.*;

public class KeyEventHandler implements KeyListener {
  // displays the key code of the key that has been pressed
  public void keyPressed(KeyEvent e) {
    System.out.println("Key with keycode " +e.getKeyCode() +" pressed");
  }

  // displays the key code of the key that has been released
  public void keyReleased(KeyEvent e) {
    System.out.println("Key with keycode " +e.getKeyCode() +" released");
  }

  // displays the character for the key that has been pressed
  public void keyTyped(KeyEvent e) {
    System.out.println("Key with char " +e.getKeyChar() +" typed");
  }

  public static void main(String[] args) {
    JFrame window = new JFrame();
    JPanel panel = new JPanel();

    // create a key listener
    KeyEventHandler eventHandler = new KeyEventHandler();

    // make panel focusable so it can receive keyboard events
    panel.setFocusable(true);

    // add a key listener to panel
    panel.addKeyListener(eventHandler);
```

```
        window.setContentPane(panel);
        window.setDefaultCloseOperation(JFrame.EXIT_ON_CLOSE);
        window.setSize(500, 500);
        window.setVisible(true);
    }
}
```

The following sample program output shows the results when the keys "d," "1," and "↑" are pressed on the keyboard:

```
Key with keycode 68 pressed
Key with char d typed
Key with keycode 68 released
Key with keycode 49 pressed
Key with char 1 typed
Key with keycode 49 released
Key with keycode 38 pressed
Key with keycode 38 released
```

Note that when an alphanumeric key, such as *d* (key code 68) or 1 (key code 49), is pressed, both the keyTyped and keyPressed methods are executed, whereas when the arrow key ↑ (key code 38) is pressed, only the keyPressed method is executed.

13.3   The Swing Timer

A Swing timer is used to perform some action at regular intervals of time. For example, a timer can be used to display a message at 1-second intervals. The class Timer (see Figure 13–4) is defined in the package javax.swing. The constructor creates a timer that has a single listener attached to it. Multiple

Figure 13–4

The Swing timer.

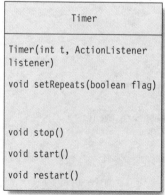

Timer	
Timer(int t, ActionListener listener)	Constructor creates a timer that repeatedly notifies its listener after a delay of t milliseconds.
void setRepeats(boolean flag)	If flag is false, this timer notifies its listeners only once after the initial delay specified in its constructor; otherwise, it notifies them repeatedly.
void stop()	Stops this timer from notifying its listeners.
void start()	Starts this timer.
void restart()	Restarts this timer after it was stopped.

listeners can be attached to a timer using the addActionListener method. Using its setRepeats method, the timer can be programmed to periodically send an ActionEvent to all of its listeners. Alternately, it can be programmed to execute only once (instead of periodically) after a specified time delay.

Example 4

Write a program, using a timer, that displays the time at intervals of 1 second.

Solution: We write an event handler that prints out the time in milliseconds using the currentTimeMillis method provided in class System. (The System class in the java.lang package contains methods for printing time in milliseconds and nanoseconds, among others.) The method currentTimeMillis returns the number of milliseconds that have elapsed since midnight on January 1, 1970 (Universal Coordinated Time) and the current time on your computer. The complete code for this example is shown here:

```java
package moreguiprogramming;
import java.awt.*;
import java.awt.event.*;
import javax.swing.*;

public class TimerEventHandler implements ActionListener {
  JTextArea textArea;

  TimerEventHandler(JTextArea t) {
    textArea = t;
  }

  public void actionPerformed(ActionEvent e) {
    textArea.append("Current time is " +System.currentTimeMillis() +"\n");
  }

  public static void main(String[] args) {
    JFrame f = new JFrame();
    JPanel topPanel = new JPanel();
    final JTextArea textArea = new JTextArea();
    topPanel.add(textArea);

    // listener for the timer
    TimerEventHandler eventHandler = new TimerEventHandler(textArea);
```

```
// create a timer that fires an action event every 1 second
Timer timer = new Timer(1000, eventHandler);
timer.start();

// create the scroll pane and add topPanel to it
JScrollPane scrollPane = new JScrollPane(topPanel);

// add the scroll pane to the content pane
f.getContentPane().add(scrollPane, BorderLayout.CENTER);
f.setSize(500, 500);
f.setTitle("Swing Timer Demo");
f.setDefaultCloseOperation(JFrame.EXIT_ON_CLOSE);
f.setVisible(true);
  }
}
```

The time is printed out in the `actionPerformed` method of the `TimerEvent-Handler` class. An instance of this class `eventHandler` is created in `main`:

```
TimerEventHandler eventHandler = new TimerEventHandler(textArea);
```

This statement creates a timer that notifies its listener `eventHandler` every 1000 milliseconds:

```
Timer timer = new Timer(1000, eventHandler);
```

The listener executes its `actionPerformed` method each time it is notified. This action prints out the time on a scrollable text area in a window. The program output is shown in Figure 13–5. Check the accuracy of the timer. What happens if the period of the timer is reduced to 500 milliseconds? 100 milliseconds?   ■

Timers are used in animation to draw some objects at regular time intervals. In the class `BallGame`, you will see how to use a timer to control the animation in the ball game.

13.4   The JDialog Class

When a dialog box that is created using the `JOptionPane` class is displayed, user input to the windows in that program is blocked. The `JDialog` class creates custom dialog boxes that do not block user input to the other windows. Figure 13–6 shows some constructors and methods for this class. To create a custom dialog box using `JDialog`, create a custom panel with other components and add it to a dialog box as shown here:

```
JDialog dialog = new Dialog(frame, "Program Message");
dialog.setContentPane(customPanel); // customPanel is a custom panel
```

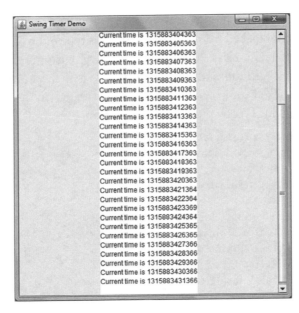

Figure 13-5

Sample output of the
TimerEventHandler
program.

JDialog	
JDialog(Frame window)	Constructor creates a dialog box attached to the given window.
JDialog(Frame window, String title)	Constructor creates a dialog box with the given title and attached to the given window.
Container getContentPane()	Returns the content pane for this dialog box.
void setContentPane(Container pane)	Sets the content pane for this dialog box.
void setVisible(boolean flag)	Makes this dialog box visible if flag is true.
void dispose()	Removes this dialog box.
void setUndecorated(boolean flag)	Removes the decorations from this dialog box if flag is true.

Figure 13-6

Some constructors and
methods in the JDialog
class.

Example 5

Write a program to create a dialog box that appears when the user clicks a button, with the text "Click me" inside a window. The window should also contain a text field, and the user should be able to type in the text field while the dialog box is displayed. The dialog box should display the text "Game has ended," and then close when the user clicks a button on it.

Solution: It is necessary to create a JDialog dialog box because windows are not blocked from the user when this type of box is displayed. The following code in class JDialogDemo creates a custom dialog box with a yellow background and an OK button. When the button labeled "Click me" is clicked, an instance of this class is created on the screen. You can close this dialog box by pressing its OK button.

```java
package moreguiprogramming;
import javax.swing.*;
import java.awt.*;
import java.awt.event.*;

public class JDialogDemo {
  JDialog dialog;
  JPanel dialogPanel;
  JButton button;
  JLabel label;

  JDialogDemo(JFrame window) {
    dialog = new JDialog(window);
    dialogPanel = new JPanel();
    button = new JButton("OK");
    label = new JLabel("Game has ended");

    // remove the dialog box when its OK button is clicked
    button.addActionListener( new ActionListener() {
      public void actionPerformed(ActionEvent e) {
        dialog.setVisible(false);
        dialog.dispose();  // removes the dialog box
      }
    });

    dialogPanel.add(label);
    dialogPanel.add(button);
    dialog.setSize(150, 80);
    dialogPanel.setBackground(Color.yellow);
    dialog.setUndecorated(true);
    dialog.setContentPane(dialogPanel);
    dialog.setVisible(true);
  }

  public static void main(String[] args) {
    final JFrame window = new JFrame();
    JPanel topPanel = new JPanel(new BorderLayout());
    JButton dialogButton = new JButton("Click me");
```

```
    // creates a dialog box when this button is clicked
    dialogButton.addActionListener(new ActionListener() {
      public void actionPerformed(ActionEvent e) {
        new JDialogDemo(window);
      }
    });

    // add a text field and button to topPanel
    JTextField textField = new JTextField();
    topPanel.add(textField, BorderLayout.CENTER);
    topPanel.add(dialogButton, BorderLayout.NORTH);

    window.setContentPane(topPanel);
    window.setSize(500, 500);
    window.setTitle("JDialog Demo");
    window.setDefaultCloseOperation(JFrame.EXIT_ON_CLOSE);
    window.setVisible(true);
  }
}
```

Figure 13–7 shows the dialog box that is displayed when the button is clicked in the window. Note that it is possible to write in the text field while the dialog box is displayed.   ■

Figure 13–7

The dialog box is created when the button labeled "Click me" is pressed. You can type in the text area while the dialog box is displayed.

13.5   A 2D Animation Game—Ball Game

In this section, you will see how to use mouse listeners and a timer to create a 2D animation game. In this game, the player tries to hit a set of balls in a window using a bat. Each time a ball is hit, the score is incremented by 5 points. A ball can be hit by the bat only while the ball is moving down, not up. Each time a ball falls to the bottom of the window, the number of lives left is decremented by 1 and a new ball is added to the window. The objective of this game is to reach the maximum score without losing all lives. The game starts at level 1 with a single ball and 3 lives. The number of balls in the window and the number of lives is incremented by 1 with each new level. Thus, at level 9, there will be 9 balls in the window, and to avoid losing a life, the player must hit all of them to prevent them from reaching the bottom of the window.

The requirements for the game are as follows:

- Maintain an array of balls, where each ball knows its current *x*- and *y*-coordinates in the window.

- Display an animation of the balls using their velocity.

- Be able to detect whether the bat has made contact with a ball.

- Determine whether a ball has reached the upper or side edge of the window and make it bounce off this edge.

- Be able to move the bat inside the window using the mouse.

We will use the Model View Controller (MVC) pattern in our program. The **model** comprises the classes Ball, Bat, and BallGameRules, which describe the ball, bat, and rules of the game, respectively. The **view** displays the animation, as well as the score and lives fields and the number of levels in the game. The view comprises the classes BallGameView and BallGameDrawingPanel. The **controller** (class BallGameController) contains a timer that fires off an event periodically to redraw the view at regular time intervals so that the positions of the balls in the window are updated according to the rules. It also contains a mouse listener that listens to mouse clicks, and the bat is moved to the position where the mouse is clicked in the window by the user. Each of these classes is discussed in more detail in the following sections. The complete code for all of these classes is provided in the Jav-aBook/src/ballgame directory on the CD-ROM.

13.5.1 Ball Game—Class Bat

Class Bat maintains information about the shape and current position of the bat. It contains the following fields:

```
private int x;          // bat's current x position
private int y;          // bat's current y position
private int length;     // length of the bat
private int width;      // width of the bat
private int corner=20;  // corner width
```

Two methods in this class are described next. This first method draws the shape of the bat:

```
public void drawShape(Graphics2D myGraphics) {
    RoundRectangle2D rect = new RoundRectangle2D.Float(x, y, length, width,
corner, corner);
    myGraphics.fill(rect);
}
```

The second method initializes the starting position and size of the bat:

```
public void reset() {
    x = 100;
    y = 200;
    setLength(100);
    setWidth(10);
}
```

This class also contains accessor and mutator methods for its fields.

13.5.2 Ball Game—Class Ball

A ball moves up or down with a certain velocity. Therefore, class Ball con-tains accessor and mutator methods for these fields:

```
private float x, y;       // current position of ball
private float velX, velY; // velocity of ball in pixels per second
private int direction;    // UP or DOWN
private float width;      // ball's width
```

The velocity of the ball in the y direction velY is negative when the ball is moving up, and it is positive when the ball is moving down. Similarly, the velocity in the *x* direction velX is positive or negative depending on whether the ball is moving to the right or to the left. The following three constants are also defined in Ball:

```
public static final int UP = 0;
public static final int DOWN = 1;
public static final float GRAVITY = 0.05f;
```

A ball's direction is represented by the constants UP and DOWN. The constant GRAVITY is used to simulate the effect of gravity.

The method step in class Ball updates the position of the ball based on how much it has moved in the specified time interval:

```
public void step(float timeInterval) {
  x += velX * timeInterval;
  y += velY * timeInterval;
  updateSpeed(timeInterval);
}
```

To simulate the effect of gravity, when a ball moves up or down, its velocity decreases or increases, respectively. The updateSpeed method in Ball modifies the velocity of a ball using the constant GRAVITY:

```
public void updateSpeed(float timeInterval) {
    velY += GRAVITY * timeInterval;
}
```

This class also contains a method to draw a ball, along with accessor and mutator methods for its fields.

13.5.3   Ball Game—Class BallGameRules

This class contains the rules of the games. It determines whether the ball has collided with the edge of a window or the bat, whether a miss has occurred, and whether the game has been won or lost. It also keeps track of the current game score, level, and lives left. It is provided with the window coordinates of the upper-left (lowX, lowY) and lower-right corners (highX, highY), but is not aware of the BallGameView and BallGameController classes.

The boolean methods atTop, atBottom, atLeft, and atRight determine whether the ball is at the top, bottom, left, or right edge of the window. For example, the ball is at the left corner of the window if its field x is less than or equal to lowX, as shown in Figure 13–8. The code for these methods follows:

```
// check if ball is at top
public boolean atTop() {
```

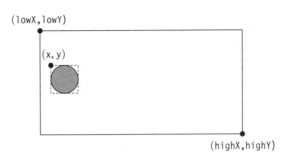

Figure 13–8
Window and ball
coordinates.

```
    if (ball.getY() <= lowY)
      return true;
    else
      return false;
}

// check if ball is at bottom
public boolean atBottom() {
  if (ball.getY() >= highY)
    return true;
  else
    return false;
}

// check if ball is at left
public boolean atLeft() {
  if (ball.getX() < lowX)
    return true;
  else
    return false;
}

// check if ball is at right
public boolean atRight() {
  if (ball.getX() + ball.getWidth() >= highX)
    return true;
  else
    return false;
}
```

The method batTouched determines whether the ball has collided with the
bat. One simple scheme that is commonly employed in games to detect collision between objects is to determine whether the *bounding rectangles* of

Figure 13–9

Bounding rectangles of two irregularly shaped objects.

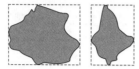

the objects intersect. The **bounding rectangle** of an object is the smallest rectangle that completely encloses that object. Figure 13–9 shows the bounding rectangles (dotted lines) of two objects with an irregular shape.

The two objects are determined to have collided when their bounding rectangles overlap. (A problem with this approach is that it can lead to false positives because the bounding rectangles may intersect slightly even when the objects have not collided.) We can use the method intersects in Rectangle2D.Float to determine whether two rectangles overlap:

> **public boolean intersects(double x, double y, double w, double h)**—a method that returns true if this rectangle overlaps the rectangle with coordinates (x, y), width w, and height h.

The code for method batTouched follows:

```
// check if ball touched bat
public boolean batTouched() {
  Rectangle2D ballBoundingRect = new Rectangle2D.Float(ball.getX(),
ball.getY(), ball.getWidth(), ball.getWidth());

  if (ballBoundingRect.intersects(bat.getX(), bat.getY(), bat.getLength(),
bat.getWidth()))
    return true;

  return false;
}
```

This next method called update sets the new direction and speed of the ball when it collides with a side of the window or the bat. If the ball collides with the left end of the window with velocity −velX, it bounces back with the same speed in the opposite direction; that is, with a velocity of velX. If the ball collides with the bat when it is moving down, it rebounds back up with a velocity of −velY. To prevent all balls from moving in the same direction, a ball is deflected to the left (right) if it makes contact with the left (right) end of the bat. When a ball reaches the bottom of the window, it is added back to the game from a random location at the top of the window and the number of lives left is decremented. This method also updates the current score and levels of the game:

```
// rules of the ball game go here
public int update(Ball ball) {
  this.ball = ball;

  if (atTop() && ball.getDirection() == Ball.UP) {
    // ball is at top of window, set velY positive
    ball.setSpeedY(Math.abs(ball.getSpeedY()));
    ball.setDirection(Ball.DOWN);
  } else if (atBottom()) {
    // ball is at bottom, missed!
    decrementLives();

    // return ball to a random location at top of window
    ball.reset(rand.nextInt((int)(highX - lowX)/2), 0);
    return (-1);
  } else if (atLeft()) {
    // ball is at left end of window, set velX positive
    ball.setSpeedX(Math.abs(ball.getSpeedX()));
  } else if (atRight()) {
    // ball is at right end of window, set velX negative
    ball.setSpeedX(-Math.abs(ball.getSpeedX()));
  } else if (batTouched()) {
    // ball has made contact with the bat
    if (ball.getDirection() == Ball.DOWN) {
      ball.setSpeedY(-Math.abs(ball.getSpeedY()));
      ball.setDirection(Ball.UP);

      if (atBatRight())  {
       // move ball to upper left corner
        ball.setSpeedX(-Math.abs(ball.getSpeedX()));
      } else {
        // move ball toward upper right corner
        ball.setSpeedX(Math.abs(ball.getSpeedX()));
      }

      // update the game score and level
```

```
        incrementScore();
        updateLevel();
     }
   }
   return 0;
}
```

Other methods in this class include `incrementScore` that adds `POINTS_PER_MOVE` to the current score, `wonGame` that returns `true` if the current score is greater than `MAX_SCORE`, and `lostGame` that returns `true` if the number of lives left is equal to zero.

13.5.4   Ball Game—Class `BallGameDrawingPanel`

The classes `BallGameView` and `BallGameDrawingPanel` provide a GUI for the game. Here, we describe the class `BallGameDrawingPanel` that is used to create a panel for the animation. We draw balls and a bat in the `paintComponent` method of this class using the `drawShape` methods in classes `Bat` and `Ball`. We also display the image stored in the file `bricks.jpg` in the `JavaBook/image` directory as the background of a panel. This process takes two steps:

1. First, read the image from the file and store it into the computer's memory. The reason for reading the image from the file into memory is that reading files that are stored on disk is a slow process, whereas reading images stored in the computer's memory is faster because the images can be accessed much more quickly. We discussed earlier how you could use methods in the `ImageIcon` and `Toolkit` classes to read an image. Another way to perform this task is by using the `read` method in class `javax.imageio.ImageIO`:

   public static BufferedImage read(File input) throws IOException—a method that returns the image stored in the file `input` as a `BufferedImage`.

2. Draw this image on the window in the component's `paintComponent` method by using the `drawImage` method of that component's graphics context.

The following code segment in the constructor of class `BallGameDrawingPanel` reads the image stored in file `bricks.jpg` into the `BufferedImage` called background Image:

```
    File filename = new File("image/bricks.jpg");
    try {
      backgroundImage = ImageIO.read(filename);
    } catch (IOException e) {
    System.out.println("An error has occurred while reading image file.
Check that file exists and is in the correct directory.");
      System.exit(1);
    }
```

The paintComponent method in BallGameDrawingPanel to draw the background image, bat, and balls is shown here:

```
public void paintComponent(Graphics g) {
  super.paintComponent(g);
  Graphics2D g2 = (Graphics2D) g;

  // draw the background image
  g2.drawImage(backgroundImage, 0, 0, this);

  // draw the bat and balls
  bat.drawShape(g2);
  for (int i = 0; i < level; i++)
    balls[i].drawShape(g2);
}
```

The array balls contains the balls, which are instances of class Ball.

The complete code for this class is provided in the JavaBook/src/ballgame directory on the CD-ROM.

13.5.5 Ball Game—Class BallGameView

The class BallGameView creates a GUI. It contains a pause button, as well as three text fields with their corresponding labels to display the score, level, and lives in the game. The button, labels, and text fields are directly added to the drawing panel, which is set as the content pane for the window. The borders around the button and text fields are removed by creating an empty border around these components. The fonts and sizes of the text fields and labels are specified using the setFont method. We have added two methods, getWindowWidth and getWindowHeight, that return the width and height of the drawing panel. The drawing panel (called drawingPanel) is an instance of class BallGameDrawingPanel. The pause button is created using an image stored in a file called pauseIcon.gif in the JavaBook/image directory on the CD-ROM.

A portion of the code for class BallGameView is shown here:

```java
public class BallGameView extends JFrame {
  // components
  private JButton pauseButton;      // button to pause the animation
  private JLabel levelLabel;        // displays label level
  private JLabel scoreLabel;        // displays label score
  private JLabel livesLabel;        // displays label lives
  private JTextField scoreField;    // displays score
  private JTextField levelField;    // displays level
  private JTextField livesField;    // displays number of lives left

  // panel
  private BallGameDrawingPanel drawingPanel;

  public BallGameView(Ball[] b, Bat t, int windowWidth, int windowHeight) {
    // create the panels
    drawingPanel = new BallGameDrawingPanel(b, t);

    // create the labels
    levelLabel = new JLabel("level", JLabel.LEFT);
    scoreLabel = new JLabel("score", JLabel.RIGHT);
    livesLabel = new JLabel("lives", JLabel.RIGHT);

    // create and initialize the text fields
    levelField = new JTextField(3);
    scoreField = new JTextField(3);
    livesField = new JTextField(4);
    levelField.setEditable(false);
    scoreField.setEditable(false);
    livesField.setEditable(false);
    levelField.setText("1");
    scoreField.setText("0");
    livesField.setText("0");

    // add pauseButton to buttonPanel
    pauseButton = new JButton(new ImageIcon("image/pauseIcon.gif"));
    pauseButton.setEnabled(true);

    // add the level, score and lives fields to textFieldPanel
    drawingPanel.add(levelLabel);
    drawingPanel.add(levelField);
    drawingPanel.add(scoreLabel);
```

```
    drawingPanel.add(scoreField);
    drawingPanel.add(livesLabel);
    drawingPanel.add(livesField);
    drawingPanel.add(pauseButton);

    // format the button and fields
    levelField.setBorder(BorderFactory.createEmptyBorder(0,0,0,0));
    scoreField.setBorder(BorderFactory.createEmptyBorder(0,0,0,0));
    livesField.setBorder(BorderFactory.createEmptyBorder(0,0,0,0));
    pauseButton.setBorder(BorderFactory.createEmptyBorder(0,0,0,0));
    levelLabel.setFont(new Font("Lucida Sans", Font.ITALIC, 25));
    levelField.setFont(new Font("Lucida Sans", Font.ITALIC, 25));
    scoreField.setFont(new Font("Lucida Sans", Font.ITALIC, 25));
    livesField.setFont(new Font("Lucida Sans", Font.ITALIC, 25));
    scoreLabel.setFont(new Font("Lucida Sans", Font.ITALIC, 25));
    livesLabel.setFont(new Font("Lucida Sans", Font.ITALIC, 25));

    // allow the background to show through these fields
    levelField.setOpaque(false);
    scoreField.setOpaque(false);
    livesField.setOpaque(false);

    // add the panel to this window
    setContentPane(drawingPanel);
    setDefaultCloseOperation(JFrame.EXIT_ON_CLOSE);
    setUndecorated(true);
    setTitle("Ball Game");
    setSize(windowWidth, windowHeight);
  }
}
```

The size of the window (windowWidth and windowHeight) is specified by the user and passed in as arguments to the constructor of this class. This class contains several methods to update the display, such as setLevel, setScore, setLives, and redraw.

The redraw method displays the bat and balls at updated positions in the window. This process is done by invoking drawingPanel's repaint method, which clears drawingPanel and then calls its paintComponent method:

```
public void redraw() {
  drawingPanel.repaint();
}
```

The following method uses a technique called **clipping** to redraw only a portion of drawingPanel instead of its entire contents. The portion of the window that lies within a rectangle with its upper-left corner at (x, y), width w, and height h is updated:

```
public void redraw(int x, int y, int w, int h) {
    drawingPanel.repaint(x, y, w, h);
}
```

Using clipping, only that part of the window that has changed is redrawn, instead of the entire window. In the ball game, for example, suppose that the ball moves from location (oldx, oldy) to (newx, newy), as shown in Figure 13–10. We only have to repaint the area that consists of two (imaginary) rectangles that enclose the ball in its old and new locations; the rest of the window is unchanged.

Clipping can be implemented quite easily using these overloaded repaint methods in JComponent:

> **public void repaint(int x, int y, int w, int h)**—a method that repaints the area occupied by a rectangle having its upper-left corner at (x, y) with width w and height h.
>
> **public void repaint(Rectangle r)**—a method that repaints only the region that is contained in the rectangle r.

For example, in Figure 13–10, assume that the two rectangles have height and width diameter. Thus, the the areas occupied by the two rectangles in Figure 13–10 can be repainted in component comp as follows:

```
comp.repaint(oldx, oldy, diameter, diameter);
comp.repaint(newx, newy, diameter, diameter);
```

Figure 13–10

The two rectangles show the areas that must be redrawn when the ball moves from location (oldx, oldy) to (newx, newy) in the window.

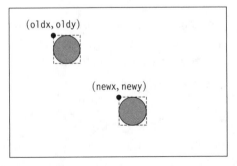

If the ball has already moved to the new position, the first call to repaint will clear the drawing of the ball from the position (oldx, oldy), and the second call to repaint will draw the ball at the new position (newx, newy).

Examine the complete code for this class in the JavaBook/src/ballgame directory on the CD-ROM.

13.5.6 Ball Game—Class BallGameController

The BallGameController class is the glue between the model and the view. This class contains the code to animate the ball, as well as update the position of the bat and the score, level, and lives fields on the view.

The controller is aware of the BallGameView and BallGameRules classes; therefore, it can update the view based on the game rules.

In our ball game, we want to be able to control the position of the bat using the mouse so that whenever the player clicks on the drawing panel with the mouse, the bat is moved to that location. We create a mouse listener that listens to mouse button presses. The mousePressed method moves the bat to the new location where the mouse button was pressed. This is done as follows in the constructor for this class:

```
// add a listener to move the bat to where the mouse was clicked
view.addMouseListener( new MouseAdapter() {
  public void mousePressed(MouseEvent e) {
    updateBatPosition(e.getX(), e.getY());
  }
} );
```

To add animation, we create a timer in the constructor of BallGameController:

```
timer = new Timer(delay, this);
timer.start();
```

Whenever the timer is fired, the actionPerformed method in BallGameController is executed. This method does the following:

1. Updates the speed and direction of all the balls based on their positions. For example, if a ball is at one of the edges of the window, it should rebound back. This is done using the update method in the BallGameRules class.

2. Records the old position of each ball.

3. Moves each ball by a small amount that depends on the time that has elapsed since the timer was last fired. This is done by calling the step method in the Ball class.

4. Records the new position of each ball.

5. Clears the window, and redraws drawingPanel using the clipping method described earlier. This method only clears and redraws those portions of the drawingPanel that have changed.

6. Updates the score, level, and lives fields of the view.

7. Checks whether the game has ended.

The actionPerformed method of BallGameController is shown here:

```
public void actionPerformed(ActionEvent e) {
  // update the speed & direction of the ball
  for (int i = 0; i < rules.getLevel(); i++) {
    rules.update(balls[i]);

    // record position of ball before it moves
    int oldx = (int) balls[i].getX();
    int oldy = (int) balls[i].getY();

    // move the ball to a new position
    balls[i].step(delay/1000.0f);

    // record position of ball after it moves
    int newx = (int) balls[i].getX();
    int newy = (int) balls[i].getY();
    int width = (int) balls[i].getWidth();

    // use clipping to redraw the ball in the window
    view.redraw(oldx, oldy, width+2, width+2);
    view.redraw(newx, newy, width+2, width+2);
  }

  // update score, level and lives fields
  updateView();

  // check whether game has ended
  checkEndOfGame();
}
```

We would also like to be able to pause the game by pressing the pause button. We do so by creating an action listener that calls the `stop` method of `timer`:

```
view.addPauseListener(new ActionListener() {
  public void actionPerformed(ActionEvent e) {
    // stop the timer to pause the game
    timer.stop();

    if(!view.displayConfirmGameEndMessage())
      System.exit(0);

    timer.start();
  }
});
```

13.5.7   Compiling the Source Code and Running the Ball Game

The complete code for the ball game is provided in the JavaBook/src/ballgame directory on the CD-ROM. It comprises the classes `Ball`, `Bat`, `BallGameView`, `BallGameDrawingPanel`, `BallGameRules`, `BallGameController`, and `BallGame`. The `BallGame` class is shown here:

```
public class BallGame {
  public void play() {
    // create the model (bat, balls, and rules)
    Bat bat = new Bat();

    // create the balls
    Ball[] balls = new Ball[BallGameRules.MAX_BALLS];
    for (int i = 0; i < BallGameRules.MAX_BALLS; i++) {
      balls[i] = new Ball();
    }

    // set the window size to that of the computer screen
    Toolkit tkit = Toolkit.getDefaultToolkit();
    int windowWidth = tkit.getScreenSize().width;
    int windowHeight = tkit.getScreenSize().height;

    // create the rules
    BallGameRules rules = new BallGameRules(0, 0, windowWidth,
windowHeight, bat);

    // create the view
```

```
    BallGameView view = new BallGameView(balls, bat, windowWidth,
windowHeight);

    // create the controller
    BallGameController controller = new BallGameController(balls, bat,
view, rules);

    view.setVisible(true);
  }

  public static void main(String[] args) {
    BallGame game = new BallGame();
    game.play();
  }
}
```

The main program has only two statements that create the game and begin its play.

The ball objects are created and stored in an array named balls in class BallGame:

```
Ball[] balls;
```

Although you can set the window size using the setSize method, you can also make the window as large as your computer's screen. How can you determine the size of the screen? Every system contains a toolkit that provides information about your computer's display. You can access this toolkit using the getDefaultToolkit method of the java.awt.Toolkit class:

```
Toolkit tkit = Toolkit.getDefaultToolkit();
```

The toolkit is queried with the getScreenSize method to determine the screen size as follows:

```
int screenWidth = tkit.getScreenSize().width; // screen width
int screenHeight = tkit.getScreenSize().height; // screen height
```

You can compile and run this program as follows:

```
C:\JavaBook>javac -d bin src\ballgame\*
```

```
C:\JavaBook>java -classpath bin ballgame.BallGame
```

When you run the program, you will notice that the movement of the ball is slightly jerky. The reason for this is that the Swing timer does not run at regular intervals as expected. In fact, if you print out the times at which the actionPerformed method is executed, you will observe that the time interval between consecutive firings of the timer can vary considerably.

Figure 13–11
Playing a ball game.

bricks.jpg © Dariusz Gudowicz, 123RF.com

Figure 13–11 shows a snapshot of the game in progress. You can change the speed of the balls, the number of levels, or any of the other rules, to create your own version of this game. With this background, you are ready to start creating your own games!

13.6 Summary

In this chapter, we discussed how you can write listeners to handle mouse and key events. The JDialog class can be used to create custom dialog boxes. A Swing timer can be used to perform a task periodically. We also explored the basics of creating a simple game. A mouse listener is used in this game to move the bat to the location where the mouse is clicked in the window. The Swing timer is used to redraw the graphics in the window periodically, giving the impression that the balls are moving. The Model View Controller architecture introduced earlier was explained in more detail using the ball game program.

Exercises

1. What is the purpose of the MouseEvent class?

2. Which listener interfaces are provided to handle mouse events?

3. Use an example to explain how you can create a listener that listens to mouse clicks by implementing the interface MouseListener.

4. Use an example to explain how you can create a listener that listens to mouse presses by implementing the interface MouseListener.

5. Use an example to explain how you can create a listener that listens to mouse clicks by inheriting from the class MouseAdapter.

6. Which of the following statements are true?

    a.   Multiple listeners can be attached to a component.
    b.   A listener can handle events from only a single event source.
    c.   A button cannot fire a MouseEvent.
    d.   A Swing timer can be used to perform a task only once.
    e.   A Swing timer can have multiple listeners.

7. What is the error in the following code segment?

```
JFrame f = new JFrame();
f.addMouseListener(new MouseAdapter() {
  public void MousePressed(MouseEvent e) {
    System.out.println("Mouse pressed");
  }
});
f.setDefaultCloseOperation(JFrame.EXIT_ON_CLOSE);
f.setSize(500, 500);
f.setVisible(true);
```

8. Write a program that draws a small geometrical shape at the position where the mouse is clicked in a window.

9. Write a program that writes the text "Mouse pressed" in a window when the mouse is pressed, and erases it when the mouse is released.

10. Write a program that changes the color of a panel to white when a mouse enters it, and to black when the mouse exits it.

11. Write a program to move a line of text up, down, or sideways in a window using the arrow keys.

12. Modify the code in the ball game (provided in the JavaBook/src/ball-game directory on the CD-ROM) so that the bat can be controlled using the arrow keys.

13. Modify the code in the ball game (provided in the JavaBook/src/ball-game directory on the CD-ROM) to create custom dialog boxes using JDialog instead of JOptionPane.

14. Examine the Controller and View classes (in the JavaBook/src/com/programwithjava/animation directory on the CD-ROM) that were used to animate the car and airplane in Chapter 6.

Image Manipulation

15. Write a program to display a photograph in a window. Clicking a corner of the photograph and dragging it with the mouse should resize the photograph.

16. Write a program to display a set of photographs as a slide show. The viewer should be able to specify the duration for which each photograph should be displayed.

References

1. "Java™ Platform, Standard Edition 6, API Specification." Web. <http://download.oracle.com/javase/6/docs/api/>.

2. "The Java™ Tutorials." Web. <http://download.oracle.com/javase/tutorial/>.

3. Eckel, Bruce. *Thinking in Java.* Upper Saddle River, NJ: Prentice Hall, 2006. Print.

4. Anderson, Julie, and Herve Franceschi. *Java 6 Illuminated: An Active Learning Approach.* Sudbury, MA: Jones and Bartlett, 2008. Print.

5. Knudsen, Jonathan. *Java 2D Graphics.* Beijing: O'Reilly, 1999. Print.

CHAPTER 14

Multithreaded Programming

CHAPTER CONTENTS

In this chapter, you will learn how to create and run multiple threads in a program. The examples explain thread programming concepts using audio and video. In order to run these examples, you must install QuickTime and QuickTime for Java (QTJ) on your computer. The instructions for installing these tools are provided in this chapter.

14.1   What Is Multithreading?

Even if you have never worked with threads, the programs that you have been writing contain at least two threads: main and **garbage collector**. The main thread executes the code in the main method from the beginning to the end of this method. The garbage collector thread runs only occasionally; it executes a garbage collection algorithm that removes unused objects from the heap. Both of these threads are created automatically by the JVM.

A **thread** is a flow of execution in a program. Consider the sequence in which the statements in the main method are executed—this represents the flow of execution of the main thread. A multithreaded program has multiple threads, each with its own flow of execution. The threads share resources and can execute independently of each other. As an analogy, a single-threaded program is like a kitchen with one cook, whereas a multithreaded program is like a kitchen with many cooks. The cooks share the resources in the kitchen, but each cook can work independently to carry out a certain task.

One reason why threads are useful is because there can be a division of tasks between different threads in a program. There is a separate thread for garbage collection; as a result, the programmer is freed from having to worry about how and when the garbage collection takes place. But why not use a different program for this purpose instead? Threads have the advantage that all of the threads in a program share the heap. Therefore, they share the objects that are created by other threads in the same program. Threads also share files that have been opened in the program. Different programs, however, have different heaps, and so sharing data between programs requires more effort from the programmer.

Another reason for using threads is to improve the responsiveness of a program. For example, when a GUI is created, an **event dispatch thread** is created automatically. This thread waits until the user performs some action on a component (such as clicks a button on the GUI), and then executes the associated event-handling code for that component. If a GUI-based program contains a single thread, and this thread is tied up performing a lengthy computation, the program will take a long time to respond to a user action. With multithreading, however, separate threads can be used for computation-intensive tasks and GUI event handling.

If the computer has a single processor, only one thread can execute on it at a time and other threads must wait. This is like a kitchen with many cooks but a single stove. Threads take turns to run on the processor so that their execution can be interleaved. This gives the impression that the threads are running in parallel, but the program cannot run any faster than it would with a single thread. On a system with more than one processor, a multithreaded program can run faster because the threads can execute in parallel on the different processors, in the same manner that meals could be prepared faster in a kitchen with multiple cooks and stoves.

The programmer can explicitly create and manipulate multiple threads in a program using the methods in the `Thread` class. In this chapter, we will discuss this class using media-based examples.

14.2   Playing Movies on the QuickTime Player

A custom class called `MoviePlayer` is provided in the `com.programwithjava .movie` package to make it easy to play audio and video from a Java program on Apple's QuickTime player. The class `MoviePlayer` is written using **QuickTime for Java** (**QTJ**), which is a Java-like multimedia framework that provides access to QuickTime. You will need to install QTJ, if it is not already installed on your computer. You do not have to learn QTJ, however, unless you wish to extend the functionality of the `MoviePlayer` class. An excellent reference on QTJ is provided at the end of this chapter.

14.2.1   Installing QuickTime and QTJ

Before you start working on the examples in this chapter, you must have QuickTime and QTJ installed on your computer. QuickTime is available for Mac OS X and Windows but not Linux. You can download QuickTime from this link:

```
http://www.apple.com/quicktime/
```

Follow the instructions to install QuickTime (doing so will install QTJ as well). You should install QuickTime only after you have installed the Java runtime environment.

On the Windows system, you can verify that QTJ is installed by checking that the file QTJava.zip is present in the lib/ext directory of the Java installation in your computer. For example, if the Java runtime environment is installed in C:/Program Files/jdk1.6.0_21, you will find the file QTJava.zip in the following directory:

```
C:/Program Files/jdk1.6.0_21/jre/lib/ext/QTJava.zip
```

Alternately, if the file is placed elsewhere, you can copy it manually to this same location. (Do not try to unzip this file.) You must also update the PATH environment variable on your Windows computer (if it not automatically updated) so that it contains the path C:/Program Files/jdk1.6.0_21/jre/lib/ext. On Mac OS X, the QTJava.zip file is placed in the System/Library/Java/Extensions directory.

14.2.2   The MoviePlayer Class

We will use the methods provided in the MoviePlayer class to play media on a QuickTime player from our programs. These methods are shown in Figure 14–1. In our programs, we will use media objects of type Movie, which is a class defined in the quicktime.std.movies package. (In QuickTime, a "movie" refers to any type of media, such as audio, video, text, and graphics.)

Suppose that you want to play a video. First, you create a player using the constructor:

```
MoviePlayer player = new MoviePlayer("");
```

The next step is to create a Movie object of the video that you want to play. Suppose that the video is stored in the file myVideo.mov. This step creates a movie:

```
Movie movie = player.createMovie("myVideo.mov");
```

Calling the playVideo method of MoviePlayer creates a window (with the argument to its constructor set as the name of the window) in which the video is displayed:

```
player.playVideo(movie);
```

You can use the playAudio method similarly to play audio files.

MoviePlayer	
MoviePlayer(String title) throws Exception	Constructor creates a player that can play movies.
Movie createMovie(String filename) throws Exception	Creates an object of type Movie from the media file whose name is passed in as an argument to this method.
void playVideo(Movie m) throws Exception	Starts playing the video m in a window.
void playAudio(Movie m) throws Exception	Starts playing the audio m.
void stop(Movie m) throws Exception	Stops playing the movie m.
void setStartTime(Movie m, int startTime) throws Exception	Specifies the time duration in seconds (startTime) from the current time when the movie m should start playing.
void setStopTime(Movie m, int stopTime) throws Exception	Specifies the duration in seconds (stopTime) from the current time when the movie m should stop playing.
long getStopTime(Movie m) throws Exception	Returns the time (in seconds) when the movie m will stop.
long getStartTime(Movie m) throws Exception	Returns the time (in seconds) when the movie m will start.
void close()	Closes the program.

Figure 14–1

Class MoviePlayer in the com.programwithjava. movie package.

14.3 The Thread Class

The java.lang.Thread class contains many constructors and methods for creating and using threads. Two methods in this class are shown in Figure 14–2.

We first explain how you can use these two methods, and then we introduce additional methods and constructors throughout the chapter.

Thread	
static Thread currentThread()	Returns a reference to the thread that calls this method.
String getName()	Returns the name of this thread.

Figure 14–2

Some methods in the Thread class.

As mentioned earlier, the `main` thread is created automatically and executes all the statements in the `main` method sequentially. After the last statement has been executed, the `main` thread terminates. Consider the following program:

```
package multithreadedprogramming;

public class MainThreadDemo {
   public static void main(String[] args) {
     System.out.println("Hello");
     System.out.println("This is " +Thread.currentThread().getName());
     System.out.println("Goodbye");
   }
}
```

The thread executing the `main` method prints out its name when the `getName` method is called in the second line. The following output shows that this is the thread named `main`:

```
Hello
This is main
Goodbye
```

A program can contain multiple threads in which each thread executes a different piece of code; it can also contain multiple threads that are executing the same code. An existing thread can create a new thread. For example, the `main` thread can create other threads, which in turn can create still other threads.

14.4   Simplified Model of a Computer

Before we discuss the rest of the `Thread` API, it will be helpful to examine a simplified model of the computer. The computer has a processor with three queues called **ready**, **sleep**, and **blocked**, as shown in Figure 14–3. Each queue can hold multiple threads. A thread is either running on the processor or waiting in one of these three queues.

Threads take turns running on the processor, waiting in the **ready queue** while the processor is busy with another thread. A thread that is running on the processor can **suspend** itself for a specified duration of time. A suspended thread releases the processor and moves to the **sleep queue**. It stays in this queue until the specified time duration has elapsed, after which the thread is moved back to the ready queue. There may be several other threads in the ready queue waiting for the processor, and so the thread that

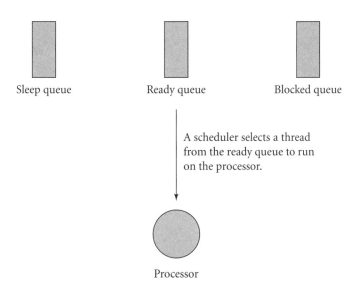

Figure 14–3
Simplified model of processor with three queues.

was woken up might have to wait until it is scheduled to run on the processor again. A thread that is executing on the processor might need a resource (such as an I/O device) that is not available. This thread is removed from the processor and put in the **blocked queue**. It is then moved into the ready queue when the resource becomes available.

A **scheduler** decides which thread in the ready queue should run next on the processor. The scheduling algorithm used depends on the JVM and the operating system on which the code will be run. Therefore, threads in a program might run in different orders on different platforms. Every thread has a priority assigned to it, where the priorities usually range from 1 (lowest) to 10 (highest). On some platforms, one thread is selected from among several threads having the same priority to run until it completes execution or blocks. Other platforms might have a variation in which threads with the same priority take turns to execute for a fixed amount of time on the processor, instead of waiting for a particular thread to finish execution first.

With this background, we are now ready to examine the Thread class.

14.5 The sleep Method

A thread can suspend itself for a certain amount of time by calling the sleep method in the Thread class. The sleep method is shown in Figure 14–4. It is especially useful to suspend a thread that must carry out a task periodically.

Figure 14–4

The sleep method.

Thread	
static void sleep(long milliseconds) throws InterruptedException	Suspends the calling thread for the specified number of milliseconds.

Figure 14–5

A thread that invokes its sleep method is removed from the processor and put into the sleep queue.

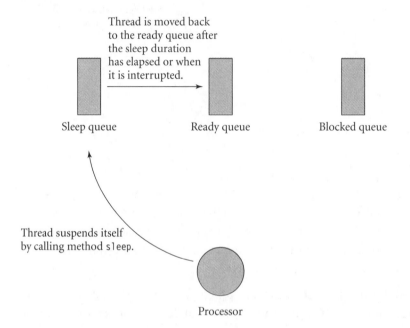

For example, consider a thread that needs to print out messages at regular intervals. It can do so by displaying the message and then sleeping for the required duration. The thread calling sleep is put in the *sleep* queue, as shown in Figure 14–5. The processor can now execute another thread selected by the scheduler, and thus it can be used efficiently by multiple threads.

Example 1

In this example, the sleep method is used to prevent a thread from closing a program prematurely.

```
package multithreadedprogramming;
import com.programwithjava.movie.MoviePlayer;
import quicktime.std.movies.*;
```

```
public class ThreadSleep {
  public static void main(String[] args) {
    try {
      // create a movie player
      MoviePlayer player = new MoviePlayer("");

      // create a Movie object
      Movie video = player.createMovie("video/SanFrancisco.mov");

      System.out.println("Playing video");
      // play the video
      player.playVideo(video);

      // main thread waits for 142 seconds
      Thread.sleep(142000);

      // close the program
      player.close();
    } catch(Exception e) {
      e.printStackTrace();
    }
  }
}
```

The main thread executes each of the statements in main. The first statement in main creates a movie player called player:

```
MoviePlayer player = new MoviePlayer("");
```

A Movie object called video is created next from the SanFrancisco.mov file:

```
Movie video = player.createMovie("video/SanFrancisco.mov");
```

The player can start playing the movie using the playVideo method:

```
player.playVideo(video);
```

After the main thread has executed the preceding statement, it can execute the next statement without waiting for the video display to finish:

```
Thread.sleep(142000);
```

This will suspend the main thread for 142,000 milliseconds, or 142 seconds. The unit of time provided as an argument to method sleep is in milliseconds. Finally, after this time duration has elapsed, the main thread executes the last statement, which will close the program. It is important to note that a thread can only suspend itself and not any other thread by calling the method sleep.

Before running the program, copy the file SanFrancisco.mov from the JavaBook/video library on the CD-ROM into a new directory called video that is created inside the JavaBook directory on your computer. Run the program to view the video. To understand how suspending the thread affects the program, comment out the Thread.sleep statement in main, and rerun the program. You will see that the window flashes on the screen very briefly and then closes. Why does this happen? The main thread is not suspended now; thus it executes the statement to close the program right after it has started the video display. As a result, the video does not play. ■

Although the sleep time is specified as *t* milliseconds, a thread might also have to wait longer than *t* milliseconds to run again on the processor if other threads in the ready queue are scheduled ahead of it. A thread that is sleeping can be woken up before *t* milliseconds have elapsed, using an interrupt. We will discuss the use of interrupts later in the chapter.

> A thread that calls *sleep* with an argument of *t* milliseconds will be suspended for **at least** *t* milliseconds (unless it is interrupted).

As an exercise, write a program in which the main thread displays a message every 1 second.

14.6   Creating a New Thread

An existing thread can create a new thread using the constructors shown in Figure 14–6. For example, the following statement creates a thread with the name "New thread":

```
Thread t1 = new Thread("New thread");
```

You will see how to use the constructors that take a Runnable interface as an argument a little later.

After a thread has been created, it is put in the *ready* queue by calling its start method, as shown in Figure 14–7. These two statements create a new thread t1 and start it:

```
Thread t1 = new Thread();
t1.start();
```

Figure 14–6

Constructors and methods to create and run a new thread.

Thread	
Thread()	Constructor creates a thread without a name.
Thread(String name)	Constructor creates a thread with the given name.
Thread(Runnable obj)	Constructor creates a thread that executes the run method of obj.
Thread(Runnable obj, String name)	Constructor creates a thread with the given name that executes the run method of obj.
void start()	Puts this thread in the ready queue.
void run()	Empty method that must be overridden by descendants of Thread.

Figure 14–7

Starting a new thread.

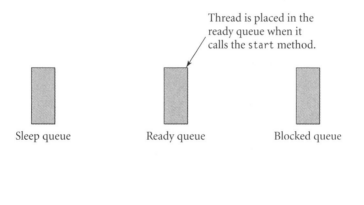

Thread is placed in the ready queue when it calls the start method.

Sleep queue   Ready queue   Blocked queue

Processor

A thread must not invoke its start method more than once or after it has completed execution.

When the thread is scheduled to run on the processor, it executes the code in its run method. The run method in class Thread is an empty method. The programmer must override this method in the new class so that a thread that executes this method does some useful work. The next example shows how to do this.

Example 2

The class TwoThreadsDemo extends Thread and overrides the run method of the latter. The main thread creates an instance of TwoThreadsDemo called newThread. Can you determine which thread (main or newThread) executes the code to play the video in the following program?

```java
package multithreadedprogramming;
import com.programwithjava.movie.MoviePlayer;
import quicktime.std.movies.*;

public class TwoThreadsDemo extends Thread {
  public void run() {
    try {
      // create a movie player
      MoviePlayer player = new MoviePlayer("");

      // create a Movie object
      Movie video = player.createMovie("video/SanFrancisco.mov");

      System.out.println("Playing video");
      // play the video
      player.playVideo(video);

      // wait for 30 seconds
      Thread.sleep(30000);

      // close the program
      player.close();
    } catch (Exception e) {
      e.printStackTrace();
    }
  }

  public static void main(String[] args) {
    // main Thread executes this code
    TwoThreadsDemo newThread = new TwoThreadsDemo();
    newThread.start();

    for (int i = 0; i < 100; i++) {
      System.out.println( "Main thread writes to console");
    }
  }
}
```

Solution: When newThread is run on the processor, it will execute the code inside the run method of class TwoThreadsDemo. The main thread, on the other hand, will execute the for loop in main and then exit the system. Therefore, newThread plays the video in class TwoThreadsDemo, whereas the main thread plays it in class ThreadSleep.   ∎

Never write code assuming that threads will execute in a certain order because doing so will affect the portability, and even the *correctness*, of your program. For example, in the preceding program, the main thread could execute before newThread, or vice versa. If we created multiple threads that were writing to the console, their execution could be interleaved, or they could execute sequentially in some arbitrary order. The important point to remember is that the programmer must not make any assumptions about the execution order.

> A key point to remember when writing a multithreaded program is that the program must run correctly regardless of the order in which the threads are scheduled.

14.7   Thread Names

Threads are given names such as *Thread-0, Thread-1, Thread-2,* and so forth at the time they are created. You can assign a different name to a thread when it is created by using the constructor that takes a parameter of type String. The two methods shown in Figure 14–8 can be used to modify or get an existing thread's name.

The following example shows how to use these methods.

```
              Thread

void setName(String n)    Changes the name of this thread to n.
String getName()          Returns the name of this thread.
```

Figure 14–8

Methods to set or get a thread's name.

Example 3

Examine the code in ThreadNamesDemo. You will see that two threads of this type are created in main. Both of these threads execute the same code in the run method of ThreadNamesDemo. Why does each window have a different title?

```java
package multithreadedprogramming;
import com.programwithjava.movie.MoviePlayer;
import quicktime.std.movies.*;

public class ThreadNamesDemo extends Thread {
  public void run() {
    try {
      // create a movie player
      MoviePlayer player = new MoviePlayer("Thread name:"
+Thread.currentThread().getName());

      // create a Movie object
      Movie video = player.createMovie("video/SanFrancisco.mov");

      System.out.println("Playing video");
      // play the video
      player.playVideo(video);

      // wait for 30 seconds
      Thread.sleep(30000);

      // close the program
      player.close();
    } catch (Exception e) {
      e.printStackTrace();
    }
  }

  public static void main(String[] args) {
    // main Thread executes this code
    ThreadNamesDemo newThreadA = new ThreadNamesDemo();
    newThreadA.start();

    ThreadNamesDemo newThreadB = new ThreadNamesDemo();
    newThreadB.start();

    for (int i = 0; i < 100; i++)
      System.out.println( Thread.currentThread().getName() +" writes to
console");
    System.out.println("Main thread exits");
  }
}
```

Figure 14–9

The two windows display the same output but have different titles.

Solution: The `main` thread creates two new threads, both of which execute the `run` method of the class `ThreadNamesDemo`. What each thread does differently, however, is create a player with the same name as itself. This is done using the `getName` method in the following statement:

```
MoviePlayer player = new MoviePlayer("Thread name:"
+Thread.currentThread().getName());
```

Therefore, each video is played in a window that is labeled with the name of the thread that created it. When you run the program, both windows are created at the same location in the screen, and you must move the top window to a different location on the screen to see the one below it. Check that the titles of the two windows are different. Figure 14–9 shows a snapshot of the output.

Use the `setName` method to change the name of the `main` thread before the second `for` loop and rerun the program. Observe how the output changes.   ∎

14.8   More on the Thread Class

Some other methods in the `Thread` class are shown in Figure 14–10. The `isAlive` method determines whether or not a thread has terminated. The `getPriority` method returns the thread's priority, and `setPriority` changes the priority to the desired value, which should lie in the range 1 to 10. A thread that is currently executing on the processor can call the `yield`

Figure 14–10

Some other methods in the Thread class.

Thread	
`void interrupt()`	Interrupts this thread.
`boolean isAlive()`	Returns true only if this thread has not terminated.
`final void join() throws InterruptedException`	Suspends the thread that is currently executing until this thread exits.
`boolean isInterrupted()`	Returns true if this thread has been interrupted; otherwise, it returns false.
`int getPriority()`	Returns the priority of this thread.
`void setPriority(int priority)`	Sets the priority of this thread.
`static void yield()`	Suspends this thread, which is currently executing, by putting it back in the ready queue.

method to release the processor voluntarily so that other threads can run on it. This is especially useful if a thread performs lengthy computations on the processor because it gives other waiting threads a chance to run as well. The suspended thread is then put back in the ready queue. A thread that performs a long computation (without invoking sleep) can call the isInterruped method periodically to determine whether it has been interrupted.

We discuss the interrupt and join methods next.

14.9   Interrupting a Thread

A thread terminates after it has completed executing its run method. Sometimes it might be necessary to terminate a thread prematurely, or otherwise change what the thread is doing. These tasks can be accomplished using interrupts. (The interrupt method in class Thread was shown in Figure 14–10.)

A thread t1 that is executing on the processor can interrupt another thread t2 by executing this statement:

```
t2.interrupt();
```

Thread t2 receives the interrupt when it executes a method such as sleep or join. (You will see how join works a little later in the chapter.) These two methods throw an exception of type InterruptedException. The interrupted thread then executes the exception-handling code. For example, suppose that thread t2 is executing the code in this try block:

```
try {
  // statements before sleep
```

```
  Thread.sleep(5000);
  // statements after sleep
} catch (InterruptedException e) {
  // thread executes this code after it receives the interrupt
}
```

Furthermore, suppose that t1 interrupts t2 before the latter has executed its sleep method. Thread t2 will continue executing all of the statements until it reaches method sleep. This method will throw an InterruptedException because t2 has been interrupted. Hence, t2 will then skip the remaining code after this method in the try block and execute the interrupt-handling code in the catch block instead.

A thread is allowed to interrupt itself. Interrupting a thread that has already terminated has no effect.

Example 4

Examine the class ThreadInterruptDemo to understand how interrupts work. Two threads are created here: main and audioThread. The main thread sleeps for 35 seconds after it has created and started audioThread. The thread audio-Thread is suspended using the sleep method after it has created a player to play an audio file. The main thread interrupts audioThread after 35 seconds have elapsed. When audioThread is interrupted, it will execute the exception-handling code to close the program. If the main thread did not interrupt audioThread, the audio would continue playing for up to an hour or until its end.

```
package multithreadedprogramming;
import com.programwithjava.movie.MoviePlayer;
import quicktime.std.movies.*;

public class ThreadInterruptDemo {
  public static void main(String[] args) {
    // create a thread to play audio
    Thread audioThread = new Thread() {
      MoviePlayer player;
      Movie audio;
      public void run() {
        try {
          // create a movie player and play audio
          player = new MoviePlayer("");
          audio = player.createMovie("audio/hammockFight.mp3");
          this.setName("AudioThread");
          player.playAudio(audio);
```

hammockFight.mp3 courtesy of
Kevin MacLeod (incompetech.com)

```
        Thread.sleep(3600000); // play time is one hour
        System.out.println("Thread " +Thread.currentThread().getName() +
" is terminating normally");
      } catch (InterruptedException e) {
        System.out.println("Thread " +Thread.currentThread().getName()
+ " is interrupted");
        player.close();
      } catch (Exception e) {
        e.printStackTrace();
      }
    }
  };

  // start the new thread
  audioThread.start();

  try {
    // main thread waits for 35 seconds
    Thread.sleep(35000);
    System.out.println("main thread is interrupting AudioThread");
    audioThread.interrupt();
  } catch (InterruptedException e) {
    e.printStackTrace();
  }
  }
}
```

Before running this program, copy the file hammockFight.mp3 from the Jav-
aBook/audio directory on the CD-ROM into the JavaBook/audio directory on
your computer. The program plays the audio and displays this output:

```
main thread is interrupting AudioThread
Thread AudioThread is interrupted
```

The main thread creates and starts audioThread and then waits for 35 seconds
before interrupting it. As a result, audioThread executes the code in the catch
block and this statement is never executed:

```
System.out.println("Thread " +Thread.currentThread().getName() + " is
terminating normally");
```

Note that we have created a new thread in this example using an anonymous class. Here, audioThread references an instance of an anonymous class

that extends class Thread. The run method of this anonymous class overrides that of class Thread.   ∎

14.10   The join Method

The join method is used to make one thread wait until another thread exits. Suppose that thread t1 is currently executing on the processor, and it executes the following statement:

```
t2.join();
```

This will cause t1 to pause execution until t2 terminates.

Example 5

The program ThreadJoinDemo shows how join works. Two threads, videoThread and audioThread, are created in main. The thread videoThread plays video for a random amount of time. The main thread waits until videoThread quits using the following statement:

```
videoThread.join();
```

The main thread then interrupts audioThread to stop the audio. Although videoThread and audioThread execute independently of each other, their activities are coordinated by the main thread using the method join:

```
package multithreadedprogramming;
import com.programwithjava.movie.MoviePlayer;
import java.util.*;
import quicktime.std.movies.*;

public class ThreadJoinDemo {
  public static void main(String[] args) {
    // create a thread to play video
    Thread videoThread = new Thread() {
      public void run() {
        try {
          MoviePlayer player = new MoviePlayer("Movie Player");
          Movie video = player.createMovie("video/SanFrancisco.mov");
          player.playVideo(video);

          // wait for a random number of seconds, then close video
          Random r = new Random();
          int time = r.nextInt(30);
```

```
            System.out.println("Video display time in seconds = " +time);
            Thread.sleep(time * 1000);
            player.close();
          } catch (Exception e) {
            e.printStackTrace();
          }
        }
      };

      // create another thread to play audio
      Thread audioThread = new Thread() {
        MoviePlayer player;
        Movie audio;
        public void run() {
          try {
            // create a movie player and play audio
            player = new MoviePlayer("");
            audio = player.createMovie("audio/ecossaiseInEFlat.mp3");
            this.setName("Audio Thread");
            player.playAudio(audio);
            Thread.sleep(3600000); // sleep time is one hour
          } catch (InterruptedException e) {
            System.out.println("Thread " +Thread.currentThread().getName() +
" is interrupted");

            // close the player when the interrupt is received
            player.close();
          } catch (Exception e) {
            e.printStackTrace();
          }
        }
      };

      // start the threads
      videoThread.start();
      audioThread.start();

      try {
        System.out.println("main thread is waiting for videoThread to
exit..");
        videoThread.join();

        System.out.println("main thread is interrupting audioThread");
        audioThread.interrupt();
```

ecossaiseInEFlat.mp3
courtesy of Kevin MacLeod
(incompetech.com)

```
    } catch (InterruptedException e) {
      e.printStackTrace();
    }
  }
}
```

14.11   Creating a New Thread Using the Runnable Interface

As you have already seen in the TwoThreadsDemo class, one way to create a thread is by extending class Thread. However, if a class already extends another class, it cannot also extend Thread because Java does not allow multiple inheritance. The Runnable interface provides another way to create a thread:

```
public interface Runnable {
  public void run();
}
```

A class that implements Runnable must implement the run method in this interface. A thread can be created by passing an instance of this class to the following thread constructor:

> **Thread (Runnable obj)**—a constructor that creates a thread that executes the run method of obj.

For example, suppose you want to create a thread that executes the code in a class called NewClass, defined here:

```
class NewClass extends SomeClass {
  // code
}
```

First, you modify NewClass to implement the Runnable interface:

```
class NewClass extends SomeClass implements Runnable {
  // code
  public void run {
    // code
  }
}
```

Next, you create an instance of NewClass and pass it to the Thread(Runnable) constructor:

```
NewClass object = new NewClass();
Thread t1 = new Thread (object);
```

This will create a new thread t1 that executes the run method of object. We say that t1 executes in the *body* of object. There can be *multiple* threads executing in the body of an object, as this next example shows.

Example 6

How many threads execute in the body of object that is of type Runnable? What does this program do?

```
package multithreadedprogramming;
import com.programwithjava.movie.MoviePlayer;
import quicktime.std.movies.Movie;

public class RunnableDemo implements Runnable {
  public void run() {
    try {
      // every thread that executes this code creates a separate player
      MoviePlayer player = new MoviePlayer("");

      // create a Movie object
      Movie video = player.createMovie("video/SanFrancisco.mov");

      System.out.println("Playing video");
      // play the video
      player.playVideo(video);

      // wait for 10 seconds
      Thread.sleep(10000);

      // close the program
      player.close();
    } catch (Exception e) {
      e.printStackTrace();
    }
  }

  public static void main(String[] args) {
    Runnable object = new RunnableDemo();

    for (int i = 0; i < 2; i++) {
      // uses the Thread(Runnable) constructor
      Thread newThread = new Thread(object);
```

```
        newThread.start();
    }
  }
}
```

Solution: The `main` thread first creates `object` that is of type `Runnable`. It then creates two threads that execute in the body of this object that is, execute the object's `run` method. Each of the two threads creates a different player, so that each video displays in a different window. Note that both windows are created at the same location in the screen, and so you must move the window on the top to a different location to view the one below it.   ■

14.12   Local Versus Instance Variables

You already know that there are three types of variables in a class: local, instance, and static. When multiple threads execute a program, these variables are either private to a thread or shared between threads, as described here:

- Local variables are *private* to a thread. Every thread has a separate copy of a local variable.

- Instance variables are *shared between threads of an object.* When one thread modifies an instance variable, the changes are visible to all of the other threads in that object.

- Static variables are *shared among all threads in a program.*

Examine the code in the `run` method of the class `RunnableDemo`. Note that `player` and `video` are local variables in this class because they are declared inside a method. Therefore, when the two threads execute this code, each thread creates its own player. As a result, the video appears in two different windows.

The `SharedVariablesDemo` class shows how instance variables are shared between threads. The code is nearly the same as in `RunnableDemo`, with the difference that `filename` is an instance variable in this class.

Example 7

Why is the same filename displayed in separate windows?

```
package multithreadedprogramming;
import com.programwithjava.movie.MoviePlayer;
```

```
import quicktime.std.movies.Movie;

public class SharedVariablesDemo implements Runnable {
  private String filename;

  public void setFile(String s) {
    filename = s;
  }

  public void run() {
    try {

      MoviePlayer player = new MoviePlayer(filename);

      // create a Movie object
      Movie video = player.createMovie(filename);

      System.out.println("Playing video");
      // play the video
      player.playVideo(video);

      // wait for 10 seconds
      Thread.sleep(10000);

      // close the program
      player.close();
    } catch (Exception e) {
      e.printStackTrace();
    }
  }

  public static void main(String[] args) {
    SharedVariablesDemo object = new SharedVariablesDemo();
    object.setFile("video/SanFrancisco.mov");

    for (int i = 0; i < 2; i++) {
      Thread newThread = new Thread(object);
      newThread.start();
    }
  }
}
```

Solution: Both videos are displayed in separate windows because the local variable player is not shared between the two threads. However, the instance field filename *is* shared between the two threads. This field is passed to the MoviePlayer constructor; thus, both the window titles are the same.

As an exercise, modify this program so that each thread plays a different video by prompting the user to enter the name of a video file and storing it in filename. Declare filename as a local variable instead of an instance field.   ∎

14.13   Synchronizing Threads

Java has a mechanism, known as *monitor lock*, that coordinates access to resources shared by multiple threads. A **monitor lock** is an internal lock possessed by every object. A thread that wants exclusive access to an object must acquire this lock. Only one thread can lock an object at a time, and contending threads must wait for the lock to be released by the thread that holds it.

The monitor lock can be acquired using a *synchronized statement.* A **synchronized statement** contains the keyword synchronized followed by the name of the object that a thread wants to lock:

```
synchronized (objectName) {
  // only one thread at a time can execute
  // the code in this block
}
```

To lock the object that a thread currently executes in, replace the object's name with the this keyword:

```
synchronized (this) {
  // code
}
```

A thread releases the lock automatically once it exits the synchronized block.

Example 8

The SynchronizationDemo program shows how synchronized statements can be used to ensure that only one thread at a time can play audio. Two threads, named red and blue, execute in the body of an object named obj. The red thread runs first, acquires obj's lock, and starts playing audio. The blue thread runs 2 seconds later and tries to acquire obj's lock as well, but is blocked by red. The thread red plays audio for 5 seconds and then exits the synchronized block, at which point it releases obj's lock. Now, thread blue acquires the lock and enters the synchronized block to play the audio. Note that blue and red cannot play audio simultaneously. Check what happens if the synchronized statement is removed:

```
package multithreadedprogramming;
import com.programwithjava.movie.MoviePlayer;
import quicktime.std.movies.Movie;

public class SynchronizationDemo implements Runnable {
  private MoviePlayer player; // shared between threads

  public SynchronizationDemo() {
    try {
      player = new MoviePlayer("Thread name:"
+Thread.currentThread().getName());
    } catch (Exception e) {
      e.printStackTrace();
    }
  }

  public void run() {
    try {
      // create a Movie object
      Movie audio = player.createMovie("audio/groovy.wav");

      synchronized(this) {
        // play audio for 5 seconds and then
        // stop it and wait another 5 seconds
        player.playAudio(audio);
        Thread.sleep(5000);
        player.stop(audio);
        Thread.sleep(5000);
        System.out.println("Thread "+Thread.currentThread().getName() +" is
exiting");
      }
    } catch (Exception e) {
      e.printStackTrace();
    }
  }

  public static void main(String[] args) {
```

```
    Runnable obj = new SynchronizationDemo();

    Thread red = new Thread(obj, "red");
    red.start();

    // main thread waits for 2 seconds
    try {
      Thread.sleep(2000);
    } catch (InterruptedException e) {
      e.printStackTrace();
    }

    Thread blue = new Thread(obj, "blue");
    blue.start();

    // main thread waits for blue thread to exit
    try {
      blue.join();
    } catch (InterruptedException e) {
      e.printStackTrace();
    }

    System.exit(0);
  }
}
```

Solution: In the main method, the main thread first creates the thread red, and then waits for 2 seconds before creating thread blue. Thread red executes the run method of obj, and acquires the monitor lock of this object in the synchronized statement. This prevents thread blue from playing the audio until red releases the lock. If you comment out the synchronized statement and rerun the program, you will hear both threads play the audio together for some time. ∎

A method is synchronized by adding the synchronized keyword before the method's return type. Only one thread can be executing a **synchronized method** at a time. For example, we can use this synchronized method in SynchronizationDemo instead of the synchronized statement:

```
public synchronized void playMusic() throws Exception {
  player.playAudio(audio);
  Thread.sleep(5000);
  player.stop(audio);
  Thread.sleep(5000);
}
```

A thread can acquire exclusive access to static fields using the **static synchronized** statement or method:

```
public static synchronized methodName () {
  // shared static fields can be modified here
}
```

The run method should not be synchronized. What are the implications of using a synchronized run method?

In the next section, we discuss why (and when) it is necessary to synchronize threads.

14.14   Problems with Threads

Although multithreading has its advantages, it can also lead to problems. We have seen that threads share instance variables of a class. Threads share static fields as well. When multiple threads try to *modify* an instance variable or a static field at the same time without using synchronization, a problem known as a **race condition** can occur. Race conditions result in unpredictable program outputs, as the next example shows.

Example 9

RaceConditionDemo shows an example of a race condition. It contains a boolean variable called flag. Several threads call the method playMusic in run. In playMusic, a thread sets the value of flag to false at the start of the method, sleeps for some time, and then checks whether the value of flag is true. (The music is played only if flag is true.) flag had previously been set to false; as a result, it appears that flag can never be true, and so each thread should exit the method without playing any music. Run the program and check what happens.

```
package multithreadedprogramming;
import com.programwithjava.movie.MoviePlayer;
import quicktime.std.movies.Movie;

public class RaceConditionDemo extends Thread {
  private MoviePlayer player;
  private Movie audio;
  private boolean flag;

  public RaceConditionDemo() {
    try {
```

```
      player = new MoviePlayer("Thread name:"
+Thread.currentThread().getName());
      audio = player.createMovie("audio/blues.wav");
    } catch (Exception e) {
      e.printStackTrace();
    }
  }

  public void run() {
    try {
      playMusic();
    } catch (Exception e) {
      e.printStackTrace();
    }
  }

  public void playMusic() throws Exception {
    flag = false;
    Thread.sleep(2000);
    if (flag == true){
      player.playAudio(audio);
      // play for 10 seconds
      Thread.sleep(10000);
      player.stop(audio);
    }
    System.out.println("Thread "+Thread.currentThread().getName() +" is
exiting");
    flag = true; // set flag to true before exiting method
  }

  public static void main(String[] args) {
    RaceConditionDemo obj = new RaceConditionDemo();
    for (int i = 0; i < 10; i++) {
      Thread newThread = new Thread(obj);
      newThread.start();
      try {
        Thread.sleep(1000);
      } catch (InterruptedException e) {
        e.printStackTrace();
      }
    }
    // main thread waits for 20 seconds
    try {
        Thread.sleep(20000);
```

```
    } catch (InterruptedException e) {
       e.printStackTrace();
    }
    System.exit(0);
  }
}
```

Solution: Upon running the program, you will note that some, but not all, of the threads are able to play music. The problem is that when multiple threads are modifying the same variable together, their operations might be interleaved so that the output is unpredictable. In this program, flag is a shared variable. Suppose that Thread2 sets the value of flag to false and goes to sleep. Thread1, which is also executing the same method, wakes up and sets flag to true before exiting the method. When Thread2 wakes up and checks flag, it will see that flag is true and start playing the audio. If we vary the number of threads and their sleep times in this program, the output changes *unpredictably* due to the race condition.

To correct this problem, either make playMusic a synchronized method, or enclose all of its statements within a synchronized block.   ∎

> It is important to remember threads must modify shared variables only inside *synchronized blocks* or *synchronized methods* so that race conditions can be prevented.

Two other types of problems that can occur in a multithreaded program are *deadlock* and *starvation*. A **deadlock** is said to have occurred when all threads are holding a resource, as well as waiting for a resource that is held by another thread, such that no thread is able to execute. Figure 14–11 shows an example of a deadlock. Thread1 holds Lock1 and is blocked waiting for Lock2. On the other hand, Thread2 holds Lock2 and is blocked waiting for Lock1. Neither thread can proceed; thus a deadlock has occurred.

Starvation occurs when a thread is not in a deadlock but is unable to run on the processor for other reasons, such as the priority level of other threads in that program. If higher priority threads are always selected to run on the processor, a low priority thread may never get a chance to do so, resulting in starvation.

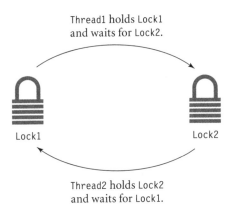

Thread1 holds Lock1
and waits for Lock2.

Lock1   Lock2

Thread2 holds Lock2
and waits for Lock1.

Figure 14–11

Two threads in a deadlock.

14.15 . Summary

In this chapter, we discussed the basics of multithreaded programming in Java. A new thread can be created by extending class Thread and overriding its run method. Another way to create a thread is by implementing the Runnable interface. This thread will execute the run method of the Runnable object. A thread that needs to run periodically can suspend itself by calling the sleep method. Shared resources must be accessed within synchronized blocks or methods. The programmer should be aware of potential problems in a multithreaded program, such as race conditions, deadlocks, and starvation.

Exercises

1. What is a thread?

2. Name two threads that are created automatically in a Java program. What is the purpose of each?

3. Explain the two ways in which a thread can be created.

4. What is the job of a scheduler? Why is it critical to ensure that the multithreaded program run correctly regardless of the order in which threads are scheduled?

5. What does the sleep method do? Why is this method declared as static?

6. What is a monitor? Explain how the synchronization keyword is used.

7. What is a race condition? How can it be prevented?

8. What is the difference between yield and sleep?

9. Write a program to check whether two or more threads can be given the same name.

10. Write a program in which the main thread creates a new thread. Both threads should print out their names 20 times using the getName method. Run the program several times on different platforms. Does the output vary?

11. Write a program in which the main thread plays video for 5 seconds, after which it closes the QuickTime player and terminates.

12. Write a program in which the main thread creates a new thread named videoThread. The thread videoThread should play video for 5 seconds, after which it closes the QuickTime player and terminates.

13. Write a program in which a thread plays audio for a random amount of time (between 10 and 15 seconds) and then terminates. After the first thread has terminated, a second thread should start playing audio for 5 seconds.

14. What is a deadlock? Write a program that demonstrates how a deadlock can occur.

15. Write a program to show how a thread can be terminated using a shared variable that it repeatedly checks.

16. Write a program to show how a thread can be terminated using an interrupt.

Further Reading

An in-depth discussion on multithreading is provided in [3]. If you would like to extend the functionality of the MoviePlayer class that we have used in the programs in this chapter or to write your own class to play media, you will need to learn QuickTime for Java [4].

References

1. "Java™ Platform, Standard Edition 6, API Specification." Web. <http://download.oracle.com/javase/6/docs/api/>.

2. "The Java™ Tutorials." Web. <http://download.oracle.com/javase/tutorial/>.

3. Hyde, Paul. *Java Thread Programming.* Indianapolis, IN: Sams Publishing., 1999. Print.

4. Adamson, Chris. *QuickTime for Java: A Developer's Notebook.* Sebastopol, CA: O'Reilly, 2005. Print.

Index